Essential Proudhon

Compiled and Edited by J. Bates

CONTENTS

God is Evil, Man is Free

Introduction
by Shawn P. Wilbur

Proudhon was fond of scandal and provocation — and it got him, and his friends, into hot water. In his *System of Economic Contradictions*, he wrapped his already provocative thesis about the evolution of institutions around a scandalous narrative about "the hypothesis of God." Proudhon was fascinated with Christianity, and wrote about it from a variety of perspectives and in a variety of tones, but he is probably best remembered for writings like his "Hymn to Satan" and the final chapter of the first volumes of the *Economic Contradictions*, where he worked himself up to a sort of declaration of war against the very idea of God:

"If God did not exist" — it is Voltaire, the enemy of religions, who says so, — "it would be necessary to invent him." Why? "Because," adds the same Voltaire, "if I were dealing with an atheist prince whose interest it might be to have me pounded in a mortar, I am very sure that I should be pounded." Strange aberration of a great mind! And if you were dealing with a pious prince, whose confessor, speaking in the name of God, should command that you be burned alive, would you not be very sure of being burned also? Do you forget, then, anti-Christ, the Inquisition, and the Saint Bartholomew, and the stakes of Vanini and Bruno, and the tortures of Galileo, and the martyrdom of so many free thinkers? Do not try to distinguish here between use and abuse: for I should reply to you that from a mystical and supernatural principle, from a principle which embraces everything, which explains everything, which justifies everything, such as the idea of God, all consequences are legitimate, and that the zeal of the believer is the sole judge of their propriety.

"I once believed," says Rousseau, "that it was possible to be an honest man and dispense with God; but I have recovered from that error." Fundamentally the same argument as that. of Voltaire, the same justification of intolerance: Man does good and abstains from evil only through consideration of a Providence which watches over him; a curse on those who deny its existence! And, to cap the climax of absurdity, the man who thus seeks for our virtue the sanction of a Divinity who rewards and punishes is the same man who teaches the native goodness of man as a religious dogma.

1

And for my part I say: The first duty of man, on becoming intelligent and free, is to continually hunt the idea of God out of his mind and conscience. For God, if he exists, is essentially hostile to our nature, and we do not depend at all upon his authority. We arrive at knowledge in spite of him, at comfort in spite of him, at society in spite of him; every step we take in advance is a victory in which we crush Divinity.

Let it no longer be said that the ways of God are impenetrable. We have penetrated these ways, and there we have read in letters of blood the proofs of God's impotence, if not of his malevolence. My reason, long humiliated, is gradually rising to a level with the infinite; with time it will discover all that its inexperience hides from it; with time I shall be less and less a worker of misfortune, and by the light that I shall have acquired, by the perfection of my liberty, I shall purify myself, idealize my being, and become the chief of creation, the equal of God. A single moment of disorder which the Omnipotent might have prevented and did not prevent accuses his Providence and shows him lacking in wisdom; the slightest progress which man, ignorant, abandoned, and betrayed, makes towards good honors him immeasurably. By what right should God still say to me: Be holy, for I am holy? Lying spirit, I will answer him, imbecile God, your reign is over; look to the beasts for other victims. I know that I am not holy and never can become so; and how could you be holy, if I resemble you? Eternal father, Jupiter or Jehovah, we have learned to know you; you are, you were, you ever will be, the jealous rival of Adam, the tyrant of Prometheus.

So I do not fall into the sophism refuted by St. Paul, when he forbids the vase to say to the potter: Why hast thou made me thus? I do not blame the author of things for having made me an inharmonious creature, an incoherent assemblage; I could exist only in such a condition. I content myself with crying out to him: Why do you deceive me? Why, by your silence, have you unchained egoism within me? Why have you submitted me to the torture of universal doubt by the bitter illusion of the antagonistic ideas which you have put in my mind? Doubt of truth, doubt of justice, doubt of my conscience and my liberty, doubt of yourself, O God! and, as a result of this doubt, necessity of war with myself and with my neighbor! That, supreme Father, is what you have done for our happiness and your glory; such, from the beginning, have been your will and your government; such the bread, kneaded in blood and tears, upon which you have fed us. The sins which we ask you to forgive, you caused us to commit; the traps from which we implore you to deliver us, you set for us; and the Satan who besets us is yourself.

2

You triumphed, and no one dared to contradict you, when, after having tormented in his body and in his soul the righteous Job, a type of our humanity, you insulted his candid piety, his prudent and respectful ignorance. We were as naught before your invisible majesty, to whom we gave the sky for a canopy and the earth for a footstool. And now here you are dethroned and broken. Your name, so long the last word of the savant, the sanction of the judge, the force of the prince, the hope of the poor, the refuge of the repentant sinner, — this incommunicable name, I say, henceforth an object of contempt and curses, shall be a hissing among men. For God is stupidity and cowardice; God is hypocrisy and falsehood; God is tyranny and misery; God is evil. As long as humanity shall bend before an altar, humanity, the slave of kings and priests, will be condemned; as long as one man, in the name of God, shall receive the oath of another man, society will be founded on perjury; peace and love will be banished from among mortals. God, take yourself away! for, from this day forth, cured of your fear and become wise, I swear, with hand extended to heaven, that you are only the tormentor of my reason, the spectre of my conscience.

Naturally, this riled folks up. And Proudhon wasn't the only to feel the heat. The perception was that his friends, and socialism in general, were getting a black eye from his provocative writing. So he was under some pressure to clear things up. But Proudhon wasn't always real good at giving the people what they wanted, so his reply (*le Peuple*, May 6, 1849) may not have exactly smoothed things over. But it's a lot of fun...

God is Evil

My friends beg me, in the interest of our common ideas, and to remove any pretext for slander, to make my opinion known on the divinity and Providence, and at the same time to explain certain passages from the *System of [Economic] Contradictions*, that the reactionary tartuffes have for a year constantly exploited against socialism with simple and credulous souls.

I surrender to their solicitations. I will even say that if I have for so long let the *Constitutionnel* and its consorts make of me a Vanini even more ferocious that the original, attacking at once God and the Devil, — the family and property, — I had my reasons for that. First I wanted to lead certain schools, up to then considered enemies, to confess themselves their perfect resemblance; I wanted, in a word, it to be

3

demonstrated to the eyes of all that doctrinaire and Jesuit, it is all one. Also, as a metaphysician by profession, I was not unhappy to take advantage of the circumstances in order to judge, by a decisive test, where our century really is with regard to religion. It is not given to everyone to engage in such experiments in social psychology, and to examine, as I have for six months, public reason. Few men are in a position for that; and besides, it is too costly. Thus I was curious to know if, among a people such as our own, who, for two centuries, have banished religious disputes from among them; who have posited in principle the absolute liberty of conscience, that is to say the most determined skepticism; who, through the mouthpiece of the present head of the ministry, M. Odilon-Barrot, have put God and religion beyond the law; who salary all the faiths existing in their territory, while waiting for them to fade away; among a people where one no longer swears but by *honor* and *conscience;* where education, justice, power, literature and art, everything, finally, is religious indifference, if not atheism, the minds of the citizens were on a level with the institutions.

There is, I said to myself, a man who exactly fulfills his civic duties; who, above all things, respects the family of his fellow man; who keeps himself pure for the good of others; who makes a rule of never disguising his thoughts, even at the risk of his respect; who has sworn himself to the improvement of his fellows; well! What could it matter to the people to know if this man is or is not an atheist? How could that modify their opinion? Especially if one considers that the word *atheist* is as poorly defined, as obscure, as the word *God*, of which it is the negation.

For a mind enamored with philosophical and social trifles, the question deserves to be examined deeply.

Now, I have seen that, thank God! — if you'll excuse the expression — the bulk of the people in France have been stirred very little by the transcendent interests of the supreme being, and that there remains hardly anyone but the *Constitutionnel* and the Jesuits, M. Thiers and M. de Montalembert, to take up the cause of the divinity. Here, in order to conceal nothing, is all that I gathered from my researches.

1. Four petitions have arrived at the National Assembly, holding thirty to forty signatures, and demanding my expulsion from the Assembly for cause of atheism. As if I did not have the right to be atheist!... If the National Assembly ever occupies

4

itself with these petitions, my honorable colleagues will laugh about it like the gods.

2. I have received two anonymous letters in which I have been warned, with plenty of biblical citations in support, that if I continue, as I have, to blaspheme, the heavens will strike me. — OK! I say, If the heavens intervene, I am a goner!

3. Finally, here is the *Constitutionnel*, number of May 3, which tells me to *beware*, that *if I push Providence too far, she will chastise me*, delivering me up to the delirium of my pride. — Indeed, merely to be occupied with her, that is good reason to become mad.

That is all that I have been able to gather of the indignation of the devout; the rest, the immense majority of the French people, jeer at the Providence of Constitutionnel and of the good God of the Jesuits, like an ass with a fistful of nettles.

However, it is time that the comedy finishes; and, since my friends wish it and our colleagues in socialism desire it, I will address to them my profession of faith. God and the people pardon me! What I am going to say is a serious thing; but such is the sacrilegious hypocrisy of my adversaries, that I am almost ashamed of my action, as if I had just taken the holy water.

Man is Free

There is my first proposition. Liberty is thought; I only translate the *Cogito, ergo sum*, of Descartes. I am free, therefore I am. All the propositions that will follow, follow from that one, with the rigor of a geometric demonstration.

By virtue of his liberty, man adheres to or resists the *divine order*, which is nothing but the order of *nature* delivered to itself.

By his adhesion to the divine order, as by the modifications that it imposes on him, man enters into a share of government of the universe. He becomes himself, like God, of whom he is the eternal reflection, *creator* and *revealer;* he is a form of the divinity.

All that which does not come to modify the free action of man falls exclusively under the law of God.

Reciprocally, all that which surpasses the force of nature is the proper work of the will of man.

God is *eternal reason;* man is *progressive reason.*

These two reasons are necessary to one another; they complete one another.

Their *agreement* constitutes what I call the government of Providence.

Providence is not, then, like God and man, whose convergence it represents, a simple idea; it is a complex idea. — It is the harmony between the order of nature and the order of liberty, a thing that the popular proverb expresses by saying: *Help yourself, heaven will aid you!*

All that man does on encountering the divine law is *arbitrary;* all that happens without man's knowledge, or despite it, is a matter of *fatality.*

Depending on whether Humanity is more or less *autonomous*, that is to say mistress and legislator of itself; whether its share of initiative is more or less great and reasoned, and the course of events more or less freed from the unconscious laws of nature, the amount of *good* increased or diminished in the world. So that order, in its highest expression, or, as the ancient philosophers said, the Sovereign Good, results from the perfect accord between the two sovereign powers, God and man, and the extreme *wretchedness* of their complete scission.

The *progress* in Humanity can then be defined, the incessant struggle of man with nature, eternal opposition, producing and eternal conciliation.

Everywhere where man misunderstood the law of nature where it is lacking, it is inevitable that nature and society fall into dissolution. The perfection of the physical world is linked to the perfection of the social world, and *vice versa.* A God, a world, without humanity, is impossible; a Humanity-God is a contradiction. Confusion, exclusion, there is (the) evil.

God, eternal and infinite, is *everywhere*, Humanity, immortal and progressive, is *somewhere.*

Neither can the divine order be fully absorbed in human law, nor can free will resolve itself entirely in fatalism. These two orders should develop in parallel, sustain one another, harmonize, not blend: the *antinomy* between man and God is unsolvable.

The *absolute* is a conception necessary for the reason, not without reality. In other terms, God, considered as the synthesis of the faculties of the finite and infinite, does not exist. From yet another point of view, man is not the *weakened* image, but the *reversed* image of God.

The *equality* of relations between God and man; the distinction and the *antagonism* of their natures; the obligatory *convergence* of their wills; the progress of their agreement, are the fundamental dogmas of the *democratic and social philosophy*.

Christianity has been the *prophecy*, and socialism is the *realization*.

Atheism is the negation of Providence, as it results from the agreement between the inflexible laws of nature and the incessant aspirations of liberty, and as I have attempted to define it.

Atheism is, in general, the doctrine that, in an infinite variety of forms, materialism and spiritualism, Catholicism and paganism, deism, pantheism, idealism, skepticism and mysticism, etc., denies by turns equality, la contemporaneity, the necessity of the two powers, God and man, their distinction, their solidarity, tends continually either to subordinate one to the other, or to isolate them, or to resolve them.

God, eternal and inevitable reason, not being conceivable without man; and man, progressive and free reason, not being conceivable without God; and that duality being inconvertible and insoluble, every theory that detracts from it is atheism.

Thus, atheism is the opposite of *anti-theism*, which is nothing other than socialism itself, which is to say the theory Providence, or, as St. Augustine would have said, the organization of the *City of God*.

After that, the vulgar who relate everything to a superior will, to a *Supreme Being*, of which man will only be the creature and plaything, profoundly religious as to consciousness, is atheist in beliefs. The supremacy of God is a mutilation of Humanity: it is atheism.

7

It is as true today to say that the world does not know God, as it was at the birth of Jesus Christ.

Bossuet, in his *Discours sur l'histoire universelle*, where he glorifies the creator to the detriment of humanity, attributing everything to God, and making man the passive instrument of his designs, Bossuet, without wanting or knowing it, is an atheist.

Jean-Jacques Rousseau is an atheist, when, after having misanthropically denied civilization, that is, the participation of humanity in the government of the universe, he prostrates himself before nature and returns civilized society to the savage state. The philosopher of Geneva has not seen that the knowledge of God is progressive like society, that it is really because of the progress of that society.

And as in every state of civilization the *political* form has for point of departure the theological or metaphysical idea, — as in society *government* is produced according to the example of religion, — we constantly see the varieties of atheism become so many varieties of *despotism*.

Thus Bossuet, after having made the theory of divine absolutism in his *Discours sur l'histoire universelle*, has been carried by the force of his principle to make the theory of monarchical absolutism in his *Politique tirée de l'Écriture sainte*. Thus Jean-Jacques Rousseau, the theoretician of deism, a kind of compromise between reason and faith, can be considered as the father of *constitutionalism*, an arbitrary transaction between monarchy and democracy. Rousseau is the predecessor of M. Guizot: besides, the *Social Contract* is only a contradiction on the part of the philosopher of Geneva. And as deism is the worst of hypocrisies, constitutionalism is the worst of governments.

The present society, finally, a society without energy, without philosophy, without an idea of God or of itself, living from day to day on some extinct traditions, rejecting every intervention of free will in its industrial economy, awaiting its salvation only from the fatality of nature, as it awaits the sun and rain, is profoundly atheist.

And the most detestable of atheists, although they do not cease to claim to follow God and Church, are those who envy the people liberty and knowledge; who make them march at the points of their bayonets, who preach resignation and renunciation to them, the respect of parasitism and submission to the foreigner. — It is those who say to them: Make

8

love but do not make children, because you cannot feed them; labor, but save, because you are not certain that you can always work.

It is time that we knew them, these detractors of divine and human Providence, who pose as defenders of religion, and who always deny one of the faces of the infinite; who award themselves the title of *party of order*, but who have never organized anything but conspiracies...

The readers of the *Peuple* understand at present why, in a recent article, where I brought out the deep and incurable powerlessness of these men, I called their tyrannical domination the *reign of God!* Aren't they fatalists, indeed? Don't they oppose every effort of liberty! Don't they want us to relate it exclusively to the force of things? Don't they have, as maxims, these simple phrases:

Laissez faire, laissez passer!

Chacun chez soi, chacun pour soi! [Every one for his home, every one for himself]

Qui vivra verra! [Time will tell!]

and a thousand others, which are so many acts of despair, so many professions of atheism?

Similarly, the readers of the *Peuple* will understand how, in a work where I will proceeded to the determination of the socialist dogma by the analysis of the contradictions, I have successively been able to make the critique of God and Humanity, and to show that, either by one, or by the other, the order in society, or what I today call *Providence*, was impossible: the convergence of both is required. I showed on that occasion that the God of the deists and of the Catholics, the God of the *Constitutionnel* and the *Univers*, is as impossible, as contradictory and immoral as the man of Rousseau or Lamettrie; that such a God would be the negation of God himself, and would deserve to be called *Satan* or *Evil*. In what sense have I failed my principles? How have I offended the intimate belief of Humanity?

One has so often cited, in horror of socialism, that passage of the *Economic Contradictions*, that the readers of the *Peuple* will be grateful to have me explain it. The true ideas could not be spread about too much or too early: it is the remedy against atheism, against superstition, oppression and exploitation in all its forms.

9

The author of the *Economic Contradictions* begins by positioning himself in the catholic hypothesis, namely that God's reason is like that of man, although infinitely superior, and he addresses this question to his adversaries:

Would God be guilty if, after having created the world according to the laws of geometry, he had put it into our minds, or even allowed us to believe without fault of our own, that a circle may be square or a square circular, though, in consequence of this false opinion, we should have to suffer an incalculable series of evils? Again, undoubtedly.

Well! that is exactly what God, the God of Providence, has done in the government of humanity; it is of that that I accuse him. He knew from all eternity — inasmuch as we mortals have discovered it after six thousand years of painful experience — that order in society — that is, liberty, wealth, science — is realized by the reconciliation of opposite ideas which, were each to be taken as absolute in itself, would precipitate us into an abyss of misery: why did he not warn us? Why did he not correct our judgment at the start? Why did he abandon us to our imperfect logic, especially when our egoism must find a pretext in his acts of injustice and perfidy? He knew, this jealous God, that, if he exposed us to the hazards of experience, we should not find until very late that security of life which constitutes our entire happiness: why did he not abridge this long apprenticeship by a revelation of our own laws? Why, instead of fascinating us with contradictory opinions, did he not reverse experience by causing us to reach the antinomies by the path of analysis of synthetic ideas, instead of leaving us to painfully clamber up the steeps of antinomy to synthesis?

The reasoning is this: If God is such as the theists claim, sovereignly good, fair and provident, how has he not prevented evil? That is the standard argument of the materialists. Now what with the conclusion of the author be? It is here that he completely separates himself from his precursors.

If, as was formerly thought, the evil from which humanity suffers arose solely from the imperfection inevitable in every creature, or better, if this evil were caused only by the antagonism of the potentialities and inclinations which constitute our being, and which reason should teach us to master and guide, we should have no right to complain. Our condition being all that it could be, God would be justified.

But, in view of this willful delusion of our minds, a delusion which it was so easy to dissipate and the effects of which must be so terrible, where is the excuse of Providence? Is it not true that grace failed man here? God, whom faith represents as a tender father and a prudent master, abandons us to the fatality of our incomplete conceptions; he digs the ditch under our feet; he causes us to move blindly: and then, at every fall, he punishes us as rascals. What do I say? It seems as if it were in spite of him that at last, covered with bruises from our journey, we recognize our road; as if we offended his glory in becoming more intelligent and free through the trials which he imposes upon us. What need, then, have we to continually invoke Divinity, and what have we to do with those satellites of a Providence which for sixty centuries, by the aid of a thousand religions, has deceived and misled us?

What does that argumentation mean? Nothing but this: Reason, in God, is constructed otherwise than it *becomes* each day in man; apart from that, God would be inexcusable. — Note that the author guards himself well from concluding after the manner of the atheist materialists: Providence is unjustifiable; thus there is no God. He says on the contrary: If God and Providence are not justified, it is because we do not understand them; it is because God and Providence are different than the priests and philosophers say that they are.

The discussion continues on this terrain, and soon we see that not only does reason, in God, not *resemble* that of man, but that it is precisely the *inverse* of man's intelligence.

When the theists, in order to establish their dogma of Providence, cite the order of nature as a proof, although this argument is only a begging of the question, at least it cannot be said that it involves a contradiction, and that the fact cited bears witness against the hypothesis. In the system of the world, for instance, nothing betrays the smallest anomaly, the slightest lack of foresight, from which any prejudice whatever can be drawn against the idea of a supreme, intelligent, personal motor. In short, though the order of nature does not prove the reality of a Providence, it does not contradict it.

It is a very different thing with the government of humanity. Here order does not appear at the same time as matter; it was not created, as in the system of the world, once and for eternity. It is gradually developed according to an inevitable series of principles and consequences which the human being himself, the being to be ordered, must disengage spontaneously, by his own energy and at the solicitation of experience. No revelation regarding this is given him. Man is submitted at his origin to a pre-established necessity, to an absolute and irresistible order. That this order may be realized, man must discover it; that it may exist, he must have divined it. This labor of invention might be abridged; no one, either in heaven or on earth, will come to man's aid; no one will instruct him. Humanity, for hundreds of centuries, will devour its generations; it will exhaust itself in blood and mire, without the God whom it worships coming once to illuminate its reason and abridge its time of trial. Where is divine action here? Where is Providence?

What, then, is the progression of this discussion?

It is: 1° that before an error, invincible and that it was so easy to dissipate, the inaction of Providence (as the catholic atheists understand it) is not justified; 2° that from this it is necessary to conclude, not that God does not exist, but that we do not understand God; 3° that in fact, the reason that has presided over the order of nature is obviously otherwise, the reason that presides over the development of human destinies is otherwise. Soon we will see, and that will be the conclusion of the chapter, that reason in God is different from that in man, not in its *extent*, but it is *quality;* from which this consequence, that God and man, necessary to one another, contemporary with one another, at once inseparable and irreducible, are in a state of perpetual antagonism, so that the supreme perfection in the one is adequate to the supreme infirmity in the other, and that the destiny of man is, by unceasingly studying Divinity, to resemble it as little as possible.

Here is the passage where that consequence is found developed, and which has so scandalized the devout:

And for my part I say: The first duty of man, on becoming intelligent and free, is to continually hunt the idea of God out of his mind and conscience. For God, if he exists, is essentially hostile to our nature, and we do not depend at all upon his authority. We arrive at knowledge in spite of him, at comfort in spite of him, at society in spite of him; every step we take in advance is a victory in which we crush Divinity.

Let it no longer be said that the ways of God are impenetrable. We have penetrated these ways, and there we have read in letters of blood the proofs of God's impotence, if not of his malevolence. My reason, long humiliated, is gradually rising to a level with the infinite; with time it will discover all that its inexperience hides from it; with time I shall be less and less a worker of misfortune, and by the light that I shall have acquired, by the perfection of my liberty, I shall purify myself, idealize my being, and become the chief of creation, the equal of God.

12

It is impossible to better bring to light, on the one hand, the *progressivity* of human reason, and, on the other, the *immobility* of divine reason. How have some serious men been able to see, in all that, only an atheistic declamation, in the style of those by Diderot or the Baron d'Holbach?

A single moment of disorder which the Omnipotent might have prevented and did not prevent accuses his Providence and shows him lacking in wisdom; the slightest progress which man, ignorant, abandoned, and betrayed, makes towards good honors him immeasurably. By what right should God still say to me: *Be holy, for I am holy?* Lying spirit, I will answer him, imbecile God, your reign is over; look to the beasts for other victims. I know that I am not holy and never can become so; and how could you be holy, if I resemble you? Eternal father, Jupiter or Jehovah, we have learned to know you; you are, you were, you ever will be, the jealous rival of Adam, the tyrant of Prometheus.

So I do not fall into the sophism refuted by St. Paul, when he forbids the vase to say to the potter: Why hast thou made me thus? I do not blame the author of things for having made me an inharmonious creature, an incoherent assemblage; I could exist only in such a condition. I content myself with crying out to him: Why do you deceive me? Why, by your silence, have you unchained egoism within me? Why have you submitted me to the torture of universal doubt by the bitter illusion of the antagonistic ideas which you have put in my mind? Doubt of truth, doubt of justice, doubt of my conscience and my liberty, doubt of yourself, O God! and, as a result of this doubt, necessity of war with myself and with my neighbor!

Is there need at present to warn the reader that this does not really fall on God and Providence? — How, if the author was atheist, would he reproach God for having made him *doubt him*, and then to have made him fall into sin! That would not make sense. Under the names of God and Providence, it is Catholicism and deism, principles of Malthusian economy and of the constitutional theory, that the writer attacks. The catholic papers are not mistaken. The lines that follow, and which are the paraphrase of the Sunday oration, could not in that regard leave them in doubt.

That, supreme Father, is what you have done for our happiness and your glory (*Ad majorent Dei gloriam!*); such, from the beginning, have been your will and your government; such the bread, kneaded in blood and tears, upon which you have fed us. The sins which we ask you to

13

forgive, you caused us to commit; the traps from which we implore you to deliver us, you set for us; and the Satan who besets us is yourself.

On the one hand, capital, authority, wealth, science; on the other, poverty, obedience, ignorance: that is the fatal antagonism that it is a question of bringing to an end; that is Malthusian fatalism, that is Catholicism! That is all that socialism has sworn to lay waste. Listen to his oath:

You triumphed, and no one dared to contradict you, when, after having tormented in his body and in his soul the righteous Job, a type of our humanity, you insulted his candid piety, his prudent and respectful ignorance. We were as naught before your invisible majesty, to whom we gave the sky for a canopy and the earth for a footstool. And now here you are dethroned and broken. Your name, so long the last word of the savant, the sanction of the judge, the force of the prince, the hope of the poor, the refuge of the repentant sinner, — this incommunicable name, I say, henceforth an object of contempt and curses, shall be a hissing among men. For God is stupidity and cowardice; God is hypocrisy and falsehood; God is tyranny and misery; God is evil.

As long as humanity shall bend before an altar, humanity, the slave of kings and priests, will be condemned; as long as one man, in the name of God, shall receive the oath of another man, society will be founded on perjury; peace and love will be banished from among mortals. God, take yourself away! for, from this day forth, cured of your fear and become wise, I swear, with hand extended to heaven, that you are only the tormentor of my reason, the specter of my conscience.

It is useless to prolong this citation, the sense of which can no longer be in doubt.

A few weeks ago, at the news of the liquidation of the Bank of the People, the *Constitutionnel* let out a cry of joy and nearly presented me as a huckster. — I responded by producing my resources and my accounts: the Constitutionnel was silent.

Some time after, I published in the *Peuple* a plan for a *Code de la résistance*; and *Constitutionnel* cried out that this was the organization of social disorganization. I then demonstrated that the organization of the resistance, the right of insurrection and conspiracy was the pure spirit of the constitutional system: the *Constitutionnel* was silent.

14

The other day, I proved, by a review of the year 1848, that all the evil that has been produced from February 22 until May 1, 1849, was due to the providential theory, current in the world of the Catholics and doctrinaires. The *Constitutionnel* accused me on that occasion of atheism, and found nothing better, to justify its dire, than to cite a passage were I had intended precisely to establish that the true atheism is Catholicism, the religion of the *Univers* and the *Constitutionnel*.

Will the *Constitutionnel* deign just once, instead of always slandering, to seriously discuss the Bank of the People, doctrinaire theory, and the Catholic faith?

Letter of Proudhon To Marx

Lyon, 17 May 1846

My dear Monsieur Marx,

I gladly agree to become one of the recipients of your correspondence, whose aims and organization seem to me most useful. Yet I cannot promise to write often or at great length: my varied occupations, combined with a natural idleness, do not favour such epistolary efforts. I must also take the liberty of making certain qualifications which are suggested by various passages of your letter.

First, although my ideas in the matter of organization and realization are at this moment more or less settled, at least as regards principles, I believe it is my duty, as it is the duty of all socialists, to maintain for some time yet the critical or dubitive form; in short, I make profession in public of an almost absolute economic anti-dogmatism.

Let us seek together, if you wish, the laws of society, the manner in which these laws are realized, the process by which we shall succeed in discovering them; but, for God's sake, after having demolished all the *a priori* dogmatisms, do not let us in our turn dream of indoctrinating the people; do not let us fall into the contradiction of your compatriot Martin Luther, who, having overthrown Catholic theology, at once set about, with excommunication and anathema, the foundation of a Protestant theology. For the last three centuries Germany has been mainly occupied in undoing Luther's shoddy work; do not let us leave humanity with a similar mess to clear up as a result of our efforts. I applaud with all my heart your thought of bringing all opinions to light; let us carry on a good and loyal polemic; let us give the world an example of learned and far-sighted tolerance, but let us not, merely because we are at the head of a movement, make ourselves the leaders of a new intolerance, let us not pose as the apostles of a new religion, even if it be the religion of logic, the religion of reason. Let us gather together and encourage all protests, let us brand all exclusiveness, all mysticism; let us never regard a question as exhausted, and when we have used our last argument, let us begin again, if need be, with eloquence and irony. On that condition, I will gladly enter your association. Otherwise — no!

I have also some observations to make on this phrase of your letter: *at the moment of action*. Perhaps you still retain the opinion that no

16

reform is at present possible without a *coup de main*, without what was formerly called a revolution and is really nothing but a shock. That opinion, which I understand, which I excuse, and would willingly discuss, having myself shared it for a long time, my most recent studies have made me abandon completely. I believe we have no need of it in order to succeed; and that consequently we should not put forward *revolutionary action* as a means of social reform, because that pretended means would simply be an appeal to force, to arbitrariness, in brief, a contradiction. I myself put the problem in this way: *to bring about the return to society, by an economic combination, of the wealth which was withdrawn from society by another economic combination.* In other words, through Political Economy to turn the theory of Property against Property in such a way as to engender what you German socialists call *community* and what I will limit myself for the moment to calling *liberty* or *equality*. But I believe that I know the means of solving this problem with only a short delay; I would therefore prefer to burn Property by a slow fire, rather than give it new strength by making a St Bartholomew's night of the proprietors

Your very devoted
Pierre-Joseph Proudhon

The Malthusians

Dr. Malthus, an economist, an Englishman, once wrote the following words:

"A man who is born into a world already occupied, his family unable to support him, and society not requiring his labor, such a man, I say, has not the least legal right to claim any nourishment whatever; he is really one too many on the earth. At the great banquet of Nature there is no plate laid for him. Nature commands him to take himself away, and she will not be slow to put her order into execution."

As a consequence of this great principle, Malthus recommends, with the most terrible threats, every man who has neither labor nor income upon which to live to take himself away, or at any rate to have no more children. A family, — that is, love, — like bread, is forbidden such a man by Malthus.

Dr. Malthus was, while living, a minister of the Holy Gospel, a mild-mannered philanthropist, a good husband, a good father, a good citizen, believing in God us firmly as any man in France. He died (heaven grant him peace) in 1834. It may be said that he was the first, without doubt, to reduce to absurdity all political economy, and state the great revolutionary question, the question between labor and capital. With us, whose faith in Providence still lives, in spite of the century's indifference, it is proverbial — and herein consists the difference between the English and ourselves — that "everybody must live." And our people, in saying this, think themselves as truly Christian, as conservative of good morals and the family, as the late Malthus.

Now, what the people say in France, the economists deny; the lawyers and the litterateurs deny; the Church, which pretends to be Christian, and also Gallican, denies; the press denies; the large proprietors deny; the government which endeavors to represent them, denies.

The press, the government, the Church, literature, economy, wealth, — everything in France has become English; everything is Malthusian. It is in the name of God and his holy providence, in the name of morality, in the name of the sacred interests of the family, that they maintain that there is not room in the country for all the children of the country, and that they warn our women to be less prolific. In France, in spite of the desire of the people, in spite of the national belief, eating and drinking are regarded as privileges, labor a privilege, family a privilege, country a privilege.

M. Antony Thouret said recently that property, without which there is neither country, nor family, nor labor, nor morality, would be irreproachable as soon as it should cease to be a privilege; a clear statement of the fact that, to abolish all the privileges which, so to speak, exclude a portion of the people from the law, from humanity, we must abolish, first of all, the fundamental privilege, and change the constitution of property.

M. A. Thouret, in saying that, agreed with us and with the people. The State, the press, political economy, do not view the matter in that light; they agree in the hope that property, without which, as M. Thouret says, there is no labor, no family, no Republic, may remain what it always has been, — a privilege.

All that has been done, said, and printed today and for the last twenty years, has been done, said, and printed in consequence of the theory of Malthus.

The theory of Malthus is the theory of political murder; of murder from motives of philanthropy and for love of God. There are too many people in the world; that is the first article of faith of all those who, at present, in the name of the people, reign and govern. It is for this reason that they use their best efforts to diminish the population. Those who best acquit themselves of this duty, who practice with piety, courage, and fraternity the maxims of Malthus, are good citizens, religious men, those who protest against such conduct are anarchists, socialists, atheists.

That the Revolution of February was the result of this protest constitutes its inexpiable crime. Consequently, it shall be taught its business, this Revolution which promised that all should live. The original, indelible stain on this Republic is that the people have pronounced it anti-Malthusian. That is why the Republic is so especially obnoxious to those who were, and would become again, the toadies and accomplices of kings — grand eaters of men, as Cato called them. They would make monarchy of your Republic; they would devour its children.

There lies the whole secret of the sufferings, the agitations, and the contradictions of our country.

The economists are the first among us, by an inconceivable blasphemy, to establish as a providential dogma the theory of Malthus. I do not reproach them; neither do I abuse them. On this point the economists act in good faith and from the best intentions in the world. They would like nothing better than to make the human race happy; but they cannot conceive how, without some sort of an organization of homicide, a balance between population and production can exist.

Ask the Academy of Moral Sciences. One of its most honorable members, whose name I will not call, — though he is proud of his opinions, as every honest man should be, — being the prefect of I know not which department, saw fit one day, in a proclamation, to advise those within his province to have thenceforth fewer children by their wives. Great was the scandal among the priests and gossips, who looked upon this academic morality as the morality of swine! The savant of whom I speak was none the less, like all his fellows, a zealous defender of the family and of morality; but, he observed with Malthus, at the banquet of Nature there is not room for all.

M. Thiers, also a member of the Academy of Moral Sciences, lately told the committee on finance that, if he were minister, he would confine himself to courageously and stoically passing through the crisis, devoting himself to the expenses of his budget, enforcing a respect for order, and carefully guarding against every financial innovation, every socialistic idea, — especially such as the right to labor, — as well as every revolutionary expedient. And the whole committee applauded him.

In giving this declaration of the celebrated historian and statesman, I have no desire to accuse his intentions. In the present state of the public mind, I should succeed only in serving the ambition of M. Thiers, if he has any left. What I wish to call attention to is that M. Thiers, in expressing himself in this wise, testified, perhaps unconsciously, to his faith in Malthus.

Mark this well, I pray you. There are two millions, four millions of men who will die of misery and hunger, if some means be not found of giving them work. This is a great misfortune, surely, and we are the first to lament it, the Malthusians tell you; but what is to be done? It is better that four millions of men should die than that privilege should be compromised; it is not the fault of capital, if labor is idle; at the banquet of credit there is not room for all.

They are courageous, they are stoical, these statesmen of the school of Malthus, when it is a matter of sacrificing laborers by the millions. Thou hast killed the poor man, said the prophet Elias to the king of Israel, and then thou hast taken away his inheritance. *Occidisti et possedisti.* To-day we must reverse the phrase, and say to those who possess and govern: You have the privilege of labor, the privilege of credit, the privilege of property, as M. Thouret says; and it is because you do not wish to be deprived of these privileges, that you shed the blood of the poor like water: *Possedisti et occidisti!*

And the people, under the pressure of bayonets, are being eaten slowly; they die without a sigh or a murmur; the sacrifice is effected in silence. Courage, laborers! sustain each other: Providence will finally conquer fate. Courage! the condition of your fathers, the soldiers of the republic, at the sieges of Genes and Mayence, was even worse than yours.

M. Leon Faucher, in contending that journals should be forced to furnish securities and in favoring the maintenance of taxes on the press, reasoned also after the manner of Malthus. The serious journal, said he, the journal that deserves consideration and esteem, is that which is established on a capital of from four to five hundred thousand francs. The journalist who has only his pen is like the workman who has only his arms. If he can find no market for his services or get no credit with which to carry on his enterprise, it is a sign that public opinion is against him; he has not the least right to address the country: at the banquet of public life there is not room for all.

Listen to Lacordaire, that light of the Church, that chosen vessel of Catholicism. He will tell you that socialism is antichrist. And why is socialism antichrist? Because socialism is the enemy of Malthus, whereas Catholicism, by a final transformation, has become Malthusian.

The gospel tells us, cries the priest, that there will always be poor people, *Pauperes semper habebitis vobsicum*, and that property, consequently in so far as it is a privilege and makes poor people, is sacred. Poverty is necessary to the exercise of evangelical charity; at the banquet of this world here below there cannot be room for all.

He feigns ignorance, the infidel, of the fact that poverty, in Biblical language, signified every sort of affliction and pain, not hard times and the condition of the proletaire. And how could he who went up and down Judea crying, Woe to the rich! be understood differently? In the thought of Jesus Christ, woe to the rich means woe to the Malthusians.

21

If Christ were living today, he would say to Lacordaire and his companions: "You are of the race of those who, in all ages, have shed the blood of the just, from Abel unto Zacharias. Your law is not my law; your God is not my God!..." And the Lacordaires would crucify Christ as a seditious person and an atheist.

Almost the whole of journalism is infected with the same ideas. Let "Le National," for example, tell us whether it has not always believed, whether it does not still believe, that pauperism is a permanent element of civilization; that the enslavement of one portion of humanity is necessary to the glory of another; that those who maintain the contrary are dangerous dreamers who deserve to be shot; that such is the basis of the State. For, if this be not the secret thought of "Le National," if "Le National" sincerely and resolutely desires the emancipation of laborers, why these anathemas against, why this anger with, the genuine socialists — those who, for ten and twenty years, have demanded this emancipation?

Further, let the Bohemian of literature, today the myrmidons of Journalism, paid slanderers, courtiers of the privileged classes, eulogists of all the vices, parasites living upon other parasites, who prate so much of God only to dissemble their materialism, of the family only to conceal their adulteries, and whom we shall see, out of disgust for marriage, caressing monkeys when Malthusian women fail, — let these, I say, publish their economic creed, in order that the people may know them.

Faites des filles, nous les aimons, — beget girls, we love them, — sing these wretches, parodying the poet. But abstain from begetting boys; at the banquet of sensualism there is not room for all.

The government was inspired by Malthus when, having a hundred thousand laborers at its disposal, to whom it gave gratuitous support, it refused to employ them at useful labor, and when, after the civil war, it asked that a law be passed for their transportation. With the expenses of the pretended national workshops, with the costs of war, lawsuits, imprisonment, and transportation, it might have given the insurgents six months income, and thus changed our whole economic system. But labor is a monopoly; the government does not wish revolutionary industry to compete with privileged industry; at the workbench of the nation there is not room for all.

Large industrial establishments ruin small ones; that is the law of capital, that is Malthus.

22

Wholesale trade gradually swallows the retail; again Malthus.

Large estates encroach upon and consolidate the smallest possessions: still Malthus.

Soon one half of the people will say to the other:

The earth and its products are my property.
Industry and its products are my property.
Commerce and transportation are my property.
The State is my property.

You who possess nether reserve nor property, who hold no public offices and whose labor is useless to us, **take yourselves away!** You have really no business on the earth; beneath the sunshine of the Republic there is not room for all.

Who will tell me that the right to labor and to live is not the whole of the Revolution?

Who will tell me that the principle of Malthus is not the whole of the counter-Revolution?

And it is for having published such things as these, — for having exposed the evil boldly and sought the remedy in good faith, that speech has been forbidden me by the government, the government that represents the Revolution!

That is why I have been deluged with the slanders, treacheries, cowardice, hypocrisy, outrages, desertions, and failings of all those who hate or love the people! That is why I have been given over; for a whole month, to the mercy of the jackals of the press and the screech-owls of the platform! Never was a man, either in the past or in the present, the object of so much execration as I have become, for the simple reason that I wage war upon cannibals.

To slander one who could not reply was to shoot a prisoner. Malthusian carnivora, I discover you there! Go on, then; we have more than one account to settle yet. And, if calumny is not sufficient for you, use iron and lead. You may kill me; no one can avoid his fate, and I am at your discretion. But you shall not conquer me; you shall never persuade the people, while I live and hold a pen, that, with the exception of

23

yourselves, there is one too many on the earth. I swear it before the people and in the name of the Republic!

System of Economical Contradictions: or, The Philosophy of Poverty

Introduction. The hypothesis of a God

Before entering upon the subject-matter of these new memoirs, I must explain an hypothesis which will undoubtedly seem strange, but in the absence of which it is impossible for me to proceed intelligibly: I mean the hypothesis of a God.

To suppose God, it will be said, is to deny him. Why do you not affirm him?

Is it my fault if belief in Divinity has become a suspected opinion; if the bare suspicion of a Supreme Being is already noted as evidence of a weak mind; and if, of all philosophical Utopias, this is the only one which the world no longer tolerates? Is it my fault if hypocrisy and imbecility everywhere hide behind this holy formula?

Let a public teacher suppose the existence, in the universe, of an unknown force governing suns and atoms, and keeping the whole machine in motion. With him this supposition, wholly gratuitous, is perfectly natural; it is received, encouraged: witness attraction — an hypothesis which will never be verified, and which, nevertheless, is the glory of its originator. But when, to explain the course of human events, I suppose, with all imaginable caution, the intervention of a God, I am sure to shock scientific gravity and offend critical ears: to so wonderful an extent has our piety discredited Providence, so many tricks have been played by means of this dogma or fiction by charlatans of every stamp! I have seen the theists of my time, and blasphemy has played over my lips; I have studied the belief of the people, — this people that Brydaine called the best friend of God, — and have shuddered at the negation which was about to escape me. Tormented by conflicting feelings, I appealed to reason; and it is reason which, amid so many dogmatic contradictions, now forces the hypothesis upon me. A priori dogmatism, applying itself to God, has proved fruitless: who knows whither the hypothesis, in its turn, will lead us?

I will explain therefore how, studying in the silence of my heart, and far from every human consideration, the mystery of social revolutions, God, the great unknown, has become for me an hypothesis, — I mean a necessary dialectical tool.

I.

If I follow the God-idea through its successive transformations, I find that this idea is preeminently social: I mean by this that it is much more a collective act of faith than an individual conception. Now, how and under what circumstances is this act of faith produced? This point it is important to determine.

From the moral and intellectual point of view, society, or the collective man, is especially distinguished from the individual by spontaneity of action, — in other words, instinct. While the individual obeys, or imagines he obeys, only those motives of which he is fully conscious, and upon which he can at will decline or consent to act; while, in a word, he thinks himself free, and all the freer when he knows that he is possessed of keener reasoning faculties and larger information, — society is governed by impulses which, at first blush, exhibit no deliberation and design, but which gradually seem to be directed by a superior power, existing outside of society, and pushing it with irresistible might toward an unknown goal. The establishment of monarchies and republics, caste-distinctions, judicial institutions, etc., are so many manifestations of this social spontaneity, to note the effects of which is much easier than to point out its principle and show its cause. The whole effort, even of those who, following Bossuet, Vico, Herder, Hegel, have applied themselves to the philosophy of history, has been hitherto to establish the presence of a providential destiny presiding over all the movements of man. And I observe, in this connection, that society never fails to evoke its genius previous to action: as if it wished the powers above to ordain what its own spontaneity has already resolved on. Lots, oracles, sacrifices, popular acclamation, public prayers, are the commonest forms of these tardy deliberations of society.

This mysterious faculty, wholly intuitive, and, so to speak, super-social, scarcely or not at all perceptible in persons, but which hovers over humanity like an inspiring genius, is the primordial fact of all psychology.

Now, unlike other species of animals, which, like him, are governed at the same time by individual desires and collective impulses, man has the privilege of perceiving and designating to his own mind the instinct or fatum which leads him; we shall see later that he has also the power of foreseeing and even influencing its decrees. And the first act of man, filled and carried away with enthusiasm (of the divine breath), is to adore the invisible Providence on which he feels that he depends,

26

and which he calls GOD, — that is, Life, Being, Spirit, or, simpler still, Me; for all these words, in the ancient tongues, are synonyms and homophones.

"I am Me," God said to Abraham, "and I covenant with Thee.".... And to Moses: "I am the Being. Thou shalt say unto the children of Israel, 'The Being hath sent me unto you.'" These two words, the Being and Me, have in the original language — the most religious that men have ever spoken — the same characteristic. [1] Elsewhere, when Ie-hovah, acting as law-giver through the instrumentality of Moses, attests his eternity and swears by his own essence, he uses, as a form of oath, I; or else, with redoubled force, I, the Being. Thus the God of the Hebrews is the most personal and wilful of all the gods, and none express better than he the intuition of humanity.

God appeared to man, then, as a me, as a pure and permanent essence, placing himself before him as a monarch before his servant, and expressing himself now through the mouth of poets, legislators, and soothsayers, musa, nomos, numen; now through the popular voice, vox populi vox Dei. This may serve, among other things, to explain the existence of true and false oracles; why individuals secluded from birth do not attain of themselves to the idea of God, while they eagerly grasp it as soon as it is presented to them by the collective mind; why, finally, stationary races, like the Chinese, end by losing it. [2] In the first place, as to oracles, it is clear that all their accuracy depends upon the universal conscience which inspires them; and, as to the idea of God, it is easily seen why isolation and statu quo are alike fatal to it. On the one hand, absence of communication keeps the mind absorbed in animal self-contemplation; on the other, absence of motion, gradually changing social life into mechanical routine, finally eliminates the idea of will and providence. Strange fact! religion, which perishes through progress, perishes also through quiescence.

Notice further that, in attributing to the vague and (so to speak) objectified consciousness of a universal reason the first revelation of Divinity, we assume absolutely nothing concerning even the reality or non-reality of God. In fact, admitting that God is nothing more than collective instinct or universal reason, we have still to learn what this universal reason is in itself. For, as we shall show directly, universal reason is not given in individual reason, in other words, the knowledge of social laws, or the theory of collective ideas, though deduced from the fundamental concepts of pure reason, is nevertheless wholly empirical, and never would have been discovered a priori by means of deduction, induction, or synthesis. Whence it follows that universal

27

reason, which we regard as the origin of these laws; universal reason, which exists, reasons, labors, in a separate sphere and as a reality distinct from pure reason, just as the planetary system, though created according to the laws of mathematics, is a reality distinct from mathematics, whose existence could not have been deduced from mathematics alone: it follows, I say, that universal reason is, in modern languages, exactly what the ancients called God. The name is changed: what do we know of the thing?

Let us now trace the evolution of the Divine idea.

The Supreme Being once posited by a primary mystical judgment, man immediately generalizes the subject by another mysticism, — analogy. God, so to speak, is as yet but a point: directly he shall fill the world.

As, in sensing his social me, man saluted his Author, so, in finding evidence of design and intention in animals, plants, springs, meteors, and the whole universe, he attributes to each special object, and then to the whole, a soul, spirit, or genius presiding over it; pursuing this inductive process of apotheosis from the highest summit of Nature, which is society, down to the humblest forms of life, to inanimate and inorganic matter. From his collective me, taken as the superior pole of creation, to the last atom of matter, man extends, then, the idea of God, — that is, the idea of personality and intelligence, — just as God himself extended heaven, as the book of Genesis tells us; that is, created space and time, the conditions of all things.

Thus, without a God or master-builder, the universe and man would not exist: such is the social profession of faith. But also without man God would not be thought, or — to clear the interval — God would be nothing. If humanity needs an author, God and the gods equally need a revealer; theogony, the history of heaven, hell, and their inhabitants, — those dreams of the human mind, — is the counterpart of the universe, which certain philosophers have called in return the dream of God. And how magnificent this theological creation, the work of society! The creation of the demiourgos was obliterated; what we call the Omnipotent was conquered; and for centuries the enchanted imagination of mortals was turned away from the spectacle of Nature by the contemplation of Olympian marvels.

Let us descend from this fanciful region: pitiless reason knocks at the door; her terrible questions demand a reply.

28

"What is God?" she asks; "where is he? what is his extent? what are his wishes? what his powers? what his promises?" — and here, in the light of analysis, all the divinities of heaven, earth, and hell are reduced to an incorporeal, insensible, immovable, incomprehensible, undefinable I-know-not-what; in short, to a negation of all the attributes of existence. In fact, whether man attributes to each object a special spirit or genius, or conceives the universe as governed by a single power, he in either case but SUPPOSES an unconditioned, that is, an impossible, entity, that he may deduce therefrom an explanation of such phenomena as he deems inconceivable on any other hypothesis. The mystery of God and reason! In order to render the object of his idolatry more and more rational, the believer despoils him successively of all the qualities which would make him real; and, after marvellous displays of logic and genius, the attributes of the Being par excellence are found to be the same as those of nihility. This evolution is inevitable and fatal: atheism is at the bottom of all theodicy.

Let us try to understand this progress.

God, creator of all things, is himself no sooner created by the conscience, — in other words, no sooner have we lifted God from the idea of the social me to the idea of the cosmic me, — than immediately our reflection begins to demolish him under the pretext of perfecting him. To perfect the idea of God, to purify the theological dogma, was the second hallucination of the human race.

The spirit of analysis, that untiring Satan who continually questions and denies, must sooner or later look for proof of religious dogmas. Now, whether the philosopher determine the idea of God, or declare it indeterminable; whether he approach it with his reason, or retreat from it, — I say that this idea receives a blow; and, as it is impossible for speculation to halt, the idea of God must at last disappear. Then the atheistic movement is the second act of the theologic drama; and this second act follows from the first, as effect from cause. "The heavens declare the glory of God," says the Psalmist. Let us add, And their testimony dethrones him.

Indeed, in proportion as man observes phenomena, he thinks that he perceives, between Nature and God, intermediaries; such as relations of number, form, and succession; organic laws, evolutions, analogies, — forming an unmistakable series of manifestations which invariably produce or give rise to each other. He even observes that, in the development of this society of which he is a part, private wills and associative deliberations have some influence; and he says to himself

29

that the Great Spirit does not act upon the world directly and by himself, or arbitrarily and at the dictation of a capricious will, but mediately, by perceptible means or organs, and by virtue of laws. And, retracing in his mind the chain of effects andcauses, he places clear at the extremity, as a balance, God.

A poet has said, —

Par dela tous les cieux, le Dieu des cieux reside.

Thus, at the first step in the theory, the Supreme Being is reduced to the function of a motive power, a mainspring, a corner-stone, or, if a still more trivial comparison may be allowed me, a constitutional sovereign, reigning but not governing, swearing to obey the law and appointing ministers to execute it. But, under the influence of the mirage which fascinates him, the theist sees, in this ridiculous system, only a new proof of the sublimity of his idol; who, in his opinion, uses his creatures as instruments of his power, and causes the wisdom of human beings to redound to his glory.

Soon, not content with limiting the power of the Eternal, man, increasingly deicidal in his tendencies, insists on sharing it.

If I am a spirit, a sentient me giving voice to ideas, continues the theist, I consequently am a part of absolute existence; I am free, creative, immortal, equal with God. Cogito, ergo sum, — I think, therefore I am immortal, that is the corollary, the translation of Ego sum qui sum: philosophy is in accord with the Bible. The existence of God and the immortality of the soul are posited by the conscience in the same judgment: there, man speaks in the name of the universe, to whose bosom he transports his me; here, he speaks in his own name, without perceiving that, in this going and coming, he only repeats himself.

The immortality of the soul, a true division of divinity, which, at the time of its first promulgation, arriving after a long interval, seemed a heresy to those faithful to the old dogma, has been none the less considered the complement of divine majesty, necessarily postulated by eternal goodness and justice. Unless the soul is immortal, God is incomprehensible, say the theists; resembling in this the political theorists who regard sovereign representation and perpetual tenure of office as essential conditions of monarchy. But the inconsistency of the ideas is as glaring as the parity of the doctrines is exact: consequently the dogma of immortality soon became the stumbling-block of philosophical theologians, who, ever since the days of Pythagoras and

Orpheus, have been making futile attempts to harmonize divine attributes with human liberty, and reason with faith. A subject of triumph for the impious!.... But the illusion could not yield so soon: the dogma of immortality, for the very reason that it was a limitation of the uncreated Being, was a step in advance. Now, though the human mind deceives itself by a partial acquisition of the truth, it never retreats, and this perseverance in progress is proof of its infallibility. Of this we shall soon see fresh evidence.

In making himself like God, man made God like himself: this correlation, which for many centuries had been execrated, was the secret spring which determined the new myth. In the days of the patriarchs God made an alliance with man; now, to strengthen the compact, God is to become a man. He will take on our flesh, our form, our passions, our joys, and our sorrows; will be born of woman, and die as we do. Then, after this humiliation of the infinite, man will still pretend that he has elevated the ideal of his God in making, by a logical conversion, him whom he had always called creator, a saviour, a redeemer. Humanity does not yet say, I am God: such a usurpation would shock its piety; it says, God is in me, IMMANUEL, nobiscum Deus. And, at the moment when philosophy with pride, and universal conscience with fright, shouted with unanimous voice, The gods are departing! excedere deos! a period of eighteen centuries of fervent adoration and superhuman faith was inaugurated.

But the fatal end approaches. The royalty which suffers itself to be limited will end by the rule of demagogues; the divinity which is defined dissolves in a pandemonium. Christolatry is the last term of this long evolution of human thought. The angels, saints, and virgins reign in heaven with God, says the catechism; and demons and reprobates live in the hells of eternal punishment. Ultramundane society has its left and its right: it is time for the equation to be completed; for this mystical hierarchy to descend upon earth and appear in its real character.

When Milton represents the first woman admiring herself in a fountain, and lovingly extending her arms toward her own image as if to embrace it, he paints, feature for feature, the human race. — This God whom you worship, O man! this God whom you have made good, just, omnipotent, omniscient, immortal, and holy, is yourself: this ideal of perfection is your image, purified in the shining mirror of your conscience. God, Nature, and man are three aspects of one and the same being; man is God himself arriving at self-consciousness through a thousand evolutions. In Jesus Christ man recognized himself as God;

and Christianity is in reality the religion of God-man. There is no other God than he who in the beginning said, ME; there is no other God than THEE.

Such are the last conclusions of philosophy, which dies in unveiling religion's mystery and its own.

II.

It seems, then, that all is ended; it seems that, with the cessation of the worship and mystification of humanity by itself, the theological problem is for ever put aside. The gods have gone: there is nothing left for man but to grow weary and die in his egoism. What frightful solitude extends around me, and forces its way to the bottom of my soul! My exaltation resembles annihilation; and, since I made myself a God, I seem but a shadow. It is possible that I am still a me, but it is very difficult to regard myself as the absolute; and, if I am not the absolute, I am only half of an idea.

Some ironical thinker, I know not who, has said: "A little philosophy leads away from religion, and much philosophy leads back to it." This proposition is humiliatingly true.

Every science develops in three successive periods, which may be called — comparing them with the grand periods of civilization — the religious period, the sophistical period, the scientific period. [3] Thus, alchemy represents the religious period of the science afterwards called chemistry, whose definitive plan is not yet discovered; likewise astrology was the religious period of another science, since established, — astronomy.

Now, after being laughed at for sixty years about the philosopher's stone, chemists, governed by experience, no longer dare to deny the transmutability of bodies; while astronomers are led by the structure of the world to suspect also an organism of the world; that is, something precisely like astrology. Are we not justified in saying, in imitation of the philosopher just quoted, that, if a little chemistry leads away from the philosopher's stone, much chemistry leads back to it; and similarly, that, if a little astronomy makes us laugh at astrologers, much astronomy will make us believe in them? [4]

I certainly have less inclination to the marvellous than many atheists, but I cannot help thinking that the stories of miracles, prophecies, charms, etc., are but distorted accounts of the extraordinary effects produced by certain latent forces, or, as was formerly said, by occult powers. Our science is still so brutal and unfair; our professors exhibit so much impertinence with so little knowledge; they deny so impudently facts which embarrass them, in order to protect the opinions which they champion, — that I distrust strong minds equally with superstitious ones. Yes, I am convinced of it; our gross rationalism is the inauguration of a period which, thanks to science, will become truly prodigious; the universe, to my eyes, is only a laboratory of magic, from which anything may be expected.... This said, I return to my subject.

They would be deceived, then, who should imagine, after my rapid survey of religious progress, that metaphysics has uttered its last word upon the double enigma expressed in these four words, — the existence of God, the immortality of the soul. Here, as elsewhere, the most advanced and best established conclusions, those which seem to have settled for ever the theological question, lead us back to primeval mysticism, and involve the new data of an inevitable philosophy. The criticism of religious opinions makes us smile today both at ourselves and at religions; and yet the resume of this criticism is but a reproduction of the problem. The human race, at the present moment, is on the eve of recognizing and affirming something equivalent to the old notion of Divinity; and this, not by a spontaneous movement as before, but through reflection and by means of irresistible logic. I will try, in a few words, to make myself understood.

If there is a point on which philosophers, in spite of themselves, have finally succeeded in agreeing, it is without doubt the distinction between intelligence and necessity, the subject of thought and its object, the me and the not-me; in ordinary terms, spirit and matter. I know well that all these terms express nothing that is real and true; that each of them designates only a section of the absolute, which alone is true and real; and that, taken separately, they involve, all alike, a contradiction. But it is no less certain also that the absolute is completely inaccessible to us; that we know it only by its opposite extremes, which alone fall within the limits of our experience; and that, if unity only can win our faith, duality is the first condition of science.

Thus, who thinks, and what is thought? What is a soul? what is a body? I defy any one to escape this dualism. It is with essences as with ideas: the former are seen separated in Nature, as the latter in the understanding; and just as the ideas of God and immortality, in spite of their identity, are posited successively and contradictorily in

33

philosophy, so, in spite of their fusion in the absolute, the me and the not-me posit themselves separately and contradictorily in Nature, and we have beings who think, at the same time with others which do not think.

Now, whoever has taken pains to reflect knows today that such a distinction, wholly realized though it be, is the most unintelligible, most contradictory, most absurd thing which reason can possibly meet. Being is no more conceivable without the properties of spirit than without the properties of matter: so that if you deny spirit, because, included in none of the categories of time, space, motion, solidity, etc., it seems deprived of all the attributes which constitute reality, I in my turn will deny matter, which, presenting nothing appreciable but its inertia, nothing intelligible but its forms, manifests itself nowhere as cause (voluntary and free), and disappears from view entirely as substance; and we arrive at pure idealism, that is, nihility. But nihility is inconsistent with the existence of living, reasoning — I know not what to call them — uniting in themselves, in a state of commenced synthesis or imminent dissolution, all the antagonistic attributes of being. We are compelled, then, to end in a dualism whose terms we know perfectly well to be false, but which, being for us the condition of the truth, forces itself irresistibly upon us; we are compelled, in short, to commence, like Descartes and the human race, with the me; that is, with spirit.

But, since religions and philosophies, dissolved by analysis, have disappeared in the theory of the absolute, we know no better than before what spirit is, and in this differ from the ancients only in the wealth of language with which we adorn the darkness that envelops us. With this exception, however; that while, to the ancients, order revealed intelligence outside of the world, to the people of today it seems to reveal it rather within the world. Now, whether we place it within or without, from the moment we affirm it on the ground of order, we must admit it wherever order is manifested, or deny it altogether. There is no more reason for attributing intelligence to the head which produced the "Iliad" than to a mass of matter which crystallizes in octahedrons; and, reciprocally, it is as absurd to refer the system of the world to physical laws, leaving out an ordaining ME, as to attribute the victory of Marengo to strategic combinations, leaving out the first consul. The only distinction that can be made is that, in the latter case, the thinking ME is located in the brain of a Bonaparte, while, in the case of the universe, the ME has no special location, but extends everywhere.

The materialists think that they have easily disposed of their opponents by saying that man, having likened the universe to his body, finishes the comparison by presuming the existence in the universe of a soul similar to that which he supposes to be the principle of his own life and thought; that thus all the arguments in support of the existence of God are reducible to an analogy all the more false because the term of comparison is itself hypothetical.

It is certainly not my intention to defend the old syllogism: Every arrangement implies an ordaining intelligence; there is wonderful order in the world; then the world is the work of an intelligence. This syllogism, discussed so widely since the days of Job and Moses, very far from being a solution, is but the statement of the problem which it assumes to solve. We know perfectly well what order is, but we are absolutely ignorant of the meaning of the words Soul, Spirit, Intelligence: how, then, can we logically reason from the presence of the one to the existence of the other? I reject, then, even when advanced by the most thoroughly informed, the pretended proof of the existence of God drawn from the presence of order in the world; I see in it at most only an equation offered to philosophy. Between the conception of order and the affirmation of spirit there is a deep gulf of metaphysics to be filled up; I am unwilling, I repeat, to take the problem for the demonstration.

But this is not the point which we are now considering. I have tried to show that the human mind was inevitably and irresistibly led to the distinction of being into me and not-me, spirit and matter, soul and body. Now, who does not see that the objection of the materialists proves the very thing it is intended to deny? Man distinguishing within himself a spiritual principle and a material principle, — what is this but Nature herself, proclaiming by turns her double essence, and bearing testimony to her own laws? And notice the inconsistency of materialism: it denies, and has to deny, that man is free; now, the less liberty man has, the more weight is to be attached to his words, and the greater their claim to be regarded as the expression of truth. When I hear this machine say to me, "I am soul and I am body," though such a revelation astonishes and confounds me, it is invested in my eyes with an authority incomparably greater than that of the materialist who, correcting conscience and Nature, undertakes to make them say, "I am matter and only matter, and intelligence is but the material faculty of knowing."

What would become of this assertion, if, assuming in my turn the offensive, I should demonstrate that belief in the existence of bodies, or, in other words, in the reality of a purely corporeal nature, is untenable? Matter, they say, is impenetrable. — Impenetrable by what? I ask. Itself, undoubtedly; for they would not dare to say spirit, since they would therein admit what they wish to set aside. Whereupon I raise this double question: What do you know about it, and what does it signify?

1. Impenetrability, which is pretended to be the definition of matter, is only an hypothesis of careless naturalists, a gross conclusion deduced from a superficial judgment. Experience shows that matter possesses infinite divisibility, infinite expansibility, porosity without assignable limits, and permeability by heat, electricity, and magnetism, together with a power of retaining them indefinitely; affinities, reciprocal influences, and transformations without number: qualities, all of them, hardly compatible with the assumption of an impenetrable aliquid. Elasticity, which, better than any other property of matter, could lead, through the idea of spring or resistance, to that of impenetrability, is subject to the control of a thousand circumstances, and depends entirely on molecular attraction: now, what is more irreconcilable with impenetrability than this attraction? Finally, there is a science which might be defined with exactness as the science of penetrability of matter: I mean chemistry. In fact, how does what is called chemical composition differ from penetration? [5].... In short, we know matter only through its forms; of its substance we know nothing. How, then, is it possible to affirm the reality of an invisible, impalpable, incoercible being, ever changing, ever vanishing, impenetrable to thought alone, to which it exhibits only its disguises? Materialist! I permit you to testify to the reality of your sensations; as to what occasions them, all that you can say involves this reciprocity: something (which you call matter) is the occasion of sensations which are felt by another something (which I call spirit).

2. But what, then, is the source of this supposition that matter is impenetrable, which external observation does not justify and which is not true; and what is its meaning?

Here appears the triumph of dualism. Matter is pronounced impenetrable, not, as the materialists and the vulgar fancy, by the testimony of the senses, but by the conscience. The me, an incomprehensible nature, feeling itself free, distinct, and permanent, and meeting outside of itself another nature equally incomprehensible, but also distinct and permanent in spite of its metamorphoses, declares, on the strength of the sensations and ideas which this essence suggests to it, that the not-me is extended and impenetrable. Impenetrability is a figurative term, an image by which thought, a division of the absolute, pictures to itself material reality, another division of the absolute; but this impenetrability, without which matter disappears, is, in the last analysis, only a spontaneous judgment of inward sensation, a metaphysical a priori, an unverified hypothesis of spirit.

Thus, whether philosophy, after having overthrown theological dogmatism, spiritualizes matter or materializes thought, idealizes being or realizes ideas; or whether, identifying substance and cause, it everywhere substitutes FORCE, phrases, all, which explain and signify nothing, — it always leads us back to this everlasting dualism, and, in summoning us to believe in ourselves, compels us to believe in God, if not in spirits. It is true that, making spirit a part of Nature, in distinction from the ancients, who separated it, philosophy has been led to this famous conclusion, which sums up nearly all the fruit of its researches: In man spirit knows itself, while everywhere else it seems not to know itself — "That which is awake in man, which dreams in the animal, and sleeps in the stone," said a philosopher.

Philosophy, then, in its last hour, knows no more than at its birth: as if it had appeared in the world only to verify the words of Socrates, it says to us, wrapping itself solemnly around with its funeral pall, "I know only that I know nothing." What do I say? Philosophy knows today that all its judgments rest on two equally false, equally impossible, and yet equally necessary and inevitable hypotheses, — matter and spirit. So that, while in former times religious intolerance and philosophic disputes, spreading darkness everywhere, excused doubt and tempted to libidinous indifference, the triumph of negation on all points no longer permits even this doubt; thought, freed from every barrier, but conquered by its own successes, is forced to affirm what seems to it clearly contradictory and absurd. The savages say that the world is a great fetich watched over by a great manitou. For thirty centuries the poets, legislators, and sages of civilization, handing down from age to age the philosophic lamp, have written nothing more sublime than this profession of faith. And here, at the end of this long conspiracy against God, which has called itself philosophy, emancipated reason concludes with savage reason, The universe is a not-me, objectified by a me.

Humanity, then, inevitably supposes the existence of God: and if, during the long period which closes with our time, it has believed in the reality of its hypothesis; if it has worshipped the inconceivable object; if, after being apprehended in this act of faith, it persists knowingly, but no longer voluntarily, in this opinion of a sovereign being which it knows to be only a personification of its own thought; if it is on the

37

point of again beginning its magic invocations, — we must believe that so astonishing an hallucination conceals some mystery, which deserves to be fathomed.

I say hallucination and mystery, but without intending to deny thereby the superhuman content of the God-idea, and without admitting the necessity of a new symbolism, — I mean a new religion. For if it is indisputable that humanity, in affirming God, — or all that is included in the word me or spirit, — only affirms itself, it is equally undeniable that it affirms itself as something other than its own conception of itself, as all mythologies and theologies show. And since, moreover, this affirmation is incontestable, it depends, without doubt, upon hidden relations, which ought, if possible, to be determined scientifically.

In other words, atheism, sometimes called humanism, true in its critical and negative features, would be, if it stopped at man in his natural condition, if it discarded as an erroneous judgment the first affirmation of humanity, that it is the daughter, emanation, image, reflection, or voice of God, -humanism, I say, if it thus denied its past, would be but one contradiction more. We are forced, then, to undertake the criticism of humanism; that is, to ascertain whether humanity, considered as a whole and throughout all its periods of development, satisfies the Divine idea, after eliminating from the latter the exaggerated and fanciful attributes of God; whether it satisfies the perfection of being; whether it satisfies itself. We are forced, in short, to inquire whether humanity tends toward God, according to the ancient dogma, or is itself becoming God, as modern philosophers claim. Perhaps we shall find in the end that the two systems, despite their seeming opposition, are both true and essentially identical: in that case, the infallibility of human reason, in its collective manifestations as well as its studied speculations, would be decisively confirmed. — In a word, until we have verified to man the hypothesis of God, there is nothing definitive in the atheistic negation.

It is, then, a scientific, that is, an empirical demonstration of the idea of God, that we need: now, such a demonstration has never been attempted. Theology dogmatizing on the authority of its myths, philosophy speculating by the aid of categories, God has existed as a transcendental conception, incognizable by the reason, and the hypothesis always subsists.

It subsists, I say, this hypothesis, more tenacious, more pitiless than ever. We have reached one of those prophetic epochs when society, scornful of the past and doubtful of the future, now distractedly clings to the present, leaving a few solitary thinkers to establish the new faith; now cries to God from the depths of its enjoyments and asks for a sign of salvation, or seeks in the spectacle of its revolutions, as in the entrails of a victim, the secret of its destiny.

Why need I insist further? The hypothesis of God is allowable, for it forces itself upon every man in spite of himself: no one, then, can take exception to it. He who believes can do no less than grant me the supposition that God exists; he who denies is forced to grant it to me also, since he entertained it before me, every negation implying a previous affirmation; as for him who is in doubt, he needs but to reflect a moment to understand that his doubt necessarily supposes an unknown something, which, sooner or later, he will call God.

But if I possess, through the fact of my thought, the right to suppose God, I must abandon the right to affirm him. In other words, if my hypothesis is irresistible, that, for the present, is all that I can pretend. For to affirm is to determine; now, every determination, to be true, must be reached empirically. In fact, whoever says determination, says relation, conditionality, experience. Since, then, the determination of the idea of God must result from an empirical demonstration, we must abstain from everything which, in the search for this great unknown, not being established by experience, goes beyond the hypothesis, under penalty of relapsing into the contradictions of theology, and consequently arousing anew atheistic dissent.

III.

It remains for me to tell why, in a work on political economy, I have felt it necessary to start with the fundamental hypothesis of all philosophy.

And first, I need the hypothesis of God to establish the authority of social science. — When the astronomer, to explain the system of the world, judging solely from appearance, supposes, with the vulgar, the sky arched, the earth flat, the sun much like a football, describing a curve in the air from east to west, he supposes the infallibility of the senses, reserving the right to rectify subsequently, after further observation, the data with which he is obliged to start. Astronomic philosophy, in fact, could not admit a priori that the senses deceive us, and that we do not see what we do see: admitting such a principle, what would become of the certainty of astronomy? But the evidence of the senses being able, in certain cases, to rectify and complete itself, the authority of the senses remains unshaken, and astronomy is possible.

So social philosophy does not admit a priori that humanity can err or be deceived in its actions: if it should, what would become of the authority of the human race, that is, the authority of reason, synonymous at bottom with the sovereignty of the people? But it thinks that human judgments, always true at the time they are pronounced, can successively complete and throw light on each other, in proportion to the acquisition of ideas, in such a way as to maintain continual harmony between universal reason and individual speculation, and indefinitely extend the sphere of certainty: which is always an affirmation of the authority of human judgments.

Now, the first judgment of the reason, the preamble of every political constitution seeking a sanction and a principle, is necessarily this: There is a God; which means that society is governed with design, premeditation, intelligence. This judgment, which excludes chance, is, then, the foundation of the possibility of a social science; and every historical and positive study of social facts, undertaken with a view to amelioration and progress, must suppose, with the people, the existence of God, reserving the right to account for this judgment at a later period.

Thus the history of society is to us but a long determination of the idea of God, a progressive revelation of the destiny of man. And while ancient wisdom made all depend on the arbitrary and fanciful notion of Divinity, oppressing reason and conscience, and arresting progress through fear of an invisible master, the new philosophy, reversing the method, trampling on the authority of God as well as that of man, and accepting no other yoke than that of fact and evidence, makes all converge toward the theological hypothesis, as toward the last of its problems.

Humanitarian atheism is, therefore, the last step in the moral and intellectual enfranchisement of man, consequently the last phase of philosophy, serving as a pathway to the scientific reconstruction and verification of all the demolished dogmas.

I need the hypothesis of God, not only, as I have just said, to give a meaning to history, but also to legitimate the reforms to be effected, in the name of science, in the State.

Whether we consider Divinity as outside of society, whose movements it governs from on high (a wholly gratuitous and probably illusory opinion); or whether we deem it immanent in society and identical with that impersonal and unconscious reason which, acting instinctively, makes civilization advance (although impersonality and ignorance of self are contrary to the idea of intelligence); or whether, finally, all that is accomplished in society results from the relation of its elements (a system whose whole merit consists in changing an active into a passive, in making intelligence necessity, or, which amounts to the same thing, in taking law for cause), — it always follows that the manifestations of social activity, necessarily appearing to us either as indications of the will of the Supreme Being, or as a sort of language typical of general and impersonal reason, or, finally, as landmarks of necessity, are absolute authority for us. Being connected in time as well as in spirit, the facts accomplished determine and legitimate the facts to be accomplished; science and destiny are in accord; everything which happens resulting from reason, and, reciprocally, reason judging only from experience of that which happens, science has a right to participate in government, and that which establishes its competency as a counsellor justifies its intervention as a sovereign.

Science, expressed, recognized, and accepted by the voice of all as divine, is queen of the world. Thus, thanks to the hypothesis of God, all conservative or retrogressive opposition, every dilatory plea offered by theology, tradition, or selfishness, finds itself peremptorily and irrevocably set aside.

I need the hypothesis of God to show the tie which unites civilization with Nature.

In fact, this astonishing hypothesis, by which man is assimilated to the absolute, implying identity of the laws of Nature and the laws of reason, enables us to see in human industry the complement of creative action, unites man with the globe which he inhabits, and, in the cultivation of the domain in which Providence has placed us, which thus becomes in part our work, gives us a conception of the principle and end of all things. If, then, humanity is not God, it is a continuation of God; or, if a different phraseology be preferred, that which humanity does today by design is the same thing that it began by instinct, and which Nature seems to accomplish by necessity. In all these cases, and whichever opinion we may choose, one thing remains certain: the unity of action and law. Intelligent beings, actors in an intelligently-devised fable, we may fearlessly reason from ourselves to the universe and the eternal; and, when we shall have completed the organization of labor, may say with pride, The creation is explained.

Thus philosophy's field of exploration is fixed; tradition is the starting-point of all speculation as to the future; utopia is forever exploded; the

41

study of the me, transferred from the individual conscience to the manifestations of the social will, acquires the character of objectivity of which it has been hitherto deprived; and, history becoming psychology, theology anthropology, the natural sciences metaphysics, the theory of the reason is deduced no longer from the vacuum of the intellect, but from the innumerable forms of a Nature abundantly and directly observable.

I need the hypothesis of God to prove my good-will towards a multitude of sects, whose opinions I do not share, but whose malice I fear: — theists; I know one who, in the cause of God, would be ready to draw sword, and, like Robespierre, use the guillotine until the last atheist should be destroyed, not dreaming that that atheist would be himself; — mystics, whose party, largely made up of students and women marching under the banner of MM. Lamennais, Quinet, Leroux, and others, has taken for a motto, "Like master, like man;" like God, like people; and, to regulate the wages of the workingman, begins by restoring religion; — spiritualists, who, should I overlook the rights of spirit, would accuse me of establishing the worship of matter, against which I protest with all the strength of my soul; — sensualists and materialists, to whom the divine dogma is the symbol of constraint and the principle of enslavement of the passions, outside of which, they say, there is for man neither pleasure, nor virtue, nor genius; — eclectics and sceptics, sellers and publishers of all the old philosophies, but not philosophers themselves, united in one vast brotherhood, with approbation and privilege, against whoever thinks, believes, or affirms without their permission; -conservatives finally, retrogressives, egotists, and hypocrites, preaching the love of God by hatred of their neighbor, attributing to liberty the world's misfortunes since the deluge, and scandalizing reason by their foolishness.

Is it possible, however, that they will attack an hypothesis which, far from blaspheming the revered phantoms of faith, aspires only to exhibit them in broad daylight; which, instead of rejecting traditional dogmas and the prejudices of conscience, asks only to verify them; which, while defending itself against exclusive opinions, takes for an axiom the infallibility of reason, and, thanks to this fruitful principle, will doubtless never decide against any of the antagonistic sects? Is it possible that the religious and political conservatives will charge me with disturbing the order of society, when I start with the hypothesis of a sovereign intelligence, the source of every thought of order; that the semi-Christian democrats will curse me as an enemy of God, and consequently a traitor to the republic, when I am seeking for the meaning and content of the idea of God; and that the tradesmen of the

42

university will impute to me the impiety of demonstrating the non-value of their philosophical products, when I am especially maintaining that philosophy should be studied in its object, — that is, in the manifestations of society and Nature?....

I need the hypothesis of God to justify my style.

In my ignorance of everything regarding God, the world, the soul, and destiny; forced to proceed like the materialist, — that is, by observation and experience, — and to conclude in the language of the believer, because there is no other; not knowing whether my formulas, theological in spite of me, would be taken literally or figuratively; in this perpetual contemplation of God, man, and things, obliged to submit to the synonymy of all the terms included in the three categories of thought, speech, and action, but wishing to affirm nothing on either one side or the other, — rigorous logic demanded that I should suppose, no more, no less, this unknown that is called God. We are full of Divinity, Jovis omnia plena; our monuments, our traditions, our laws, our ideas, our languages, and our sciences, all are infected by this indelible superstition outside of which we can neither speak nor act, and without which we do not even think.

Finally, I need the hypothesis of God to explain the publication of these new memoirs.

Our society feels itself big with events, and is anxious about the future: how account for these vague presentiments by the sole aid of a universal reason, immanent if you will, and permanent, but impersonal, and therefore dumb, or by the idea of necessity, if it implies that necessity is self-conscious, and consequently has presentiments? There remains then, once more, an agent or nightmare which weighs upon society, and gives it visions.

Now, when society prophesies, it puts questions in the mouths of some, and answers in the mouths of others. And wise, then, he who can listen and understand; for God himself has spoken, quia locutus est Deus.

The Academy of Moral and Political Sciences has proposed the following question: —

"To determine the general facts which govern the relations of profits to wages, and to explain their respective oscillations."

A few years ago the same Academy asked, "What are the causes of misery?" The nineteenth century has, in fact, but one idea, — equality and reform. But the wind bloweth where it listeth: many began to reflect upon the question, no one answered it. The college of aruspices has, therefore, renewed its question, but in more significant terms. It wishes to know whether order prevails in the workshop; whether wages are equitable; whether liberty and privilege compensate each other justly; whether the idea of value, which controls all the facts of exchange, is, in the forms in which the economists have represented it, sufficiently exact; whether credit protects labor; whether circulation is regular; whether the burdens of society weigh equally on all, etc.

And, indeed, insufficiency of income being the immediate cause of misery, it is fitting that we should know why, misfortune and malevolence aside, the workingman's income is insufficient. It is still the same question of inequality of fortunes, which has made such a stir for a century past, and which, by a strange fatality, continually reappears in academic programmes, as if there lay the real difficulty of modern times.

Equality, then, — its principle, its means, its obstacles, its theory, the motives of its postponement, the cause of social and providential iniquities, — these the world has got to learn, in spite of the sneers of incredulity.

I know well that the views of the Academy are not thus profound, and that it equals a council of the Church in its horror of novelties; but the more it turns towards the past, the more it reflects the future, and the more, consequently, must we believe in its inspiration: for the true prophets are those who do not understand their utterances. Listen further.

"What," the Academy has asked, "are the most useful applications of the principle of voluntary and private association that we can make for the alleviation of misery?"

And again: —

"To expound the theory and principles of the contract of insurance, to give its history, and to deduce from its rationale and the facts the developments of which this contract is capable, and the various useful applications possible in the present state of commercial and industrial progress."

44

Publicists admit that insurance, a rudimentary form of commercial solidarity, is an association in things, *societas in re*; that is, a society whose conditions, founded on purely economical relations, escape man's arbitrary dictation. So that a philosophy of insurance or mutual guarantee of security, which shall be deduced from the general theory of real (*in re*) societies, will contain the formula of universal association, in which no member of the Academy believes. And when, uniting subject and object in the same point of view, the Academy demands, by the side of a theory of association of interests, a theory of voluntary association, it reveals to us the most perfect form of society, and thereby affirms all that is most at variance with its convictions. Liberty, equality, solidarity, association! By what inconceivable blunder has so eminently conservative a body offered to the citizens this new programme of the rights of man? It was in this way that Caiaphas prophesied redemption by disowning Jesus Christ.

Upon the first of these questions, forty-five memoirs were addressed to the Academy within two years, — a proof that the subject was marvellously well suited to the state of the public mind. But among so many competitors no one having been deemed worthy of the prize, the Academy has withdrawn the question; alleging as a reason the incapacity of the competitors, but in reality because, the failure of the contest being the sole object that the Academy had in view, it behooved it to declare, without further delay, that the hopes of the friends of association were groundless.

Thus, then, the gentlemen of the Academy disavow, in their session-chamber, their announcements from the tripod! There is nothing in such a contradiction astonishing to me; and may God preserve me from calling it a crime! The ancients believed that revolutions announced their advent by dreadful signs, and that among other prodigies animals spoke. This was a figure, descriptive of those unexpected ideas and strange words which circulate suddenly among the masses at critical moments, and which seem to be entirely without human antecedent, so far removed are they from the sphere of ordinary judgment. At the time in which we live, such a thing could not fail to occur. After having, by a prophetic instinct and a mechanical spontaneity, *pecudesque locutae*, proclaimed association, the gentlemen of the Academy of Moral and Political Sciences have returned to their ordinary prudence; and with them custom has conquered inspiration. Let us learn, then, how to distinguish heavenly counsel from the interested judgments of men, and hold it for certain that, in the discourse of sages, that is the most trustworthy to which they have given the least reflection.

Nevertheless the Academy, in breaking so rudely with its intuitions, seems to have felt some remorse. In place of a theory of association in which, after reflection, it no longer believes, it asks for a "Critical examination of Pestalozzi's system of instruction and education, considered mainly in its relation to the well-being and morality of the poor classes." Who knows? perchance the relation between profits and wages, association, the organization of labor indeed, are to be found at the bottom of a system of instruction. Is not man's life a perpetual apprenticeship? Are not philosophy and religion humanity's education? To organize instruction, then, would be to organize industry and fix the theory of society: the Academy, in its lucid moments, always returns to that.

"What influence," the Academy again asks, "do progress and a desire for material comfort have upon a nation's morality?"

Taken in its most obvious sense, this new question of the Academy is commonplace, and fit at best to exercise a rhetorisian's skill. But the Academy, which must continue till the end in its ignorance of the revolutionary significance of its oracles, has drawn aside the curtain in its commentary. What, then, so profound has it discovered in this Epicurean thesis?

"The desire for luxury and its enjoyments," it tells us; "the singular love of it felt by the majority; the tendency of hearts and minds to occupy themselves with it exclusively; the agreement of individuals AND THE STATE in making it the motive and the end of all their projects, all their efforts, and all their sacrifices, — engender general or individual feelings which, beneficent or injurious, become principles of action more potent, perhaps, than any which have heretofore governed men."

Never had moralists a more favorable opportunity to assail the sensualism of the century, the venality of consciences, and the corruption instituted by the government: instead of that, what does the Academy of Moral Sciences do? With the most automatic calmness, it establishes a series in which luxury, so long proscribed by the stoics and ascetics, — those masters of holiness, — must appear in its turn as a principle of conduct as legitimate, as pure, and as grand as all those formerly invoked by religion and philosophy. Determine, it tells us, the motives of action (undoubtedly now old and worn-out) of which LUXURY is historically the providential successor, and, from the results of the former, calculate the effects of the latter. Prove, in short,

46

that Aristippus was only in advance of his century, and that his system of morality must have its day, as well as that of Zeno and A Kempis.

We are dealing, then, with a society which no longer wishes to be poor; which mocks at everything that was once dear and sacred to it, — liberty, religion, and glory, — so long as it has not wealth; which, to obtain it, submits to all outrages, and becomes an accomplice in all sorts of cowardly actions: and this burning thirst for pleasure, this irresistible desire to arrive at luxury, — a symptom of a new period in civilization, — is the supreme commandment by virtue of which we are to labor for the abolition of poverty: thus saith the Academy. What becomes, then, of the doctrine of expiation and abstinence, the morality of sacrifice, resignation, and happy moderation? What distrust of the compensation promised in the other life, and what a contradiction of the Gospel! But, above all, what a justification of a government which has adopted as its system the golden key! Why have religious men, Christians, Senecas, given utterance in concert to so many immoral maxims?

The Academy, completing its thought, will reply to us: —

"Show how the progress of criminal justice, in the prosecution and punishment of attacks upon persons and property, follows and marks the ages of civilization from the savage condition up to that of the best-governed nations."

Is it possible that the criminal lawyers in the Academy of Moral Sciences foresaw the conclusion of their premises? The fact whose history is now to be studied, and which the Academy describes by the words "progress of criminal justice," is simply the gradual mitigation which manifests itself, both in the forms of criminal examinations and in the penalties inflicted, in proportion as civilization increases in liberty, light, and wealth. So that, the principle of repressive institutions being the direct opposite of all those on which the welfare of society depends, there is a constant elimination of all parts of the penal system as well as all judicial paraphernalia, and the final inference from this movement is that the guarantee of order lies neither in fear nor punishment; consequently, neither in hell nor religion.

What a subversion of received ideas! What a denial of all that it is the business of the Academy of Moral Sciences to defend! But, if the guarantee of order no longer lies in the fear of a punishment to be suffered, either in this life or in another, where then are to be found the guarantees protective of persons and property? Or rather, without repressive institutions, what becomes of property? And without property, what becomes of the family?

The Academy, which knows nothing of all these things, replies without agitation: —

"Review the various phases of the organization of the family upon the soil of France from ancient times down to our day."

Which means: Determine, by the previous progress of family organization, the conditions of the existence of the family in a state of equality of fortunes, voluntary and free association, universal solidarity, material comfort and luxury, and public order without prisons, courts, police, or hangmen.

There will be astonishment, perhaps, at finding that the Academy of Moral and Political Sciences, after having, like the boldest innovators, called in question all the principles of social order, — religion, family, property, justice, — has not also proposed this problem: What is the best form of government? In fact, government is for society the source of all initiative, every guarantee, every reform. It would be, then, interesting to know whether the government, as constituted by the Charter, is adequate to the practical solution of the Academy's questions.

But it would be a misconception of the oracles to imagine that they proceed by induction and analysis; and precisely because the political problem was a condition or corollary of the demonstrations asked for, the Academy could not offer it for competition. Such a conclusion would have opened its eyes, and, without waiting for the memoirs of the competitors, it would have hastened to suppress its entire programme. The Academy has approached the question from above. It has said: —

The works of God are beautiful in their own essence, justificata in semet ipsa; they are true, in a word, because they are his. The thoughts of man resemble dense vapors pierced by long and narrow flashes. What, then, is the truth in relation to us, and what is the character of certainty?

As if the Academy had said to us: You shall verify the hypothesis of your existence, the hypothesis of the Academy which interrogates you, the hypotheses of time, space, motion, thought, and the laws of thought.

48

Then you may verify the hypothesis of pauperism, the hypothesis of inequality of conditions, the hypothesis of universal association, the hypothesis of happiness, the hypotheses of monarchy and republicanism, the hypothesis of Providence!....

A complete criticism of God and humanity.

I point to the programme of the honorable society: it is not I who have fixed the conditions of my task, it is the Academy of Moral and Political Sciences. Now, how can I satisfy these conditions, if I am not myself endowed with infallibility; in a word, if I am not God or divine? The Academy admits, then, that divinity and humanity are identical, or at least correlative; but the question now is in what consists this correlation: such is the meaning of the problem of certainty, such is the object of social philosophy.

Thus, then, in the name of the society that God inspires, an Academy questions.

In the name of the same society, I am one of the prophets who attempt to answer. The task is an immense one, and I do not promise to accomplish it: I will go as far as God shall give me strength. But, whatever I may say, it does not come from me: the thought which inspires my pen is not personal, and nothing that I write can be attributed to me. I shall give the facts as I have seen them; I shall judge them by what I shall have said; I shall call everything by its strongest name, and no one will take offence. I shall inquire freely, and by the rules of divination which I have learned, into the meaning of the divine purpose which is now expressing itself through the eloquent lips of sages and the inarticulate wailings of the people: and, though I should deny all the prerogatives guaranteed by our Constitution, I shall not be factious. I shall point my finger whither an invisible influence is pushing us; and neither my action nor my words shall be irritating. I shall stir up the cloud, and, though I should cause it to launch the thunderbolt, I should be innocent. In this solemn investigation to which the Academy invites me, I have more than the right to tell the truth, — I have the right to say what I think: may my thought, my words, and the truth be but one and the same thing!

And you, reader, — for without a reader there is no writer, — you are half of my work. Without you, I am only sounding brass; with the aid of your attention, I will speak marvels. Do you see this passing whirlwind called SOCIETY, from which burst forth, with startling brilliancy, lightnings, thunders, and voices? I wish to cause you to place your finger on the hidden springs which move it; but to that end you must reduce yourself at my command to a state of pure intelligence. The eyes of love and pleasure are powerless to recognize beauty in a skeleton, harmony in naked viscera, life in dark and coagulated blood: consequently the secrets of the social organism are a sealed letter to the man whose brain is beclouded by passion and prejudice. Such sublimities are unattainable except by cold and silent contemplation. Suffer me, then, before revealing to your eyes the leaves of the book of life, to prepare your soul by this sceptical purification which the great teachers of the people — Socrates, Jesus Christ, St. Paul, St. Remi, Bacon, Descartes, Galileo, Kant, etc. — have always claimed of their disciples.

Whoever you may be, clad in the rags of misery or decked in the sumptuous vestments of luxury, I restore you to that state of luminous nudity which neither the fumes of wealth nor the poisons of envious poverty dim. How persuade the rich that the difference of conditions arises from an error in the accounts; and how can the poor, in their beggary, conceive that the proprietor possesses in good faith? To investigate the sufferings of the laborer is to the idler the most intolerable of amusements; just as to do justice to the fortunate is to the miserable the bitterest of draughts.

You occupy a high position: I strip you of it; there you are, free. There is too much optimism beneath this official costume, too much subordination, too much idleness. Science demands an insurrection of thought: now, the thought of an official is his salary.

Your mistress, beautiful, passionate, artistic, is, I like to believe, possessed only by you. That is, your soul, your spirit, your conscience, have passed into the most charming object of luxury that nature and art have produced for the eternal torment of fascinated mortals. I separate you from this divine half of yourself: at the present day it is too much to wish for justice and at the same time to love a woman. To think with grandeur and clearness, man must remove the lining of his nature and hold to his masculine hypostasis. Besides, in the state in which I have put you, your lover would no longer know you: remember the wife of Job.

What is your religion?.... Forget your faith, and, through wisdom, become an atheist. — What! you say; an atheist in spite of our hypothesis! — No, but because of our hypothesis. One's thought must have been raised above divine things for a long time to be entitled to suppose a personality beyond man, a life beyond this life. For the rest,

50

have no fears for your salvation. God is not angry with those who are led by reason to deny him, any more than he is anxious for those who are led by faith to worship him; and, in the state of your conscience, the surest course for you is to think nothing about him. Do you not see that it is with religion as with governments, the most perfect of which would be the denial of all? Then let no political or religious fancy hold your soul captive; in this way only can you now keep from being either a dupe or a renegade. Ah! said I in the days of my enthusiastic youth, shall I not hear the tolling for the second vespers of the republic, and our priests, dressed in white tunics, singing after the Doric fashion the returning hymn: Change, ô Dieu, notre servitude, comme le vent du desert en un souffle rafraîchissan!..... But I have despaired of republicans, and no longer know either religion or priests.

I should like also, in order to thoroughly secure your judgment, dear reader, to render your soul insensible to pity, superior to virtue, indifferent to happiness. But that would be too much to expect of a neophyte. Remember only, and never forget, that pity, happiness, and virtue, like country, religion, and love, are masks....

Chapter I. Of the Economic Science.

1. — Opposition between FACT and RIGHT in social economy.

I AFFIRM the REALITY of an economic science.

This proposition, which few economists now dare to question, is the boldest, perhaps, that a philosopher ever maintained; and the inquiries to follow will prove, I hope, that its demonstration will one day be deemed the greatest effort of the human mind.

I affirm, on the other hand, the absolute certainty as well as the progressive nature of economic science, of all the sciences in my opinion the most comprehensive, the purest, the best supported by facts: a new proposition, which alters this science into logic or metaphysics in concreto, and radically changes the basis of ancient philosophy. In other words, economic science is to me the objective form and realization of metaphysics; it is metaphysics in action, metaphysics projected on the vanishing plane of time; and whoever studies the laws of labor and exchange is truly and specially a metaphysician.

51

After what I have said in the introduction, there is nothing in this which should surprise any one. The labor of man continues the work of God, who, in creating all beings, did but externally realize the eternal laws of reason. Economic science is, then, necessarily and at once a theory of ideas, a natural theology, and a psychology. This general outline alone would have sufficed to explain why, having to treat of economic matters, I was obliged previously to suppose the existence of God, and by what title I, a simple economist, aspire to solve the problem of certainty.

But I hasten to say that I do not regard as a science the incoherent ensemble of theories to which the name political economy has been officially given for almost a hundred years, and which, in spite of the etymology of the name, is after ail but the code, or immemorial routine, of property. These theories offer us only the rudiments, or first section, of economic science; and that is why, like property, they are all contradictory of each other, and half the time inapplicable. The proof of this assertion, which is, in one sense, a denial of political economy as handed down to us by Adam Smith, Ricardo, Malthus, and J. B. Say, and as we have known it for half a century, will be especially developed in this treatise.

The inadequacy of political economy has at all times impressed thoughtful minds, who, too fond of their dreams for practical investigation, and confining themselves to the estimation of apparent results, have constituted from the beginning a party of opposition to the statu quo, and have devoted themselves to persevering, and systematic ridicule of civilization and its customs. Property, on the other hand, the basis of all social institutions, has never lacked zealous defenders, who, proud to be called practical, have exchanged blow for blow with the traducers of political economy, and have labored with a courageous and often skilful hand to strengthen the edifice which general prejudice and individual liberty have erected in concert. The controversy between conservatives and reformers, still pending, finds its counterpart, in the history of philosophy, in the quarrel between realists and nominalists; it is almost useless to add that, on both sides, right and wrong are equal, and that the rivalry, narrowness, and intolerance of opinions have been the sole cause of the misunderstanding.

Thus two powers are contending for the government of the world, and cursing each other with the fervor of two hostile religions: political economy, or tradition; and socialism, or utopia.

What is, then, in more explicit terms, political economy? What is socialism?

Political economy is a collection of the observations thus far made in regard to the phenomena of the production and distribution of wealth; that is, in regard to the most common, most spontaneous, and therefore most genuine, forms of labor and exchange.

The economists have classified these observations as far as they were able; they have described the phenomena, and ascertained their contingencies and relations; they have observed in them, in many cases, a quality of necessity which has given them the name of laws; and this ensemble of information, gathered from the simplest manifestations of society, constitutes political economy.

Political economy is, therefore, the natural history of the most apparent and most universally accredited customs, traditions, practices, and methods of humanity in all that concerns the production and distribution of wealth. By this title, political economy considers itself legitimate in fact and in right: in fact, because the phenomena which it studies are constant, spontaneous, and universal; in right, because these phenomena rest on the authority of the human race, the strongest authority possible. Consequently, political economy calls itself a science; that is, a rational and systematic knowledge of regular and necessary facts.

Socialism, which, like the god Vishnu, ever dying and ever returning to life, has experienced within a score of years its ten-thousandth incarnation in the persons of five or six revelators, — socialism affirms the irregularity of the present constitution of society, and, consequently, of all its previous forms. It asserts, and proves, that the order of civilization is artificial, contradictory, inadequate; that it engenders oppression, misery, and crime; it denounces, not to say calumniates, the whole past of social life, and pushes on with all its might to a reformation of morals and institutions.

Socialism concludes by declaring political economy a false and sophistical hypothesis, devised to enable the few to exploit the many; and applying the maxim A fructibus cognoscetis, it ends with a demonstration of the impotence and emptiness of political economy by the list of human calamities for which it makes it responsible.

But if political economy is false, jurisprudence, which in all countries is the science of law and custom, is false also; since, founded on the

53

distinction of thine and mine, it supposes the legitimacy of the facts described and classified by political economy. The theories of public and international law, with all the varieties of representative government, are also false, since they rest on the principle of individual appropriation and the absolute sovereignty of wills.

All these consequences socialism accepts. To it, political economy, regarded by many as the physiology of wealth, is but the organization of robbery and poverty; just as jurisprudence, honored by legists with the name of written reason, is, in its eyes, but a compilation of the rubrics of legal and official spoliation, — in a word, of property. Considered in their relations, these two pretended sciences, political economy and law, form, in the opinion of socialism, the complete theory of iniquity and discord. Passing then from negation to affirmation, socialism opposes the principle of property with that of association, and makes vigorous efforts to reconstruct social economy from top to bottom; that is, to establish a new code, a new political system, with institutions and morals diametrically opposed to the ancient forms.

Thus the line of demarcation between socialism and political economy is fixed, and the hostility flagrant.

Political economy tends toward the glorification of selfishness; socialism favors the exaltation of communism.

The economists, saving a few violations of their principles, for which they deem it their duty to blame governments, are optimists with regard to accomplished facts; the socialists, with regard to facts to be accomplished.

The first affirm that that which ought to be is; the second, that that which ought to be is not. Consequently, while the first are defenders of religion, authority, and the other principles contemporary with, and conservative of, property, — although their criticism, based solely on reason, deals frequent blows at their own prejudices, — the second reject authority and faith, and appeal exclusively to science, — although a certain religiosity, utterly illiberal, and an unscientific disdain for facts, are always the most obvious characteristics of their doctrines.

For the rest, neither party ever ceases to accuse the other of incapacity and sterility.

The socialists ask their opponents to account for the inequality of conditions, for those commercial debaucheries in which monopoly and competition, in monstrous union, perpetually give birth to luxury and misery; they reproach economic theories, always modeled after the past, with leaving the future hopeless; in short, they point to the regime of property as a horrible hallucination, against which humanity has protested and struggled for four thousand years.

The economists, on their side, defy socialists to produce a system in which property, competition, and political organization can be dispensed with; they prove, with documents in hand, that all reformatory projects have ever been nothing but rhapsodies of fragments borrowed from the very system that socialism sneers at, — plagiarisms, in a word, of political economy, outside of which socialism is incapable of conceiving and formulating an idea.

Every day sees the proofs in this grave suit accumulating, and the question becoming confused.

While society has traveled and stumbled, suffered and thrived, in pursuing the economic routine, the socialists, since Pythagoras, Orpheus, and the unfathomable Hermes, have labored to establish their dogma in opposition to political economy. A few attempts at association in accordance with their views have even been made here and there: but as yet these exceptional undertakings, lost in the ocean of property, have been without result; and, as if destiny had resolved to exhaust the economic hypothesis before attacking the socialistic utopia, the reformatory party is obliged to content itself with pocketing the sarcasms of its adversaries while waiting for its own turn to come.

This, then, is the state of the cause: socialism incessantly denounces the crimes of civilization, verifies daily the powerlessness of political economy to satisfy the harmonic attractions of man, and presents petition after petition; political economy fills its brief with socialistic systems, all of which, one after another, pass away and die, despised by common sense. The persistence of evil nourishes the complaint of the one, while the constant succession of reformatory checks feeds the malicious irony of the other. When will judgment be given? The tribunal is deserted; meanwhile, political economy improves its opportunities, and, without furnishing bail, continues to lord it over the world; possideo quia possideo.

If we descend from the sphere of ideas to the realities of the world, the antagonism will appear still more grave and threatening.

When, in these recent years, socialism, instigated by prolonged convulsions, made its fantastic appearance in our midst, men whom all controversy had found until then indifferent and lukewarm went back in fright to monarchical and religious ideas; democracy, which was charged with being developed at last to its ultimate, was cursed and driven back. This accusation of the conservatives against the democrats was a libel. Democracy is by nature as hostile to the socialistic idea as incapable of filling the place of royalty, against which it is its destiny endlessly to conspire. This soon became evident, and we are witnesses of it daily in the professions of Christian and proprietary faith by democratic publicists, whose abandonment by the people began at that moment.

On the other hand, philosophy proves no less distinct from socialism, no less hostile to it, than politics and religion.

For just as in politics the principle of democracy is the sovereignty of numbers, and that of monarchy the sovereignty of the prince; just as likewise in affairs of conscience religion is nothing but submission to a mystical being, called God, and to the priests who represent him; just as finally in the economic world property — that is, exclusive control by the individual of the instruments of labor — is the point of departure of every theory, — so philosophy, in basing itself upon the a priori assumptions of reason, is inevitably led to attribute to the me alone the generation and autocracy of ideas, and to deny the metaphysical value of experience; that is, universally to substitute, for the objective law, absolutism, despotism.

Now, a doctrine which, springing up suddenly in the heart of society, without antecedents and without ancestors, rejected from every department of conscience and society the arbitrary principle, in order to substitute as sole truth the relation of facts; which broke with tradition, and consented to make use of the past only as a point from which to launch forth into the future, — such a doctrine could not fail to stir up against it the established AUTHORITIES; and we can see today how, in spite of their internal discords, the said AUTHORITIES, which are but one, combine to fight the monster that is ready to swallow them.

To the workingmen who complain of the insufficiency of wages and the uncertainty of labor, political economy opposes the liberty of commerce; to the citizens who are seeking for the conditions of liberty and order, the ideologists respond with representative systems; to the tender souls who, having lost their ancient faith, ask the reason and end of their existence, religion proposes the unfathomable secrets of

56

Providence, and philosophy holds doubt in reserve. Subterfuges always; complete ideas, in which heart and mind find rest, never! Socialism cries that it is time to set sail for the mainland, and to enter port: but, say the antisocialists, there is no port; humanity sails onward in God's care, under the command of priests, philosophers, orators, economists, and our circumnavigation is eternal.

Thus society finds itself, at its origin, divided into two great parties: the one traditional and essentially hierarchical, which, according to the object it is considering, calls itself by turns royalty or democracy, philosophy or religion, in short, property; the other socialism, which, coming to life at every crisis of civilization, proclaims itself preeminently anarchical and atheistic; that is, rebellious against all authority, human and divine.

Now, modern civilization has demonstrated that in a conflict of this nature the truth is found, not in the exclusion of one of the opposites, but wholly and solely in the reconciliation of the two; it is, I say, a fact of science that every antagonism, whether in Nature or in ideas, is resolvable in a more general fact or in a complex formula, which harmonizes the opposing factors by absorbing them, so to speak, in each other. Can we not, then, men of common sense, while awaiting the solution which the future will undoubtedly bring forth, prepare ourselves for this great transition by an analysis of the struggling powers, as well as their positive and negative qualities? Such a work, performed with accuracy and conscientiousness, even though it should not lead us directly to the solution, would have at least the inestimable advantage of revealing to us the conditions of the problem, and thereby putting us on our guard against every form of utopia.

What is there, then, in political economy that is necessary and true; whither does it tend; what are its powers; what are its wishes? It is this which I propose to determine in this work. What is the value of socialism? The same investigation will answer this question also.

For since, after all, socialism and political economy pursue the same end, — namely, liberty, order, and well-being among men, — it is evident that the conditions to be fulfilled — in other words, the difficulties to be overcome — to attain this end, are also the same for both, and that it remains only to examine the methods attempted or proposed by either party. But since, moreover, it has been given thus far to political economy alone to translate its ideas into acts, while socialism has scarcely done more than indulge in perpetual satire, it is no less clear that, in judging the works of economy according to their merit, we at the same time shall reduce to its just value the invective of the socialists: so that our criticism, though apparently special, will lead to absolute and definitive conclusions.

This it is necessary to make clearer by a few examples, before entering fully upon the examination of political economy.

2. — Inadequacy of theories and criticisms.

We will record first an important observation: the contending parties agree in acknowledging a common authority, whose support each claims, -SCIENCE.

Plato, a utopian, organized his ideal republic in the name of science, which, through modesty and euphemism, he called philosophy. Aristotle, a practical man, refuted the Platonic utopia in the name of the same philosophy. Thus the social war has continued since Plato and Aristotle. The modern socialists refer all things to science one and indivisible, but without power to agree either as to its content, its limits, or its method; the economists, on their side, affirm that social science in no wise differs from political economy.

It is our first business, then, to ascertain what a science of society must be.

Science, in general, is the logically arranged and systematic knowledge of that which IS.

Applying this idea to society, we will say: Social science is the logically arranged and systematic knowledge, not of that which society has been, nor of that which it will be, but of that which it IS in its whole life; that is, in the sum total of its successive manifestations: for there alone can it have reason and system. Social science must include human order, not alone in such or such a period of duration, nor in a few of its elements; but in all its principles and in the totality of its existence: as if social evolution, spread throughout time and space, should find itself suddenly gathered and fixed in a picture which, exhibiting the series of the ages and the sequence of phenomena, revealed their connection and unity. Such must be the science of every living and progressive reality; such social science indisputably is.

It may be, then, that political economy, in spite of its individualistic tendency and its exclusive affirmations, is a constituent part of social science, in which the phenomena that it describes are like the starting-points of a vast triangulation and the elements of an organic and complex whole. From this point of view, the progress of humanity, proceeding from the simple to the complex, would be entirely in harmony with the progress of science; and the conflicting and so often desolating facts, which are today the basis and object of political economy, would have to be considered by us as so many special hypotheses, successively realized by humanity in view of a superior hypothesis, whose realization would solve all difficulties, and satisfy socialism without destroying political economy. For, as I said in my introduction, in no case can we admit that humanity, however it expresses itself, is mistaken.

Let us now make this clearer by facts.

The question now most disputed is unquestionably that of the organization of labor.

As John the Baptist preached in the desert, Repent ye so the socialists go about proclaiming everywhere this novelty old as the world, Organize labor, though never able to tell what, in their opinion, this organization should be. However that may be, the economists have seen that this socialistic clamor was damaging their theories: it was, indeed, a rebuke to them for ignoring that which they ought first to recognize, — labor. They have replied, therefore, to the attack of their adversaries, first by maintaining that labor is organized, that there is no other organization of labor than liberty to produce and exchange, either on one's own personal account, or in association with others, — in which case the course to be pursued has been prescribed by the civil and commercial codes. Then, as this argument served only to make them the laughing-stock of their antagonists, they assumed the offensive; and, showing that the socialists understood nothing at all themselves of this organization that they held up as a scarecrow, they ended by saying that it was but a new socialistic chimera, a word without sense, — an absurdity. The latest writings of the economists are full of these pitiless conclusions.

Nevertheless, it is certain that the phrase organization of labor contains as clear and rational a meaning as these that follow: organization of the workshop, organization of the army, organization of police, organization of charity, organization of war. In this respect, the argument of the economists is deplorably irrational. No less certain is it that the organization of labor cannot be a utopia and chimera; for at the moment that labor, the supreme condition of civilization, begins to

59

exist, it follows that it is already submitted to an organization, such as it is, which satisfies the economists, but which the socialists think detestable.

There remains, then, relatively to the proposal to organize labor formulated by socialism, this objection, — that labor is organized. Now, this is utterly untenable, since it is notorious that in labor, supply, demand, division, quantity, proportion, price, and security, nothing, absolutely nothing is regulated; on the contrary, everything is given up to the caprices of free-will; that is, to chance.

As for us, guided by the idea that we have formed of social science, we shall affirm, against the socialists and against the economists, not that labor must he organized, nor that it is organized but that it is being organized.

Labor, we say, is being organized: that is, the process of organization has been going on from the beginning of the world, and will continue till the end. Political economy teaches us the primary elements of this organization; but socialism is right in asserting that, in its present form, the organization is inadequate and transitory; and the whole mission of science is continually to ascertain, in view of the results obtained and the phenomena in course of development, what innovations can be immediately effected.

Socialism and political economy, then, while waging a burlesque war, pursue in reality the same idea, — the organization of labor.

But both are guilty of disloyalty to science and of mutual calumny, when on the one hand political economy, mistaking for science its scraps of theory, denies the possibility of further progress; and when socialism, abandoning tradition, aims at reestablishing society on undiscoverable bases.

Thus socialism is nothing but a profound criticism and continual development of political economy; and, to apply here the celebrated aphorism of the school, Nihil est in intellectu, quod non prius fuerit in sensu, there is nothing in the socialistic hypotheses which is not duplicated in economic practice. On the other hand, political economy is but an impertinent rhapsody, so long as it affirms as absolutely valid the facts collected by Adam Smith and J. B. Say.

Another question, no less disputed than the preceding one, is that of usury, or lending at interest.

Usury, or in other words the price of use, is the emolument, of whatever nature, which the proprietor derives from the loan of his property. Quidquid sorti accrescit usura est, say the theologians. Usury, the foundation of credit, was one of the first of the means which social spontaneity employed in its work of organization, and whose analysis discloses the profound laws of civilization. The ancient philosophers and the Fathers of the Church, who must be regarded here as the representatives of socialism in the early centuries of the Christian era, by a singular fallacy, — which arose however from the paucity of economic knowledge in their day, — allowed farm-rent and condemned interest on money, because, as they believed, money was unproductive. They distinguished consequently between the loan of things which are consumed by use — among which they included money — and the loan of things which, without being consumed, yield a product to the user.

The economists had no difficulty in showing, by generalizing the idea of rent, that in the economy of society the action of capital, or its productivity, was the same whether it was consumed in wages or retained the character of an instrument; that, consequently, it was necessary either to prohibit the rent of land or to allow interest on money, since both were by the same title payment for privilege, indemnity for loan. It required more than fifteen centuries to get this idea accepted, and to reassure the consciences that had been terrified by the anathemas pronounced by Catholicism against usury. But finally the weight of evidence and the general desire favored the usurers: they won the battle against socialism; and from this legitimation of usury society gained some immense and unquestionable advantages. Under these circumstances socialism, which had tried to generalize the law enacted by Moses for the Israelites alone, Non foeneraberis proximo tuo, sed alieno, was beaten by an idea which it had accepted from the economic routine, — namely, farm-rent, — elevated into the theory of the productivity of capital.

But the economists in their turn were less fortunate, when they were afterwards called upon to justify farm-rent in itself, and to establish this theory of the product of capital. It may be said that, on this point, they have lost all the advantage they had at first gained against socialism.

Undoubtedly — and I am the first to recognize it — the rent of land, like that of money and all personal and real property, is a spontaneous and universal fact, which has its source in the depths of our nature, and which soon becomes, by its natural development, one of the most potent means of organization. I shall prove even that interest on capital is but the materialization of the apllorism, All labor should leave an excess. But in the face of this theory, or rather this fiction, of the productivity of capital, arises another thesis no less certain, which in these latter days has struck the ablest economists: it is that all value is born of labor, and is composed essentially of wages; in other words, that no wealth has its origin in privilege, or acquires any value except through work; and that, consequently, labor alone is the source of revenue among men. How, then, reconcile the theory of farm-rent or productivity of capital — a theory confirmed by universal custom, which conservative political economy is forced to accept but cannot justify — with this other theory which shows that value is normally composed of wages, and which inevitably ends, as we shall demonstrate, in an equality in society between net product and raw product?

The socialists have not wasted the opportunity. Starting with the principle that labor is the source of all income, they began to call the holders of capital to account for their farm-rents and emoluments; and, as the economists won the first victory by generalizing under a common expression farm-rent and usury, so the socialists have taken their revenge by causing the seignorial rights of capital to vanish before the still more general principle of labor. Property has been demolished from top to bottom: the economists could only keep silent; but, powerless to arrest itself in this new descent, socialism has slipped clear to the farthest boundaries of communistic utopia, and, for want of a practical solution, society is reduced to a position where it can neither justify its tradition, nor commit itself to experiments in which the least mistake would drive it backward several thousand years.

In such a situation what is the mandate of science?

Certainly not to halt in an arbitrary, inconceivable, and impossible juste milieu; it is to generalize further, and discover a third principle, a fact, a superior law, which shall explain the fiction of capital and the myth of property, and reconcile them with the theory which makes labor the origin of all wealth. This is what socialism, if it wishes to proceed logically, must undertake. In fact, the theory of the real productivity of labor, and that of the fictitious productivity of capital, are both essentially economical: socialism has endeavored only to show the contradiction between them, without regard to experience or logic; for it appears to be as destitute of the one as of the other. Now, in law, the litigant who accepts the authority of a title in one particular must accept it in all; it is not allowable to divide the documents and proofs. Had socialism the right to decline the authority of political economy in relation to usury, when it appealed for support to this same authority in relation to the analysis of value? By no means. All that socialism could demand in such a case was, either that political economy should be directed to reconcile its theories, or that it might be itself intrusted with this difficult task.

The more closely we examine these solemn discussions, the more clearly we see that the whole trouble is due to the fact that one of the parties does not wish to see, while the other refuses to advance.

It is a principle of our law that no one can be deprived of his property except for the sake of general utility, and in consideration of a fair indemnity payable in advance.

This principle is eminently an economic one; for, on the one hand, it assumes the right of eminent domain of the citizen expropriated, whose consent, according to the democratic spirit of the social compact, is necessarily presupposed. On the other hand, the indemnity, or the price of the article taken, is fixed, not by the intrinsic value of the article, but by the general law of commerce, — supply and demand; in a word, by opinion. Expropriation in the name of society may be likened to a contract of convenience, agreed to by each with all; not only then must the price be paid, but the convenience also must be paid for: and it is thus, in reality, that the indemnity is estimated. If the Roman legists had seen this analogy, they undoubtedly would have hesitated less over the question of expropriation for the sake of public utility.

Such, then, is the sanction of the social right of expropriation: indemnity.

Now, practically, not only is the principle of indemnity not applied in all cases where it ought to be, but it is impossible that it should be so applied. Thus, the law which established railways provided indemnity for the lands to be occupied by the rails; it did nothing for the multitude of industries dependent upon the previous method of conveyance, whose losses far exceeded the value of the lands whose owners received compensation. Similarly, when the question of indemnifying the manufacturers of beet-root sugar was under consideration, it occurred to no one that the State ought to indemnify also the large number of laborers and employees who earned their livelihood in the beet-root industry, and who were, perhaps, to be reduced to want.

Nevertheless, it is certain, according to the idea of capital and the theory of production, that as the possessor of land, whose means of labor is taken from him by the railroad, has a right to be indemnified, so also the manufacturer, whose capital is rendered unproductive by the same railroad, is entitled to indemnification. Why, then, is he not indemnified? Alas! because to indemnify him is impossible. With such a system of justice and impartiality society would be, as a general thing, unable to act, and would return to the fixedness of Roman justice. There must be victims. The principle of indemnity is consequently abandoned; to one or more classes of citizens the State is inevitably bankrupt.

At this point the socialists appear. They charge that the sole object of political economy is to sacrifice the interests of the masses and create privileges; then, finding in the law of expropriation the rudiment of an agrarian law, they suddenly advocate universal expropriation; that is, production and consumption in common.

But here socialism relapses from criticism into utopia, and its incapacity becomes freshly apparent in its contradictions. If the principle of expropriation for the sake of public utility, carried to its logical conclusion, leads to a complete reorganization of society, before commencing the work the character of this new organization must be understood; now, socialism, I repeat, has no science save a few bits of physiology and political economy. Further, it is necessary in accordance with the principle of indemnity, if not to compensate citizens, at least to guarantee to them the values which they part with; it is necessary, in short, to insure them against loss. Now, outside of the public fortune, the management of which it demands, where will socialism find security for this same fortune?

It is impossible, in sound and honest logic, to escape this circle. Consequently the communists, more open in their dealings than certain other sectarians of flowing and pacific ideas, decide the difficulty; and promise, the power once in their hands, to expropriate all and indemnify and guarantee none. At bottom, that would be neither unjust nor disloyal. Unfortunately, to burn is not to reply, as the interesting

Desmoulins said to Robespierre; and such a discussion ends always in fire and the guillotine. Here, as everywhere, two rights, equally sacred, stand in the presence of each other, the right of the citizen and the right of the State; it is enough to say that there is a superior formula which reconciles the socialistic utopias and the mutilated theories of political economy, and that the problem is to discover it. In this emergency what

64

are the contending parties doing? Nothing. We might say rather that they raise questions only to get an opportunity to redress injuries. What do I say? The questions are not even understood by them; and, while the public is considering the sublime problems of society and human destiny, the professors of social science, orthodox and heretics, do not agree on principles. Witness the question which occasioned these inquiries, and which its authors certainly understand no better than its disparagers, — the relation of profits and wages.

What! an Academy of economists has offered for competition a question the terms of which it does not understand! How, then, could it have conceived the idea?

Well! I know that my statement is astonishing and incredible; but it is true. Like the theologians, who answer metaphysical problems only by myths and allegories, which always reproduce the problems but never solve them, the economists reply to the questions which they ask only by relating how they were led to ask them: should they conceive that it was possible to go further, they would cease to be economists.

For example, what is profit? That which remains for the manager after he has paid all the expenses. Now, the expenses consist of the labor performed and the materials consumed; or, in fine, wages. What, then, is the wages of a workingman? The least that can be given him; that is, we do not know. What should be the price of the merchandise put upon the market by the manager? The highest that he can obtain; that is, again, we do not know. Political economy prohibits the supposition that the prices of merchandise and labor can be fixed, although it admits that they can be estimated; and that for the reason, say the economists, that estimation is essentially an arbitrary operation, which never can lead to sure and certain conclusions. How, then, shall we find the relation between two unknowns which, according to political economy, cannot be determined? Thus political economy proposes insolvable problems; and yet we shall soon see that it must propose them, and that our century must solve them. That is why I said that the Academy of Moral Sciences, in offering for competition the question of the relation of profits and wages, spoke unconsciously, spoke prophetically.

But it will be said, Is it not true that, if labor is in great demand and laborers are scarce, wages will rise, while profits on the other hand will decrease; that if, in the press of competition, there is an excess of production, there will be a stoppage and forced sales, consequently no profit for the manager and a danger of idleness for the laborer; that then the latter will offer his labor at a reduced price; that, if a machine is invented, it will first extinguish the fires of its rivals; then, a monopoly established, and the laborer made dependent on the employer, profits and wages will be inversely proportional? Cannot all these causes, and others besides, be studied, ascertained, counterbalanced, etc.?

Oh, monographs, histories! — we have been saturated with them since the days of Adam Smith and J. B. Say, and they are scarcely more than variations of these authors' words.

But it is not thus that the question should be understood, although the Academy has given it no other meaning. The relation of profits end wages should be considered in an absolute sense, and not from the inconclusive point of view of the accidents of commerce and the division of interests: two things which must ultimately receive their interpretation. Let me explain myself.

Considering producer and consumer as a single individual, whose recompense is naturally equal to his product; then dividing this product into two parts, one which rewards the producer for his outlay, another which represents his profit, according to the axiom that all labor should leave an excess, -we have to determine the relation of one of these parts to the other. This done, it will be easy to deduce the ratio of the fortunes of these two classes of men, employers and wage-laborers, as well as account for all commercial oscillations. This will be a series of corollaries to add to the demonstration.

Now, that such a relation may exist and be estimated, there must necessarily be a law, internal or external, which governs wages and prices; and since, in the present state of things, wages and prices vary and oscillate continually, we must ask what are the general facts, the causes, which make value vary and oscillate, and within what limits this oscillation takes place.

But this very question is contrary to the accepted principles; for whoever says oscillation necessarily supposes a mean direction toward which value's centre of gravity continually tends; and when the Academy asks that we determine the oscillations of profit and wages, it asks thereby that we determine value. Now that is precisely what the gentlemen of the Academy deny: they are unwilling to admit that, if value is variable, it is for that very reason determinable; that variability is the sign and condition of determinability. They pretend that value, ever varying, can never be determined. This is like maintaining that, given the number of oscillations of a pendulum per second, their amplitude, and the latitude and elevation of the spot where the experiment is performed, the length of the pendulum cannot be determined because the pendulum is in motion. Such is political economy's first article of faith.

As for socialism, it does not appear to have understood the question, or to be concerned about it. Among its many organs, some simply and merely put aside the problem by substituting division for distribution, — that is, by banishing number and measure from the social organism: others relieve themselves of the embarrassment by applying universal suffrage to the wages question. It is needless to say that these platitudes find dupes by thousands and hundreds of thousands.

The condemnation of political economy has been formulated by Malthus in this famous passage: —

A man who is born into a world already occupied, his family unable to support him, and society not requiring his labor, — such a man, I say, has not the least right to claim any nourishment whatever: he is really one too many on the earth. At the great banquet of Nature there is no plate laid for him. Nature commands him to take himself away, and she will not be slow to put her order into execution. [6]

This then is the necessary, the fatal, conclusion of political economy, — a conclusion which I shall demonstrate by evidence hitherto unknown in this field of inquiry, — Death to him who does not possess!

In order better to grasp the thought of Malthus, let us translate it into philosophical propositions by stripping it of its rhetorical gloss: —

"Individual liberty, and property, which is its expression, are economical data; equality and solidarity are not.

"Under this system, each one by himself, each one for himself: labor, like all merchandise, is subject to fluctuation: hence the risks of the proletariat.

"Whoever has neither income nor wages has no right to demand anything of others: his misfortune falls on his own head; in the game of fortune, luck has been against him."

From the point of view of political economy these propositions are irrefutable; and Malthus, who has formulated them with such alarming exactness, is secure against all reproach. From the point of view of the conditions of social science, these same propositions are radically false, and even contradictory.

The error of Malthus, or rather of political economy, does not consist in saying that a man who has nothing to eat must die; or in maintaining that, under the system of individual appropriation, there is no course for him who has neither labor nor income but to withdraw from life by suicide, unless he prefers to be driven from it by starvation: such is, on the one hand, the law of our existence; such is, on the other, the consequence of property; and M. Rossi has taken altogether too much trouble to justify the good sense of Malthus on this point. I suspect, indeed, that M. Rossi, in making so lengthy and loving an apology for Malthus, intended to recommend political economy in the same way that his fellow-countryman Machiavel, in his book entitled "The Prince," recommended despotism to the admiration of the world. In pointing out misery as the necessary condition of industrial and commercial absolutism, M. Rossi seems to say to us: There is your law, your justice, your political economy; there is property.

But Gallic simplicity does not understand artifice; and it would have been better to have said to France, in her immaculate tongue: The error of Malthus, the radical vice of political economy, consists, in general terms, in affirming as a definitive state a transitory condition, — namely, the division of society into patricians and proletaires; and, particularly, in saying that in an organized, and consequently solidaire, society, there may be some who possess, labor, and consume, while others have neither possession, nor labor, nor bread. Finally Malthus, or political economy, reasons erroneously when seeing in the faculty of indefinite reproduction — which the human race enjoys in neither greater nor less degree than all animal and vegetable species — a permanent danger of famine; whereas it is only necessary to show the necessity, and consequently the existence, of a law of equilibrium between population and production.

In short, the theory of Malthus — and herein lies the great merit of this writer, a merit which none of his colleagues has dreamed of attributing to him — is a reductio ad absurdum of all political economy.

As for socialism, that was summed up long since by Plato and Thomas More in a single word, UTOPIA, — that is, no-place, a chimera.

Nevertheless, for the honor of the human mind and that justice may be done to all, this must be said: neither could economic and legislative science have had any other beginning than they did have, nor can society remain in this original position.

Every science must first define its domain, produce and collect its materials: before system, facts; before the age of art, the age of learning. The economic science, subject like every other to the law of time and the conditions of experience, before seeking to ascertain how things ought to take place in society, had to tell us how things do take place; and all these processes which the authors speak of so pompously in their books as laws, principles, and theories, in spite of their incoherence and inconsistency, had to be gathered up with scrupulous diligence, and described with strict impartiality. The fulfilment of this task called for more genius perhaps, certainly for more self-sacrifice, than will be demanded by the future progress of the science.

If, then, social economy is even yet rather an aspiration towards the future than a knowledge of reality, it must be admitted that the elements of this study are all included in political economy; and I believe that I express the general sentiment in saying that this opinion has become that of the vast majority of minds. The present finds few defenders, it is true; but the disgust with utopia is no less universal: and everybody understands that the truth lies in a formula which shall reconcile these two terms: CONSERVATION and MOTION.

Thus, thanks to Adam Smith, J. B. Say, Ricardo, and Malthus, as well as their rash opponents, the mysteries of fortune, atria Ditis, are uncovered; the power of capital, the oppression of the laborer, the machinations of monopoly, illumined at all points, shun the public gaze. Concerning the facts observed and described by the economists, we reason and conjecture: abusive laws, iniquitous customs, respected so long as the obscurity which sustained their life lasted, with difficulty dragged to the daylight, are expiring beneath the general reprobation; it is suspected that the government of society must be learned no longer from an empty ideology, after the fashion of the Contrat social, but, as Montesquieu foresaw, from the relation of things; and already a Left of eminently socialistic tendencies, composed of savants, magistrates, legists, professors, and even capitalists and manufacturers, — all born representatives and defenders of privilege, — and of a million of adepts, is forming in the nation above and outside of parliamentary opinions, and seeking, by an analysis of economic facts, to capture the secrets of the life of societies.

Let us represent political economy, then, as an immense plain, strewn with materials prepared for an edifice. The laborers await the signal, full of ardor, and burning to commence the work: but the architect has disappeared without leaving the plan. The economists have stored their memories with many things: unhappily they have not the shadow of an estimate. They know the origin and history of each piece; what it cost to make it; what wood makes the best joists, and what clay the best bricks; what has been expended in tools and carts; how much the carpenters earned, and how much the stone-cutters: they do not know the destination and the place of anything. The economists cannot deny that they have before them the fragments, scattered pell-mell, of a chef-d'oeuvre, disjecti membra poetae; but it has been impossible for them as yet to recover the general design, and, whenever they have attempted any comparisons, they have met only with incoherence. Driven to despair at last by their fruitless combinations, they have erected as a dogma the architectural incongruity of the science, or, as they say, the inconveniences of its principles; in a word, they have denied the science. [7]

Thus the division of labor, without which production would be almost nothing, is subject to a thousand inconveniences, the worst of which is the demoralization of the laborer; machinery causes, not only cheapness, but obstruction of the market and stoppage of business; competition ends in oppression; taxation, the material bond of society, is generally a scourge dreaded equally with fire and hail; credit is necessarily accompanied by bankruptcy; property is a swarm of abuses; commerce degenerates into a game of chance, in which it is sometimes allowable even to cheat: in short, disorder existing everywhere to an equal extent with order, and no one knowing how the latter is to banish the former, taxis ataxien diokein, the economists have decided that all is for the best, and regard every reformatory proposition as hostile to political economy.

The social edifice, then, has been abandoned; the crowd has burst into the wood-yard; columns, capitals, and plinths, wood, stone, and metal, have been distributed in portions and drawn by lot: and, of all these materials collected for a magnificent temple, property, ignorant and barbarous, has built huts. The work before us, then, is not only to recover the plan of the edifice, but to dislodge the occupants, who maintain that their city is superb, and, at the very mention of restoration, appear in battle-array at their gates. Such confusion was not seen of old at Babel: happily we speak French, and are more courageous than the companions of Nimrod.

But enough of allegory: the historical and descriptive method, successfully employed so long as the work was one of examination

70

only, is henceforth useless: after thousands of monographs and tables, we are no further advanced than in the age of Xenophon and Hesiod. The Phenicians, the Greeks, the Italians, labored in their day as we do in ours: they invested their money, paid their laborers, extended their domains, made their expeditions and recoveries, kept their books, speculated, dabbled in stocks, and ruined themselves according to all the rules of economic art; knowing as well as ourselves how to gain monopolies and fleece the consumer and laborer. Of all this accounts are only too numerous; and, though we should rehearse forever our statistics and our figures, we should always have before our eyes only chaos, — chaos constant and uniform.

It is thought, indeed, that from the era of mythology to the present year 57 of our great revolution, the general welfare has improved: Christianity has long been regarded as the chief cause of this amelioration, but now the economists claim all the honor for their own principles. For after all, they say, what has been the influence of Christianity upon society? Thoroughly utopian at its birth, it has been able to maintain and extend itself only by gradually adopting all the economic categories, — labor, capital, farm-rent, usury, traffic, property; in short, by consecrating the Roman law, the highest expression of political economy.

Christianity, a stranger in its theological aspect to the theories of production and consumption, has been to European civilization what the trades-unions and free-masons were not long since to itinerant workmen, — a sort of insurance company and mutual aid society; in this respect, it owes nothing to political economy, and the good which it has done cannot be invoked by the latter in its own support. The effects of charity and self-sacrifice are outside of the domain of economy, which must bring about social happiness through justice and the organization of labor. For the rest, I am ready to admit the beneficial effects of the system of property; but I observe that these effects are entirely balanced by the misery which it is the nature of this system to produce; so that, as an illustrious minister recently confessed before the English Parliament, and as we shall soon show, the increase of misery in the present state of society is parallel and equal to the increase of wealth, — which completely annuls the merits of political economy.

Thus political economy is justified neither by its maxims nor by its works; and, as for socialism, its whole value consists in having established this fact. We are forced, then, to resume the examination of political economy, since it alone contains, at least in part, the materials of social science; and to ascertain whether its theories do not conceal some error, the correction of which would reconcile fact and right, reveal the organic law of humanity, and give the positive conception of order.

Chapter II. Of Value.

1. — Opposition of value in USE and value in EXCHANGE.

Value is the corner-stone of the economic edifice. The divine artist who has intrusted us with the continuation of his work has explained himself on this point to no one; but the few indications given may serve as a basis of conjecture. Value, in fact, presents two faces: one, which the economists call value in use, or intrinsic value; another, value in exchange, or of opinion. The effects which are produced by value under this double aspect, and which are very irregular so long as it is not established, — or, to use a more philosophical expression, so long as it is not constituted, -are changed totally by this constitution.

Now, in what consists the correlation between useful value and value in exchange? What is meant by constituted value, and by what sudden change is this constitution effected? To answer these questions is the object and end of political economy. I beg the reader to give his whole attention to what is to follow, this chapter being the only one in the work which will tax his patience. For my part, I will endeavor to be more and more simple and clear.

Everything which can be of any service to me is of value to me, and the more abundant the useful thing is the richer I am: so far there is no difficulty. Milk and flesh, fruits and grains, wool, sugar, cotton, wine, metals, marble; in fact, land, water, air, fire, and sunlight, — are, relatively to me, values of use, values by nature and function. If all the things which serve to sustain my life were as abundant as certain of them are, light for instance, — in other words, if the quantity of every valuable thing was inexhaustible, — my welfare would be forever assured: I should not have to labor; I should not even think. In such a state, things would always be useful, but it would be no longer true to say that they ARE VALUABLE; for value, as we shall soon see, indicates an essentially social relation; and it is solely through exchange, reverting as it were from society to Nature, that we have acquired the idea of utility. The whole development of civilization originates, then, in the necessity which the human race is under of continually causing the creation of new values; just as the evils of society are primarily caused by the perpetual struggle which we maintain against our own inertia. Take away from man that desire which leads him to think and fits him for a life of contemplation, and the lord of creation stands on a level with the highest of the beasts.

But how does value in use become value in exchange? For it should be noticed that the two kinds of value, although coexisting in thought (since the former becomes apparent only in the presence of the latter), nevertheless maintain a relation of succession: exchangeable value is a sort of reflex of useful value; just as the theologians teach that in the Trinity the Father, contemplating himself through all eternity, begets the Son. This generation of the idea of value has not been noted by the economists with sufficient care: it is important that we should tarry over it.

Since, then, of the objects which I need, a very large number exist in Nature only in moderate quantities, or even not at all, I am forced to assist in the production of that which I lack; and, as I cannot turn my hand to so many things, I propose to other men, my collaborators in various functions, to yield me a portion of their products in exchange for mine. I shall then always have in my possession more of my own special product than I consume; just as my fellows will always have in their possession more of their respective products than they use. This tacit agreement is fulfilled by commerce. Here we may observe that the logical succession of the two kinds of value is even more apparent in history than in theory, men having spent thousands of years in disputing over natural wealth (this being what is called primitive communism) before their industry afforded opportunity for exchange.

Now, the capacity possessed by all products, whether natural or the result of labor, of serving to maintain man, is called distinctively value in use; their capacity of purchasing each other, value in exchange. At bottom this is the same thing, since the second case only adds to the first the idea of substitution, which may seem an idle subtlety; practically, the consequences are surprising, and beneficial or fatal by turns.

Consequently, the distinction established in value is based on facts, and is not at all arbitrary: it is for man, in submitting to this law, to use it to increase his welfare and liberty. Labor, as an author (M. Walras) has beautifully expressed it, is a war declared against the parsimony of Nature; by it wealth and society are simultaneously created. Not only does labor produce incomparably more wealth than Nature gives us, — for instance, it has been remarked that the shoemakers alone in France produce ten times more than the mines of Peru, Brazil, and Mexico combined, — but, labor infinitely extending and multiplying its rights by the changes which it makes in natural values, it gradually comes about that all wealth, in running the gauntlet of labor, falls wholly into the hands of him who creates it, and that nothing, or almost nothing, is left for the possessor of the original material.

Such, then, is the path of economic progress: at first, appropriation of the land and natural values; then, association and distribution through labor until complete equality is attained. Chasms are scattered along our road, the sword is suspended over our heads; but, to avert all dangers, we have reason, and reason is omnipotence.

It results from the relation of useful value to exchangeable value that if, by accident or from malice, exchange should be forbidden to a single producer, or if the utility of his product should suddenly cease, though his storehouses were full, he would possess nothing. The more sacrifices he had made and the more courage he had displayed in producing, the greater would be his misery. If the utility of the product, instead of wholly disappearing, should only diminish, — a thing which may happen in a hundred ways, — the laborer, instead of being struck down and ruined by a sudden catastrophe, would be impoverished only; obliged to give a large quantity of his own value for a small quantity of the values of others, his means of subsistence would be reduced by an amount equal to the deficit in his sale: which would lead by degrees from competency to want. If, finally, the utility of the product should increase, or else if its production should become less costly, the balance of exchange would turn to the advantage of the producer, whose condition would thus be raised from fatiguing mediocrity to idle opulence. This phenomenon of depreciation and enrichment is manifested under a thousand forms and by a thousand combinations; it is the essence of the passional and intriguing game of commerce and industry. And this is the lottery, full of traps, which the economists think ought to last forever, and whose suppression the Academy of Moral and Political Sciences unwittingly demands, when, under the names of profit and wages, it asks us to reconcile value in use and value in exchange; that is, to find the method of rendering all useful values equally exchangeable, and, vice versa, all exchangeable values equally useful.

The economists have very clearly shown the double character of value, but what they have not made equally plain is its contradictory nature. Here begins our criticism.

Utility is the necessary condition of exchange; but take away exchange, and utility vanishes: these two things are indissolubly connected. Where, then, is the contradiction?

Since all of us live only by labor and exchange, and grow richer as production and exchange increase, each of us produces as much useful value as possible, in order to increase by that amount his exchanges, and consequently his enjoyments. Well, the first effect, the inevitable effect, of the multiplication of values is to LOWER them: the more abundant is an article of merchandise, the more it loses in exchange and depreciates commercially. Is it not true that there is a contradiction between the necessity of labor and its results?

I adjure the reader, before rushing ahead for the explanation, to arrest his attention upon the fact.

A peasant who has harvested twenty sacks of wheat, which he with his family proposes to consume, deems himself twice as rich as if he had harvested only ten; likewise a housewife who has spun fifty yards of linen believes that she is twice as rich as if she had spun but twenty-five. Relatively to the household, both are right; looked at in their external relations, they may be utterly mistaken. If the crop of wheat is double throughout the whole country, twenty sacks will sell for less than ten would have sold for if it had been but half as great; so, under similar circumstances, fifty yards of linen will be worth less than twenty-five: so that value decreases as the production of utility increases, and a producer may arrive at poverty by continually enriching himself. And this seems unalterable, inasmuch as there is no way of escape except all the products of industry become infinite in quantity, like air and light, which is absurd. God of my reason! Jean Jacques would have said: it is not the economists who are irrational; it is political economy itself which is false to its definitions. Mentita est iniquitas sibi.

In the preceding examples the useful value exceeds the exchangeable value: in other cases it is less. Then the same phenomenon is produced, but in the opposite direction: the balance is in favor of the producer, while the consumer suffers. This is notably the case in seasons of scarcity, when the high price of provisions is always more or less factitious. There are also professions whose whole art consists in giving to an article of minor usefulness, which could easily be dispensed with, an exaggerated value of opinion: such, in general, are the arts of luxury. Man, through his aesthetic passion, is eager for the trifles the possession of which would highly satisfy his vanity, his innate desire for luxury, and his more noble and more respectable love of the beautiful: upon this the dealers in this class of articles speculate. To tax fancy and elegance is no less odious or absurd than to tax circulation: but such a tax is collected by a few fashionable merchants, whom general infatuation protects, and whose whole merit generally consists in warping taste and generating fickleness. Hence no one complains; and all the maledictions of opinion are reserved for the monopolists who, through genius, succeed in raising by a few cents the price of linen and bread.

It is little to have pointed out this astonishing contrast between useful value and exchangeable value, which the economists have been in the habit of regarding as very simple: it must be shown that this pretended simplicity conceals a profound mystery, which it is our duty to fathom.

I summon, therefore, every serious economist to tell me, otherwise than by transforming or repeating the question, for what reason value decreases in proportion as production augments, and reciprocally what causes this same value to increase in proportion as production diminishes. In technical terms, useful value and exchangeable value, necessary to each other, are inversely proportional to each other; I ask, then, why scarcity, instead of utility, is synonymous with dearness. For — mark it well — the price of merchandise is independent of the amount of labor expended in production; and its greater or less cost does not serve at all to explain the variations in its price. Value is capricious, like liberty: it considers neither utility nor labor; on the contrary, it seems that, in the ordinary course of affairs, and exceptional derangements aside, the most useful objects are those which are sold at the lowest price; in other words, that it is just that the men who perform the most attractive labor should be the best rewarded, while those whose tasks demand the most exertion are paid the least. So that, in following the principle to its ultimate consequences, we reach the most logical of conclusions: that things whose use is necessary and quantity infinite must be gratuitous, while those which are without utility and extremely scarce must bear an inestimable price. But, to complete the embarrassment, these extremes do not occur in practice: on the one hand, no human product can ever become infinite in quantity; on the other, the rarest things must be in some degree useful, else they would not be susceptible of value. Useful value and exchangeable value remain, then, in inevitable attachment, although it is their nature continually to tend towards mutual exclusion.

I shall not fatigue the reader with a refutation of the logomachies which might be offered in explanation of this subject: of the contradiction inherent in the idea of value there is no assignable cause, no possible explanation. The fact of which I speak is one of those called primitive, — that is, one of those which may serve to explain others, but which in themselves, like the bodies called simple, are inexplicable. Such is the dualism of spirit and matter. Spirit and matter are two terms each of which, taken separately, indicates a special aspect of spirit, but corresponds to no reality. So, given man's needs of a great variety of products together with the obligation of procuring them by his labor, the opposition of useful value to exchangeable value necessarily results; and from this opposition a contradiction on the very threshold of political economy. No intelligence, no will, divine or human, can prevent it.

Therefore, instead of searching for a chimerical explanation, let us content ourselves with establishing the necessity of the contradiction. Whatever the abundance of created values and the proportion in which they exchange for each other, in order that we may exchange our products, mine must suit you when you are the buyer, and I must be satisfied with yours when you are the seller. For no one has a right to impose his own merchandise upon another: the sole judge of utility, or in other words the want, is the buyer. Therefore, in the first case, you have the deciding power; in the second, I have it. Take away reciprocal liberty, and exchange is no longer the expression of industrial solidarity: it is robbery. Communism, by the way, will never surmount this difficulty.

But, where there is liberty, production is necessarily undetermined, either in quantity or in quality; so that from the point of view of economic progress, as from that of the relation of consumers, valuation always is an arbitrary matter, and the price of merchandise will ever fluctuate. Suppose for a moment that all producers should sell at a fixed price: there would be some who, producing at less cost and in better quality, would get much, while others would get nothing. In every way equilibrium would be destroyed. Do you wish, in order to prevent business stagnation, to limit production strictly to the necessary amount? That would be a violation of liberty: for, in depriving me of the power of choice, you condemn me to pay the highest price; you destroy competition, the sole guarantee of cheapness, and encourage smuggling. In this way, to avoid commercial absolutism, you would rush into administrative absolutism; to create equality, you would destroy liberty, which is to deny equality itself. Would you group producers in a single workshop (supposing you to possess this secret)? That again does not suffice: it would be necessary also to group consumers in a common household, whereby you would abandon the

77

point. We are not to abolish the idea of value, which is as impossible as to abolish labor, but to determine it; we are not to kill individual liberty, but to socialize it. Now, it is proved that it is the free will of man that gives rise to the opposition between value in use and value in exchange: how reconcile this opposition while free will exists? And how sacrifice the latter without sacrificing man?

Then, from the very fact that I, as a free purchaser, am judge of my own wants, judge of the fitness of the object, judge of the price I wish to pay, and that you on the other hand, as a free producer, control the means of production, and consequently have the power to reduce your expenses, absolutism forces itself forward as an element of value, and causes it to oscillate between utility and opinion.

But this oscillation, clearly pointed out by the economists, is but the effect of a contradiction which, repeating itself on a vast scale, engenders the most unexpected phenomena. Three years of fertility, in certain provinces of Russia, are a public calamity, just as, in our vineyards, three years of abundance are a calamity to the wine-grower I know well that the economists attribute this distress to a lack of markets; wherefore this question of markets is an important one with them. Unfortunately the theory of markets, like that of emigration with which they attempted to meet Malthus, is a begging of the question. The States having the largest market are as subject to over-production as the most isolated countries: where are high and low prices better known than in the stock-exchanges of Paris and London?

From the oscillation of value and the irregular effects resulting therefrom the socialists and economists, each in their own way, have reasoned to opposite, but equally false, conclusions: the former have made it a text for the slander of political economy and its exclusion from social science; the latter, for the denial of all possibility of reconciliation, and the affirmation of the incommensurability of values, and consequently the inequality of fortunes, as an absolute law of commerce.

I say that both parties are equally in error.

1. The contradictory idea of value, so clearly exhibited by the inevitable distinction between useful value and value in exchange does not arise from a false mental perception, or from a vicious terminology, or from any practical error; it lies deep in the nature of things, and forces itself upon the mind as a general form of thought, — that is, as a category. Now, as the idea of value is the point of departure of political economy,

78

it follows that all the elements of the science — I use the word science in anticipation — are contradictory in themselves and opposed to each other: so truly is this the case that on every question the economist finds himself continually placed between an affirmation and a negation alike irrefutable. ANTINOMY, in fine, to use a word sanctioned by modern philosophy, is the essential characteristic of political economy; that is to say, it is at once its death-sentence and its justification.

Antinomy, literally counter-law, means opposition in principle or antagonism in relation, just as contradiction or antilogy indicates opposition or discrepancy in speech. Antinomy, — I ask pardon for entering into these scholastic details, comparatively unfamiliar as yet to most economists, — antinomy is the conception of a law with two faces, the one positive, the other negative. Such, for instance, is the law called attraction, by which the planets revolve around the sun, and which mathematicians have analyzed into centripetal force and centrifugal force. Such also is the problem of the infinite divisibility of matter, which, as Kant has shown, can be denied and affirmed successively by arguments equally plausible and irrefutable.

Antinomy simply expresses a fact, and forces itself imperatively on the mind; contradiction, properly speaking, is an absurdity. This distinction between antinomy (contra-lex) and contradiction (contra-dictio) shows in what sense it can be said that, in a certain class of ideas and facts, the argument of contradiction has not the same value as in mathematics.

In mathematics it is a rule that, a proposition being proved false, its opposite is true, and vice versa. In fact, this is the principal method of mathematical demonstration. In social economy, it is not the same: thus we see, for example, that property being proved by its results to be false, the opposite formula, communism, is none the truer on this account, but is deniable at the same time and by the same title as property. Does it follow, as has been said with such ridiculous emphasis, that every truth, every idea, results from a contradiction, — that is, from a something which is affirmed and denied at the same moment and from the same point of view, — and that it may be necessary to abandon wholly the old-fashioned logic, which regards contradiction as the infallible sign of error? This babble is worthy of sophists who, destitute of faith and honesty, endeavor to perpetuate scepticism in order to maintain their impertinent uselessness. Because antinomy, immediately it is misunderstood, leads inevitably to contradiction, these have been mistaken for each other, especially among the French, who like to judge everything by its effects. But neither contradiction nor antinomy, which analysis discovers at the bottom of every simple idea, is the principle of truth. Contradiction is always synonymous with nullity; as for antinomy, sometimes called by the same name, it is indeed the forerunner of truth, the material of which, so to speak, it supplies; but it is not truth, and, considered in itself, it is the efficient cause of disorder, the characteristic form of delusion and evil.

An antinomy is made up of two terms, necessary to each other, but always opposed, and tending to mutual destruction. I hardly dare to add, as I must, that the first of these terms has received the name thesis, position, and the second the name anti-thesis, counter-position. This method of thought is now so well-known that it will soon figure, I hope, in the text-books of the primary schools. We shall see directly how from the combination of these two zeros unity springs forth, or the idea which dispels the antinomy.

Thus, in value, there is nothing useful that cannot be exchanged, nothing exchangeable if it be not useful: value in use and value in exchange are inseparable. But while, by industrial progress, demand varies and multiplies to an infinite extent, and while manufactures tend in consequence to increase the natural utility of things, and finally to convert all useful value into exchangeable value, production, on the other hand, continually increasing the power of its instruments and always reducing its expenses, tends to restore the venal value of things to their primitive utility: so that value in use and value in exchange are in perpetual struggle.

The effects of this struggle are well-known: the wars of commerce and of the market; obstructions to business; stagnation; prohibition; the massacres of competition; monopoly; reductions of wages; laws fixing maximum prices; the crushing inequality of fortunes; misery, — all these result from the antinomy of value. The proof of this I may be excused from giving here, as it will appear naturally in the chapters to follow.

The socialists, while justly demanding that this antagonism be brought to an end, have erred in mistaking its source, and in seeing in it only a mental oversight, capable of rectification by a legal decree. Hence this lamentable outbreak of sentimentalism, which has rendered socialism so insipid to positive minds, and which, spreading the absurdest delusions, makes so many fresh dupes every day. My complaint of socialism is not that it has appeared among us without cause, but that it has clung so long and so obstinately to its silliness.

2. But the economists have erred no less gravely in rejecting a priori, and just because of the contradictory, or rather antinomical, nature of value, every idea and hope of reform, never desiring to understand that, for the very reason that society has arrived at its highest point of antagonism, reconciliation and harmony are at hand. This, nevertheless, is what a close study of political economy would have shown to its adepts, had they paid more attention to the lights of modern metaphysics. It is indeed demonstrated, by the most positive evidence known to the human mind, that wherever an antinomy appears there is a promise of a resolution of its terms, and consequently an announcement of a coming change. Now, the idea of value, as developed by J. B. Say among others, satisfies exactly these conditions. But the economists, who have remained for the most part by an inconceivable fatality ignorant of the movement of philosophy, have guarded against the supposition that the essentially contradictory, or, as they say, variable, character of value might be at the same time the authentic sign of its constitutionality, — that is, of its eminently harmonious and determinable nature. However dishonorable it may be to the economists of the various schools, it is certain that their opposition to socialism results solely from this false conception of their own principles; one proof, taken from a thousand, will suffice.

The Academy of Sciences (not that of Moral Sciences, but the other), going outside of its province one day, listened to a paper in which it was proposed to calculate tables of value for all kinds of merchandise upon the basis of the average product per man and per day's labor in each branch of industry. "Le Journal des Economistes" (August, 1845) immediately made this communication, intrusive in its eyes, the text of a protest against the plan of tariff which was its object, and the occasion of a reestablishment of what it called true principles: —

"There is no measure of value, no standard of value," it said in its conclusions; "economic science tells us this, just as mathematical science tells us that there is no perpetual motion or quadrature of the circle, and that these never will be found. Now, if there is no standard of value, if the measure of value is not even a metaphysical illusion, what then is the law which governs exchanges?..... As we have said before, it is, in a general way, supply and demand: that is the last word of science."

Now, how did "Le Journal des Economistes" prove that there is no measure of value? I use the consecrated expression: though I shall show directly that this phrase, measure of value, is somewhat ambiguous, and

81

does not convey the exact meaning which it is intended, and which it ought, to express.

This journal repeated, with accompanying examples, the exposition that we have just given of the variability of value, but without arriving, as we did, at the contradiction. Now, if the estimable editor, one of the most distinguished economists of the school of Say, had had stricter logical habits; if he had been long used, not only to observing facts, but to seeking their explanation in the ideas which produce them, — I do not doubt that he would have expressed himself more cautiously, and that, instead of seeing in the variability of value the last word of science, he would have recognized unaided that it is the first. Seeing that the variability of value proceeds not from things, but from the mind, he would have said that, as human liberty has its law, so value must have its law; consequently, that the hypothesis of a measure of value, this being the common expression, is not at all irrational; quite the contrary, that it is the denial of this measure that is illogical, untenable.

And indeed, what is there in the idea of measuring, and consequently of fixing, value, that is unscientific? All men believe in it; all wish it, search for it, suppose it: every proposition of sale or purchase is at bottom only a comparison between two values, — that is, a determination, more or less accurate if you will, but nevertheless effective. The opinion of the human race on the existing difference between real value and market price may be said to be unanimous. It is for this reason that so many kinds of merchandise are sold at a fixed price; there are some, indeed, which, even in their variations, are always fixed, — bread, for instance. It will not be denied that, if two manufacturers can supply one another by an account current, and at a settled price, with quantities of their respective products, ten, a hundred, a thousand manufacturers can do the same. Now, that would be a solution of the problem of the measure of value. The price of everything would be debated upon, I allow, because debate is still our only method of fixing prices; but yet, as all light is the result of conflict, debate, though it may be a proof of uncertainty, has for its object, setting aside the greater or less amount of good faith that enters into it, the discovery of the relation of values to each other, — that is, their measurement, their law.

Ricardo, in his theory of rent, has given a magnificent example of the commensurability of values. He has shown that arable lands are to each other as the crops which they yield with the same outlay; and here universal practice is in harmony with theory. Now who will say that

82

this positive and sure method of estimating the value of land, and in general of all engaged capital, cannot be applied to products also?.....

They say: Political economy is not affected by a priori arguments; it pronounces only upon facts. Now, facts and experience teach us that there is no measure of value and can be none, and prove that, though the conception of such an idea was necessary in the nature of things, its realization is wholly chimerical. Supply and demand is the sole law of exchange.

I will not repeat that experience proves precisely the contrary; that everything, in the economic progress of society, denotes a tendency toward the constitution and establishment of value; that that is the culminating point of political economy — which by this constitution becomes transformed — and the supreme indication of order in society: this general outline, reiterated without proof, would become tiresome. I confine myself for the moment within the limits of the discussion, and say that supply and demand, held up as the sole regulators of value, are nothing more than two ceremonial forms serving to bring useful value and exchangeable value face to face, and to provoke their reconciliation. They are the two electric poles, whose connection must produce the economical phenomenon of affinity called EXCHANGE. Like the poles of a battery, supply and demand are diametrically opposed to each other, and tend continually to mutual annihilation; it is by their antagonism that the price of things is either increased, or reduced to nothing: we wish to know, then, if it is not possible, on every occasion, so to balance or harmonize these two forces that the price of things always may be the expression of their true value, the expression of justice. To say after that that supply and demand is the law of exchange is to say that supply and demand is the law of supply and demand; it is not an explanation of the general practice, but a declaration of its absurdity; and I deny that the general practice is absurd.

I have just quoted Ricardo as having given, in a special instance, a positive rule for the comparison of values: the economists do better still. Every year they gather from tables of statistics the average prices of the various grains. Now, what is the meaning of an average? Every one can see that in a single operation, taken at random from a million, there is no means of knowing which prevailed, supply — that is, useful value — or exchangeable value, — that is, demand. But as every increase in the price of merchandise is followed sooner or later by a proportional reduction; as, in other words, in society the profits of speculation are equal to the losses, — we may regard with good reason the average of prices during a complete period as indicative of the real and legitimate value of products. This average, it is true, is ascertained too late: but who knows that we could not discover it in advance? Is there an economist who dares to deny it?

Nolens volens, then, the measure of value must be sought for: logic commands it, and her conclusions are adverse to economists and socialists alike. The opinion which denies the existence of this measure is irrational, unreasonable. Say as often as you please, on the one hand, that political economy is a science of facts, and that the facts are contrary to the hypothesis of a determination of value, or, on the other, that this troublesome question would not present itself in a system of universal association, which would absorb all antagonism, — I will reply still, to the right and to the left: —

1. That as no fact is produced which has not its cause, so none exists which has not its law; and that, if the law of exchange is not discovered, the fault is, not with the facts, but with the savants.

2. That, as long as man shall labor in order to live, and shall labor freely, justice will be the condition of fraternity and the basis of association; now, without a determination of value, justice is imperfect, impossible.

2. — Constitution of value; definition of wealth.

We know value in its two opposite aspects; we do not know it in its TOTALITY. If we can acquire this new idea, we shall have absolute value; and a table of values, such as was called for in the memoir read to the Academy of Sciences, will be possible.

Let us picture wealth, then, as a mass held by a chemical force in a permanent state of composition, in which new elements, continually entering, combine in different proportions, but according to a certain law: value is the proportional relation (the measure) in which each of these elements forms a part of the whole.

From this two things result: one, that the economists have been wholly deluded when they have looked for the general measure of value in wheat, specie, rent, etc., and also when, after having demonstrated that this standard of measure was neither here nor there, they have concluded that value has neither law nor measure; the other, that the proportion of values may continually vary without ceasing on that account to be subject to a law, whose determination is precisely the solution sought.

This idea of value satisfies, as we shall see, all the conditions: for it includes at once both the positive and fixed element in useful value and the variable element in exchangeable value; in the second place, it puts an end to the contradiction which seemed an insurmountable obstacle in the way of the determination of value; further, we shall show that value thus understood differs entirely from a simple juxtaposition of the two ideas of useful and exchangeable value, and that it is endowed with new properties.

The proportionality of products is not a revelation that we pretend to offer to the world, or a novelty that we bring into science, any more than the division of labor was an unheard-of thing when Adam Smith explained its marvels. The proportionality of products is, as we might prove easily by innumerable quotations, a common idea running through the works on political economy, but to which no one as yet has dreamed of attributing its rightful importance: and this is the task which we undertake today. We feel bound, for the rest, to make this declaration in order to reassure the reader concerning our pretensions to originality, and to satisfy those minds whose timidity leads them to look with little favor upon new ideas.

The economists seem always to have understood by the measure of value only a standard, a sort of original unit, existing by itself, and applicable to all sorts of merchandise, as the yard is applicable to all lengths. Consequently, many have thought that such a standard is furnished by the precious metals. But the theory of money has proved that, far from being the measure of values, specie is only their arithmetic, and a conventional arithmetic at that. Gold and silver are to value what the thermometer is to heat. The thermometer, with its arbitrarily graduated scale, indicates clearly when there is a loss or an increase of heat: but what the laws of heat-equilibrium are; what is its proportion in various bodies; what amount is necessary to cause a rise of ten, fifteen, or twenty degrees in the thermometer, — the thermometer does not tell us; it is not certain even that the degrees of the scale, equal to each other, correspond to equal additions of heat.

The idea that has been entertained hitherto of the measure of value, then, is inexact; the object of our inquiry is not the standard of value, as has been said so often and so foolishly, but the law which regulates the proportions of the various products to the social wealth; for upon the knowledge of this law depends the rise and fall of prices in so far as it is normal and legitimate. In a word, as we understand by the measure of celestial bodies the relation resulting from the comparison of these bodies with each other, so, by the measure of values, we must understand the relation which results from their comparison. Now, I say that this relation has its law, and this comparison its principle.

I suppose, then, a force which combines in certain proportions the elements of wealth, and makes of them a homogeneous whole: if the constituent elements do not exist in the desired proportion, the combination will take place nevertheless; but, instead of absorbing all the material, it will reject a portion as useless. The internal movement by which the combination is produced, and which the affinities of the various substances determine — this movement in society is exchange; exchange considered no longer simply in its elementary form and between man and man, but exchange considered as the fusion of all values produced by private industry in one and the same mass of social wealth. Finally, the proportion in which each element enters into the compound is what we call value; the excess remaining after the combination is non-value, until the addition of a certain quantity of other elements causes further combination and exchange.

We will explain later the function of money.

This determined, it is conceivable that at a given moment the proportions of values constituting the wealth of a country may be determined, or at least empirically approximated, by means of statistics and inventories, in nearly the same way that the chemists have discovered by experience, aided by analysis, the proportions of hydrogen and oxygen necessary to the formation of water. There is nothing objectionable in this method of determining values; it is, after all, only a matter of accounts. But such a work, however interesting it might be, would teach us nothing very useful. On the one hand, indeed, we know that the proportion continually varies; on the other, it is clear that from a statement of the public wealth giving the proportions of values only for the time and place when and where the statistics should be gathered we could not deduce the law of proportionality of wealth. For that, a single operation of this sort would not be sufficient; thousands and millions of similar ones would be necessary, even admitting the method to be worthy of confidence.

Now, here there is a difference between economic science and chemistry. The chemists, who have discovered by experience such beautiful proportions, know no more of their how or why than of the force which governs them. Social economy, on the contrary, to which no a posteriori investigation could reveal directly the law of proportionality of values, can grasp it in the very force which produces it, and which it is time to announce.

This force, which Adam Smith has glorified so eloquently, and which his successors have misconceived (making privilege its equal), — this force is LABOR. Labor differs in quantity and quality with the producer; in this respect it is like all the great principles of Nature and the most general laws, simple in their action and formula, but infinitely modified by a multitude of special causes, and manifesting themselves under an innumerable variety of forms. It is labor, labor alone, that produces all the elements of wealth, and that combines them to their last molecules according to a law of variable, but certain, proportionality. It is labor, in fine, that, as the principle of life, agitates (mens agitat) the material (molem) of wealth, and proportions it.

Society, or the collective man, produces an infinitude of objects, the enjoyment of which constitutes its well-being. This well-being is developed not only in the ratio of the quantity of the products, but also in the ratio of their variety (quality) and proportion. From this fundamental datum it follows that society always, at each instant of its life, must strive for such proportion in its products as will give the greatest amount of well-being, considering the power and means of production. Abundance, variety, and proportion in products are the three factors which constitute WEALTH: wealth, the object of social economy, is subject to the same conditions of existence as beauty, the object of art; virtue, the object of morality; and truth, the object of metaphysics.

But how establish this marvelous proportion, so essential that without it a portion of human labor is lost, — that is, useless, inharmonious, untrue, and consequently synonymous with poverty and annihilation?

Prometheus, according to the fable, is the symbol of human activity. Prometheus steals the fire of heaven, and invents the early arts; Prometheus foresees the future, and aspires to equality with Jupiter; Prometheus is God. Then let us call society Prometheus.

Prometheus devotes, on an average, ten hours a day to labor, seven to rest, and seven to pleasure. In order to gather from his toil the most useful fruit, Prometheus notes the time and trouble that each object of his consumption costs him. Only experience can teach him this, and this experience lasts throughout his life. While laboring and producing, then, Prometheus is subject to an infinitude of disappointments. But, as

87

a final result, the more he labors, the greater is his well-being and the more idealized his luxury; the further he extends his conquests over Nature, the more strongly he fortifies within him the principle of life and intelligence in the exercise of which he alone finds happiness; till finally, the early education of the Laborer completed and order introduced into his occupations, to labor, with him, is no longer to suffer, — it is to live, to enjoy. But the attractiveness of labor does not nullify the rule, since, on the contrary, it is the fruit of it; and those who, under the pretext that labor should be attractive, reason to the denial of justice and to communism, resemble children who, after having gathered some flowers in the garden, should arrange a flower-bed on the staircase.

In society, then, justice is simply the proportionality of values; its guarantee and sanction is the responsibility of the producer.

Prometheus knows that such a product costs an hour's labor, such another a day's, a week's, a year's; he knows at the same time that all these products, arranged according to their cost, form the progression of his wealth. First, then, he will assure his existence by providing himself with the least costly, and consequently most necessary, things; then, as fast as his position becomes secure, he will look forward to articles of luxury, proceeding always, if he is wise, according to the natural position of each article in the scale of prices. Sometimes Prometheus will make a mistake in his calculations, or else, carried away by passion, he will sacrifice an immediate good to a premature enjoyment, and, after having toiled and moiled, he will starve. Thus, the law carries with it its own sanction; its violation is inevitably accompanied by the immediate punishment of the transgressor.

Say, then, was right in saying: "The happiness of this class (the consumers), composed of all the others, constitutes the general well-being, the state of prosperity of a country." Only he should have added that the happiness of the class of producers, which also is composed of all the others, equally constitutes the general well-being, the state of prosperity of a country. So, when he says: "The fortune of each consumer is perpetually at war with all that he buys," he should have added again: "The fortune of each producer is incessantly attacked by all that he sells." In the absence of a clear expression of this reciprocity, most economical phenomena become unintelligible; and I will soon show how, in consequence of this grave omission, most economists in writing their books have talked wildly about the balance of trade.

88

I have just said that society produces first the least costly, and consequently most necessary, things. Now, is it true that cheapness of products is always a correlative of their necessity, and vice versa; so that these two words, necessity and cheapness, like the following ones, costliness and superfluity, are synonymes?

If each product of labor, taken alone, would suffice for the existence of man, the synonymy in question would not be doubtful; all products having the same qualities, those would be most advantageously produced, and therefore the most necessary, which cost the least. But the parallel between the utility and price of products is not characterized by this theoretical precision: either through the foresight of Nature or from some other cause, the balance between needs and productive power is more than a theory, — it is a fact, of which daily practice, as well as social progress, gives evidence.

Imagine ourselves living in the day after the birth of man at the beginning of civilization: is it not true that the industries originally the simplest, those which required the least preparation and expense, were the following: gathering, pasturage, hunting, and fishing, which were followed long afterwards by agriculture? Since then, these four primitive industries have been perfected, and moreover appropriated: a double circumstance which does not change the meaning of the facts, but, on the contrary, makes it more manifest. In fact, property has always attached itself by preference to objects of the most immediate utility, to made values, if I may so speak; so that the scale of values might be fixed by the progress of appropriation.

In his work on the "Liberty of Labor" M. Dunoyer has positively accepted this principle by distinguishing four great classes of industry, which he arranges according to the order of their development, — that is, from the least labor-cost to the greatest. These are extractive industry, — including all the semi-barbarous functions mentioned above, — commercial industry, manufacturing, industry, agricultural industry. And it is for a profound reason that the learned author placed agriculture last in the list. For, despite its great antiquity, it is certain that this industry has not kept pace with the others, and the succession of human affairs is not decided by their origin, but by their entire development. It may be that agricultural industry was born before the others, and it may be that all were contemporary; but that will be deemed of the latest date which shall be perfected last.

Thus the very nature of things, as well as his own wants, indicates to the laborer the order in which he should effect the production of the values that make up his well-being. Our law of proportionality, then, is at once physical and logical, objective and subjective; it has the highest degree of certainty. Let us pursue the application.

Of all the products of labor, none perhaps has cost longer and more patient efforts than the calendar. Nevertheless, there is none the enjoyment of which can now be procured more cheaply, and which, consequently, by our own definitions, has become more necessary. How, then, shall we explain this change? Why has the calendar, so useless to the early hordes, who only needed the alternation of night and day, as of winter and summer, become at last so indispensable, so unexpensive, so perfect? For, by a marvelous harmony, in social economy all these adjectives are interconvertible. How account, in short, by our law of proportion, for the variability of the value of the calendar?

In order that the labor necessary to the production of the calendar might be performed, might be possible, man had to find means of gaining time from his early occupations and from those which immediately followed them. In other words, these industries had to become more productive, or less costly, than they were at the beginning: which amounts to saying that it was necessary first to solve the problem of the production of the calendar from the extractive industries themselves.

Suppose, then, that suddenly, by a fortunate combination of efforts, by the division of labor, by the use of some machine, by better management of the natural resources, — in short, by his industry, — Prometheus finds a way of producing in one day as much of a certain object as he formerly produced in ten: what will follow? The product will change its position in the table of the elements of wealth; its power of affinity for other products, so to speak, being increased, its relative value will be proportionately diminished, and, instead of being quoted at one hundred, it will thereafter be quoted only at ten. But this value will still and always be none the less accurately determined, and it will still be labor alone which will fix the degree of its importance. Thus value varies, and the law of value is unchangeable: further, if value is susceptible of variation, it is because it is governed by a law whose principle is essentially inconstant, — namely, labor measured by time.

The same reasoning applies to the production of the calendar as to that of all possible values. I do not need to explain how — civilization (that is, the social fact of the increase of life) multiplying our tasks, rendering our moments more and more precious, and obliging us to keep a perpetual and detailed record of our whole life — the calendar has become to all one of the most necessary things. We know, moreover, that this wonderful discovery has given rise, as its natural complement, to one of our most valuable industries, the manufacture of clocks and watches.

At this point there very naturally arises an objection, the only one that can be offered against the theory of the proportionality of values.

Say and the economists who have succeeded him have observed that, labor being itself an object of valuation, a species of merchandise indeed like any other, to take it as the principal and efficient cause of value is to reason in a vicious circle. Therefore, they conclude, it is necessary to fall back on scarcity and opinion.

These economists, if they will allow me to say it, herein have shown themselves wonderfully careless. Labor is said to have value, not as merchandise itself, but in view of the values supposed to be contained in it potentially. The value of labor is a figurative expression, an anticipation of effect from cause.

It is a fiction by the same title as the productivity of capital. Labor produces, capital has value: and when, by a sort of ellipsis, we say the value of labor, we make an enjambement which is not at all contrary to the rules of language, but which theorists ought to guard against mistaking for a reality. Labor, like liberty, love, ambition, genius, is a thing vague and indeterminate in its nature, but qualitatively defined by its object, — that is, it becomes a reality through its product. When, therefore, we say: This man's labor is worth five francs per day, it is as if we should say: The daily product of this man's labor is worth five francs.

Now, the effect of labor is continually to eliminate scarcity and opinion as constitutive elements of value, and, by necessary consequence, to transform natural or indefinite utilities (appropriated or not) into measurable or social utilities: whence it follows that labor is at once a war declared upon the parsimony of Nature and a permanent conspiracy against property.

According to this analysis, value, considered from the point of view of the association which producers, by division of labor and by exchange, naturally form among themselves, is the proportional relation of the products which constitute wealth, and what we call the value of any special product is a formula which expresses, in terms of money, the proportion of this product to the general wealth. — Utility is the basis of value; labor fixes the relation; the price is the expression which, barring the fluctuations that we shall have to consider, indicates this relation.

Such is the centre around which useful and exchangeable value oscillate, the point where they are finally swallowed up and disappear: such is the absolute, unchangeable law which regulates economic disturbances and the freaks of industry and commerce, and governs progress. Every effort of thinking and laboring humanity, every individual and social speculation, as an integrant part of collective wealth, obeys this law. It was the destiny of political economy, by successively positing all its contradictory terms, to make this law known; the object of social economy, which I ask permission for a moment to distinguish from political economy, although at bottom there is no difference between them, will be to spread and apply it universally.

The theory of the measure or proportionality of values is, let it be noticed, the theory of equality itself. Indeed, just as in society, where we have seen that there is a complete identity between producer and consumer, the revenue paid to an idler is like value cast into the flames of Etna, so the laborer who receives excessive wages is like a gleaner to whom should be given a loaf of bread for gathering a stalk of grain: and all that the economists have qualified as unproductive consumption is in reality simply a violation of the law of proportionality.

We shall see in the sequence how, from these simple data, the social genius gradually deduces the still obscure system of organization of labor, distribution of wages, valuation of products, and universal solidarity. For social order is established upon the basis of inexorable justice, not at all upon the paradisical sentiments of fraternity, self-sacrifice, and love, to the exercise of which so many honorable socialists are endeavoring now to stimulate the people. It is in vain that, following Jesus Christ, they preach the necessity, and set the example, of sacrifice; selfishness is stronger, and only the law of severity, economic fatality, is capable of mastering it. Humanitarian enthusiasm may produce shocks favorable to the progress of civilization; but these crises of sentiment, like the oscillations of value, must always result only in a firmer and more absolute establishment of justice. Nature, or Divinity, we distrust in our hearts: she has never believed in the love of man for his fellow; and all that science reveals to us of the ways of Providence in the progress of society — I say it to the shame of the human conscience, but our hypocrisy must be made aware of it — shows a profound misanthropy on the part of God. God helps us, not from motives of goodness, but because order is his essence; God promotes the welfare of the world, not because he deems it worthy, but because the religion of his supreme intelligence lays the obligation upon him: and while the vulgar give him the sweet name Father, it is impossible for the historian, for the political economist, to believe that he either loves or esteems us.

Let us imitate this sublime indifference, this stoical ataraxia, of God; and, since the precept of charity always has failed to promote social welfare, let us look to pure reason for the conditions of harmony and virtue.

Value, conceived as the proportionality of products, otherwise called CONSTITUTED VALUE, necessarily implies in an equal degree utility and venality, indivisibly and harmoniously united. It implies utility, for, without this condition, the product would be destitute of that affinity which renders it exchangeable, and consequently makes it an element of wealth; it implies venality, since, if the product was not acceptable in the market at any hour and at a known price, it would be only a non-value, it would be nothing.

But, in constituted value, all these properties acquire a broader, more regular, truer significance than before. Thus, utility is no longer that inert capacity, so to speak, which things possess of serving for our enjoyments and in our researches; venality is no longer the exaggeration of a blind fancy or an unprincipled opinion; finally, variability has ceased to explain itself by a disingenuous discussion between supply and demand: all that has disappeared to give place to a positive, normal, and, under all possible circumstances, determinable idea. By the constitution of values each product, if it is allowable to establish such an analogy, becomes like the nourishment which, discovered by the alimentary instinct, then prepared by the digestive organs, enters into the general circulation, where it is converted, according to certain proportions, into flesh, bone, liquid, etc., and gives to the body life, strength, and beauty.

Now, what change does the idea of value undergo when we rise from the contradictory notions of useful value and exchangeable value to that of constituted value or absolute value? There is, so to speak, a joining together, a reciprocal penetration, in which the two elementary concepts, grasping each other like the hooked atoms of Epicurus, absorb one another and disappear, leaving in their place a compound possessed, but in a superior degree, of all their positive properties, and divested of all their negative properties. A value really such — like

93

money, first-class business paper, government annuities, shares in a well-established enterprise — can neither be increased without reason nor lost in exchange: it is governed only by the natural law of the addition of special industries and the increase of products. Further, such a value is not the result of a compromise, — that is, of eclecticism, juste-milieu, or mixture; it is the product of a complete fusion, a product entirely new and distinct from its components, just as water, the product of the combination of hydrogen and oxygen, is a separate body, totally distinct from its elements.

The resolution of two antithetical ideas in a third of a superior order is what the school calls synthesis. It alone gives the positive and complete idea, which is obtained, as we have seen, by the successive affirmation or negation — for both amount to the same thing — of two diametrically opposite concepts. Whence we deduce this corollary, of the first importance in practice as well as in theory: wherever, in the spheres of morality, history, or political economy, analysis has established the antinomy of an idea, we may affirm on a priori grounds that this antinomy conceals a higher idea, which sooner or later will make its appearance.

I am sorry to have to insist at so great length on ideas familiar to all young college graduates: but I owed these details to certain economists, who, apropos of my critique of property, have heaped dilemmas on dilemmas to prove that, if I was not a proprietor, I necessarily must be a communist; all because they did not understand thesis, antithesis, and synthesis.

The synthetic idea of value, as the fundamental condition of social order and progress, was dimly seen by Adam Smith, when, to use the words of M. Blanqui, "he showed that labor is the universal and invariable measure of values, and proved that everything has its natural price, toward which it continually gravitates amid the fluctuations of the market, occasioned by accidental circumstances foreign to the venal value of the thing."

But this idea of value was wholly intuitive with Adam Smith, and society does not change its habits upon the strength of intuitions; it decides only upon the authority of facts. The antinomy had to be expressed in a plainer and clearer manner: J. B. Say was its principal interpreter. But, in spite of the imaginative efforts and fearful subtlety of this economist, Smith's definition controls him without his knowledge, and is manifest throughout his arguments.

94

"To put a value on an article," says Say, "is to declare that it should be estimated equally with some other designated article...... The value of everything is vague and arbitrary until it is RECOGNIZED......" There is, therefore, a method of recognizing the value of things, — that is, of determining it; and, as this recognition or determination results from the comparison of things with each other, there is, further, a common feature, a principle, by means of which we are able to declare that one thing is worth more or less than, or as much as, another.

Say first said: "The measure of value is the value of an other product." Afterwards, having seen that this phrase was but a tautology, he modified it thus: "The measure of value is the quantity of another product," which is quite as unintelligible. Moreover, this writer, generally so clear and decided, embarrasses himself with vain distinctions: "We may appreciate the value of things; we cannot measure it, — that is, compare it with an invariable and known standard, for no such standard exists. We can do nothing but estimate the value of things by comparing them." At other times he distinguishes between real values and relative values: "The former are those whose value changes with the cost of production; the latter are those whose value changes relatively to the value of other kinds of merchandise."

Singular prepossession of a man of genius, who does not see that to compare, to appraise, to appreciate, is to MEASURE; that every measure, being only a comparison, indicates for that very reason a true relation, provided the comparison is accurate; that, consequently, value, or real measure, and value, or relative measure, are perfectly identical; and that the difficulty is reduced, not to the discovery of a standard of measure, since all quantities may serve each other in that capacity, but to the determination of a point of comparison. In geometry the point of comparison is extent, and the unit of measure is now the division of the circle into three hundred and sixty parts, now the circumference of the terrestrial globe, now the average dimension of the human arm, hand, thumb, or foot. In economic science, we have said after Adam Smith, the point of view from which all values are compared is labor; as for the unit of measure, that adopted in France is the FRANC. It is incredible that so many sensible men should struggle for forty years against an idea so simple. But no: The comparison of values is effected without a point of comparison between them, and without a unit of measure, — such is the proposition which the economists of the nineteenth century, rather than accept the revolutionary idea of equality, have resolved to maintain against all comers. What will posterity say?

I shall presently show, by striking examples, that the idea of the measure or proportion of values, theoretically necessary, is constantly realized in every-day life.

3. — Application of the law of proportionality of values.

Every product is a representative of labor.

Every product, therefore, can be exchanged for some other, as universal practice proves.

But abolish labor, and you have left only articles of greater or less usefulness, which, being stamped with no economic character, no human seal, are without a common measure, — that is, are logically unexchangeable.

Gold and silver, like other articles of merchandise, are representatives of value; they have, therefore, been able to serve as common measures and mediums of exchange. But the special function which custom has allotted to the precious metals, — that of serving as a commercial agent, — is purely conventional, and any other article of merchandise, less conveniently perhaps, but just as authentically, could play this part: the economists admit it, and more than one example of it can be cited. What, then, is the reason of this preference generally accorded to the metals for the purpose of money, and how shall we explain this speciality of function, unparalleled in political economy, possessed by specie? For every unique thing incomparable in kind is necessarily very difficult of comprehension, and often even fails of it altogether. Now, is it possible to reconstruct the series from which money seems to have been detached, and, consequently, restore the latter to its true principle?

In dealing with this question the economists, following their usual course, have rushed beyond the limits of their science; they have appealed to physics, to mechanics, to history, etc.; they have talked of all things, but have given no answer. The precious metals, they have said, by their scarcity, density, and incorruptibility, are fitted to serve as money in, a degree unapproached by other kinds of merchandise. In short, the economists, instead of replying to the economic question put to them, have set themselves to the examination of a question of art. They have laid great stress on the mechanical adaptation of gold and silver for the purpose of money; but not one of them has seen or understood the economic reason which gave to the precious metals the privilege they now enjoy.

Now, the point that no one has noticed is that, of all the various articles of merchandise, gold and silver were the first whose value was determined. In the patriarchal period, gold and silver still were bought and sold in ingots, but already with a visible tendency to superiority and with a marked preference. Gradually sovereigns took possession of them and stamped them with their seal; and from this royal consecration was born money, — that is, the commodity par excellence; that which, notwithstanding all commercial shocks, maintains a determined proportional value, and is accepted in payment for all things.

That which distinguishes specie, in fact, is not the durability of the metal, which is less than that of steel, nor its utility, which is much below that of wheat, iron, coal, and numerous other substances, regarded as almost vile when compared with gold; neither is it its scarcity or density, for in both these respects it might be replaced, either by labor spent upon other materials, or, as at present, by bank notes representing vast amounts of iron or copper. The distinctive feature of gold and silver, I repeat, is the fact that, owing to their metallic properties, the difficulties of their production, and, above all, the intervention of public authority, their value as merchandise was fixed and authenticated at an early date.

I say then that the value of gold and silver, especially of the part that is made into money, although perhaps it has not yet been calculated accurately, is no longer arbitrary; I add that it is no longer susceptible of depreciation, like other values, although it may vary continually nevertheless. All the logic and erudition that has been expended to prove, by the example of gold and silver, that value is essentially indeterminable, is a mass of paralogisms, arising from a false idea of the question, ab ignorantia elenchi.

Philip I, King of France, mixed with the livre tournois of Charlemagne one-third alloy, imagining that, since he held the monopoly of the power of coining money, he could do what every merchant does who holds the monopoly of a product. What was, in fact, this adulteration of money, for which Philip and his successors are so severely blamed? A very sound argument from the standpoint of commercial routine, but wholly false in the view of economic science, — namely, that, supply and demand being the regulators of value, we may, either by causing an artificial scarcity or by monopolizing the manufacture, raise the estimation, and consequently the value, of things, and that this is as true of gold and silver as of wheat, wine, oil, tobacco. Nevertheless, Philip's fraud was no sooner suspected than his money was reduced to its true value, and he lost himself all that he had expected to gain from his subjects. The same thing happened after all similar attempts. What was the reason of this disappointment?

Because, say the economists, the quantity of gold and silver in reality being neither diminished nor increased by the false coinage, the proportion of these metals to other merchandise was not changed, and consequently it was not in the power of the sovereign to make that which was worth but two worth four. For the same reason, if, instead of debasing the coin, it had been in the king's power to double its mass, the exchangeable value of gold and silver would have decreased one-half immediately, always on account of this proportionality and equilibrium. The adulteration of the coin was, then, on the part of the king, a forced loan, or rather, a bankruptcy, a swindle.

Marvelous! the economists explain very clearly, when they choose, the theory of the measure of value; that they may do so, it is necessary only to start them on the subject of money. Why, then, do they not see that money is the written law of commerce, the type of exchange, the first link in that long chain of creations all of which, as merchandise, must receive the sanction of society, and become, if not in fact, at least in right, acceptable as money in settlement of all kinds of transactions?

"Money," M. Augier very truly says, "can serve, either as a means of authenticating contracts already made, or as a good medium of exchange, only so far as its value approaches the ideal of permanence; for in all cases it exchanges or buys only the value which it possesses." [8]

Let us turn this eminently judicious observation into a general formula.

Labor becomes a guarantee of well-being and equality only so far as the product of each individual is in proportion with the mass; for in all cases it exchanges or buys a value equal only to its own.

Is it not strange that the defence of speculative and fraudulent commerce is undertaken boldly, while at the same time the attempt of a royal counterfeiter, who, after all, did but apply to gold and silver the fundamental principle of political economy, the arbitrary instability of values, is frowned down? If the administration should presume to give twelve ounces of tobacco for a pound, [9] the economists would cry robbery; but, if the same administration, using its privilege, should increase the price a few cents a pound, they would regard it as dear, but would discover no violation of principles. What an imbroglio is political economy!

There is, then, in the monetization of gold and silver something that the economists have given no account of; namely, the consecration of the law of proportionality, the first act in the constitution of values. Humanity does all things by infinitely small degrees: after comprehending the fact that all products of labor must be submitted to a proportional measure which makes all of them equally exchangeable, it begins by giving this attribute of absolute exchangeability to a special product, which shall become the type and model of all others. In the same way, to lift its members to liberty and equality, it begins by creating kings. The people have a confused idea of this providential progress when, in their dreams of fortune and in their legends, they speak continually of gold and royalty; and the philosophers only do homage to universal reason when, in their so-called moral homilies and their socialistic utopias, they thunder with equal violence against gold and tyranny. Auri sacra fames! Cursed gold! ludicrously shouts some communist. As well say cursed wheat, cursed vines, cursed sheep; for, like gold and silver, every commercial value must reach an exact and accurate determination. The work was begun long since; today it is making visible progress.

Let us pass to other considerations.

It is an axiom generally admitted by the economists that all labor should leave an excess.

I regard this proposition as universally and absolutely true; it is a corollary of the law of proportionality, which may be regarded as an epitome of the whole science of economy. But — I beg pardon of the economists -the principle that all labor should leave an excess has no meaning in their theory, and is not susceptible of demonstration. If supply and demand alone determine value, how can we tell what is an excess and what is a sufficiency? If neither cost, nor market price, nor wages can be mathematically determined, how is it possible to conceive of a surplus, a profit? Commercial routine has given us the idea of profit as well as the word; and, since we are equal politically, we infer that every citizen has an equal right to realize profits in his personal industry. But commercial operations are essentially irregular, and it has been proved beyond question that the profits of commerce are but an arbitrary discount forced from the consumer by the producer, — in short, a displacement, to say the least. This we should soon see, if it was possible to compare the total amount of annual losses with the amount of profits. In the thought of political economy, the principle that all labor should leave an excess is simply the consecration of the constitutional right which all of us gained by the revolution, — the right of robbing one's neighbor.

The law of proportionality of values alone can solve this problem. I will approach the question a little farther back: its gravity warrants me in treating it with the consideration that it merits.

Most philosophers, like most philologists, see in society only a creature of the mind, or rather, an abstract name serving to designate a collection of men. It is a prepossession which all of us received in our infancy with our first lessons in grammar, that collective nouns, the names of genera and species, do not designate realities. There is much to say under this head, but I confine myself to my subject. To the true economist, society is a living being, endowed with an intelligence and an activity of its own, governed by special laws discoverable by observation alone, and whose existence is manifested, not under a material aspect, but by the close concert and mutual interdependence of all its members. Therefore, when a few pages back, adopting the allegorical method, we used a fabulous god as a symbol of society, our language in reality was not in the least metaphorical: we only gave a name to the social being, an organic and synthetic unit. In the eyes of any one who has reflected upon the laws of labor and exchange (I disregard every other consideration), the reality, I had almost said the personality, of the collective man is as certain as the reality and the personality of the individual man. The only difference is that the latter appears to the senses as an organism whose parts are in a state of material coherence, which is not true of society. But intelligence, spontaneity, development, life, all that constitutes in the highest degree the reality of being, is as essential to society as to man: and hence it is that the government of societies is a science, — that is, a study of natural relations, — and not an art, — that is, good pleasure and absolutism. Hence it is, finally, that every society declines the moment it falls into the hands of the ideologists.

The principle that all labor should leave an excess, undemonstrable by political economy, — that is, by proprietary routine, — is one of those which bear strongest testimony to the reality of the collective person: for, as we shall see, this principle is true of individuals only because it emanates from society, which thus confers upon them the benefit of its own laws.

Let us turn to facts. It has been observed that railroad enterprises are a source of wealth to those who control them in a much less degree than to the State. The observation is a true one; and it might have been added that it applies, not only to railroads, but to every industry. But this phenomenon, which is essentially the result of the law of proportionality of values and of the absolute identity of production and consumption, is at variance with the ordinary notion of useful value and exchangeable value.

The average price charged for the transportation of merchandise by the old method is eighteen centimes per ton and kilometer, the merchandise taken and delivered at the warehouses. It has been calculated that, at this price, an ordinary railroad corporation would net a profit of not quite ten per cent., nearly the same as the profit made by the old method. But let us admit that the rapidity of transportation by rail is to that by wheels, all allowances made, as four to one: in society time itself being value, at the same price the railroad would have an advantage over the stage-wagon of four hundred per cent. Nevertheless, this enormous advantage, a very real one so far as society is concerned, is by no means realized in a like proportion by the carrier, who, while he adds four hundred per cent. to the social value, makes personally less than ten per cent. Suppose, in fact, to make the thing still clearer, that the railroad should raise its price to twenty-five centimes, the rate by the old method remaining at eighteen; it would lose immediately all its consignments; shippers, consignees, everybody would return to the stage-wagon, if necessary. The locomotive would be abandoned; a social advantage of four hundred per cent. would be sacrificed to a private loss of thirty-three per cent.

The reason of this is easily seen. The advantage which results from the rapidity of the railroad is wholly social, and each individual participates in it only in a very slight degree (do not forget that we are speaking now only of the transportation of merchandise); while the loss falls directly and personally on the consumer. A special profit of four hundred per cent. in a society composed of say a million of men represents four ten-thousandths for each individual; while a loss to the consumer of thirty-three per cent means a social deficit of thirty-three millions. Private interest and collective interest, seemingly so divergent at first blush, are therefore perfectly identical and equal: and this example may serve to show already how economic science reconciles all interests.

Consequently, in order that society may realize the profit above supposed, it is absolutely necessary that the railroad's prices shall not exceed, or shall exceed but very little, those of the stage-wagon.

But, that this condition may be fulfilled, — in other words, that the railroad may be commercially possible, — the amount of matter transported must be sufficiently great to cover at least the interest on the capital invested and the running expenses of the road. Then a railroad's first condition of existence is a large circulation, which implies a still larger production and a vast amount of exchanges.

But production, circulation, and exchange are not self-creative things; again, the various kinds of labor are not developed in isolation and independently of each other: their progress is necessarily connected, solidary, proportional. There may be antagonism among manufacturers; but, in spite of them, social action is one, convergent, harmonious, — in a word, personal. Further, there is a day appointed for the creation of great instruments of labor: it is the day when general consumption shall be able to maintain their employment, — that is, for all these propositions are interconvertible, the day when ambient labor can feed new machinery. To anticipate the hour appointed by the progress of labor would be to imitate the fool who, going from Lyons to Marseilles, chartered a steamer for himself alone.

These points cleared up, nothing is easier than to explain why labor must leave an excess for each producer.

And first, as regards society: Prometheus, emerging from the womb of Nature, awakens to life in a state of inertia which is very charming, but which would soon become misery and torture if he did not make haste to abandon it for labor. In this original idleness, the product of Prometheus being nothing, his well-being is the same as that of the brute, and may be represented by zero.

Prometheus begins to work: and from his first day's labor, the first of the second creation, the product of Prometheus — that is, his wealth, his well-being — is equal to ten.

The second day Prometheus divides his labor, and his product increases to one hundred.

The third day, and each following day, Prometheus invents machinery, discovers new uses in things, new forces in Nature; the field of his existence extends from the domain of the senses to the sphere of morals and intelligence, and with every step that his industry takes the amount of his product increases, and assures him additional happiness. And since, finally, with him, to consume is to produce, it is clear that each day's consumption, using up only the product of the day before, leaves a surplus product for the day after.

But notice also — and give especial heed to this all-important fact — that the well-being of man is directly proportional to the intensity of labor and the multiplicity of industries: so that the increase of wealth and the increase of labor are correlative and parallel.

To say now that every individual participates in these general conditions of collective development would be to affirm a truth which, by reason of the evidence in its support, would appear silly. Let us point out rather the two general forms of consumption in society.

Society, like the individual, has first its articles of personal consumption, articles which time gradually causes it to feel the need of, and which its mysterious instincts command it to create. Thus in the middle ages there was, with a large number of cities, a decisive moment when the building of city halls and cathedrals became a violent passion, which had to be satisfied at any price; the life of the community depended upon it. Security and strength, public order, centralization, nationality, country, independence, these are the elements which make up the life of society, the totality of its mental faculties; these are the sentiments which must find expression and representation. Such formerly was the object of the temple of Jerusalem, real palladium of the Jewish nation; such was the temple of Jupiter Capitolinus of Rome. Later, after the municipal palace and the temple, — organs, so to speak, of centralization and progress, — came the other works of public utility, — bridges, theatres, schools, hospitals, roads, etc.

The monuments of public utility being used essentially in common, and consequently gratuitously, society is rewarded for its advances by the political and moral advantages resulting from these great works, and which, furnishing security to labor and an ideal to the mind, give fresh impetus to industry and the arts.

But it is different with the articles of domestic consumption, which alone fall within the category of exchange. These can be produced only upon the conditions of mutuality which make consumption possible, — that is, immediate payment with advantage to the producers. These conditions we have developed sufficiently in the theory of proportionality of values, which we might call as well the theory of the gradual reduction of cost.

I have demonstrated theoretically and by facts the principle that all labor should leave an excess; but this principle, as certain as any proposition in arithmetic, is very far from universal realization. While, by the progress of collective industry, each individual day's labor yields a greater and greater product, and while, by necessary consequence, the laborer, receiving the same wages, must grow ever richer, there exist in society classes which thrive and classes which perish; laborers paid twice, thrice, a hundred times over, and laborers continually out of pocket; everywhere, finally, people who enjoy and people who suffer, and, by a monstrous division of the means of industry, individuals who consume and do not produce. The distribution of well-being follows all the movements of value, and reproduces them in misery and luxury on a frightful scale and with terrible energy. But everywhere, too, the progress of wealth — that is, the proportionality of values — is the dominant law; and when the economists combat the complaints of the socialists with the progressive increase of public wealth and the alleviations of the condition of even the most unfortunate classes, they proclaim, without suspecting it, a truth which is the condemnation of their theories.

For I entreat the economists to question themselves for a moment in the silence of their hearts, far from the prejudices which disturb them, and regardless of the employments which occupy them or which they wait for, of the interests which they serve, of the votes which they covet, of the distinctions which tickle their vanity: let them tell me whether, hitherto, they have viewed the principle that all labor should leave an excess in connection with this series of premises and conclusions which we have elaborated, and whether they ever have understood these words to mean anything more than the right to speculate in values by manipulating supply and demand; whether it is not true that they affirm at once, on the one hand the progress of wealth and well-being, and consequently the measure of values, and on the other the arbitrariness of commercial transactions and the incommensurability of values, — the flattest of contradictions? Is it not because of this contradiction that we continually hear repeated in lectures, and read in the works on political economy, this absurd hypothesis: If the price of ALL things was doubled...... ? As if the price of all things was not the proportion of things, and as if we could double a proportion, a relation, a law! Finally, is it not because of the proprietary and abnormal routine upheld by political economy that every one, in commerce, industry, the arts,

104

and the State, on the pretended ground of services rendered to society, tends continually to exaggerate his importance, and solicits rewards, subsidies, large pensions, exorbitant fees: as if the reward of every service was not determined necessarily by the sum of its expenses? Why do not the economists, if they believe, as they appear to, that the labor of each should leave an excess, use all their influence in spreading this truth, so simple and so luminous: Each man's labor can buy only the value which it contains, and this value is proportional to the services of all other laborers?

But here a last consideration presents itself, which I will explain in a few words.

J. B. Say, who of all the economists has insisted the most strenuously upon the absolute indeterminability of value, is also the one who has taken the most pains to refute that idea. He, if I am not mistaken, is the author of the formula: Every product is worth what it costs; or, what amounts to the same thing: Products are bought with products. This aphorism, which leads straight to equality, has been controverted since by other economists; we will examine in turn the affirmative and the negative.

When I say that every product is worth the products which it has cost, I mean that every product is a collective unit which, in a new form, groups a certain number of other products consumed in various quantities. Whence it follows that the products of human industry are, in relation to each other, genera and species, and that they form a series from the simple to the composite, according to the number and proportion of the elements, all equivalent to each other, which constitute each product. It matters little, for the present, that this series, as well as the equivalence of its elements, is expressed in practice more or less exactly by the equilibrium of wages and fortunes; our first business is with the relation of things, the economic law. For here, as ever, the idea first and spontaneously generates the fact, which, recognized then by the thought which has given it birth, gradually rectifies itself and conforms to its principle. Commerce, free and competitive, is but a long operation of redressal, whose object is to define more and more clearly the proportionality of values, until the civil law shall recognize it as a guide in matters concerning the condition of persons. I say, then, that Say's principle, Every product is worth what it costs, indicates a series in human production analogous to the animal and vegetable series, in which the elementary units (day's works) are regarded as equal. So that political economy affirms at its birth, but by a contradiction, what neither Plato, nor Rousseau, nor any ancient or modern publicist has thought possible, -equality of conditions and fortunes.

Prometheus is by turns husbandman, wine-grower, baker, weaver. Whatever trade he works at, laboring only for himself, he buys what he consumes (his products) with one and the same money (his products), whose unit of measurement is necessarily his day's work. It is true that labor itself is liable to vary; Prometheus is not always in the same condition, and from one moment to another his enthusiasm, his fruitfulness, rises and falls. But, like everything that is subject to variation, labor has its average, which justifies us in saying that, on the whole, day's work pays for day's work, neither more nor less. It is quite true that, if we compare the products of a certain period of social life with those of another, the hundred millionth day's work of the human race will show a result incomparably superior to that of the first; but it must be remembered also that the life of the collective being can no more be divided than that of the individual; that, though the days may not resemble each other, they are indissolubly united, and that in the sum total of existence pain and pleasure are common to them. If, then, the tailor, for rendering the value of a day's work, consumes ten times the product of the day's work of the weaver, it is as if the weaver gave ten days of his life for one day of the tailor's. This is exactly what happens when a peasant pays twelve francs to a lawyer for a document which it takes him an hour to prepare; and this inequality, this iniquity in exchanges, is the most potent cause of misery that the socialists have unveiled, — as the economists confess in secret while awaiting a sign from the master that shall permit them to acknowledge it openly.

Every error in commutative justice is an immolation of the laborer, a transfusion of the blood of one man into the body of another..... Let no one be frightened; I have no intention of fulminating against property an irritating philippic; especially as I think that, according to my principles, humanity is never mistaken; that, in establishing itself at first upon the right of property, it only laid down one of the principles of its future organization; and that, the pre-ponderance of property once destroyed, it remains only to reduce this famous antithesis to unity. All the objections that can be offered in favor of property I am as well acquainted with as any of my critics, whom I ask as a favor to show their hearts when logic fails them. How can wealth that is not measured by labor be valuable? And if it is labor that creates wealth and legitimates property, how explain the consumption of the idler? Where is the honesty in a system of distribution in which a product is worth, according to the person, now more, now less, than it costs.

106

Say's ideas led to an agrarian law; therefore, the conservative party hastened to protest against them. "The original source of wealth," M. Rossi had said, "is labor. In proclaiming this great principle, the industrial school has placed in evidence not only an economic principle, but that social fact which, in the hands of a skilful historian, becomes the surest guide in following the human race in its marchings and haltings upon the face of the earth."

Why, after having uttered these profound words in his lectures, has M. Rossi thought it his duty to retract them afterwards in a review, and to compromise gratuitously his dignity as a philosopher and an economist?

"Say that wealth is the result of labor alone; affirm that labor is always the measure of value, the regulator of prices; yet, to escape one way or another the objections which these doctrines call forth on all hands, some incomplete, others absolute, you will be obliged to generalize the idea of labor, and to substitute for analysis an utterly erroneous synthesis."

I regret that a man like M. Rossi should suggest to me so sad a thought; but, while reading the passage that I have just quoted, I could not help saying: Science and truth have lost their influence: the present object of worship is the shop, and, after the shop, the desperate constitutionalism which represents it. To whom, then, does M. Rossi address himself? Is he in favor of labor or something else; analysis or synthesis? Is he in favor of all these things at once? Let him choose, for the conclusion is inevitably against him.

If labor is the source of all wealth, if it is the surest guide in tracing the history of human institutions on the face of the earth, why should equality of distribution, equality as measured by labor, not be a law?

If, on the contrary, there is wealth which is not the product of labor, why is the possession of it a privilege? Where is the legitimacy of monopoly? Explain then, once for all, this theory of the right of unproductive consumption; this jurisprudence of caprice, this religion of idleness, the sacred prerogative of a caste of the elect.

What, now, is the significance of this appeal from analysis to the false judgments of the synthesis? These metaphysical terms are of no use, save to indoctrinate simpletons, who do not suspect that the same proposition can be construed, indifferently and at will, analytically or synthetically. Labor is the principle of value end the source of wealth:

an analytic proposition such as M. Rossi likes, since it is the summary of an analysis in which it is demonstrated that the primitive notion of labor is identical with the subsequent notions of product, value, capital, wealth, etc. Nevertheless, we see that M. Rossi rejects the doctrine which results from this analysis. Labor, capital, and land are the sources of wealth: a synthetic proposition, precisely such as M. Rossi does not like. Indeed, wealth is considered here as a general notion, produced in three distinct, but not identical, ways. And yet the doctrine thus formulated is the one that M. Rossi prefers. Now, would it please M. Rossi to have us render his theory of monopoly analytically and ours of labor synthetically? I can give him the satisfaction..... But I should blush, with so earnest a man, to prolong such badinage. M. Rossi knows better than any one that analysis and synthesis of themselves prove absolutely nothing, and that the important work, as Bacon said, is to make exact comparisons and complete enumerations.

Since M. Rossi was in the humor for abstractions, why did he not say to the phalanx of economists who listen so respectfully to the least word that falls from his lips:

"Capital is the material of wealth, as gold and silver are the material of money, as wheat is the material of bread, and, tracing the series back to the end, as earth, water, fire, and air are the material of all our products. But it is labor, labor alone, which successively creates each utility given to these materials, and which consequently transforms them into capital and wealth. Capital is the result of labor, — that is, realized intelligence and life, — as animals and plants are realizations of the soul of the universe, and as the chefs d'oeuvre of Homer, Raphael, and Rossini are expressions of their ideas and sentiments. Value is the proportion in which all the realizations of the human soul must balance each other in order to produce a harmonious whole, which, being wealth, gives us well-being, or rather is the token, not the object, of our happiness.

"The proposition, there is no measure of value, is illogical and contradictory, as is shown by the very arguments which have been offered in its support.

"The proposition, labor is the principle of proportionality of values, not only is true, resulting as it does from an irrefutable analysis, but it is the object of progress, the condition and form of social well-being, the beginning and end of political economy. From this proposition and its corollaries, every product is worth what it costs, and products are bought with products, follows the dogma of equality of conditions.

"The idea of value socially constituted, or of proportionality of values, serves to explain further: (a) how a mechanical invention, notwithstanding the privilege which it temporarily creates and the disturbances which it occasions, always produces in the end a general amelioration; (b) how the value of an economical process to its discoverer can never equal the profit which it realizes for society; (c) how, by a series of oscillations between supply and demand, the value of every product constantly seeks a level with cost and with the needs of consumption, and consequently tends to establish itself in a fixed and positive manner; (d) how, collective production continually increasing the amount of consumable things, and the day's work constantly obtaining higher and higher pay, labor must leave an excess for each producer; (e) how the amount of work to be done, instead of being diminished by industrial progress, ever increases in both quantity and quality — that is, in intensity and difficulty — in all branches of industry; (f) how social value continually eliminates fictitious values, — in other words, how industry effects the socialization of capital and property; (g) finally, how the distribution of products, growing in regularity with the strength of the mutual guarantee resulting from the constitution of value, pushes society onward to equality of conditions and fortunes.

"Finally, the theory of the successive constitution of all commercial values implying the infinite progress of labor, wealth, and well-being, the object of society, from the economic point of view, is revealed to us: To produce incessantly, with thee least possible amount of labor for each product, the greatest possible quantity and variety of values, in such a way as to realize, for each individual, the greatest amount of physical, moral, and intellectual well-being, and, for the race, the highest perfection and infinite glory.

Now that we have determined, not without difficulty, the meaning of the question asked by the Academy of Moral Sciences touching the oscillations of profit and wages, it is time to begin the essential part of our work. Wherever labor has not been socialized, — that is, wherever value is not synthetically determined, — there is irregularity and dishonesty in exchange; a war of stratagems and ambuscades; an impediment to production, circulation, and consumption; unproductive labor; insecurity; spoliation; insolidarity; want; luxury: but at the same time an effort of the genius of society to obtain justice, and a constant tendency toward association and order. Political economy is simply the history of this grand struggle. On the one hand, indeed, political economy, in so far as it sanctions and pretends to perpetuate the anomalies of value and the prerogatives of selfishness, is truly the theory of misfortune and the organization of misery; but in so far as it explains the means invented by civilization to abolish poverty, although these means always have been used exclusively in the interest of monopoly, political economy is the preamble of the organization of wealth.

It is important, then, that we should resume the study of economic facts and practices, discover their meaning, and formulate their philosophy. Until this is done, no knowledge of social progress can be acquired, no reform attempted. The error of socialism has consisted hitherto in perpetuating religious reverie by launching forward into a fantastic future instead of seizing the reality which is crushing it; as the wrong of the economists has been in regarding every accomplished fact as an injunction against any proposal of reform.

For my own part, such is not my conception of economic science, the true social science. Instead of offering a priori arguments as solutions of the formidable problems of the organization of labor and the distribution of wealth, I shall interrogate political economy as the depositary of the secret thoughts of humanity; I shall cause it to disclose the facts in the order of their occurrence, and shall relate their testimony without intermingling it with my own. It will be at once a triumphant and a lamentable history, in which the actors will be ideas, the episodes theories, and thc dates formulas.

Chapter III. Economic Evolutions. — First Period. — The Division of Labor.

The fundamental idea, the dominant category, of political economy is VALUE.

Value reaches its positive determination by a series of oscillations between supply and demand.

Consequently, value appears successively under three aspects: useful value, exchangeable value, and synthetic, or social, value, which is true value. The first term gives birth to the second in contradiction to it, and the two together, absorbing each other in reciprocal penetration, produce the third: so that the contradiction or antagonism of ideas appears as the point of departure of all economic science, allowing us to say of it, parodying the sentence of Tertullian in relation to the Gospel, Credo quia absurdum: There is, in social economy, a latent

110

truth wherever there is an apparent contradiction, Credo quia contrarium.

From the point of view of political economy, then, social progress consists in a continuous solution of the problem of the constitution of values, or of the proportionality and solidarity of products.

But while in Nature the synthesis of opposites is contemporary with their opposition, in society the antithetic elements seem to appear at long intervals, and to reach solution only after long and tumultuous agitation. Thus there is no example — the idea even is inconceivable — of a valley without a hill, a left without a right, a north pole without a south pole, a stick with but one end, or two ends without a middle, etc. The human body, with its so perfectly antithetic dichotomy, is formed integrally at the very moment of conception; it refuses to be put together and arranged piece by piece, like the garment patterned after it which, later, is to cover it. [10]

In society, on the contrary, as well as in the mind, so far from the idea reaching its complete realization at a single bound, a sort of abyss separates, so to speak, the two antinomical positions, and even when these are recognized at last, we still do not see what the synthesis will be. The primitive concepts must be fertilized, so to speak, by burning controversy and passionate struggle; bloody battles will be the preliminaries of peace. At the present moment, Europe, weary of war and discussion, awaits a reconciling principle; and it is the vague perception of this situation which induces the Academy of Moral and Political Sciences to ask, "What are the general facts which govern the relations of profits to wages and determine their oscillations?" in other words, what are the most salient episodes and the most remarkable phases of the war between labor and capital?

If, then, I demonstrate that political economy, with all its contradictory hypotheses and equivocal conclusions, is nothing but an organization of privilege and misery, I shall have proved thereby that it contains by implication the promise of an organization of labor and equality, since, as has been said, every systematic contradiction is the announcement of a composition; further, I shall have fixed the bases of this composition. Then, indeed, to unfold the system of economical contradictions is to lay the foundations of universal association; to show how the products of collective labor come out of society is to explain how it will be possible to make them return to it; to exhibit the genesis of the problems of production and distribution is to prepare the way for their solution. All these propositions are identical and equally evident.

111

1. — Antagonistic effects of the principle of division.

All men are equal in the state of primitive communism, equal in their nakedness and ignorance, equal in the indefinite power of their faculties. The economists generally look at only the first of these aspects; they neglect or overlook the second. Nevertheless, according to the profoundest philosophers of modern times, La Rochefoucault, Helvetius, Kant, Fichte, Hegel, Jacotot, intelligence differs in individuals only qualitatively, each having thereby his own specialty or genius; in its essence, — namely, judgment, — it is quantitatively equal in all. Hence it follows that, a little sooner or a little later, according as circumstances shall be more or less favorable, general progress must lead all men from original and negative equality to a positive equivalence of talents and acquirements.

I insist upon this precious datum of psychology, the necessary consequence of which is that the hierarchy of capacities henceforth cannot be allowed as a principle and law of organization: equality alone is our rule, as it is also our ideal. Then, just as the equality of misery must change gradually into equality of well-being, as we have proved by the theory of value, so the equality of minds, negative in the beginning, since it represents only emptiness, must reappear in a positive form at the completion of humanity's education. The intellectual movement proceeds parallelly with the economic movement; they are the expression, the translation, of each other; psychology and social economy are in accord, or rather, they but unroll the same history, each from a different point of view. This appears especially in Smith's great law, the division of labor.

Considered in its essence, the division of labor is the way in which equality of condition and intelligence is realized. Through diversity of function, it gives rise to proportionality of products and equilibrium in exchange, and consequently opens for us the road to wealth; as also, in showing us infinity everywhere in art and Nature, it leads us to idealize our acts, and makes the creative mind — that is, divinity itself, mentem diviniorem — immanent and perceptible in all laborers.

Division of labor, then, is the first phase of economic evolution as well as of intellectual development: our point of departure is true as regards both man and things, and the progress of our exposition is in no wise arbitrary.

But, at this solemn hour of the division of labor, tempestuous winds begin to blow upon humanity. Progress does not improve the condition

112

of all equally and uniformly, although in the end it must include and transfigure every intelligent and industrious being. It commences by taking possession of a small number of privileged persons, who thus compose the elite of nations, while the mass continues, or even buries itself deeper, in barbarism. It is this exception of persons on the part of progress which has perpetuated the belief in the natural and providential inequality of conditions, engendered caste, and given an hierarchical form to all societies. It has not been understood that all inequality, never being more than a negation, carries in itself the proof of its illegitimacy and the announcement of its downfall: much less still has it been imagined that this same inequality proceeds accidentally from a cause the ulterior effect of which must be its entire disappearance.

Thus, the antinomy of value reappearing in the law of division, it is found that the first and most potent instrument of knowledge and wealth which Providence has placed in our hands has become for us an instrument of misery and imbecility. Here is the formula of this new law of antagonism, to which we owe the two oldest maladies of civilization, aristocracy and the proletariat: Labor, in dividing itself according to the law which is peculiar to it, and which is the primary condition of its productivity, ends in the frustration of its own objects, and destroys itself, in other words: Division, in the absence of which there is no progress, no wealth, no equality, subordinates the workingman, and renders intelligence useless, wealth harmful, and equality impossible.

All the economists, since Adam Smith, have pointed out the advantages and the inconveniences of the law of division, but at the same time insisting much more strenuously upon the first than the second, because such a course was more in harmony with their optimistic views, and not one of them ever asking how a law can have inconveniences. This is the way in which J. B. Say summed up the question: —

"A man who during his whole life performs but one operation, certainly acquires the power to execute it better and more readily than another; but at the same time he becomes less capable of any other occupation, whether physical or moral; his other faculties become extinct, and there results a degeneracy in the individual man. That one has made only the eighteenth part of a pin is a sad account to give of one's self: but let no one imagine that it is the workingman who spends his life in handling a file or a hammer that alone degenerates in this way from the dignity of his nature; it is the same with the man whose position leads him to exercise the most subtle faculties of his mind... On the whole, it may be said that the separation of tasks is an advantageous use of human forces; that it increases enormously the products of society; but that it takes something from the capacity of each man taken individually." [11]

What, then, after labor, is the primary cause of the multiplication of wealth and the skill of laborers? Division.

What is the primary cause of intellectual degeneracy and, as we shall show continually, civilized misery? Division.

How does the same principle, rigorously followed to its conclusions, lead to effects diametrically opposite? There is not an economist, either before or since Adam Smith, who has even perceived that here is a problem to be solved. Say goes so far as to recognize that in the division of labor the same cause which produces the good engenders the evil; then, after a few words of pity for the victims of the separation of industries, content with having given an impartial and faithful exhibition of the facts, he leaves the matter there. "You know," he seems to say, "that the more we divide the workmen's tasks, the more we increase the productive power of labor; but at the same time the more does labor, gradually reducing itself to a mechanical operation, stupefy intelligence."

In vain do we express our indignation against a theory which, creating by labor itself an aristocracy of capacities, leads inevitably to political inequality; in vain do we protest in the name of democracy and progress that in the future there will be no nobility, no bourgeoisie no pariahs. The economist replies, with the impassibility of destiny: You are condemned to produce much, and to produce cheaply; otherwise your industry will be always insignificant, your commerce will amount to nothing, and you will drag in the rear of civilization instead of taking the lead. — What! among us, generous men, there are some predestined to brutishness; and the more perfect our industry becomes, the larger will grow the number of our accursed brothers!..... — Alas!..... That is the last word of the economist.

We cannot fail to recognize in the division of labor, as a general fact and as a cause, all the characteristics of a LAW; but as this law governs two orders of phenomena radically opposite and destructive of each other, it must be confessed also that this law is of a sort unknown in the exact sciences, — that it is, strange to say, a contradictory law, a counter-law an antinomy. Let us add, in anticipation, that such appears

114

to be the identifying feature of social economy, and consequently of philosophy.

Now, without a RECOMPOSITION of labor which shall obviate the inconveniences of division while preserving its useful effects, the contradiction inherent in the principle is irremediable. It is necessary, — following the style of the Jewish priests, plotting the death of Christ, — it is necessary that the poor should perish to secure the proprietor his for tune, expedit unum hominem pro populo mori. I am going to demonstrate the necessity of this decree; after which, if the parcellaire laborer still retains a glimmer of intelligence, he will console himself with the thought that he dies according to the rules of political economy.

Labor, which ought to give scope to the conscience and render it more and more worthy of happiness, leading through parcellaire division to prostration of mind, dwarfs man in his noblest part, minorat capitis, and throws him back into animality. Thenceforth the fallen man labors as a brute, and consequently must be treated as a brute. This sentence of Nature and necessity society will execute.

The first effect of parcellaire labor, after the depravation of the mind, is the lengthening of the hours of labor, which increase in inverse proportion to the amount of intelligence expended. For, the product increasing in quantity and quality at once, if, by any industrial improvement whatever, labor is lightened in one way, it must pay for it in another. But as the length of the working-day cannot exceed from sixteen to eighteen hours, when compensation no longer can be made in time, it will be taken from the price, and wages will decrease. And this decrease will take place, not, as has been foolishly imagined, because value is essentially arbitrary, but because it is essentially determinable. Little matters it that the struggle between supply and demand ends, now to the advantage of the employer, now to the benefit of the employee; such oscillations may vary in amplitude, this depending on well-known accessory circumstances which have been estimated a thousand times. The certain point, and the only one for us to notice now, is that the universal conscience does not set the same price upon the labor of an overseer and the work of a hod-carrier. A reduction in the price of the day's work, then, is necessary: so that the laborer, after having been afflicted in mind by a degrading function, cannot fail to be struck also in his body by the meagreness of his reward. This is the literal application of the words of the Gospel: He that hath not, from him shall be taken even that which he hath.

There is in economic accidents a pitiless reason which laughs at religion and equity as political aphorisms, and which renders man happy or unhappy according as he obeys or escapes the prescriptions of destiny. Certainly this is far from that Christian charity with which so many honorable writers today are inspired, and which, penetrating to the heart of the bourgeoisie, endeavors to temper the rigors of the law by numerous religious institutions. Political economy knows only justice, justice as inflexible and unyielding as the miser's purse; and it is because political economy is the effect of social spontaneity and the expression of the divine will that I have been able to say: God is man's adversary, and Providence a misanthrope. God makes us pay, in weight of blood and measure of tears, for each of our lessons; and to complete the evil, we, in our relations with our fellows, all act like him. Where, then, is this love of the celestial father for his creatures? Where is human fraternity?

Can he do otherwise? say the theists. Man falling, the animal remains: how could the Creator recognize in him his own image? And what plainer than that he treats him then as a beast of burden? But the trial will not last for ever, and sooner or later labor, having been particularized, will be synthetized.

Such is the ordinary argument of all those who seek to justify Providence, but generally succeed only in lending new weapons to atheism. That is to say, then, that God would have envied us, for six thousand years, an idea which would have saved millions of victims, a distribution of labor at once special and synthetic! In return, he has given us, through his servants Moses, Buddha, Zoroaster, Mahomet, etc., those insipid writings, the disgrace of our reason, which have killed more men than they contain letters! Further, if we must believe primitive revelation, social economy was the cursed science, the fruit of the tree reserved for God, which man was forbidden to touch! Why this religious depreciation of labor, if it is true, as economic science already shows, that labor is the father of love and the organ of happiness? Why this jealousy of our advancement? But if, as now sufficiently appears, our progress depends upon ourselves alone, of what use is it to adore this phantom of divinity, and what does he still ask of us through the multitude of inspired persons who pursue us with their sermons? All of you, Christians, protestant and orthodox, neo-revelators, charlatans and dupes, listen to the first verse of the humanitarian hymn upon God's mercy: "In proportion as the principle of division of labor receives complete application, the worker becomes weaker, narrower, and more dependent. Art advances: the artisan recedes!" [12]

116

Then let us guard against anticipating conclusions and prejudging the latest revelation of experience. At present God seems less favorable than hostile: let us confine ourselves to establishing the fact.

Just as political economy, then, at its point of departure, has made us understand these mysterious and dismal words: In proportion as the production of utility increases, venality decreases; so arrived at its first station, it warns us in a terrible voice: In proportion as art advances, the artisan recedes. To fix the ideas better, let us cite a few examples.

In all the branches of metal-working, who are the least industrious of the wage-laborers? Precisely those who are called machinists. Since tools have been so admirably perfected, a machinist is simply a man who knows how to handle a file or a plane: as for mechanics, that is the business of engineers and foremen. A country blacksmith often unites in his own person, by the very necessity of his position, the various talents of the locksmith, the edge-tool maker, the gunsmith, the machinist, the wheel-wright, and the horse-doctor: the world of thought would be astonished at the knowledge that is under the hammer of this man, whom the people, always inclined to jest, nickname brule-fer. A workingman of Creuzot, who for ten years has seen the grandest and finest that his profession can offer, on leaving his shop, finds himself unable to render the slightest service or to earn his living. The incapacity of the subject is directly proportional to the perfection of the art; and this is as true of all the trades as of metal-working.

The wages of machinists are maintained as yet at a high rate: sooner or later their pay must decrease, the poor quality of the labor being unable to maintain it.

I have just cited a mechanical art; let us now cite a liberal industry.

Would Gutenburg and his industrious companions, Faust and Schoffer, ever have believed that, by the division of labor, their sublime invention would fall into the domain of ignorance — I had almost said idiocy? There are few men so weak-minded, so unlettered, as the mass of workers who follow the various branches of the typographic industry, — compositors, pressmen, type-founders, book-binders, and paper-makers. The printer, as he existed even in the days of the Estiennes, has become almost an abstraction. The employment of women in type-setting has struck this noble industry to the heart, and consummated its degradation. I have seen a female compositor — and she was one of the best — who did not know how to read, and was acquainted only with the forms of the letters. The whole art has been

117

withdrawn into the hands of foremen and proof-readers, modest men of learning whom the impertinence of authors and patrons still humiliates, and a few workmen who are real artists. The press, in a word, fallen into mere mechanism, is no longer, in its personnel, at the level of civilization: soon there will be left of it but a few souvenirs.

I am told that the printers of Paris are endeavoring by association to rise again from their degradation: may their efforts not be exhausted in vain empiricism or misled into barren utopias!

After private industries, let us look at public administration.

In the public service, the effects of parcellaire labor are no less frightful, no less intense: in all the departments of administration, in proportion as the art develops, most of the employees see their salaries diminish. A letter-carrier receives from four hundred to six hundred francs per annum, of which the administration retains about a tenth for the retiring pension. After thirty years of labor, the pension, or rather the restitution, is three hundred francs per annum, which, when given to an alms-house by the pensioner, entitles him to a bed, soup, and washing. My heart bleeds to say it, but I think, nevertheless, that the administration is generous: what reward would you give to a man whose whole function consists in walking? The legend gives but five sous to the Wandering Jew; the letter-carriers receive twenty or thirty; true, the greater part of them have a family. That part of the service which calls into exercise the intellectual faculties is reserved for the postmasters and clerks: these are better paid; they do the work of men.

Everywhere, then, in public service as well as free industry, things are so ordered that nine-tenths of the laborers serve as beasts of burden for the other tenth: such is the inevitable effect of industrial progress and the indispensable condition of all wealth. It is important to look well at this elementary truth before talking to the people of equality, liberty, democratic institutions, and other utopias, the realization of which involves a previous complete revolution in the relations of laborers.

The most remarkable effect of the division of labor is the decay of literature.

In the Middle Ages and in antiquity the man of letters, a sort of encyclopaedic doctor, a successor of the troubadour and the poet, all-knowing, was almighty. Literature lorded it over society with a high hand; kings sought the favor of authors, or revenged themselves for their contempt by burning them, — them and their books. This, too, was a way of recognizing literary sovereignty.

Today we have manufacturers, lawyers, doctors, bankers, merchants, professors, engineers, librarians, etc.; we have no men of letters. Or rather, whoever has risen to a remarkable height in his profession is thereby and of necessity lettered: literature, like the baccalaureate, has become an elementary part of every profession. The man of letters, reduced to his simplest expression, is the public writer, a sort of writing commissioner in the pay of everybody, whose best-known variety is the journalist.

It was a strange idea that occurred to the Chambers four years ago, -that of making a law on literary property! As if henceforth the idea was not to become more and more the all-important point, the style nothing. Thanks to God, there is an end of parliamentary eloquence as of epic poetry and mythology; the theatre rarely attracts business men and savants; and while the connoisseurs are astonished at the decline of art, the philosophic observer sees only the progress of manly reason, troubled rather than rejoiced at these dainty trifles. The interest in romance is sustained only as long as it resembles reality; history is reducing itself to anthropological exegesis; everywhere, indeed, the art of talking well appears as a subordinate auxiliary of the idea, the fact. The worship of speech, too mazy and slow for impatient minds, is neglected, and its artifices are losing daily their power of seduction. The language of the nineteenth century is made up of facts and figures, and he is the most eloquent among us who, with the fewest words, can say the most things. Whoever cannot speak this language is mercilessly relegated to the ranks of the rhetoricians; he is said to have no ideas.

In a young society the progress of letters necessarily outstrips philosophical and industrial progress, and for a long time serves for the expression of both. But there comes a day when thought leaves language in the rear, and when, consequently, the continued preeminence of literature in a society becomes a sure symptom of decline. Language, in fact, is to every people the collection of its native ideas, the encyclopædia which Providence first reveals to it; it is the field which its reason must cultivate before directly attacking Nature through observation and experience. Now, as soon as a nation, after having exhausted the knowledge contained in its vocabulary, instead of pursuing its education by a superior philosophy, wraps itself in its poetic mantle, and begins to play with its periods and its hemistichs, we may safely say that such a society is lost. Everything in it will become subtle, narrow, and false; it will not have even the advantage of maintaining in its splendor the language of which it is foolishly enamored; instead of going forward in the path of the geniuses of transition, the Tacituses, the Thucydides, the Machiavels, and the Montesquieus, it will be seen to fall, with irresistible force, from the majesty of Cicero to the subtleties of Seneca, the antitheses of St. Augustine, and the puns of St. Bernard.

Let no one, then, be deceived: from the moment that the mind, at first entirely occupied with speech, passes to experience and labor, the man of letters, properly speaking, is simply the puny personification of the least of our faculties; and literature, the refuse of intelligent industry, finds a market only with the idlers whom it amuses and the proletaires whom it fascinates, the jugglers who besiege power and the charlatans who shelter themselves behind it, the hierophants of divine right who blow the trumpet of Sinai, and the fanatical proclaimers of the sovereignty of the people, whose few mouth-pieces, compelled to practise their tribunician eloquence from tombs until they can shower it from the height of rostrums, know no better than to give to the public parodies of Gracchus and Demosthenes.

All the powers of society, then, agree in indefinitely deteriorating the condition of the parcellaire laborer; and experience, universally confirming the theory, proves that this worker is condemned to misfortune from his mother's womb, no political reform, no association of interests, no effort either of public charity or of instruction, having the power to aid him. The various specifics proposed in these latter days, far from being able to cure the evil, would tend rather to inflame it by irritation; and all that has been written on this point has only exhibited in a clear light the vicious circle of political economy.

This we shall demonstrate in a few words.

2. — Impotence of palliatives. — MM. Blanqui, Chevalier, Dunoyer, Rossi, and Passy.

All the remedies proposed for the fatal effects of parcellaire division may be reduced to two, which really are but one, the second being the inversion of the first: to raise the mental and moral condition of the workingman by increasing his comfort and dignity; or else, to prepare the way for his future emancipation and happiness by instruction.

We will examine successively these two systems, one of which is represented by M. Blanqui, the other by M. Chevalier.

120

M. Blanqui is a friend of association and progress, a writer of democratic tendencies, a professor who has a place in the hearts of the proletariat. In his opening discourse of the year 1845, M. Blanqui proclaimed, as a means of salvation, the association of labor and capital, the participation of the working man in the profits, — that is, a beginning of industrial solidarity. "Our century," he exclaimed, "must witness the birth of the collective producer." M. Blanqui forgets that the collective producer was born long since, as well as the collective consumer, and that the question is no longer a genetic, but a medical, one. Our task is to cause the blood proceeding from the collective digestion, instead of rushing wholly to the head, stomach, and lungs, to descend also into the legs and arms. Besides, I do not know what method M. Blanqui proposes to employ in order to realize his generous thought, — whether it be the establishment of national workshops, or the loaning of capital by the State, or the expropriation of the conductors of business enterprises and the substitution for them of industrial associations, or, finally, whether he will rest content with a recommendation of the savings bank to workingmen, in which case the participation would be put off till doomsday.

However this may be, M. Blanqui's idea amounts simply to an increase of wages resulting from the copartnership, or at least from the interest in the business, which he confers upon the laborers. What, then, is the value to the laborer of a participation in the profits?

A mill with fifteen thousand spindles, employing three hundred hands, does not pay at present an annual dividend of twenty thousand francs. I am informed by a Mulhouse manufacturer that factory stocks in Alsace are generally below par and that this industry has already become a means of getting money by stock-jobbing instead of by labor. To SELL; to sell at the right time; to sell dear, — is the only object in view; to manufacture is only to prepare for a sale. When I assume, then, on an average, a profit of twenty thousand francs to a factory employing three hundred persons, my argument being general, I am twenty thousand francs out of the way. Nevertheless, we will admit the correctness of this amount. Dividing twenty thousand francs, the profit of the mill, by three hundred, the number of persons, and again by three hundred, the number of working days, I find an increase of pay for each person of twenty-two and one-fifth centimes, or for daily expenditure an addition of eighteen centimes, just a morsel of bread. Is it worth while, then, for this, to expropriate mill-owners and endanger the public welfare, by erecting establishments which must be insecure, since, property being divided into infinitely small shares, and being no longer supported by profit, business enterprises would lack ballast, and would be unable to weather commercial gales. And even if no expropriation was involved, what a poor prospect to offer the working class is an increase of eighteen centimes in return for centuries of economy; for no less time than this would be needed to accumulate the requisite capital, supposing that periodical suspensions of business did not periodically consume its savings!

The fact which I have just stated has been pointed out in several ways. M. Passy [13] himself took from the books of a mill in Normandy where the laborers were associated with the owner the wages of several families for a period of ten years, and he found that they averaged from twelve to fourteen hundred francs per year. He then compared the situation of mill-hands paid in proportion to the prices obtained by their employers with that of laborers who receive fixed wages, and found that the difference is almost imperceptible. This result might easily have been foreseen. Economic phenomena obey laws as abstract and immutable as those of numbers: it is only privilege, fraud, and absolutism which disturb the eternal harmony.

M. Blanqui, repentant, as it seems, at having taken this first step toward socialistic ideas, has made haste to retract his words. At the same meeting in which M. Passy demonstrated the inadequacy of cooperative association, he exclaimed: "Does it not seem that labor is a thing susceptible of organization, and that it is in the power of the State to regulate the happiness of humanity as it does the march of an army, and with an entirely mathematical precision? This is an evil tendency, a delusion which the Academy cannot oppose too strongly, because it is not only a chimera, but a dangerous sophism. Let us respect good and honest intentions; but let us not fear to say that to publish a book upon the organization of labor is to rewrite for the fiftieth time a treatise upon the quadrature of the circle or the philosopher's stone."

Then, carried away by his zeal, M. Blanqui finishes the destruction of his theory of cooperation, which M. Passy already had so rudely shaken, by the following example: "M. Dailly, one of the most enlightened of farmers, has drawn up an account for each piece of land and an account for each product; and he proves that within a period of thirty years the same man has never obtained equal crops from the same piece of land. The products have varied from twenty-six thousand francs to nine thousand or seven thousand francs, sometimes descending as low as three hundred francs. There are also certain products — potatoes, for instance — which fail one time in ten. How, then, with these variations and with revenues so uncertain, can we establish even distribution and uniform wages for laborers?...."

It might be answered that the variations in the product of each piece of land simply indicate that it is necessary to associate proprietors with each other after having associated laborers with proprietors, which would establish a more complete solidarity: but this would be a prejudgment on the very thing in question, which M. Blanqui definitively decides, after reflection, to be unattainable, — namely, the organization of labor. Besides, it is evident that solidarity would not add an obolus to the common wealth, and that, consequently, it does not even touch the problem of division.

In short, the profit so much envied, and often a very uncertain matter with employers, falls far short of the difference between actual wages and the wages desired; and M. Blanqui's former plan, miserable in its results and disavowed by its author, would be a scourge to the manufacturing industry. Now, the division of labor being henceforth universally established, the argument is generalized, and leads us to the conclusion that misery is an effect of labor, as well as of idleness.

The answer to this is, and it is a favorite argument with the people: Increase the price of services; double and triple wages.

I confess that if such an increase was possible it would be a complete success, whatever M. Chevalier may have said, who needs to be slightly corrected on this point.

According to M. Chevalier, if the price of any kind of merchandise whatever is increased, other kinds will rise in a like proportion, and no one will benefit thereby.

This argument, which the economists have rehearsed for more than a century, is as false as it is old, and it belonged to M. Chevalier, as an engineer, to rectify the economic tradition. The salary of a head clerk being ten francs per day, and the wages of a workingman four, if the income of each is increased five francs, the ratio of their fortunes, which was formerly as one hundred to forty, will be thereafter as one hundred to sixty. The increase of wages, necessarily taking place by addition and not by proportion, would be, therefore, an excellent method of equalization; and the economists would deserve to have thrown back at them by the socialists the reproach of ignorance which they have bestowed upon them at random.

But I say that such an increase is impossible, and that the supposition is absurd: for, as M. Chevalier has shown very clearly elsewhere, the figure which indicates the price of the day's labor is only an algebraic

123

exponent without effect on the reality: and that which it is necessary first to endeavor to increase, while correcting the inequalities of distribution, is not the monetary expression, but the quantity of products. Till then every rise of wages can have no other effect than that produced by a rise of the price of wheat, wine, meat, sugar, soap, coal, etc., — that is, the effect of a scarcity. For what is wages?

It is the cost price of wheat, wine, meat, coal; it is the integrant price of all things. Let us go farther yet: wages is the proportionality of the elements which compose wealth, and which are consumed every day reproductively by the mass of laborers. Now, to double wages, in the sense in which the people understand the words, is to give to each producer a share greater than his product, which is contradictory: and if the rise pertains only to a few industries, a general disturbance in exchange ensues, — that is, a scarcity. God save me from predictions! but, in spite of my desire for the amelioration of the lot of the working class, I declare that it is impossible for strikes followed by an increase of wages to end otherwise than in a general rise in prices: that is as certain as that two and two make four. It is not by such methods that the workingmen will attain to wealth and — what is a thousand times more precious than wealth — liberty. The workingmen, supported by the favor of an indiscreet press, in demanding an increase of wages, have served monopoly much better than their own real interests: may they recognize, when their situation shall become more painful, the bitter fruit of their inexperience!

Convinced of the uselessness, or rather, of the fatal effects, of an increase of wages, and seeing clearly that the question is wholly organic and not at all commercial, M. Chevalier attacks the problem at the other end. He asks for the working class, first of all, instruction, and proposes extensive reforms in this direction.

Instruction! this is also M. Arago's word to the workingmen; it is the principle of all progress. Instruction!.... It should be known once for all what may be expected from it in the solution of the problem before us; it should be known, I say, not whether it is desirable that all should receive it, — this no one doubts, — but whether it is possible.

To clearly comprehend the complete significance of M. Chevalier's views, a knowledge of his methods is indispensable.

M. Chevalier, long accustomed to discipline, first by his polytechnic studies, then by his St. Simonian connections, and finally by his position in the University, does not seem to admit that a pupil can have any other inclination than to obey the regulations, a sectarian any other thought than that of his chief, a public functionary any other opinion than that of the government. This may be a conception of order as respectable as any other, and I hear upon this subject no expressions of approval or censure. Has M. Chevalier an idea to offer peculiar to himself? On the principle that all that is not forbidden by law is allowed, he hastens to the front to deliver his opinion, and then abandons it to give his adhesion, if there is occasion, to the opinion of authority. It was thus that M. Chevalier, before settling down in the bosom of the Constitution, joined M. Enfantin: it was thus that he gave his views upon canals, railroads, finance, property, long before the administration had adopted any system in relation to the construction of railways, the changing of the rate of interest on bonds, patents, literary property, etc.

M. Chevalier, then, is not a blind admirer of the University system of instruction, — far from it; and until the appearance of the new order of things, he does not hesitate to say what he thinks. His opinions are of the most radical.

M. Villemain had said in his report: "The object of the higher education is to prepare in advance a choice of men to occupy and serve in all the positions of the administration, the magistracy, the bar and the various liberal professions, including the higher ranks and learned specialties of the army and navy."

"The higher education," thereupon observes M. Chevalier, [14] "is designed also to prepare men some of whom shall be farmers, others manufacturers, these merchants, and those private engineers. Now, in the official programme, all these classes are forgotten. The omission is of considerable importance; for, indeed, industry in its various forms, agriculture, commerce, are neither accessories nor accidents in a State: they are its chief dependence.... If the University desires to justify its name, it must provide a course in these things; else an industrial university will be established in opposition to it.... We shall have altar against altar, etc...."

And as it is characteristic of a luminous idea to throw light on all questions connected with it, professional instruction furnishes M. Chevalier with a very expeditious method of deciding, incidentally, the quarrel between the clergy and the University on liberty of education.

"It must be admitted that a very great concession is made to the clergy in allowing Latin to serve as the basis of education. The clergy know

125

Latin as well as the University; it is their own tongue. Their tuition, moreover, is cheaper; hence they must inevitably draw a large portion of our youth into their small seminaries and their schools of a higher grade...."

The conclusion of course follows: change the course of study, and you decatholicize the realm; and as the clergy know only Latin and the Bible, when they have among them neither masters of art, nor farmers, nor accountants; when, of their forty thousand priests, there are not twenty, perhaps, with the ability to make a plan or forge a nail, — we soon shall see which the fathers of families will choose, industry or the breviary, and whether they do not regard labor as the most beautiful language in which to pray to God.

Thus would end this ridiculous opposition between religious education and profane science, between the spiritual and the temporal, between reason and faith, between altar and throne, old rubrics henceforth meaningless, but with which they still impose upon the good nature of the public, until it takes offence.

M. Chevalier does not insist, however, on this solution: he knows that religion and monarchy are two powers which, though continually quarrelling, cannot exist without each other; and that he may not awaken suspicion, he launches out into another revolutionary idea, — equality.

"France is in a position to furnish the polytechnic school with twenty times as many scholars as enter at present (the average being one hundred and seventy-six, this would amount to three thousand five hundred and twenty). The University has but to say the word.... If my opinion was of any weight, I should maintain that mathematical capacity is much less special than is commonly supposed. I remember the success with which children, taken at random, so to speak, from the pavements of Paris, follow the teaching of La Martiniere by the method of Captain Tabareau."

If the higher education, reconstructed according to the views of M. Chevalier, was sought after by all young French men instead of by only ninety thousand as commonly, there would be no exaggeration in raising the estimate of the number of minds mathematically inclined from three thousand five hundred and twenty to ten thousand; but, by the same argument, we should have ten thousand artists, philologists, and philosophers; ten thousand doctors, physicians, chemists, and naturalists; ten thousand economists, legists, and administrators; twenty

126

thousand manufacturers, foremen, merchants, and accountants; forty thousand farmers, wine-growers, miners, etc., — in all, one hundred thousand specialists a year, or about one-third of our youth. The rest, having, instead of special adaptations, only mingled adaptations, would be distributed indifferently elsewhere.

It is certain that so powerful an impetus given to intelligence would quicken the progress of equality, and I do not doubt that such is the secret desire of M. Chevalier. But that is precisely what troubles me: capacity is never wanting, any more than population, and the problem is to find employment for the one and bread for the other. In vain does M. Chevalier tell us: "The higher education would give less ground for the complaint that it throws into society crowds of ambitious persons without any means of satisfying their desires, and interested in the overthrow of the State; people without employment and unable to get any, good for nothing and believing themselves fit for anything, especially for the direction of public affairs. Scientific studies do not so inflate the mind. They enlighten and regulate it at once; they fit men for practical life...." Such language, I reply, is good to use with patriarchs: a professor of political economy should have more respect for his position and his audience. The government has only one hundred and twenty offices annually at its disposal for one hundred and seventy-six students admitted to the polytechnic school: what, then, would be its embarrassment if the number of admissions was ten thousand, or even, taking M. Chevalier's figures, three thousand five hundred? And, to generalize, the whole number of civil positions is sixty thousand, or three thousand vacancies annually; what dismay would the government be thrown into if, suddenly adopting the reformatory ideas of M. Chevalier, it should find itself besieged by fifty thousand office-seekers! The following objection has often been made to republicans without eliciting a reply: When everybody shall have the electoral privilege, will the deputies do any better, and will the proletariat be further advanced? I ask the same question of M. Chevalier: When each academic year shall bring you one hundred thousand fitted men, what will you do with them?

To provide for these interesting young people, you will go down to the lowest round of the ladder. You will oblige the young man, after fifteen years of lofty study, to begin, no longer as now with the offices of aspirant engineer, sub-lieutenant of artillery, second lieutenant, deputy, comptroller, general guardian, etc., but with the ignoble positions of pioneer, train-soldier, dredger, cabin-boy, fagot-maker, and exciseman. There he will wait, until death, thinning the ranks, enables him to advance a step. Under such circumstances a man, a graduate of the

127

polytechnic school and capable of becoming a Vauban, may die a laborer on a second class road, or a corporal in a regiment

Oh! how much more prudent Catholicism has shown itself, and how far it has surpassed you all, St. Simonians, republicans, university men, economists, in the knowledge of man and society! The priest knows that our life is but a voyage, and that our perfection cannot be realized here below; and he contents himself with outlining on earth an education which must be completed in heaven. The man whom religion has moulded, content to know, do, and obtain what suffices for his earthly destiny, never can become a source of embarrassment to the government: rather would he be a martyr. O beloved religion! is it necessary that a bourgeoisie which stands in such need of you should disown you?...

Into what terrible struggles of pride and misery does this mania for universal instruction plunge us! Of what use is professional education, of what good are agricultural and commercial schools, if your students have neither employment nor capital? And what need to cram one's self till the age of twenty with all sorts of knowledge, then to fasten the threads of a mule-jenny or pick coal at the bottom of a pit? What! you have by your own confession only three thousand positions annually to bestow upon fifty thousand possible capacities, and yet you talk of establishing schools! Cling rather to your system of exclusion and privilege, a system as old as the world, the support of dynasties and patriciates, a veritable machine for gelding men in order to secure the pleasures of a caste of Sultans. Set a high price upon your teaching, multiply obstacles, drive away, by lengthy tests, the son of the proletaire whom hunger does not permit to wait, and protect with all your power the ecclesiastical schools, where the students are taught to labor for the other life, to cultivate resignation, to fast, to respect those in high places, to love the king, and to pray to God. For every useless study sooner or later becomes an abandoned study: knowledge is poison to slaves.

Surely M. Chevalier has too much sagacity not to have seen the consequences of his idea. But he has spoken from the bottom of his heart, and we can only applaud his good intentions: men must first be men; after that, he may live who can.

Thus we advance at random, guided by Providence, who never warns us except with a blow: this is the beginning and end of political economy.

Contrary to M. Chevalier, professor of political economy at the College of France, M. Dunoyer, an economist of the Institute, does not wish instruction to be organized. The organization of instruction is a species of organization of labor; therefore, no organization. Instruction, observes M. Dunoyer, is a profession, not a function of the State; like all professions, it ought to be and remain free. It is communism, it is socialism, it is the revolutionary tendency, whose principal agents have been Robespierre, Napoleon, Louis XVIII, and M. Guizot, which have thrown into our midst these fatal ideas of the centralization and absorption of all activity in the State. The press is very free, and the pen of the journalist is an object of merchandise; religion, too, is very free, and every wearer of a gown, be it short or long, who knows how to excite public curiosity, can draw an audience about him. M. Lacordaire has his devotees, M. Leroux his apostles, M. Buchez his convent. Why, then, should not instruction also be free? If the right of the instructed, like that of the buyer, is unquestionable, and that of the instructor, who is only a variety of the seller, is its correlative, it is impossible to infringe upon the liberty of instruction without doing violence to the most precious of liberties, that of the conscience. And then, adds M. Dunoyer, if the State owes instruction to everybody, it will soon be maintained that it owes labor; then lodging; then shelter.... Where does that lead to?

The argument of M. Dunoyer is irrefutable: to organize instruction is to give to every citizen a pledge of liberal employment and comfortable wages; the two are as intimately connected as the circulation of the arteries and the veins. But M. Dunoyer's theory implies also that progress belongs only to a certain select portion of humanity, and that barbarism is the eternal lot of nine-tenths of the human race. It is this which constitutes, according to M. Dunoyer, the very essence of society, which manifests itself in three stages, religion, hierarchy, and beggary. So that in this system, which is that of Destutt de Tracy, Montesquieu, and Plato, the antinomy of division, like that of value, is without solution.

It is a source of inexpressible pleasure to me, I confess, to see M. Chevalier, a defender of the centralization of instruction, opposed by M. Dunoyer, a defender of liberty; M. Dunoyer in his turn antagonized by M. Guizot; M. Guizot, the representative of the centralizers, contradicting the Charter, which posits liberty as a principle; the Charter trampled under foot by the University men, who lay sole claim to the privilege of teaching, regardless of the express command of the Gospel to the priests: Go and teach. And above all this tumult of economists, legislators, ministers, academicians, professors, and priests, economic Providence giving the lie to the Gospel, and shouting: Pedagogues! what use am I to make of your instruction?

Who will relieve us of this anxiety? M. Rossi leans toward eclecticism: Too little divided, he says, labor remains unproductive; too much divided, it degrades man. Wisdom lies between these extremes; in medio virtus. Unfortunately this intermediate wisdom is only a small amount of poverty joined with a small amount of wealth, so that the condition is not modified in the least. The proportion of good and evil, instead of being as one hundred to one hundred, becomes as fifty to fifty: in this we may take, once for all, the measure of eclecticism. For the rest, M. Rossi's juste-milieu is in direct opposition to the great economic law: To produce with the least possible expense the greatest possible quantity of values.... Now, how can labor fulfil its destiny without an extreme division? Let us look farther, if you please.

"All economic systems and hypotheses," says M. Rossi, "belong to the economist, but the intelligent, free, responsible man is under the control of the moral law... Political economy is only a science which examines the relations of things, and draws conclusions therefrom. It examines the effects of labor; in the application of labor, you should consider the importance of the object in view. When the application of labor is unfavorable to an object higher than the production of wealth, it should not be applied... Suppose that it would increase the national wealth to compel children to labor fifteen hours a day: morality would say that that is not allowable. Does that prove that political economy is false? No; that proves that you confound things which should be kept separate."

If M. Rossi had a little more of that Gallic simplicity so difficult for foreigners to acquire, he would very summarily have thrown his tongue to the dogs, as Madame de Sevigne said. But a professor must talk, talk, talk, not for the sake of saying anything, but in order to avoid silence. M. Rossi takes three turns around the question, then lies down: that is enough to make certain people believe that he has answered it.

It is surely a sad symptom for a science when, in developing itself according to its own principles, it reaches its object just in time to be contradicted by another; as, for example, when the postulates of political economy are found to be opposed to those of morality, for I suppose that morality is a science as well as political economy. What, then, is human knowledge, if all its affirmations destroy each other, and on what shall we rely? Divided labor is a slave's occupation, but it alone is really productive; undivided labor belongs to the free man, but

130

it does not pay its expenses. On the one hand, political economy tells us to be rich; on the other, morality tells us to be free; and M. Rossi, speaking in the name of both, warns us at the same time that we can be neither free nor rich, for to be but half of either is to be neither. M. Rossi's doctrine, then, far from satisfying this double desire of humanity, is open to the objection that, to avoid exclusiveness, it strips us of everything: it is, under another form, the history of the representative system.

But the antagonism is even more profound than M. Rossi has supposed. For since, according to universal experience (on this point in harmony with theory), wages decrease in proportion to the division of labor, it is clear that, in submitting ourselves to parcellaire slavery, we thereby shall not obtain wealth; we shall only change men into machines: witness the laboring population of the two worlds. And since, on the other hand, without the division of labor, society falls back into barbarism, it is evident also that, by sacrificing wealth, we shall not obtain liberty: witness all the wandering tribes of Asia and Africa. Therefore it is necessary — economic science and morality absolutely command it — for us to solve the problem of division: now, where are the economists? More than thirty years ago, Lemontey, developing a remark of Smith, exposed the demoralizing and homicidal influence of the division of labor. What has been the reply; what investigations have been made; what remedies proposed; has the question even been understood?

Every year the economists report, with an exactness which I would commend more highly if I did not see that it is always fruitless, the commercial condition of the States of Europe. They know how many yards of cloth, pieces of silk, pounds of iron, have been manufactured; what has been the consumption per head of wheat, wine, sugar, meat: it might be said that to them the ultimate of science is to publish inventories, and the object of their labor is to become general comptrollers of nations. Never did such a mass of material offer so fine a field for investigation. What has been found; what new principle has sprung from this mass; what solution of the many problems of long standing has been reached; what new direction have studies taken?

One question, among others, seems to have been prepared for a final judgment, — pauperism. Pauperism, of all the phenomena of the civilized world, is today the best known: we know pretty nearly whence it comes, when and how it arrives, and what it costs; its proportion at various stages of civilization has been calculated, and we have convinced ourselves that all the specifics with which it hitherto has

131

been fought have been impotent. Pauperism has been divided into genera, species, and varieties: it is a complete natural history, one of the most important branches of anthropology. Well I the unquestionable result of all the facts collected, unseen, shunned, covered by the economists with their silence, is that pauperism is constitutional and chronic in society as long as the antagonism between labor and capital continues, and that this antagonism can end only by the absolute negation of political economy. What issue from this labyrinth have the economists discovered?

This last point deserves a moment's attention.

In primitive communism misery, as I have observed in a preceding paragraph, is the universal condition.

Labor is war declared upon this misery.

Labor organizes itself, first by division, next by machinery, then by competition, etc.

Now, the question is whether it is not in the essence of this organization, as given us by political economy, at the same time that it puts an end to the misery of some, to aggravate that of others in a fatal and unavoidable manner. These are the terms in which the question of pauperism must be stated, and for this reason we have undertaken to solve it.

What means, then, this eternal babble of the economists about the improvidence of laborers, their idleness, their want of dignity, their ignorance, their debauchery, their early marriages, etc.? All these vices and excesses are only the cloak of pauperism; but the cause, the original cause which inexorably holds four-fifths of the human race in disgrace, — what is it? Did not Nature make all men equally gross, averse to labor, wanton, and wild? Did not patrician and proletaire spring from the same clay? Then how happens it that, after so many centuries, and in spite of so many miracles of industry, science, and art, comfort and culture have not become the inheritance of all? How happens it that in Paris and London, centres of social wealth, poverty is as hideous as in the days of Caesar and Agricola? Why, by the side of this refined aristocracy, has the mass remained so uncultivated? It is laid to the vices of the people: but the vices of the upper class appear to be no less; perhaps they are even greater. The original stain affected all alike: how happens it, once more, that the baptism of civilization has not been equally efficacious for all? Does this not show that progress

132

itself is a privilege, and that the man who has neither wagon nor horse is forced to flounder about for ever in the mud? What do I say? The totally destitute man has no desire to improve: he has fallen so low that ambition even is extinguished in his heart.

"Of all the private virtues," observes M. Dunoyer with infinite reason, "the most necessary, that which gives us all the others in succession, is the passion for well-being, is the violent desire to extricate one's self from misery and abjection, is that spirit of emulation and dignity which does not permit men to rest content with an inferior situation.... But this sentiment, which seems so natural, is unfortunately much less common than is thought. There are few reproaches which the generality of men deserve less than that which ascetic moralists bring against them of being too fond of their comforts: the opposite reproach might be brought against them with infinitely more justice.... There is even in the nature of men this very remarkable feature, that the less their knowledge and resources, the less desire they have of acquiring these. The most miserable savages and the least enlightened of men are precisely those in whom it is most difficult to arouse wants, those in whom it is hardest to inspire the desire to rise out of their condition; so that man must already have gained a certain degree of comfort by his labor, before he can feel with any keenness that need of improving his condition, of perfecting his existence, which I call the love of well-being." [15]

Thus the misery of the laboring classes arises in general from their lack of heart and mind, or, as M. Passy has said somewhere, from the weakness, the inertia of their moral and intellectual faculties. This inertia is due to the fact that the said laboring classes, still half savage, do not have a sufficiently ardent desire to ameliorate their condition: this M. Dunoyer shows. But as this absence of desire is itself the effect of misery, it follows that misery and apathy are each other's effect and cause, and that the proletariat turns in a circle.

To rise out of this abyss there must be either well-being, — that is, a gradual increase of wages, — or intelligence and courage, — that is, a gradual development of faculties: two things diametrically opposed to the degradation of soul and body which is the natural effect of the division of labor. The misfortune of the proletariat, then, is wholly providential, and to undertake to extinguish it in the present state of political economy would be to produce a revolutionary whirlwind.

For it is not without a profound reason, rooted in the loftiest considerations of morality, that the universal conscience, expressing

133

itself by turns through the selfishness of the rich and the apathy of the proletariat, denies a reward to the man whose whole function is that of a lever and spring. If, by some impossibility, material well-being could fall to the lot of the parcellaire laborer, we should see something monstrous happen: the laborers employed at disagreeable tasks would become like those Romans, gorged with the wealth of the world, whose brutalized minds became incapable of devising new pleasures. Well-being without education stupefies people and makes them insolent: this was noticed in the most ancient times. Incrassatus est, et recalcitravit, says

Deuteronomy. For the rest, the parcellaire laborer has judged himself: he is content, provided he has bread, a pallet to sleep on, and plenty of liquor on Sunday. Any other condition would be prejudicial to him, and would endanger public order.

At Lyons there is a class of men who, under cover of the monopoly given them by the city government, receive higher pay than college professors or the head-clerks of the government ministers: I mean the porters. The price of loading and unloading at certain wharves in Lyons, according to the schedule of the Rigues or porters' associations, is thirty centimes per hundred kilogrammes. At this rate, it is not seldom that a man earns twelve, fifteen, and even twenty francs a day: he only has to carry forty or fifty sacks from a vessel to a warehouse. It is but a few hours' work. What a favorable condition this would be for the development of intelligence, as well for children as for parents, if, of itself and the leisure which it brings, wealth was a moralizing principle! But this is not the case: the porters of Lyons are today what they always have been, drunken, dissolute, brutal, insolent, selfish, and base. It is a painful thing to say, but I look upon the following declaration as a duty, because it is the truth: one of the first reforms to be effected among the laboring classes will be the reduction of the wages of some at the same time that we raise those of others. Monopoly does not gain in respectability by belonging to the lowest classes of people, especially when it serves to maintain only the grossest individualism. The revolt of the silk-workers met with no sympathy, but rather hostility, from the porters and the river population generally. Nothing that happens off the wharves has any power to move them. Beasts of burden fashioned in advance for despotism, they will not mingle with politics as long as their privilege is maintained. Nevertheless, I ought to say in their defence that, some time ago, the necessities of competition having brought their prices down, more social sentiments began to awaken in these gross natures: a few more reductions seasoned with a little poverty, and the Rigues of Lyons will

134

be chosen as the storming-party when the time comes for assaulting the bastilles.

In short, it is impossible, contradictory, in the present system of society, for the proletariat to secure well-being through education or education through well-being. For, without considering the fact that the proletaire, a human machine, is as unfit for comfort as for education, it is demonstrated, on the one hand, that his wages continually tend to go down rather than up, and, on the other, that the cultivation of his mind, if it were possible, would be useless to him; so that he always inclines towards barbarism and misery. Everything that has been attempted of late years in France and England with a view to the amelioration of the condition of the poor in the matters of the labor of women and children and of primary instruction, unless it was the fruit of some hidden thought of radicalism, has been done contrary to economic ideas and to the prejudice of the established order. Progress, to the mass of laborers, is always the book sealed with the seven seals; and it is not by legislative misconstructions that the relentless enigma will be solved.

For the rest, if the economists, by exclusive attention to their old routine, have finally lost all knowledge of the present state of things, it cannot be said that the socialists have better solved the antinomy which division of labor raised. Quite the contrary, they have stopped with negation; for is it not perpetual negation to oppose, for instance, the uniformity of parcellaire labor with a so-called variety in which each one can change his occupation ten, fifteen, twenty times a day at will?

As if to change ten, fifteen, twenty times a day from one kind of divided labor to another was to make labor synthetic; as if, consequently, twenty fractions of the day's work of a manual laborer could be equal to the day's work of an artist! Even if such industrial vaulting was practicable, — and it may be asserted in advance that it would disappear in the presence of the necessity of making laborers responsible and therefore functions personal, — it would not change at all the physical, moral, and intellectual condition of the laborer; the dissipation would only be a surer guarantee of his incapacity and, consequently, his dependence. This is admitted, moreover, by the organizers, communists, and others. So far are they from pretending to solve the antinomy of division that all of them admit, as an essential condition of organization, the hierarchy of labor, — that is, the classification of laborers into parcellaires and generalizers or organizers, — and in all utopias the distinction of capacities, the basis or everlasting excuse for inequality of goods, is admitted as a pivot. Those reformers whose schemes have nothing to recommend them but

135

logic, and who, after having complained of the simplism, monotony, uniformity, and extreme division of labor, then propose a plurality as a SYNTHESIS, — such inventors, I say, are judged already, and ought to be sent back to school.

But you, critic, the reader undoubtedly will ask, what is your solution? Show us this synthesis which, retaining the responsibility, the personality, in short, the specialty of the laborer, will unite extreme division and the greatest variety in one complex and harmonious whole.

My reply is ready: Interrogate facts, consult humanity: we can choose no better guide. After the oscillations of value, division of labor is the economic fact which influences most perceptibly profits and wages. It is the first stake driven by Providence into the soil of industry, the starting-point of the immense triangulation which finally must determine the right and duty of each and all. Let us, then, follow our guides, without which we can only wander and lose ourselves.

Tu longe seggere, et vestigia semper adora.

Chapter IV. Second Period. — Machinery.

"I HAVE witnessed with profound regret the CONTINUANCE OF DISTRESS in the manufacturing districts of the country."

Words of Queen Victoria on the reassembling of parliament.

If there is anything of a nature to cause sovereigns to reflect, it is that, more or less impassible spectators of human calamities, they are, by the very constitution of society and the nature of their power, absolutely powerless to cure the sufferings of their subjects; they are even prohibited from paying any attention to them. Every question of labor and wages, say with one accord the economic and representative theorists, must remain outside of the attributes of power. From the height of the glorious sphere where religion has placed them, thrones, dominations, principalities, powers, and all the heavenly host view the torment of society, beyond the reach of its stress; but their power does not extend over the winds and floods. Kings can do nothing for the salvation of mortals. And, in truth, these theorists are right: the prince is established to maintain, not to revolutionize; to protect reality, not to bring about utopia. He represents one of the antagonistic principles: hence, if he were to establish harmony, he would eliminate himself, which on his part would be sovereignly unconstitutional and absurd.

But as, in spite of theories, the progress of ideas is incessantly changing the external form of institutions in such a way as to render continually necessary exactly that which the legislator neither desires nor foresees, — so that, for instance, questions of taxation become questions of distribution; those of public utility, questions of national labor and industrial organization; those of finance, operations of credit; and those of international law, questions of customs duties and markets, — it stands as demonstrated that the prince, who, according to theory, should never interfere with things which nevertheless, without theory's foreknowledge, are daily and irresistibly becoming matters of government, is and can be henceforth, like Divinity from which he emanates, whatever may be said, only an hypothesis, a fiction.

And finally, as it is impossible that the prince and the interests which it is his mission to defend should consent to diminish and disappear before emergent principles and new rights posited, it follows that progress, after being accomplished in the mind insensibly, is realized in society by leaps, and that force, in spite of the calumny of which it is the object, is the necessary condition of reforms. Every society in which the power of insurrection is suppressed is a society dead to progress: there is no truth of history better proven.

And what I say of constitutional monarchies is equally true of representative democracies: everywhere the social compact has united power and conspired against life, it being impossible for the legislator either to see that he was working against his own ends or to proceed otherwise.

Monarchs and representatives, pitiable actors in parliamentary comedies, this in the last analysis is what you are: talismans against the future! Every year brings you the grievances of the people; and when you are asked for the remedy, your wisdom covers its face! Is it necessary to support privilege, — that is, that consecration of the right of the strongest which created you and which is changing every day? Promptly, at the slightest nod of your head, a numerous army starts up, runs to arms, and forms in line of battle. And when the people complain that, in spite of their labor and precisely because of their labor, misery devours them, when society asks you for life, you recite acts of mercy! All your energy is expended for conservatism, all your virtue vanishes in aspirations! Like the Pharisee, instead of feeding your father, you pray for him! Ah! I tell you, we possess the secret of your mission: you exist only to prevent us from living. Nolite ergo imperare, get you gone!

137

As for us, who view the mission of power from quite another standpoint, and who wish the special work of government to be precisely that of exploring the future, searching for progress, and securing for all liberty, equality, health, and wealth, we continue our task of criticism courageously, entirely sure that, when we have laid bare the cause of the evils of society, the principle of its fevers, the motive of its disturbances, we shall not lack the power to apply the remedy.

1. — Of the function of machinery in its relations to liberty.

The introduction of machinery into industry is accomplished in opposition to the law of division, and as if to reestablish the equilibrium profoundly compromised by that law. To truly appreciate the significance of this movement and grasp its spirit, a few general considerations become necessary.

Modern philosophers, after collecting and classifying their annals, have been led by the nature of their labors to deal also with history: then it was that they saw, not without surprise, that the history of philosophy was the same thing at bottom as the philosophy of history; further, that these two branches of speculation, so different in appearance, the history of philosophy and the philosophy of history, were also only the stage representation of the concepts of metaphysics, which is philosophy entire.

Now, dividing the material of universal history among a certain number of frames, such as mathematics, natural history, social economy, etc., it will be found that each of these divisions contains also metaphysics. And it will be the same down to the last subdivision of the totality of history: so that entire philosophy lies at the bottom of every natural or industrial manifestation; that it is no respecter of degrees or qualities; that, to rise to its sublimest conceptions, all prototypes may be employed equally well; and, finally, that, all the postulates of reason meeting in the most modest industry as well as in the most general sciences, to make every artisan a philosopher, — that is, a generalizing and highly synthetic mind, — it would be enough to teach him — what? his profession.

Hitherto, it is true, philosophy, like wealth, has been reserved for certain classes: we have the philosophy of history, the philosophy of law, and some other philosophies also; this is a sort of appropriation which, like many others of equally noble origin, must disappear. But, to consummate this immense equation, it is necessary to begin with the

138

philosophy of labor, after which each laborer will be able to attempt in his turn the philosophy of his trade.

Thus every product of art and industry, every political and religious constitution, like every creature organized or unorganized, being only a realization, a natural or practical application, of philosophy, the identity of the laws of nature and reason, of being and idea, is demonstrated; and when, for our own purpose, we establish the constant conformity of economic phenomena to the pure laws of thought, the equivalence of the real and the ideal in human facts, we only repeat in a particular case this eternal demonstration.

What do we say, in fact?

To determine value, — in other words, to organize within itself the production and distribution of wealth, — society proceeds exactly as the mind does in the generation of concepts. First it posits a primary fact, acts upon a primary hypothesis, the division of labor, a veritable antinomy, the antagonistic results of which are evolved in social economy, just as the consequences might have been deduced in the mind: so that the industrial movement, following in all respects the deduction of ideas, is divided into a double current, one of useful effects, the other of subversive results, all equally necessary and legitimate products of the same law. To harmonically establish this two-faced principle and solve this antinomy, society evokes a second, soon to be followed by a third; and such will be the progress of the social genius until, having exhausted all its contradictions, — supposing, though it is not proved, that there is an end to contradiction in humanity, — it shall cover with one backward leap all its previous positions and in a single formula solve all problems.

In following in our exposition this method of the parallel development of the reality and the idea, we find a double advantage: first, that of escaping the reproach of materialism, so often applied to economists, to whom facts are truth simply because they are facts, and material facts. To us, on the contrary, facts are not matter, — for we do not know what the word matter means, — but visible manifestations of invisible ideas. So viewed, the value of facts is measured by the idea which they represent; and that is why we have rejected as illegitimate and non-conclusive useful value and value in exchange, and later the division of labor itself, although to the economists all these have an absolute authority.

On the other hand, it is as impossible to accuse us of spiritualism, idealism, or mysticism: for, admitting as a point of departure only the external manifestation of the idea, — the idea which we do not know, which does not exist, as long as it is not reflected, like light, which would be nothing if the sun existed by itself in an infinite void, — and brushing aside all a prori reasoning upon theogony and cosmogony, all inquiry into substance, cause, the me and the not-me, we confine ourselves to searching for the laws of being and to following the order of their appearance as far as reason can reach.

Doubtless all knowledge brings up at last against a mystery: such, for instance, as matter and mind, both of which we admit as two unknown essences, upon which all phenomena rest. But this is not to say that mystery is the point of departure of knowledge, or that mysticism is the necessary condition of logic: quite the contrary, the spontaneity of our reason tends to the perpetual rejection of mysticism; it makes an a priori protest against all mystery, because it has no use for mystery except to deny it, and because the negation of mysticism is the only thing for which reason has no need of experience.

In short, human facts are the incarnation of human ideas: therefore, to study the laws of social economy is to constitute the theory of the laws of reason and create philosophy. We may now pursue the course of our investigation.

At the end of the preceding chapter we left the laborer at loggerheads with the law of division: how will this indefatigable OEdipus manage to solve this enigma?

In society the incessant appearance of machinery is the antithesis, the inverse formula, of the division of labor; it is the protest of the industrial genius against parcellaire and homicidal labor. What is a machine, in fact? A method of reuniting divers particles of labor which division had separated. Every machine may be defined as a summary of several operations, a simplification of powers, a condensation of labor, a reduction of costs. In all these respects machinery is the counterpart of division. Therefore through machinery will come a restoration of the parcellaire laborer, a decrease of toil for the workman, a fall in the price of his product, a movement in the relation of values, progress towards new discoveries, advancement of the general welfare.

As the discovery of a formula gives a new power to the geometer, so the invention of a machine is an abridgment of manual labor which multiplies the power of the producer, from which it may be inferred that the antinomy of the division of labor, if not entirely destroyed, will be balanced and neutralized. No one should fail to read the lectures of M. Chevalier setting forth the innumerable advantages resulting to society from the intervention of machinery; they make a striking picture to which I take pleasure in referring my reader.

Machinery, positing itself in political economy in opposition to the division of labor, represents synthesis opposing itself in the human mind to analysis; and just as in the division of labor and in machinery, as we shall soon see, political economy entire is contained, so with analysis and synthesis goes the possession of logic entire, of philosophy. The man who labors proceeds necessarily and by turns by division and the aid of tools; likewise, he who reasons performs necessarily and by turns the operations of synthesis and analysis, nothing more, absolutely nothing. And labor and reason will never get beyond this: Prometheus, like Neptune, attains in three strides the confines of the world.

From these principles, as simple and as luminous as axioms, immense consequences follow.

As in the operation of the mind analysis and synthesis are essentially inseparable, and as, looking at the matter from another point, theory becomes legitimate only on condition of following experience foot by foot, it follows that labor, uniting analysis and synthesis, theory and experience, in a continuous action, — labor, the external form of logic and consequently a summary of reality and idea, — appears again as a universal method of instruction. Fit fabricando faber: of all systems of education the most absurd is that which separates intelligence from activity, and divides man into two impossible entities, theorizer and automaton. That is why we applaud the just complaints of M. Chevalier, M. Dunoyer, and all those who demand reform in university education; on that also rests the hope of the results that we have promised ourselves from such reform. If education were first of all experimental and practical, reserving speech only to explain, summarize, and coordinate work; if those who cannot learn with imagination and memory were permitted to learn with their eyes and hands, — soon we should witness a multiplication, not only of the forms of labor, but of capacities; everybody, knowing the theory of something, would thereby possess the language of philosophy; on occasion he could, were it only for once in his life, create, modify, perfect, give proof of intelligence and comprehension, produce his master-piece, in a word, show himself a man. The inequality in the acquisitions of memory would not affect the equivalence of faculties, and genius would no longer seem to us other than what it really is, — mental health.

The fine minds of the eighteenth century went into extended disputations about what constitutes genius, wherein it differs from talent, what we should understand by mind, etc. They had transported into the intellectual sphere the same distinctions that, in society, separate persons. To them there were kings and rulers of genius, princes of genius, ministers of genius; and then there were also noble minds and bourgeois minds, city talents and country talents. Clear at the foot of the ladder lay the gross industrial population, souls imperfectly outlined, excluded from the glory of the elect. All rhetorics are still filled with these impertinences, which monarchical interests, literary vanity, and socialistic hypocrisy strain themselves to sanction, for the perpetual slavery of nations and the maintenance of the existing order.

But, if it is demonstrated that all the operations of the mind are reducible to two, analysis and synthesis, which are necessarily inseparable, although distinct; if, by a forced consequence, in spite of the infinite variety of tasks and studies, the mind never does more than begin the same canvas over again, — the man of genius is simply a man with a good constitution, who has worked a great deal, thought a great deal, analyzed, compared, classified, summarized, and concluded a great deal; while the limited being, who stagnates in an endemic routine, instead of developing his faculties, has killed his intelligence through inertia and automatism. It is absurd to distinguish as differing in nature that which really differs only in age, and then to convert into privilege and exclusion the various degrees of a development or the fortunes of a spontaneity which must gradually disappear through labor and education.

The psychological rhetoricians who have classified human souls into dynasties, noble races, bourgeois families, and the proletariat observed nevertheless that genius was not universal, and that it had its specialty; consequently Homer, Plato, Phidias, Archimedes, Caesar, etc., all of whom seemed to them first in their sort, were declared by them equals and sovereigns of distinct realms. How irrational! As if the specialty of genius did not itself reveal the law of the equality of minds! As if, looking at it in another light, the steadiness of success in the product of genius were not a proof that it works according to principles outside of itself, which are the guarantee of the perfection of its work, as long as it follows them with fidelity and certainty! This apotheosis of genius, dreamed of with open eyes by men whose chatter will remain forever barren, would warrant a belief in the innate stupidity of the majority of mortals, if it were not a striking proof of their perfectibility.

Labor, then, after having distinguished capacities and arranged their equilibrium by the division of industries, completes the armament of intelligence, if I may venture to say so, by machinery. According to the testimony of history as well as according to analysis, and notwithstanding the anomalies caused by the antagonism of economic principles, intelligence differs in men, not by power, clearness, or reach, but, in the first place, by specialty, or, in the language of the schools, by qualitative determination, and, in the second place, by exercise and education. Hence, in the individual as in the collective man, intelligence is much more a faculty which comes, forms, and develops, quae fit, than an entity or entelechy which exists, wholly formed, prior to apprenticeship. Reason, by whatever name we call it, — genius, talent, industry, — is at the start a naked and inert potentiality, which gradually grows in size and strength, takes on color and form, and shades itself in an infinite variety of ways. By the importance of its acquirements, by its capital, in a word, the intelligence of one individual differs and will always differ from that of another; but, being a power equal in all at the beginning, social progress must consist in rendering it, by an ever increasing perfection of methods, again equal in all at the end. Otherwise labor would remain a privilege for some and a punishment for others.

But the equilibrium of capacities, the prelude of which we have seen in the division of labor, does not fulfil the entire destiny of machinery, and the views of Providence extend far beyond. With the introduction of machinery into economy, wings are given to LIBERTY.

The machine is the symbol of human liberty, the sign of our domination over nature, the attribute of our power, the expression of our right, the emblem of our personality. Liberty, intelligence, — those constitute the whole of man: for, if we brush aside as mystical and unintelligible all speculation concerning the human being considered from the point of view of substance (mind or matter), we have left only two categories of manifestations, — the first including all that we call sensations, volitions, passions, attractions, instincts, sentiments; the other, all phenomena classed under the heads of attention, perception, memory, imagination, comparison, judgment, reasoning, etc. As for the organic apparatus, very far from being the principle or base of these two orders of faculties, it must be considered as their synthetic and positive realization, their living and harmonious expression. For just as from the long-continued issue by humanity of its antagonistic principles

143

must some day result social organization, so man must be conceived as the result of two series of potentialities.

Thus, after having posited itself as logic, social economy, pursuing its work, posits itself as psychology. The education of intelligence and liberty, — in a word, the welfare of man, — all perfectly synonymous expressions, — such is the common object of political economy and philosophy. To determine the laws of the production and distribution of wealth will be to demonstrate, by an objective and concrete exposition, the laws of reason and liberty; it will be to create philosophy and right a posteriori: whichever way we turn, we are in complete metaphysics.

Let us try, now, with the joint data of psychology and political economy, to define liberty.

If it is allowable to conceive of human reason, in its origin, as a lucid and reflecting atom, capable of some day representing the universe, but at first giving no image at all, we may likewise consider liberty, at the birth of conscience, as a living point, punctum saliens, a vague, blind, or, rather, indifferent spontaneity, capable of receiving all possible impressions, dispositions, and inclinations. Liberty is the faculty of acting and of not acting, which, through any choice or determination whatever (I use the word determination here both passively and actively), abandons its indifference and becomes will.

I say, then, that liberty, like intelligence, is naturally an undetermined, unformed faculty, which gets its value and character later from external impressions, — a faculty, therefore, which is negative at the beginning, but which gradually defines and outlines itself by exercise, — I mean, by education.

The etymology of the word liberty, at least as I understand it, will serve still better to explain my thought. The root is lib-et, he pleases (German, lieben, to love); whence have been constructed lib-eri, children, those dear to us, a name reserved for the children of the father of a family; lib-ertas, the condition, character, or inclination of children of a noble race; lib-ido, the passion of a slave, who knows neither God nor law nor country, synonymous with licentia, evil conduct. When spontaneity takes a useful, generous, or beneficent direction, it is called libertas; when, on the contrary, it takes a harmful, vicious, base, or evil direction, it is called libido.

144

A learned economist, M. Dunoyer, has given a definition of liberty which, by its likeness to our own, will complete the demonstration of its exactness.

I call liberty that power which man acquires of using his forces more easily in proportion as he frees himself from the obstacles which originally hindered the exercise thereof. I say that he is the freer the more thoroughly delivered he is from the causes which prevented him from making use of his forces, the farther from him he has driven these causes, the more he has extended and cleared the sphere of his action.... Thus it is said that a man has a free mind, that he enjoys great liberty of mind, not only when his intelligence is not disturbed by any external violence, but also when it is neither obscured by intoxication, nor changed by disease, nor kept in impotence by lack of exercise.

M. Dunoyer has here viewed liberty only on its negative side, — that is, as if it were simply synonymous with freedom from obstacles. At that rate liberty would not be a faculty of man; it would be nothing. But immediately M. Dunoyer, though persisting in his incomplete definition, seizes the true side of the matter: then it is that it occurs to him to say that man, in inventing a machine, serves his liberty, not, as we express ourselves, because he determines it, but, in M. Dunoyer's style, because he removes a difficulty from its path.

Thus articulate language is a better instrument than language by sign; therefore one is freer to express his thought and impress it upon the mind of another by speech than by gesture. The written word is a more potent instrument than the spoken word; therefore one is freer to act on the mind of his fellows when he knows how to picture the word to their eyes than when he simply knows how to speak it. The press is an instrument two or three hundred times more potent than the pen; therefore one is two or three hundred times freer to enter into relation with other men when he can spread his ideas by printing than when he can publish them only by writing.

I will not point out all that is inexact and illogical in this fashion of representing liberty. Since Destutt de Tracy, the last representative of the philosophy of Condillac, the philosophical spirit has been obscured among economists of the French school; the fear of ideology has perverted their language, and one perceives, in reading them, that adoration of fact has caused them to lose even the perception of theory. I prefer to establish the fact that M. Dunoyer, and political economy with him, is not mistaken concerning the essence of liberty, a force, energy, or spontaneity indifferent in itself to every action, and

145

consequently equally susceptible of any determination, good or bad, useful or harmful. M. Dunoyer has had so strong a suspicion of the truth that he writes himself:

Instead of considering liberty as a dogma, I shall present it as a result; instead of making it the attribute of man, I shall make it the attribute of civilization; instead of imagining forms of government calculated to establish it, I shall do my best to explain how it is born of every step of our progress.

Then he adds, with no less reason:

It will be noticed how much this method differs from that of those dogmatic philosophers who talk only of rights and duties; of what it is the duty of governments to do and the right of nations to demand, etc. I do not say sententiously: men have a right to be free; I confine myself to asking: how does it happen that they are so?

In accordance with this exposition one may sum up in four lines the work that M. Dunoyer has tried to do: A REVIEW of the obstacles that impede liberty and the means (instruments, methods, ideas, customs, religions, governments, etc.) that favor it. But for its omissions, the work of M. Dunoyer would have been the very philosophy of political economy.

After having raised the problem of liberty, political economy furnishes us, then, with a definition conforming in every point to that given by psychology and suggested by the analogies of language: and thus we see how, little by little, the study of man gets transported from the contemplation of the me to the observation of realities.

Now, just as the determinations of man's reason have received the name of ideas (abstract, supposed a priori ideas, or principles, conceptions, categories; and secondary ideas, or those more especially acquired and empirical), so the determinations of liberty have received the name of volitions, sentiments, habits, customs. Then, language, figurative in its nature, continuing to furnish the elements of primary psychology, the habit has been formed of assigning to ideas, as the place or capacity where they reside, the intelligence, and to volitions, sentiments, etc., the conscience. All these abstractions have been long taken for realities by the philosophers, not one of whom has seen that all distribution of the faculties of the soul is necessarily a work of caprice, and that their psychology is but an illusion.

146

However that may be, if we now conceive these two orders of determinations, reason and liberty, as united and blended by organization in a living, reasonable, and free person, we shall understand immediately that they must lend each other mutual assistance and influence each other reciprocally. If, through an error or oversight of the reason, liberty, blind by nature, acquires a false and fatal habit, the reason itself will not be slow to feel the effects; instead of true ideas, conforming to the natural relations of things, it will retain only prejudices, as much more difficult to root out of the intelligence afterwards, as they have become dearer to the conscience through age. In this state of things reason and liberty are impaired; the first is disturbed in its development, the second restricted in its scope, and man is led astray, becomes, that is, wicked and unhappy at once.

Thus, when, in consequence of a contradictory perception and an incomplete experience, reason had pronounced through the lips of the economists that there was no regulating principle of value and that the law of commerce was supply and demand, liberty abandoned itself to the passion of ambition, egoism, and gambling; commerce was thereafter but a wager subjected to certain police regulations; misery developed from the sources of wealth; socialism, itself a slave of routine, could only protest against effects instead of rising against causes; and reason was obliged, by the sight of so many evils, to recognize that it had taken a wrong road.

Man can attain welfare only in proportion as his reason and his liberty not only progress in harmony, but never halt in their development. Now, as the progress of liberty, like that of reason, is indefinite, and as, moreover, these two powers are closely connected and solidary, it must be concluded that liberty is the more perfect the more closely it defines itself in conformity with the laws of reason, which are those of things, and that, if this reason were infinite, liberty itself would become infinite. In other words, the fullness of liberty lies in the fullness of reason: summa lex summa libertas.

These preliminaries were indispensable in order to clearly appreciate the role of machinery and to make plain the series of economic evolutions. And just here I will remind the reader that we are not constructing a history in accordance with the order of events, but in accordance with the succession of ideas. The economic phases or categories are now contemporary, now inverted, in their manifestation; hence the extreme difficulty always felt by the economists in systematizing their ideas; hence the chaos of their works, even those most to be commended in every other respect, such as Adam Smith's,

147

Ricardo's, and J. B. Say's. But economic theories none the less have their logical succession and their series in the mind: it is this order which we flatter ourselves that we have discovered, and which will make this work at once a philosophy and a history.

2. — Machinery's contradiction. — Origin of capital and wages.

From the very fact that machinery diminishes the workman's toil, it abridges and diminishes labor, the supply of which thus grows greater from day to day and the demand less. Little by little, it is true, the reduction in prices causing an increase in consumption, the proportion is restored and the laborer set at work again: but as industrial improvements steadily succeed each other and continually tend to substitute mechanical operations for the labor of man, it follows that there is a constant tendency to cut off a portion of the service and consequently to eliminate laborers from production. Now, it is with the economic order as with the spiritual order: outside of the church there is no salvation; outside of labor there is no subsistence. Society and nature, equally pitiless, are in accord in the execution of this new decree.

"When a new machine, or, in general, any process whatever that expedites matters," says J. B. Say, "replaces any human labor already employed, some of the industrious arms, whose services are usefully supplanted, are left without work. A new machine, therefore, replaces the labor of a portion of the laborers, but does not diminish the amount of production, for, if it did, it would not be adopted; it displaces revenue. But the ultimate advantage is wholly on the side of machinery, for, if abundance of product and lessening of cost lower the venal value, the consumer — that is, everybody — will benefit thereby."

Say's optimism is infidelity to logic and to facts. The question here is not simply one of a small number of accidents which have happened during thirty centuries through the introduction of one, two, or three machines; it is a question of a regular, constant, and general phenomenon. After revenue has been displaced as Say says, by one machine, it is then displaced by another, and again by another, and always by another, as long as any labor remains to be done and any exchanges remain to be effected. That is the light in which the phenomenon must be presented and considered: but thus, it must be admitted, its aspect changes singularly. The displacement of revenue, the suppression of labor and wages, is a chronic, permanent, indelible plague, a sort of cholera which now appears wearing the features of

Gutenberg, now assumes those of Arkwright; here is called Jacquard, there James Watt or Marquis de Jouffroy. After carrying on its ravages for a longer or shorter time under one form, the monster takes another, and the economists, who think that he has gone, cry out: "It was nothing!" Tranquil and satisfied, provided they insist with all the weight of their dialectics on the positive side of the question, they close their eyes to its subversive side, notwithstanding which, when they are spoken to of poverty, they again begin their sermons upon the improvidence and drunkenness of laborers.

In 1750, — M. Dunoyer makes the observation, and it may serve as a measure of all lucubrations of the same sort, — "in 1750 the population of the duchy of Lancaster was 300,000 souls. In 1801, thanks to the development of spinning machines, this population was 672,000 souls. In 1831 it was 1,336,000 souls. Instead of the 40,000 workmen whom the cotton industry formerly employed, it now employs, since the invention of machinery, 1,500,000."

M. Dunoyer adds that at the time when the number of workmen employed in this industry increased in so remarkable a manner, the price of labor rose one hundred and fifty per cent. Population, then, having simply followed industrial progress, its increase has been a normal and irreproachable fact, — what do I say? — a happy fact, since it is cited to the honor and glory of the development of machinery. But suddenly M. Dunoyer executes an about-face: this multitude of spinning-machines soon being out of work, wages necessarily declined; the population which the machines had called forth found itself abandoned by the machines, at which M. Dunoyer declares: Abuse of marriage is the cause of poverty.

English commerce, in obedience to the demand of the immense body of its patrons, summons workmen from all directions, and encourages marriage; as long as labor is abundant, marriage is an excellent thing, the effects of which they are fond of quoting in the interest of machinery; but, the patronage fluctuating, as soon as work and wages are not to be had, they denounce the abuse of marriage, and accuse laborers of improvidence. Political economy — that is, proprietary despotism — can never be in the wrong: it must be the proletariat.

The example of printing has been cited many a time, always to sustain the optimistic view. The number of persons supported today by the manufacture of books is perhaps a thousand times larger than was that of the copyists and illuminators prior to Gutenberg's time; therefore, they conclude with a satisfied air, printing has injured nobody. An infinite number of similar facts might be cited, all of them indisputable, but not one of which would advance the question a step. Once more, no one denies that machines have contributed to the general welfare; but I affirm, in regard to this incontestable fact, that the economists fall short of the truth when they advance the absolute statement that the simplification of processes has nowhere resulted in a diminution of the number of hands employed in any industry whatever. What the economists ought to say is that machinery, like the division of labor, in the present system of social economy is at once a source of wealth and a permanent and fatal cause of misery.

In 1836, in a Manchester mill, nine frames, each having three hundred and twenty-four spindles, were tended by four spinners. Afterwards the mules were doubled in length, which gave each of the nine six hundred and eighty spindles and enabled two men to tend them.

There we have the naked fact of the elimination of the workman by the machine. By a simple device three workmen out of four are evicted; what matters it that fifty years later, the population of the globe having doubled and the trade of England having quadrupled, new machines will be constructed and the English manufacturers will reemploy their workmen? Do the economists mean to point to the increase of population as one of the benefits of machinery? Let them renounce, then, the theory of Malthus, and stop declaiming against the excessive fecundity of marriage.

They did not stop there: soon a new mechanical improvement enabled a single worker to do the work that formerly occupied four.

A new three-fourths reduction of manual work: in all, a reduction of human labor by fifteen-sixteenths.

A Bolton manufacturer writes: "The elongation of the mules of our frames permits us to employ but twenty-six spinners where we employed thirty-five in 1837."

Another decimation of laborers: one out of four is a victim.

These facts are taken from the "Revue Economique" of 1842; and there is nobody who cannot point to similar ones. I have witnessed the introduction of printing machines, and I can say that I have seen with my own eyes the evil which printers have suffered thereby. During the fifteen or twenty years that the machines have been in use a portion of the workmen have gone back to composition, others have abandoned their trade, and some have died of misery: thus laborers are continually crowded back in consequence of industrial innovations. Twenty years ago eighty canal-boats furnished the navigation service between Beaucaire and Lyons; a score of steam-packets has displaced them all. Certainly commerce is the gainer; but what has become of the boating-population? Has it been transferred from the boats to the packets? No: it has gone where all superseded industries go, — it has vanished.

For the rest, the following documents, which I take from the same source, will give a more positive idea of the influence of industrial improvements upon the condition of the workers.

The average weekly wages, at Manchester, is ten shillings. Out of four hundred and fifty workers there are not forty who earn twenty shillings.

The author of the article is careful to remark that an Englishman consumes five times as much as a Frenchman; this, then, is as if a French workingman had to live on two francs and a half a week.

"Edinburgh Review," 1835: "To a combination of workmen (who did not want to see their wages reduced) we owe the mule of Sharpe and Roberts of Manchester; and this invention has severely punished the imprudent unionists."

Punished should merit punishment. The invention of Sharpe and Roberts of Manchester was bound to result from the situation; the refusal of the workmen to submit to the reduction asked of them was only its determining occasion. Might not one infer, from the air of vengeance affected by the "Edinburgh Review," that machines have a retroactive effect?

An English manufacturer: "The insubordination of our workmen has given us the idea of dispensing with them. We have made and stimulated every imaginable effort of the mind to replace the service of men by tools more docile, and we have achieved our object. Machinery has delivered capital from the oppression of labor. Wherever we still employ a man, we do so only temporarily, pending the invention for us of some means of accomplishing his work without him."

What a system is that which leads a business man to think with delight that society will soon be able to dispense with men! Machinery has delivered capital from the oppression of labor! That is exactly as if the cabinet should undertake to deliver the treasury from the oppression of the taxpayers. Fool! though the workmen cost you something, they are your customers: what will you do with your products, when, driven away by you, they shall consume them no longer? Thus machinery, after crushing the workmen, is not slow in dealing employers a counter-blow; for, if production excludes consumption, it is soon obliged to stop itself.

During the fourth quarter of 1841 four great failures, happening in an English manufacturing city, threw seventeen hundred and twenty people on the street.

These failures were caused by over-production, — that is, by an inadequate market, or the distress of the people. What a pity that machinery cannot also deliver capital from the oppression of consumers! What a misfortune that machines do not buy the fabrics which they weave! The ideal society will be reached when commerce, agriculture, and manufactures can proceed without a man upon earth!

In a Yorkshire parish for nine months the operatives have been working but two days a week.

Machines!

At Geston two factories valued at sixty thousand pounds sterling have been sold for twenty-six thousand. They produced more than they could sell.

Machines!

In 1841 the number of children under thirteen years of age engaged in manufactures diminishes, because children over thirteen take their place.

Machines! The adult workman becomes an apprentice, a child, again: this result was foreseen from the phase of the division of labor, during which we saw the quality of the workman degenerate in the ratio in which industry was perfected.

In his conclusion the journalist makes this reflection: "Since 1836 there has been a retrograde movement in the cotton industry"; — that is, it no longer keeps up its relation with other industries: another result foreseen from the theory of the proportionality of values.

152

Today workmen's coalitions and strikes seem to have stopped throughout England, and the economists rightly rejoice over this return to order, — let us say even to common sense. But because laborers henceforth — at least I cherish the hope — will not add the misery of their voluntary periods of idleness to the misery which machines force upon them, does it follow that the situation is changed? And if there is no change in the situation, will not the future always be a deplorable copy of the past?

The economists love to rest their minds on pictures of public felicity: it is by this sign principally that they are to be recognized, and that they estimate each other. Nevertheless there are not lacking among them, on the other hand, moody and sickly imaginations, ever ready to offset accounts of growing prosperity with proofs of persistent poverty.

M. Theodore Fix thus summed up the general situation in December, 1844:

The food supply of nations is no longer exposed to those terrible disturbances caused by scarcities and famines, so frequent up to the beginning of the nineteenth century. The variety of agricultural growths and improvements has abolished this double scourge almost absolutely. The total wheat crop in France in 1791 was estimated at about 133,000,000 bushels, which gave, after deducting seed, 2.855 bushels to each inhabitant. In 1840 the same crop was estimated at 198,590,000 bushels, or 2.860 bushels to each individual, the area of cultivated surface being almost the same as before the Revolution.... The rate of increase of manufactured goods has been at least as high as that of food products; and we are justified in saying that the mass of textile fabrics has more than doubled and perhaps tripled within fifty years. The perfecting of technical processes has led to this result....

Since the beginning of the century the average duration of life has increased by two or three years, — an undeniable sign of greater comfort, or, if you will, a diminution of poverty.

Within twenty years the amount of indirect revenue, without any burdensome change in legislation, has risen from $40,000,000 francs to 720,000,000, — a symptom of economic, much more than of fiscal, progress.

On January 1, 1844, the deposit and consignment office owed the savings banks 351,500,000 francs, and Paris figured in this sum for 105,000,000. Nevertheless the development of the institution has taken

153

place almost wholly within twelve years, and it should be noticed that the 351,500,000 francs now due to the savings banks do not constitute the entire mass of economies effected, since at a given time the capital accumulated is disposed of otherwise.... In 1843, out of 320,000 workmen and 80,000 house-servants living in the capital, 90,000 workmen have deposited in the savings banks 2,547,000 francs, and 34,000 house-servants 1,268,000 francs.

All these facts are entirely true, and the inference to be drawn from them in favor of machines is of the exactest, — namely, that they have indeed given a powerful impetus to the general welfare. But the facts with which we shall supplement them are no less authentic, and the inference to be drawn from these against machines will be no less accurate, — to wit, that they are a continual cause of pauperism. I appeal to the figures of M. Fix himself.

Out of 320,000 workmen and 80,000 house-servants residing in Paris, there are 230,000 of the former and 46,000 of the latter — a total of 276,000 — who do not deposit in the savings banks. No one would dare pretend that these are 276,000 spendthrifts and ne'er-do-weels who expose themselves to misery voluntarily. Now, as among the very ones who make the savings there are to be found poor and inferior persons for whom the savings bank is but a respite from debauchery and misery, we may conclude that, out of all the individuals living by their labor, nearly three-fourths either are imprudent, lazy, and depraved, since they do not deposit in the savings banks, or are too poor to lay up anything. There is no other alternative. But common sense, to say nothing of charity, permits no wholesale accusation of the laboring class: it is necessary, therefore, to throw the blame back upon our economic system. How is it that M. Fix did not see that his figures accused themselves?

They hope that, in time, all, or almost all, laborers will deposit in the savings banks. Without awaiting the testimony of the future, we may test the foundations of this hope immediately.

According to the testimony of M. Vee, mayor of the fifth arrondissement of Paris, "the number of needy families inscribed upon the registers of the charity bureaus is 30,000, — which is equivalent to 65,000 individuals." The census taken at the beginning of 1846 gave 88,474. And poor families not inscribed, — how many are there of those? As many. Say, then, 180,000 people whose poverty is not doubtful, although not official. And all those who live in straitened circumstances, though keeping up the appearance of comfort, — how many are there of those? Twice as many, — a total of 360,000 persons, in Paris, who are somewhat embarrassed for means.

"They talk of wheat," cries another economist, M. Louis Leclerc, "but are there not immense populations which go without bread? Without leaving our own country, are there not populations which live exclusively on maize, buckwheat, chestnuts?"

M. Leclerc denounces the fact: let us interpret it. If, as there is no doubt, the increase of population is felt principally in the large cities, — that is, at those points where the most wheat is consumed, — it is clear that the average per head may have increased without any improvement in the general condition. There is no such liar as an average.

"They talk," continues the same writer, "of the increase of indirect consumption. Vain would be the attempt to acquit Parisian adulteration: it exists; it has its masters, its adepts, its literature, its didactic and classic treatises.... France possessed exquisite wines; what has been done with them? What has become of this splendid wealth? Where are the treasures created since Probus by the national genius? And yet, when one considers the excesses to which wine gives rise wherever it is dear, wherever it does not form a part of the regular life of the people; when in Paris, capital of the kingdom of good wines, one sees the people gorging themselves with I know not what, — stuff that is adulterated, sophisticated, sickening, and sometimes execrable, — and well-to-do persons drinking at home or accepting without a word, in famous restaurants, so-called wines, thick, violet-colored, and insipid, flat, and miserable enough to make the poorest Burgundian peasant shudder, — can one honestly doubt that alcoholic liquids are one of the most imperative needs of our nature?

I quote this passage at length, because it sums up in relation to a special case all that could be said upon the inconveniences of machinery. To the people it is with wine as with fabrics, and generally with all goods and merchandise created for the consumption of the poor. It is always the same deduction: to reduce by some process or other the cost of manufacture, in order, first, to maintain advantageously competition with more fortunate or richer rivals; second, to serve the vast numbers of plundered persons who cannot disregard price simply because the quality is good. Produced in the ordinary ways, wine is too expensive for the mass of consumers; it is in danger of remaining in the cellars of the retailers. The manufacturer of wines gets around the difficulty: unable to introduce machinery into the cultivation of the vine, he finds

155

a means, with the aid of some accompaniments, of placing the precious liquid within the reach of all. Certain savages, in their periods of scarcity, eat earth; the civilized workman drinks water. Malthus was a great genius.

As far as the increase of the average duration of life is concerned, I recognize the fact, but at the same time I declare the observation incorrect. Let us explain that. Suppose a population of ten million souls: if, from whatever cause you will, the average life should increase five years for a million individuals, mortality continuing its ravages at the same rate as before among the nine other millions, it would be found, on distributing this increase among the whole, that on an average six months had been added to the life of each individual. It is with the average length of life, the so-called indicator of average comfort, as with average learning: the level of knowledge does not cease to rise, which by no means alters the fact that there are today in France quite as many barbarians as in the days of Francois I. The charlatans who had railroad speculation in view made a great noise about the importance of the locomotive in the circulation of ideas; and the economists, always on the lookout for civilized stupidities, have not failed to echo this nonsense. As if ideas, in order to spread, needed locomotives! What, then, prevents ideas from circulating from the Institute to the Faubourgs Saint-Antoine and Saint-Marceau, in the narrow and wretched streets of Old Paris and the Temple Quarter, everywhere, in short, where dwells this multitude even more destitute of ideas than of bread? How happens it that between a Parisian and a Parisian, in spite of the omnibus and the letter-carrier, the distance is three times greater today than in the fourteenth century?

The ruinous influence of machinery on social economy and the condition of the laborers is exercised in a thousand ways, all of which are bound together and reciprocally labelled: cessation of labor, reduction of wages, over-production, obstruction of the market, alteration and adulteration of products, failures, displacement of laborers, degeneration of the race, and, finally, diseases and death.

M. Théodore Fix has remarked himself that in the last fifty years the average stature of man, in France, has diminished by a considerable fraction of an inch. This observation is worth his previous one: upon whom does this diminution take effect?

In a report read to the Academy of Moral Sciences on the results of the law of March 22, 1841, M. Leon Faucher expressed himself thus:

156

Young workmen are pale, weak, short in stature, and slow to think as well as to move. At fourteen or fifteen years they seem no more developed than children of nine or ten years in the normal state. As for their intellectual and moral development, there are some to be found who, at the age of thirteen, have no notion of God, who have never heard of their duties, and whose first school of morality was a prison.

That is what M. Léon Faucher has seen, to the great displeasure of M. Charles Dupin, and this state of things he declares that the law of March 22 is powerless to remedy. And let us not get angry over this impotence of the legislator: the evil arises from a cause as necessary for us as the sun; and in the path upon which we have entered, anger of any kind, like palliatives of any kind, could only make our situation worse. Yes, while science and industry are making such marvellous progress, it is a necessity, unless civilization's centre of gravity should suddenly change, that the intelligence and comfort of the proletariat be diminished; while the lives of the well-to-do classes grow longer and easier, it is inevitable that those of the needy should grow harder and shorter. This is established in the writings of the best — I mean, the most optimistic — thinkers.

According to M. de Morogues, 7,500,000 men in France have only ninety-one francs a year to spend, 25 centimes a day. Cing sous! cing sous! (Five cents! five cents!). There is something prophetic, then, in this odious refrain.

In England (not including Scotland and Ireland) the poor-rate was:

1801. £4,078,891 for a population of 8,872,980

1818. £7,870,801 " " " "   11,978,875

1833. £8,000,000 " " " "   14,000,000

The progress of poverty, then, has been more rapid than that of population; in face of this fact, what becomes of the hypotheses of Malthus? And yet it is indisputable that during the same period the average comfort increased: what, then, do statistics signify?

The death-rate for the first arrondissement of Paris is one to every fifty-two inhabitants, and for the twelfth one to every twenty-six. Now, the latter contains one needy person to every seven inhabitants, while the former has only one to every twenty-eight. That does not prevent the average duration of life, even in Paris, from increasing, as M. Fix has very correctly observed.

At Mulhouse the probabilities of average life are twenty-nine years for children of the well-to-do class and TWO years for those of the workers; in 1812 the average life in the same locality was twenty-five years, nine months, and twelve days, while in 1827 it was not over twenty-one years and nine months. And yet throughout France the average life is longer. What does this mean?

M. Blanqui, unable to explain so much prosperity and so much poverty at once, cries somewhere: "Increased production does not mean additional wealth.... Poverty, on the contrary, becomes the wider spread in proportion to the concentration of industries. There must be some radical vice in a system which guarantees no security either to capital or labor, and which seems to multiply the embarrass-ments of producers at the same time that it forces them to multiply their products."

There is no radical vice here. What astonishes M. Blanqui is simply that of which the Academy to which he belongs has asked a determination, — namely, the oscillations of the economic pendulum, VALUE, beating alternately and in regular time good and evil, until the hour of the universal equation shall strike. If I may be permitted another comparison, humanity in its march is like a column of soldiers, who, starting in the same step and at the same moment to the measured beating of the drum, gradually lose their distances. The whole body advances, but the distance from head to tail grows ever longer; and it is a necessary effect of the movement that there should be some laggards and stragglers.

But it is necessary to penetrate still farther into the antinomy. Machines promised us an increase of wealth; they have kept their word, but at the same time endowing us with an increase of poverty. They promised us liberty; I am going to prove that they have brought us slavery.

I have stated that the determination of value, and with it the tribulations of society, began with the division of industries, without which there could be no exchange, or wealth, or progress. The period through which we are now passing — that of machinery — is distinguished by a special characteristic, — WAGES.

158

Wages issued in a direct line from the employment of machinery, — that is, to give my thought the entire generality of expression which it calls for, from the economic fiction by which capital becomes an agent of production. Wages, in short, coming after the division of labor and exchange, is the necessary correlative of the theory of the reduction of costs, in whatever way this reduction may be accomplished. This genealogy is too interesting to be passed by without a few words of explanation.

The first, the simplest, the most powerful of machines is the workshop.

Division simply separates the various parts of labor, leaving each to devote himself to the specialty best suited to his tastes: the workshop groups the laborers according to the relation of each part to the whole. It is the most elementary form of the balance of values, undiscoverable though the economists suppose this to be. Now, through the workshop, production is going to increase, and at the same time the deficit.

Somebody discovered that, by dividing production into its various parts and causing each to be executed by a separate workman, he would obtain a multiplication of power, the product of which would be far superior to the amount of labor given by the same number of workmen when labor is not divided.

Grasping the thread of this idea, he said to himself that, by forming a permanent group of laborers assorted with a view to his special purpose, he would produce more steadily, more abundantly, and at less cost. It is not indispensable, however, that the workmen should be gathered into one place: the existence of the workshop does not depend essentially upon such contact. It results from the relation and proportion of the different tasks and from the common thought directing them. In a word, concentration at one point may offer its advantages, which are not to be neglected; but that is not what constitutes the workshop

This, then, is the proposition which the speculator makes to those whose collaboration he desires: I guarantee you a perpetual market for your products, if you will accept me as purchaser or middle-man. The bargain is so clearly advantageous that the proposition cannot fail of acceptance. The laborer finds in it steady work, a fixed price, and security; the employer, on the other hand, will find a readier sale for his goods, since, producing more advantageously, he can lower the price; in short, his profits will be larger because of the mass of his investments. All, even to the public and the magistrate, will

159

congratulate the employer on having added to the social wealth by his combinations, and will vote him a reward.

But, in the first place, whoever says reduction of expenses says reduction of services, not, it is true, in the new shop, but for the workers at the same trade who are left outside, as well as for many others whose accessory services will be less needed in future. Therefore every establishment of a workshop corresponds to an eviction of workers: this assertion, utterly contradictory though it may appear, is as true of the workshop as of a machine.

The economists admit it: but here they repeat their eternal refrain that, after a lapse of time, the demand for the product having increased in proportion to the reduction of price, labor in turn will come finally to be in greater demand than ever. Undoubtedly, WITH TIME, the equilibrium will be restored; but, I must add again, the equilibrium will be no sooner restored at this point than it will be disturbed at another, because the spirit of invention never stops, any more than labor. Now, what theory could justify these perpetual hecatombs?" When we have reduced the number of toilers," wrote Sismondi, "to a fourth or a fifth of what it is at present, we shall need only a fourth or a fifth as many priests, physicians, etc. When we have cut them off altogether, we shall be in a position to dispense with the human race." And that is what really would happen if, in order to put the labor of each machine in proportion to the needs of consumption, — that is, to restore the balance of values continually destroyed, — it were not necessary to continually create new machines, open other markets, and consequently multiply services and displace other arms. So that on the one hand industry and wealth, on the other population and misery, advance, so to speak, in procession, one always dragging the other after it.

I have shown the contractor, at the birth of industry, negotiating on equal terms with his comrades, who have since become his workmen. It is plain, in fact, that this original equality was bound to disappear through the advantageous position of the master and the dependence of the wage-workers. In vain does the law assure to each the right of enterprise, as well as the faculty to labor alone and sell one's products directly. According to the hypothesis, this last resource is impracticable, since it was the object of the workshop to annihilate isolated labor. And as for the right to take the plough, as they say, and go at speed, it is the same in manufactures as in agriculture; to know how to work is nothing, it is necessary to arrive at the right time; the shop, as well as the land, is to the first comer. When an establishment has had the leisure to develop itself, enlarge its foundations, ballast

160

itself with capital, and assure itself a body of patrons, what can the workman who has only his arms do against a power so superior? Hence it was not by an arbitrary act of sovereign power or by fortuitous and brutal usurpation that the guilds and masterships were established in the Middle Ages: the force of events had created them long before the edicts of kings could have given them legal consecration; and, in spite of the reform of '89, we see them reestablishing themselves under our eyes with an energy a hundred times more formidable. Abandon labor to its own tendencies, and the subjection of three-fourths of the human race is assured.

But this is not all. The machine, or the workshop, after having degraded the laborer by giving him a master, completes his degeneracy by reducing him from the rank of artisan to that of common workman.

Formerly the population on the banks of the Saone and Rhone was largely made up of watermen, thoroughly fitted for the conduct of canal-boats or row-boats. Now that the steam-tug is to be found almost everywhere, most of the boatmen, finding it impossible to get a living at their trade, either pass three-fourths of their life in idleness, or else become stokers.

If not misery, then degradation: such is the last alternative which machinery offers to the workman. For it is with a machine as with a piece of artillery: the captain excepted, those whom it occupies are servants, slaves.

Since the establishment of large factories, a multitude of little industries have disappeared from the domestic hearth: does any one believe that the girls who work for ten and fifteen cents have as much intelligence as their ancestors?

"After the establishment of the railway from Paris to Saint Germain," M. Dunoyer tells us, "there were established between Pecq and a multitude of places in the more or less immediate vicinity such a number of omnibus and stage lines that this establishment, contrary to all expectation, has considerably increased the employment of horses."

Contrary to all expectation! It takes an economist not to expect these things. Multiply machinery, and you increase the amount of arduous and disagreeable labor to be done: this apothegm is as certain as any of those which date from the deluge. Accuse me, if you choose, of ill-will towards the most precious invention of our century, — nothing shall prevent me from saying that the principal result of railways, after the

161

subjection of petty industry, will be the creation of a population of degraded laborers, — signalmen, sweepers, loaders, lumpers, draymen, watchmen, porters, weighers, greasers, cleaners, stokers, firemen, etc. Two thousand miles of railway will give France an additional fifty thousand serfs: it is not for such people, certainly, that M. Chevalier asks professional schools.

Perhaps it will be said that, the mass of transportation having increased in much greater proportion than the number of day-laborers, the difference is to the advantage of the railway, and that, all things considered, there is progress. The observation may even be generalized and the same argument applied to all industries.

But it is precisely out of this generality of the phenomenon that springs the subjection of laborers. Machinery plays the leading role in industry, man is secondary: all the genius displayed by labor tends to the degradation of the proletariat. What a glorious nation will be ours when, among forty millions of inhabitants, it shall count thirty-five millions of drudges, paper-scratchers, and flunkies!

With machinery and the workshop, divine right — that is, the principle of authority — makes its entrance into political economy. Capital, Mastership, Privilege, Monopoly, Loaning, Credit, Property, etc., — such are, in economic language, the various names of I know not what, but which is otherwise called Power, Authority, Sovereignty, Written Law, Revelation, Religion, God in short, cause and principle of all our miseries and all our crimes, and who, the more we try to define him, the more eludes us.

Is it, then, impossible that, in the present condition of society, the workshop with its hierarchical organization, and machinery, instead of serving exclusively the interests of the least numerous, the least industrious, and the wealthiest class, should be employed for the benefit of all?

That is what we are going to examine.

3. — Of preservatives against the disastrous influence of machinery.

Reduction of manual labor is synonymous with lowering of price, and, consequently, with increase of exchange, since, if the consumer pays less, he will buy more.

But reduction of manual labor is synonymous also with restriction of market, since, if the producer earns less, he will buy less. And this is the course that things actually take. The concentration of forces in the workshop and the intervention of capital in production, under the name of machinery, engender at the same time overproduction and destitution; and everybody has witnessed these two scourges, more to be feared than incendiarism and plague, develop in our day on the vastest scale and with devouring intensity. Nevertheless it is impossible for us to retreat: it is necessary to produce, produce always, produce cheaply; otherwise, the existence of society is compromised. The laborer, who, to escape the degradation with which the principle of division threatened him, had created so many marvellous machines, now finds himself either prohibited or subjugated by his own works. Against this alternative what means are proposed?

M. de Sismondi, like all men of patriarchal ideas, would like the division of labor, with machinery and manufactures, to be abandoned, and each family to return to the system of primitive indivision, — that is, to each one by himself, each one for himself, in the most literal meaning of the words. That would be to retrograde; it is impossible.

M. Blanqui returns to the charge with his plan of participation by the workman, and of consolidation of all industries in a joint-stock company for the benefit of the collective laborer. I have shown that this plan would impair public welfare without appreciably improving the condition of the laborers; and M. Blanqui himself seems to share this sentiment. How reconcile, in fact, this participation of the workman in the profits with the rights of inventors, contractors, and capitalists, of whom the first have to reimburse themselves for large outlays, as well as for their long and patient efforts; the second continually endanger the wealth they have acquired, and take upon themselves alone the chances of their enterprises, which are often very hazardous; and the third could sustain no reduction of their dividends without in some way losing their savings? How harmonize, in a word, the equality desirable to establish between laborers and employers with the preponderance which cannot be taken from heads of establishments, from loaners of capital, and from inventors, and which involves so clearly their exclusive appropriation of the profits? To decree by a law the admission of all workmen to a share of the profits would be to pronounce the dissolution of society: all the economists have seen this so clearly that they have finally changed into an exhortation to employers what had first occurred to them as a project. Now, as long as the wage-worker gets no profit save what may be allowed him by the contractor, it is

163

perfectly safe to assume that eternal poverty will be his lot: it is not in the power of the holders of labor to make it otherwise.

For the rest, the idea, otherwise very laudable, of associating workmen with employers tends to this communistic conclusion, evidently false in its premises: The last word of machinery is to make man rich and happy without the necessity of labor on his part. Since, then, natural agencies must do everything for us, machinery ought to belong to the State, and the goal of progress is communism.

I shall examine the communistic theory in its place.

But I believe that I ought to immediately warn the partisans of this utopia that the hope with which they flatter themselves in relation to machinery is only an illusion of the economists, something like perpetual motion, which is always sought and never found, because asked of a power which cannot give it. Machines do not go all alone: to keep them in motion it is necessary to organize an immense service around them; so that in the end, man creating for himself an amount of work proportional to the number of instruments with which he surrounds himself, the principal consideration in the matter of machinery is much less to divide its products than to see that it is fed, — that is, to continually renew the motive power. Now, this motive power is not air, water, steam, electricity; it is labor, — that is, the market.

A railroad suppresses all along its line conveyances, stages, harness-makers, saddlers, wheelwrights, inn-keepers: I take facts as they are just after the establishment of the road. Suppose the State, as a measure of preservation or in obedience to the principle of indemnity, should make the laborers displaced by the railroad its proprietors or operators: the transportation rates, let us suppose, being reduced by twenty-five per cent. (otherwise of what use is the railroad?), the income of all these laborers united will be diminished by a like amount, — which is to say that a fourth of the persons formerly living by conveyances will find themselves literally without resources, in spite of the munificence of the State. To meet their deficit they have but one hope, — that the mass of transportation effected over the line may be increased by twenty-five per cent, or else that they may find employment in other lines of industry, — which seems at first impossible, since, by the hypothesis and in fact, places are everywhere filled, proportion is maintained everywhere, and the supply is sufficient for the demand.

Moreover it is very necessary, if it be desired to increase the mass of transportation, that a fresh impetus be given to labor in other industries. Now, admitting that the laborers displaced by this over-production find employment, and that their distribution among the various kinds of labor proves as easy in practice as in theory, the difficulty is still far from settled. For the number of those engaged in circulation being to the number of those engaged in production as one hundred to one thousand, in order to obtain, with a circulation one-fourth less expensive, — in other words, one-fourth more powerful, — the same revenue as before, it will be necessary to strengthen production also by one-fourth, — that is, to add to the agricultural and industrial army, not twenty-five, — the figure which indicates the proportionality of the carrying industry, — but two hundred and fifty. But, to arrive at this result, it will be necessary to create machines, — what is worse, to create men: which continually brings the question back to the same point. Thus contradiction upon contradiction: now not only is labor, in consequence of machinery, lacking to men, but also men, in consequence of their numerical weakness and the insufficiency of their consumption, are lacking to machinery: so that, pending the establishment of equilibrium, there is at once a lack of work and a lack of arms, a lack of products and a lack of markets. And what we say of the railroad is true of all industries: always the man and the machine pursue each other, the former never attaining rest, the latter never attaining satisfaction.

Whatever the pace of mechanical progress; though machines should be invented a hundred times more marvellous than the mule-jenny, the knitting-machine, or the cylinder press; though forces should be discovered a hundred times more powerful than steam, — very far from freeing humanity, securing its leisure, and making the production of everything gratuitous, these things would have no other effect than to multiply labor, induce an increase of population, make the chains of serfdom heavier, render life more and more expensive, and deepen the abyss which separates the class that commands and enjoys from the class that obeys and suffers.

Suppose now all these difficulties overcome; suppose the laborers made available by the railroad adequate to the increase of service demanded for the support of the locomotive, — compensation being effected without pain, nobody will suffer; on the contrary, the well-being of each will be increased by a fraction of the profit realized by the substitution of the railway for the stage-coach. What then, I shall be asked, prevents these things from taking place with such regularity and

165

precision? And what is easier than for an intelligent government to so manage all industrial transitions?

I have pushed the hypothesis as far as it could go in order to show, on the one hand, the end to which humanity is tending, and, on the other, the difficulties which it must overcome in order to attain it. Surely the providential order is that progress should be effected, in so far as machinery is concerned, in the way that I have just spoken of: but what embarrasses society's march and makes it go from Charybdis to Scylla is precisely the fact that it is not organized. We have reached as yet only the second phase of its evolution, and already we have met upon our road two chasms which seem insuperable, — division of labor and machinery. How save the parcellaire workman, if he is a man of intelligence, from degradation, or, if he is degraded already, lift him to intellectual life? How, in the second place, give birth among laborers to that solidarity of interest without which industrial progress counts its steps by its catastrophes, when these same laborers are radically divided by labor, wages, intelligence, and liberty, — that is, by egoism? How, in short, reconcile what the progress already accomplished has had the effect of rendering irreconcilable? To appeal to communism and fraternity would be to anticipate dates: there is nothing in common, there can exist no fraternity, between such creatures as the division of labor and the service of machinery have made. It is not in that direction — at least for the present — that we must seek a solution.

Well! it will be said, since the evil lies still more in the minds than in the system, let us come back to instruction, let us labor for the education of the people.

In order that instruction may be useful, in order that it may even be received, it is necessary, first of all, that the pupil should be free, just as, before planting a piece of ground, we clear it of thorns and dog-grass. Moreover, the best system of education, even so far as philosophy and morality are concerned, would be that of professional education: once more, how reconcile such education with parcellaire division and the service of machinery? How shall the man who, by the effect of his labor, has become a slave, — that is, a chattel, a thing, — again become a person by the same labor, or in continuing the same exercise? Why is it not seen that these ideas are mutually repellent, and that, if, by some impossibility, the proletaire could reach a certain degree of intelligence, he would make use of it in the first place to revolutionize society and change all civil and industrial relations? And what I say is no vain exaggeration. The working class, in Paris and the large cities, is vastly superior in point of ideas to what it was twenty-five years ago; now, let them tell me if this class is not decidedly, energetically revolutionary! And it will become more and more so in proportion as it shall acquire the ideas of justice and order, in proportion especially as it shall reach an understanding of the mechanism of property.

Language, — I ask permission to recur once more to etymology, — language seems to me to have clearly expressed the moral condition of the laborer, after he has been, if I may so speak, depersonalized by industry. In the Latin the idea of servitude implies that of subordination of man to things; and when later feudal law declared the serf attached to the glebe, it only periphrased the literal meaning of the word servus. [16] Spontaneous reason, oracle of fate itself, had therefore condemned the subaltern workman, before science had established his debasement. Such being the case, what can the efforts of philanthropy do for beings whom Providence has rejected?

Labor is the education of our liberty. The ancients had a profound perception of this truth when they distinguished the servile arts from the liberal arts. For, like profession, like ideas; like ideas, like morals. Everything in slavery takes on the character of degradation, — habits, tastes, inclinations, sentiments, pleasures: it involves universal subversion. Occupy one's self with the education of the poor! But that would create the most cruel antagonism in these degenerate souls; that would inspire them with ideas which labor would render intolerable to them, affections incompatible with the brutishness of their condition, pleasures of which the perception is dulled in them. If such a project could succeed, instead of making a man of the laborer, it would make a demon of him. Just study those faces which people the prisons and the galleys, and tell me if most of them do not belong to subjects whom the revelation of the beautiful, of elegance, of wealth, of comfort, of honor, and of science, of all that makes the dignity of man, has found too weak, and so has demoralized and killed.

At least wages should be fixed, say the less audacious; schedules of rates should be prepared in all industries, to be accepted by employers and workmen.

This hypothesis of salvation is cited by M. Fix. And he answers victoriously:

Such schedules have been made in England and elsewhere; their value is known; everywhere they have been violated as soon as accepted, both by employers and by workmen.

The causes of the violation of the schedules are easy to fathom: they are to be found in machinery, in the incessant processes and combinations of industry. A schedule is agreed upon at a given moment: but suddenly there comes a new invention which gives its author the power to lower the price of merchandise. What will the other employers do? They will cease to manufacture and will discharge their workmen, or else they will propose to them a reduction. It is the only course open to them, pending a discovery by them in turn of some process by means of which, without lowering the rate of wages, they will be able to produce more cheaply than their competitors: which will be equivalent again to a suppression of workmen.

M. Léon Faucher seems inclined to favor a system of indemnity. He says:

We readily conceive that, in some interest or other, the State, representing the general desire, should command the sacrifice of an industry.

It is always supposed to command it, from the moment that it grants to each the liberty to produce, and protects and defends this liberty against all encroachment.

But this is an extreme measure, an experiment which is always perilous, and which should be accompanied by all possible consideration for individuals. The State has no right to take from a class of citizens the labor by which they live, before otherwise providing for their subsistence or assuring itself that they will find in some new industry employment for their minds and arms. It is a principle in civilized countries that the government cannot seize a piece of private property, even on grounds of public utility, without first buying out the proprietor by a just indemnity paid in advance. Now, labor seems to us property quite as legitimate, quite as sacred, as a field or a house, and we do not understand why it should be expropriated without any sort of compensation....

As chimerical as we consider the doctrines which represent government as the universal purveyor of labor in society, to the same extent does it seem to us just and necessary that every displacement of labor in the name of public utility should be effected only by means of a compensation or a transition, and that neither individuals nor classes should be sacrificed to State considerations. Power, in well-constituted nations, has always time and money to give for the mitigation of these partial sufferings. And it is precisely because industry does not emanate from it, because it is born and developed under the free and individual initiative of citizens, that the government is bound, when it disturbs its course, to offer it a sort of reparation or indemnity.

There's sense for you: whatever M. Léon Faucher may say, he calls for the organization of labor. For government to see to it that every displacement of labor is effected only by means of a compensation or a transition, and that individuals and classes are never sacrificed to State considerations, — that is, to the progress of industry and the liberty of enterprise, the supreme law of the State, — is without any doubt to constitute itself, in some way that the future shall determine, the purveyor of labor in society and the guardian of wages. And, as we have many times repeated, inasmuch as industrial progress and consequently the work of disarranging and rearranging classes in society is continual, it is not a special transition for each innovation that needs to be discovered, but rather a general principle, an organic law of transition, applicable to all possible cases and producing its effect itself. Is M. Léon Faucher in a position to formulate this law and reconcile the various antagonisms which we have described? No, since he prefers to stop at the idea of an indemnity. Power, he says, in well-organized nations, has always time and money to give for the mitigation of these partial sufferings. I am sorry for M. Faucher's generous intentions, but they seem to me radically impracticable.

Power has no time and money save what it takes from the taxpayers. To indemnify by taxation laborers thrown out of work would be to visit ostracism upon new inventions and establish communism by means of the bayonet; that is no solution of the difficulty. It is useless to insist further on indemnification by the State. Indemnity, applied according to M. Faucher's views, would either end in industrial despotism, in something like the government of Mohammed-Ali, or else would degenerate into a poor-tax, — that is, into a vain hypocrisy. For the good of humanity it were better not to indemnify, and to let labor seek its own eternal constitution.

There are some who say: Let government carry laborers thrown out of work to points where private industry is not established, where individual enterprise cannot reach. We have mountains to plant again with trees, ten or twelve million acres of land to clear, canals to dig, in short, a thousand things of immediate and general utility to undertake.

"We certainly ask our readers' pardon for it," answers M. Fix; "but here again we are obliged to call for the intervention of capital. These surfaces, certain communal lands excepted, are fallow, because, if

169

cultivated, they would yield no net product, and very likely not even the costs of cultivation. These lands are possessed by proprietors who either have or have not the capital necessary to cultivate them. In the former case, the proprietor would very probably content himself, if he cultivated these lands, with a very small profit, and perhaps would forego what is called the rent of the land: but he has found that, in undertaking such cultivation, he would lose his original capital, and his other calculations have shown him that the sale of the products would not cover the costs of cultivation.... All things considered, therefore, this land will remain fallow, because capital that should be put into it would yield no profit and would be lost. If it were otherwise, all these lands would be immediately put in cultivation; the savings now disposed of in another direction would necessarily gravitate in a certain proportion to the cultivation of land; for capital has no affections: it has interests, and always seeks that employment which is surest and most lucrative."

This argument, very well reasoned, amounts to saying that the time to cultivate its waste lands has not arrived for France, just as the time for railroads has not arrived for the Kaffres and the Hottentots. For, as has been said in the second chapter, society begins by working those sources which yield most easily and surely the most necessary and least expensive products: it is only gradually that it arrives at the utilization of things relatively less productive. Since the human race has been tossing about on the face of its globe, it has struggled with no other task; for it the same care is ever recurrent, — that of assuring its subsistence while going forward in the path of discovery. In order that such clearing of land may not become a ruinous speculation, a cause of misery, in other words, in order that it may be possible, it is necessary, therefore, to multiply still further our capital and machinery, discover new processes, and more thoroughly divide labor. Now, to solicit the government to take such an initiative is to imitate the peasants who, on seeing the approach of a storm, begin to pray to God and to invoke their saint. Governments — today it cannot be too often repeated — are the representatives of Divinity, — I had almost said executors of celestial vengeance: they can do nothing for us. Does the English government, for instance, know any way of giving labor to the unfortunates who take refuge in its workhouses? And if it knew, would it dare? Aid yourself, and Heaven will aid you! This note of popular distrust of Divinity tells us also what we must expect of power, — nothing.

Arrived at the second station of our Calvary, instead of abandoning ourselves to sterile contemplations, let us be more and more attentive to the teachings of destiny. The guarantee of our liberty lies in the progress of our torture.

Chapter V. Third Period. — Competition.

BETWEEN the hundred-headed hydra, division of labor, and the unconquered dragon, machinery, what will become of humanity? A prophet has said it more than two thousand years ago: Satan looks on his victim, and the fires of war are kindled, Aspexit gentes, et dissolvit. To save us from two scourges, famine and pestilence, Providence sends us discord.

Competition represents that philosophical era in which, a semi-understanding of the antinomies of reason having given birth to the art of sophistry, the characteristics of the false and the true were confounded, and in which, instead of doctrines, they had nothing but deceptive mental tilts. Thus the industrial movement faithfully reproduces the metaphysical movement; the history of social economy is to be found entire in the writings of the philosophers. Let us study this interesting phase, whose most striking characteristic is to take away the judgment of those who believe as well as those who protest.

1. — Necessity of competition.

M. Louis Reybaud, novelist by profession, economist on occasion, breveted by the Academy of Moral and Political

Sciences for his anti-reformatory caricatures, and become, with the lapse of time, one of the writers most hostile to social ideas, — M. Louis Reybaud, whatever he may do, is none the less profoundly imbued with these same ideas: the opposition which he thus exhibits is neither in his heart nor in his mind; it is in the facts.

In the first edition of his "Studies of Contemporary Reformers," M. Reybaud, moved by the sight of social sufferings as well as the courage of these founders of schools, who believed that they could reform the world by an explosion of sentimentalism, had formally expressed the opinion that the surviving feature of all their systems was ASSOCIATION. M. Dunoyer, one of M. Reybaud's judges, bore this testimony, the more flattering to M. Reybaud from being slightly ironical in form:

M. Reybaud, who has exposed with so much accuracy and talent, in a book which the French Academy has crowned, the vices of the three principal reformatory systems, holds fast to the principle common to them, which serves as their base, — association. Association in his eyes, he declares, is the greatest problem of modern times. It is called, he says, to solve that of the distribution of the fruits of labor. Though authority can do nothing towards the solution of this problem, association could do everything. M. Reybaud speaks here like a writer of the phalansterian school....

M. Reybaud had advanced a little, as one may see. Endowed with too much good sense and good faith not to perceive the precipice, he soon felt that he was straying, and began a retrograde movement. I do not call this about-face a crime on his part: M. Reybaud is one of those men who cannot justly be held responsible for their metaphors. He had spoken before reflecting, he retracted: what more natural! If the socialists must blame any one, let it be M. Dunoyer, who had prompted M. Reybaud's recantation by this singular compliment.

M. Dunoyer was not slow in perceiving that his words had not fallen on closed ears. He relates, for the glory of sound principles, that, "in a second edition of the 'Studies of Reformers,' M. Reybaud has himself tempered the absolute tone of his expressions. He has said, instead of could do everything, could do much."

It was an important modification, as M. Dunoyer brought clearly to his notice, but it still permitted M. Reybaud to write at the same time:

These symptoms are grave; they may be considered as prophecies of a confused organization, in which labor would seek an equilibrium and a regularity which it now lacks.... At the bottom of all these efforts is hidden a principle, association, which it would be wrong to condemn on the strength of irregular manifestations.

Finally M. Reybaud has loudly declared himself a partisan of competition, which means that he has decidedly abandoned the principle of association. For if by association we are to understand only the forms of partnership fixed by the commercial code, the philosophy of which has been summarized for us by MM. Troplong and Delangle, it is no longer worth while to distinguish between socialists and economists, between one party which seeks association and another which maintains that association exists.

Let no one imagine, because M. Reybaud has happened to say heedlessly yes and no to a question of which he does not seem to have yet formed a clear idea, that I class him among those speculators of socialism, who, after having launched a hoax into the world, begin immediately to make their retreat, under the pretext that, the idea now belonging to the public domain, there is nothing more for them to do but to leave it to make its way. M. Reybaud, in my opinion, belongs rather to the category of dupes, which includes in its bosom so many honest people and people of so much brains. M. Reybaud will remain, then, in my eyes, the vir probus dicendi peritus, the conscientious and skilful writer, who may easily be caught napping, but who never expresses anything that he does not see or feel. Moreover, M. Reybaud, once placed on the ground of economic ideas, would find the more difficulty in being consistent with himself because of the clearness of his mind and the accuracy of his reasoning. I am going to make this curious experiment under the reader's eyes.

If I could be understood by M. Reybaud, I would say to him: Take your stand in favor of competition, you will be wrong; take your stand against competition, still you will be wrong: which signifies that you will always be right. After that, if, convinced that you have not erred either in the first edition of your book or in the fourth, you should succeed in formulating your sentiment in an intelligible manner, I will look upon you as an economist of as great genius as Turgot and A. Smith; but I warn you that then you will resemble the latter, of whom you doubtless know little; you will be a believer in equality. Do you accept the wager?

To better prepare M. Reybaud for this sort of reconciliation with himself, let us show him first that this versatility of judgment, for which anybody else in my place would reproach him with insulting bitterness, is a treason, not on the part of the writer, but on the part of the facts of which he has made himself the interpreter.

In March, 1844, M. Reybaud published on oleaginous seeds — a subject which interested the city of Marseilles, his birthplace — an article in which he took vigorous ground in favor of free competition and the oil of sesame. According to the facts gathered by the author, which seem authentic, sesame would yield from forty-five to forty-six per cent of oil, while the poppy and the colza yield only twenty-five to thirty per cent, and the olive simply twenty to twenty-two. Sesame, for this reason, is disliked by the northern manufacturers, who have asked and obtained its prohibition. Nevertheless the English are on the watch, ready to take possession of this valuable branch of commerce. Let them prohibit the seed, says M. Reybaud, the oil will reach us mixed, in soap, or in some other way: we shall have lost the profit of manufacture. Moreover, the interest of our marine service requires the protection of this trade; it is a matter of no less than forty thousand casks of seed, which implies a maritime outfit of three hundred vessels and three thousand sailors.

These facts are conclusive: forty-five per cent. of oil instead of twenty-five; in quality superior to all the oils of France; reduction in the price of an article of prime necessity; a saving to consumers; three hundred ships, three thousand sailors, — such would be the value to us of liberty of commerce. Therefore, long live competition and sesame!

Then, in order to better assure these brilliant results, M. Reybaud, impelled by his patriotism and going straight in pursuit of his idea, observes — very judiciously in our opinion — that the government should abstain henceforth from all treaties of reciprocity in the matter of transportation: he asks that French vessels may carry the imports as well as the exports of French commerce.

"What we call reciprocity," he says, "is a pure fiction, the advantage of which is reaped by whichever of the parties can furnish navigation at the smallest expense. Now, as in France the elements of navigation, such as the purchase of the ships, the wages of the crews, and the costs of outfit, rise to an excessive figure, higher than in any of the other maritime nations, it follows that every reciprocity treaty is equivalent on our part to a treaty of abdication, and that, instead of agreeing to an act of mutual convenience, we resign ourselves, knowingly or involuntarily, to a sacrifice."

And M. Reybaud then points out the disastrous consequences of reciprocity:

France consumes five hundred thousand bales of cotton, and the Americans land them on our wharves; she uses enormous quantities of coal, and the English do the carrying thereof; the Swedes and Norwegians deliver to us themselves their iron and wood; the Dutch, their cheeses; the Russians, their hemp and wheat; the Genoese, their rice; the Spaniards, their oils; the Sicilians, their sulphur; the Greeks and Armenians, all the commodities of the Mediterranean and Black seas."

Evidently such a state of things is intolerable, for it ends in rendering our merchant marine useless. Let us hasten back, then, into our ship

174

yards, from which the cheapness of foreign navigation tends to exclude us. Let us close our doors to foreign vessels, or at least let us burden them with a heavy tax. Therefore, down with competition and rival marines!

Does M. Reybaud begin to understand that his economico-socialistic oscillations are much more innocent than he would have believed? What gratitude he owes me for having quieted his conscience, which perhaps was becoming alarmed!

The reciprocity of which M. Reybaud so bitterly complains is only a form of commercial liberty. Grant full and entire liberty of trade, and our flag is driven from the surface of the seas, as our oils would be from the continent. Therefore we shall pay dearer for our oil, if we insist on making it ourselves; dearer for our colonial products, if we wish to carry them ourselves. To secure cheapness it would be necessary, after having abandoned our oils, to abandon our marine: as well abandon straightway our cloths, our linens, our calicoes, our iron products, and then, as an isolated industry necessarily costs too much, our wines, our grains, our forage! Whichever course you may choose, privilege or liberty, you arrive at the impossible, at the absurd.

Undoubtedly there exists a principle of reconciliation; but, unless it be utterly despotic, it must be derived from a law superior to liberty itself: now, it is this law which no one has yet defined, and which I ask of the economists, if they really are masters of their science. For I cannot consider him a savant who, with the greatest sincerity and all the wit in the world, preaches by turns, fifteen lines apart, liberty and monopoly.

Is it not immediately and intuitively evident that COMPETITION DESTROYS COMPETITION? Is there a theorem in geometry more certain, more peremptory, than that? How then, upon what conditions, in what sense, can a principle which is its own denial enter into science? How can it become an organic law of society? If competition is necessary; if, as the school says, it is a postulate of production, — how does it become so devastating in its effects? And if its most certain effect is to ruin those whom it incites, how does it become useful? For the inconveniences which follow in its train, like the good which it procures, are not accidents arising from the work of man: both follow logically from the principle, and subsist by the same title and face to face.

And, in the first place, competition is as essential to labor as division, since it is division itself returning in another form, or rather, raised to its second power; division, I say, no longer, as in the first period of economic evolution, adequate to collective force, and consequently absorbing the personality of the laborer in the workshop, but giving birth to liberty by making each subdivision of labor a sort of sovereignty in which man stands in all his power and independence. Competition, in a word, is liberty in division and in all the divided parts: beginning with the most comprehensive functions, it tends toward its realization even in the inferior operations of parcellaire labor.

Here the communists raise an objection. It is necessary, they say, in all things, to distinguish between use and abuse. There is a useful, praiseworthy, moral competition, a competition which enlarges the heart and the mind, a noble and generous competition, — it is emulation; and why should not this emulation have for its object the advantage of all? There is another competition, pernicious, immoral, unsocial, a jealous competition which hates and which kills, — it is egoism.

So says communism; so expressed itself, nearly a year ago, in its social profession of faith, the journal, "La Reforme."

Whatever reluctance I may feel to oppose men whose ideas are at bottom my own, I cannot accept such dialectics. "La Reforme," in believing that it could reconcile everything by a distinction more grammatical than real, has made use, without suspecting it, of the golden mean, — that is, of the worst sort of diplomacy. Its argument is exactly the same as that of M. Rossi in regard to the division of labor: it consists in setting competition and morality against each other, in order to limit them by each other, as M. Rossi pretended to arrest and restrict economic inductions by morality, cutting here, lopping there, to suit the need and the occasion. I have refuted M. Rossi by asking him this simple question: How can science be in disagreement with itself, the science of wealth with the science of duty? Likewise I ask the communists: How can a principle whose development is clearly useful be at the same time pernicious?

They say: emulation is not competition. I note, in the first place, that this pretended distinction bears only on the divergent effects of the principle, which leads one to suppose that there were two principles which had been confounded. Emulation is nothing but competition itself; and, since they have thrown themselves into abstractions, I willingly plunge in also. There is no emulation without an object, just as there is no passional initiative without an object; and as the object of every passion is necessarily analogous to the passion itself, — woman to the lover, power to the ambitious, gold to the miser, a crown to the poet, — so the object of industrial emulation is necessarily profit.

No, rejoins the communist, the laborer's object of emulation should be general utility, fraternity, love.

But society itself, since, instead of stopping at the individual man, who is in question at this moment, they wish to attend only to the collective man, — society, I say, labors only with a view to wealth; comfort, happiness, is its only object. Why, then, should that which is true of society not be true of the individual also, since, after all, society is man and entire humanity lives in each man? Why substitute for the immediate object of emulation, which in industry is personal welfare, that far-away and almost metaphysical motive called general welfare, especially when the latter is nothing without the former and can result only from the former?

Communists, in general, build up a strange illusion: fanatics on the subject of power, they expect to secure through a central force, and in the special case in question, through collective wealth, by a sort of reversion, the welfare of the laborer who has created this wealth: as if the individual came into existence after society, instead of society after the individual. For that matter, this is not the only case in which we shall see the socialists unconsciously dominated by the traditions of the regime against which they protest.

But what need of insisting? From the moment that the communist changes the name of things, vera rerum vocabala, he tacitly admits his powerlessness, and puts himself out of the question. That is why my sole reply to him shall be: In denying competition, you abandon the thesis; henceforth you have no place in the discussion. Some other time we will inquire how far man should sacrifice himself in the interest of all: for the moment the question is the solution of the problem of competition, — that is, the reconciliation of the highest satisfaction of egoism with social necessities; spare us your moralities.

Competition is necessary to the constitution of value, — that is, to the very principle of distribution, and consequently to the advent of equality. As long as a product is supplied only by a single manufacturer, its real value remains a mystery, either through the producer's misrepresentation or through his neglect or inability to reduce the cost of production to its extreme limit. Thus the privilege of production is a real loss to society, and publicity of industry, like competition between laborers, a necessity. All the utopias ever imagined or imaginable cannot escape this law.

Certainly I do not care to deny that labor and wages can and should be guaranteed; I even entertain the hope that the time of such guarantee is not far off: but I maintain that a guarantee of wages is impossible without an exact knowledge of value, and that this value can be discovered only by competition, not at all by communistic institutions or by popular decree. For in this there is something more powerful than the will of the legislator and of citizens, — namely, the absolute impossibility that man should do his duty after finding himself relieved of all responsibility to himself: now, responsibility to self, in the matter of labor, necessarily implies competition with others. Ordain that, beginning January 1, 1847, labor and wages are guaranteed to all: immediately an immense relaxation will succeed the extreme tension to which industry is now subjected; real value will fall rapidly below nominal value; metallic money, in spite of its effigy and stamp, will experience the fate of the assignats; the merchant will ask more and give less; and we shall find ourselves in a still lower circle in the hell of misery in which competition is only the third turn.

Even were I to admit, with some socialists, that the attractiveness of labor may some day serve as food for emulation without any hidden thought of profit, of what utility could this utopia be in the phase which we are studying? We are yet only in the third period of economic evolution, in the third age of the constitution of labor, — that is, in a period when it is impossible for labor to be attractive. For the attractiveness of labor can result only from a high degree of physical, moral, and intellectual development of the laborer. Now, this development itself, this education of humanity by industry, is precisely the object of which we are in pursuit through the contradictions of social economy. How, then, could the attractiveness of labor serve us as a principle and lever, when it is still our object and our end?

But, if it is unquestionable that labor, as the highest manifestation of life, intelligence, and liberty, carries with it its own attractiveness, I deny that this attractiveness can ever be wholly separated from the motive of utility, and consequently from a return of egoism; I deny, I say, labor for labor, just as I deny style for style, love for love, art for art. Style for style has produced in these days hasty literature and thoughtless improvisation; love for love leads to unnatural vice, onanism, and prostitution; art for art ends in Chinese knick-knacks, caricature, the worship of the ugly. When man no longer looks to labor for anything but the pleasure of exercise, he soon ceases to labor, he plays. History is full of facts which attest this degradation. The games of Greece, Isthmian, Olympic, Pythian, Nemean, exercises of a society which produced everything by its slaves; the life of the Spartans and the ancient Cretans, their models; the gymnasiums, playgrounds, horse-races, and disorders of the market-place among the Athenians; the occupations which Plato assigns to the warriors in his Republic, and which but represent the tastes of his century; finally, in our feudal society, the tilts and tourneys, — all these inventions, as well as many others which I pass in silence, from the game of chess, invented, it is said, at the siege of Troy by Palamedes, to the cards illustrated for Charles VI. by Gringonneur, are examples of what labor becomes as soon as the serious motive of utility is separated from it. Labor, real labor, that which produces wealth and gives knowledge, has too much need of regularity and perseverance and sacrifice to be long the friend of passion, fugitive in its nature, inconstant, and disorderly; it is something too elevated, too ideal, too philosophical, to become exclusively pleasure and enjoyment, — that is, mysticism and sentiment. The faculty of laboring, which distinguishes man from the brutes, has its source in the profoundest depths of the reason: how could it become in us a simple manifestation of life, a voluptuous act of our feeling?

But if now they fall back upon the hypothesis of a transformation of our nature, unprecedented in history, and of which there has been nothing so far that could have expressed the idea, it is nothing more than a dream, unintelligible even to those who defend it, an inversion of progress, a contradiction given to the most certain laws of economic science; and my only reply is to exclude it from the discussion.

Let us stay in the realm of facts, since facts alone have a meaning and can aid us. The French Revolution was effected for industrial liberty as well as for political liberty: and although France in 1789 had not seen all the consequences of the principle for the realization of which she asked, — let us say it boldly, — she was mistaken neither in her wishes nor in her expectation. Whoever would try to deny it would lose in my eyes the right to criticism: I will never dispute with an adversary who would posit as a principle the spontaneous error of twenty-five millions of men.

At the end of the eighteenth century France, wearied with privileges, desired at any price to shake off the torpor of her corporations, and restore the dignity of the laborer by conferring liberty upon him. Everywhere it was necessary to emancipate labor, stimulate genius, and render the manufacturer responsible by arousing a thousand

179

competitors and loading upon him alone the consequences of his indolence, ignorance, and insincerity. Before '89 France was ripe for the transition; it was Turgot who had the glory of effecting the first passage.

Why then, if competition had not been a principle of social economy, a decree of destiny, a necessity of the human soul, why, instead of abolishing corporations, masterships, and wardenships, did they not think rather of repairing them all? Why, instead of a revolution, did they not content themselves with a reform? Why this negation, if a modification was sufficient? Especially as this middle party was entirely in the line of conservative ideas, which the bourgeoisie shared. Let communism, let quasi-socialistic democracy, which, in regard to the principle of competition, represent — though they do not suspect it — the system of the golden mean, the counter-revolutionary idea, explain to me this unanimity of the nation, if they can!

Moreover the event confirmed the theory. Beginning with the Turgot ministry, an increase of activity and well-being manifested itself in the nation. The test seemed so decisive that it obtained the approval of all legislatures. Liberty of industry and commerce figure in our constitutions on a level with political liberty. To this liberty, in short, France owes the growth of her wealth during the last sixty years.

After this capital fact, which establishes so triumphantly the necessity of competition, I ask permission to cite three or four others, which, being less general in their nature, will throw into bolder relief the influence of the principle which I defend.

Why is our agriculture so prodigiously backward? How is it that routine and barbarism still hover, in so many localities, over the most important branch of national labor? Among the numerous causes that could be cited, I see, in the front rank, the absence of competition. The peasants fight over strips of ground; they compete with each other before the notary; in the fields, no. And speak to them of emulation, of the public good, and with what amazement you fill them! Let the king, they say (to them the king is synonymous with the State, with the public good, with society), let the king attend to his business, and we will attend to ours! Such is their philosophy and their patriotism. Ah! if the king could excite competition with them! Unfortunately it is impossible. While in manufactures competition follows from liberty and property, in agriculture liberty and property are a direct obstacle to competition. The peasant, rewarded, not according to his labor and intelligence, but according to the quality of the land and the caprice of God, aims, in cultivating, to pay the lowest possible wages and to make the least possible advance outlays. Sure of always finding a market for his goods, he is much more solicitous about reducing his expenses than about improving the soil and the quality of its products. He sows, and Providence does the rest. The only sort of competition known to the agricultural class is that of rents; and it cannot be denied that in France, and for instance in Beauce, it has led to useful results. But as the principle of this competition takes effect only at second hand, so to speak, as it does not emanate directly from the liberty and property of the cultivators, it disappears with the cause that produces it, so that, to insure the decline of agricultural industry in many localities, or at least to arrest its progress, perhaps it would suffice to make the farmers proprietors.

Another branch of collective labor, which of late years has given rise to sharp debates, is that of public works. "To manage the building of a road, M. Dunoyer very well says, "perhaps a pioneer and a postilion would be better than an engineer fresh from the School of Roads and Bridges." There is no one who has not had occasion to verify the correctness of this remark.

On one of our finest rivers, celebrated by the importance of its navigation, a bridge was being built. From the beginning of the work the rivermen had seen that the arches would be much too low to allow the circulation of boats at times when the river was high: they pointed this out to the engineer in charge of the work. Bridges, answered the latter with superb dignity, are made for those who pass over, not for those who pass under. The remark has become a proverb in that vicinity. But, as it is impossible for stupidity to prevail forever, the government has felt the necessity of revising the work of its agent, and as I write the arches of the bridge are being raised. Does any one believe that, if the merchants interested in the course of the navigable way had been charged with the enterprise at their own risk and peril, they would have had to do their work twice? One could fill a book with masterpieces of the same sort achieved by young men learned in roads and bridges, who, scarcely out of school and given life positions, are no longer stimulated by competition.

In proof of the industrial capacity of the State, and consequently of the possibility of abolishing competition altogether, they cite the administration of the tobacco industry. There, they say, is no adulteration, no litigation, no bankruptcy, no misery. The condition of the workmen, adequately paid, instructed, sermonized, moralized, and assured of a retiring pension accumulated by their savings, is incomparably superior to that of the immense majority of workmen engaged in free industry.

All this may be true: for my part, I am ignorant on the subject. I know nothing of what goes on in the administration of the tobacco factories; I have procured no information either from the directors or the workmen, and I have no need of any. How much does the tobacco sold by the administration cost? How much is it worth? You can answer the first of these questions: you only need to call at the first tobacco shop you see. But you can tell me nothing about the second, because you have no standard of comparison and are forbidden to verify by experiment the items of cost of administration, which it is consequently impossible to accept. Therefore the tobacco business, made into a monopoly, necessarily costs society more than it brings in; it is an industry which, instead of subsisting by its own product, lives by subsidies, and which consequently, far from furnishing us a model, is one of the first abuses which reform should strike down.

And when I speak of the reform to be introduced in the production of tobacco, I do not refer simply to the enormous tax which triples or quadruples the value of this product; neither do I refer to the hierarchical organization of its employees, some of whom by their salaries are made aristocrats as expensive as they are useless, while others, hopeless receivers of petty wages, are kept forever in the situation of subalterns. I do not even speak of the privilege of the tobacco shops and the whole world of parasites which they support: I have particularly in view the useful labor, the labor of the workmen. From the very fact that the administration's workman has no competitors and is interested neither in profit nor loss, from the fact that he is not free, in a word, his product is necessarily less, and his service too expensive. This being so, let them say that the government treats its employees well and looks out for their comfort: what wonder? Why do not people see that liberty bears the burdens of privilege, and that, if, by some impossibility, all industries were to be treated like the tobacco industry, the source of subsidies failing, the nation could no longer balance its receipts and its expenses, and the State would become a bankrupt?

Foreign products: I cite the testimony of an educated man, though not a political economist, — M. Liebig.

Formerly France imported from Spain every year soda to the value of twenty or thirty millions of francs; for Spanish soda was the best. All through the war with England the price of soda, and consequently that of soap and glass, constantly rose. French manufacturers therefore had to suffer considerably from this state of things. Then it was that Leblanc discovered the method of extracting soda from common salt. This process was a source of wealth to France; the manufacture of soda acquired extraordinary proportions; but neither Leblanc nor Napoleon enjoyed the profit of the invention. The Restoration, which took advantage of the wrath of the people against the author of the continental blockade, refused to pay the debt of the emperor, whose promises had led to Leblanc's discoveries....

A few years ago, the king of Naples having undertaken to convert the Sicilian sulphur trade into a monopoly, England, which consumes an immense quantity of this sulphur, warned the king of Naples that, if the monopoly were maintained, it would be considered a casus belli. While the two governments were exchanging diplomatic notes, fifteen patents were taken out in England for the extraction of sulphuric acid from the limestones, iron pyrites, and other mineral substances in which England abounds. But the affair being arranged with the king of Naples, nothing came of these exploitations: it was simply established, by the attempts which were made, that the extraction of sulphuric acid by the new processes could have been carried on successfully, which perhaps would have annihilated Sicily's sulphur trade.

Had it not been for the war with England, had not the king of Naples had a fancy for monopoly, it would have been a long time before any one in France would have thought of extracting soda from sea salt, or any one in England of getting sulphuric acid from the mountains of lime and pyrites which she contains. Now, that is precisely the effect of competition upon industry. Man rouses from his idleness only when want fills him with anxiety; and the surest way to extinguish his genius is to deliver him from all solicitude and take away from him the hope of profit and of the social distinction which results from it, by creating around him peace everywhere, peace always, and transferring to the State the responsibility of his inertia.

Yes, it must be admitted, in spite of modern quietism, — man's life is a permanent war, war with want, war with nature, war with his fellows, and consequently war with himself. The theory of a peaceful equality, founded on fraternity and sacrifice, is only a counterfeit of the Catholic doctrine of renunciation of the goods and pleasures of this world, the principle of beggary, the panegyric of misery. Man may love his fellow well enough to die for him; he does not love him well enough to work for him.

To the theory of sacrifice, which we have just refuted in fact and in right, the adversaries of competition add another, which is just the opposite of the first: for it is a law of the mind that, when it does not know the truth, which is its point of equilibrium, it oscillates between two contradictions. This new theory of anti-competitive socialism is that of encouragements.

What more social, more progressive in appearance, than encouragement of labor and of industry? There is no democrat who does not consider it one of the finest attributes of power, no utopian theorist who does not place it in the front rank as a means of organizing happiness. Now, government is by nature so incapable of directing labor that every reward bestowed by it is a veritable larceny from the common treasury. M. Reybaud shall furnish us the text of this induction.

"The premiums granted to encourage exportation," observes M. Reybaud somewhere, "are equivalent to the taxes paid for the importation of raw material; the advantage remains absolutely null, and serves to encourage nothing but a vast system of smuggling."

This result is inevitable. Abolish customs duties, and national industry suffers, as we have already seen in the case of sesame; maintain the duties without granting premiums for exportation, and national commerce will be beaten in foreign markets. To obviate this difficulty do you resort to premiums? You but restore with one hand what you have received with the other, and you provoke fraud, the last result, the caput mortuum, of all encouragements of industry. Hence it follows that every encouragement to labor, every reward bestowed upon industry, beyond the natural price of its product, is a gratuitous gift, a bribe taken out of the consumer and offered in his name to a favorite of power, in exchange for zero, for nothing. To encourage industry, then, is synonymous at bottom with encouraging idleness: it is one of the forms of swindling.

In the interest of our navy the government had thought it best to grant to outfitters of transport-ships a premium for every man employed on their vessels. Now, I continue to quote M. Reybaud:

On every vessel that starts for Newfoundland from sixty to seventy men embark. Of this number twelve are sailors: the balance consists of villagers snatched from their work in the fields, who, engaged as day laborers for the preparation of fish, remain strangers to the rigging, and have nothing that is marine about them except their feet and stomach.

184

Nevertheless, these men figure on the rolls of the naval inscription, and there perpetuate a deception. When there is occasion to defend the institution of premiums, these are cited in its favor; they swell the numbers and contribute to success.

Base jugglery! doubtless some innocent reformer will exclaim. Be it so: but let us analyze the fact, and try to disengage the general idea to be found therein.

In principle the only encouragement to labor that science can admit is profit. For, if labor cannot find its reward in its own product, very far from encouraging it, it should be abandoned as soon as possible, and, if this same labor results in a net product, it is absurd to add to this net product a gratuitous gift, and thus overrate the value of the service. Applying this principle, I say then: If the merchant service calls only for ten thousand sailors, it should not be asked to support fifteen thousand; the shortest course for the government is to put five thousand conscripts on State vessels, and send them on their expeditions, like princes. Every encouragement offered to the merchant marine is a direct invitation to fraud, — what do I say? — a proposal to pay wages for an impossible service. Do the handling and discipline of vessels and all the conditions of maritime commerce accommodate themselves to these adjuncts of a useless persononel? What, then, can the ship-owner do in face of a government which offers him a bonus to embark on his vessel people of whom he has no need? If the ministry throws the money of the treasury into the street, am I guilty if I pick it up?

Thus — and it is a point worthy of notice — the theory of encouragements emanates directly from the theory of sacrifice; and, in order to avoid holding man responsible, the opponents of competition, by the fatal contradiction of their ideas, are obliged to make him now a god, now a brute. And then they are astonished that society is not moved by their appeal! Poor children! men will never be better or worse than you see them now and than they always have been. As soon as their individual welfare solicits them, they desert the general welfare: in which I find them, if not honorable, at least worthy of excuse. It is your fault if you now demand of them more than they owe you and now stimulate their greed with rewards which they do not deserve. Man has nothing more precious than himself, and consequently no other law than his responsibility. The theory of self-sacrifice, like that of rewards, is a theory of rogues, subversive of society and morality; and by the very fact that you look either to sacrifice or to privilege for the maintenance of order, you create a new antagonism in society. Instead of causing the birth of harmony from the

185

free activity of persons, you render the individual and the State strangers to each other; in commanding union, you breathe discord.

To sum up, outside of competition there remains but this alternative, — encouragement, which is a mystification, or sacrifice, which is hypocrisy.

Therefore competition, analyzed in its principle, is an inspiration of justice; and yet we shall see that competition, in its results, is unjust.

2. — Subversive effects of competition, and the destruction of liberty thereby.

The kingdom of heaven suffereth violence, says the Gospel, and the violent take it by force. These words are the allegory of society. In society regulated by labor, dignity, wealth, and glory are objects of competition; they are the reward of the strong, and competition may be defined as the regime of force. The old economists did not at first perceive this contradiction: the moderns have been forced to recognize it.

"To elevate a State from the lowest degree of barbarism to the highest degree of opulence," wrote A. Smith, "but three things are necessary, — peace, moderate taxes, and a tolerable administration of justice. All the rest is brought about by the natural course of things."

On which the last translator of Smith, M. Blanqui, lets fall this gloomy comment:

We have seen the natural course of things produce disastrous effects, and create anarchy in production, war for markets, and piracy in competition. The division of labor and the perfecting of machinery, which should realize for the great working family of the human race the conquest of a certain amount of leisure to the advantage of its dignity, have produced at many points nothing but degradation and misery..... When A. Smith wrote, liberty had not yet come with its embarrassments and its abuses, and the Glasgow professor foresaw only its blessings... Smith would have written like M. de Sismondi, if he had been a witness of the sad condition of Ireland and the manufacturing districts of England in the times in which we live.

Now then, litterateurs, statesmen, daily publicists, believers and half-believers, all you who have taken upon yourselves the mission of

186

indoctrinating men, do you hear these words which one would take for a translation from Jeremiah? Will you tell us at last to what end you pretend to be conducting civilization? What advice do you offer to society, to the country, in alarm?

But to whom do I speak? Ministers, journalists, sextons, and pedants! Do such people trouble themselves about the problems of social economy? Have they ever heard of competition?

A citizen of Lyons, a soul hardened to mercantile war, travelled in Tuscany. He observes that from five to six hundred thousand straw hats are made annually in that country, the aggregate value of which amounts to four or five millions of francs. This industry is almost the sole support of the people of the little State. "How is it," he says to himself, "that so easily conducted a branch of agriculture and manufactures has not been transported into Provence and Languedoc, where the climate is the same as in Tuscany?" But, thereupon observes an economist, if the industry of the peasants of Tuscany is taken from them, how will they contrive to live?

The manufacture of black silks had become for Florence a specialty the secret of which she guarded preciously.

A shrewd Lyons manufacturer, the tourist notices with satisfaction, has come to set up an establishment in Florence, and has finally got possession of the peculiar processes of dyeing and weaving. Probably this discovery will diminish Florentine exportation. — A Journey in Italy, by M. FULCHIRON.

Formerly the breeding of the silk-worm was abandoned to the peasants of Tuscany; whom it aided to live.

Agricultural societies have been formed; they have represented that the silk-worm, in the peasant's sleeping-room, did not get sufficient ventilation or sufficient steadiness of temperature, or as good care as it would have if the laborers who breed them made it their sole business. Consequently rich, intelligent, and generous citizens have built, amid the applause of the public, what are called bigattieres (from bigatti, silk-worm). — M. DE SISMONDI.

And then, you ask, will these breeders of silk-worms, these manufacturers of silks and hats, lose their work? Precisely: it will even be proved to them that it is for their interest that they should, since they

187

will be able to buy the same products for less than it costs them to manufacture them. Such is competition.

Competition, with its homicidal instinct, takes away the bread of a whole class of laborers, and sees in it only an improvement, a saving; it steals a secret in a cowardly manner, and glories in it as a discovery; it changes the natural zones of production to the detriment of an entire people, and pretends to have done nothing but utilize the advantages of its climate. Competition overturns all notions of equity and justice; it increases the real cost of production by needlessly multiplying the capital invested, causes by turns the dearness of products and their depreciation, corrupts the public conscience by putting chance in the place of right, and maintains terror and distrust everywhere.

But what! Without this atrocious characteristic, competition would lose its happiest effects; without the arbitrary element in exchange and the panics of the market, labor would not continually build factory against factory, and, not being maintained in such good working order, production would realize none of its marvels. After having caused evil to arise from the very utility of its principle, competition again finds a way to extract good from evil; destruction engenders utility, equilibrium is realized by agitation, and it may be said of competition, as Samson said of the lion which he had slain: De comedente cibus exiit, et de forti dulcedo. Is there anything, in all the spheres of human knowledge, more surprising than political economy?

Let us take care, nevertheless, not to yield to an impulse of irony, which would be on our part only unjust invective. It is characteristic of economic science to find its certainty in its contradictions, and the whole error of the economists consists in not having understood this. Nothing poorer than their criticism, nothing more saddening than their mental confusion, as soon as they touch this question of competition: one would say that they were witnesses forced by torture to confess what their conscience would like to conceal. The reader will take it kindly if I put before his eyes the arguments for laissez-passer, introducing him, so to speak, into the presence of a secret meeting of economists.

M. Dunoyer opens the discussion.

Of all the economists M. Dunoyer has most energetically embraced the positive side of competition, and consequently, as might have been expected, most ineffectually grasped the negative side. M. Dunoyer, with whom nothing can be done when what he calls principles are under discussion, is very far from believing that in matters of political economy yes and no may be true at the same moment and to the same extent; let it be said even to his credit, such a conception is the more repugnant to him because of the frankness and honesty with which he holds his doctrines. What would I not give to gain an entrance into this pure but so obstinate soul for this truth as certain to me as the existence of the sun, — that all the categories of political economy are contradictions! Instead of uselessly exhausting himself in reconciling practice and theory; instead of contenting himself with the ridiculous excuse that everything here below has its advantages and its inconveniences, — M. Dunoyer would seek the synthetic idea which solves all the antinomies, and, instead of the paradoxical conservative which he now is, he would become with us an inexorable and logical revolutionist.

"If competition is a false principle," says M. Dunoyer, "it follows that for two thousand years humanity has been pursuing the wrong road."

No, what you say does not follow, and your prejudicial remark is refuted by the very theory of progress. Humanity posits its principles by turns, and sometimes at long intervals: never does it give them up in substance, although it destroys successively their expressions and formulas. This destruction is called negation; because the general reason, ever progressive, continually denies the completeness and sufficiency of its prior ideas. Thus it is that, competition being one of the periods in the constitution of value, one of the elements of the social synthesis, it is true to say at the same time that it is indestructible in its principle, and that nevertheless in its present form it should be abolished, denied. If, then, there is any one here who is in opposition to history, it is you.

I have several remarks to make upon the accusations of which competition has been the object. The first is that this regime, good or bad, ruinous or fruitful, does not really exist as yet; that it is established nowhere except in a partial and most incomplete manner.

This first observation has no sense. Competition kills competition, as we said at the outset; this aphorism may be taken for a definition. How, then, could competition ever be complete? Moreover, though it should be admitted that competition does not yet exist in its integrity, that would simply prove that competition does not act with all the power of elimination that there is in it; but that will not change at all its contradictory nature. What need have we to wait thirty centuries longer to find out that, the more competition develops, the more it tends to reduce the number of competitors?

The second is that the picture drawn of it is unfaithful; and that sufficient heed is not paid to the extension which the general welfare has undergone, including even that of the laboring classes.

If some socialists fail to recognize the useful side of competition, you on your side make no mention of its pernicious effects. The testimony of your opponents coming to complete your own, competition is shown in the fullest light, and from a double falsehood we get the truth as a result. As for the gravity of the evil, we shall see directly what to think about that.

The third is that the evil experienced by the laboring classes is not referred to its real causes.

If there are other causes of poverty than competition, does that prevent it from contributing its share? Though only one manufacturer a year were ruined by competition, if it were admitted that this ruin is the necessary effect of the principle, competition, as a principle, would have to be rejected.

The fourth is that the principal means proposed for obviating it would be inexpedient in the extreme.

Possibly: but from this I conclude that the inadequacy of the remedies proposed imposes a new duty upon you, — precisely that of seeking the most expedient means of preventing the evil of competition.

The fifth, finally, is that the real remedies, in so far as it is possible to remedy the evil by legislation, would be found precisely in the regime which is accused of having produced it, — that is, in a more and more real regime of liberty and competition.

Well! I am willing. The remedy for competition, in your opinion, is to make competition universal. But, in order that competition may be universal, it is necessary to procure for all the means of competing; it is necessary to destroy or modify the predominance of capital over labor, to change the relations between employer and workman, to solve, in a word, the antinomy of division and that of machinery; it is necessary to ORGANIZE LABOR: can you give this solution?

M. Dunoyer then develops, with a courage worthy of a better cause, his own utopia of universal competition: it is a labyrinth in which the author stumbles and contradicts himself at every step.

"Competition," says M. Dunoyer, "meets a multitude of obstacles."

In fact, it meets so many and such powerful ones that it becomes impossible itself. For how is triumph possible over obstacles inherent in the constitution of society and consequently inseparable from competition itself?

In addition to the public services, there is a certain number of professions the practice of which the government has seen fit to more or less exclusively reserve; there is a larger number of which legislation has given a monopoly to a restricted number of individuals. Those which are abandoned to competition are subjected to formalities and restrictions, to numberless barriers, which keep many from approaching, and in these consequently competition is far from being unlimited. In short, there are few which are not submitted to varied taxes, necessary doubtless, etc.

What does all this mean? M. Dunoyer doubtless does not intend that society shall dispense with government, administration, police, taxes, universities, in a word, with everything that constitutes a society. Then, inasmuch as society necessarily implies exceptions to competition, the hypothesis of universal competition is chimerical, and we are back again under the regime of caprice, — a result foretold in the definition of competition. Is there anything serious in this reasoning of M. Dunoyer?

Formerly the masters of the science began by putting far away from them every preconceived idea, and devoted themselves to tracing facts back to general laws, without ever altering or concealing them. The researches of Adam Smith, considering the time of their appearance, are a marvel of sagacity and lofty reasoning. The economic picture presented by Quesnay, wholly unintelligible as it appears, gives evidence of a profound sentiment of the general synthesis. The introduction to J. B. Say's great treatise dwells exclusively upon the scientific characteristics of political economy, and in every line is to be seen how much the author felt the need of absolute ideas. The economists of the last century certainly did not constitute the science, but they sought this constitution ardently and honestly.

191

How far we are today from these noble thoughts! No longer do they seek a science; they defend the interests of dynasty and caste. The more powerless routine becomes, the more stubbornly they adhere to it; they make use of the most venerated names to stamp abnormal phenomena with a quality of authenticity which they lack; they tax accusing facts with heresy; they calumniate the tendencies of the century; and nothing irritates an economist so much as to pretend to reason with him.

"The peculiar characteristic of the present time," cries M. Dunoyer, in a tone of keen discontent, "is the agitation of all classes; their anxiety, their inability to ever stop at anything and be contented; the infernal labor performed upon the less fortunate that they may become more and more discontented in proportion to the increased efforts of society to make their lot really less pitiful."

Indeed! Because the socialists goad political economy, they are incarnate devils! Can there be anything more impious, in fact, than to teach the proletaire that he is wronged in his labor and his wages, and that, in the surroundings in which he lives, his poverty is irremediable?

M. Reybaud repeats, with greater emphasis, the wail of his master, M. Dunoyer: one would think them the two seraphim of Isaiah chanting a Sanctus to competition. In June, 1844, at the time when he published the fourth edition of his "Contemporary Reformers," M. Reybaud wrote, in the bitterness of his soul:

To socialists we owe the organization of labor, the right to labor; they are the promoters of the regime of surveillance.... The legislative chambers on either side of the channel are gradually succumbing to their influence.... Thus utopia is gaining ground....

And M. Reybaud more and more deplores the secret influence of socialism on the best minds, and stigmatizes — see the malice! — the unperceived contagion with which even those who have broken lances against socialism allow themselves to be inoculated. Then he announces, as a last act of his high justice against the wicked, the approaching publication, under the title of "Laws of Labor," of a work in which he will prove (unless some new evolution takes place in his ideas) that the laws of labor have nothing in common, either with the right to labor or with the organization of labor, and that the best of reforms is laissez-faire.

"Moreover," adds M. Reybaud, "the tendency of political economy is no longer to theory, but to practice. The abstract portions of the science seem henceforth fixed. The controversy over definitions is exhausted, or nearly so. The works of the great economists on value, capital, supply and demand, wages, taxes, machinery, farm-rent, increase of population, over-accumulation of products, markets, banks, monopolies, etc., seem to have set the limit of dogmatic researches, and form a body of doctrine beyond which there is little to hope."

Facility of speech, impotence in argument, — such would have been the conclusion of Montesquieu upon this strange panegyric of the founders of social economy. THE SCIENCE IS COMPLETE! M. Reybaud makes oath to it; and what he proclaims with so much authority is repeated at the Academy, in the professors' chairs, in the councils of State, in the legislative halls; it is published in the journals; the king is made to say it in his New Year's addresses; and before the courts the cases of claimants are decided accordingly.

THE SCIENCE IS COMPLETE! What fools we are, then, socialists, to hunt for daylight at noonday, and to protest, with our lanterns in our hands, against the brilliancy of these solar rays!

But, gentlemen, it is with sincere regret and profound distrust of myself that I find myself forced to ask you for further light. If you cannot cure our ills, give us at least kind words, give us evidence, give us resignation.

"It is obvious," says M. Dunoyer, "that wealth is infinitely better distributed in our day than it ever has been."

"The equilibrium of pains and pleasures," promptly continues M. Reybaud, "ever tends to restore itself on earth."

What, then! What do you say? Wealth better distributed, equilibrium restored! Explain yourselves, please, as to this better distribution. Is equality coming, or inequality going? Is solidarity becoming closer, or competition diminishing? I will not quit you until you have answered me, non missura cutem.... For, whatever the cause of the restoration of equilibrium and of the better distribution which you point out, I embrace it with ardor, and will follow it to its last consequences. Before 1830 — I select the date at random — wealth was not so well distributed: how so? Today, in your opinion, it is better distributed: why? You see what I am coming at: distribution being not yet perfectly equitable and the equilibrium not absolutely perfect, I ask, on the one hand, what obstacle it is that disturbs the equilibrium, and, on the other, by virtue of what principle humanity continually passes from the greater to the less evil and from the good to the better? For, in fact, this secret principle of amelioration can be neither competition, nor machinery, nor division of labor, nor supply and demand: all these principles are but levers which by turns cause value to oscillate, as the Academy of Moral Sciences has very clearly seen. What, then, is the sovereign law of well-being? What is this rule, this measure, this criterion of progress, the violation of which is the perpetual cause of poverty? Speak, and quit your haranguing.

Wealth is better distributed, you say. Show us your proofs.

M. Dunoyer:

According to official documents, taxes are assessed on scarcely less than eleven million separate parcels of landed property. The number of proprietors by whom these taxes are paid is estimated at six millions; so that, assuming four individuals to a family, there must be no less than twenty-four million inhabitants out of thirty-four who participate in the ownership of the soil.

Then, according to the most favorable figures, there must be ten million proletaires in France, or nearly one-third of the population. Now, what have you to say to that? Add to these ten millions half of the twenty-four others, whose property, burdened with mortgages, parcelled out, impoverished, wretched, gives them no support, and still you will not have the number of individuals whose living is precarious.

The number of twenty-four million proprietors perceptibly tends to increase.

I maintain that it perceptibly tends to decrease. Who is the real proprietor, in your opinion, — the nominal holder, assessed, taxed, pawned, mortgaged, or the creditor who collects the rent? Jewish and Swiss money-lenders are today the real proprietors of Alsace; and proof of their excellent judgment is to be found in the fact that they have no thought of acquiring landed estates: they prefer to invest their capital.

To the landed proprietors must be added about fifteen hundred thousand holders of patents and licenses, or, assuming four persons to a family, six million individuals interested as leaders in industrial enterprises.

But, in the first place, a great number of these licensed individuals are landed proprietors, and you count them twice. Further, it may be safely said that, of the whole number of licensed manufacturers and merchants, a fourth at most realize profits, another fourth hold their own, and the rest are constantly running behind in their business. Take, then, half at most of the six million so-called leaders in enterprises, which we will add to the very problematical twelve million landed proprietors, and we shall attain a total of fifteen million Frenchmen in a position, by their education, their industry, their capital, their credit, their property, to engage in competition. For the rest of the nation, or nineteen million souls, competition, like Henri IV.'s pullet in the pot, is a dish which they produce for the class which can pay for it, but which they never touch.

Another difficulty. These nineteen million men, within whose reach competition never comes, are hirelings of the competitors. In the same way formerly the serfs fought for the lords, but without being able themselves to carry a banner or put an army on foot. Now, if competition cannot by itself become the common condition, why should not those for whom it offers nothing but perils, exact guarantees from the barons whom they serve? And if these guarantees can not be denied them, how could they be other than barriers to competition, just as the truce of God, invented by the bishops, was a barrier to feudal wars? By the constitution of society, I said a little while ago, competition is an exceptional matter, a privilege; now I ask how it is possible for this privilege to coexist with equality of rights?

And think you, when I demand for consumers and wage-receivers guarantees against competition, that it is a socialist's dream? Listen to two of your most illustrious confreres, whom you will not accuse of performing an infernal work.

M. Rossi (Volume I, Lecture 16) recognizes in the State the right to regulate labor, when the danger is too great and the guarantees insufficient, which means always. For the legislator must secure public order by principles and laws: he does not wait for unforeseen facts to arise in order that he may drive them back with an arbitrary hand. Elsewhere (Volume II, pp. 73–77) the same professor points out, as consequences of exaggerated competition, the incessant formation of a financial and landed aristocracy and the approaching downfall of small holders, and he raises the cry of alarm. M. Blanqui, on his side, declares that the organization of labor is recognized by economic science as in the order of the day (he has since retracted the statement), urges the participation of workers in the profits and the advent of the collective laborer, and thunders continually against the monopolies, prohibitions, and tyranny of capital. Qui habet aures audiendi audiat! M. Rossi, as a writer on criminal law, decrees against the robberies of competition; M. Blanqui, as examining magistrate, proclaims the guilty parties: it is the counterpart of the duet sung just now by MM. Reybaud and Dunoyer. When the latter cry Hosanna, the former respond, like the Fathers in the Councils, Anathema.

But, it will be said, MM. Blanqui and Rossi mean to strike only the abuses of competition; they have taken care not to proscribe the principle, and in that they are thoroughly in accord with MM. Reybaud and Dunoyer.

I protest against this distinction, in the interest of the fame of the two professors.

In fact, abuse has invaded everything, and the exception has become the rule. When M. Troplong, defending, with all the economists, the liberty of commerce, admitted that the coalition of the cab companies was one of those facts against which the legislator finds himself absolutely powerless, and which seem to contradict the sanest notions of social economy, he still had the consolation of saying to himself that such a fact was wholly exceptional, and that there was reason to believe that it would not become general. Now, this fact has become general: the most conservative jurisconsult has only to put his head out of his window to see that today absolutely everything has been monopolized through competition, — transportation (by land, rail, and water), wheat and flour, wine and brandy, wood, coal, oil, iron, fabrics, salt, chemical products, etc. It is sad for jurisprudence, that twin sister of political economy, to see its grave anticipations contradicted in less than a lustre, but it is sadder still for a great nation to be led by such poor geniuses and to glean the few ideas which sustain its life from the brushwood of their writings.

In theory we have demonstrated that competition, on its useful side, should be universal and carried to its maximum of intensity; but that, viewed on its negative side, it must be everywhere stifled, even to the last vestige. Are the economists in a position to effect this elimination? Have they foreseen the consequences, calculated the difficulties? If the answer should be affirmative, I should have the boldness to propose the following case to them for solution.

A treaty of coalition, or rather of association, — for the courts would be greatly embarrassed to define either term, — has just united in one company all the coal mines in the basin of the Loire. On complaint of the municipalities of Lyons and Saint Etienne, the ministry has appointed a commission charged with examining the character and tendencies of this frightful society. Well, I ask, what can the intervention of power, with the assistance of civil law and political economy, accomplish here?

They cry out against coalition. But can the proprietors of mines be prevented from associating, from reducing their general expenses and costs of exploitation, and from working their mines to better advantage by a more perfect understanding with each other? Shall they be ordered to begin their old war over again, and ruin themselves by increased expenses, waste, over-production, disorder, and decreased prices? All that is absurd.

Shall they be prevented from increasing their prices so as to recover the interest on their capital? Then let them be protected themselves against any demands for increased wages on the part of the workmen; let the law concerning joint-stock companies be reenacted; let the sale of shares be prohibited; and when all these measures shall have been taken, as the capitalist-proprietors of the basin cannot justly be forced to lose capital invested under a different condition of things, let them be indemnified.

Shall a tariff be imposed upon them? That would be a law of maximum. The State would then have to put itself in the place of the exploiters; keep the accounts of their capital, interest, and office expenses; regulate the wages of the miners, the salaries of the engineers and directors, the price of the wood employed in the extraction of the coal, the expenditure for material; and, finally, determine the normal and legitimate rate of profit. All this cannot be done by ministerial decree: a law is necessary. Will the legislator dare, for the sake of a special industry, to change the public law of the French, and put power in the place of property? Then of two things one: either commerce in coals will fall into the hands of the State, or else the State must find some means of reconciling liberty and order in carrying on the mining industry, in which case the socialists will ask that what has been executed at one point be imitated at all points.

The coalition of the Loire mines has posited the social question in terms which permit no more evasion. Either competition, — that is, monopoly and what follows; or exploitation by the State, — that is, dearness of labor and continuous impoverishment; or else, in short, a solution based upon equality, — in other words, the organization of

197

labor, which involves the negation of political economy and the end of property.

But the economists do not proceed with this abrupt logic: they love to bargain with necessity. M. Dupin (session of the Academy of Moral and Political Sciences, June 10, 1843) expresses the opinion that, "though competition may be useful within the nation, it must be prevented between nations."

To prevent or to let alone, — such is the eternal alternative of the economists: beyond it their genius does not go. In vain is it cried out at them that it is not a question of preventing anything or of permitting everything; that what is asked of them, what society expects of them, is a reconciliation: this double idea does not enter their head.

"It is necessary," M. Dunoyer replies to M. Dupin, "to distinguish theory from practice."

My God! everybody knows that M. Dunoyer, inflexible as to principles in his works, is very accommodating as to practice in the Council of State. But let him condescend to once ask himself this question: Why am I obliged to continually distinguish practice from theory? Why do they not harmonize?

M. Blanqui, as a lover of peace and harmony, supports the learned M. Dunoyer, — that is, theory. Nevertheless he thinks, with M. Dupin, — that is, with practice, — that competition is not exempt from reproach. So afraid is M. Blanqui of calumniating and stirring up the fire!

M. Dupin is obstinate in his opinion. He cites, as evils for which competition is responsible, fraud, sale by false weights, the exploitation of children. All doubtless in order to prove that competition within the nation may be useful!

M. Passy, with his usual logic, observes that there will always be dishonest people who, etc. Accuse human nature, he cries, but not competition.

At the very outset M. Passy's logic wanders from the question. Competition is reproached with the inconveniences which result from its nature, not with the frauds of which it is the occasion or pretext. A manufacturer finds a way of replacing a workman who costs him three francs a day by a woman to whom he gives but one franc. This expedient is the only one by which he can meet a falling market and keep his establishment in motion. Soon to the working women he will add children. Then, forced by the necessities of war, he will gradually reduce wages and add to the hours of labor. Where is the guilty party here? This argument may be turned about in a hundred ways and applied to all industries without furnishing any ground for accusing human nature.

M. Passy himself is obliged to admit it when he adds: "As for the compulsory labor of children, the fault is on the parents." Exactly. And the fault of the parents on whom?

"In Ireland," continues this orator, "there is no competition, and yet poverty is extreme."

On this point M. Passy's ordinary logic has been betrayed by an extraordinary lack of memory. In Ireland there is a complete, universal monopoly of the land, and unlimited, desperate competition for farms. Competition-monopoly are the two balls which unhappy Ireland drags, one after each foot.

When the economists are tired of accusing human nature, the greed of parents, and the turbulence of radicals, they find delectation in picturing the felicity of the proletariat. But there again they cannot agree with each other or with themselves; and nothing better depicts the anarchy of competition than the disorder of their ideas.

Today the wife of the workingman dresses in elegant robes which in a previous century great ladies would not have disdained. — M. Chevalier: Lecture 4.

And this is the same M. Chevalier who, according to his own calculation, estimates that the total national income would give thirteen cents a day to each individual. Some economists even reduce this figure to eleven cents. Now, as all that goes to make up the large fortunes must come out of this sum, we may accept the estimate of M. de Morogues that the daily income of half the French people does not exceed five cents each.

"But," continues M. Chevalier, with mystical exaltation, "does not happiness consist in the harmony of desires and enjoyments, in the balance of needs and satisfactions? Does it not consist in a certain condition of soul, the conditions of which it is not the function of political economy to prevent, and which it is not its mission to engender? This is the work of religion and philosophy."

Economist, Horace would say to M: Chevalier, if he were living at the present day, attend simply to my income, and leave me to take care of my soul: Det vitam, det opes; oequum mi animum ipse parabo.

M. Dunoyer again has the floor:

It would be easy, in many cities, on holidays, to confound the working class with the bourgeois class [why are there two classes?], so fine is the dress of the former. No less has been the progress in nourishment. Food is at once more abundant, more substantial, and more varied. Bread is better everywhere. Meat, soup, white bread, have become, in many factory towns, infinitely more common than they used to be. In short, the average duration of life has been raised from thirty-five years to forty.

Farther on M. Dunoyer gives a picture of English fortunes according to Marshall. It appears from this picture that in England two million five hundred thousand families have an income of only two hundred and forty dollars. Now, in England an income of two hundred and forty dollars corresponds to an income of one hundred and forty-six dollars in our country, which, divided between four persons, gives each thirty-six dollars and a half, or ten cents a day. That is not far from the thirteen cents which M. Chevalier allows to each individual in France: the difference in favor of the latter arises from the fact that, the progress of wealth being less advanced in France, poverty is likewise less. What must one think of the economists' luxuriant descriptions or of their figures?

"Pauperism has increased to such an extent in England," confesses M. Blanqui, "that the English government has had to seek a refuge in those frightful work-houses"....

As a matter of fact, those pretended work-houses, where the work consists in ridiculous and fruitless occupations, are, whatever may be said, simply torture-houses. For to a reasonable being there is no torture like that of turning a mill without grain and without flour, with the sole purpose of avoiding rest, without thereby escaping idleness.

"This organization [the organization of competition]," continues M. Blanqui, "tends to make all the profits of labor pass into the hands of capital.... It is at Reims, at Mulhouse, at Saint-Quentin, as at Manchester, at Leeds, at Spitalfields, that the existence of the workers is most precarious"....

Then follows a frightful picture of the misery of the work-ers. Men, women, children, young girls, pass before you, starved, blanched, ragged, wan, and wild. The description ends with this stroke:

The workers in the mechanical industries can no longer supply recruits for the army.

It would seem that these do not derive much benefit from M. Dunoyer's white bread and soup.

M. Villerme regards the licentiousness of young working girls as inevitable. Concubinage is their customary status; they are entirely subsidized by employers, clerks, and students. Although as a general thing marriage is more attractive to the people than to the bourgeoisie, there are many proletaires, Malthusians without knowing it, who fear the family and go with the current. Thus, as workingmen are flesh for cannon, workingwomen are flesh for prostitution: that explains the elegant dressing on Sunday. After all, why should these young women be expected to be more virtuous than their mistresses?

M. Buret, crowned by the Academy:

I affirm that the working class is abandoned body and soul to the good pleasure of industry.

The same writer says elsewhere:

The feeblest efforts of speculation may cause the price of bread to vary a cent a pound and more: which represents $124,100 for thirty-four million men.

I may remark, in passing, that the much-lamented Buret regarded the idea of the existence of monopolists as a popular prejudice. Well, sophist! monopolist or speculator, what matters the name, if you admit the thing?

Such quotations would fill volumes. But the object of this treatise is not to set forth the contradictions of the economists and to wage fruitless war upon persons. Our object is loftier and worthier: it is to unfold the

System of Economical Contradictions, which is quite a different matter. Therefore we will end this sad review here; and, before concluding, we will throw a glance at the various means proposed whereby to remedy the inconveniences of competition.

3. — Remedies against competition.

Can competition in labor be abolished?

It would be as well worth while to ask if personality, liberty, individual responsibility can be suppressed.

Competition, in fact, is the expression of collective activity; just as wages, considered in its highest acceptation, is the expression of the merit and demerit, in a word, the responsibility, of the laborer. It is vain to declaim and revolt against these two essential forms of liberty and discipline in labor. Without a theory of wages there is no distribution, no justice; without an organization of competition there is no social guarantee, consequently no solidarity.

The socialists have confounded two essentially distinct things when, contrasting the union of the domestic hearth with industrial competition, they have asked themselves if society could not be constituted precisely like a great family all of whose members would be bound by ties of blood, and not as a sort of coalition in which each is held back by the law of his own interests.

The family is not, if I may venture to so speak, the type, the organic molecule, of society. In the family, as M. de Bonald has very well observed, there exists but one moral being, one mind, one soul, I had almost said, with the Bible, one flesh. The family is the type and the cradle of monarchy and the patriciate: in it resides and is preserved the idea of authority and sovereignty, which is being obliterated more and more in the State. It was on the model of the family that all the ancient and feudal societies were organized, and it is precisely against this old patriarchal constitution that modern democracy protests and revolts.

The constitutive unit of society is the workshop.

Now, the workshop necessarily implies an interest as a body and private interests, a collective person and individuals. Hence a system of relations unknown in the family, among which the opposition of the collective will, represented by the employer, and individual wills,

202

represented by the wage-receivers, figures in the front rank. Then come the relations from shop to shop, from capital to capital, — in other words, competition and association. For competition and association are supported by each other; they do not exist independently; very far from excluding each other, they are not even divergent. Whoever says competition already supposes a common object; competition, then, is not egoism, and the most deplorable error of socialism consists in having regarded it as the subversion of society.

Therefore there can be no question here of destroying competition, as impossible as to destroy liberty; the problem is to find its equilibrium, I would willingly say its police. For every force, every form of spontaneity, whether individual or collective, must receive its determination: in this respect it is the same with competition as with intelligence and liberty. How, then, will competition be harmoniously determined in society?

We have heard the reply of M. Dunoyer, speaking for political economy: Competition must be determined by itself. In other words, according to M. Dunoyer and all the economists, the remedy for the inconveniences of competition is more competition; and, since political economy is the theory of property, of the absolute right of use and abuse, it is clear that political economy has no other answer to make. Now, this is as if it should be pretended that the education of liberty is effected by liberty, the instruction of the mind by the mind, the determination of value by value, all of which propositions are evidently tautological and absurd.

And, in fact, to confine ourselves to the subject under discussion, it is obvious that competition, practised for itself and with no other object than to maintain a vague and discordant independence, can end in nothing, and that its oscillations are eternal. In competition the struggling elements are capital, machinery, processes, talent, and experience, — that is, capital again; victory is assured to the heaviest battalions. If, then, competition is practised only to the advantage of private interests, and if its social effects have been neither determined by science nor reserved by the State, there will be in competition, as in democracy, a continual tendency from civil war to oligarchy, from oligarchy to despotism, and then dissolution and return to civil war, without end and without rest. That is why competition, abandoned to itself, can never arrive at its own constitution: like value, it needs a superior principle to socialize and define it. These facts are henceforth well enough established to warrant us in considering them above criticism, and to excuse us from returning to them. Political economy, so far as the police of competition is concerned, having no means but competition itself, and unable to have any other, is shown to be powerless.

It remains now to inquire what solution socialism contem-plates. A single example will give the measure of its means, and will permit us to come to general conclusions regarding it.

Of all modern socialists M. Louis Blanc, perhaps, by his remarkable talent, has been most successful in calling public attention to his writings. In his "Organization of Labor," after having traced back the problem of association to a single point, competition, he unhesitatingly pronounces in favor of its abolition. From this we may judge to what an extent this writer, generally so cautious, is deceived as to the value of political economy and the range of socialism. On the one hand, M. Blanc, receiving his ideas ready made from I know not what source, giving everything to his century and nothing to history, rejects absolutely, in substance and in form, political economy, and deprives himself of the very materials of organization; on the other, he attributes to tendencies revived from all past epochs, which he takes for new, a reality which they do not possess, and misconceives the nature of socialism, which is exclusively critical. M. Blanc, therefore, has given us the spectacle of a vivid imagination ready to confront an impossibility; he has believed in the divination of genius; but he must have perceived that science does not improvise itself, and that, be one's name Adolphe Boyer, Louis Blanc, or J. J. Rousseau, provided there is nothing in experience, there is nothing in the mind.

M. Blanc begins with this declaration:

We cannot understand those who have imagined I know not what mysterious coupling of two opposite principles. To graft association upon competition is a poor idea: it is to substitute hermaphrodites for eunuchs.

These three lines M. Blanc will always have reason to regret. They prove that, when he published the fourth edition of his book, he was as little advanced in logic as in political economy, and that he reasoned about both as a blind man would reason about colors. Hermaphrodism, in politics, consists precisely in exclusion, because exclusion always restores, in some form or other and in the same degree, the idea excluded; and M. Blanc would be greatly surprised were he to be shown, by his continual mixture in his book of the most contrary principles, — authority and right, property and communism, aristocracy

204

and equality, labor and capital, reward and sacrifice, liberty and dictatorship, free inquiry and religious faith, — that the real hermaphrodite, the double-sexed publicist, is himself. M. Blanc, placed on the borders of democracy and socialism, one degree lower than the Republic, two degrees beneath M. Barrot, three beneath M. Thiers, is also, whatever he may say and whatever he may do, a descendant through four generations from M. Guizot, a doctrinaire.

"Certainly," cries M. Blanc, "we are not of those who anathematize the principle of authority. This principle we have a thousand times had occasion to defend against attacks as dangerous as absurd. We know that, when organized force exists nowhere in a society, despotism exists everywhere."

Thus, according to M. Blanc, the remedy for competition, or rather, the means of abolishing it, consists in the intervention of authority, in the substitution of the State for individual liberty: it is the inverse of the system of the economists.

I should dislike to have M. Blanc, whose social tendencies are well known, accuse me of making impolitic war upon him in refuting him. I do justice to M. Blanc's generous intentions; I love and I read his works, and I am especially thankful to him for the service he has rendered in revealing, in his "History of Ten Years," the hopeless poverty of his party. But no one can consent to seem a dupe or an imbecile: now, putting personality entirely aside, what can there be in common between socialism, that universal protest, and the hotch-potch of old prejudices which make up M. Blanc's republic? M. Blanc is never tired of appealing to authority, and socialism loudly declares itself anarchistic; M. Blanc places power above society, and socialism tends to subordinate it to society; M. Blanc makes social life descend from above, and socialism maintains that it springs up and grows from below; M. Blanc runs after politics, and socialism is in quest of science. No more hypocrisy, let me say to M. Blanc: you desire neither Catholicism nor monarchy nor nobility, but you must have a God, a religion, a dictatorship, a censorship, a hierarchy, distinctions, and ranks. For my part, I deny your God, your authority, your sovereignty, your judicial State, and all your representative mystifications; I want neither Robespierre's censer nor Marat's rod; and, rather than submit to your androgynous democracy, I would support the status quo. For sixteen years your party has resisted progress and blocked opinion; for sixteen years it has shown its despotic origin by following in the wake of power at the extremity of the left centre: it is time for it to abdicate or undergo a metamorphosis. Implacable theorists of authority, what

205

then do you propose which the government upon which you make war cannot accomplish in a fashion more tolerable than yours?

M. Blanc's SYSTEM may be summarized in three points:

1. To give power a great force of initiative, — that is, in plain English, to make absolutism omnipotent in order to realize a utopia.

2. To establish public workshops, and supply them with capital, at the State's expense.

3. To extinguish private industry by the competition of national industry.

And that is all.

Has M. Blanc touched the problem of value, which involves in itself alone all others? He does not even suspect its existence. Has he given a theory of distribution? No. Has he solved the antinomy of the division of labor, perpetual cause of the workingman's ignorance, immorality, and poverty? No. Has he caused the contradiction of machinery and wages to disappear, and reconciled the rights of association with those of liberty? On the contrary, M. Blanc consecrates this contradiction. Under the despotic protection of the State, he admits in principle the inequality of ranks and wages, adding thereto, as compensation, the ballot. Are not workingmen who vote their regulations and elect their leaders free? It may very likely happen that these voting workingmen will admit no command or difference of pay among them: then, as nothing will have been provided for the satisfaction of industrial capacities, while maintaining political equality, dissolution will penetrate into the workshop, and, in the absence of police intervention, each will return to his own affairs. These fears seem to M. Blanc neither serious nor well-founded: he awaits the test calmly, very sure that society will not go out of his way to contradict him.

And such complex and intricate questions as those of taxation, credit, international trade, property, heredity, — has M. Blanc fathomed them? Has he solved the problem of population? No, no, no, a thousand times no: when M. Blanc cannot solve a difficulty, he eliminates it. Regarding population, he says:

As only poverty is prolific, and as the social workshop will cause poverty to disappear, there is no reason for giving it any thought.

In vain does M. de Sismondi, supported by universal ex-perience, cry out to him:

We have no confidence in those who exercise delegated powers. We believe that any corporation will do its business worse than those who are animated by individual interest; that on the part of the directors there will be negligence, display, waste, favoritism, fear of compromise, all the faults, in short, to be noticed in the administration of the public wealth as contrasted with private wealth. We believe, further, that in an assembly of stockholders will be found only carelessness, caprice, negligence, and that a mercantile enterprise would be constantly compromised and soon ruined, if it were dependent upon a deliberative commercial assembly.

M. Blanc hears nothing; he drowns all other sounds with his own sonorous phrases; private interest he replaces by devotion to the public welfare; for competition he substitutes emulation and rewards. After having posited industrial hierarchy as a principle, it being a necessary consequence of his faith in God, authority, and genius, he abandons himself to mystic powers, idols of his heart and his imagination.

Thus M. Blanc begins by a coup d'État, or rather, according to his original expression, by an application of the force of initiative which he gives to power; and he levies an extraordinary tax upon the rich in order to supply the proletariat with capital. M. Blanc's logic is very simple, — it is that of the Republic: power can accomplish what the people want, and what the people want is right. A singular fashion of reforming society, this of repressing its most spontaneous tendencies, denying its most authentic manifestations, and, instead of generalizing comfort by the regular development of traditions, displacing labor and income! But, in truth, what is the good of these disguises? Why so much beating about the bush? Was it not simpler to adopt the agrarian law straightway? Could not power, by virtue of its force of initiative, at once declare all capital and tools the property of the State, save an indemnity to be granted to the present holders as a transitional measure? By means of this peremptory, but frank and sincere, policy, the economic field would have been cleared away; it would not have cost utopia more, and M. Blanc could then have proceeded at his ease, and without any hindrance, to the organization of society.

But what do I say? organize! The whole organic work of M. Blanc consists in this great act of expropriation, or substitution, if you prefer: industry once displaced and republicanized and the great monopoly established, M. Blanc does not doubt that production will go on exactly as one would wish; he does not conceive it possible that any one can raise even a single difficulty in the way of what he calls his system. And, in fact, what objection can be offered to a conception so radically null, so intangible as that of M. Blanc? The most curious part of his book is in the select collection which he has made of objections proposed by certain incredulous persons, which he answers, as may be imagined, triumphantly. These critics had not seen that, in discussing M. Blanc's system, they were arguing about the dimensions, weight, and form of a mathematical point. Now, as it has happened, the controversy maintained by M. Blanc has taught him more than his own meditations had done; and one can see that, if the objections had continued, he would have ended by discovering what he thought he had invented, — the organization of labor.

But, in fine, has the aim, however narrow, which M. Blanc pursued, — namely, the abolition of competition and the guarantee of success to an enterprise patronized and backed by the State, — been attained? On this subject I will quote the reflections of a talented economist, M. Joseph Garnier, to whose words I will permit myself to add a few comments.

The government, according to M. Blanc, would choose moral workmen, and would give them good wages.

So M. Blanc must have men made expressly for him: he does not flatter himself that he can act on any sort of temperaments. As for wages, M. Blanc promises that they shall be good; that is easier than to define their measure.

M. Blanc admits by his hypothesis that these workshops would yield a net product, and, further, would compete so successfully with private industry that the latter would change into national workshops.

How could that be, if the cost of the national workshops is higher than that of the free workshops? I have shown in the third chapter that three hundred workmen in a mill do not produce for their employer, among them all, a regular net income of twenty thousand francs, and that these twenty thousand francs, distributed among the three hundred laborers, would add but eighteen centimes a day to their income. Now, this is true of all industries. How will the national workshop, which owes its workmen good wages, make up this deficit? By emulation, says M. Blanc.

M. Blanc points with extreme complacency to the Leclaire establishment, a society of house-painters doing a very successful business, which he regards as a living demonstration of his system. M. Blanc might have added to this example a multitude of similar societies, which would prove quite as much as the Leclaire establishment, — that is, no more. The Leclaire establishment is a collective monopoly, supported by the great society which envelops it. Now, the question is whether entire society can become a monopoly, in M. Blanc's sense and patterned after the Leclaire establishment: I deny it positively. But a fact touching more closely the question before us, and which M. Blanc has not taken into consideration, is that it follows from the distribution accounts furnished by the Leclaire establishment that, the wages paid being much above the general average, the first thing to do in a reorganization of society would be to start up competition with the Leclaire establishment, either among its own workmen or outside.

Wages would be regulated by the government. The members of the social workshop would dispose of them as they liked, and the indisputable excellence of life in common would not be long in causing association in labor to give birth to voluntary association in pleasure.

Is M. Blanc a communist, yes or no? Let him declare himself once for all, instead of holding off; and if communism does not make him more intelligible, we shall at least know what he wants.

In reading the supplement in which M. Blanc has seen fit to combat the objections which some journals have raised, we see more clearly the incompleteness of his conception, daughter of at least three fathers, — Saint-Simonism, Fourierism, and communism, — with the aid of politics and a little, a very little, political economy.

According to his explanations, the State would be only the regulator, legislator, protector of industry, not the universal manufacturer or producer. But as he exclusively protects the social workshops to destroy private industry, he necessarily brings up in monopoly and falls back into the Saint-Simonian theory in spite of himself, at least so far as production is concerned.

M. Blanc cannot deny it: his system is directed against private industry; and with him power, by its force of initiative, tends to extinguish all individual initiative, to proscribe free labor. The coupling of contraries is odious to M. Blanc: accordingly we see that, after having sacrificed competition to association, he sacrifices to it liberty also. I am waiting for him to abolish the family.

Nevertheless hierarchy would result from the elective principle, as in Fouricrism, as in constitutional politics. But these social workshops again, regulated by law, — will they be anything but corporations? What is the bond of corporations? The law. Who will make the law? The government. You suppose that it will be good? Well, experience has shown that it has never been a success in regulating the innumerable accidents of industry. You tell us that it will fix the rate of profits, the rate of wages; you hope that it will do it in such a way that laborers and capital will take refuge in the social workshop. But you do not tell us how equilibrium will be established between these workshops which will have a tendency to life in common, to the phalanstery; you do not tell us how these workshops will avoid competition within and without; how they will provide for the excess of population in relation to capital; how the manufacturing social workshops will differ from those of the fields; and many other things besides. I know well that you will answer: By the specific virtue of the law! And if your government, your State, knows not how to make it? Do you not see that you are sliding down a declivity, and that you are obliged to grasp at something similar to the existing law? It is easy to see by reading you that you are especially devoted to the invention of a power susceptible of application to your system; but I declare, after reading you carefully, that in my opinion you have as yet no clear and precise idea of what you need. What you lack, as well as all of us, is the true conception of liberty and equality, which you would not like to disown, and which you are obliged to sacrifice, whatever precautions you may take.

Unacquainted with the nature and functions of power, you have not dared to stop for a single explanation; you have not given the slightest example.

Suppose we admit that the workshops succeed as producers; there will also be commercial workshops to put products in circulation and effect exchanges. And who then will regulate the price? Again the law? In truth, I tell you, you will need a new appearance on Mount Sinai; otherwise you will never get out of your difficulties, you, your Council of State, your chamber of representatives, or your areopagus of senators.

The correctness of these reflections cannot be questioned. M. Blanc, with his organization by the State, is obliged always to end where he should have begun (so beginning, he would have been saved the trouble of writing his book), — that is, in the study of economic science. As his critic very well says: "M. Blanc has made the grave mistake of using political strategy in dealing with questions which are not amenable to such treatment"; he has tried to summon the government to a fulfillment of its obligations, and he has succeeded only in demonstrating more clearly than ever the incompatibility of socialism with haranguing and parliamentary democracy. His pamphlet, all enamelled with eloquent pages, does honor to his literary capacity: as for the philosophical value of the book, it would be absolutely the same if the author had confined himself to writing on each page, in large letters, this single phrase: I PROTEST.

To sum up:

Competition, as an economic position or phase, considered in its origin, is the necessary result of the intervention of machinery, of the establishment of the workshop, and of the theory of reduction of general costs; considered in its own significance and in its tendency, it is the mode by which collective activity manifests and exercises itself, the expression of social spontaneity, the emblem of democracy and equality, the most energetic instrument for the constitution of value, the support of association. As the essay of individual forces, it is the guarantee of their liberty, the first moment of their harmony, the form of responsibility which unites them all and makes them solidary.

But competition abandoned to itself and deprived of the direction of a superior and efficacious principle is only a vague movement, an endless oscillation of industrial power, eternally tossed about between those two equally disastrous extremes, — on the one hand, corporations and patronage, to which we have seen the workshop give birth, and, on the other, monopoly, which will be discussed in the following chapter.

Socialism, while protesting, and with reason, against this anarchical competition, has as yet proposed nothing satisfactory for its regulation, as is proved by the fact that we meet everywhere, in the utopias which have seen the light, the determination or socialization of value abandoned to arbitrary control, and all reforms ending, now in hierarchical corporation, now in State monopoly, or the tyranny of communism.

Chapter VI. Fourth Period. — Monopoly

MONOPOLY, the exclusive commerce, exploitation, or enjoyment of a thing.

Monopoly is the natural opposite of competition. This simple observation suffices, as we have remarked, to overthrow the utopias based upon the idea of abolishing competition, as if its contrary were association and fraternity. Competition is the vital force which animates the collective being: to destroy it, if such a supposition were possible, would be to kill society.

But, the moment we admit competition as a necessity, it implies the idea of monopoly, since monopoly is, as it were, the seat of each competing individuality. Accordingly the economists have demonstrated — and M. Rossi has formally admitted it — that monopoly is the form of social possession, outside of which there is no labor, no product, no exchange, no wealth. Every landed possession is a monopoly; every industrial utopia tends to establish itself as a monopoly; and the same must be said of other functions not included in these two categories.

Monopoly in itself, then, does not carry the idea of injustice; in fact, there is something in it which, pertaining to society as well as to man, legitimates it: that is the positive side of the principle which we are about to examine.

But monopoly, like competition, becomes anti-social and disastrous: how does this happen? By abuse, reply the economists. And it is to defining and repressing the abuses of monopoly that the magistrates apply themselves; it is in denouncing them that the new school of economists glories.

We shall show that the so-called abuses of monopoly are only the effects of the development, in a negative sense, of legal monopoly; that they cannot be separated from their principle without ruining this principle; consequently, that they are inaccessible to the law, and that all repression in this direction is arbitrary and unjust. So that monopoly, the constitutive principle of society and the condition of wealth, is at the same time and in the same degree a principle of spoliation and pauperism; that, the more good it is made to produce, the more evil is received from it; that without it progress comes to a standstill, and that with it labor becomes stationary and civilization disappears.

1. — Necessity of monopoly.

Thus monopoly is the inevitable end of competition, which engenders it by a continual denial of itself: this generation of monopoly is already its justification. For, since competition is inherent in society as motion is in living beings, monopoly which comes in its train, which is its object and its end, and without which competition would not have been accepted, — monopoly is and will remain legitimate as long as competition, as long as mechanical processes and industrial combinations, as long, in fact, as the division of labor and the constitution of values shall be necessities and laws.

Therefore by the single fact of its logical generation monopoly is justified. Nevertheless this justification would seem of little force and would end only in a more energetic rejection of competition than ever, if monopoly could not in turn posit itself by itself and as a principle.

In the preceding chapters we have seen that division of labor is the specification of the workman considered especially as intelligence; that the creation of machinery and the organization of the workshop express his liberty; and that, by competition, man, or intelligent liberty, enters into action. Now, monopoly is the expression of victorious liberty, the prize of the struggle, the glorification of genius; it is the strongest stimulant of all the steps in progress taken since the beginning of the world: so true is this that, as we said just now, society, which cannot exist with it, would not have been formed without it.

Where, then, does monopoly get this singular virtue, which the etymology of the word and the vulgar aspect of the thing would never lead us to suspect?

Monopoly is at bottom simply the autocracy of man over himself: it is the dictatorial right accorded by nature to every producer of using his faculties as he pleases, of giving free play to his thought in whatever direction it prefers, of speculating, in such specialty as he may please to choose, with all the power of his resources, of disposing sovereignly of the instruments which he has created and of the capital accumulated by his economy for any enterprise the risks of which he may see fit to accept on the express condition of enjoying alone the fruits of his discovery and the profits of his venture.

This right belongs so thoroughly to the essence of liberty that to deny it is to mutilate man in his body, in his soul, and in the exercise of his faculties, and society, which progresses only by the free initiative of individuals, soon lacking explorers, finds itself arrested in its onward march.

It is time to give body to all these ideas by the testimony of facts.

I know a commune where from time immemorial there had been no roads either for the clearing of lands or for communication with the outside world. During three-fourths of the year all importation or exportation of goods was prevented; a barrier of mud and marsh served as a protection at once against any invasion from without and any excursion of the inhabitants of the holy and sacred community. Six horses, in the finest weather, scarcely sufficed to move a load that any jade could easily have taken over a good road. The mayor resolved, in spite of the council, to build a road through the town. For a long time he was derided, cursed, execrated. They had got along well enough without a road up to the time of his administration: why need he spend the money of the commune and waste the time of farmers in road-duty, cartage, and compulsory service? It was to satisfy his pride that Monsieur the Mayor desired, at the expense of the poor farmers, to open such a fine avenue for his city friends who would come to visit him! In spite of everything the road was made and the peasants applauded! What a difference! they said: it used to take eight horses to carry thirty sacks to market, and we were gone three days; now we start in the morning with two horses, and are back at night. But in all these remarks nothing further was heard of the mayor. The event having justified him, they spoke of him no more: most of them, in fact, as I found out, felt a spite against him.

This mayor acted after the manner of Aristides. Suppose that, wearied by the absurd clamor, he had from the beginning proposed to his constituents to build the road at his expense, provided they would pay him toll for fifty years, each, however, remaining free to travel through the fields, as in the past: in what respect would this transaction have been fraudulent?

That is the history of society and monopolists.

Everybody is not in a position to make a present to his fellow-citizens of a road or a machine: generally the inventor, after exhausting his health and substance, expects reward. Deny then, while still scoffing at them, to Arkwright, Watt, and Jacquard the privilege of their discoveries; they will shut themselves up in order to work, and possibly

214

will carry their secret to the grave. Deny to the settler possession of the soil which he clears, and no one will clear it.

But, they say, is that true right, social right, fraternal right? That which is excusable on emerging from primitive communism, an effect of necessity, is only a temporary expedient which must disappear in face of a fuller understanding of the rights and duties of man and society.

I recoil from no hypothesis: let us see, let us investigate. It is already a great point that the opponents confess that, during the first period of civilization, things could not have gone otherwise. It remains to ascertain whether the institutions of this period are really, as has been said, only temporary, or whether they are the result of laws immanent in society and eternal. Now, the thesis which I maintain at this moment is the more difficult because in direct opposition to the general tendency, and because I must directly overturn it myself by its contradiction.

I pray, then, that I may be told how it is possible to make appeal to the principles of sociability, fraternity, and solidarity, when society itself rejects every solidary and fraternal transaction? At the beginning of each industry, at the first gleam of a discovery, the man who invents is isolated; society abandons him and remains in the background. To put it better, this man, relatively to the idea which he has conceived and the realization of which he pursues, becomes in himself alone entire society. He has no longer any associates, no longer any collaborators, no longer any sureties; everybody shuns him: on him alone falls the responsibility; to him alone, then, the advantages of the speculation.

But, it is insisted, this is blindness on the part of society, an abandonment of its most sacred rights and interests, of the welfare of future generations; and the speculator, better informed or more fortunate, cannot fairly profit by the monopoly which universal ignorance gives into his hands.

I maintain that this conduct on the part of society is, as far as the present is concerned, an act of high prudence; and, as for the future, I shall prove that it does not lose thereby. I have already shown in the second chapter, by the solution of the antinomy of value, that the advantage of every useful discovery is incomparably less to the inventor, whatever he may do, than to society; I have carried the demonstration of this point even to mathematical accuracy. Later I shall show further that, in addition to the profit assured it by every discovery, society exercises over the privileges which it concedes, whether

215

temporarily or perpetually, claims of several kinds, which largely palliate the excess of certain private fortunes, and the effect of which is a prompt restoration of equilibrium. But let us not anticipate.

I observe, then, that social life manifests itself in a double fashion, — preservation and development.

Development is effected by the free play of individual energies; the mass is by its nature barren, passive, and hostile to everything new. It is, if I may venture to use the comparison, the womb, sterile by itself, but to which come to deposit themselves the germs created by private activity, which, in hermaphroditic society, really performs the function of the male organ.

But society preserves itself only so far as it avoids solidarity with private speculations and leaves every innovation absolutely to the risk and peril of individuals. It would take but a few pages to contain the list of useful inventions. The enterprises that have been carried to a successful issue may be numbered; no figure would express the multitude of false ideas and imprudent ventures which every day are hatched in human brains. There is not an inventor, not a workman, who, for one sane and correct conception, has not given birth to thousands of chimeras; not an intelligence which, for one spark of reason, does not emit whirlwinds of smoke. If it were possible to divide all the products of the human reason into two parts, putting on one side those that are useful, and on the other those on which strength, thought, capital, and time have been spent in error, we should be startled by the discovery that the excess of the latter over the former is perhaps a billion per cent. What would become of society, if it had to discharge these liabilities and settle all these bankruptcies? What, in turn, would become of the responsibility and dignity of the laborer, if, secured by the social guarantee, he could, without personal risk, abandon himself to all the caprices of a delirious imagination and trifle at every moment with the existence of humanity?

Wherefore I conclude that what has been practised from the beginning will be practised to the end, and that, on this point, as on every other, if our aim is reconciliation, it is absurd to think that anything that exists can be abolished. For, the world of ideas being infinite, like nature, and men, today as ever, being subject to speculation, — that is, to error, — individuals have a constant stimulus to speculate and society a constant reason to be suspicious and cautious, wherefore monopoly never lacks material.

To avoid this dilemma what is proposed? Compensation? In the first place, compensation is impossible: all values being monopolized, where would society get the means to indemnify the monopolists? What would be its mortgage? On the other hand, compensation would be utterly useless: after all the monopolies had been compensated, it would remain to organize industry. Where is the system? Upon what is opinion settled? What problems have been solved? If the organization is to be of the hierarchical type, we reenter the system of monopoly; if of the democratic, we return to the point of departure, for the compensated industries will fall into the public domain, — that is, into competition, — and gradually will become monopolies again; if, finally, of the communistic, we shall simply have passed from one impossibility to another, for, as we shall demonstrate at the proper time, communism, like competition and monopoly, is antinomical, impossible.

In order not to involve the social wealth in an unlimited and consequently disastrous solidarity, will they content themselves with imposing rules upon the spirit of invention and enterprise? Will they establish a censorship to distinguish between men of genius and fools? That is to suppose that society knows in advance precisely that which is to be discovered. To submit the projects of schemers to an advance examination is an a priori prohibition of all movement. For, once more, relatively to the end which he has in view, there is a moment when each manufacturer represents in his own person society itself, sees better and farther than all other men combined, and frequently without being able to explain himself or make himself understood. When Copernicus, Kepler, and Galileo, Newton's predecessors, came to the point of saying to Christian society, then represented by the Church: "The Bible is mistaken; the earth revolves, and the sun is stationary," they were right against society, which, on the strength of its senses and traditions, contradicted them. Could society then have accepted solidarity with the Copernican system? So little could it do it that this system openly denied its faith, and that, pending the accord of reason and revelation, Galileo, one of the responsible inventors, underwent torture in proof of the new idea. We are more tolerant, I presume; but this very toleration proves that, while according greater liberty to genius, we do not mean to be less discreet than our ancestors. Patents rain, but without governmental guarantee. Property titles are placed in the keeping of citizens, but neither the property list nor the charter guarantee their value: it is for labor to make them valuable. And as for the scientific and other missions which the government sometimes takes a notion to entrust to penniless explorers, they are so much extra robbery and corruption.

In fact, society can guarantee to no one the capital necessary for the testing of an idea by experiment; in right, it cannot claim the results of an enterprise to which it has not subscribed: therefore monopoly is indestructible. For the rest, solidarity would be of no service: for, as each can claim for his whims the solidarity of all and would have the same right to obtain the government's signature in blank, we should soon arrive at the universal reign of caprice, — that is, purely and simply at the statu quo.

Some socialists, very unhappily inspired — I say it with all the force of my conscience — by evangelical abstractions, believe that they have solved the difficulty by these fine maxims: "Inequality of capacities proves the inequality of duties"; "You have received more from nature, give more to your brothers," and other high-sounding and touching phrases, which never fail of their effect on empty heads, but which nevertheless are as simple as anything that it is possible to imagine. The practical formula deduced from these marvellous adages is that each laborer owes all his time to society, and that society should give back to him in exchange all that is necessary to the satisfaction of his wants in proportion to the resources at its disposal.

May my communistic friends forgive me! I should be less severe upon their ideas if I were not irreversibly convinced, in my reason and in my heart, that communism, republicanism, and all the social, political, and religious utopias which disdain facts and criticism, are the greatest obstacle which progress has now to conquer. Why will they never understand that fraternity can be established only by justice; that justice alone, the condition, means, and law of liberty and fraternity, must be the object of our study; and that its determination and formula must be pursued without relaxation, even to the minutest details? Why do writers familiar with economic language forget that superiority of talents is synonymous with superiority of wants, and that, instead of expecting more from vigorous than from ordinary personalities, society should constantly look out that they do not receive more than they render, when it is already so hard for the mass of mankind to render all that it receives? Turn which way you will, you must always come back to the cash book, to the account of receipts and expenditures, the sole guarantee against large consumers as well as against small producers. The workman continually lives in advance of his production; his tendency is always to get credit contract debts and go into bankruptcy; it is perpetually necessary to remind him of Say's aphorism: Products are bought only with products.

To suppose that the laborer of great capacity will content himself, in favor of the weak, with half his wages, furnish his services gratuitously, and produce, as the people say, for the king of Prussia — that is, for that abstraction called society, the sovereign, or my brothers, — is to base society on a sentiment, I do not say beyond the reach of man, but one which, erected systematically into a principle, is only a false virtue, a dangerous hypocrisy. Charity is recommended to us as a reparation of the infirmities which afflict our fellows by accident, and, viewing it in this light, I can see that charity may be organized; I can see that, growing out of solidarity itself, it may become simply justice. But charity taken as an instrument of equality and the law of equilibrium would be the dissolution of society. Equality among men is produced by the rigorous and inflexible law of labor, the proportionality of values, the sincerity of exchanges, and the equivalence of functions, — in short, by the mathematical solution of all antagonisms.

That is why charity, the prime virtue of the Christian, the legitimate hope of the socialist, the object of all the efforts of the economist, is a social vice the moment it is made a principle of constitution and a law; that is why certain economists have been able to say that legal charity had caused more evil in society than proprietary usurpation. Man, like the society of which he is a part, has a perpetual account current with himself; all that he consumes he must produce. Such is the general rule, which no one can escape without being, ipso facto struck with dishonor or suspected of fraud. Singular idea, truly, — that of decreeing, under pretext of fraternity, the relative inferiority of the majority of men! After this beautiful declaration nothing will be left but to draw its consequences; and soon, thanks to fraternity, aristocracy will be restored.

Double the normal wages of the workman, and you invite him to idleness, humiliate his dignity, and demoralize his conscience; take away from him the legitimate price of his efforts, and you either excite his anger or exalt his pride. In either case you damage his fraternal feelings. On the contrary, make enjoyment conditional upon labor, the only way provided by nature to associate men and make them good and happy, and you go back under the law of economic distribution, products are bought with products. Communism, as I have often complained, is the very denial of society in its foundation, which is the progressive equivalence of functions and capacities. The communists, toward whom all socialism tends, do not believe in equality by nature and education; they supply it by sovereign decrees which they cannot carry out, whatever they may do. Instead of seeking justice in the harmony of facts, they take it from their feelings, calling justice everything that seems to them to be love of one's neighbor, and incessantly confounding matters of reason with those of sentiment.

Why then continually interject fraternity, charity, sacrifice, and God into the discussion of economic questions? May it not be that the utopists find it easier to expatiate upon these grand words than to seriously study social manifestations?

Fraternity! Brothers as much as you please, provided I am the big brother and you the little; provided society, our common mother, honors my primogeniture and my services by doubling my portion. You will provide for my wants, you say, in proportion to your resources. I intend, on the contrary, that such provision shall be in proportion to my labor; if not, I cease to labor.

Charity! I deny charity; it is mysticism. In vain do you talk to me of fraternity and love: I remain convinced that you love me but little, and I feel very sure that I do not love you. Your friendship is but a feint, and, if you love me, it is from self-interest. I ask all that my products cost me, and only what they cost me: why do you refuse me?

Sacrifice! I deny sacrifice; it is mysticism. Talk to me of debt and credit, the only criterion in my eyes of the just and the unjust, of good and evil in society. To each according to his works, first; and if, on occasion, I am impelled to aid you, I will do it with a good grace; but I will not be constrained. To constrain me to sacrifice is to assassinate me.

God! I know no God; mysticism again. Begin by striking this word from your remarks, if you wish me to listen to you; for three thousand years of experience have taught me that whoever talks to me of God has designs on my liberty or on my purse. How much do you owe me? How much do I owe you? That is my religion and my God.

Monopoly owes its existence both to nature and to man: it has its source at once in the profoundest depths of our conscience and in the external fact of our individualization. Just as in our body and our mind everything has its specialty and property, so our labor presents itself with a proper and specific character, which constitutes its quality and value. And as labor cannot manifest itself without material or an object for its exercise, the person necessarily attracting the thing, monopoly is established from subject to object as infallibly as duration is constituted from past to future. Bees, ants, and other animals living in society seem endowed individually only with automatism; with them soul and instinct are almost exclusively collective. That is why, among such animals, there can be no room for privilege and monopoly; why, even in their most volitional operations, they neither consult nor deliberate. But, humanity being individualized in its plurality, man becomes inevitably a monopolist, since, if not a monopolist, he is nothing; and the social problem is to find out, not how to abolish, but how to reconcile, all monopolies.

The most remarkable and the most immediate effects of monopoly are:

1. In the political order, the classification of humanity into families, tribes, cities, nations, States: this is the elementary division of humanity into groups and sub-groups of laborers, distinguished by race, language, customs, and climate. It was by monopoly that the human race took possession of the globe, as it will be by association that it will become complete sovereign thereof.

Political and civil law, as conceived by all legislators with-out exception and as formulated by jurists, born of this patriotic and national organization of societies, forms, in the series of social contradictions, a first and vast branch, the study of which by itself alone would demand four times more time than we can give it in discussing the question of industrial economy propounded by the Academy.

2. In the economic order, monopoly contributes to the increase of comfort, in the first place by adding to the general wealth through the perfecting of methods, and then by CAPITALIZING, — that is, by consolidating the conquests of labor obtained by division, machinery, and competition. From this effect of monopoly has resulted the economic fiction by which the capitalist is considered a producer and capital an agent of production; then, as a consequence of this fiction, the theory of net product and gross product.

On this point we have a few considerations to present. First let us quote J. B. Say:

The value produced is the gross product: after the costs of production have been deducted, this value is the net product.

Considering a nation as a whole, it has no net product; for, as products have no value beyond the costs of production, when these costs are cut off, the entire value of the product is cut off. National production, annual production, should always therefore be understood as gross production.

The annual revenue is the gross revenue.

The term net production is applicable only when considering the interests of one producer in opposition to those of other producers. The manager of an enterprise gets his profit from the value produced after deducting the value consumed. But what to him is value consumed, such as the purchase of a productive service, is so much income to the performer of the service. — Treatise on Political Economy: Analytical Table.

These definitions are irreproachable. Unhappily J. B. Say did not see their full bearing, and could not have foreseen that one day his immediate successor at the College of France would attack them. M. Rossi has pretended to refute the proposition of J. B. Say that to a nation net product is the same thing as gross product by this consideration, — that nations, no more than individuals of enterprise, can produce without advances, and that, if J. B. Say's formula were true, it would follow that the axiom, Ex nihilo nihil fit, is not true

Now, that is precisely what happens. Humanity, in imitation of God, produces everything from nothing, de nihilo hilum just as it is itself a product of nothing, just as its thought comes out of the void; and M. Rossi would not have made such a mistake, if, like the physiocrats, he had not confounded the products of the industrial kingdom with those of the animal, vegetable, and mineral kingdoms. Political economy begins with labor; it is developed by labor; and all that does not come from labor, falling into the domain of pure utility, — that is, into the category of things submitted to man's action, but not yet rendered exchangeable by labor, — remains radically foreign to political economy. Monopoly itself, wholly established as it is by a pure act of collective will, does not change these relations at all, since, according to history, and according to the written law, and according to economic theory, monopoly exists, or is reputed to exist, only after labor's appearance.

Say's doctrine, therefore, is unassailable. Relatively to the man of enterprise, whose specialty always supposes other manufacturers cooperating with him, profit is what remains of the value produced after deducting the values consumed, among which must be included the salary of the man of enterprise, — in other words, his wages.

222

Relatively to society, which contains all possible specialties, net product is identical with gross product.

But there is a point the explanation of which I have vainly sought in Say and in the other economists, — to wit, how the reality and legitimacy of net product is established. For it is plain that, in order to cause the disappearance of net product, it would suffice to increase the wages of the workmen and the price of the values consumed, the selling-price remaining the same. So that, there being nothing seemingly to distinguish net product from a sum withheld in paying wages or, what amounts to the same thing, from an assessment laid upon the consumer in advance, net product has every appearance of an extortion effected by force and without the least show of right.

This difficulty has been solved in advance in our theory of the proportionality of values.

According to this theory, every exploiter of a machine, of an idea, or of capital should be considered as a man who increases with equal outlay the amount of a certain kind of products, and consequently increases the social wealth by economizing time. The principle of the legitimacy of the net product lies, then, in the processes previously in use: if the new device succeeds, there will be a surplus of values, and consequently a profit, -that is, net product; if the enterprise rests on a false basis, there will be a deficit in the gross product, and in the long run failure and bankruptcy. Even in the case — and it is the most frequent — where there is no innovation on the part of the man of enterprise, the rule of net product remains applicable, for the success of an industry depends upon the way in which it is carried on. Now, it being in accordance with the nature of monopoly that the risk and peril of every enterprise should be taken by the initiator, it follows that the net product belongs to him by the most sacred title recognized among men, — labor and intelligence.

It is useless to recall the fact that the net product is often exaggerated, either by fraudulently secured reductions of wages or in some other way. These are abuses which proceed, not from the principle, but from human cupidity, and which remain outside the domain of the theory. For the rest, I have shown, in discussing the constitution of value (Chapter II, section 2): 1, how the net product can never exceed the difference resulting from inequality of the means of production; 2, how the profit which society reaps from each new invention is incomparably greater than that of its originator. As these points have been exhausted once for all, I will not go over them again; I will simply remark that, by industrial progress, the net product of the ingenious tends steadily to decrease, while, on the other hand, their comfort increases, as the concentric layers which make up the trunk of a tree become thinner as the tree grows and as they are farther removed from the centre.

By the side of net product, the natural reward of the laborer, I have pointed out as one of the happiest effects of monopoly the capitalization of values, from which is born another sort of profit, — namely, interest, or the hire of capital. As for rent, although it is often confounded with interest, and although, in ordinary language, it is included with profit and interest under the common expression REVENUE, it is a different thing from interest; it is a consequence, not of monopoly, but of property; it depends on a special theory., of which we will speak in its place.

What, then, is this reality, known to all peoples, and never-theless still so badly defined, which is called interest or the price of a loan, and which gives rise to the fiction of the productivity of capital?

Everybody knows that a contractor, when he calculates his costs of production, generally divides them into three classes: 1, the values consumed and services paid for; 2, his personal salary; 3, recovery of his capital with interest. From this last class of costs is born the distinction between contractor and capitalist, although these two titles always express but one faculty, monopoly.

Thus an industrial enterprise which yields only interest on capital and nothing for net product, is an insignificant enterprise, which results only in a transformation of values without adding anything to wealth, — an enterprise, in short, which has no further reason for existence and is immediately abandoned. Why is it, then, that this interest on capital is not regarded as a sufficient supplement of net product? Why is it not itself the net product?

Here again the philosophy of the economists is wanting. To defend usury they have pretended that capital was productive, and they have changed a metaphor into a reality. The anti-proprietary socialists have had no difficulty in overturning their sophistry; and through this controversy the theory of capital has fallen into such disfavor that today, in the minds of the people, capitalist and idler are synonymous terms. Certainly it is not my intention to retract what I myself have maintained after so many others, or to rehabilitate a class of citizens which so strangely misconceives its duties: but the interests of science and of the proletariat itself oblige me to complete my first assertions and maintain true principles.

1. All production is effected with a view to consumption, — that is, to enjoyment. In society the correlative terms production and consumption, like net product and gross product, designate identically the same thing. If, then, after the laborer has realized a net product, instead of using it to increase his comfort, he should confine himself to his wages and steadily apply his surplus to new production, as so many people do who earn only to buy, production would increase indefinitely, while comfort and, reasoning from the standpoint of society, population would remain unchanged. Now, interest on capital which has been invested in an industrial enterprise and which has been gradually formed by the accumulation of net product, is a sort of compromise between the necessity of increasing production, on the one hand, and, on the other, that of increasing comfort; it is a method of reproducing and consuming the net product at the same time. That is why certain industrial societies pay their stockholders a dividend even before the enterprise has yielded anything. Life is short, success comes slowly; on the one hand labor commands, on the other man wishes to enjoy. To meet all these exigencies the net product shall be devoted to production, but meantime (inter-ea, inter-esse) — that is, while waiting for the new product — the capitalist shall enjoy.

Thus, as the amount of net product marks the progress of wealth, interest on capital, without which net product would be useless and would not even exist, marks the progress of comfort. Whatever the form of government which may be established among men; whether they live in monopoly or in communism; whether each laborer keeps his account by credit and debit, or has his labor and pleasure parcelled out to him by the community, — the law which we have just disengaged will always be fulfilled. Our interest accounts do nothing else than bear witness to it.

2. Values created by net product are classed as savings and capitalized in the most highly exchangeable form, the form which is freest and least susceptible of depreciation, — in a word, the form of specie, the only constituted value. Now, if capital leaves this state of freedom and engages itself, — that is, takes the form of machines, buildings, etc., — it will still be susceptible of exchange, but much more exposed than before to the oscillations of supply and demand. Once engaged, it cannot be disenaged without difficulty; and the sole resource of its owner will be exploitation. Exploitation alone is capable of maintaining engaged capital at its nominal value; it may increase it, it may diminish

it. Capital thus transformed is as if it had been risked in a maritime enterprise: the interest is the insurance premium paid on the capital. And this premium will be greater or less according to the scarcity or abundance of capital.

Later a distinction will also be established between the insurance premium and interest on capital, and new facts will result from this subdivision: thus the history of humanity is simply a perpetual distinction of the mind's concepts.

3. Not only does interest on capital cause the laborer to enjoy the fruit of his toil and insure his savings, but — and this is the most marvellous effect of interest — while rewarding the producer, it obliges him to labor incessantly and never stop.

If a contractor is his own capitalist, it may happen that he will content himself with a profit equal to the interest on his investment: but in that case it is certain that his industry is no longer making progress and consequently is suffering. This we see when the capitalist is distinct from the contractor: for then, after the interest is paid, the manufacturer's profit is absolutely nothing; his industry becomes a perpetual peril to him, from which it is important that he should free himself as soon as possible. For as society's comfort must develop in an indefinite progression, so the law of the producer is that he should continually realize a surplus: otherwise his existence is precarious, monotonous, fatiguing. The interest due to the capitalist by the producer therefore is like the lash of the planter cracking over the head of the sleeping slave; it is the voice of progress crying: "On, on! Toil, toil!" Man's destiny pushes him to happiness: that is why it denies him rest.

4. Finally, interest on money is the condition of capital's circulation and the chief agent of industrial solidarity. This aspect has been seized by all the economists, and we shall give it special treatment when we come to deal with credit.

I have proved, and better, I imagine, than it has ever been proved before:

That monopoly is necessary, since it is the antagonism of competition;

That it is essential to society, since without it society would never have emerged from the primeval forests and without it would rapidly go backwards;

Finally, that it is the crown of the producer, when, whether by net product or by interest on the capital which he devotes to production, it brings to the monopolist that increase of comfort which his foresight and his efforts deserve.

Shall we, then, with the economists, glorify monopoly, and consecrate it to the benefit of well-secured conservatives? I am willing, provided they in turn will admit my claims in what is to follow, as I have admitted theirs in what has preceded.

2. — The disasters in labor and the perversion of ideas caused by monopoly.

Like competition, monopoly implies a contradiction in its name and its definition. In fact, since consumption and production are identical things in society, and since selling is synonymous with buying, whoever says privilege of sale or exploitation necessarily says privilege of consumption and purchase: which ends in the denial of both. Hence a prohibition of consumption as well as of production laid by monopoly upon the wage-receivers. Competition was civil war, monopoly is the massacre of the prisoners.

These various propositions are supported by all sorts of evidence, — physical, algebraic, and metaphysical. What I shall add will be only the amplified exposition: their simple announcement demonstrates them.

Every society considered in its economic relations naturally divides itself into capitalists and laborers, employers and wage-receivers, distributed upon a scale whose degrees mark the income of each, whether this income be composed of wages, profit, interest, rent, or dividends.

From this hierarchical distribution of persons and incomes it follows that Say's principle just referred to: In a nation the net product is equal to the gross product, is no longer true, since, in consequence of monopoly, the selling price is much higher than the cost price. Now, as it is the cost price nevertheless which must pay the selling price, since a nation really has no market but itself, it follows that exchange, and consequently circulation and life, are impossible.

227

In France, twenty millions of laborers, engaged in all the branches of science, art, and industry, produce everything which is useful to man. Their aggregate annual wages amount, it is estimated, to twenty thousand millions; but, in consequence of the profit (net product and interest) accruing to monopolists, twenty-five thousand millions must be paid for their products. Now, as the nation has no other buyers than its wage-receivers and wage-payers, and as the latter do not pay for the former, and as the selling-price of merchandise is the same for all, it is clear that, to make circulation possible, the laborer would have to pay five for that for which he has received but four. — What is Property: Chapter IV. [17]

This, then, is the reason why wealth and poverty are correlative, inseparable, not only in idea, but in fact; this is the reason why they exist concurrently; this is what justifies the pretension of the wage-receiver that the rich man possesses no more than the poor man, except that of which the latter has been defrauded. After the monopolist has drawn up his account of cost, profit, and interest, the wage-paid consumer draws up his; and he finds that, though promised wages stated in the contract as one hundred, he has really been given but seventy-five. Monopoly, therefore, puts the wage-receivers into bankruptcy, and it is strictly true that it lives upon the spoils.

Six years ago I brought out this frightful contradiction: why has it not been thundered through the press? Why have no teachers of renown warned public opinion? Why have not those who demand political rights for the workingman proclaimed that he is robbed? Why have the economists kept silent? Why?

Our revolutionary democracy is so noisy only because it fears revolutions: but, by ignoring the danger which it dares not look in the face, it succeeds only in increasing it. "We resemble," says M. Blanqui, "firemen who increase the quantity of steam at the same time that they place weights on the safety-valve." Victims of monopoly, console yourselves! If your tormentors will not listen, it is because Providence has resolved to strike them: Non audierunt, says the Bible, quia Deus volebat occidere eos.

Sale being unable to fulfil the conditions of monopoly, merchandise accumulates; labor has produced in a year what its wages will not allow it to consume in less than fifteen months: hence it must remain idle one-fourth of the year. But, if it remains idle, it earns nothing: how will it ever buy? And if the monopolist cannot get rid of his products, how will his enterprise endure? Logical impossibility multiplies around the workshop; the facts which translate it are everywhere.

"The hosiers of England," says Eugene Buret, "had come to the point where they did not eat oftener than every other day. This state of things lasted eighteen months." And he cites a multitude of similar cases.

But the distressing feature in the spectacle of monopoly's effects is the sight of the unfortunate workingmen blaming each other for their misery and imagining that by uniting and supporting each other they will prevent the reduction of wages.

"The Irish," says an observer, "have given a disastrous lesson to the working classes of Great Britain..... They have taught our laborers the fatal secret of confining their needs to the maintenance of animal life alone, and of contenting themselves, like savages, with the minimum of the means of subsistence sufficient to prolong life..... Instructed by this fatal example, yielding partly to necessity, the working classes have lost that laudable pride which led them to furnish their houses properly and to multiply about them the decent conveniences which contribute to happiness."

I have never read anything more afflicting and more stupid. And what would you have these workingmen do? The Irish came: should they have been massacred? Wages were reduced: should death have been accepted in their stead? Necessity commanded, as you say yourselves. Then followed the interminable hours, disease, deformity, degradation, debasement, and all the signs of industrial slavery: all these calamities are born of monopoly and its sad predecessors, — competition, machinery, and the division of labor: and you blame the Irish!

At other times the workingmen blame their luck, and exhort themselves to patience: this is the counterpart of the thanks which they address to Providence, when labor is abundant and wages are sufficient.

I find in an article published by M. Leon Faucher, in the "Journal des Economistes" (September, 1845), that the English workingmen lost some time ago the habit of combining, which is surely a progressive step on which they are only to be congratulated, but that this improvement in the morale of the workingmen is due especially to their economic instruction.

"It is not upon the manufacturers," cried a spinner at the meeting in Bolton, "that wages depend. In periods of depression the employers, so to speak, are only the lash with which necessity is armed; and whether they will or no, they have to strike. The regulative principle is the relation of supply to demand; and the employers have not this power.... Let us act prudently, then; let us learn to be resigned to bad luck and to make the most of good luck: by seconding the progress of our industry, we shall be useful not only to ourselves, but to the entire country." [Applause.]

Very good: well-trained, model workmen, these! What men these spinners must be that they should submit without complaint to the lash of necessity, because the regulative principle of wages is supply and demand! M. Leon Faucher adds with a charming simplicity:

English workingmen are fearless reasoners. Give them a false principle, and they will push it mathematically to absurdity, without stopping or getting frightened, as if they were marching to the triumph of the truth.

For my part, I hope that, in spite of all the efforts of economic propagandism, French workingmen will never become reasoners of such power. Supply and demand, as well as the lash of necessity, has no longer any hold upon their minds. This was the one misery that England lacked: it will not cross the channel.

By the combined effect of division, machinery, net product, and interest, monopoly extends its conquests in an increasing progression; its developments embrace agriculture as well as commerce and industry, and all sorts of products. Everybody knows the phrase of Pliny upon the landed monopoly which determined the fall of Italy, latifundia perdidere Italiam. It is this same monopoly which still impoverishes and renders uninhabitable the Roman Campagna and which forms the vicious circle in which England moves convulsively; it is this monopoly which, established by violence after a war of races, produces all the evils of Ireland, and causes so many trials to O'Connell, powerless, with all his eloquence, to lead his repealers through this labyrinth. Grand sentiments and rhetoric are the worst remedy for social evils: it would be easier for O'Connell to transport Ireland and the Irish from the North Sea to the Australian Ocean than to overthrow with the breath of his harangues the monopoly which holds them in its grasp. General communions and sermons will do no more: if the religious sentiment still alone maintains the morale of the Irish people, it is high time that a little of that profane science, so much

230

disdained by the Church, should come to the aid of the lambs which its crook no longer protects.

The invasion of commerce and industry by monopoly is too well known to make it necessary that I should gather proofs: moreover, of what use is it to argue so much when results speak so loudly? E. Buret's description of the misery of the working-classes has something fantastic about it, which oppresses and frightens you. There are scenes in which the imagination refuses to believe, in spite of certificates and official reports. Couples all naked, hidden in the back of an unfurnished alcove, with their naked children; entire populations which no longer go to church on Sunday, because they are naked; bodies kept a week before they are buried, because the deceased has left neither a shroud in which to lay him out nor the wherewithal to pay for the coffin and the undertaker (and the bishop enjoys an income of from four to five hundred thousand francs); families heaped up over sewers, living in rooms occupied by pigs, and beginning to rot while yet alive, or dwelling in holes, like Albinoes; octogenarians sleeping naked on bare boards; and the virgin and the prostitute expiring in the same nudity: everywhere despair, consumption, hunger, hunger!.. And this people, which expiates the crimes of its masters, does not rebel! No, by the flames of Nemesis! when a people has no vengeance left, there is no longer any Providence for it.

Exterminations en masse by monopoly have not yet found their poets. Our rhymers, strangers to the things of this world, without bowels for the proletaire, continue to breathe to the moon their melancholy delights. What a subject for meditations, nevertheless, is the miseries engendered by monopoly!

It is Walter Scott who says:

Formerly, though many years since, each villager had his cow and his pig, and his yard around his house. Where a single farmer cultivates today, thirty small farmers lived formerly; so that for one individual, himself alone richer, it is true, than the thirty farmers of old times, there are now twenty-nine wretched day-laborers, without employment for their minds and arms, and whose number is too large by half. The only useful function which they fulfil is to pay, when they can, a rent of sixty shillings a year for the huts in which they dwell. [18]

A modern ballad, quoted by E. Buret, sings the solitude of monopoly:

231

Le rouet est silencieux dans la vallee:
C'en est fait des sentiments de famille.
Sur un peu de fumee le vieil aieul
Etend ses mains pales; et le foyer vide
Est aussi desole que son coeur. [19]

The reports made to parliament rival the novelist and the poet:

The inhabitants of Glensheil, in the neighborhood of the valley of Dundee, were formerly distinguished from all their neighbors by the superiority of their physical qualities. The men were of high stature, robust, active, and courageous; the women comely and graceful. Both sexes possessed an extraordinary taste for poetry and music. Now, alas! a long experience of poverty, prolonged privation of sufficient food and suitable clothing, have profoundly deteriorated this race, once so remarkably fine.

This is a notable instance of the inevitable degradation pointed out by us in the two chapters on division of labor and machinery. And our litterateurs busy themselves with the pretty things of the past, as if the present were not adequate to their genius! The first among them to venture on these infernal paths has created a scandal in the coterie! Cowardly parasites, vile venders of prose and verse, all worthy of the wages of Marsyas! Oh! if your punishment were to last as long as my contempt, you would be forced to believe in the eternity of hell.

Monopoly, which just now seemed to us so well founded in justice, is the more unjust because it not only makes wages illusory, but deceives the workman in the very valuation of his wages by assuming in relation to him a false title, a false capacity.

M. de Sismondi, in his "Studies of Social Economy," observes somewhere that, when a banker delivers to a merchant bank-notes in exchange for his values, far from giving credit to the merchant, he receives it, on the contrary, from him.

"This credit," adds M. de Sismondi, "is in truth so short that the merchant scarcely takes the trouble to inquire whether the banker is worthy, especially as the former asks credit instead of granting it."

So, according to M. de Sismondi, in the issue of bank paper, the functions of the merchant and the banker are inverted: the first is the creditor, and the second is the credited.

232

Something similar takes place between the monopolist and wage-receiver.

In fact, the workers, like the merchant at the bank, ask to have their labor discounted; in right, the contractor ought to furnish them bonds and security. I will explain myself.

In any exploitation, no matter of what sort, the contractor cannot legitimately claim, in addition to his own personal labor, anything but the IDEA: as for the EXECUTION, the result of the cooperation of numerous laborers, that is an effect of collective power, with which the authors, as free in their action as the chief, can produce nothing which should go to him gratuitously. Now, the question is to ascertain whether the amount of individual wages paid by the contractor is equivalent to the collective effect of which I speak: for, were it otherwise, Say's axiom, Every product is worth what it costs, would be violated.

"The capitalist," they say, "has paid the laborers their daily wages at a rate agreed upon; consequently he owes them nothing." To be accurate, it must be said that he has paid as many times one day's wage as he has employed laborers, — which is not at all the same thing. For he has paid nothing for that immense power which results from the union of laborers and the convergence and harmony of their efforts; that saving of expense, secured by their formation into a workshop; that multiplication of product, foreseen, it is true, by the capitalist, but realized by free forces. Two hundred grenadiers, working under the direction of an engineer, stood the obelisk upon its base in a few hours; do you think that one man could have accomplished the same task in two hundred days? Nevertheless, on the books of the capitalist, the amount of wages is the same in both cases, because he allots to himself the benefit of the collective power. Now, of two things one: either this is usurpation on his part, or it is error. -What is Property: Chapter III.

To properly exploit the mule-jenny, engineers, builders, clerks, brigades of workingmen and workingwomen of all sorts, have been needed. In the name of their liberty, of their security, of their future, and of the future of their children, these workmen, on engaging to work in the mill, had to make reserves; where are the letters of credit which they have delivered to the employers? Where are the guarantees which they have received? What! millions of men have sold their arms and parted with their liberty without knowing the import of the contract; they have engaged themselves upon the promise of continuous work and adequate reward; they have executed with their hands what the thought of the employers had conceived; they have become, by this collaboration, associates in the enterprise: and when monopoly, unable or unwilling to make further exchanges, suspends its manufacture and leaves these millions of laborers without bread, they are told to be resigned! By the new processes they have lost nine days of their labor out of ten; and for reward they are pointed to the lash of necessity flourished over them! Then, if they refuse to work for lower wages, they are shown that they punish themselves. If they accept the rate offered them, they lose that noble pride, that taste for decent conveniences which constitute the happiness and dignity of the workingman and entitle him to the sympathies of the rich. If they combine to secure an increase of wages, they are thrown into prison! Whereas they ought to prosecute their exploiters in the courts, on them the courts will avenge the violations of liberty of commerce! Victims of monopoly, they will suffer the penalty due to the monopolists! O justice of men, stupid courtesan, how long, under your goddess's tinsel, will you drink the blood of the slaughtered proletaire?

Monopoly has invaded everything, — land, labor, and the instruments of labor, products and the distribution of pro ducts. Political economy itself has not been able to avoid admitting it.

"You almost always find across your path," says M. Rossi, "some monopoly. There is scarcely a product that can be regarded as the pure and simple result of labor; accordingly the economic law which proportions price to cost of production is never completely realized. It is a formula which is profoundly modified by the intervention of one or another of the monopolies to which the instruments of production are subordinated. — Course in Political Economy: Volume I., page 143.

M. Rossi holds too high an office to give his language all the precision and exactness which science requires when monopoly is in question. What he so complacently calls a modification of economic formulas is but a long and odious violation of the fundamental laws of labor and exchange. It is in consequence of monopoly that in society, net product being figured over and above gross product, the collective laborer must repurchase his own product at a price higher than that which this product costs him, — which is contradictory and impossible; that the natural balance between production and consumption is destroyed; that the laborer is deceived not only in his settlements, but also as to the amount of his wages; that in his case progress in comfort is changed into an incessant progress in misery: it is by monopoly, in short, that all notions of commutative justice are perverted, and that social economy, instead of the positive science that it is, becomes a veritable utopia.

234

This disguise of political economy under the influence of monopoly is a fact so remarkable in the history of social ideas that we must not neglect to cite a few instances.

Thus, from the standpoint of monopoly, value is no longer that synthetic conception which serves to express the relation of a special object of utility to the sum total of wealth: monopoly estimating things, not in their relation to society, but in their relation to itself, value loses its social character, and is nothing but a vague, arbitrary, egoistic, and essentially variable thing. Starting with this principle, the monopolist extends the term product to cover all sorts of servitude, and applies the idea of capital to all the frivolous and shameful industries which his passions and vices exploit. The charms of a courtesan, says Say, are so much capital, of which the product follows the general law of values, — namely, supply and demand. Most of the works on political economy are full of such applications. But as prostitution and the state of dependence from which it emanates are condemned by morality, M. Rossi will bid us observe the further fact that political economy, after having modified its formula in consequence of the intervention of monopoly, will have to submit to a new corrective, although its conclusions are in themselves irreproachable. For, he says, political economy has nothing in common with morality: it is for us to accept it, to modify or correct its formulas, whenever our welfare, that of society, and the interests of morality call for it. How many things there are between political economy and truth!

Likewise, the theory of net product, so highly social, progressive, and conservative, has been individualized, if I may say so, by monopoly, and the principle which ought to secure society's welfare causes its ruin. The monopolist, always striving for the greatest possible net product, no longer acts as a member of society and in the interest of society; he acts with a view to his exclusive interest, whether this interest be contrary to the social interest or not. This change of perspective is the cause to which M. de Sismondi attributes the depopulation of the Roman Campagna. From the comparative researches which he has made regarding the product of the agro romano when in a state of cultivation and its product when left as pasture-land, he has found that the gross product would be twelve times larger in the former case than in the latter; but, as cultivation demands relatively a greater number of hands, he has discovered also that in the former case the net product would be less. This calculation, which did not escape the proprietors, sufficed to confirm them in the habit of leaving their lands uncultivated, and hence the Roman Campagna is uninhabited.

"All parts of the Roman States," adds M. de Sismondi, "present the same contrast between the memories of their prosperity in the Middle Ages and their present desolation. The town of Ceres, made famous by Renzo da Ceri, who defended by turns Marseilles against Charles V. and Geneva against the Duke of Savoy, is nothing but a solitude. In all the fiefs of the Orsinis and the Colonnes not a soul. From the forests which surround the pretty Lake of Vico the human race has disappeared; and the soldiers with whom the formidable prefect of Vico made Rome tremble so often in the fourteenth century have left no descendants. Castro and Ronciglione are desolated." — Studies in Political Economy.

In fact, society seeks the greatest possible gross product, and consequently the greatest possible population, because with it gross product and net product are identical. Monopoly, on the contrary, aims steadily at the greatest net product, even though able to obtain it only at the price of the extermination of the human race.

Under this same influence of monopoly, interest on capital, perverted in its idea, has become in turn a principle of death to society. As we have explained it, interest on capital is, on the one hand, the form under which the laborer enjoys his net product, while utilizing it in new creations; on the other, this interest is the material bond of solidarity between producers, viewed from the standpoint of the increase of wealth. Under the first aspect, the aggregate interest paid can never exceed the amount of the capital itself; under the second, interest allows, in addition to reimbursement, a premium as a reward of service rendered. In no case does it imply perpetuity.

But monopoly, confounding the idea of capital, which is attributable only to the creations of human industry, with that of the exploitable material which nature has given us, and which belongs to all, and favored moreover in its usurpation by the anarchical condition of a society in which possession can exist only on condition of being exclusive, sovereign, and perpetual, — monopoly has imagined and laid it down as a principle that capital, like land, animals, and plants, had in itself an activity of its own, which relieved the capitalist of the necessity of contributing anything else to exchange and of taking any part in the labors of the workshop. From this false idea of monopoly has come the Greek name of usury, tokos, as much as to say the child or the increase of capital, which caused Aristotle to perpetrate this witticism: coins beget no children. But the metaphor of the usurers has prevailed over the joke of the Stagyrite; usury, like rent, of which it is an imitation, has been declared a perpetual right; and only very lately,

236

by a half-return to the principle, has it reproduced the idea of redemption.

Such is the meaning of the enigma which has caused so many scandals among theologians and legists, and regarding which the Christian Church has blundered twice, — first, in condemning every sort of interest, and, second, in taking the side of the economists and thus contradicting its old maxims. Usury, or the right of increase, is at once the expression and the condemnation of monopoly; it is the spoliation of labor by organized and legalized capital; of all the economic subversions it is that which most loudly accuses the old society, and whose scandalous persistence would justify an unceremonious and uncompensated dispossession of the entire capitalistic class.

Finally, monopoly, by a sort of instinct of self-preservation, has perverted even the idea of association, as something that might infringe upon it, or, to speak more accurately, has not permitted its birth.

Who could hope today to define what association among men should be? The law distinguishes two species and four varieties of civil societies, and as many commercial societies, from the simple partnership to the joint-stock company. I have read the most respectable commentaries that have been written upon all these forms of association, and I declare that I have found in them but one application of the routine practices of monopoly between two or more partners who unite their capital and their efforts against everything that produces and consumes, that invents and exchanges, that lives and dies. The sine qua non of all these societies is capital, whose presence alone constitutes them and gives them a basis; their object is monopoly, — that is, the exclusion of all other laborers and capitalists, and consequently the negation of social universality so far as persons are concerned.

Thus, according to the definition of the statute, a commercial society which should lay down as a principle the right of any stranger to become a member upon his simple request, and to straightway enjoy the rights and prerogatives of associates and even managers, would no longer be a society; the courts would officially pronounce its dissolution, its nonexistence. So, again, articles of association in which the contracting parties should stipulate no contribution of capital, but, while reserving to each the express right to compete with all, should confine themselves to a reciprocal guarantee of labor and wages, saying nothing of the branch of exploitation, or of capital, or of interest, or of profit and loss, — such articles would seem contradictory in their tenor, as destitute of purpose as of reason, and would be annulled by the judge on the complaint of the first rebellious associate. Covenants thus drawn up could give rise to no judicial action; people calling themselves the associates of everybody would be considered associates of nobody; treatises contemplating guarantee and competition between associates at the same time, without any mention of social capital and without any designation of purpose, would pass for a work of transcendental charlatanism, whose author could readily be sent to a madhouse, provided the magistrates would consent to regard him as only a lunatic.

And yet it is proved, by the most authentic testimony which history and social economy furnish, that humanity has been thrown naked and without capital upon the earth which it cultivates; consequently that it has created and is daily creating all the wealth that exists; that monopoly is only a relative view serving to designate the grade of the laborer, with certain conditions of enjoyment; and that all progress consists, while indefinitely multiplying products, in determining their proportionality, — that is, in organizing labor and comfort by division, machinery, the workshop, education, and competition. On the other hand, it is evident that all the tendencies of humanity, both in its politics and in its civil laws, are towards universalization, — that is, towards a complete transformation of the idea of society as determined by our statutes.

Whence I conclude that articles of association which should regulate, no longer the contribution of the associates, — since each associate, according to the economic theory, is supposed to possess absolutely nothing upon his entrance into society, — but the conditions of labor and exchange, and which should allow access to all who might present themselves, — I conclude, I say, that such articles of association would contain nothing that was not rational and scientific, since they would be the very expression of progress, the organic formula of labor, and since they would reveal, so to speak, humanity to itself by giving it the rudiment of its constitution.

Now, who, among the jurisconsults and economists, has ever approached even within a thousand leagues of this magnificent and yet so simple idea?

"I do not think," says M. Troplong, "that the spirit of association is called to greater destinies than those which it has accomplished in the past and up to the present time... ; and I confess that I have made no attempt to realize such hopes, which I believe exaggerated.... There are well-defined limits which association should not overstep. No! association is not called upon in France to govern everything. The spontaneous impulse of the individual mind is also a living force in our nation and a cause of its originality....

"The idea of association is not new.... Even among the Romans we see the commercial society appear with all its paraphernalia of monopolies, corners, collusions, combinations, piracy, and venality.... The joint-stock company realizes the civil, commercial, and maritime law of the Middle Ages: at that epoch it was the most active instrument of labor organized in society.... From the middle of the fourteenth century we see societies form by stock subscriptions; and up to the time of Law's discomfiture, we see their number continually increase.... What! we marvel at the mines, factories, patents, and newspapers owned by stock companies! But two centuries ago such companies owned islands, kingdoms, almost an entire hemisphere. We proclaim it a miracle that hundreds of stock subscribers should group themselves around an enterprise; but as long ago as the fourteenth century the entire city of Florence was in similar silent partnership with a few merchants, who pushed the genius of enterprise as far as possible. Then, if our speculations are bad, if we have been rash, imprudent, or credulous, we torment the legislator with our cavilling complaints; we call upon him for prohibitions and nullifications. In our mania for regulating everything, even that which is already codified; for enchaining everything by texts reviewed, corrected, and added to; for administering everything, even the chances and reverses of commerce, — we cry out, in the midst of so many existing laws: 'There is still something to do!'"

M. Troplong believes in Providence, but surely he is not its man. He will not discover the formula of association clamored for today by minds disgusted with all the protocols of combination and rapine of which M. Troplong unrolls the picture in his commentary. M. Troplong gets impatient, and rightly, with those who wish to enchain everything in texts of laws; and he himself pretends to enchain the future in a series of fifty articles, in which the wisest mind could not discover a spark of economic science or a shadow of philosophy. In our mania, he cries, for regulating everything, EVEN THAT WHICH IS ALREADY CODIFIED!.... I know nothing more delicious than this stroke, which paints at once the jurisconsult and the economist. After the Code Napoleon, take away the ladder!...

"Fortunately," M. Troplong continues, "all the projects of change so noisily brought to light in 1837 and 1838 are forgotten today. The conflict of propositions and the anarchy of reformatory opinions have led to negative results. At the same time that the reaction against speculators was effected, the common sense of the public did justice to the numerous official plans of organization, much inferior in wisdom to the existing law, much less in harmony with the usages of commerce, much less liberal, after 1830, than the conceptions of the imperial Council of State! Now order is restored in everything, and the commercial code has preserved its integrity, its excellent integrity. When commerce needs it, it finds, by the side of partnership, temporary partnership, and the joint-stock company, the free silent partnership, tempered only by the prudence of the silent partners and by the provisions of the penal code regarding swindling." — Troplong: Civil and Commercial Societies: Preface.

What a philosophy is that which rejoices in the miscarriage of reformatory endeavors, and which counts its triumphs by the negative results of the spirit of inquiry! We cannot now enter upon a more fundamental criticism of the civil and commercial societies, which have furnished M. Troplong material for two volumes. We will reserve this subject for the time when, the theory of economic contradictions being finished, we shall have found in their general equation the programme of association, which we shall then publish in contrast with the practice and conceptions of our predecessors.

A word only as to silent partnership.

One might think at first blush that this form of joint-stock company, by its expansive power and by the facility for change which it offers, could be generalized in such a way as to take in an entire nation in all its commercial and industrial relations. But the most superficial examination of the constitution of this society demonstrates very quickly that the sort of enlargement of which it is susceptible, in the matter of the number of stockholders, has nothing in common with the extension of the social bond.

In the first place, like all other commercial societies, it is necessarily limited to a single branch of exploitation: in this respect it is exclusive of all industries foreign to that peculiarly its own. If it were otherwise, it would have changed its nature; it would be a new form of society, whose statutes would regulate, no longer the profits especially, but the distribution of labor and the conditions of exchange; it would be exactly such an association as M. Troplong denies and as the jurisprudence of monopoly excludes.

As for the personal composition of the company, it naturally divides itself into two categories, — the managers and the stockholders. The

240

managers, very few in number, are chosen from the promoters, organizers, and patrons of the enterprise: in truth, they are the only associates. The stockholders, compared with this little government, which administers the society with full power, are a people of taxpayers who, strangers to each other, without influence and without responsibility, have nothing to do with the affair beyond their investments. They are lenders at a premium, not associates.

One can see from this how all the industries of the kingdom could be carried on by such companies, and each citizen, thanks to the facility for multiplying his shares, be interested in all or most of these companies without thereby improving his condition: it might happen even that it would be more and more compromised. For, once more, the stockholder is the beast of burden, the exploitable material of the company: not for him is this society formed. In order that association may be real, he who participates in it must do so, not as a gambler, but as an active factor; he must have a deliberative voice in the council; his name must be expressed or implied in the title of the society; everything regarding him, in short, should be regulated in accordance with equality. But these conditions are precisely those of the organization of labor, which is not taken into consideration by the code; they form the ULTERIOR object of political economy, and consequently are not to be taken for granted, but to be created, and, as such, are radically incompatible with monopoly. [20]

Socialism, in spite of its high-sounding name, has so far been no more fortunate than monopoly in the definition of society: we may even assert that, in all its plans of organization, it has steadily shown itself in this respect a plagiarist of political economy. M. Blanc, whom I have already quoted in discussing competition, and whom we have seen by turns as a partisan of the hierarchical principle, an officious defender of inequality, preaching communism, denying with a stroke of the pen the law of contradiction because he cannot conceive it, aiming above all at power as the final sanction of his system, — M. Blanc offers us again the curious example of a socialist copying political economy without suspecting it, and turning continually in the vicious circle of proprietary routine. M. Blanc really denies the sway of capital; he even denies that capital is equal to labor in production, in which he is in accord with healthy economic theories. But he can not or does not know how to dispense with capital; he takes capital for his point of departure; he appeals to the State for its silent partnership: that is, he gets down on his knees before the capitalists and recognizes the sovereignty of monopoly. Hence the singular contortions of his dialectics. I beg the reader's pardon for these eternal personalities: but since socialism, as well as political economy, is personified in a certain number of writers, I cannot do otherwise than quote its authors.

"Has or has not capital," said "La Phalange," "in so far as it is a faculty in production, the legitimacy of the other productive faculties? If it is illegitimate, its pretensions to a share of the product are illegitimate; it must be excluded; it has no interest to receive: if, on the contrary, it is legitimate, it cannot be legitimately excluded from participation in the profits, in the increase which it has helped to create."

The question could not be stated more clearly. M. Blanc holds, on the contrary, that it is stated in a very confused manner, which means that it embarrasses him greatly, and that he is much worried to find its meaning.

In the first place, he supposes that he is asked "whether it is equitable to allow the capitalist a share of the profits of production equal to the laborer's." To which M. Blanc answers unhesitatingly that that would be unjust. Then follows an outburst of eloquence to establish this injustice.

Now, the phalansterian does not ask whether the share of the capitalist should or should not be equal to the laborer's; he wishes to know simply whether he is to have a share. And to this M. Blanc makes no reply.

Is it meant, continues M. Blanc, that capital is indispensable to production, like labor itself? Here M. Blanc distinguishes: he grants that capital is indispensable, as labor is, but not to the extent that labor is.

Once again, the phalansterian does not dispute as to quantity, but as to right.

Is it meant — it is still M. Blanc who interrogates — that all capitalists are not idlers? M. Blanc, generous to capitalists who work, asks why so large a share should be given to those who do not work? A flow of eloquence as to the impersonal services of the capitalist and the personal services of the laborer, terminated by an appeal to Providence.

For the third time, you are asked whether the participation of capital in profits is legitimate, since you admit that it is indispensable in production.

242

At last M. Blanc, who has understood all the time, decides to reply that, if he allows interest to capital, he does so only as a transitional measure and to ease the descent of the capitalists. For the rest, his project leading inevitably to the absorption of private capital in association, it would be folly and an abandonment of principle to do more. M. Blanc, if he had studied his subject, would have needed to say but a single phrase: "I deny capital."

Thus M. Blanc, — and under his name I include the whole of socialism, — after having, by a first contradiction of the title of his book, "ORGANIZATION OF LABOR," declared that capital was indispensable in production, and consequently that it should be organized and participate in profits like labor, by a second contradiction rejects capital from organization and refuses to recognize it: by a third contradiction he who laughs at decorations and titles of nobility distributes civic crowns, rewards, and distinctions to such litterateurs inventors, and artists as shall have deserved well of the country; he allows them salaries according to their grades and dignities; all of which is the restoration of capital as really, though not with the same mathematical precision, as interest and net product: by a fourth contradiction M. Blanc establishes this new aristocracy on the principle of equality, — that is, he pretends to vote masterships to equal and free associates, privileges of idleness to laborers, spoliation in short to the despoiled: by a fifth contradiction he rests this equalitarian aristocracy on the basis of a power endowed with great force, — that is, on despotism, another form of monopoly: by a sixth contradiction, after having, by his encouragements to labor and the arts, tried to proportion reward to service, like monopoly, and wages to capacity, like monopoly, he sets himself to eulogize life in common, labor and consumption in common, which does not prevent him from wishing to withdraw from the effects of common indifference, by means of national encouragements taken out of the common product, the grave and serious writers whom common readers do not care for: by a seventh contradiction.... but let us stop at seven, for we should not have finished at seventy-seven.

It is said that M. Blanc, who is now preparing a history of the French Revolution, has begun to seriously study political economy. The first fruit of this study will be, I do not doubt, a repudiation of his pamphlet on "Organization of Labor," and consequently a change in all his ideas of authority and government. At this price the "History of the French Revolution," by M. Blanc, will be a truly useful and original work.

All the socialistic sects, without exception, are possessed by the same prejudice; all, unconsciously, inspired by the economic contradiction, have to confess their powerlessness in presence of the necessity of capital; all are waiting, for the realization of their ideas, to hold power and money in their hands. The utopias of socialism in the matter of association make more prominent than ever the truth which we announced at the beginning: There is nothing in socialism which is not found in political economy; and this perpetual plagiarism is the irrevocable condemnation of both. Nowhere is to be seen the dawn of that mother-idea, which springs with so much eclat from the generation of the economic categories, — that the superior formula of association has nothing to do with capital, a matter for individual accounts, but must bear solely upon equilibrium of production, the conditions of exchange, the gradual reduction of cost, the one and only source of the increase of wealth. Instead of determining the relations of industry to industry, of laborer to laborer, of province to province, and of people to people, the socialists dream only of providing themselves with capital, always conceiving the problem of the solidarity of laborers as if it were a question of founding some new institution of monopoly. The world, humanity, capital, industry, business machinery, exist; it is a matter now simply of finding their philosophy, — in other words, of organizing them: and the socialists are in search of capital! Always outside of reality, is it astonishing that they miss it?

Thus M. Blanc asks for State aid and the establishment of national workshops; thus Fourier asked for six million francs, and his followers are still engaged today in collecting that sum; thus the communists place their hope in a revolution which shall give them authority and the treasury, and exhaust themselves in waiting for useless subscriptions. Capital and power, secondary organs in society, are always the gods whom socialism adores: if capital and power did not exist, it would invent them. Through its anxieties about power and capital, socialism has completely overlooked the meaning of its own protests: much more, it has not seen that, in involving itself, as it has done, in the economic routine, it has deprived itself of the very right to protest. It accuses society of antagonism, and through the same antago-nism it goes in pursuit of reform. It asks capital for the poor laborers, as if the misery of laborers did not come from the competition of capitalists as well as from the factitious opposition of labor and capital; as if the question were not today precisely what it was before the creation of capital, — that is, still and always a question of equilibrium; as if, in short, — let us repeat it incessantly, let us repeat it to satiety, — the question were henceforth of something other than a synthesis of all the principles brought to light by civilization, and as if, provided this synthesis, the idea which leads the world, were known, there would be any need of the intervention of capital and the State to make them evident.

Socialism, in deserting criticism to devote itself to decla-mation and utopia and in mingling with political and religious intrigues, has betrayed its mission and misunderstood the character of the century. The revolution of 1830 demoralized us; socialism is making us effeminate. Like political economy, whose contradictions it simply sifts again, socialism is powerless to satisfy the movement of minds: it is henceforth, in those whom it subjugates, only a new prejudice to destroy, and, in those who propagate it, a charlatanism to unmask, the more dangerous because almost always sincere.

Chapter VII. Fifth Period. — Police, Or Taxation.

In positing its principles humanity, as if in obedience to a sovereign order, never goes backward. Like the traveller who by oblique windings rises from the depth of the valley to the mountain-top, it follows intrepidly its zigzag road, and marches to its goal with confident step, without repentance and without pause. Arriving at the angle of monopoly, the social genius casts backward a melancholy glance, and, in a moment of profound reflection, says to itself:

"Monopoly has stripped the poor hireling of everything, — bread, clothing, home, education, liberty, and security. I will lay a tax upon the monopolist; at this price I will save him his privilege.

"Land and mines, woods and waters, the original domain of man, are forbidden to the proletaire. I will intervene in their exploitation, I will have my share of the products, and land monopoly shall be respected.

"Industry has fallen into feudalism, but I am the suzerain. The lords shall pay me tribute, and they shall keep the profit of their capital.

"Commerce levies usurious profits on the consumer. I will strew its road with toll-gates, I will stamp its checks and indorse its invoices, and it shall pass.

"Capital has overcome labor by intelligence. I will open schools, and the laborer, made intelligent himself, shall become a capitalist in his turn.

"Products lack circulation, and social life is cramped. I will build roads, bridges, canals, marts, theatres, and temples, and thus furnish at one stroke work, wealth, and a market.

"The rich man lives in plenty, while the workman weeps in famine. I will establish taxes on bread, wine, meat, salt, and honey, on articles of necessity and on objects of value, and these shall supply alms for my poor.

"And I will set guards over the waters, the woods, the fields, the mines, and the roads; I will send collectors to gather the taxes and teachers to instruct the children; I will have an army to put down refractory subjects, courts to judge them, prisons to punish them, and priests to curse them. All these offices shall be given to the proletariat and paid by the monopolists.

"Such is my certain and efficacious will."

We have to prove that society could neither think better nor act worse: this will be the subject of a review which, I hope, will throw new light upon the social problem.

Every measure of general police, every administrative and commercial regulation, like every law of taxation, is at bottom but one of the innumerable articles of this ancient bargain, ever violated and ever renewed, between the patriciate and the proletariat. That the parties or their representatives knew nothing of it, or even that they frequently viewed their political constitutions from another standpoint, is of little consequence to us: not to the man, legislator, or prince do we look for the meaning of his acts, but to the acts themselves.

1. — Synthetic idea of the tax. — Point of departure and development of this idea.

In order to render that which is to follow more intelligible, I will explain, inverting, as it were, the method which we have followed hitherto, the superior theory of the tax; then I will give its genesis; finally I will show the contradiction and results. The synthetic idea of the tax, as well as its original conception, would furnish material for the most extensive developments. I shall confine myself to a simple announcement of the propositions, with a summary indication of the proofs.

246

The tax, in its essence and positive destiny, is the form of distribution among that species of functionaries which Adam Smith has designated by the word unproductive, although he admits as much as any one the utility and even the necessity of their labor in society. By this adjective, unproductive, Adam Smith, whose genius dimly foresaw everything and left us to do everything, meant that the product of these laborers is negative, which is a very different thing from null, and that consequently distribution so far as they are concerned follows a method other than exchange.

Let us consider, in fact, what takes place, from the point of view of distribution, in the four great divisions of collective labor, — extraction, [21] manufactures, commerce, agriculture. Each producer brings to market a real product whose quantity can be measured, whose quality can be estimated, whose price can be debated, and, finally, whose value can be discounted, either in other services or merchandise, or else in money. In all these industries distribution, therefore, is nothing but the mutual exchange of products according to the law of proportionality of values.

Nothing like this takes place with the functionaries called public. These obtain their right to subsistence, not by the production of real utilities, but by the very state of unproductivity in which, by no fault of their own, they are kept. For them the law of proportionality is inverted: while social wealth is formed and increased in the direct ratio of the quantity, variety, and proportion of the effective products furnished by the four great industrial categories, the development of this same wealth, the perfecting of social order, suppose, on the contrary, so far as the personnel of police is concerned, a progressive and indefinite reduction. State functionaries, therefore, are very truly unproductive. On this point J. B. Say agreed with A. Smith, and all that he has written on this subject in correction of his master, and which has been stupidly included among his titles to glory, arises entirely, it is easy to see, from a misunderstanding. In a word, the wages of the government's employees constitute a social deficit; they must be carried to the account of losses, which it must be the object of industrial organization to continually diminish: in this view what other adjective could be used to describe the men of power than that of Adam Smith?

Here, then, is a category of services which, furnishing no real products, cannot be rewarded in the ordinary way; services which do not fall under the law of exchange, which cannot become the object of private speculation, competition, joint-stock association, or any sort of commerce, but which, theoretically regarded as performed gratuitously by all, but entrusted, by virtue of the law of division of labor, to a small number of special men who devote themselves exclusively to them, must consequently be paid for. History confirms this general datum. The human mind, which tries all solutions of every problem, has tried accordingly to submit public functions to exchange; for a long time French magistrates, like notaries, etc., lived solely by their fees. But experience has proved that this method of distribution applied to unproductive laborers was too expensive and subject to too many disadvantages, and it became necessary to abandon it.

The organization of the unproductive services contributes to the general welfare in several ways: first, by relieving producers of public cares, in which all must participate, and to which, consequently, all are more or less slaves; secondly, by establishing in society an artificial centralization, the image and prelude of the future solidarity of industries; and, finally, by furnishing a first attempt at balance and discipline.

So we admit, with J. B. Say, the usefulness of magistrates and the other agents of public authority; but we hold that this usefulness is wholly negative, and we insist, therefore, on describing these functionaries by the adjective unproductive which A. Smith applied to them, not to bring them into discredit, but because they really cannot be classed in the category of producers. "Taxation," very well says an economist of Say's school, M. J. Garnier, — "taxation is a privation which we should try to reduce to the furthest point of compatibility with the needs of society." If the writer whom I quote has reflected upon the meaning of his words, he has seen that the word privation which he uses is synonymous with non-production, and that consequently those for whose benefit taxes are collected are very truly unproductive laborers.

I insist upon this definition, which seems to me the less questionable from the fact that, however much they may dispute over the word, all agree upon the thing, because it contains the germ of the greatest revolution yet to be accomplished in the world, — I mean the subordination of the unproductive functions to the productive functions, in a word, the effective submission, always asked and never obtained, of authority to the citizens.

It is a consequence of the development of the economical contradictions that order in society first shows itself inverted; that that which should be above is placed below, that which should be in relief seems sunken, and that which should receive the light is thrown into the shadow. Thus power, which, in its essence, is, like capital, the auxiliary and subordinate of labor, becomes, through the antagonism of society, the spy, judge, and tyrant of the productive functions; power, whose original inferiority lays upon it the duty of obedience, is prince and sovereign.

In all ages the laboring classes have pursued against the office-holding class the solution of this antinomy, of which economic science alone can give the key. The oscillations — that is, the political agitations which result from this struggle of labor against power — now lead to a depression of the central force, which compromises the very existence of society; now, exaggerating this same force beyond measure, give birth to despotism. Then, the privileges of command, the infinite joy which it gives to ambition and pride, making the unproductive functions an object of universal lust, a new leaven of discord penetrates society, which, divided already in one direction into capitalists and wage-workers, and in another into producers and non-producers, is again divided as regards power into monarchists and democrats. The conflicts between royalty and the republic would furnish us most marvellous and interesting material for our episodes. The confines of this work do not permit us so long an excursion; and after having pointed out this new branch in the vast network of human aberrations, we shall confine ourselves exclusively, in dealing with taxation, to the economic question.

Such, then, in succinctest statement, is the synthetic theory of the tax, — that is, if I may venture to use the familiar comparison, of this fifth wheel of the coach of humanity, which makes so much noise, and which, in governmental parlance, is styled the State. The State, the police, or their means of existence, the tax, is, I repeat, the official name of the class designated in political economy as nonproducers, — in short, as the domestics of society.

But public reason does not attain at a single bound this simple idea, which for centuries had to remain in the state of a transcendental conception. Before civilization can mount to such a height, it must pass through frightful tempests and innumerable revolutions, in each of which, one might say, it renews its strength in a bath of blood. And when at last production, represented by capital, seems on the point of thoroughly subordinating the unproductive organ, the State, then society rises in indignation, labor weeps at the prospect of its immediate freedom, democracy shudders at the abasement of power, justice cries out as if scandalized, and all the oracles of the departing gods exclaim with terror that the abomination of desolation is in the holy places and that the end of the world has come. So true is it that humanity never desires what it seeks, and that the slightest progress cannot be realized without spreading panic among the peoples.

What, then, in this evolution, is the point of departure of society, and by what circuitous route does it reach political reform, — that is, economy in its expenditures, equality in the assessment of its taxes, and the subordination of power to industry? That is what we are about to state in a few words, reserving developments for the sequel.

The original idea of the tax is that of REDEMPTION.

As, by the law of Moses, each first-born was supposed to belong to Jehovah, and had to be redeemed by an offering, so the tax everywhere presents itself in the form of a tithe or royal prerogative by which the proprietor annually redeems from the sovereign the profit of exploitation which he is supposed to hold only by his pleasure. This theory of the tax, moreover, is but one of the special articles of what is called the social contract.

Ancients and moderns all agree, in terms more or less explicit, in regarding the juridical status of societies as a reaction of weakness against strength. This idea is uppermost in all the works of Plato, notably in the "Gorgias," where he maintains, with more subtlety than logic, the cause of the laws against that of violence, — that is, legislative absolutism against aristocratic and military absolutism. In this knotty dispute, in which the weight of evidence is equal on both sides, Plato simply expresses the sentiment of entire antiquity. Long before him, Moses, in making a distribution of lands, declaring patrimony inalienable, and ordering a general and uncompensated cancellation of all mortgages every fiftieth year, had opposed a barrier to the invasions of force. The whole Bible is a hymn to JUSTICE, — that is, in the Hebrew style, to charity, to kindness to the weak on the part of the strong, to voluntary renunciation of the privilege of power. Solon, beginning his legislative mission by a general abolition of debts, and creating rights and reserves, — that is, barriers to prevent their return, — was no less reactionary. Lycurgus went farther; he forbade individual possession, and tried to absorb the man in the State, annihilating liberty the better to preserve equilibrium. Hobbes, deriving, and with great reason, legislation from the state of war, arrived by another road at the establishment of equality upon an exception, — despotism. His book, so much calumniated, is only a development of this famous antithesis. The charter of 1830, consecrating the insurrection made in '89 by the plebeians against the nobility, and decreeing the abstract equality of persons before the law, in spite of the real inequality of powers and talents which is the veritable basis of the social system now in force, is also but a protest of society in favor of the poor against the rich, of the small against the great. All the laws of the human race regarding sale, purchase, hire, property, loans, mortgages, prescription, inheritance, donation, wills, wives' dowries, minority, guardianship, etc., etc., are real barriers erected by judicial absolutism against the absolutism of force. Respect for contracts, fidelity to promises, the religion of the oath, are fictions, osselets, [22] as the famous Lysander aptly said, with which society deceives the strong and brings them under the yoke.

The tax belongs to that great family of preventive, coercive, repressive, and vindictive institutions which A. Smith designated by the generic term police, and which is, as I have said, in its original conception, only the reaction of weakness against strength. This follows, independently of abundant historical testimony which we will put aside to confine ourselves exclusively to economic proof, from the distinction naturally arising between taxes.

All taxes are divisible into two great categories: (1) taxes of assessment, or of privilege: these are the oldest taxes; (2) taxes of consumption, or of quotité, [23] whose tendency is, by absorbing the former, to make public burdens weigh equally upon all.

The first sort of taxes — including in France the tax on land, the tax on doors and windows, the poll-tax, the tax on personal property, the tax on tenants, license-fees, the tax on transfers of property, the tax on officials' fees, road-taxes, and brevets — is the share which the sovereign reserves for himself out of all the monopolies which he concedes or tolerates; it is, as we have said, the indemnity of the poor, the permit granted to property. Such was the form and spirit of the tax in all the old monarchies: feudalism was its beau ideal. Under that regime the tax was only a tribute paid by the holder to the universal proprietor or sleeping-partner (commanditaire), the king.

When later, by the development of public right, royalty, the patriarchal form of sovereignty, begins to get impregnated by the democratic spirit, the tax becomes a quota which each voter owes to the COMMONWEALTH, and which, instead of falling into the hand of the prince, is received into the State treasury. In this evolution the principle of the tax remains intact; as yet there is no transformation of the institution; the real sovereign simply succeeds the figurative sovereign. Whether the tax enters into the peculium of the prince or serves to liquidate a common debt, it is in either case only a claim of society against privilege; otherwise, it is impossible to say why the tax is levied in the ratio of fortunes.

Let all contribute to the public expenses: nothing more just. But why should the rich pay more than the poor? That is just, they say, because they possess more. I confess that such justice is beyond my comprehension.... One of two things is true: either the proportional tax guarantees a privilege to the larger tax-payers, or else it is a wrong. Because, if property is a natural right, as the Declaration of '93 declares, all that belongs to me by virtue of this right is as sacred as my person; it is my blood, my life, myself: whoever touches it offends the apple of my eye. My income of one hundred thousand francs is as inviolable a the grisette's daily wage of seventy-five centimes; her attic is no more sacred than my suite of apartments. The tax is not levied in proportion to physical strength, size, or skill: no more should it be levied in proportion to property. — What is Property: Chapter II.

These observations are the more just because the principle which it was their purpose to oppose to that of proportional assessment has had its period of application. The proportional tax is much later in history than liege-homage, which consisted in a simple officious demonstration without real payment.

The second sort of taxes includes in general all those designated, by a sort of antiphrasis, by the term indirect, such as taxes on liquor, salt, and tobacco, customs duties, and, in short, all the taxes which DIRECTLY affect the only thing which should be taxed, — product. The principle of this tax, whose name is an actual misnomer, is unquestionably better founded in theory and more equitable in tendency than the preceding: accordingly, in spite of the opinion of the mass, always deceived as to that which serves it as well as to that which is prejudicial to it, I do not hesitate to say that this tax is the only normal one, barring its assessment and collection, with which it is not my purpose now to deal.

For, if it is true, as we have just explained, that the real nature of the tax is to pay, according to a particular form of wages, for certain services which elude the usual form of exchange, it follows that all producers, enjoying these services equally as far as personal use is concerned, should contribute to their payment in equal portions. The share for each, therefore, would be a fraction of his exchangeable product, or, in other words, an amount taken from the values delivered by him for purposes of consumption. But, under the monopoly system, and with collection upon land, the treasury strikes the product before it has

252

entered into exchange, even before it is produced, — a circumstance which results in throwing back the amount of the tax into the cost of production, and consequently puts the burden upon the consumer and lifts it from monopoly.

Whatever the significance of the tax of assessment or the tax of quotité, one thing is sure, and this is the thing which it is especially important for us to know, — namely, that, in making the tax proportional, it was the intention of the sovereign to make citizens contribute to the public expenses, no longer, according to the old feudal principle, by means of a poll-tax, which would involve the idea of an assessment figured in the ratio of the number of persons taxed, and not in the ratio of their possessions, but so much per franc of capital, which supposes that capital has its source in an authority superior to the capitalists. Everybody, spontaneously and with one accord, considers such an assessment just; everybody, therefore, spontaneously and with one accord, looks upon the tax as a resumption on the part of society, a sort of redemption exacted from monopoly. This is especially striking in England, where, by a special law, the proprietors of the soil and the manufacturers pay, in proportion to their incomes, a tax of forty million dollars, which is called the poor-rate.

In short, the practical and avowed object of the tax is to effect upon the rich, for the benefit of the people, a proportional resumption of their capital.

Now, analysis and the facts demonstrate:

That the tax of assessment, the tax upon monopoly, instead of being paid by those who possess, is paid almost entirely by those who do not possess;

That the tax of quotité, separating the producer from the consumer, falls solely upon the latter, thereby taking from the capitalist no more than he would have to pay if fortunes were absolutely equal;

Finally, that the army, the courts, the police, the schools, the hospitals, the almshouses, the houses of refuge and correction, public functions, religion itself, all that society creates for the protection, emancipation, and relief of the proletaire, paid for in the first place and sustained by the proletaire, is then turned against the proletaire or wasted as far as he is concerned; so that the proletariat, which at first labored only for the class that devours it, — that of the capitalists, — must labor also for the class that flogs it, — that of the nonproducers.

253

These facts are henceforth so well known, and the economists — I owe them this justice — have shown them so clearly, that I shall abstain from correcting their demonstrations, which, for the rest, are no longer contradicted by anybody. What I propose to bring to light, and what the economists do not seem to have sufficiently understood, is that the condition in which the laborer is placed by this new phase of social economy is susceptible of no amelioration; that, unless industrial organization, and therefore political reform, should bring about an equality of fortunes, evil is inherent in police institutions as in the idea of charity which gave them birth; in short, that the STATE, whatever form it affects, aristocratic or theocratic, monarchical or republican, until it shall have become the obedient and submissive organ of a society of equals, will be for the people an inevitable hell, — I had almost said a deserved damnation.

2. — Antinomy of the tax.

I sometimes hear the champions of the statu quo maintain that for the present we enjoy liberty enough, and that, in spite of the declamation against the existing order, we are below the level of our institutions. So far at least as taxation is concerned, I am quite of the opinion of these optimists.

According to the theory that we have just seen, the tax is the reaction of society against monopoly. Upon this point opinions are unanimous: citizens and legislators, economists, journalists, and ballad-writers, rendering, each in their own tongue, the social thought, vie with each other in proclaiming that the tax should fall upon the rich, strike the superfluous and articles of luxury, and leave those of prime necessity free. In short, they have made the tax a sort of privilege for the privileged: a bad idea, since it involved a recognition of the legitimacy of privilege, which in no case, whatever shape it may take, is good for anything. The people had to be punished for this egoistic inconsistency: Providence did not fail in its duty.

From the moment, then, of the conception of the tax as a counter-claim, it had to be fixed proportionally to means, whether it struck capital or affected income more especially. Now, I will point out that the levying of the tax at so much a franc being precisely that which should be adopted in a country where all fortunes were equal, saving the differences in the cost of assessment and collection, the treasury is the most liberal feature of our society, and that on this point our morals are really behind our institutions. But as with the wicked the best things cannot fail to be detestable, we shall see the equalitarian tax crush the people precisely because the people are not up to it.

I will suppose that the gross income in France, for each family of four persons, is 1,000 francs: this is a little above the estimate of M. Chevalier, who places it at only 63 centimes a day for each individual, or 919 francs 80 centimes for each household. The tax being today more than a thousand millions, or about an eighth of the total income, each family, earning 1,000 francs a year, is taxed 125 francs.

Accordingly, an income of 2,000 francs pays 250 francs; an income of 3,000 francs, 375; an income of 4,000 francs, 500, etc. The proportion is strict and mathematically irreproachable; the treasury, by arithmetic, is sure of losing nothing.

But on the side of the taxpayers the affair totally changes its aspect. The tax, which, in the intention of the legislator, was to have been proportioned to fortune, is, on the contrary, progressive in the ratio of poverty, so that, the poorer the citizen is, the more he pays. This I shall try to make plain by a few figures.

According to the proportional tax, there is due to the treasury:

for an income of 1,000 2,000 3,000 4,000 5,000 6,000 francs, etc.

a tax of   125   250   375   500   625   750

According to this series, then, the tax seems to increase proportionally to income.

But when it is remembered that each annual income is made up of 365 units, each of which represents the daily income of the taxpayer, the tax will no longer be found proportional; it will be found equal. In fact, if the State levies a tax of 125 francs on an income of 1,000 francs, it is as if it took from the taxed family 45 days' subsistence; likewise the assessments of 250, 375, 500, 625, and 750 francs, corresponding to incomes of 2,000, 3,000, 4,000, 5,000, and 6,000 francs, constitute in each case a tax of 45 days' pay upon each of those who enjoy these incomes.

I say now that this equality of taxation is a monstrous inequality, and that it is a strange illusion to imagine that, because the daily income is

255

larger, the tax of which it is the base is higher. Let us change our point of view from that of personal to that of collective income.

As an effect of monopoly social wealth abandoning the laboring class to go to the capitalistic class, the object of taxation has been to moderate this displacement and react against usurpation by enforcing a proportional replevin upon each privileged person. But proportional to what? To the excess which the privileged person has received undoubtedly, and not to the fraction of the social capital which his income represents. Now, the object of taxation is missed and the law turned into derision when the treasury, instead of taking its eighth where this eighth exists, asks it precisely of those to whom it should be restored. A final calculation will make this evident.

Setting the daily income of each person in France at 68 centimes, the father of a family who, whether as wages or as income from his capital, receives 1,000 francs a year receives four shares of the national income; he who receives 2,000 francs has eight shares; he who receives 4,000 francs has sixteen, etc. Hence it follows that the workman who, on an income of 1,000 francs, pays 125 francs into the treasury renders to public order half a share, or an eighth of his income and his family's subsistence; whereas the capitalist who, on an income of 6,000 francs, pays only 750 francs realizes a profit of 17 shares out of the collective income, or, in other words, gains by the tax 425 per cent.

Let us reproduce the same truth in another form.

The voters of France number about 200,000. I do not know the total amount of taxes paid by these 200,000 voters, but I do not believe that I am very far from the truth in supposing an average of 300 francs each, or a total of 60,000,000 for the 200,000 voters, to which we will add twenty-five per cent. to represent their share of indirect taxes, making in all 75,000,000, or 75 francs for each person (supposing the family of each voter to consist of five persons), which the electoral class pays to the State. The appropriations, according to the "Annuaire Economique" for 1845, being 1,106,000,000, there remains 1,031,000,000, which makes the tax paid by each non-voting citizen 31 francs 30 centimes, — two-fifths of the tax paid by the wealthy class. Now, for this proportion to be equitable, the average welfare of the non-voting class would have to be two-fifths of the average welfare of the voting class: but such is not the truth, as it falls short of this by more than three-fourths.

256

But this disproportion will seem still more shocking when it is remembered that the calculation which we have just made concerning the electoral class is altogether wrong, altogether in favor of the voters.

In fact, the only taxes which are levied for the enjoyment of the right of suffrage are: (1) the land tax; (2) the tax on polls and personal property; (3) the tax on doors and windows; (4) license-fees. Now, with the exception of the tax on polls and personal property, which varies little, the three other taxes are thrown back on the consumers; and it is the same with all the indirect taxes, for which the holders of capital are reimbursed by the consumers, with the exception, however, of the taxes on property transfers, which fall directly on the proprietor and amount in all to 150,000,000. Now, if we estimate that in this last amount the property of voters figures as one-sixth, which is placing it high, the portion of direct taxes (409,000,000) being 12 francs for each person, and that of indirect taxes (547,000,000) 16 francs, the average tax paid by each voter having a household of five will reach a total of 265 francs, while that paid by the laborer, who has only his arms to support himself, his wife, and two children, will be 112 francs. In more general terms, the average tax upon each person belonging to the upper classes will be 53 francs; upon each belonging to the lower, 28. Whereupon I renew my question: Is the welfare of those below the voting standard half as great as that of those above it?

It is with the tax as with periodical publications, which really cost more the less frequently they appear. A daily journal costs forty francs, a weekly ten francs, a monthly four. Supposing other things to be equal, the subscription prices of these journals are to each other as the numbers forty, seventy, and one hundred and twenty, the price rising with the infrequency of publication. Now, this exactly represents the increase of the tax: it is a subscription paid by each citizen in exchange for the right to labor and to live. He who uses this right in the smallest proportion pays much; he who uses it a little more pays less; he who uses it a great deal pays little.

The economists are generally in agreement about all this. They have attacked the proportional tax, not only in its principle, but in its application; they have pointed out its anomalies, almost all of which arise from the fact that the relation of capital to income, or of cultivated surface to rent, is never fixed.

Given a levy of one-tenth on the income from lands, and lands of different qualities producing, the first eight francs' worth of grain, the second six francs' worth, the third five francs' worth, the tax will call

257

for one-eighth of the income from the most fertile land, one-sixth from that a little less fertile, and, finally, one-fifth from that less fertile still. [24] Will not the tax thus established be just the reverse of what it should be? Instead of land, we may suppose other instruments of production, and compare capitals of the same value, or amounts of labor of the same order, applied to branches of industry differing in productivity: the conclusion will be the same. There is injustice in requiring the same poll-tax of ten francs from the laborer who earns one thousand francs and from the artist or physician who has an income of sixty thousand. — J. Garnier: Principles of Political Economy.

These reflections are very sound, although they apply only to collection or assessment, and do not touch the principle of the tax itself. For, in supposing the assessment to be made upon income instead of upon capital, the fact always remains that the tax, which should be proportional to fortunes, is borne by the consumer.

The economists have taken a resolve; they have squarely recognized the iniquity of the proportional tax.

"The tax," says Say, "can never be levied upon the necessary." This author, it is true, does not tell us what we are to understand by the necessary, but we can supply the omission. The necessary is what each individual gets out of the total product of the country, after deducting what must be taken for taxes. Thus, making the estimate in round numbers, the production of France being eight thousand millions and the tax one thousand millions, the necessary in the case of each individual amounts to fifty-six and a half centimes a day. Whatever is in excess of this income is alone susceptible of being taxed, according to J. B. Say; whatever falls short of it must be regarded by the treasury as inviolable.

The same author expresses this idea in other words when he says: "The proportional tax is not equitable." Adam Smith had already said before him: "It is not unreasonable that the rich man should contribute to the public expenses, not only in proportion to his income, but something more." "I will go further," adds Say; "I will not fear to say that the progressive tax is the only equitable tax." And M. J. Garnier, the latest abridger of the economists, says: "Reforms should tend to establish a progressional equality, if I may use the phrase, much more just, much more equitable, than the pretended equality of taxation, which is only a monstrous inequality."

258

So, according to general opinion and the testimony of the economists, two things are acknowledged: one, that in its principle the tax is a reaction against monopoly and directed against the rich; the other, that in practice this same tax is false to its object; that, in striking the poor by preference, it commits an injustice; and that the constant effort of the legislator must be to distribute its burden in a more equitable fashion.

I needed to establish this double fact solidly before passing to other considerations: now commences my criticism.

The economists, with that simplicity of honest folk which they have inherited from their elders and which even today is all that stands to their credit, have taken no pains to see that the progressional theory of the tax, which they point out to governments as the ne plus ultra of a wise and liberal administration, was contradictory in its terms and pregnant with a legion of impossibilities. They have attributed the oppression of the treasury by turns to the barbarism of the time, the ignorance of princes, the prejudices of caste, the avarice of collectors, everything, in short, which, in their opinion, preventing the progression of the tax, stood in the way of the sincere practice of equality in the distribution of public burdens; they have not for a moment suspected that what they asked under the name of progressive taxation was the overturn of all economic ideas.

Thus they have not seen, for instance, that the tax was progressive from the very fact that it was proportional, the only difference being that the progression was in the wrong direction, the percentage being, as we have said, not directly, but inversely proportional to fortunes. If the economists had had a clear idea of this overturn, invariable in all countries where taxation exists, so singular a phenomenon would not have failed to draw their attention; they would have sought its causes, and would have ended by discovering that what they took for an accident of civilization, an effect of the inextricable difficulties of human government, was the product of the contradiction inherent in all political economy.

The progressive tax, whether applied to capital or to income, is the very negation of monopoly, of that monopoly which is met everywhere, according to M. Rossi, across the path of social economy; which is the true stimulant of industry, the hope of economy, the preserver and parent of all wealth; of which we have been able to say, in short, that society cannot exist without it, but that, except for it, there would be no society. Let the tax become suddenly what it unquestionably must

259

sometime be, — namely, the proportional (or progressional, which is the same thing) contribution of each producer to the public expenses, and straightway rent and profit are confiscated everywhere for the benefit of the State; labor is stripped of the fruits of its toil; each individual being reduced to the proper allowance of fifty-six and a half centimes, poverty becomes general; the compact formed between labor and capital is dissolved, and society, deprived of its rudder, drifts back to its original state.

It will be said, perhaps, that it is easy to prevent the absolute annihilation of the profits of capital by stopping the progression at any moment.

Eclecticism, the golden mean, compromise with heaven or with morality: is it always to be the same philosophy, then? True science is repugnant to such arrangements. All invested capital must return to the producer in the form of interest; all labor must leave a surplus, all wages be equal to product. Under the protection of these laws society continually realizes, by the greatest variety of production, the highest possible degree of welfare. These laws are absolute; to violate them is to wound, to mutilate society. Capital, accordingly, which, after all, is nothing but accumulated labor, is inviolable. But, on the other hand, the tendency to equality is no less imperative; it is manifested at each economic phase with increasing energy and an invincible authority. Therefore you must satisfy labor and justice at once; you must give to the former guarantees more and more real, and secure the latter without concession or ambiguity.

Instead of that, you know nothing but the continual substitution of the good pleasure of the prince for your theories, the arrest of the course of economic law by arbitrary power, and, under the pretext of equity, the deception of the wage worker and the monopolist alike! Your liberty is but a half-liberty, your justice but a half-justice, and all your wisdom consists in those middle terms whose iniquity is always twofold, since they justify the pretensions of neither one party nor the other! No, such cannot be the science which you have promised us, and which, by unveiling for us the secrets of the production and consumption of wealth, must unequivocally solve the social antinomies. Your semi-liberal doctrine is the code of despotism, and shows that you are powerless to advance as well as ashamed to retreat.

If society, pledged by its economic antecedents, can never retrace its steps; if, until the arrival of the universal equation, monopoly must be maintained in its possession, — no change is possible in the laying of taxes: only there is a contradiction here, which, like every other, must be pushed till exhausted. Have, then, the courage of your opinions, — respect for wealth, and no pity for the poor, whom the God of monopoly has condemned. The less the hireling has wherewith to live, the more he must pay: qui minus habet, etiam quod habet auferetur ab eo. This is necessary, this is inevitable; in it lies the safety of society.

Let us try, nevertheless, to reverse the progression of the tax, and so arrange it that the capitalist, instead of the laborer, will pay the larger share.

I observe, in the first place, that with the usual method of collection, such a reversal is impracticable.

In fact, if the tax falls on exploitable capital, this tax, in its entirety, is included among the costs of production, and then of two things one: either the product, in spite of the increase in its selling value, will be bought by the consumer, and consequently the producer will be relieved of the tax; or else this same product will be thought too dear, and in that case the tax, as J. B. Say has very well said, acts like a tithe levied on seed, -it prevents production. Thus it is that too high a tax on the transfer of titles arrests the circulation of real property, and renders estates less productive by keeping them from changing hands.

If, on the contrary, the tax falls on product, it is nothing but a tax of quotité, which each pays in the ratio of his consumption, while the capitalist, whom it is purposed to strike, escapes.

Moreover, the supposition of a progressive tax based either on product or on capital is perfectly absurd. How can we imagine the same product paying a duty of ten per cent at the store of one dealer and a duty of but five at another's? How are estates already encumbered with mortgages and which change owners every day, how is a capital formed by joint investment or by the fortune of a single individual, to be distinguished upon the official register, and taxed, not in the ratio of their value or rent, but in the ratio of the fortune or presumed profits of the proprietor?

There remains, then, a last resource, — to tax the net income of each tax-payer, whatever his method of getting it. For instance, an income of one thousand francs would pay ten per cent.; an income of two thousand francs, twenty per cent.; an income of three thousand francs, thirty per cent., etc. We will set aside the thousand difficulties and annoyances that must be met in ascertaining these incomes, and

261

suppose the operation as easy as you like. Well! that is exactly the system which I charge with hypocrisy, contradiction, and injustice.

I say in the first place that this system is hypocritical, because, instead of taking from the rich that entire portion of their income in excess of the average national product per family, which is inadmissible, it does not, as is imagined, reverse the order of progression in the direction of wealth; at most it changes the rate of progression. Thus the present progression of the tax, for fortunes yielding incomes of a thousand francs and UNDER, being as that of the numbers 10, 11, 12, 13, etc., and, for fortunes yielding incomes of a thousand francs and OVER, as that of the numbers 10, 9, 8, 7, 6, etc., — the tax always increasing with poverty and decreasing with wealth, — if we should confine ourselves to lifting the indirect tax which falls especially on the poorer class and imposing a corresponding tax upon the incomes of the richer class, the progression thereafter, it is true, would be, for the first, only as that of the numbers 10, 10.25, 10.50, 10.75, 11, 11.25, etc., and, for the second, as 10, 9.75, 9.50, 9.25, 9, 8.75, etc. But this progression, although less rapid on both sides, would still take the same direction nevertheless, would still be a reversal of justice; and it is for this reason that the so-called progressive tax, capable at most of giving the philanthropist something to babble about, is of no scientific value. It changes nothing in fiscal jurisprudence; as the proverb says, it is always the poor man who carries the pouch, always the rich man who is the object of the solicitude of power.

I add that this system is contradictory.

In fact, one cannot both give and keep, say the jurisconsults. Instead, then, of consecrating monopolies from which the holders are to derive no privilege save that of straightway losing, with the income, all the enjoyment thereof, why not decree the agrarian law at once? Why provide in the constitution that each shall freely enjoy the fruit of his labor and industry, when, by the fact or the tendency of the tax, this permission is granted only to the extent of a dividend of fifty-six and a half centimes a day, — a thing, it is true, which the law could not have foreseen, but which would necessarily result from progression? The legislator, in confirming us in our monopolies, intended to favor production, to feed the sacred fire of industry: now, what interest shall we have to produce, if, though not yet associated, we are not to produce for ourselves alone? After we have been declared free, how can we be made subject to conditions of sale, hire, and exchange which annul our liberty?

A man possesses government securities which bring him an income of twenty thousand francs. The tax, under the new system of progression, will take fifty per cent. of this from him. At this rate it is more advantageous to him to withdraw his capital and consume the principal instead of the income. Then let him be repaid. What! repaid! The State cannot be obliged to repay; and, if it consents to redeem, it will do so in proportion to the net income. Therefore a bond for twenty thousand francs will be worth not more than ten thousand to the bondholder, because of the tax, if he wishes to get it redeemed by the State: unless he divides it into twenty lots, in which case it will return him double the amount. Likewise an estate which rents for fifty thousand francs, the tax taking two-thirds of the income, will lose two-thirds of its value. But let the proprietor divide this estate into a hundred lots and sell it at auction, and then, the terror of the treasury no longer deterring purchasers, he can get back his entire capital. So that, with the progressive tax, real estate no longer follows the law of supply and demand and is not valued according to the real income which it yields, but according to the condition of the owner. The consequence will be that large capitals will depreciate in value, and mediocrity be brought to the front; land-owners will hasten to sell, because it will be better for them to consume their property than to get an insufficient rent from it; capitalists will recall their investments, or will invest only at usurious rates; all exploitation on a large scale will be prohibited, every visible fortune proceeded against, and all accumulation of capital in excess of the figure of the necessary proscribed. Wealth, driven back, will retire within itself and never emerge except by stealth; and labor, like a man attached to a corpse, will embrace misery in an endless union. Does it not well become the economists who devise such reforms to laugh at the reformers?

After having demonstrated the contradiction and delusion of the progressive tax, must I prove its injustice also? The progressive tax, as understood by the economists and, in their wake, by certain radicals, is impracticable, I said just now, if it falls on capital and product: consequently I have supposed it to fall on incomes. But who does not see that this purely theoretical distinction between capital, product, and income falls so far as the treasury is concerned, and that the same impossibilities which we have pointed out reappear here with all their fatal character?

A manufacturer discovers a process by means of which, saving twenty per cent of his cost of production, he secures an income of twenty-five thousand francs. The treasury calls on him for fifteen thousand. He is obliged, therefore, to raise his prices, since, by the fact of the tax, his process, instead of saving twenty per cent, saves only eight per cent. Is not this as if the treasury prevented cheapness? Thus, in trying to reach the rich, the progressive tax always reaches the consumer; and it is impossible for it not to reach him without suppressing production altogether: what a mistake!

It is a law of social economy that all invested capital must return continually to the capitalist in the form of interest. With the progressive tax this law is radically violated, since, by the effect of progression, interest on capital is so reduced that industries are established only at a loss of a part or the whole of the capital. To make it otherwise, interest on capital would have to increase progressively in the same ratio as the tax itself, which is absurd. Therefore the progressive tax stops the creation of capital; furthermore it hinders its circulation. Whoever, in fact, should want to buy a plant for any enterprise or a piece of land for cultivation would have to consider, under the system of progressive taxation, not the real value of such plant or land, but rather the tax which it would bring upon him; so that, if the real income were four per cent., and, by the effect of the tax or the condition of the buyer, must go down to three, the purchase could not be effected. After having run counter to all interests and thrown the market into confusion by its categories, the progressive tax arrests the development of wealth and reduces venal value below real value; it contracts, it petrifies society. What tyranny! What derision!

The progressive tax resolves itself, then, whatever may be done, into a denial of justice, prohibition of production, confiscation. It is unlimited and unbridled absolutism, given to power over everything which, by labor, by economy, by improvements, contributes to public wealth.

But what is the use of wandering about in chimerical hypotheses when the truth is at hand. It is not the fault of the proportional principle if the tax falls with such shocking inequality upon the various classes of society; the fault is in our prejudices and our morals. The tax, as far as is possible in human operations, proceeds with equity, precision. Social economy commands it to apply to product; it applies to product. If product escapes it, it strikes capital: what more natural! The tax, in advance of civilization, supposes the equality of laborers and capitalists: the inflexible expression of necessity, it seems to invite us to make ourselves equals by education and labor, and, by balancing our functions and associating our interests, to put ourselves in accord with it. The tax refuses to distinguish between one man and another: and we blame its mathematical severity for the differences in our fortunes! We ask equality itself to comply with our injustice! Was I not right in saying at the outset that, relatively to the tax, we are behind our institutions?

Accordingly we always see the legislator stopping, in his fiscal laws, before the subversive consequences of the progressive tax, and consecrating the necessity, the immutability of the proportional tax. For equality in well-being cannot result from the violation of capital: the antinomy must be methodically solved, under penalty, for society, of falling back into chaos. Eternal justice does not accommodate itself to all the whims of men: like a woman, whom one may outrage, but whom one does not marry without a solemn alienation of one's self, it demands on our part, with the abandonment of our egoism, the recognition of all its rights, which are those of science.

The tax, whose final purpose, as we have shown, is the reward of the non-producers, but whose original idea was a restoration of the laborer, — the tax, under the system of monopoly, reduces itself therefore to a pure and simple protest, a sort of extra-judicial act, the whole effect of which is to aggravate the situation of the wage-worker by disturbing the monopolist in his possession. As for the idea of changing the proportional tax into a progressive tax, or, to speak more accurately, of reversing the order in which the tax progresses, that is a blunder the entire responsibility for which belongs to the economists.

But henceforth menace hovers over privilege. With the power of modifying the proportionality of the tax, government has under its hand an expeditious and sure means of dispossessing the holders of capital when it will; and it is a frightful thing to see everywhere that great institution, the basis of society, the object of so many controversies, of so many laws, of so many cajoleries, and of so many crimes, PROPERTY, suspended at the end of a thread over the yawning mouth of the proletariat.

3. — Disastrous and inevitable consequences of the tax. (Provisions, sumptuary laws, rural and industrial police, patents, trade-marks, etc.)

M. Chevalier addressed to himself, in July, 1843, on the subject of the tax, the following questions:

(1) Is it asked of all or by preference of a part of the nation? (2) Does the tax resemble a levy on polls, or is it exactly proportioned to the fortunes of the tax-payers? (3) Is agriculture more or less burdened than

265

manufactures or commerce? (4) Is real estate more or less spared than personal property? (5) Is he who produces more favored than he who consumes? (6) Have our taxation laws the character of sumptuary laws?

To these various questions M. Chevalier makes the reply which I am about to quote, and which sums up all of the most philosophical considerations upon the subject which I have met:

(a) The tax affects the universality, applies to the mass, takes the nation as a whole; nevertheless, as the poor are the most numerous, it taxes them willingly, certain of collecting more. (b) By the nature of things the tax sometimes takes the form of a levy on polls, as in the case of the salt tax. (c, d, e) The treasury addresses itself to labor as well as to consumption, because in France everybody labors, to real more than to personal property, and to agriculture more than to manufactures. (f) By the same reasoning, our laws partake little of the character of sumptuary laws.

What, professor! is that all that science has taught you? The tax applies to the mass, you say; it takes the nation as a whole. Alas! we know it only too well; but it is this which is iniquitous, and which we ask you to explain. The government, when engaged in the assessment and distribution of the tax, could not have believed, did not believe, that all fortunes were equal; consequently it could not have wished, did not wish, the sums paid to be equal. Why, then, is the practice of the government always the opposite of its theory? Your opinion, if you please, on this difficult matter? Explain; justify or condemn the exchequer; take whatever course you will, provided you take some course and say something. Remember that your readers are men, and that they cannot excuse in a doctor, speaking ex cathedra, such propositions as this: as the poor are the most numerous, it taxes them willingly, certain of collecting more. No, Monsieur: numbers do not regulate the tax; the tax knows perfectly well that millions of poor added to millions of poor do not make one voter. You render the treasury odious by making it absurd, and I maintain that it is neither the one nor the other. The poor man pays more than the rich because Providence, to whom misery is odious like vice, has so ordered things that the miserable must always be the most ground down. The iniquity of the tax is the celestial scourge which drives us towards equality. God! if a professor of political economy, who was formerly an apostle, could but understand this revelation!

By the nature of things, says M. Chevalier, the tax sometimes takes the form of a levy on polls. Well, in what case is it just that the tax should

266

take the form of a levy on polls? Is it always, or never? What is the principle of the tax? What is its object? Speak, answer.

And what instruction, pray, can we derive from the remark, scarcely worthy of quotation, that the treasury addresses itself to labor as well as to consumption, to real more than to personal property, to agriculture more than to manufactures? Of what consequence to science is this interminable recital of crude facts, if your analysis never extracts a single idea from them?

All the deductions made from consumption by taxation, rent, interest on capital, etc., enter into the general expense account and figure in the selling price, so that nearly always the consumer pays the tax: that we know. And as the goods most consumed are also those which yield the most revenue, it necessarily follows that the poorest people are the most heavily burdened: this consequence, like the first, is inevitable. Once more, then, of what importance to us are your fiscal distinctions? Whatever the classification of taxable material, as it is impossible to tax capital beyond its income, the capitalist will be always favored, while the proletaire will suffer iniquity, oppression. The trouble is not in the distribution of taxes; it is in the distribution of goods. M. Chevalier cannot be ignorant of this: why, then, does not M. Chevalier, whose word would carry more weight than that of a writer suspected of not loving the existing order, say as much?

From 1806 to 1811 (this observation, as well as the following, is M. Chevalier's) the annual consumption of wine in Paris was one hundred and forty quarts for each individual; now it is not more than eighty-three. Abolish the tax of seven or eight cents a quart collected from the retailer, and the consumption of wine will soon rise from eighty-three quarts to one hundred and seventy-five; and the wine industry, which does not know what to do with its products, will have a market. Thanks to the duties laid upon the importation of cattle, the consumption of meat by the people has diminished in a ratio similar to that of the falling-off in the consumption of wine; and the economists have recognized with fright that the French workman does less work than the English workman, because he is not as well fed.

Out of sympathy for the laboring classes M. Chevalier would like our manufacturers to feel the goad of foreign competition a little. A reduction of the tax on woollens to the extent of twenty cents on each pair of pantaloons would leave six million dollars in the pockets of the consumers, — half enough to pay the salt tax. Four cents less in the price of a shirt would effect a saving probably sufficient to keep a force of twenty thousand men under arms.

In the last fifteen years the consumption of sugar has risen from one hundred and sixteen million pounds to two hundred and sixty million, which gives at present an average of seven pounds and three-quarters for each individual. This progress demonstrates that sugar must be classed henceforth with bread, wine, meat, wool, cotton, wood, and coal, among the articles of prime necessity. To the poor man sugar is a whole medicine-chest: would it be too much to raise the average individual consumption of this article from seven pounds and three-quarters to fifteen pounds? Abolish the tax, which is about four dollars and a half on a hundred pounds, and your consumption will double.

Thus the tax on provisions agitates and tortures the poor proletaire in a thousand ways: the high price of salt hinders the production of cattle; the duties on meat diminish also the rations of the laborer. To satisfy at once the tax and the need of fermented beverages which the laboring class feels, they serve him with mixtures unknown to the chemist as well as to the brewer and the wine-grower. What further need have we of the dietary prescriptions of the Church? Thanks to the tax, the whole year is Lent to the laborer, and his Easter dinner is not as good as Monseigneur's Good Friday lunch. It is high time to abolish everywhere the tax on consumption, which weakens and starves the people: this is the conclusion of the economists as well as of the radicals.

But if the proletaire does not fast to feed Caesar, what will Caesar eat? And if the poor man does not cut his cloak to cover Caesar's nudity, what will Caesar wear?

That is the question, the inevitable question, the question to be solved.

M. Chevalier, then, having asked himself as his sixth question whether our taxation laws have the character of sumptuary laws, has answered: No, our taxation laws have not the character of sumptuary laws. M. Chevalier might have added — and it would have been both new and true — that that is the best thing about our taxation laws. But M. Chevalier, who, whatever he may do, always retains some of the old leaven of radicalism, has preferred to declaim against luxury, whereby he could not compromise himself with any party. "If in Paris," he cries, "the tax collected from meat should be laid upon private carriages, saddle-horses and carriage-horses, servants, and dogs, it would be a perfectly equitable operation."

Does M. Chevalier, then, sit in the College of France to expound the politics of Masaniello? I have seen the dogs at Basle wearing the treasury badge upon their necks as a sign that they had been taxed, and I looked upon the tax on dogs, in a country where taxation is almost nothing, as rather a moral lesson and a hygienic precaution than a source of revenue. In 1844 the dog tax of forty-two cents a head gave a revenue of $12,600 in the entire province of Brabant, containing 667,000 inhabitants. From this it may be estimated that the same tax, producing in all France $600,000, would lighten the taxes of quotité less than two cents a year for each individual. Certainly I am far from pretending that $600,000 is a sum to be disdained, especially with a prodigal ministry; and I regret that the Chamber should have rejected the dog tax, which would always have served to endow half a dozen highnesses. But I remember that a tax of this nature is levied much less in the interest of the treasury than as a promoter of order; that consequently it is proper to look upon it, from the fiscal point of view, as of no importance; and that it will even have to be abolished as an annoyance when the mass of the people, having become a little more humanized, shall feel a disgust for the companionship of beasts. Two cents a year, what a relief for poverty!

But M. Chevalier has other resources in reserve, — horses, carriages, servants, articles of luxury, luxury at last! How much is contained in that one word, LUXURY!

Let us cut short this phantasmagoria by a simple calculation; reflections will be in order later. In 1842 the duties collected on imports amounted to $25,800,000. In this sum of $25,800,000, sixty-one articles in common use figure for $24,800,000, and one hundred and seventy-seven, used only by those who enjoy a high degree of luxury, for ten thousand dollars. In the first class sugar yielded a revenue of $8,600,000, coffee $2,400,000, cotton $2,200,000, woollens $2,000,000, oils $1,600,000, coal $800,000, linens and hemp $600,000, — making a total of $18,200,000 on seven articles. The amount of revenue, then, is lower in proportion as the article of merchandise from which it is derived is less generally used, more rarely consumed, and found accompanying a more refined degree of luxury. And yet articles of luxury are subject to much the highest taxes. Therefore, even though, to obtain an appreciable reduction upon articles of primary necessity, the duties upon articles of luxury should be made a hundred times higher, the only result would be the suppression of a branch of commerce by a prohibitory tax. Now, the economists all favor the abolition of custom-houses; doubtless they do not wish them replaced by city toll-gates? Let us generalize this example: salt brings the treasury $11,400,000, tobacco $16,800,000. Let them show me, figures in hand, by what taxes upon articles of luxury, after having abolished the taxes on salt and tobacco, this deficit will be made up.

You wish to strike articles of luxury; you take civilization at the wrong end. I maintain, for my part, that articles of luxury should be free. In economic language what are luxuries? Those products which bear the smallest ratio to the total wealth, those which come last in the industrial series and whose creation supposes the preexistence of all the others. From this point of view all the products of human labor have been, and in turn have ceased to be, articles of luxury, since we mean by luxury nothing but a relation of succession, whether chronological or commercial, in the elements of wealth. Luxury, in a word, is synonymous with progress; it is, at each instant of social life, the expression of the maximum of comfort realized by labor and at which it is the right and destiny of all to arrive. Now, just as the tax respects for a time the newly-built house and the newly-cleared field, so it should freely welcome new products and precious articles, the latter because their scarcity should be continually combatted, the former because every invention deserves encouragement. What! under a pretext of luxury would you like to establish new classes of citizens? And do you take seriously the city of Salente and the prosopopoeia of Fabricius?

Since the subject leads us to it, let us talk of morality. Doubtless you will not deny the truth so often dwelt upon by the Senecas of all ages, — that luxury corrupts and weakens morals: which means that it humanizes, elevates, and ennobles habits, and that the first and most effective education for the people, the stimulant of the ideal in most men, is luxury. The Graces were naked, according to the ancients; where has it ever been said that they were needy? It is the taste for luxury which in our day, in the absence of religious principles, sustains the social movement and reveals to the lower classes their dignity. The Academy of Moral and Political Sciences clearly understood this when it chose luxury as the subject of one of its essays, and I applaud its wisdom from the bottom of my heart. Luxury, in fact, is already more than a right in our society, it is a necessity; and he is truly to be pitied who never allows himself a little luxury. And it is when universal effort tends to popularize articles of luxury more and more that you would confine the enjoyment of the people to articles which you are pleased to describe as articles of necessity! It is when ranks approach and blend into each other through the generalization of luxury that you would dig the line of demarcation deeper and increase the height of your steps! The workman sweats and sacrifices and grinds in order to buy a set of jewelry for his sweetheart, a necklace for his granddaughter, or a watch for his son; and you would deprive him of this happiness, unless he pays your tax, — that is, your fine.

But have you reflected that to tax articles of luxury is to prohibit the luxurious arts? Do you think that the silk-workers, whose average wages does not reach forty cents; the milliners at ten cents; the jewellers, goldsmiths, and clockmakers, with their interminable periods of idleness; servants at forty dollars, — do you think that they earn too much?

Are you sure that the tax on luxuries would not be paid by the worker in the luxurious arts, as the tax on beverages is paid by the consumer of beverages? Do you even know whether higher prices for articles of luxury would not be an obstacle to the cheapness of necessary objects, and whether, in trying to favor the most numerous class, you would not render the general condition worse? A fine speculation, in truth! Four dollars to be returned to the laborer on his wine and sugar, and eight to be taken from him in the cost of his pleasures! He shall gain fifteen cents on the leather in his boots, and, to take his family into the country four times a year, he shall pay one dollar and twenty cents more for carriage-hire! A small bourgeois spends one hundred and twenty dollars for a housekeeper, laundress, linen-tender, and errand-boys; but if, by a wiser economy which works for the interest of all, he takes a domestic, the exchequer, in the interest of articles of subsistence, will punish this plan of economy! What an absurd thing is the philanthropy of the economists, when closely scrutinized!

Nevertheless I wish to satisfy your whim; and, since you absolutely must have sumptuary laws, I undertake to give you the receipt. And I guarantee that in my system collection shall be easy: no comptrollers, assessors, tasters, assayers, inspectors, receivers; no watching, no office expenses; not the smallest annoyance or the slightest indiscretion; no constraint whatever. Let it be decreed by a law that no one in future shall receive two salaries at the same time, and that the highest fees, in any situation, shall not exceed twelve hundred dollars in Paris and eight hundred in the departments. What! you lower your eyes! Confess, then, that your sumptuary laws are but hypocrisy.

To relieve the people some would apply commercial practices to taxation. If, for instance, they say, the price of salt were reduced one-half, if letter-postage were lightened in the same proportion, consumption would not fail to increase, the revenue would be more than doubled, the treasury would gain, and so would the consumer.

Let us suppose the event to confirm this anticipation. Then I say: If letter-postage should be reduced three-fourths, and if salt should be given away, would the treasury still gain? Certainly not. What, then, is the significance of what is called the postal reform? That for every kind of product there is a natural rate, ABOVE which profit becomes usurious and tends to decrease consumption, but BELOW which the producer suffers loss. This singularly resembles the determination of value which the economists reject, and in relation to which we said: There is a secret force that fixes the extreme limits between which value oscillates, of which there is a mean term that expresses true value.

Surely no one wishes the postal service to be carried on at a loss; the opinion, therefore, is that this service should be performed at cost. This is so rudimentary in its simplicity that one is astonished that it should have been necessary to resort to a laborious investigation of the results of reducing letter-postage in England; to pile up frightful figures and probabilities beyond the limit of vision, to put the mind to torture, all to find out whether a reduction in France would lead to a surplus or a deficit, and finally to be unable to agree upon anything! What! there was not a man to be found in the Chamber with sense enough to say: There is no need of an ambassador's report or examples from England; letter-postage should be gradually reduced until receipts reach the level of expenditures. [25] What, then, has become of our old Gallic wit?

But, it will be said, if the tax should furnish salt, tobacco, letter-carriage, sugar, wines, meat, etc., at cost, consumption would undoubtedly increase, and the improvement would be enormous; but then how would the State meet its expenses? The amount of indirect taxes is nearly one hundred and twenty million dollars; upon what would you have the State levy this sum? If the treasury makes nothing out of the postal service, it will have to increase the tax on salt; if the tax on salt be lifted also, it will have to throw the burden back upon drinks; there would be no end to this litany. Therefore the supply of products at cost, whether by the State or by private industry, is impossible.

Therefore, I will reply in turn, relief of the unfortunate classes by the State is impossible, as sumptuary laws are impossible, as the progressive tax is impossible; and all your irrelevancies regarding the tax are lawyer's quibbles. You have not even the hope that the increase of population, by dividing the assessments, may lighten the burden of each; because with population misery increases, and with misery the work and the personnel of the State are augmented.

272

The various fiscal laws voted by the Chamber of Deputies during the session of 1845–46 are so many examples of the absolute incapacity of power, whatever it may be and however it may go to work, to procure the comfort of the people. From the very fact that it is power, — that is, the representative of divine right and of property, the organ of force, — it is necessarily sterile, and all its acts are stamped in the corner with a fatal deception.

I referred just now to the reform in the postage rates, which reduces the price of letter-carriage about one-third. Surely, if motives only are in question, I have no reason to reproach the government which has effected this useful reduction; much less still will I seek to diminish its merit by miserable criticisms upon matters of detail, the vile pasturage of the daily press. A tax, considerably burdensome, is reduced thirty per cent.; its distribution is made more equitable and more regular; I see only the fact, and I applaud the minister who has accomplished it. But that is not the question.

In the first place, the advantage which the government gives us by changing the tax on letters leaves the proportional — that is, the unjust — character of this tax intact: that scarcely requires demonstration. The inequality of burdens, so far as the postal tax is concerned, stands as before, the advantage of the reduction going principally, not to the poorest, but to the richest. A certain business house which paid six hundred dollars for letter-postage will pay hereafter only four hundred; it will add, then, a net profit of two hundred dollars to the ten thousand which its business brings it, and it will owe this to the munificence of the treasury. On the other hand, the peasant, the laborer, who shall write twice a year to his son in the army, and shall receive a like number of replies, will have saved ten cents. Is it not true that the postal reform acts in direct opposition to the equitable distribution of the tax? that if, according to M. Chevalier's wish, the government had desired to strike the rich and spare the poor, the tax on letters was the last that it would have needed to reduce? Does it not seem that the treasury, false to the spirit of its institution, has only been awaiting the pretext of a reduction inappreciable by poverty in order to seize the opportunity to make a present to wealth?

That is what the critics of the bill should have said, and that is what none of them saw. It is true that then the criticism, instead of applying to the minister, struck power in its essence, and with power property, which was not the design of the opponents. Truth today has all opinions against it.

And now could it have been otherwise? No, since, if they kept the old tax, they injured all without relieving any; and, if they reduced it, they could not make different rates for classes of citizens without violating the first article of the Charter, which says: "All Frenchmen are equal before the law," — that is, before the tax. Now, the tax on letters is necessarily personal; therefore it is a capitation-tax; therefore, that which is equity in this respect being iniquity from another standpoint, an equilibrium of burdens is impossible.

At the same time another reform was effected by the care of the government, — that of the tax on cattle. Formerly the duties on cattle, whether on importation from foreign countries, or from the country into the cities, were collected at so much a head; henceforth they will be collected according to weight. This useful reform, which has been clamored for so long, is due in part to the influence of the economists, who, on this occasion as on many others which I cannot recall, have shown the most honorable zeal, and have left the idle declamations of socialism very far in the rear. But here again the good resulting from the law for the amelioration of the condition of the poor is wholly illusory. They have equalized, regulated, the collection from beasts; they have not distributed it equitably among men. The rich man, who consumes twelve hundred pounds of meat a year, will feel the effects of the new condition laid upon the butchers; the immense majority of the people, who never eat meat, will not notice it. And I renew my question of a moment ago: Could the government, the Chamber, do otherwise than as it has done? No, once more; for you cannot say to the butcher: You shall sell your meat to the rich man for twenty cents a pound and to the poor man for five cents. It would be rather the contrary that you would obtain from the butcher.

So with salt. The government has reduced four-fifths the tax on salt used in agriculture, on condition of its undergoing a transformation. A certain journalist, having no better objection to raise, has made thereupon a complaint in which he grieves over the lot of those poor peasants who are more maltreated by the law than their cattle. For the third time I ask: Could it be otherwise? Of two things one: either the reduction will be absolute, and then the tax on salt must be replaced by a tax on something else; now I defy entire French journalism to invent a tax which will bear two minutes' examination; or else the reduction will be partial, whether by maintaining a portion of the duties on salt in all its uses, or by abolishing entirely the duties on salt used in certain ways. In the first case, the reduction is insufficient for agriculture and the poor; in the second, the capitation-tax still exists, in its enormous disproportion. Whatever may be done, it is the poor man, always the poor man, who is struck, since, in spite of all theories, the tax can never be laid except in the ratio of the capital possessed or consumed, and since, if the treasury should try to proceed otherwise, it would arrest progress, prohibit wealth, and kill capital.

The democrats, who reproach us with sacrificing the revolutionary interest (what is the revolutionary interest?) to the socialistic interest, ought really to tell us how, without making the State the sole proprietor and without decreeing the community of goods and gains, they mean, by any system of taxation whatever, to relieve the people and restore to labor what capital takes from it. In vain do I rack my brains; on all questions I see power placed in the falsest situation, and the opinion of journals straying into limitless absurdity.

In 1842 M. Arago was in favor of the administration of railways by corporations, and the majority in France thought with him. In 1846 he has announced a change in his opinion; and, apart from the speculators in railways, it may be said again that the majority of citizens have changed as M. Arago has. What is to be believed and what is to be done amid this see-sawing of the savants and of France?

State administration, it would seem, ought to better assure the interests of the country; but it is slow, expensive, and unintelligent. Twenty-five years of mistakes, miscalculations, improvidence, hundreds of millions thrown away, in the great work of canalizing the country, have proved it to the most incredulous. We have even seen engineers, members of the administration, loudly proclaiming the incapacity of the State in the matter of public works as well as of industry.

Administration by corporations is irreproachable, it is true, from the standpoint of the interest of the stockholders; but with these the general interest is sacrificed, the door opened to speculation, and the exploitation of the public by monopoly organized.

The ideal system would be one uniting the advantages of both methods without presenting any of their shortcomings. Now, the means of realizing these contradictory characteristics? the means of breathing zeal, economy, penetration into these irremovable officers who have nothing to gain or to lose? the means of rendering the interests of the public as dear to a corporation as its own, of making these interests veritably its own, and still keeping it distinct from the State and having consequently its private interests? Who is there, in the official world, that conceives the necessity and therefore the possibility of such a reconciliation? much more, then, who possesses its secret?

275

In such an emergency the government, as usual, has chosen the course of eclecticism; it has taken a part of the administration for itself and left the rest to the corporations; that is, instead of reconciling the contraries, it has placed them exactly in conflict. And the press, which in all things is precisely on a par with power in the matter of wit, — the press, dividing itself into three fractions, has decided, one for the ministerial compromise, another for the exclusion of the State, and the third for the exclusion of the corporations. So that today no more than before do the public or M. Arago, in spite of their somersault, know what they want.

What a herd is the French nation in this nineteenth century, with its three powers, its press, its scientific bodies, its literature, its instruction! A hundred thousand men, in our country, have their eyes constantly open upon everything that interests national progress and the country's honor. Now, propound to these hundred thousand men the simplest question of public order, and you may be assured that all will rush pell-mell into the same absurdity.

Is it better that the promotion of officials should be governed by merit or by length of service?

Certainly there is no one who would not like to see this double method of estimating capacities blended into one. What a society it would be in which the rights of talent would be always in harmony with those of age! But, they say, such perfection is utopian, for it is contradictory in its statement. And instead of seeing that it is precisely the contradiction which makes the thing possible, they begin to dispute over the respective value of the two opposed systems, which, each leading to the absurd, equally give rise to intolerable abuses.

Who shall be the judge of merit? asks one: the government. Now, the government recognizes merit only in its creatures. Therefore no promotion by choice, none of that immoral system which destroys the independence and the dignity of the office-holder.

But, says another, length of service is undoubtedly very respectable. It is a pity that it has the disadvantage of rendering stagnant things which are essentially voluntary and free, — labor and thought; of creating obstacles to power even among its agents, and of bestowing upon chance, often upon incapacity, the reward of genius and audacity.

Finally they compromise: to the government is accorded the power of appointing arbitrarily to a certain number of offices pretended men of merit, who are supposed to have no need of experience, while the rest, apparently deemed incapable, are promoted in turn. And the press, that ambling old nag of all presumptuous mediocrities, which generally lives only by the gratuitous compositions of young people as destitute of talent as of acquired knowledge, hastens to begin again its attacks upon power, accusing it, — not without reason too, — here of favoritism, there of routine.

Who could hope ever to do anything to the satisfaction of the press? After having declaimed and gesticulated against the enormous size of the budget, here it is clamoring for increased salaries for an army of officials, who, to tell the truth, really have not the wherewithal to live. Now it is the teachers, of high and low grade, who make their complaints heard through its columns; now it is the country clergy, so insufficiently paid that they have been forced to maintain their fees, a fertile source of scandal and abuse. Then it is the whole administrative nation, which is neither lodged, nor clothed, nor warmed, nor fed: it is a million men with their families, nearly an eighth of the population, whose poverty brings shame upon France and for whom one hundred million dollars should at once be added to the budget. Note that in this immense personnel there is not one man too many; on the contrary, if the population grows, it will increase proportionally. Are you in a position to tax the nation to the extent of four hundred million dollars? Can you take, out of an average income of $184 for four persons, $47.25 -more than one-fourth — to pay, together with the other expenses of the State, the salaries of the non-productive laborers? And if you cannot, if you can neither pay your expenses nor reduce them, what do you want? of what do you complain?

Let the people know it, then, once for all: all the hopes of reduction and equity in taxation, with which they are lulled by turns by the harangues of power and the diatribes of party leaders, are so many mystifications; the tax cannot be reduced, nor can its assessment be more equitable, under the monopoly system. On the contrary, the lower the condition of the citizen becomes, the heavier becomes his tax; that is inevitable, irresistible, in spite of the avowed design of the legislator and the repeated efforts of the treasury. Whoever cannot become or remain rich, whoever has entered the cavern of misfortune, must make up his mind to pay in proportion to his poverty: Lasciate ogni speranza, voi ch' entrate.

Taxation, then, police, — henceforth we shall not separate these two ideas, — is a new source of pauperism; taxation aggravates the subversive effects of the preceding antinomies, — division of labor, machinery, competition, monopoly. It attacks the laborer in his liberty and in his conscience, in his body and in his soul, by parasitism, vexations, the frauds which it prompts, and the punishments which follow them.

Under Louis XIV. the smuggling of salt alone caused annually thirty-seven hundred domiciliary seizures, two thousand arrests of men, eighteen hundred of women, sixty-six hundred of children, eleven hundred seizures of horses, fifty confiscations of carriages, and three hundred condemnations to the galleys. And this, observes the historian, was the result of one tax alone, — the salt-tax. What, then, was the total number of unfortunates imprisoned, tortured, expropriated, on account of the tax?

In England, out of every four families, one is unproductive, and that is the family which enjoys an abundance. What an advantage it would be for the working-class, you think, if this leprosy of parasitism should be removed! Undoubtedly, in theory, you are right; in practice, the suppression of parasitism would be a calamity. Though one-fourth of the population of England is unproductive, another fourth of the same population is at work for it: now, what would these laborers do, if they should suddenly lose the market for their products? An absurd supposition, you say. Yes, an absurd supposition, but a very real supposition, and one which you must admit precisely because it is absurd. In France a standing army of five hundred thousand men, forty thousand priests, twenty thousand doctors, eighty thousand lawyers, and I know not how many hundred thousand other nonproducers of every sort, constitute an immense market for our agriculture and our manufactures. Let this market suddenly close, and manufactures will stop, commerce will go into bankruptcy, and agriculture will be smothered beneath its products.

But how is it conceivable that a nation should find its market clogged because of having got rid of its useless mouths? Ask rather why an engine, whose consumption has been figured at six hundred pounds of coal an hour, loses its power if it is given only three hundred. But again, might not these non-producers be made producers, since we cannot get rid of them? Eh! child: tell me, then, how you will do without police, and monopoly, and competition, and all the contradictions, in short, of which your order of things is made up. Listen.

In 1844, at the time of the troubles in Rive-de-Gier, M. Anselme Petetin published in the "Revue Independante" two articles, full of reason and sincerity, concerning the anarchy prevailing in the conduct

278

of the coal mines in the basin of the Loire. M. Petetin pointed out the necessity of uniting the mines and centralizing their administration. The facts which he laid before the public were not unknown to power; has power troubled itself about the union of the mines and the organization of that industry? Not at all. Power has followed the principle of free competition; it has let alone and looked on.

Since that time the mining companies have combined, not without causing some anxiety to consumers, who have seen in this combination a plot to raise the price of fuel. Will power, which has received numerous complaints upon this subject, intervene to restore competition and prevent monopoly? It cannot do it; the right of combination is identical in law with the right of association; monopoly is the basis of our society, as competition is its conquest; and, provided there is no riot, power will let alone and look on. What other course could it pursue? Can it prohibit a legally established commercial association? Can it oblige neighbors to destroy each other? Can it forbid them to reduce their expenses? Can it establish a maximum? If power should do any one of these things, it would overturn the established order. Power, therefore, can take no initiative: it is instituted to defend and protect monopoly and competition at once, within the limitations of patents, licenses, land taxes, and other bonds which it has placed upon property. Apart from these limitations power has no sort of right to act in the name of society. The social right is not defined; moreover, it would be a denial of monopoly and competition. How, then, could power take up the defence of that which the law did not foresee or define, of that which is the opposite of the rights recognized by the legislator?

Consequently, when the miner, whom we must consider in the events of Rive-de-Gier as the real representative of society against the mine-owners, saw fit to resist the scheme of the monopolists by defending his wages and opposing combination to combination, power shot the miner down. And the political brawlers accused authority, saying it was partial, ferocious, sold to monopoly, etc. For my part, I declare that this way of viewing the acts of authority seems to me scarcely philosophical, and I reject it with all my energies. It is possible that they might have killed fewer people, possible also that they might have killed more: the fact to be noticed here is not the number of dead and wounded, but the repression of the workers. Those who have criticised authority would have done as it did, barring perhaps the impatience of its bayonets and the accuracy of its aim: they would have repressed, I say; they would not have been able to do anything else. And the reason, which it would be vain to try to brush aside, is that competition is legal,

279

joint-stock association is legal, supply and demand are legal, and all the consequences which flow directly from competition, joint-stock association, and free commerce are legal, whereas workingmen's strikes are ILLEGAL. And it is not only the penal code which says this, but the economic system, the necessity of the established order. As long as labor is not sovereign, it must be a slave; society is possible only on this condition. That each worker individually should have the free disposition of his person and his arms may be tolerated; [26] but that the workers should undertake, by combinations, to do violence to monopoly society cannot permit. Crush monopoly, and you abolish competition, and you disorganize the workshop, and you sow dissolution everywhere. Authority, in shooting down the miners, found itself in the position of Brutus placed between his paternal love and his consular duties: he had to sacrifice either his children or the republic. The alternative was horrible, I admit; but such is the spirit and letter of the social compact, such is the tenor of the charter, such is the order of Providence.

Thus the police function, instituted for the defence of the proletariat, is directed entirely against the proletariat. The proletaire is driven from the forests, from the rivers, from the mountains; even the cross-roads are forbidden him; soon he will know no road save that which leads to prison.

The advance in agriculture has made the advantage of artificial meadows and the necessity of abolishing common land generally felt. Everywhere communal lands are being cleared, let, enclosed; new advances, new wealth. But the poor day-laborer, whose only patrimony is the communal land and who supports a cow and several sheep in summer by letting them feed along the roads, through the underbrush, and over the stripped fields, will lose his sole and last resource. The landed proprietor, the purchaser or farmer of the communal lands, will alone thereafter sell, with his wheat and vegetables, milk and cheese. Instead of weakening an old monopoly, they create a new one. Even the road-laborers reserve for themselves the edges of the roads as a meadow belonging to them, and drive off all non-administrative cattle. What follows? That the day-laborer, before abandoning his cow, lets it feed in contravention of the law, becomes a marauder, commits a thousand depredations, and is punished by fine and imprisonment: of what use to him are police and agricultural progress? Last year the mayor of Mulhouse, to prevent grape-stealing, forbade every individual not an owner of vines to travel by day or night over roads running by or through vineyards, — a charitable precaution, since it prevented even desires and regrets. But if the public highway is nothing but an accessory of private property; if the communal lands are converted into private property; if the public domain, in short, assimilated to private property, is guarded, exploited, leased, and sold like private property, — what remains for the proletaire? Of what advantage is it to him that society has left the state of war to enter the regime of police?

Industry, as well as land, has its privileges, — privileges consecrated by the law, as always, under conditions and reservations, but, as always also, to the great disadvantage of the consumer. The question is interesting; we will say a few words upon it.

I quote M. Renouard.

"Privileges," says M. Renouard, "were a corrective of regulation."

I ask M. Renouard's permission to translate his thought by reversing his phrase: Regulation was a corrective of privilege. For whoever says regulation says limitation: now, how conceive of limiting privilege before it existed? I can conceive a sovereign submitting privileges to regulations; but I cannot at all understand why he should create privileges expressly to weaken the effect of regulations. There is nothing to prompt such a concession; it would be an effect without a cause. In logic as well as in history, everything is appropriated and monopolized when laws and regulations arrive: in this respect civil legislation is like penal legislation. The first results from possession and appropriation, the second from the appearance of crimes and offences. M. Renouard, preoccupied with the idea of servitude inherent in all regulation, has considered privilege as a compensation for this servitude; and it was this which led him to say that privileges are a corrective of regulation. But what M. Renouard adds proves that he meant the opposite:

The fundamental principle of our legislation, that of granting temporary monopoly as a condition of a contract between society and the laborer, has always prevailed, etc.

What is, in reality, this grant of a monopoly? A simple acknowledgment, a declaration. Society, wishing to favor a new industry and enjoy the advantages which it promises, bargains with the inventor, as it has bargained with the farmer; it guarantees him the monopoly of his industry for a time; but it does not create the monopoly. The monopoly exists by the very fact of the invention; and the acknowledgment of the monopoly is what constitutes society.

281

This ambiguity cleared up, I pass to the contradictions of the law.

All industrial nations have adopted the establishment of a temporary monopoly as a condition of a contract between society and the inventor..... I do not take readily to the belief that all legislators of all countries have committed robbery.

M. Renouard, if ever he reads this work, will do me the justice to admit that, in quoting him, I do not criticise his thought; he himself has perceived the contradictions of the patent law. All that I pretend is to connect this contradiction with the general system.

Why, in the first place, a temporary monopoly in manufacture, while land monopoly is perpetual? The Egyptians were more logical; with them these two monopolies were alike hereditary, perpetual, inviolable. I know the considerations which have prevailed against the perpetuity of literary property, and I admit them all; but these considerations apply equally well to property in land; moreover, they leave intact all the arguments brought forward against them. What, then, is the secret of all these variations of the legislator? For the rest, I do not need to say that, in pointing out this inconsistency, it is not my purpose either to slander or to satirize; I admit that the course of the legislator is determined, not by his will, but by necessity.

But the most flagrant contradiction is that which results from the enacting section of the law. Title IV, article 30, 3, reads: "If the patent relates to principles, methods, systems, discoveries, theoretical or purely scientific conceptions, without indicating their industrial applications, the patent is void."

Now, what is a principle, a method, a theoretical conception, a system? It is the especial fruit of genius, it is invention in its purity, it is the idea, it is everything. The application is the gross fact, nothing. Thus the law excludes from the benefit of the patent the very thing which deserves it, — namely, the idea; on the contrary, it grants a patent to the application, — that is, to the material fact, to a pattern of the idea, as Plato would have said. Therefore it is wrongly called a patent for invention; it should be called a patent for first occupancy.

In our day, if a man had invented arithmetic, algebra, or the decimal system, he would have obtained no patent; but Bareme would have had a right of property in his Computations. Pascal, for his theory of the weight of the atmosphere, would not have been patented; instead of

282

him, a glazier would have obtained the privilege of the barometer. I quote M. Arago:

After two thousand years it occurred to one of our fellow-countrymen that the screw of Archimedes, which is used to raise water, might be employed in forcing down gases; it suffices, without making any change, to turn it from right to left, instead of turning it, as when raising water, from left to right. Large volumes of gas, charged with foreign substances, are thus forced into water to a great depth; the gas is purified in rising again. I maintain that there was an invention; that the person who saw a way to make the screw of Archimedes a blowing machine was entitled to a patent.

What is more extraordinary is that Archimedes himself would thus be obliged to buy the right to use his screw; and M. Arago considers that just.

It is useless to multiply these examples: what the law meant to monopolize is, as I said just now, not the idea, but the fact; not the invention, but the occupancy. As if the idea were not the category which includes all the facts that express it; as if a method, a system, were not a generalization of experiences, and consequently that which properly constitutes the fruit of genius, — invention! Here legislation is more than anti-economic, it borders on the silly. Therefore I am entitled to ask the legislator why, in spite of free competition, which is nothing but the right to apply a theory, a principle, a method, a non-appropriable system, he forbids in certain cases this same competition, this right to apply a principle?" It is no longer possible," says M. Renouard, with strong reason, "to stifle competitors by combining in corporations and guilds; the loss is supplied by patents." Why has the legislator given hands to this conspiracy of monopolies, to this interdict upon theories belonging to all?

But what is the use of continually questioning one who can say nothing? The legislator did not know in what spirit he was acting when he made this strange application of the right of property, which, to be exact, we ought to call the right of priority. Let him explain himself, then, at least, regarding the clauses of the contract made by him, in our name, with the monopolists.

I pass in silence the part relating to dates and other administrative and fiscal formalities, and come to this article:

The patent does not guarantee the invention.

Doubtless society, or the prince who represents it, cannot and should not guarantee the invention, since, in granting a monopoly for fourteen years, society becomes the purchaser of the privilege, and consequently it is for the patentee to furnish the guarantee. How, then, can legislators proudly say to their constituents: "We have negotiated in your name with an inventor; he pledges himself to give you the enjoyment of his discovery on condition of having the exclusive exploitation for fourteen years. But we do not guarantee the invention"? On what, then, have you relied, legislators? How did you fail to see that, without a guarantee of the invention, you conceded a privilege, not for a real discovery, but for a possible discovery, and that thus the field of industry was given up by you before the plough was found? Certainly, your duty bade you to be prudent; but who gave you a commission to be dupes?

Thus the patent for invention is not even the fixing of a date; it is an abandonment in anticipation. It is as if the law should say: "I assure the land to the first occupant, but without guaranteeing its quality, its location, or even its existence; not even knowing whether I ought to give it up or that it falls within the domain of appropriation!" A pretty use of the legislative power!

I know that the law had excellent reasons for abstaining; but I maintain that it also had good reasons for intervening. Proof:

"It cannot be concealed," says M. Renouard, "it cannot be prevented; patents are and will be instruments of quackery as well as a legitimate reward of labor and genius.... It is for the good sense of the public to do justice to juggleries."

As well say it is for the good sense of the public to distinguish true remedies from false, pure wine from adulterated; or, it is for the good sense of the public to distinguish in a buttonhole the decoration awarded to merit from that prostituted to mediocrity and intrigue. Why, then, do you call yourselves the State, Power, Authority, Police, if the work of Police must be performed by the good sense of the public?

As the proverb says, he who owns land must defend it; likewise, he who holds a privilege is liable to attack.

Well! how will you judge the counterfeit, if you have no guarantee? In vain will they offer you the plea: in right first occupancy, in fact similarity. Where reality depends upon quality, not to demand a guarantee is to grant no right over anything, is to take away the means of comparing processes and identifying the counterfeit. In the matter of

284

industrial processes success depends upon such trifles! Now, these trifles are the whole.

I infer from all this that the law regarding patents for inventions, indispensable so far as its motives are concerned, is impossible — that is, illogical, arbitrary, disastrous — in its economy. Under the control of certain necessities the legislator has thought best, in the general interest, to grant a privilege for a definite thing; and he finds that he has given a signature-in-blank to monopoly, that he has abandoned the chances which the public had of making the discovery or some other similar to it, that he has sacrificed the rights of competitors without compensation, and abandoned the good faith of defenceless consumers to the greed of quacks. Then, in order that nothing might be lacking to the absurdity of the contract, he has said to those whom he ought to guarantee: "Guarantee yourselves!"

I do not believe, any more than M. Renouard, that the legislators of all ages and all countries have wilfully committed robbery in sanctioning the various monopolies which are pivotal in public economy. But M. Renouard might well also agree with me that the legislators of all ages and all countries have never understood at all their own decrees. A deaf and blind man once learned to ring the village bells and wind the village clock. It was fortunate for him, in performing his bell-ringer's functions, that neither the noise of the bells nor the height of the bell-tower made him dizzy. The legislators of all ages and all countries, for whom I profess, with M. Renouard, the profoundest respect, resemble that blind and deaf man; they are the Jacks-in-the-clock-house of all human follies.

What a feather it would be in my cap if I should succeed in making these automata reflect! if I could make them understand that their work is a Penelope's web, which they are condemned to unravel at one end as fast as they weave at the other!

Thus, while applauding the creation of patents, on other points they demand the abolition of privileges, and always with the same pride, the same satisfaction. M. Horace Say wishes trade in meat to be free. Among other reasons he puts forward this strictly mathematical argument:

The butcher who wants to retire from business seeks a purchaser for his investment; he figures in the account his tools, his merchandise, his reputation, and his custom; but under the present system, he adds to these the value of the bare title, — that is, the right to share in a monopoly. Now, this supplementary capital which the purchasing butcher gives for the title bears interest; it is not a new creation; this interest must enter into the price of his meat. Hence the limitation of the number of butchers' stalls has a tendency to raise the price of meat rather than lower it.

I do not fear to affirm incidentally that what I have just said about the sale of a butcher's stall applies to every charge whatever having a salable title.

M. Horace Say's reasons for the abolition of the butcher's privilege are unanswerable; moreover, they apply to printers, notaries, attorneys, process-servers, clerks of courts, auctioneers, brokers, dealers in stocks, druggists, and others, as well as to butchers. But they do not destroy the reasons which have led to the adoption of these monopolies, and which are generally deduced from the need of security, authenticity, and regularity in business, as well as from the interests of commerce and the public health. The object, you say, is not attained. My God! I know it: leave the butcher's trade to competition, and you will eat carrion; establish a monopoly in the butcher's trade, and you will eat carrion. That is the only fruit you can hope for from your monopoly and patent legislation.

Abuses! cry the protective economists. Establish over commerce a supervisory police, make trade-marks obligatory, punish the adulteration of products, etc.

In the path upon which civilization has entered, whichever way we turn, we always end, then, either in the despotism of monopoly, and consequently the oppression of consumers, or else in the annihilation of privilege by the action of the police, which is to go backwards in economy and dissolve society by destroying liberty. Marvellous thing! in this system of free industry, abuses, like lice, being generated by their own remedies, if the legislator should try to suppress all offences, be on the watch against all frauds, and secure persons, property, and the public welfare against any attack, going from reform to reform, he would finally so multiply the non-productive functions that the entire nation would be engaged in them, and that at last there would be nobody left to produce. Everybody would be a policeman; the industrial class would become a myth. Then, perhaps, order would reign in monopoly.

"The principle of the law yet to be made concerning trade-marks," says M. Renouard, "is that these marks cannot and should not be transformed into guarantees of quality."

This is a consequence of the patent law, which, as we have seen, does not guarantee the invention. Adopt M. Renouard's principle; after that of what use will marks be? Of what importance is it to me to read on the cork of a bottle, instead of twelve-cent wine or fifteen-cent wine, WINE-DRINKERS' COMPANY or the name of any other concern you will? What I care for is not the name of the merchant, but the quality and fair price of the merchandise.

The name of the manufacturer is supposed, it is true, to serve as a concise sign of good or bad manufacture, of superior or inferior quality. Then why not frankly take part with those who ask, besides the mark of origin, a mark significant of something? Such a reservation is incomprehensible. The two sorts of marks have the same purpose; the second is only a statement or paraphrase of the first, a condensation of the merchant's prospectus; why, once more, if the origin signifies something, should not the mark define this significance?

M. Wolowski has very clearly developed this argument in his opening lecture of 1843–44, the substance of which lies entirely in the following analogy:

Just as the government has succeeded in determining a standard of quantity, it may, it should also fix a standard of quality; one of these standards is the necessary complement of the other. The monetary unit, the system of weights and measures, have not infringed upon industrial liberty; no more would it be damaged by a system of trade-marks.

M. Wolowski then supports himself on the authority of the princes of the science, A. Smith and J. B. Say, — a precaution always useful with hearers who bow to authority much more than to reason.

I declare, for my part, that I thoroughly share M. Wolowski's idea, and for the reason that I find it profoundly revolutionary. The trade-mark, being, according to M. Wolowski's expression, nothing but a standard of qualities, is equivalent in my eyes to a general scheduling of prices. For, whether a particular administration marks in the name of the State and guarantees the quality of the merchandise, as is the case with gold and silver, or whether the matter of marking is left to the manufacturer, from the moment that the mark must give the intrinsic composition of the merchandise (these are M. Wolowski's own words) and guarantee the consumer against all surprise, it necessarily resolves itself into a fixed price. It is not the same thing as price; two similar products, but differing in origin and quality, may be of equal value, as a bottle of Burgundy may be worth a bottle of Bordeaux; but the mark, being significant, leads to an exact knowledge of the price, since it gives the analysis. To calculate the price of an article of merchandise is to decompose it into its constituent parts; now, that is exactly what the trade-mark must do, if designed to signify anything. Therefore we are on the road, as I have said, to a general scheduling of prices.

But a general scheduling of prices is nothing but a determination of all values, and here again political economy comes into conflict with its own principles and tendencies. Unfortunately, to realize M. Wolowski's reform, it is necessary to begin by solving all the previous contradictions and enter a higher sphere of association; and it is this absence of solution which has brought down upon M. Wolowski's system the condemnation of most of his fellow-economists.

In fact, the system of trade-marks is inapplicable in the existing order, because this system, contrary to the interests of the manufacturers and repugnant to their habits, could be sustained only by the energetic will of power. Suppose for a moment that the administration be charged with affixing the marks; its agents will have to interpose continually in the work of manufacture, as it interposes in the liquor business and the manufacture of beer; further, these agents, whose functions seem already so intrusive and annoying, deal only with taxable quantities, not with exchangeable qualities. These fiscal supervisors and inspectors will have to carry their investigation into all details in order to repress and prevent fraud; and what fraud? The legislator will have defined it either incorrectly or not at all; it is at this point that the task becomes appalling.

There is no fraud in selling wine of the poorest quality, but there is fraud in passing off one quality for another; then you are obliged to differentiate the qualities of wines, and consequently to guarantee them. Is it fraudulent to mix wines? Chaptal, in his treatise on the art of making wine, advises this as eminently useful; on the other hand, experience proves that certain wines, in some way antagonistic to each other or incompatible, produce by their mixture a disagreeable and unhealthy drink. Then you are obliged to say what wines can be usefully mixed, and what cannot. Is it fraudulent to aromatize, alcoholize, and water wines? Chaptal recommends this also; and everybody knows that this drugging produces sometimes advantageous results, sometimes pernicious and detestable effects. What substances will you proscribe? In what cases? In what proportion? Will you prohibit chicory in coffee, glucose in beer, water, cider, and three-six alcohol in wine?

The Chamber of Deputies, in the rude attempt at a law which it was pleased to make this year regarding the adulteration of wines, stopped in the very middle of its work, overcome by the inextricable difficulties of the question. It succeeded in declaring that the introduction of water into wine, and of alcohol above the proportion of eighteen per cent., was fraudulent, and in putting this fraud into the category of offences. It was on the ground of ideology; there one never meets an obstacle. But everybody has seen in this redoubling of severity the interest of the treasury much more than that of the consumer; the Chamber did not dare to create a whole army of wine-tasters, inspectors, etc., to watch for fraud and identify it, and thus load the budget with a few extra millions; in prohibiting watering and alcoholization, the only means left to the merchant-manufacturers of putting wine within the reach of all and realizing profits, it did not succeed in increasing the market by a decrease in production. The chamber, in a word, in prosecuting the adulteration of wines, has simply set back the limits of fraud. To make its work accomplish its purpose it would first have to show how the liquor trade is possible without adulteration, and how the people can buy unadulterated wine, — which is beyond the competency and escapes the capacity of the Chamber.

If you wish the consumer to be guaranteed, both as to value and as to healthfulness, you are forced to know and to determine all that constitutes good and honest production, to be continually at the heels of the manufacturer, and to guide him at every step. He no longer manufactures; you, the State, are the real manufacturer.

Thus you find yourself in a trap. Either you hamper the liberty of commerce by interfering in production in a thousand ways, or you declare yourself sole producer and sole merchant.

In the first case, through annoying everybody, you will finally cause everybody to rebel; and sooner or later, the State getting itself expelled, trade-marks will be abolished. In the second you substitute everywhere the action of power for individual initiative, which is contrary to the principles of political economy and the constitution of society. Do you take a middle course? It is favor, nepotism, hypocrisy, the worst of systems.

289

Suppose, now, that the marking be left to the manufacturer. I say that then the marks, even if made obligatory, will gradually lose their significance, and at last become only proofs of origin. He knows but little of commerce who imagines that a merchant, a head of a manufacturing enterprise, making use of processes that are not patentable, will betray the secret of his industry, of his profits, of his existence. The significance will then be a delusion; it is not in the power of the police to make it otherwise. The Roman emperors, to discover the Christians who dissembled their religion, obliged everybody to sacrifice to the idols. They made apostates and martyrs; and the number of Christians only increased. Likewise significant marks, useful to some houses, will engender innumerable frauds and repressions; that is all that can be expected of them. To induce the manufacturer to frankly indicate the intrinsic composition — that is, the industrial and commercial value — of his merchandise, it is necessary to free him from the perils of competition and satisfy his monopolistic instincts: can you do it? It is necessary, further, to interest the consumer in the repression of fraud, which, so long as the producer is not utterly disinterested, is at once impossible and contradictory. Impossible: place on the one hand a depraved consumer, China; on the other a desperate merchant, England; between them a venomous drug causing excitement and intoxication; and, in spite of all the police in the world, you will have trade in opium. Contradictory: in society the consumer and the producer are but one, — that is, both are interested in the production of that which it is injurious to them to consume; and as, in the case of each, consumption follows production and sale, all will combine to guard the first interest, leaving it to each to guard himself against the second.

The thought which prompted trade-marks is of the same character as that which formerly inspired the maximum laws. Here again is one of the innumerable cross-roads of political economy.

It is indisputable that maximum laws, though made and supported by their authors entirely as a relief from famine, have invariably resulted in an aggravation of famine. Accordingly it is not injustice or malice with which the economists charge these abhorred laws, but stupidity, inexpediency. But what a contradiction in the theory with which they oppose them!

To relieve famine it is necessary to call up provisions, or, to put it better, to bring them to light; so far there is nothing to reproach. To secure a supply of provisions it is necessary to attract the holders by profits, excite their competition, and assure them complete liberty in

290

the market: does not this process strike you as the absurdest homoeopathy? How is it that the more easily I can be taxed the sooner I shall be provided? Let alone, they say, let pass; let competition and monopoly act, especially in times of famine, and even though famine is the effect of competition and monopoly. What logic! but, above all, what morality!

But why, then, should there not be a tariff for farmers as well as for bakers? Why not a registration of the sowing, of the harvest, of the vintage, of the pasturage, and of the cattle, as well as a stamp for newspapers, circulars, and orders, or an administration for brewers and wine-merchants? Under the monopoly system this would be, I admit, an increase of torments; but with our tendencies to unfairness in trade and the disposition of power to continually increase its personnel and its budget, a law of inquisition regarding crops is becoming daily more indispensable.

Besides, it would be difficult to say which, free trade or the maximum, causes the more evil in times of famine.

But, whichever course you choose, — and you cannot avoid the alternative, — the deception is sure and the disaster immense. With the maximum goods seek concealment; the terror increasing from the very effect of the law, the price of provisions rises and rises; soon circulation stops, and the catastrophe follows, as prompt and pitiless as a band of plunderers. With competition the progress of the scourge is slower, but no less fatal: how many deaths from exhaustion or hunger before the high prices attract food to the market! how many victims of extortion after it has arrived! It is the story of the king to whom God, in punishment for his pride, offered the alternative of three days' pestilence, three months' famine, or three years' war. David chose the shortest; the economists prefer the longest. Man is so miserable that he would rather end by consumption than by apoplexy; it seems to him that he does not die as much. This is the reason why the disadvantages of the maximum and the benefits of free trade have been so much exaggerated.

For the rest, if France during the last twenty-five years has experienced no general famine, the cause is not in the liberty of commerce, which knows very well, when it wishes, how to produce scarcity in the midst of plenty and how to make famine prevail in the bosom of abundance; it is in the improvement in the methods of communication, which, shortening distances, soon restore the equilibrium disturbed for a moment by local penury. A striking example of that sad truth that in society the general welfare is never the effect of a conspiracy of individual wills!

The farther we delve into this system of illusory compromises between monopoly and society, — that is, as we have explained in 1 of this chapter, between capital and labor, between the patriciate and the proletariat, -the more we discover that it is all foreseen, regulated, and executed in accordance with this infernal maxim, with which Hobbes and Machiavel, those theorists of despotism, were unacquainted: EVERYTHING BY THE PEOPLE AND AGAINST THE PEOPLE. While labor produces, capital, under the mask of a false fecundity, enjoys and abuses; the legislator, in offering his mediation, thought to recall the privileged class to fraternal feelings and surround the laborer with guarantees; and now he finds, by the fatal contradiction of interests, that each of these guarantees is an instrument of torture. It would require a hundred volumes, the life of ten men, and a heart of iron, to relate from this standpoint the crimes of the State towards the poor and the infinite variety of its tortures. A summary glance at the principal classes of police will be enough to enable us to estimate its spirit and economy.

After having sown trouble in all minds by a confusion of civil, commercial, and administrative laws, made the idea of justice more obscure by multiplying contradictions, and rendered necessary a whole class of interpreters for the explanation of this system, it has been found necessary also to organize the repression of crimes and provide for their punishment. Criminal justice, that particularly rich order of the great family of non-producers, whose maintenance costs France annually more than six million dollars, has become to society a principle of existence as necessary as bread is to the life of man; but with this difference, — that man lives by the product of his hands, while society devours its members and feeds on its own flesh.

It is calculated by some economists that there is,

In London..   1 criminalto every 89 inhabitants.

In Liverpool.. 1 ” ”   45 ”

In Newcastle.. 1 ” ”   27 ”

But these figures lack accuracy, and, utterly frightful as they seem, do not express the real degree of social perversion due to the police. We have to determine here not only the number of recognized criminals, but the number of offences. The work of the criminal courts is only a special mechanism which serves to place in relief the moral destruction of humanity under the monopoly system; but this official exhibition is far from including the whole extent of the evil. Here are other figures which will lead us to a more certain approximation.

The police courts of Paris disposed,

In 1835.... of 106,467 cases.

In 1836.... " 128,489 "

In 1837.... " 140,247 "

Supposing this rate of increase to have continued up to 1846, and to this total of misdemeanors adding the cases of the criminal courts, the simple matters that go no further than the police, and all the offences unknown or left unpunished, — offences far surpassing in number, so the magistrates say, those which justice reaches, — we shall arrive at the conclusion that in one year, in the city of Paris, there are more infractions of the law committed than there are inhabitants. And as it is necessary to deduct from the presumable authors of these infractions children of seven years and under, who are outside the limits of guilt, the figures will show that every adult citizen is guilty, three or four times a year, of violating the established order.

Thus the proprietary system is maintained at Paris only by the annual consummation of one or two millions of offences! Now, though all these offences should be the work of a single man, the argument would still hold good: this man would be the scapegoat loaded with the sins of Israel: of what consequence is the number of the guilty, provided justice has its contingent?

Violence, perjury, robbery, cheating, contempt of persons and society, are so much a part of the essence of monopoly; they flow from it so naturally, with such perfect regularity, and in accordance with laws so certain, — that it is possible to submit their perpetration to calculation, and, given the number of a population, the condition of its industry, and the stage of its enlightenment, to rigorously deduce therefrom the

293

statistics of its morality. The economists do not know yet what the principle of value is; but they know, within a few decimals, the proportionality of crime. So many thousand souls, so many malefactors, so many condemnations: about that there can be no mistake. It is one of the most beautiful applications of the theory of chances, and the most advanced branch of economic science. If socialism had invented this accusing theory, the whole world would have cried calumny.

Yet, after all, what is there in it that should surprise us? As misery is a necessary result of the contradictions of society, a result which it is possible to determine mathematically from the rate of interest, the rate of wages, and the prevailing market-prices, so crimes and misdemeanors are another effect of this same antagonism, susceptible, like its cause, of estimation by figures. The materialists have drawn the silliest inferences from this subordination of liberty to the laws of numbers: as if man were not under the influence of all that surrounds him, and as if, since all that surrounds him is governed by inexorable laws, he must not experience, in his freest manifestations, the reaction of those laws!

The same character of necessity which we have just pointed out in the establishment and sustenance of criminal justice is found, but under a more metaphysical aspect, in its morality.

In the opinion of all moralists, the penalty should be such as to secure the reformation of the offender, and consequently free from everything that might cause his degradation. Far be it from me to combat this blessed tendency of minds and disparage attempts which would have been the glory of the greatest men of antiquity. Philanthropy, in spite of the ridicule which sometimes attaches to its name, will remain, in the eyes of posterity, the most honorable characteristic of our time: the abolition of the death penalty, which is merely postponed; the abolition of the stigma; the studies regarding the effects of the cellular system; the establishment of workshops in the prisons; and a multitude of other reforms which I cannot even name, — give evidence of real progress in our ideas and in our morals. What the author of Christianity, in an impulse of sublime love, related of his mystical kingdom, where the repentant sinner was to be glorified above the just and the innocent man, — that utopia of Christian charity has become the aspiration of our sceptical society; and when one thinks of the unanimity of feeling which prevails in respect to it, he asks himself with surprise who then prevents this aspiration from being realized.

294

Alas! it is because reason is still stronger than love, and logic more tenacious than crime; it is because here as everywhere in our civilization there reigns an insoluble contradiction. Let us not wander into fantastic worlds; let us embrace, in all its frightful nudity, the real one.

Le crime fait la honte, et non pas l'echafaud, [27]

says the proverb. By the simple fact that man is punished, provided he deserved to be, he is degraded: the penalty renders him infamous, not by virtue of the definition of the code, but by reason of the fault which caused the punishment. Of what importance, then, is the materiality of the punishment? of what importance all your penitentiary systems? What you do is to satisfy your feelings, but is powerless to rehabilitate the unfortunate whom your justice strikes. The guilty man, once branded by chastisement, is incapable of reconciliation; his stain is indelible, and his damnation eternal. If it were possible for it to be otherwise, the penalty would cease to be proportional to the offence; it would be no more than a fiction, it would be nothing. He whom misery has led to larceny, if he suffers himself to fall into the hands of justice, remains forever the enemy of God and men; better for him that he had never been born; it was Jesus Christ who said it: Bonum erat ei, si natus non fulsset homo ille. And what Jesus Christ declared, Christians and infidels do not dispute: the irreparability of shame is, of all the revelations of the Gospel, the only one which the proprietary world has understood. Thus, separated from nature by monopoly, cut off from humanity by poverty, the mother of crime and its punishment, what refuge remains for the plebeian whom labor cannot support, and who is not strong enough to take?

To conduct this offensive and defensive war against the proletariat a public force was indispensable: the executive power grew out of the necessities of civil legislation, administration, and justice. And there again the most beautiful hopes have changed into bitter disappointments.

As legislator, as burgomaster, and as judge, the prince has set himself up as a representative of divine authority. A defender of the poor, the widow, and the orphan, he has promised to cause liberty and equality to prevail around the throne, to come to the aid of labor, and to listen to the voice of the people. And the people have thrown themselves lovingly into the arms of power; and, when experience has made them feel that power was against them, instead of blaming the institution, they have fallen to accusing the prince, ever unwilling to understand

295

that, the prince being by nature and destination the chief of non-producers and greatest of monopolists, it was impossible for him, in spite of himself, to take up the cause of the people.

All criticism, whether of the form or the acts of government, ends in this essential contradiction. And when the self-styled theorists of the sovereignty of the people pretend that the remedy for the tyranny of power consists in causing it to emanate from popular suffrage, they simply turn, like the squirrel, in their cage. For, from the moment that the essential conditions of power — that is, authority, property, hierarchy — are preserved, the suffrage of the people is nothing but the consent of the people to their oppression, — which is the silliest charlatanism.

In the system of authority, whatever its origin, monarchical or democratic, power is the noble organ of society; by it society lives and moves; all initiative emanates from it; order and perfection are wholly its work. According to the definitions of economic science, on the contrary, — definitions which harmonize with the reality of things, — power is the series of non-producers which social organization must tend to indefinitely reduce. How, then, with the principle of authority so dear to democrats, shall the aspiration of political economy, an aspiration which is also that of the people, be realized? How shall the government, which by the hypothesis is everything, become an obedient servant, a subordinate organ? Why should the prince have received power simply to weaken it, and why should he labor, with a view to order, for his own elimination? Why should he not try rather to fortify himself, to add to his courtiers, to continually obtain new subsidies, and finally to free himself from dependence on the people, the inevitable goal of all power originating in the people?

It is said that the people, naming its legislators and through them making its will known to power, will always be in a position to arrest its invasions; that thus the people will fill at once the role of prince and that of sovereign. Such, in a word, is the utopia of democrats, the eternal mystification with which they abuse the proletariat.

But will the people make laws against power; against the principle of authority and hierarchy, which is the principle upon which society is based; against liberty and property? According to our hypothesis, this is more than impossible, it is contradictory. Then property, monopoly, competition, industrial privileges, the inequality of fortunes, the preponderance of capital, hierarchical and crushing centralization, administrative oppression, legal absolutism, will be preserved; and, as it is impossible for a government not to act in the direction of its principle, capital will remain as before the god of society, and the people, still exploited, still degraded, will have gained by their attempt at sovereignty only a demonstration of their powerlessness.

In vain do the partisans of power, all those dynastico-republican doctrinaires who are alike in everything but tactics, flatter themselves that, once in control of affairs, they will inaugurate reform everywhere. Reform what?

Reform the constitution? It is impossible. Though the entire nation should enter the constitutional convention, it would not leave it until it had either voted its servitude under another form, or decreed its dissolution.

Reconstruct the code, the work of the emperor, the pure substance of Roman law and custom? It is impossible. What have you to put in the place of your proprietary routine, outside of which you see and understand nothing? in the place of your laws of monopoly, the limits of whose circle your imagination is powerless to overstep? More than half a century ago royalty and democracy, those two sibyls which the ancient world has bequeathed to us, undertook, by a constitutional compromise, to harmonize their oracles; since the wisdom of the prince has placed itself in unison with the voice of the people, what revelation has resulted? what principle of order has been discovered? what issue from the labyrinth of privilege pointed out? Before prince and people had signed this strange compromise, in what were their ideas not similar? and now that each is trying to break the contract, in what do they differ?

Diminish public burdens, assess taxes on a more equitable basis? It is impossible: to the treasury as to the army the man of the people will always furnish more than his contingent.

Regulate monopoly, bridle competition? It is impossible; you would kill production.

Open new markets? It is impossible. [28]

Organize credit? It is impossible. [29]

Attack heredity? It is impossible. [30]

Create national workshops, assure a minimum to unemployed workmen, and assign to employees a share of the profits? It is impossible. It is in the nature of government to be able to deal with labor only to enchain laborers, as it deals with products only to levy its tithe.

Repair, by a system of indemnities, the disastrous effects of machinery? It is impossible.

Combat by regulations the degrading influence of parcellaire division? It is impossible.

Cause the people to enjoy the benefits of education? It is impossible.

Establish a tariff of prices and wages, and fix the value of things by sovereign authority? It is impossible, it is impossible.

Of all the reforms which society in its distress solicits not one is within the competence of power; not one can be realized by it, because the essence of power is repugnant to them all, and it is not given to man to unite what God has divided.

At least, the partisans of governmental initiative will say, you will admit that, in the accomplishment of the revolution promised by the development of antinomies, power would be a potent auxiliary. Why, then, do you oppose a reform which, putting power in the hands of the people, would second your views so well? Social reform is the object; political reform is the instrument: why, if you wish the end, do you reject the means?

Such is today the reasoning of the entire democratic press, which I forgive with all my heart for having at last, by this quasi-socialistic confession of faith, itself proclaimed the emptiness of its theories. It is in the name of science, then, that democracy calls for a political reform as a preliminary to social reform. But science protests against this subterfuge as an insult; science repudiates any alliance with politics, and, very far from expecting from it the slightest aid, must begin with politics its work of exclusion.

How little affinity there is between the human mind and truth! When I see the democracy, socialistic but yesterday, continually asking for capital in order to combat capital's influence; for wealth, in order to cure poverty; for the abandonment of liberty, in order to organize

298

liberty; for the reformation of government, in order to reform society, — when I see it, I say, taking upon itself the responsibility of society, provided social questions be set aside or solved, it seems to me as if I were listening to a fortune-teller who, before answering the questions of those who consult her, begins by inquiring into their age, their condition, their family, and all the accidents of their life. Eh! miserable sorceress, if you know the future, you know who I am and what I want; why do you ask me to tell you?

Likewise I will answer the democrats: If you know the use that you should make of power, and if you know how power should be organized, you possess economic science. Now, if you possess economic science, if you have the key of its contradictions, if you are in a position to organize labor, if you have studied the laws of exchange, you have no need of the capital of the nation or of public force. From this day forth you are more potent than money, stronger than power. For, since the laborers are with you, you are by that fact alone masters of production; you hold commerce, manufactures, and agriculture enchained; you have the entire social capital at your disposition; you have full control of taxation; you block the wheels of power, and you trample monopoly under foot. What other initiative, what greater authority, do you ask? What prevents you from applying your theories?

Surely not political economy, although generally followed and accredited: for, everything in political economy having a true side and a false side, your only problem is to combine the economic elements in such a way that their total shall no longer present a contradiction.

Nor is it the civil law: for that law, sanctioning economic routine solely because of its advantages and in spite of its disadvantages, is susceptible, like political economy itself, of being bent to all the exigencies of an exact synthesis, and consequently is as favorable to you as possible.

Finally, it is not power, which, the last expression of antagonism and created only to defend the law, could stand in your way only by forswearing itself.

Once more, then, what stops you?

If you possess social science, you know that the problem of association consists in organizing, not only the non-producers, — in that direction, thank heaven! little remains to be done, — but also the producers, and by this organization subjecting capital and subordinating power. Such

299

is the war that you have to sustain: a war of labor against capital; a war of liberty against authority; a war of the producer against the non-producer; a war of equality against privilege. What you ask, to conduct the war to a successful conclusion, is precisely that which you must combat. Now, to combat and reduce power, to put it in its proper place in society, it is of no use to change the holders of power or introduce some variation into its workings: an agricultural and industrial combination must be found by means of which power, today the ruler of society, shall become its slave. Have you the secret of that combination?

But what do I say? That is precisely the thing to which you do not consent. As you cannot conceive of society without hierarchy, you have made yourselves the apostles of authority; worshippers of power, you think only of strengthening it and muzzling liberty; your favorite maxim is that the welfare of the people must be achieved in spite of the people; instead of proceeding to social reform by the extermination of power and politics, you insist on a reconstruction of power and politics. Then, by a series of contradictions which prove your sincerity, but the illusory character of which is well known to the real friends of power, the aristocrats and monarchists, your competitors, you promise us, in the name of power, economy in expenditures, an equitable assessment of taxes, protection to labor, gratuitous education, universal suffrage, and all the utopias repugnant to authority and property. Consequently power in your hands has never been anything but ruinous, and that is why you have never been able to retain it; that is why, on the Eighteenth of Brumaire, [31] four men were sufficient to take it away from you, and why today the bourgeoisie, which is as fond of power as you are and which wants a strong power, will not restore it to you.

Thus power, the instrument of collective might, created in society to serve as a mediator between labor and privilege, finds itself inevitably enchained to capital and directed against the proletariat. No political reform can solve this contradiction, since, by the confession of the politicians themselves, such a reform would end only in increasing the energy and extending the sphere of power, and since power would know no way of touching the prerogatives of monopoly without overturning the hierarchy and dissolving society. The problem before the laboring classes, then, consists, not in capturing, but in subduing both power and monopoly, — that is, in generating from the bowels of the people, from the depths of labor, a greater authority, a more potent fact, which shall envelop capital and the State and subjugate them. Every proposition of reform which does not satisfy this condition is

300

simply one scourge more, a rod doing sentry duty, virgem vigilantem, as a prophet said, which threatens the proletariat.

The crown of this system is religion. There is no occasion for me to deal here with the philosophic value of religious opinions, relate their history, or seek their interpretation. I confine myself to a consideration of the economic origin of religion, the secret bond which connects it with police, the place which it occupies in the series of social manifestations.

Man, despairing of finding the equilibrium of his powers, leaps, as it were, outside of himself and seeks in infinity that sovereign harmony the realization of which is to him the highest degree of reason, power, and happiness. Unable to harmonize with himself, he kneels before God and prays. He prays, and his prayer, a hymn sung to God, is a blasphemy against society.

It is from God, man says to himself, that authority and power come to me: then, let us obey God and the prince. Obedite Deo et principibus. It is from God that law and justice come to me. Per me reges regnant et potentes decernunt justitiam. Let us respect the commands of the legislator and the magistrate. It is God who controls the prosperity of labor, who makes and unmakes fortunes: may his will be done! Dominus dedit, Dominus abstulit, sit nomen Domini benedictum. It is God who punishes me when misery devours me, and when I am persecuted for righteousness's sake: let us receive with respect the scourges which his mercy employs for our purification. Humiliamini igitur sub potenti manu Dei. This life, which God has given me, is but an ordeal which leads me to salvation: let us shun pleasure; let us love and invite pain; let us find our pleasure in doing penance. The sadness which comes from injustice is a favor from on high; blessed are they that mourn! Beati qui lugent!.... Haec est enim gratia, si quis sustinet tristitias, patiens injuste.

A century ago a missionary, preaching before an audience made up of financiers and grandees, did justice to this odious morality. "What have I done?" he cried, with tears. "I have saddened the poor, the best friends of my God! I have preached the rigors of penance to unfortunates who want for bread! It is here, where my eyes fall only on the powerful and on the rich, on the oppressors of suffering humanity, that I must launch the word of God in all the force of its thunder!"

Let us admit, nevertheless, that the theory of resignation has served society by preventing revolt. Religion, consecrating by divine right the

301

inviolability of power and of privilege, has given humanity the strength to continue its journey and exhaust its contradictions. Without this bandage thrown over the eyes of the people society would have been a thousand times dissolved. Some one had to suffer that it might be cured; and religion, the comforter of the afflicted, decided that it should be the poor man. It is this suffering which has led us to our present position; civilization, which owes all its marvels to the laborer, owes also to his voluntary sacrifice its future and its existence. Oblatus est quia ipse voluit, et livore ejus sanati sumus.

O people of laborers! disinherited, harassed, proscribed people! people whom they imprison, judge, and kill! despised people, branded people! Do you not know that there is an end, even to patience, even to devotion? Will you not cease to lend an ear to those orators of mysticism who tell you to pray and to wait, preaching salvation now through religion, now through power, and whose vehement and sonorous words captivate you? Your destiny is an enigma which neither physical force, nor courage of soul, nor the illuminations of enthusiasm, nor the exaltation of any sentiment, can solve. Those who tell you to the contrary deceive you, and all their discourses serve only to postpone the hour of your deliverance, now ready to strike. What are enthusiasm and sentiment, what is vain poesy, when confronted with necessity? To overcome necessity there is nothing but necessity itself, the last reason of nature, the pure essence of matter and spirit.

Thus the contradiction of value, born of the necessity of free will, must be overcome by the proportionality of value, another necessity produced by the union of liberty and intelligence. But, in order that this victory of intelligent and free labor might produce all its consequences, it was necessary that society should pass through a long succession of torments.

It was a necessity that labor, in order to increase its power, should be divided; and a necessity, in consequence of this division, that the laborer should be degraded and impoverished.

It was a necessity that this original division should be reconstructed by scientific instruments and combinations; and a necessity, in consequence of this reconstruction, that the subordinated laborer should lose, together with his legitimate wages, even the exercise of the industry which supported him.

It was a necessity that competition then should step in to emancipate liberty on the point of perishing; and a necessity that this deliverance should end in a vast elimination of laborers.

It was a necessity that the producer, ennobled by his art, as formerly the warrior was by arms, should bear aloft his banner, in order that the valor of man might be honored in labor as in war; and a necessity that of privilege should straightway be born the proletariat.

It was a necessity that society should then take under its protection the conquered plebeian, a beggar without a roof; and a necessity that this protection should be converted into a new series of tortures.

We shall meet on our way still other necessities, all of which will disappear, like the others, before greater necessities, until shall come at last the general equation, the supreme necessity, the triumphant fact, which must establish the kingdom of labor forever.

But this solution cannot result either from surprise or from a vain compromise. It is as impossible to associate labor and capital as to produce without labor and without capital; as impossible to establish equality by power as to suppress power and equality and make a society without people and without police.

There is a necessity, I repeat, of a MAJOR FORCE to invert the actual formulas of society; a necessity that the LABOR of the people, not their valor nor their votes, should, by a scientific, legitimate, immortal, insurmountable combination, subject capital to the people and deliver to them power.

Chapter VIII. Of the Responsibility of Man and Of God, Under the Law of Contradiction, Or a Solution of the Problem of Providence.

THE ancients blamed human nature for the presence of evil in the world.

Christian theology has only embroidered this theme in its own fashion; and, as that theology sums up the whole religious period extending from the origin of society to our own time, it may be said that the dogma of original sin, having in its favor the assent of the human race, acquires by that very fact the highest degree of probability.

So, according to all the testimony of ancient wisdom, each people defending its own institutions as excellent and glorifying them, it is not to religions, or to governments, or to traditional customs accredited by the respect of generations, that the cause of evil must be traced, but rather to a primitive perversion, to a sort of congenital malice in the will of man. As to the question how a being could have perverted and corrupted itself originally, the ancients avoided that difficulty by fables: Eve's apple and Pandora's box have remained celebrated among their symbolic solutions.

Not only, then, had antiquity posited in its myths the question of the origin of evil; it had solved it by another myth, in unhesitatingly affirming the criminality ab ovo of our race.

Modern philosophers have erected against the Christian dogma a dogma no less obscure, — that of the depravity of society. Man is born good, cries Rousseau, in his peremptory style; but society — that is, the forms and institutions of society — depraves him. In such terms was formulated the paradox, or, better, the protest, of the philosopher of Geneva.

Now, it is evident that this idea is only the ancient hypothesis turned about. The ancients accused the individual man; Rousseau accuses the collective man: at bottom, it is always the same proposition, an absurd proposition.

Nevertheless, in spite of the fundamental identity of the principle, Rousseau's formula, precisely because it was an opposition, was a step forward; consequently it was welcomed with enthusiasm, and it became the signal of a reaction full of contradictions and absurdities. Singular thing! it is to the anathema launched by the author of "Emile" against society that modern socialism is to be traced.

For the last seventy or eighty years the principle of social perversion has been exploited and popularized by various sectarians, who, while copying Rousseau, reject with all their might the anti-social philosophy of that writer, without perceiving that, by the very fact that they aspire to reform society, they are as unsocial or unsociable as he. It is a curious spectacle to see these pseudo-innovators, condemning after Jean Jacques monarchy, democracy, property, communism, thine and mine, monopoly, wages, police, taxation, luxury, commerce, money, in a word, all that constitutes society and without which society is inconceivable, and then accusing this same Jean Jacques of misanthropy and paralogism, because, after having seen the emptiness of all utopias, at the same time that he pointed out the antagonism of civilization, he sternly concluded against society, though recognizing that without society there is no humanity.

I advise those who, on the strength of what slanderers and plagiarists say, imagine that Rousseau embraced his theory only from a vain love of eccentricity, to read "Emile" and the "Social Contract" once more. That admirable dialectician was led to deny society from the standpoint of justice, although he was forced to admit it as necessary; just as we, who believe in an indefinite progress, do not cease to deny, as normal and definitive, the existing state of society. Only, whereas Rousseau, by a political combination and an educational system of his own, tried to bring man nearer to what he called nature, and what seemed to him the ideal society, we, instructed in a profounder school, say that the task of society is to continually solve its antinomies, — a matter of which Rousseau could have had no idea. Thus, apart from the now abandoned system of the "Social Contract," and so far as criticism alone is concerned, socialism, whatever it may say, is still in the same position as Rousseau, forced to reform society incessantly, — that is, to perpetually deny it.

Rousseau, in short, simply declared in a summary and definitive manner what the socialists repeat in detail and at every moment of progress, — namely, that social order is imperfect, always lacking something. Rousseau's error does not, can not lie in this negation of society: it consists, as we shall show, in his failure to follow his argument to the end and deny at once society, man, and God.

However that may be, the theory of man's innocence, corresponding to that of the depravity of society, has at last got the upper hand. The immense majority of socialists — Saint-Simon, Owen, Fourier, and their disciples; communists, democrats, progressives of all sorts — have solemnly repudiated the Christian myth of the fall to substitute there for the system of an aberration on the part of society. And, as most of these sectarians, in spite of their flagrant impiety, were still too religious, too pious, to finish the work of Jean Jacques and trace back to God the responsibility for evil, they have found a way of deducing from the hypothesis of God the dogma of the native goodness of man, and have begun to fulminate against society in the finest fashion.

The theoretical and practical consequences of this reaction were that, evil — that is, the effect of internal and external struggle — being abnormal and transitory, penal and repressive institutions are likewise transitory; that in man there is no native vice, but that his environment has depraved his inclinations; that civilization has been mistaken as to its own tendencies; that constraint is immoral, that our passions are holy; that enjoyment is holy and should be sought after like virtue itself, because God, who caused us to desire it, is holy. And, the women coming to the aid of the eloquence of the philosophers, a deluge of anti-restrictive protests has fallen, quasi de vulva erumpens, to make use of a comparison from the Holy Scriptures, upon the wonder-stricken public.

The writings of this school are recognizable by their evangelical style, their melancholy theism, and, above all, their enigmatical dialectics.

"They blame human nature," says M. Louis Blanc, "for almost all our evils; the blame should be laid upon the vicious character of social institutions. Look around you: how many talents misplaced, and CONSEQUENTLY depraved! How many activities have become turbulent for want of having found their legitimate and natural object! They force our passions to traverse an impure medium; is it at all surprising that they become altered? Place a healthy man in a pestilent atmosphere, and he will inhale death.... Civilization has taken a wrong road,... and to say that it could not have been otherwise is to lose the right to talk of equity, of morality, of progress; it is to lose the right to talk of God. Providence disappears to give place to the grossest fatalism."

The name of God recurs forty times, and always to no purpose, in M. Blanc's "Organization of Labor," which I quote from preference, because in my view it represents advanced democratic opinion better than any other work, and because I like to do it honor by refuting it.

Thus, while socialism, aided by extreme democracy, deifies man by denying the dogma of the fall, and consequently dethrones God, henceforth useless to the perfection of his creature, this same socialism, through mental cowardice, falls back upon the affirmation of Providence, and that at the very moment when it denies the providential authority of history.

And as nothing stands such chance of success among men as contradiction, the idea of a religion of pleasure, renewed from Epicurus during an eclipse of public reason, has been taken as an inspiration of the national genius; it is this that distinguishes the new theists from the Catholics, against whom the former have inveighed so loudly during the last two years only out of rivalry in fanaticism. It is the fashion today to speak of God on all occasions and to declaim against the pope;

306

to invoke Providence and to scoff at the Church. Thank God! we are not atheists, said "La Reforme" one day; all the more, it might have added by way of increasing its absurdity, we are not Christians. The word has gone forth to every one who holds a pen to bamboozle the people, and the first article of the new faith is that an infinitely good God has created man as good as himself; which does not prevent man, under the eye of God, from becoming wicked in a detestable society.

Nevertheless it is plain, in spite of these semblances of religion, we might even say these desires for it, that the quarrel between socialism and Christian tradition, between man and society, must end by a denial of Divinity. Social reason is not distinguishable by us from absolute Reason, which is no other than God himself, and to deny society in its past phases is to deny Providence, is to deny God.

Thus, then, we are placed between two negations, two contradictory affirmations: one which, by the voice of entire antiquity, setting aside as out of the question society and God which it represents, finds in man alone the principle of evil; another which, protesting in the name of free, intelligent, and progressive man, throws back upon social infirmity and, by a necessary consequence, upon the creative and inspiring genius of society all the disturbances of the universe.

Now, as the anomalies of social order and the oppression of individual liberties arise principally from the play of economic contradictions, we have to inquire, in view of the data which we have brought to light:

1. Whether fate, whose circle surrounds us, exercises a control over our liberty so imperious and compulsory that infractions of the law, committed under the dominion of antinomies, cease to be imputable to us? And, if not, whence arises this culpability peculiar to man?

2. Whether the hypothetical being, utterly good, omnipotent, omniscient, to whom faith attributes the supreme direction of human agitations, has not himself failed society at the moment of danger? And, if so, to explain this insufficiency of Divinity.

In short, we are to find out whether man is God, whether God himself is God, or whether, to attain the fullness of intelligence and liberty, we must search for a superior cause.

1. — The culpability of man. — Exposition of the myth of the fall.

As long as man lives under the law of egoism, he accuses himself; as soon as he rises to the conception of a social law, he accuses society. In both cases humanity accuses humanity; and so far the clearest result of this double accusation is the strange faculty, which we have not yet pointed out, and which religion attributes to God as well as to man, of REPENTANCE.

Of what, then, does humanity repent? For what does God, who repents as well as ourselves, desire to punish us? Poenituit Deum quod hominem fecisset in terra, et tactus dolore cordis intrinsecus, delebo, inquit, hominem....

If I demonstrate that the offences charged upon humanity are not the consequence of its economic embarrassments, although the latter result from the constitution of its ideas; that man does evil gratuitously and when not under compulsion, just as he honors himself by acts of heroism which justice does not exact, — it will follow that man, at the tribunal of his conscience, may be allowed to plead certain extenuating circumstances, but can never be entirely discharged of his guilt; that the struggle is in his heart as well as in his mind; that he deserves now praise, now blame, which is a confession, in either case, of his inharmonious state; finally, that the essence of his soul is a perpetual compromise between opposing attractions, his morality a system of seesaw, in a word, — and this word tells the whole story, — eclecticism.

My proof shall be soon made.

There exists a law, older than our liberty, promulgated from the beginning of the world, completed by Jesus Christ, preached and certified by apostles, martyrs, confessors, and virgins, graven on the heart of man, and superior to all metaphysics: it is LOVE. Love thy neighbor as thyself, Jesus Christ tells us, after Moses. That is the whole of it. Love thy neighbor as thyself, and society will be perfect; love thy neighbor as thyself, and all distinctions of prince and shepherd, of rich and poor, of learned and ignorant, disappear, all clashing of human interests ceases. Love thy neighbor as thyself, and happiness with industry, without care for the future, shall fill thy days. To fulfil this law and make himself happy man needs only to follow the inclination of his heart and listen to the voice of his sympathies. He resists; he does more: not content wtih {sic} preferring himself to his neighbor, he labors constantly to destroy his neighbor; after having betrayed love through egoism, he overturns it by injustice.

Man, I say, faithless to the law of charity, has, of himself and without any necessity, made the contradictions of society so many instruments of harm; through his egoism civilization has become a war of surprises and ambushes; he lies, he steals, he murders, when not compelled to do so, without provocation, without excuse. In short, he does evil with all the characteristics of a nature deliberately maleficent, and all the more wicked because, when it so wishes, it knows how to do good gratuitously also and is capable of self-sacrifice; wherefore it has been said of it, with as much reason as depth: Homo homini lupus, vel deus.

Not to unduly extend the subject, and especially in order to avoid prejudging the questions that I shall have to consider, I limit myself to the economic facts already analyzed.

With the fact that the division of labor is by nature, pending the attainment of a synthetic organization, an irresistible cause of physical, moral, and mental inequality among men neither society nor conscience have anything to do. That is a fact of necessity, of which the rich man is as innocent as the parcellaire workman, consigned by his position to all sorts of poverty.

But how happens it that this inevitable inequality is converted into a title of nobility for some, of abjection for others? How happens it, if man is good, that he has not succeeded in levelling by his goodness this wholly metaphysical obstacle, and that, instead of strengthening the fraternal tie that binds men, pitiless necessity breaks it? Here man cannot be excused on the ground of his economic inexperience or legislative shortsightedness; it was enough that he had a heart. Since the martyrs of the division of labor should have been helped and honored by the rich, why have they been rejected as impure? Why is it an unheard-of thing for masters to occasionally relieve their slaves, for princes, magistrates, and priests to change places with mechanics, and for nobles to assume the task of the peasants on the land? What is the reason of this brutal pride of the powerful?

And note that such conduct on their part would have been not only charitable and fraternal, but in accord with the sternest justice. By virtue of the principle of collective force, laborers are the equals and associates of their leaders; so that in the system of monopoly itself, community of action restoring the equilibrium which parcellaire individualism has disturbed, justice and charity blend. On the hypothesis of the essential goodness of man, how then is to be explained the monstrous attempt to change the authority of some into nobility and the obedience of others into plebeianism? Labor, between the serf and the free man, like color between the black and the white, has always drawn an impassable line; and we ourselves, who glory so in our philanthropy, at the bottom of our hearts are of the same opinion as our predecessors. The sympathy which we feel for the proletaire is like that with which animals inspire us; delicacy of organs, dread of misery, pride in separating ourselves from all suffering, — it is these shifts of egoism that prompt our charity.

For in fact — and I desire only this fact to confound us — is it not true that spontaneous benevolence, so pure in its primitive conception (eleemosyna, sympathy, tenderness), alms, in fine, has become for the unfortunate a sign of degradation, a public stigma? And socialists, rebuking Christianity, dare to talk to us of love! The Christian thought, the conscience of humanity, hit the mark precisely, when it founded so many institutions for the relief of misfortune. To grasp the evangelical precept in its depth and render legal charity as honorable to those who had been its objects as to those who had exercised it, there was needed — what? Less pride, less greed, less egoism. If man is good, will any one tell me how the right to alms has become the first link in the long chain of infractions, misdemeanors, and crimes? Will any one still dare to blame the misdeeds of man upon the antagonisms of social economy, when these antagonisms offered him so beautiful an opportunity of manifesting the charity of his heart, I do not say by self-sacrifice, but by the simple doing of justice?

I know — and this objection is the only one that can be offered against my position — that charity is covered with shame and dishonor because the individual who asks it is too often, alas! suspected of misconduct and rarely to be recommended on the score of dignity of morals and of labor. And statistics prove that those who are poor through cowardice and negligence outnumber ten times those who are poor through accident or mischance.

Far be it from me to challenge this observation, the truth of which is demonstrated by too many facts, and which, moreover, has received the sanction of the people. The people are the first to accuse the poor of laziness; and there is nothing more common than to meet in the lower classes men who boast, as if it were a title of nobility, that they have never been in the hospital and in their greatest distress have never been recipients of public charity. Thus, just as opulence avows its robberies, misery confesses its shame. Man is a tyrant or a slave by will before becoming so by fortune; the heart of the proletaire is like that of the rich man, — a sewer of boiling sensuality, the home of crapulence and imposture.

310

Upon this unexpected revelation I ask how it happens, if man is good and charitable, that the rich calumniate charity while the poor defile it? It is perversion of judgment on the part of the rich, say some; it is degradation of faculties on the part of the poor, say others. But how is it that judgment is perverted on the one hand, and on the other that faculties are degraded? How comes it that a true and cordial fraternity has not arrested on the one side and on the other the effects of pride and labor? Let my questions be answered by reasons, not by phrases.

Labor, in inventing processes and machines which infinitely multiply its power, and then in stimulating industrial genius by rivalry and assuring its conquests by means of the profits of capital and privileges of exploitation, has rendered the hierarchical constitution of society more profound and more inevitable; I repeat that no blame attaches to any one for this. But I call the holy law of the Gospel to witness that it was within our power to draw wholly different consequences from this subordination of man to man, or, better, of laborer to laborer.

The traditions of feudal life and of that of the patriarchs set the example for the manufacturers. The division of labor and the other accidents of production were only calls to the great family life, indications of the preparatory system in accordance with which fraternity was to appear and be developed. Masterships, corporations, and rights of primogeniture were conceived under the influence of this idea; many communists even are not hostile to this form of association; is it surprising that the ideal is so tenacious among those who, conquered but not converted, still appear as its representatives? What, then, prevented charity, union, sacrifice from maintaining themselves in the hierarchy, when the hierarchy might have been only a condition of labor? To this end it would have sufficed if men having machines, valiant knights fighting with equal weapons, had not made a mystery of their secrets or withheld them from others; if barons had set to work, not to monopolize their products, but to cheapen them; and if vassals, assured that war would result only in increasing their wealth, had always shown themselves enterprising, industrious, and faithful. The chief of the workshop would then have been simply a captain putting his men through manoeuvres in their interest as well as in his own, and maintaining them, not with his perquisites, but with their own services.

Instead of these fraternal relations, we have had pride, jealousy, and perjury; the employer, like the vampire of the fable, exploiting the degraded wage-worker, and the wage-worker conspiring against the employer; the idler devouring the substance of the laborer, and the serf, squatting in filth, having no strength left but for hatred.

311

Called on to furnish for the work of production, these tools, those labor, capitalists and laborers are today in a struggle: why? Because absolutism presides over all their relations; because the capitalist speculates on the need which the laborer feels of procuring tools, while the laborer, in turn, seeks to derive advantage from the need which the capitalist feels of fertilizing his capital. — L. Blanc: Organization of Labor.

And why this absolutism in the relations of capitalist and laborer? Why this hostility of interests? Why this reciprocal enmity? Instead of eternally explaining the fact by the fact itself, go to the bottom, and you will find everywhere, as original motive, a passion for enjoyment which neither law nor justice nor charity restrain; you will see egoism continually discounting the future, and sacrificing to its monstrous caprices labor, capital, life, and the security of all.

The theologians have given the name concupiscence or concupiscible appetite to the passionate greed for sensual things, the effect, according to them, of original sin. I trouble myself little, for the present, as to the nature of the original sin; I simply observe that the concupiscible appetite of the theologians is no other than that need of luxury pointed out by the Academy of Moral Sciences as the ruling motive of our epoch. Now, the theory of proportionality of values demonstrates that luxury is naturally measured by production; that every consumption in advance is recovered by an equivalent later privation; and that the exaggeration of luxury in a society necessarily has an increase of misery as its correlative. Now, were man to sacrifice his personal welfare for luxurious and advance enjoyments, perhaps I should accuse him only of imprudence; but, when he injures the welfare of his neighbor, — a welfare which he should regard as inviolable, both from charity and on the ground of justice, — I say then that man is wicked, inexcusably wicked.

When God, according to Bossuet, formed the bowels of man, he originally placed goodness there. Thus love is our first law; the prescriptions of pure reason, as well as the promptings of the senses, take second and third rank only. Such is the hierarchy of our faculties, — a principle of love forming the foundation of our conscience and served by an intelligence and organs. Hence of two things one: either the man who violates charity to obey his cupidity is guilty; or else, if this psychology is false, and the need of luxury in man must hold a place beside charity and reason, man is a disorderly animal, utterly wicked, and the most execrable of beings.

312

Thus the organic contradictions of society cannot cover the responsibility of man; viewed in themselves, moreover, these contradictions are only the theory of the hierarchical regime, the first form and consequently an irreproachable form of society. By the antinomy of their development labor and capital have been continually led back to equality at the same time as to subordination, to solidarity as well as to dependence; one was the agent, the other the stimulator and guardian of the common wealth. This indication has been indistinctly seen by the theorists of the feudal system; Christianity came in time to cement the compact; and it is still the sentiment of this misunderstood and broken, but in itself innocent and legitimate, organization which causes regrets among us and sustains the hope of a party. As this system was written in the book of destiny, it cannot be said to be bad in itself, just as the embryonic state cannot be called bad because it precedes adult age in physiological development.

I insist, therefore, on my accusation:

Under the regime abolished by Luther and the French Revolution man could be happy in proportion to the progress of his industry; he did not choose to be; on the contrary, he forbade himself to be.

Labor has been regarded as dishonorable; the clergy and the nobility have made themselves the devourers of the poor; to satisfy their animal passions, they have extinguished charity in their hearts; they have ruined, oppressed, assassinated the laborer. And thus it is that we see capital still hunting the proletariat. Instead of tempering the subversive tendency of economic principles by association and mutuality, the capitalist exaggerates it unnecessarily and with evil design; he abuses the senses and the conscience of the workman; he makes him a valet in his intrigues, a purveyor of his debaucheries, an accomplice in his robberies; he makes him in all respects like himself, and then it is that he can defy the justice of revolutions to touch him. Monstrous thing! the man who lives in misery, and whose soul therefore seems a nearer neighbor of charity and honor, shares his master's corruption; like him, he gives everything to pride and luxury, and if he sometimes cries out against the inequality from which he suffers, it is still less from zeal for justice than from rivalry in desire. The greatest obstacle which equality has to overcome is not the aristocratic pride of the rich man, but the ungovernable egoism of the poor man. And you rely on his native goodness to reform at once both the spontaneity and the premeditation of his malice!

"As the false and anti-social education given to the present generation," says Louis Blanc, "permits no search for any other motive for emulation and encouragement than an increase of reward, the difference of wages should be graduated according to the hierarchy of functions, an entirely new education having to change ideas and morals in this matter."

Dismissing the hierarchy of functions and the inequality of wages for what they are worth, let us consider here only the motive assigned by the author. Is it not strange to see M. Blanc affirm the goodness of our nature, and at the same time address himself to the most ignoble of our propensities, — avarice? Truly, evil must seem to you very deeply rooted, if you deem it necessary to begin the restoration of charity by a violation of charity. Jesus Christ broke openly with pride and greed; apparently the libertines whom he catechised were holy personages compared with the herd infected with socialism. But tell us then, in short, how our ideas have been warped, why our education is anti-social, since it is now demonstrated that society has followed the route traced by destiny and can no longer be charged with the crimes of man.

Really, the logic of socialism is marvellous.

Man is good, they say; but it is necessary to detach his interests from evil to secure his abstinence from it. Man is good; but he must be interested in the good, else he will not do it. For, if the interest of his passions leads him to evil, he will do evil; and, if this same interest leaves him indifferent to good, he will not do good. And society will have no right to reproach him for having listened to his passions, because it was for society to conduct him by his passions. What a rich and precious nature was that of Nero, who killed his mother because she wearied him, and who caused Rome to be burned in order to have a representation of the pillage of Troy! What an artist's soul was that of Heliogabalus, who organized prostitution! What a potent character was Tiberius! But what an abominable society was that which perverted those divine souls, and produced, moreover, Tacitus and Marcus Aurelius!

This, then, is what is called the harmlessness of man, — the holiness of his passions! An aged Sappho, abandoned by her lovers, goes back under the conjugal law; her interest detached from love, she returns to marriage, and is holy. What a pity that this word holy (saint) has not in French the double meaning which it possesses in the Hebrew language! All would be in accord regarding the holiness of Sappho.

I read in a report upon the railways of Belgium that, the Belgian administration having allowed its engineers a premium of two and one-half cents for every bushel of coke saved out of an average consumption of two hundred and ten pounds for a given distance traversed, this premium bore such fruits that the consumption fell from two hundred and ten pounds to one hundred and six. This fact sums up the whole socialistic philosophy: to gradually train the workingman to justice, encourage him to labor, lift him to the sublimity of devotion, by increase of wages, profit-sharing, distinctions, and rewards. Certainly I do not mean to blame this method, which is as old as the world: whatever way you take to tame serpents and tigers and render them useful, I applaud it. But do not say that your beasts are doves; for then, as sole reply, I shall point you to their claws and teeth. Before the Belgian engineers became interested in the economy of fuel, they burned double the quantity. Therefore on their part there was carelessness, negligence, prodigality, waste, perhaps theft, although they were bound to the administration by a contract which obliged them to practise all the contrasted virtues. It is good, you say, to interest the laborer. I say further that it is just. But I maintain that this interest, more powerful over man than voluntarily accepted obligation, more powerful, in a word, than DUTY, accuses man. Socialism goes backward in morality, and it turns up its nose at Christianity. It does not understand charity, and yet, to hear it, one would suppose that it invented charity.

See, moreover, observe the socialists, what fortunate fruits the perfecting of our social order has already borne! The present generation is undeniably better than its predecessors: are we wrong in concluding that a perfect society will produce perfect citizens? Say rather, reply the conservative believers in the dogma of the fall, that, religion having purified hearts, it is not astonishing that institutions have felt the effects. Now let religion finish its work, and have no fears about society.

So speak and retort in an endless wandering from the question the theorists of the two schools. Neither understand that humanity, to use a Biblical expression, is one and constant in its generations, — that is, that everything in it, at every period of its development, in the individual as in the mass, proceeds from the same principle, which is, not being, but becoming. They do not see, on the one hand, that progress in morality is a continual conquest of mind over animality, just as progress in wealth is the fruit of the war waged by labor upon the parsimony of nature; consequently that the idea of native goodness lost through society is as absurd as the idea of native wealth lost

315

through labor, and that a compromise with the passions should be viewed in the same light as a compromise with rest. On the other hand, they refuse to understand that, if there is progress in humanity, whether through religion or from some other cause, the hypothesis of constitutional corruption is nonsense, a contradiction.

But I anticipate the conclusions at which I must arrive: let us, for the present, establish simply that the moral perfection of humanity, like material welfare, is realized by a series of oscillations between vice and virtue, merit and demerit.

Yes, humanity grows in justice, but this growth of our liberty, due entirely to the growth of our intelligence, surely gives no proof of the goodness of our nature; and, far from authorizing us to glorify our passions, it really destroys their sway. The fashion and style of our malice change with time: the barons of the middle ages plundered the traveller on the highway, and then offered him hospitality in their castles; mercantile feudality, less brutal, exploits the proletaire and builds hospitals for him: who would dare to say which of the two has deserved the palm of virtue?

Of all the economic contradictions value is that which, dominating the others and summing them up, holds in a sense the sceptre of society, I had almost said of the moral world. Until value, oscillating between its two poles, — useful value and value in exchange, — arrives at its constitution, thine and mine remain fixed arbitrarily; the conditions of fortune are the effect of chance; property rests on a precarious title; everything in social economy is provisional. What should social, intelligent, and free beings have learned from this uncertainty of value? To make amicable regulations that should protect labor and guarantee exchange and cheapness. What a happy opportunity for all to make up, by honesty, disinterestedness, and tenderness of heart, for the ignorance of the objective laws of the just and the unjust! Instead of that, commerce has everywhere become, by spontaneous effort and unanimous consent, an uncertain operation, a venturesome enterprise, a lottery, and often a deceitful and fraudulent speculation.

What obliges the holder of provisions, the storekeeper of society, to pretend that there is a scarcity, sound the alarm, and provoke a rise of prices? Public short-sightedness places the consumer at his mercy; some change of temperature furnishes him a pretext; the assured prospect of gain finally corrupts him, and fear, skilfully spread abroad, throws the population into his toils. Certainly the motive which actuates the swindler, the thief, the assassin, those natures warped, it is said, by the social order, is the same which animates the monopolist who is not in need. How, then, does this passion for gain, abandoned to itself, turn to the prejudice of society? Why has preventive, repressive, and coercive legislation always been necessary to set a limit to liberty? For that is the accusing fact, which it is impossible to deny: everywhere the law has grown out of abuse; everywhere the legislator has found himself forced to make man powerless to harm, which is synonymous with muzzling a lion or infibulating a boar. And socialism itself, ever imitating the past, makes no other pretence: what is, indeed, the organization which it claims, if not a stronger guarantee of justice, a more complete limitation of liberty?

The characteristic trait of the merchant is to make everything either an object or an instrument of traffic. Disassociated from his fellows, his interests separated from those of others, he is for and against all deeds, all opinions, all parties. A discovery, a science, is in his eyes an instrument of war, out of the way of which he tries to keep, and which he would like to annihilate, unless he can make use of it himself to kill his competitors. An artist, an educated person, is an artilleryman who knows how to handle the weapon, and whom he tries to corrupt, if he cannot win him. The merchant is convinced that logic is the art of proving at will the true and the false; he was the inventor of political venality, traffic in consciences, prostitution of talents, corruption of the press. He knows how to find arguments and advocates for all lies, all iniquities. He alone has never deceived himself as to the value of political parties: he deems them all equally exploitable, — that is, equally absurd.

Without respect for his avowed opinions, which he abandons and resumes by turns; sharply pursuing in others those violations of faith of which he is himself guilty, — he lies in his claims, he lies in his representations, he lies in his inventories; he exaggerates, he extenuates, he over-rates; he regards himself as the centre of the world, and everything outside of him has only a relative existence, value, and truth. Subtle and shrewd in his transactions, he stipulates, he reserves, trembling always lest he may say too much or not enough; abusing words with the simple, generalizing in order not to compromise himself, specifying in order to allow nothing, he turns three times upon himself and thinks seven times under his chin before saying his last word. Has he at last concluded? He rereads himself, he interprets himself, he comments on himself; he tortures himself to find a deep meaning in every part of his contract, and in the clearest phrases the opposite of what they say.

317

What infinite art, what hypocrisy, in his relations with the manual laborer! From the simple shopkeeper to the big contractor, how skilful they are in exploiting his arms! How well they know how to contend with labor, in order to obtain it at a low price! In the first place, it is a hope for which the master receives a slight service; then it is a promise which he discounts by requiring some duty; then a trial, a sacrifice, — for he needs nobody, — which the unfortunate man must recognize by contenting himself with the lowest wages; there are endless exactions and overcharges, compensated by settlements on pay-days effected in the most rapacious and deceitful spirit. And the workman must keep silent and bend the knee, and clench his fist under his frock: for the employer has the work, and only too happy is he who can obtain the favor of his swindles. And because society has not yet found a way to prevent, repress, and punish this odious grinding process, so spontaneous, so ingenuous, so disengaged from all superior impulse, it is attributed to social constraint. What folly!

The commission-merchant is the type, the highest expression, of monopoly, the embodiment of commerce, that is, of civilization. Every function depends upon his, participates in it, or is assimilated to it: for, as from the standpoint of the distribution of wealth the relations of men with each other are all reducible to exchanges, — that is, to transfers of values, — it may be said that civilization is personified in the commission-merchant.

Now, question the commission-merchants as to the morality of their trade; they will be frank with you; all will tell you that the commission business is extortion. Complaints are made of the frauds and adulterations which disgrace manufactures: commerce — I refer especially to the commission business — is only a gigantic and permanent conspiracy of monopolists, by turns competing or joined in pools; it is not a function performed with a view to a legitimate profit, but a vast organization of speculation in all articles of consumption, as well as on the circulation of persons and products. Already swindling is tolerated in this profession: how many way-bills overcharged, erased, altered! how many stamps counterfeited! how much damage concealed or fraudulently compounded! how many lies as to quality! how many promises given and retracted! how many documents suppressed! what intrigues and combinations! and then what treasons!

The commission-merchant — that is, the merchant — that is, the man - is a gambler, a slanderer, a charlatan, a mercenary, a thief, a forger....

318

This is the effect of our antagonistic society, observe the neo-mystics. So say the commercial people, the first under all circumstances to accuse the corruption of the century. They act as they do, if we may believe them, simply to indemnify themselves and wholly against their inclination: they follow necessity; theirs is a case of legitimate defence.

Does it require an effort of genius to see that these mutual recriminations strike at the very nature of man, that the pretended perversion of society is nothing but the perversion of man, and that the opposition of principles and interests is only an external accident, so to speak, which brings into relief, but without exerting a necessitating influence, both the blackness of our egoism and the rare virtues with which our race is honored?

I understand inharmonious competition and its irresistible eliminating effects: this is inevitable. Competition, in its higher expression, is the gearing by means of which laborers reciprocally stimulate and sustain each other. But, pending the realization of that organization which must elevate competition to its veritable nature, it remains a civil war in which producers, instead of aiding each other in labor, grind and crush each other by labor. The danger here was imminent; man, to avert it, had this supreme law of love; and nothing was easier, while pushing competition to its extreme limits in the interest of production, than to then repair its murderous effects by an equitable distribution. Far from that, this anarchical competition has become, as it were, the soul and spirit of the laborer. Political economy placed in the hands of man this weapon of death, and he has struck; he has used competition, as the lion uses his paws and jaws, to kill and devour. How is it, then, I repeat, that a wholly external accident has changed the nature of man, which is supposed to be good and gentle and social?

The wine merchant calls to his aid jelly, magnin, insects, water, and poisons; by combinations of his own he adds to the destructive effects of competition. Whence comes this mania? From the fact, you say, that his competitor sets him the example! And this competitor, who incites him? Some other competitor. So that, if we make the tour of society, we shall find that it is the mass, and in the mass each particular individual, who, by a tacit agreement of their passions, — pride, indolence, greed, distrust, jealousy, — have organized this detestable war.

After having gathered about him tools, material, and workmen, the contractor must recover in the product, besides the amount of his outlay, first the interest of his capital, and then a profit. It is in

319

consequence of this principle that lending at interest has finally become established, and that gain, considered in itself, has always passed for legitimate. Under this system, the police of nations not having seen at first the essential contradiction of loans at interest, the wage-worker, instead of depending directly upon himself, had to depend upon an employer, as the soldier belonged to the count, or the tribe to the patriarch. This order of things was necessary, and, pending the establishment of complete equality, it was not impossible that the welfare of all should be secured by it. But when the master, in his disorderly egoism, has said to the servant: "You shall not share with me," and robbed him at one stroke of labor and wages, where is the necessity, where the excuse? Will it be necessary further, in order to justify the concupiscible appetite, to fall back on the irascible appetite? Take care: in drawing back in order to justify the human being in the series of his lusts, instead of saving his morality, you abandon it. For my part, I prefer the guilty man to the wild-beast man.

Nature has made man sociable: the spontaneous development of his instincts now makes him an angel of charity, now robs him even of the sentiment of fraternity and the idea of devotion. Did any one ever see a capitalist, weary of gain, conspiring for the general good and making the emancipation of the proletariat his last speculation? There are many people, favorites of fortune, to whom nothing is lacking but the crown of beneficence: now, where is the grocer who, having grown rich, begins to sell at cost? Where the baker who, retiring from business, leaves his customers and his establishment to his assistants? Where the apothecary who, under the pretence of winding up his affairs, surrenders his drugs at their true value? When charity has its martyrs, why has it not its amateurs? If there should suddenly be formed a congress of bondholders, capitalists, and men of business, retired but still fit for service, with a view to carrying on a certain number of industries gratuitously, in a short time society would be reformed from top to bottom. But work for nothing! That is for the Vincent de Pauls, the Fenelons, all those whose souls have always been weaned and whose hearts have been pure. The man enriched by gain will be a municipal councillor, a member of the committee on charities, an officer of the infant schools: he will perform all the honorary functions, barring exactly that which would be efficacious, but which is repugnant to his habits. Work without hope of profits! That cannot be, for it would be self-destruction. He would like to, perhaps; he has not the courage. Video meliora proboque, deteriora sequor. The retired proprietor is really the owl of the fable gathering beech-nuts for its mutilated mice until it is ready to devour them. Is society also to be blamed for these effects of a passion so long, so freely, so fully gratified?

320

Who, then, will explain this mystery of a manifold and discordant being, capable at once of the highest virtues and the most frightful crimes? The dog licks his master who strikes him, because the dog's nature is fidelity and this nature never leaves him. The lamb takes refuge in the arms of the shepherd who fleeces and eats him, because the sheep's inseparable characteristics are gentleness and peace. The horse dashes through flame and grape-shot without touching with his swiftly-moving feet the wounded and dead lying in his path, because the horse's soul is unalterable in its generosity. These animals are martyrs for our sakes through the constancy and devotion of their natures. The servant who defends his master at the peril of his life, for a little gold betrays and murders him; the chaste wife pollutes her bed because of some disgust or absence, and in Lucrece we find Messalina; the proprietor, by turns father and tyrant, refits and restores his ruined farmer and drives from his lands the farmer's too numerous family, which has increased on the strength of the feudal contract; the warrior, mirror and paragon of chivalry, makes the corpses of his companions a stepping-stone to advancement. Epaminondas and Regulus traffic in the blood of their soldiers, — how many instances have my own eyes witnessed! — and by a horrible contrast the profession of sacrifice is the most fruitful in cowardice. Humanity has its martyrs and its apostates: to what, I ask again, must this division be attributed?

To the antagonism of society, you always say; to the state of separation, isolation, hostility to his fellows, in which man has hitherto lived; in a word, to that alienation of his heart which has led him to mistake enjoyment for love, property for possession, pain for labor, intoxication for joy; to that warped conscience, in short, which remorse has not ceased to pursue under the name of original sin. When man, reconciled with himself, shall cease to look upon his neighbor and nature as hostile powers, then will he love and produce simply by the spontaneity of his energy; then it will be his passion to give, as it is today to acquire; and then will he seek in labor and devotion his only happiness, his supreme delight. Then, love becoming really and indivisibly the law of man, justice will thereafter be but an empty name, painful souvenir of a period of violence and tears.

Certainly I do not overlook the fact of antagonism, or, as it will please you to call it, of religious alienation, any more than the necessity of reconciling man with himself; my whole philosophy is but a perpetuity of reconciliations. You admit that the divergence of our nature is the preliminary of society, or, let us rather say, the material of civilization. This is precisely the fact, but, remember well, the indestructible fact of which I seek the meaning. Certainly we should be very near an understanding, if, instead of considering the dissidence and harmony of the human faculties as two distinct periods, clean-cut and consecutive in history, you would consent to view them with me simply as the two faces of our nature, ever adverse, ever in course of reconciliation, but never entirely reconciled. In a word, as individualism is the primordial fact of humanity, so association is its complementary term; but both are in incessant manifestation, and on earth justice is eternally the condition of love.

Thus the dogma of the fall is not simply the expression of a special and transitory state of human reason and morality: it is the spontaneous confession, in symbolic phrase, of this fact as astonishing as it is indestructible, the culpability, the inclination to evil, of our race. Curse upon me a sinner! cries on every hand and in every tongue the conscience of the human race. Voe nobis quia peccavimus! Religion, in giving this idea concrete and dramatic form, has indeed gone back of history and beyond the limits of the world for that which is essential and immanent in our soul; this, on its part, was but an intellectual mirage; it was not mistaken as to the essentiality and permanence of the fact. Now, it is this fact for which we have to account, and it is also from this point of view that we are to interpret the dogma of original sin.

All peoples have had their expiatory customs, their penitential sacrifices, their repressive and penal institutions, born of the horror and regret of sin. Catholicism, which built a theory wherever social spontaneity had expressed an idea or deposited a hope, converted into a sacrament the at once symbolic and effective ceremony by which the sinner expressed his repentance, asked pardon of God and men for his fault, and prepared himself for a better life. Consequently I do not hesitate to say that the Reformation, in rejecting contrition, cavilling over the word metanoia, attributing to faith alone the virtue of justification, deconsecrating repentance in short, took a step backward and utterly failed to recognize the law of progress. To deny was not to reply. On this point as on so many others the abuses of the Church called for reform; the theories of repentance, of damnation, of the remission of sin, and of grace contained, if I may venture to say so, in a latent state, the entire system of humanity's education; these theories needed to be developed and grown into rationalism; Luther knew nothing but their destruction. Auricular confession was a degradation of repentance, an equivocal demonstration substituted for a great act of humility; Luther surpassed papist hypocrisy by reducing the primitive confession before God and men (exomologoumai to theo.... kai humin, adelphoi) to a soliloquy. The Christian meaning then was lost, and not until three centuries later was it restored by philosophy.

Since, then, Christianity — that is, religious humanity — has not been in error as to the REALITY of a fact essential in human nature, — a fact which it has designated by the words original prevarication, let us further interrogate Christianity, humanity, as to the MEANING of this fact. Let us not be astonished either by metaphor or by allegory: truth is independent of figures. And besides, what is truth to us but the continuous progress of our mind from poetry to prose?

And first let us inquire whether this at least singular idea of original prevarication had not, somewhere in the Christian theology, its correlative. For the true idea, the generic idea, cannot result from an isolated conception; there must be a series.

Christianity, after having posited the dogma of the fall as the first term, followed up its thought by affirming, for all who should die in this state of pollution, an irrevocable separation from God, an eternity of punishment. Then it completed its theory by reconciling these two opposites by the dogma of rehabilitation or of grace, according to which every creature born in the hatred of God is reconciled by the merits of Jesus Christ, which faith and repentance render efficacious. Thus, essential corruption of our nature and perpetuity of punishment, except in the case of redemption through voluntary participation in Christ's sacrifice, — such is, in brief, the evolution of the theological idea. The second affirmation is a consequence of the first; the third is a negation and transformation of the two others: in fact, a constitutional vice being necessarily indestructible, the expiation which it involves is as eternal as itself, unless a superior power comes to break destiny and lift the anathema by an integral renovation.

The human mind, in its religious caprices as well as in its most positive theories, has always but one method; the same metaphysics produced the Christian mysteries and the contradictions of political economy; faith, without knowing it, hangs upon reason; and we, explorers of divine and human manifestations, are entitled to verify, in the name of reason, the hypotheses of theology.

What was it, then, that the universal reason, formulated in religious dogmas, saw in human nature, when, by so regular a metaphysical construction, it declared successively the ingenuousness of the offence, the eternity of the penalty, the necessity of grace? The veils of theology are becoming so transparent that it quite resembles natural history.

323

If we conceive the operation by which the supreme being is supposed to have produced all beings, no longer as an emanation, an exertion of the creative force and infinite substance, but as a division or differentiation of this substantial force, each being, organized or unorganized, will appear to us the special representative of one of the innumerable potentialities of the infinite being, as a section of the absolute; and the collection of all these individualities (fluids, minerals, plants, insects, fish, birds, and quadrupeds) will be the creation, the universe.

Man, an abridgment of the universe, sums up and syncretizes in his person all the potentialities of being, all the sections of the absolute; he is the summit at which these potentialities, which exist only by their divergence, meet in a group, but without penetrating or becoming confounded with each other. Man, therefore, by this aggregation, is at once spirit and matter, spontaneity and reflection, mechanism and life, angel and brute. He is venomous like the viper, sanguinary like the tiger, gluttonous like the hog, obscene like the ape; and devoted like the dog, generous like the horse, industrious like the bee, monogamic like the dove, sociable like the beaver and sheep. And in addition he is man, — that is, reasonable and free, susceptible of education and improvement. Man enjoys as many names as Jupiter; all these names he carries written on his face; and, in the varied mirror of nature, his infallible instinct is able to recognize them. A serpent is beautiful to the reason; it is the conscience that finds it odious and ugly. The ancients as well as the moderns grasped this idea of the constitution of man by agglomeration of all terrestrial potentialities: the labors of Gall and Lavater were, if I may say so, only attempts at disintegration of the human syncretism, and their classification of our faculties a miniature picture of nature. Man, in short, like the prophet in the lions' den, is veritably given over to the beasts; and if anything is destined to exhibit to posterity the infamous hypocrisy of our epoch, it is the fact that educated persons, spiritualistic bigots, have thought to serve religion and morality by altering the nature of our race and giving the lie to anatomy.

Therefore the only question left to decide is whether it depends upon man, notwithstanding the contradictions which the progressive emission of his ideas multiplies around him, to give more or less scope to the potentialities placed under his control, or, as the moralists say, to his passions; in other words, whether, like Hercules of old, he can conquer the animality which besets him, the infernal legion which seems ever ready to devour him.

Now, the universal consent of peoples bears witness — and we have shown it in the third and fourth chapters — that man, all his animal impulses set aside, is summed up in intelligence and liberty, — that is, first, a faculty of appreciation and choice, and, second, a power of action indifferently applicable to good and evil. We have shown further that these two faculties, which exercise a necessary influence over each other, are susceptible of indefinite development and improvement.

Social destiny, the solution of the human enigma, is found, then, in these words: EDUCATION, PROGRESS.

The education of liberty, the taming of our instincts, the enfranchisement or redemption of our soul, — this, then, as Lessing has proved, is the meaning of the Christian mystery. This education will last throughout our life and that of humanity: the contradictions of political economy may be solved; the essential contradiction of our being never will be. That is why the great teachers of humanity, Moses, Buddha, Jesus Christ, Zoroaster, were all apostles of expiation, living symbols of repentance. Man is by nature a sinner, -that is, not essentially ill-doing, but rather ill-done, — and it is his destiny to perpetually re-create his ideal in himself. That is what the greatest of painters, Raphael, felt profoundly, when he said that art consists in rendering things, not as nature made them, but as it should have made them.

Henceforth, then, it is ours to teach the theologians, for we alone continue the tradition of the Church, we alone possess the meaning of the Scriptures, of the Councils, and of the Fathers. Our interpretation rests on the most certain and most authentic grounds, on the greatest authority to which men can appeal, the metaphysical construction of ideas and facts. Yes, the human being is vicious because he is illogical, because his constitution is but an eclecticism which holds in perpetual struggle the potentialities of his being, independently of the contradictions of society. The life of man is only a continual compromise between labor and pain, love and enjoyment, justice and egoism; and the voluntary sacrifice which man makes in obedience to his inferior attractions is the baptism which prepares the way for his reconciliation with God and renders him worthy of that beatific union and eternal happiness.

The object of social economy, in incessantly securing order in labor and favoring the education of the race, is then to render charity — that charity which knows not how to rule its slaves — superfluous as far as possible by equality, or better, to make charity develop from justice, as

325

a flower from its stem. Ah! if charity had had the power to create happiness among men, it would have proved it long ago; and socialism, instead of seeking the organization of labor, would have had but to say: "Take care, you are lacking in charity."

But, alas! charity in man is stunted, sly, sluggish, and lukewarm; in order to act, it needs elixirs and aromas. That is why I have clung to the triple dogma of prevarication, damnation, and redemption, — that is, perfectibility through justice. Liberty here below is always in need of assistance, and the Catholic theory of celestial favors comes to complete this too real demonstration of the miseries of our nature.

Grace, say the theologians, is, in the order of salvation, every help or means which can conduct us to eternal life. That is to say, man perfects himself, civilizes himself, humanizes himself only by the incessant aid of experience, by industry, science, and art, by pleasure and pain, in a word, by all bodily and mental exercises.

There is an habitual grace, called also justifying and sanctifying, which is conceived as a quality residing in the soul, containing the innate virtues and gifts of the Holy Spirit, and inseparable from charity. In other words, habitual grace is the symbol of the predominance of good impulses, which lead man to order and love, and by means of which he succeeds in subduing his evil tendencies and remaining master in his own domain. As for actual grace, that indicates the external means which give scope to the orderly passions and serve to combat the subversive passions.

Grace, according to Saint Augustine, is essentially gratuitous, and precedes sin in man. Bossuet expressed the same thought in his style so full of poesy and tenderness: When God formed the bowels of man, he originally placed goodness there. In fact, the first determination of free will is in this natural goodness, by which man is continually incited to order, to labor, to study, to modesty, to charity, and to sacrifice. Therefore Saint Paul could say, without attacking free will, that, in everything concerning the accomplishment of good, God worketh in us both to will and to do. For all the holy aspirations of man are in him before he begins to think and feel; and the pangs of heart which he experiences when he violates them, the delight with which he is filled when he obeys them, all the invitations, in short, which come to him from society and his education, do not belong to him.

When grace is such that the will chooses the good with joy and love, without hesitation and without recall, it is styled efficacious. Every one has witnessed those transports of soul which suddenly decide a vocation, an act of heroism. Liberty does not perish therein; but from its predeterminations it may be said that it was inevitable that it should so decide. And the Pelagians, Lutherans, and others have been mistaken in saying that grace compromised free choice and killed the creative force of the will; since all determinations of the will come necessarily either from society which sustains it, or from nature which opens its career and points out its destiny.

But, on the other hand, the Augustinians, the Thomists, the congruists, Jansen, Thomassin, Molina, etc., were strangely mistaken when, sustaining at once free will and grace, they failed to see that between these two terms the same relation exists as between substance and form, and that they have confessed an opposition which does not exist. Liberty, like intelligence, like all substance and all force, is necessarily determined, — that is, it has its forms and its attributes. Now, while in matter the form and the attribute are inherent in and contemporary with substance, in liberty the form is given by three external agents, as it were, — the human essence, the laws of thought, exercise or education. Grace, in fine, like its opposite, temptation, indicates precisely the fact of the determination of liberty.

To sum up, all modern ideas regarding the education of humanity are only an interpretation, a philosophy of the Catholic doctrine of grace, a doctrine which seemed obscure to its authors only because of their ideas upon free will, which they supposed to be threatened as soon as grace or the source of its determinations was spoken of. We affirm, on the contrary, that liberty, indifferent in itself to all modality, but destined to act and to take shape according to a preestablished order, receives its first impulse from the Creator who inspires it with love, intelligence, courage, resolution, and all the gifts of the Holy Spirit, and then delivers it to the labor of experience. It follows from this that grace is necessarily pre-moving, that without it man is capable of no sort of good, and that nevertheless free will accomplishes its own destiny spontaneously, with reflection and choice. In all this there is neither contradiction nor mystery. Man, in so far as he is man, is good; but, like the tyrant described by Plato, who was, he too, a teacher of grace, man carries in his bosom a thousand monsters, which the worship of justice and science, music and gymnastics, all the graces of opportunity and condition, must cause him to overcome. Correct one definition in Saint Augustine, and all that doctrine of grace, famous because of the disputes which it excited and which disconcerted the Reformation, will seem to you brilliant with clearness and harmony.

And now is man God?

God, according to the theological hypothesis, being the sovereign, absolute, highly synthetic being, the infinitely wise and free, and therefore indefectible and holy, Me, it is plain that man, the syncretism of the creation, the point of union of all the potentialities manifested by the creation, physical, organic, mental, and moral; man, perfectible and fallible, does not satisfy the conditions of Divinity as he, from the nature of his mind, must conceive them. Neither is he God, nor can he, living, become God.

All the more, then, the oak, the lion, the sun, the universe itself, sections of the absolute, are not God. At the same stroke the worship of man and the worship of nature are overthrown.

Now we have to present the counter-proof of this theory.

From the standpoint of social contradictions we have judged of the morality of man. We are to judge, in its turn and from the same standpoint, the morality of Providence. In other words, is God possible, as speculation and faith offer him for the adoration of mortals?

2. — Exposition of the myth of Providence. — Retrogression of God.

Among the proofs, to the number of three, which theologians and philosophers are accustomed to bring forward to show the existence of a God, they give the foremost position to universal consent.

This argument I considered when, without rejecting or admitting it, I promptly asked myself: What does universal consent affirm in affirming a God? And in this connection I should recall the fact that the difference of religions is not a proof that the human race has fallen into error in affirming a supreme Me outside of itself, any more than the diversity of languages is a proof of the non-reality of reason. The hypothesis of God, far from being weakened, is strengthened and established by the very divergence and opposition of faiths.

An argument of another sort is that which is drawn from the order of the world. In regard to this I have observed that, nature affirming spontaneously, by the voice of man, its own distinction into mind and matter, it remained to find out whether an infinite mind, a soul of the world, governs and moves the universe, as conscience, in its obscure intuition, tells us that a mind animates man. If, then, I added, order were an infallible sign of the presence of mind, the presence of a God in the universe could not be overlooked.

Unfortunately this if is not demonstrated and cannot be. For, on the one hand, pure mind, conceived as the opposite of matter, is a contradictory entity, the reality of which, consequently, nothing can attest. On the other hand, certain beings ordered in themselves — such as crystals, plants, and the planetary system, which, in the sensations that they make us feel, do not return us sentiment for sentiment, as the animals do — seeming to us utterly destitute of conscience, there is no more reason for supposing a mind in the centre of the world than for placing one in a stick of sulphur; and it may be that, if mind, conscience, exists anywhere, it is only in man.

Nevertheless, if the order of the world can tell us nothing as to the existence of God, it reveals a thing no less precious perhaps, and which will serve us as a landmark in our inquiries, — namely, that all beings, all essences, all phenomena are bound together by a totality of laws resulting from their properties, a totality which in the third chapter I have named fatality or necessity. Whether or not there exists then an infinite intelligence, embracing the whole system of these laws, the whole field of fatalism; whether or not to this infinite intelligence is united in profound penetration a superior will, eternally determined by the totality of the cosmic laws and consequently infinitely powerful and free; whether or not, finally, these three things, fatality, intelligence, will, are contemporary in the universe, adequate to each other and identical, — it is clear that so far we find nothing repugnant to these positions; but it is precisely this hypothesis, this anthropomorphism, which is yet to be demonstrated.

Thus, while the testimony of the human race reveals to us a God, without saying what this God may be, the order of the world reveals to us a fatality, — that is, an absolute and peremptory totality of causes and effects, — in short, a system of laws, — which would be, if God exists, like the sight and knowledge of this God.

The third and last proof of the existence of God proposed by the theists and called by them the metaphysical proof is nothing but a tautological construction of categories, which proves absolutely nothing.

Something exists; therefore there is something in existence.

Something is multiple; therefore something is one.

Something comes after something; therefore something is prior to something.

Something is smaller of greater than something; therefore something is greater than all things.

Something is moved; therefore something is mover, etc., ad infinitum.

That is what is called even today, in the faculties and the seminaries, by the minister of public education and by Messeigneurs the bishops, proving the existence of God by metaphysics. That is what the elite of the French youth are condemned to bleat after their professors, for a year, or else forfeit their diplomas and the privilege of studying law, medicine, polytechnics, and the sciences. Certainly, if anything is calculated to surprise, it is that with such philosophy Europe is not yet atheistic. The persistence of the theistic idea by the side of the jargon of the schools is the greatest of miracles; it constitutes the strongest prejudice that can be cited in favor of Divinity.

I do not know what humanity calls God.

I cannot say whether it is man, the universe, or some invisible reality that we are to understand by that name; or indeed whether the word stands for anything more than an ideal, a creature of the mind.

Nevertheless, to give body to my hypothesis and influence to my inquiries, I shall consider God in accordance with the common opinion, as a being apart, omnipresent, distinct from creation, endowed with imperishable life as well as infinite knowledge and activity, but above all foreseeing and just, punishing vice and rewarding virtue. I shall put aside the pantheistic hypothesis as hypocritical and lacking courage. God is personal, or he does not exist: this alternative is the axiom from which I shall deduce my entire theodicy.

Not concerning myself therefore for the present with questions which the idea of God may raise later, the problem before me now is to decide, in view of the facts the evolution of which in society I have established, what I should think of the conduct of God, as it is held up for my faith and relatively to humanity. In short, it is from the standpoint of the demonstrated existence of evil that I, with the aid of a new dialectical process, mean to fathom the Supreme Being.

Evil exists: upon this point everybody seems to agree.

330

Now, have asked the stoics, the Epicureans, the manicheans, and the atheists, how harmonize the presence of evil with the idea of a sovereignly good, wise, and powerful God? How can God, after allowing the introduction of evil into the world, whether through weakness or negligence or malice, render responsible for their acts creatures which he himself has created imperfect, and which he thus delivers to all the dangers of their attractions? Why, finally, since he promises the just a never-ending bliss after death, or, in other words, gives us the idea and desire of happiness, does he not cause us to enjoy this life by stripping us of the temptation of evil, instead of exposing us to an eternity of torture?

Such used to be the purport of the protest of the atheists.

Today this is scarcely discussed: the theists are no longer troubled by the logical impossibilities of their system. They want a God, especially a Providence: there is competition for this article between the radicals and the Jesuits. The socialists preach happiness and virtue in the name of God; in the schools those who talk the loudest against the Church are the first of mystics.

The old theists were more anxious about their faith. They tried, if not to demonstrate it, at least to render it reasonable, feeling sure, unlike their successors, that there is neither dignity nor rest for the believer except in certainty.

The Fathers of the Church then answered the incredulous that evil is only deprivation of a greater good, and that those who always reason about the better lack a point of support upon which to establish themselves, which leads straight to absurdity. In fact, every creature being necessarily confined and imperfect, God, by his infinite power, can continually add to his perfections: in this respect there is always, in some degree, a deprivation of good in the creature. Reciprocally, however imperfect and confined the creature is supposed to be, from the moment that it exists it enjoys a certain degree of good, better for it than annihilation. Therefore, though it is a rule that man is considered good only so far as he accomplishes all the good that he can, it is not the same with God, since the obligation to do good infinitely is contradictory to the very faculty of creation, perfection and creature being two terms that necessarily exclude each other. God, then, was sole judge of the degree of perfection which it was proper to give to each creature: to prefer a charge against him under this head is to slander his justice.

331

As for sin, — that is, moral evil, — the Fathers, to reply to the objections of the atheists, had the theories of free will, redemption, justification, and grace, to the discussion of which we need not return.

I have no knowledge that the atheists have replied categorically to this theory of the essential imperfection of the creature, a theory reproduced with brilliancy by M. de Lamennais in his "Esquisse." It was impossible, indeed, for them to reply to it; for, reasoning from a false conception of evil and of free will, and in profound ignorance of the laws of humanity, they were equally without reasons by which either to triumph over their own doubts or to refute the believers.

Let us leave the sphere of the finite and infinite, and place ourselves in the conception of order. Can God make a round circle, a right-angled square? Certainly.

Would God be guilty if, after having created the world according to the laws of geometry, he had put it into our minds, or even allowed us to believe without fault of our own, that a circle may be square or a square circular, though, in consequence of this false opinion, we should have to suffer an incalculable series of evils? Again, undoubtedly.

Well! that is exactly what God, the God of Providence, has done in the government of humanity; it is of that that I accuse him. He knew from all eternity — inasmuch as we mortals have discovered it after six thousand years of painful experience — that order in society — that is, liberty, wealth, science — is realized by the reconciliation of opposite ideas which, were each to be taken as absolute in itself, would precipitate us into an abyss of misery: why did he not warn us? Why did he not correct our judgment at the start? Why did he abandon us to our imperfect logic, especially when our egoism must find a pretext in his acts of injustice and perfidy? He knew, this jealous God, that, if he exposed us to the hazards of experience, we should not find until very late that security of life which constitutes our entire happiness: why did he not abridge this long apprenticeship by a revelation of our own laws? Why, instead of fascinating us with contradictory opinions, did he not reverse experience by causing us to reach the antinomies by the path of analysis of synthetic ideas, instead of leaving us to painfully clamber up the steeps of antinomy to synthesis?

If, as was formerly thought, the evil from which humanity suffers arose solely from the imperfection inevitable in every creature, or better, if this evil were caused only by the antagonism of the potentialities and inclinations which constitute our being, and which reason should teach us to master and guide, we should have no right to complain. Our condition being all that it could be, God would be justified.

But, in view of this wilful delusion of our minds, a delusion which it was so easy to dissipate and the effects of which must be so terrible, where is the excuse of Providence? Is it not true that grace failed man here? God, whom faith represents as a tender father and a prudent master, abandons us to the fatality of our incomplete conceptions; he digs the ditch under our feet; he causes us to move blindly: and then, at every fall, he punishes us as rascals. What do I say? It seems as if it were in spite of him that at last, covered with bruises from our journey, we recognize our road; as if we offended his glory in becoming more intelligent and free through the trials which he imposes upon us. What need, then, have we to continually invoke Divinity, and what have we to do with those satellites of a Providence which for sixty centuries, by the aid of a thousand religions, has deceived and misled us?

What! God, through his gospel-bearers and by the law which he has put in our hearts, commands us to love our neighbor as ourselves, to do to others as we wish to be done by, to render each his due, not to keep back anything from the laborer's hire, and not to lend at usury; he knows, moreover, that in us charity is lukewarm and conscience vacillating, and that the slightest pretext always seems to us a sufficient reason for exemption from the law: and yet he involves us, with such dispositions, in the contradictions of commerce and property, in which, by the necessity of the theory, charity and justice are bound to perish! Instead of enlightening our reason concerning the bearing of principles which impose themselves upon it with all the power of necessity, but whose consequences, adopted by egoism, are fatal to human fraternity, he places this abused reason at the service of our passion; by seduction of the mind, he destroys our equilibrium of conscience; he justifies in our own eyes our usurpations and our avarice; he makes the separation of man from his fellow inevitable and legitimate; he creates division and hatred among us in rendering equality by labor and by right impossible; he makes us believe that this equality, the law of the world, is unjust among men; and then he proscribes us en masse for not having known how to practise his incomprehensible precepts! I believe I have proved, to be sure, that our abandonment by Providence does not justify us; but, whatever our crime, toward it we are not guilty; and if there is a being who, before ourselves and more than ourselves, is deserving of hell, — I am bound to name him, — it is God.

When the theists, in order to establish their dogma of Providence, cite the order of nature as a proof, although this argument is only a begging

333

of the question, at least it cannot be said that it involves a contradiction, and that the fact cited bears witness against the hypothesis. In the system of the world, for instance, nothing betrays the smallest anomaly, the slightest lack of foresight, from which any prejudice whatever can be drawn against the idea of a supreme, intelligent, personal motor. In short, though the order of nature does not prove the reality of a Providence, it does not contradict it.

It is a very different thing with the government of humanity. Here order does not appear at the same time as matter; it was not created, as in the system of the world, once and for eternity. It is gradually developed according to an inevitable series of principles and consequences which the human being himself, the being to be ordered, must disengage spontaneously, by his own energy and at the solicitation of experience. No revelation regarding this is given him. Man is submitted at his origin to a preestablished necessity, to an absolute and irresistible order. That this order may be realized, man must discover it; that it may exist, he must have divined it. This labor of invention might be abridged; no one, either in heaven or on earth, will come to man's aid; no one will instruct him. Humanity, for hundreds of centuries, will devour its generations; it will exhaust itself in blood and mire, without the God whom it worships coming once to illuminate its reason and abridge its time of trial. Where is divine action here? Where is Providence?

"If God did not exist," — it is Voltaire, the enemy of religions, who says so, — "it would be necessary to invent him. " Why? "Because," adds the same Voltaire, "if I were dealing with an atheist prince whose interest it might be to have me pounded in a mortar, I am very sure that I should be pounded." Strange aberration of a great mind! And if you were dealing with a pious prince, whose confessor, speaking in the name of God, should command that you be burned alive, would you not be very sure of being burned also? Do you forget, then, anti-Christ, the Inquisition, and the Saint Bartholomew, and the stakes of Vanini and Bruno, and the tortures of Galileo, and the martyrdom of so many free thinkers? Do not try to distinguish here between use and abuse: for I should reply to you that from a mystical and supernatural principle, from a principle which embraces everything, which explains everything, which justifies everything, such as the idea of God, all consequences are legitimate, and that the zeal of the believer is the sole judge of their propriety.

"I once believed," says Rousseau, "that it was possible to be an honest man and dispense with God; but I have recovered from that error."

Fundamentally the same argument as that of Voltaire, the same justification of intolerance: Man does good and abstains from evil only through consideration of a Providence which watches over him; a curse on those who deny its existence! And, to cap the climax of absurdity, the man who thus seeks for our virtue the sanction of a Divinity who rewards and punishes is the same man who teaches the native goodness of man as a religious dogma.

And for my part I say: The first duty of man, on becoming intelligent and free, is to continually hunt the idea of God out of his mind and conscience. For God, if he exists, is essentially hostile to our nature, and we do not depend at all upon his authority. We arrive at knowledge in spite of him, at comfort in spite of him, at society in spite of him; every step we take in advance is a victory in which we crush Divinity.

Let it no longer be said that the ways of God are impenetrable. We have penetrated these ways, and there we have read in letters of blood the proofs of God's impotence, if not of his malevolence. My reason, long humiliated, is gradually rising to a level with the infinite; with time it will discover all that its inexperience hides from it; with time I shall be less and less a worker of misfortune, and by the light that I shall have acquired, by the perfection of my liberty, I shall purify myself, idealize my being, and become the chief of creation, the equal of God. A single moment of disorder which the Omnipotent might have prevented and did not prevent accuses his Providence and shows him lacking in wisdom; the slightest progress which man, ignorant, abandoned, and betrayed, makes towards good honors him immeasurably. By what right should God still say to me: Be holy, for I am holy? Lying spirit, I will answer him, imbecile God, your reign is over; look to the beasts for other victims. I know that I am not holy and never can become so; and how could you be holy, if I resemble you? Eternal father, Jupiter or Jehovah, we have learned to know you; you are, you were, you ever will be, the jealous rival of Adam, the tyrant of Prometheus.

So I do not fall into the sophism refuted by St. Paul, when he forbids the vase to say to the potter: Why hast thou made me thus? I do not blame the author of things for having made me an inharmonious creature, an incoherent assemblage; I could exist only in such a condition. I content myself with crying out to him: Why do you deceive me? Why, by your silence, have you unchained egoism within me? Why have you submitted me to the torture of universal doubt by the bitter illusion of the antagonistic ideas which you have put in my mind? Doubt of truth, doubt of justice, doubt of my conscience and my liberty, doubt of yourself, O God! and, as a result of this doubt, necessity of

335

war with myself and with my neighbor! That, supreme Father, is what you have done for our happiness and your glory; such, from the beginning, have been your will and your government; such the bread, kneaded in blood and tears, upon which you have fed us. The sins which we ask you to forgive, you caused us to commit; the traps from which we implore you to deliver us, you set for us; and the Satan who besets us is yourself.

You triumphed, and no one dared to contradict you, when, after having tormented in his body and in his soul the righteous Job, a type of our humanity, you insulted his candid piety, his prudent and respectful ignorance. We were as naught before your invisible majesty, to whom we gave the sky for a canopy and the earth for a footstool. And now here you are dethroned and broken. Your name, so long the last word of the savant, the sanction of the judge, the force of the prince, the hope of the poor, the refuge of the repentant sinner, — this incommunicable name, I say, henceforth an object of contempt and curses, shall be a hissing among men. For God is stupidity and cowardice; God is hypocrisy and falsehood; God is tyranny and misery; God is evil. As long as humanity shall bend before an altar, humanity, the slave of kings and priests, will be condemned; as long as one man, in the name of God, shall receive the oath of another man, society will be founded on perjury; peace and love will be banished from among mortals. God, take yourself away! for, from this day forth, cured of your fear and become wise, I swear, with hand extended to heaven, that you are only the tormentor of my reason, the spectre of my conscience.

I deny, therefore, the supremacy of God over humanity; I reject his providential government, the non-existence of which is sufficiently established by the metaphysical and economical hallucinations of humanity, — in a word, by the martyrdom of our race; I decline the jurisdiction of the Supreme Being over man; I take away his titles of father, king, judge, good, merciful, pitiful, helpful, rewarding, and avenging. All these attributes, of which the idea of Providence is made up, are but a caricature of humanity, irreconcilable with the autonomy of civilization, and contradicted, moreover, by the history of its aberrations and catastrophes. Does it follow, because God can no longer be conceived as Providence, because we take from him that attribute so important to man that he has not hesitated to make it the synonym of God, that God does not exist, and that the theological dogma from this moment is shown to be false in its content?

Alas! no. A prejudice relative to the divine essence has been destroyed; by the same stroke the independence of man is established: that is all.

The reality of the divine Being is left intact, and our hypothesis still exists. In demonstrating that it was impossible for God to be Providence, we have taken a first step in the determination of the idea of God; the question now is to find out whether this first datum accords with the rest of the hypothesis, and consequently to determine, from the same standpoint of intelligence, what God is, if he is.

For just as, after having established the guilt of man under the influence of the economical contradictions, we have had to account for this guilt, if we would not leave man wounded after having made him a contemptible satire, likewise, after having admitted the chimerical nature of the doctrine of a Providence in God, we must inquire how this lack of Providence harmonizes with the idea of sovereign intelligence and liberty, if we would not sacrifice the proposed hypothesis, which nothing yet shows to be false.

I affirm, then, that God, if there is a God, does not resemble the effigies which philosophers and priests have made of him; that he neither thinks nor acts according to the law of analysis, foresight, and progress, which is the distinctive characteristic of man; that, on the contrary, he seems rather to follow an inverse and retrogressive course; that intelligence, liberty, personality in God are constituted not as in us; and that this originality of nature, perfectly accounted for, makes God an essentially anti-civilizing, anti-liberal, anti-human being.

I prove my proposition by going from the negative to the positive, — that is, by deducing the truth of my thesis from the progress of the objections to it.

1. God, say the believers, can be conceived only as infinitely good, infinitely wise, infinitely powerful, etc., — the whole litany of the infinites. Now, infinite perfection cannot be reconciled with the datum of a will holding an indifferent or even reactionary attitude toward progress: therefore, either God does not exist, or the objection drawn from the development of the antinomies proves only our ignorance of the mysteries of infinity.

I answer these reasoners that, if, to give legitimacy to a wholly arbitrary opinion, it suffices to fall back on the unfathomability of mysteries, I am as well satisfied with the mystery of a God without providence as with that of a Providence without efficacy. But, in view of the facts, there is no occasion to invoke such a consideration of probability; we must confine ourselves to the positive declaration of experience. Now, experience and facts prove that humanity, in its development, obeys an

337

inflexible necessity, whose laws are made clear and whose system is realized as fast as the collective reason reveals it, without anything in society to give evidence of an external instigation, either from a providential command or from any superhuman thought. The basis of the belief in Providence is this necessity itself, which is, as it were, the foundation and essence of collective humanity. But this necessity, thoroughly systematic and progressive as it may appear, does not on that account constitute providence either in humanity or in God; to become convinced thereof it is enough to recall the endless oscillations and painful gropings by which social order is made manifest.

2. Other arguers come unexpectedly across our path, and cry: What is the use of these abstruse researches? There is no more an infinite intelligence than a Providence; there is neither me nor will in the universe outside of man. All that happens, evil as well as good, happens necessarily. An irresistible ensemble of causes and effects embraces man and nature in the same fatality; and those faculties in ourselves which we call conscience, will, judgment, etc., are only particular accidents of the eternal, immutable, and inevitable whole.

This argument is the preceding one inverted. It consists in substituting for the idea of an omnipotent and omniscient author that of a necessary and eternal, but unconscious and blind, coordination. From this opposition we can already form a presentiment that the reasoning of the materialists is no firmer than that of the believers.

Whoever says necessity or fatality says absolute and inviolable order; whoever, on the contrary, says disturbance and disorder affirms that which is most repugnant to fatality. Now, there is disorder in the world, disorder produced by the play of spontaneous forces which no power enchains: how can that be, if everything is the result of fate?

But who does not see that this old quarrel between theism and materialism proceeds from a false notion of liberty and fatality, two terms which have been considered contradictory, though really they are not. If man is free, says the one party, all the more surely is God free too, and fatality is but a word; if everything is enchained in nature, answers the other party, there is neither liberty nor Providence: and so each party argues in its own direction till out of sight, never able to understand that this pretended opposition of liberty and fatality is only the natural, but not antithetical, distinction between the facts of activity and those of intelligence.

Fatality is the absolute order, the law, the code, fatum, of the constitution of the universe. But this code, very far from being exclusive in itself of the idea of a sovereign legislator, supposes it so naturally that all antiquity has not hesitated to admit it; and today the whole question is to find out whether, as the founders of religions have believed, the legislator preceded the law in the universe, — that is, whether intelligence is prior to fatality, — or whether, as the moderns claim, the law preceded the legislator, — in other words, whether mind is born of nature. BEFORE or AFTER, this alternative sums up all philosophy. To dispute over the posteriority or priority of mind is all very well, but to deny mind in the name of fatality is an exclusion which nothing justifies. To refute it, it is sufficient to recall the very fact on which it is based, — the existence of evil.

Given matter and attraction, the system of the world is their product: that is fatal. Given two correlative and contradictory ideas, a composition must follow: that also is fatal. Fatality clashes, not with liberty, whose destiny, on the contrary, is to secure the accomplishment of fatality within a certain sphere, but with disorder, with everything that acts as a barrier to the execution of the law. Is there disorder in the world, yes or no? The fatalists do not deny it, for, by the strangest blunder, it is the presence of evil which has made them fatalists. Now, I say that the presence of evil, far from giving evidence of fatality, breaks fatality, does violence to destiny, and supposes a cause whose erroneous but voluntary initiative is in discordance with the law. This cause I call liberty; and I have proved, in the fourth chapter, that liberty, like reason which serves man as a torch, is as much greater and more perfect as it harmonizes more completely with the order of nature, which is fatality.

Therefore to oppose fatality to the testimony of the conscience which feels itself free, and vice versa, is to prove that one misconstrues ideas and has not the slightest appreciation of the question. The progress of humanity may be defined as the education of reason and human liberty by fatality: it is absurd to regard these three terms as exclusive of each other and irreconcilable, when in reality they sustain each other, fatality serving as the base, reason coming after, and liberty crowning the edifice. It is to know and penetrate fatality that human reason tends; it is to conform to it that liberty aspires; and the criticism in which we are now engaged of the spontaneous development and instinctive beliefs of the human race is at bottom only a study of fatality. Let us explain this.

Man, endowed with activity and intelligence, has the power to disturb the order of the world, of which he forms a part. But all his digressions have been foreseen, and are effected within certain limits, which, after a certain number of goings and comings, lead man back to order. From these oscillations of liberty may be determined the role of humanity in the world; and, since the destiny of man is bound up with that of creatures, it is possible to go back from him to the supreme law of things and even to the sources of being.

Accordingly I will no longer ask: How is it that man has the power to violate the providential order, and how is it that Providence allows him to do so? I state the question in other terms: How is it that man, an integrant part of the universe, a product of fatality, is able to break fatality? How is it that a fatal organization, the organization of humanity, is adventitious, contradictory, full of tumult and catastrophes? Fatality is not confined to an hour, to a century, to a thousand years: if science and liberty must inevitably be ours, why do they not come sooner? For, the moment we suffer from the delay, fatality contradicts itself; evil is as exclusive of fatality as of Providence.

What sort of a fatality, in short, is that which is contradicted every instant by the facts which take place within its bosom? This the fatalists are bound to explain, quite as much as the theists are bound to explain what sort of an infinite intelligence that can be which is unable either to foresee or prevent the misery of its creatures.

But that is not all. Liberty, intelligence, fatality, are at bottom three adequate expressions, serving to designate three different faces of being. In man reason is only a defined liberty conscious of its limit. But within the circle of its limitations this liberty is also fatality, a living and personal fatality. When, therefore, the conscience of the human race proclaims that the fatality of the universe — that is, the highest, the supreme fatality — is adequate to an infinite reason as well as to an infinite liberty, it simply puts forth an hypothesis in every way legitimate, the verification of which is incumbent upon all parties.

3. Now come the humanists, the new atheists, and say:

Humanity in its ensemble is the reality sought by the social genius under the mystical name of God. This phenomenon of the collective reason, — a sort of mirage in which humanity, contemplating itself, takes itself for an external and transcendent being who considers its destinies and presides over them, — this illusion of the conscience, we say, has been analyzed and explained; and henceforth to reproduce the theological hypothesis is to take a step backward in science. We must

340

confine ourselves strictly to society, to man. God in religion, the State in politics, property in economy, such is the triple form under which humanity, become foreign to itself, has not ceased to rend itself with its own hands, and which today it must reject.

I admit that every affirmation or hypothesis of Divinity proceeds from anthropomorphism, and that God in the first place is only the ideal, or rather, the spectre of man. I admit further that the idea of God is the type and foundation of the principle of authority and absolutism, which it is our task to destroy or at least to subordinate wherever it manifests itself, in science, industry, public affairs. Consequently I do not contradict humanism; I continue it. Taking up its criticism of the divine being and applying it to man, I observe:

That man, in adoring himself as God, has posited of himself an ideal contrary to his own essence, and has declared himself an antagonist of the being supposed to be sovereignly perfect, — in short, of the infinite;

That man consequently is, in his own judgment, only a false divinity, since in setting up God he denies himself; and that humanism is a religion as detestable as any of the theisms of ancient origin;

That this phenomenon of humanity taking itself for God is not explainable in the terms of humanism, and requires a further interpretation.

God, according to the theological conception, is not only sovereign master of the universe, the infallible and irresponsible king of creatures, the intelligible type of man; he is the eternal, immutable, omnipresent, infinitely wise, infinitely free being. Now, I say that these attributes of God contain more than an ideal, more than an elevation — to whatever power you will — of the corresponding attributes of humanity; I say that they are a contradiction of them. God is contradictory of man, just as charity is contradictory of justice; as sanctity, the ideal of perfection, is contradictory of perfectibility; as royalty, the ideal of legislative power, is contradictory of law, etc. So that the divine hypothesis is reborn from its resolution into human reality, and the problem of a complete, harmonious, and absolute existence, ever put aside, ever comes back.

To demonstrate this radical antinomy it suffices to put facts in juxtaposition with definitions.

341

Of all facts the most certain, most constant, most indubitable, is certainly that in man knowledge is progressive, methodical, the result of reflection, — in short, experimental; so much so that every theory not having the sanction of experience — that is, of constancy and concatenation in its representations — thereby lacks a scientific character. In regard to this not the slightest doubt can be raised. Mathematics themselves, though called pure, are subject to the CONCATENATION of propositions, and hence depend upon experience and acknowledge its law.

Man's knowledge, starting with acquired observation, then progresses and advances in an unlimited sphere. The goal which it has in view, the ideal which it tends to realize without ever being able to attain it, — placing it on the contrary farther and farther ahead of it, — is the infinite, the absolute.

Now, what would be an infinite knowledge, an absolute knowledge, determining an equally infinite liberty, such as speculation supposes in God? It would be a knowledge not only universal, but intuitive, spontaneous, as thoroughly free from hesitation as from objectivity, although embracing at once the real and the possible; a knowledge sure, but not demonstrative; complete, not sequential; a knowledge, in short, which, being eternal in its formation, would be destitute of any progressive character in the relation of its parts.

Psychology has collected numerous examples of this mode of knowing in the instinctive and divinatory faculties of animals; in the spontaneous talent of certain men born mathematicians and artists, independent of all education; finally, in most of the primitive human institutions and monuments, products of unconscious genius independent of theories. And the regular and complex movements of the heavenly bodies; the marvellous combinations of matter, — could it not be said that these too are the effects of a special instinct, inherent in the elements?

If, then, God exists, something of him appears to us in the universe and in ourselves: but this something is in flagrant opposition with our most authentic tendencies, with our most certain destiny; this something is continually being effaced from our soul by education, and to make it disappear is the object of our care. God and man are two natures which shun each other as soon as they know each other; in the absence of a transformation of one or the other or both, how could they ever be reconciled? If the progress of reason tends to separate us from Divinity, how could God and man be identical in point of reason? How, consequently, could humanity become God by education?

Let us take another example.

The essential characteristic of religion is feeling. Hence, by religion, man attributes feeling to God, as he attributes reason to him; moreover, he affirms, following the ordinary course of his ideas, that feeling in God, like knowledge, is infinite.

Now, that alone is sufficient to change the quality of feeling in God, and make it an attribute totally distinct from that of man. In man sentiment flows, so to speak, from a thousand different sources: it contradicts itself, it confuses itself, it rends itself; otherwise, it would not feel itself. In God, on the contrary, sentiment is infinite, — that is, one, complete, fixed, clear, above all storms, and not needing irritation as a contrast in order to arrive at happiness. We ourselves experience this divine mode of feeling when a single sentiment, absorbing all our faculties, as in the case of ecstasy, temporarily imposes silence upon the other affections. But this rapture exists always only by the aid of contrast and by a sort of provocation from without; it is never perfect, or, if it reaches fulness, it is like the star which attains its apogee, for an indivisible instant.

Thus we do not live, we do not feel, we do not think, except by a series of oppositions and shocks, by an internal warfare; our ideal, then, is not infinity, but equilibrium; infinity expresses something other than ourselves.

It is said: God has no attributes peculiar to himself; his attributes are those of man; then man and God are one and the same thing.

On the contrary, the attributes of man, being infinite in God, are for that very reason peculiar and specific: it is the nature of the infinite to become speciality, essence, from the fact that the finite exists. Deny then, if you will, the reality of God, as one denies the reality of a contradictory idea; reject from science and morality this inconceivable and bloody phantom which seems to pursue us the more, the farther it gets from us; up to a certain point that may be justified, and at any rate can do no harm. But do not make God into humanity, for that would be slander of both.

Will it be said that the opposition between man and the divine being is illusory, and that it arises from the opposition that exists between the individual man and the essence of entire humanity? Then it must be maintained that humanity, since it is humanity that they deify, is neither progressive, nor contrasted in reason and feeling; in short, that it is

343

infinite in everything, — which is denied not only by history, but by psychology.

This is not a correct understanding, cry the humanists. To have the right ideal of humanity, it must be considered, not in its historic development, but in the totality of its manifestations, as if all human generations, gathered into one moment, formed a single man, an infinite and immortal man.

That is to say, they abandon the reality to seize a projection; the true man is not the real man; to find the veritable man, the human ideal, we must leave time and enter eternity, — what do I say? — desert the finite for infinity, man for God! Humanity, in the shape we know it, in the shape in which it is developed, in the only shape in fact in which it can exist, is erect; they show us its reversed image, as in a mirror, and then say to us: That is man! And I answer: It is no longer man, it is God. Humanism is the most perfect theism.

What, then, is this providence which the theists suppose in God? An essentially human faculty, an anthropomorphic attribute, by which God is thought to look into the future according to the progress of events, in the same way that we men look into the past, following the perspective of chronology and history.

Now, it is plain that, just as infinity — that is, spontaneous and universal intuition in knowledge — is incompatible with humanity, so providence is incompatible with the hypothesis of the divine being. God, to whom all ideas are equal and simultaneous; God, whose reason does not separate synthesis from antinomy; God, to whom eternity renders all things present and contemporary, — was unable, when creating us, to reveal to us the mystery of our contradictions; and that precisely because he is God, because he does not see contradiction, because his intelligence does not fall under the category of time and the law of progress, because his reason is intuitive and his knowledge infinite. Providence in God is a contradiction within a contradiction; it was through providence that God was actually made in the image of man; take away this providence, and God ceases to be man, and man in turn must abandon all his pretensions to divinity.

Perhaps it will be asked of what use it is to God to have infinite knowledge, if he is ignorant of what takes place in humanity.

Let us distinguish. God has a perception of order, the sentiment of good. But this order, this good, he sees as eternal and absolute; he does

344

not see it in its successive and imperfect aspects; he does not grasp its defects. We alone are capable of seeing, feeling, and appreciating evil, as well as of measuring duration, because we alone are capable of producing evil, and because our life is temporary. God sees and feels only order; God does not grasp what happens, because what happens is beneath him, beneath his horizon. We, on the contrary, see at once the good and the evil, the temporal and the eternal, order and disorder, the finite and the infinite; we see within us and outside of us; and our reason, because it is finite, surpasses our horizon.

Thus, by the creation of man and the development of society, a finite and providential reason, our own, has been posited in contradiction of the intuitive and infinite reason, God; so that God, without losing anything of his infinity in any direction, seems diminished by the very fact of the existence of humanity. Progressive reason resulting from the projection of eternal ideas upon the movable and inclined plane of time, man can understand the language of God, because he comes from God and his reason at the start is like that of God; but God cannot understand us or come to us, because he is infinite and cannot re-clothe himself in finite attributes without ceasing to be God, without destroying himself. The dogma of providence in God is shown to be false, both in fact and in right.

It is easy now to see how the same reasoning turns against the system of the deification of man.

Man necessarily positing God as absolute and infinite in his attributes, whereas he himself develops in a direction the inverse of this ideal, there is discord between the progress of man and what man conceives as God. On the one hand, it appears that man, by the syncretism of his constitution and the perfectibility of his nature, is not God and cannot become God; on the other, it is plain that God, the supreme Being, is the antipode of humanity, the ontological summit from which it indefinitely separates itself. God and man, having divided between them the antagonistic faculties of being, seem to be playing a game in which the control of the universe is the stake, the one having spontaneity, directness, infallibility, eternity, the other having foresight, deduction, mobility, time. God and man hold each other in perpetual check and continually avoid each other; while the latter goes ahead in reflection and theory without ever resting, the former, by his providential incapacity, seems to withdraw into the spontaneity of his nature. There is a contradiction, therefore, between humanity and its ideal, an opposition between man and God, an opposition which

345

Christian theology has allegorized and personified under the name of Devil or Satan, — that is, contradictor, enemy of God and man.

Such is the fundamental antinomy which I find that modern critics have not taken into account, and which, if neglected, having sooner or later to end in the negation of the man-God and consequently in the negation of this whole philosophical exegesis, reopens the door to religion and fanaticism.

God, according to the humanists, is nothing but humanity itself, the collective me to which the individual me is subjected as to an invisible master. But why this singular vision, if the portrait is a faithful copy of the original? Why has man, who from his birth has known directly and with out a telescope his body, his soul, his chief, his priest, his country, his condition, been obliged to see himself as in a mirror, and without recognizing himself, under the fantastic image of God? Where is the necessity of this hallucination? What is this dim and ambiguous consciousness which, after a certain time, becomes purified, rectified, and, instead of taking itself for another, definitively apprehends itself as such? Why on the part of man this transcendental confession of society, when society itself was there, present, visible, palpable, willing, and acting, — when, in short, it was known as society and named as such?

No, it is said, society did not exist; men were agglomerated, but not associated; the arbitrary constitution of property and the State, as well as the intolerant dogmatism of religion, prove it.

Pure rhetoric: society exists from the day that individuals, communicating by labor and speech, assume reciprocal obligations and give birth to laws and customs. Undoubtedly society becomes perfect in proportion to the advances of science and economy, but at no epoch of civilization does progress imply any such metamorphosis as those dreamed of by the builders of utopia; and however excellent the future condition of humanity is to be, it will be none the less the natural continuation, the necessary consequence, of its previous positions.

For the rest, no system of association being exclusive in itself, as I have shown, of fraternity and justice, it has never been possible to confound the political ideal with God, and we see in fact that all peoples have distinguished society from religion. The first was taken as end, the second regarded only as means; the prince was the minister of the collective will, while God reigned over consciences, awaiting beyond the grave the guilty who escaped the justice of men. Even the idea of progress and reform has never been anywhere absent; nothing, in short,

346

of that which constitutes social life has been entirely ignored or misconceived by any religious nation. Why, then, once more, this tautology of Society-Divinity, if it is true, as is pretended, that the theological hypothesis contains nothing other than the ideal of human society, the preconceived type of humanity transfigured by equality, solidarity, labor, and love?

Certainly, if there is a prejudice, a mysticism, which now seems to me deceptive in a high degree, it is no longer Catholicism, which is disappearing, but rather this humanitary philosophy, making man a holy and sacred being on the strength of a speculation too learned not to have something of the arbitrary in its composition; proclaiming him God, — that is, essentially good and orderly in all his powers, in spite of the disheartening evidence which he continually gives of his doubtful morality; attributing his vices to the constraint in which he has lived, and promising from him in complete liberty acts of the purest devotion, because in the myths in which humanity, according to this philosophy, has painted itself, we find described and opposed to each other, under the names of hell and paradise, a time of constraint and penalty and an era of happiness and independence! With such a doctrine it would suffice — and moreover it would be inevitable — for man to recognize that he is neither God, nor good, nor holy, nor wise, in order to fall back immediately into the arms of religion; so that in the last analysis all that the world will have gained by the denial of God will be the resurrection of God.

Such is not my view of the meaning of the religious fables. Humanity, in recognizing God as its author, its master, its alter ego, has simply determined its own essence by an antithesis, — an eclectic essence, full of contrasts, emanated from the infinite and contradictory of the infinite, developed in time and aspiring to eternity, and for all these reasons fallible, although guided by the sentiment of beauty and order. Humanity is the daughter of God, as every opposition is the daughter of a previous position: that is why humanity has formed God like itself, has lent him its own attributes, but always by giving them a specific character, — that is, by defining God in contradiction of itself. Humanity is a spectre to God, just as God is a spectre to humanity; each of the two is the other's cause, reason, and end of existence.

It was not enough, then, to have demonstrated, by criticism of religious ideas, that the conception of the divine me leads back to the perception of the human me; it was also necessary to verify this deduction by a criticism of humanity itself, and to see whether this humanity satisfies the conditions that its apparent divinity supposes. Now, such is the task

347

that we solemnly inaugurated when, starting at once with human reality and the divine hypothesis, we began to unroll the history of society in its economic institutions and speculative thoughts.

We have shown, on the one hand, that man, although incited by the antagonism of his ideas, and although up to a certain point excusable, does evil gratuitously and by the bestial impulse of his passions, which are repugnant to the character of a free, intelligent, and holy being. We have shown, on the other hand, that the nature of man is not harmoniously and synthetically constituted, but formed by an agglomeration of the potentialities specialized in each creature, — a circumstance which, in revealing to us the principle of the disorders committed by human liberty, has finished the demonstration of the non-divinity of our race. Finally, after having proved that in God providence not only does not exist, but is impossible; after having, in other words, separated the divine attributes of the infinite Being from the anthropomorphic attributes, — we have concluded, contrary to the affirmations of the old theodicy, that, relatively to the destiny of man, a destiny essentially progressive, intelligence and liberty in God suffered a contrast, a sort of limitation and diminution, resulting from his eternal, immutable, and infinite nature; so that man, instead of adoring in God his sovereign and his guide, could and should look on him only as his antagonist. And this last consideration will suffice to make us reject humanism also, as tending invincibly, by the deification of humanity, to a religious restoration. The true remedy for fanaticism, in our view, is not to identify humanity with God, which amounts to affirming, in social economy communism, in philosophy mysticism and the statu quo; it is to prove to humanity that God, in case there is a God, is its enemy.

What solution will result later from these data? Will God, in the end, be found to be a reality?

I do not know whether I shall ever know. If it is true, on the one hand, that I have today no more reason for affirming the reality of man, an illogical and contradictory being, than the reality of God, an inconceivable and unmanifested being, I know at least, from the radical opposition of these two natures, that I have nothing to hope or to fear from the mysterious author whom my consciousness involuntarily supposes; I know that my most authentic tendencies separate me daily from the contemplation of this idea; that practical atheism must be henceforth the law of my heart and my reason; that from observable necessity I must continually learn the rule of my conduct; that any mystical commandment, any divine right, which should be proposed to me, must be rejected and combatted by me; that a return to God through religion, idleness, ignorance, or submission, is an outrage upon myself; and that if I must sometime be reconciled with God, this reconciliation, impossible as long as I live and in which I should have everything to gain and nothing to lose, can be accomplished only by my destruction.

Let us then conclude, and inscribe upon the column which must serve as a landmark in our later researches:

The legislator distrusts man, an abridgment of nature and a syncretism of all beings. He does not rely on Providence, an inadmissible faculty in the infinite mind.

But, attentive to the succession of phenomena, submissive to the lessons of destiny, he seeks in necessity the law of humanity, the perpetual prophecy of his future.

He remembers also, sometimes, that, if the sentiment of Divinity is growing weaker among men; if inspiration from above is gradually withdrawing to give place to the deductions of experience; if there is a more and more flagrant separation of man and God; if this progress, the form and condition of our life, escapes the perceptions of an infinite and consequently non-historic intelligence; if, to say it all, appeal to Providence on the part of a government is at once a cowardly hypocrisy and a threat against liberty, — nevertheless the universal consent of the peoples, manifested by the establishment of so many different faiths, and the forever insoluble contradiction which strikes humanity in its ideas, its manifestations, and its tendencies indicate a secret relation of our soul, and through it of entire nature, with the infinite, — a relation the determination of which would express at the same time the meaning of the universe and the reason of our existence.

[1] Ie-hovah, and in composition Iah, the Being; Iao, ioupitur, same meaning; ha-iah, Heb., he was; ei, Gr, he is, ei-nai, to be; an-i, Heb., and in conjugation th-i, me; e-go, io, ich, i, m-i, me, t-ibi, te, and all the personal pronouns in which the vowels i, e, ei, oi, denote personality in general, and the consonants, m or n, s or t, serve to indicate the number of the person. For the rest, let who will dispute over these analogies; I have no objections: at this depth, the science of the philologist is but cloud and mystery. The important point to which I wish to call attention

is that the phonetic relation of names seems to correspond to the metaphysical relation of ideas.

[2] The Chinese have preserved in their traditions the remembrance of a religion which had ceased to exist among them five or six centuries before our era. (See Pauthier, "China," Paris, Didot.) More surprising still is it that this singular people, in losing its primitive faith, seems to have understood that divinity is simply the collective me of humanity: so that, more than two thousand years ago, China had reached, in its commonly-accepted belief, the latest results of the philosophy of the Occident. "What Heaven sees and understands," it is written in the Shu-king, "is only that which the people see and understand. What the people deem worthy of reward and punishment is that which Heaven wishes to punish and reward. There is an intimate communication between Heaven and the people: let those who govern the people, therefore, be watchful and cautious." Confucius expressed the same idea in another manner: "Gain the affection of the people, and you gain empire. Lose the affection of the people, and you lose empire." There, then, general reason was regarded as queen of the world, a distinction which elsewhere has been bestowed upon revelations. The Tao-te-king is still more explicit. In this work, which is but an outline criticism of pure reason, the philosopher Lao-tse continually identifies, under the name of TAO, universal reason and the infinite being; and all the obscurity of the book of Lao tse consists, in my opinion, of this constant identification of principles which our religious and metaphysical habits have so widely separated.

[3] See, among others, Auguste Comte, "Course of Positive Philosophy," and P. J. Proudhon, "Creation of Order in Humanity."

[4] I do not mean to affirm here in a positive manner the transmutability of bodies, or to point it out as a subject for investigation; still less do I pretend to say what ought to be the opinion of savants upon this point. I wish only to call attention to the species of scepticism generated in every uninformed mind by the most general conclusions of chemical philosophy, or, better, by the irreconcilable hypotheses which serve as the basis of its theories. Chemistry is truly the despair of reason: on all sides it mingles with the fanciful; and the more knowledge of it we gain by experience, the more it envelops itself in impenetrable mysteries. This thought was recently suggested to me by reading M. Liebig's "Letters on Chemistry" (Paris, Masgana, 1845, translation of Bertet-Dupiney and Dubreuil Helion). Thus M. Liebig, after having banished from science hypothetical causes and all the entities admitted by the ancients, — such as the creative

power of matter, the horror of a vacuum, the esprit recteur, etc. (p. 22), — admits immediately, as necessary to the comprehension of chemical phenomena, a series of entities no less obscure, — vital force, chemical force, electric force, the force of attraction, etc. (pp. 146, 149). One might call it a realization of the properties of bodies, in imitation of the psychologists' realization of the faculties of the soul under the names liberty, imagination, memory, etc. Why not keep to the elements? Why, if the atoms have weight of their own, as M. Liebig appears to believe, may they not also have electricity and life of their own? Curious thing! the phenomena of matter, like those of mind, become intelligible only by supposing them to be produced by unintelligible forces and governed by contradictory laws: such is the inference to be drawn from every page of M. Liebig's book. Matter, according to M. Liebig, is essentially inert and entirely destitute of spontaneous activity (p. 148): why, then, do the atoms have weight? Is not the weight inherent in atoms the real, eternal, and spontaneous motion of matter? And that which we chance to regard as rest, — may it not be equilibrium rather? Why, then, suppose now an inertia which definitions contradict, now an external potentiality which nothing proves?

Atoms having weight, M. Liebig infers that they are indivisible (p. 58). What logic! Weight is only force, that is, a thing hidden from the senses, whose phenomena alone are perceptible, — a thing, consequently, to which the idea of division and indivision is inapplicable; and from the presence of this force, from the hypothesis of an indeterminate and immaterial entity, is inferred an indivisible material existence!

For the rest, M. Liebig confesses that it is impossible for the mind to conceive of particles absolutely indivisible; he recognizes, further, that the fact of this indivisibility is not proved; but he adds that science cannot dispense with this hypothesis: so that, by the confession of its teachers, chemistry has for its point of departure a fiction as repugnant to the mind as it is foreign to experience. What irony! Atoms are unequal in weight, says M. Liebig, because unequal in volume: nevertheless, it is impossible to demonstrate that chemical equivalents express the relative weight of atoms, or, in other words, that what the calculation of atomic equivalents leads us to regard as an atom is not composed of several atoms. This is tantamount to saying that more matter weighs more than less matter; and, since weight is the essence of materiality, we may logically conclude that, weight being universally identical with itself, there is also an identity in matter; that the differences of simple bodies are due solely, either to different methods of atomic association, or to different degrees of molecular condensation, and that, in reality, atoms are transmutable: which M. Liebig does not admit.

"We have," he says, "no reason for believing that one element is convertible into another element" (p. 135). What do you know about it? The reasons for believing in such a conversion can very well exist and at the same time escape your attention; and it is not certain that your intelligence in this respect has risen to the level of your experience. But, admitting the negative argument of M. Liebig, what follows? That, with about fifty-six exceptions, irreducible as yet, all matter is in a condition of perpetual metamorphosis. Now, it is a law of our reason to suppose in Nature unity of substance as well as unity of force and system; moreover, the series of chemical compounds and simple substances themselves leads us irresistibly to this conclusion. Why, then, refuse to follow to the end the road opened by science, and to admit an hypothesis which is the inevitable result of experience itself? M. Liebig not only denies the transmutability of elements, but rejects the spontaneous formation of germs. Now, if we reject the spontaneous formation of germs, we are forced to admit their eternity; and as, on the other hand, geology proves that the globe has not been inhabited always, we must admit also that, at a given moment, the eternal germs of animals and plants were born, without father or mother, over the whole face of the earth. Thus, the denial of spontaneous generation leads back to the hypothesis of spontaneity: what is there in much-derided metaphysics more contradictory? Let it not be thought, however, that I deny the value and certainty of chemical theories, or that the atomic theory seems to me absurd, or that I share the Epicurean opinion as to spontaneous generation. Once more, all that I wish to point out is that, from the point of view of principles, chemistry needs to exercise extreme tolerance, since its own existence depends on a certain number of fictions, contrary to reason and experience, and destructive of each other.

[5] Chemists distinguish between mixture and composition, just as logicians distinguish between the association of ideas and their synthesis. It is true, nevertheless, that, according to the chemists, composition may be after all but a mixture, or rather an aggregation of atoms, no longer fortuitous, but systematic, the atoms forming different compounds by varying their arrangement. But still this is only an hypothesis, wholly gratuitous; an hypothesis which explains nothing, and has not even the merit of being logical. Why does a purely numerical or geometrical difference in the composition and form of atoms give rise to physiological properties so different? If atoms are indivisible and impenetrable, why does not their association, confined to mechanical effects, leave them unchanged in essence? Where is the relation between the cause supposed and the effect obtained? We must distrust our intellectual vision: it is with chemical theories as with psychological systems. The mind, in order to account for

352

phenomena, works with atoms, which it does not and can never see, as with the me, which it does not perceive: it applies its categories to everything; that is, it distinguishes, individualizes, concretes, numbers, compares, things which, material or immaterial, are thoroughly identical and indistinguishable. Matter, as well as spirit, plays, as we view it, all sorts of parts; and, as there is nothing arbitrary in its metamorphoses, we build upon them these psychologic and atomic theories, true in so far as they faithfully represent, in terms agreed upon, the series of phenomena, but radically false as soon as they pretend to realize their abstractions and are accepted literally.

[6] The passage quoted may not be given in the exact words used by Malthus, it having reached its present shape through the medium of a French rendering — Translator.

[7] "The principle which governs the life of nations is not pure science: it is the total of the complex data which depend on the state of enlightenment, on needs and interests." Thus expressed itself, in December, 1844, one of the clearest minds that France contained, M. Leon Faucher. Explain, if you can, how a man of this stamp was led by his economic convictions to declare that the complex data of society are opposed to pure science.

[8] "History of Public Credit."

[9] In France, the sale of tobacco is a government monopoly. — Translator.

[10] A subtle philologist, M. Paul Ackermann, has shown, using the French language as an illustration, that, since every word in a language has its opposite, or, as the author calls it, its antonym, the entire vocabulary might be arranged in couples, forming a vast dualistic system. (See Dictionary of Antonyms. By PAUL ACKERMAN. Paris: Brockhaus & Avenarius. 1842)

[11] "Treatise on Political Economy."

[12] Tocqueville, "Democracy in America."

[13] Meeting of the Academy of Moral and Political Sciences, September, 1845.

[14] Journal des Economistes," April, 1843.

[15] "The Liberty of Labor," Vol. II, p. 80.

[16] In spite of the most approved authorities, I cannot accept the idea that serf, in Latin servus, was so called from servare, to keep, because the slave was a prisoner of war who was kept for labor. Servitude, or at least domesticity, is certainly prior to war, although war may have noticeably strengthened it. Why, moreover, if such was the origin of the idea as well as of the thing, should they not have said, instead of serv-us, serv-atus, in conformity with grammatical deduction? To me the real etymology is revealed in the opposition of serv-are and serv-ire, the primitive theme of which is ser-o in-stro, to join, to press, whence ser-ies, joint, continuity, Ser-a, lock, sertir, insert, etc. All these words imply the idea of a principal thing, to which is joined an accessory, as an object of special usefulness. Thence serv-ire, to be an object of usefulness, a thing secondary to another; serv-are, as we say to press, to put aside, to assign a thing its utility; serv-us, a man at hand, a utility, a chattel, in short, a man of service. The opposite of servus is dem-inus (dom-us, dom-anium, and domare); that is, the head of the household, the master of the house, he who utilizes men, servat, animals, domat, and things, possidet.That consequently prisoners of war should have been reserved for slavery, servati ad servitium, or rather serti ad glebam, is perfectly conceivable; their destiny being known, they have simply taken their name from it.

[17] A comparison of this passage, as given here, with the English translation of "What is Property" will show a marked variation in the language. This is explained by the fact that the author, in reproducing the passage, modified it considerably. The same is true of another quotation from the same work which will be found a few pages farther on. — Translator.

[18] This extract from Scott, as well as that from a parliamentary report cited a few paragraphs later, is here translated from the French, and presumably differs in form somewhat, therefore, from the original English. — Translator.

[19] The spinning-wheel is silent in the valley: family feelings are at an end. Over a little smoke the aged grandsire spreads his pale hands; and the empty hearth is as desolate as his heart. — Translator.

[20] Possibly these paragraphs will not be clear to all without the explanation that the form of association discussed in them, called in French the commandite, is a joint-stock company to which the shareholders simply lend their capital, without acquiring a share in the

management or incurring responsibility for the results thereof. — Translator.

[21] Hunting, fishing, mining, — in short, the gathering of all natural products. — Translator.

[22] Little bones taken from the joints of animals and serving as playthings for children. — Translator.

[23] A tax whose total product is not fixed in advance, but depends upon the quantity of things or persons upon whom it happens to fall. — Translator.

[24] This sentence, as it stands, is unintelligible, and probably is not correctly quoted by Proudhon. At any rate, one of Garnier's works contains a similar passage, which begins thus: "Given a levy of one on the area of the land, and lands of different qualities producing, the first eight, the second six, the third five, the tax will call for one-eighth," etc. This is perfectly clear, and the circumstances supposed are aptly illustrative of Proudhon's point. I should unhesitatingly pronounce it the correct version, except for the fact that Proudhon, in the succeeding paragraph, interprets Garnier as supposing income to be assessed instead of capital. — Translator.

[25] Thank heaven! the minister has settled the question, and I tender him my very sincere compliments. By the proposed tariff letter-postage will be reduced to 2 cents for distances under 12 1/2 miles; 4 cents, for distances between 12 1/2 and 25 miles; 6 cents, between 25 and 75 miles; 8 cents, between 75 and 225 miles; 10 cents, for longer distances.]

[26] The new law regarding service-books has confined the independence of workers within narrower limits. The democratic press has again thundered its indignation this subject against those in power, as if they had been guilty of anything more than the application of the principles of authority and property, which are those of democracy. What the Chambers have done in regard to service-books was inevitable, and should have been expected. It is as impossible for a society founded on the proprietary principle not to end in class distinctions as for a democracy to avoid despotism, for a religion to be reasonable, for fanaticism to show tolerance. This is the law of contradiction: how long will it take us to understand it?

355

[27] The crime makes the shame, and not the scaffold. — Translator.

[28] See volume II, chapter IX.

[29] Ibid., chapter X.

[30] Ibid., chapter XI.

[31] Date of the Napoleonic coup d'Etat, according to the revolutionary calendar.

Toast to the Revolution

October 17, 1848

Citizens,

When our friends of the democratic republic, apprehensive of our ideas and our inclinations, cry out against the qualification of *socialist* which we add to that of *democrat*, of what do they reproach us? — They reproach us for not being revolutionaries.

Let us see then if they or we are in the tradition; whether they or we have the true revolutionary practice.

And when our adversaries of the middle class, concerned for their privileges, pour upon us calumny and insult, what is the pretext of their charges? It is that we want to totally destroy property, the family, and civilization.

Let us see then again whether we or our adversaries better deserve the title of conservatives.

Revolutions are the successive manifestation of justice in human history. — It is for this reason that all revolutions have their origins in a previous revolution.

Whoever talks about revolution necessarily talks about *progress*, but just as necessarily about *conservation*. From this it follows that revolution is always in history and that, strictly speaking, there are not several revolutions, but only one permanent revolution.

The revolution, eighteen centuries ago, called itself the gospel, the Good News. Its fundamental dogma was the *Unity of God;* its motto, *the equality of all men before God*. Ancient slavery rested on the antagonism and inequality of gods, which represented the relative inferiority of races, in the state of war. Christianity created the rights of peoples, the brotherhood of nations; it abolished simultaneously idolatry and slavery.

Certainly no one denies today that the Christians, revolutionaries who fought by testimony and by martyrdom, were men of progress. They were also conservatives.

The polytheist initiation, after civilizing the first humans, after converting these men of the woods, *sylvestres homine*, as the poet says, into men of the towns, became itself, through sensualism and privilege, a principle of corruption and enslavement. Humanity was lost, when it was saved by the Christ, who received for that glorious mission the double title of *Savior* and *Redeemer*, or as we put it in our political language, conservative and revolutionary.

That was the character of the first and greatest of revolutions. It renewed the world, and in renewing it conserved it.

But, supernatural and spiritual as it was, that revolution nevertheless only expressed the more material side of justice, the enfranchisement of bodies and the abolition of slavery. Established on faith, it left thought enslaved; it was not sufficient for the emancipation of man, who is body and spirit, matter and intelligence. It called for another revolution. A thousand years after the coming of Christ, a new upheaval began, within the religion the first revolution founded, a prelude to new progress. Scholasticism carried within it, along with the authority of the Church and the scripture, the authority of reason! In about the 16th century, the revolution burst out.

The revolution, in that epoch, without abandoning its first given, took another name, which was already celebrated. It called itself philosophy. Its dogma was *the liberty of reason*, and its motto, which follows from that, was *the equality of all before reason*.

Here then is man declared inviolable and free in his double essence, as soul and as body. Was this progress? Who but a tyrant could deny it? Was it an act of conservation? The question does not even merit a response.

The destiny of man, a wise man once said, is to contemplate the works of God. Having known God in his heart, by faith, the time had come for man to know him with his reason. The Gospel had been for man like a primary education; now grown to adulthood, he needed a higher teaching, lest he stagnate in idiocy and the servitude that follows it.

In this way, the likes of Galileo, Arnaud de Bresce, Giordano Bruno, Descartes, Luther — all that elite of thinkers, wise men and artists, who shone in the 15th, 16th and 17th centuries as great revolutionaries — were at the same time the conservatives of society, the heralds of civilization. They continued, in opposition to the representatives of

Christ, the movement started by Christ, and for it suffered no lack of persecution and martyrdom!

Here was the second great revolution, the second great manifestation of justice. It too renewed the world — and saved it.

But philosophy, adding its conquests to those of the Gospel, did not fulfill the program of that eternal justice. Liberty, called forth from the heart of God by Christ, was still only individual: it had to be established in the tribunal. Conscience was needed to make it pass into law.

About the middle of the last century then a new development commenced and, as the first revolution had been religious and the second philosophical, the third revolution was political. It called itself the social contract.

It took for its dogma *the sovereignty of the people*: it was the counterpart of the Christian dogma of *the unity of god*.

Its motto was *equality before the law*, the corollary of those which it had previously inscribed on its flag: equality before God and equality before reason.

Thus, with each revolution, liberty appeared to us always as the instrument of justice, with equality as its criterion. The third term — the aim of justice, the goal it always pursues, the end it approaches — is brotherhood.

Never let us lose sight of this order of revolutionary development. History testifies that brotherhood, supreme end of revolutions, does not impose itself. It has as conditions first liberty, then equality. It is as if just said to us all: Men, be free; citizens, become equal; brothers, embrace one another.

Who dares deny that the revolution undertaken sixty years ago by our fathers, and which the heroic memory makes our hearts beat with such force that we almost forget our own sense of duty — who denies, I ask, that that revolution was a progress? Nobody. Very well, then. But was it not both progressive and conservative? Could society have survived with its time-worn despotism, its degraded nobility, its corrupt clergy, with its egotistical and undisciplined parliament, so given to intrigue, with a people in rags, a race which can be exploited at will?

359

Is it necessary to blot out the sun, in order to make the case? The revolution of '89 was the salvation of humanity; it is for that reason that it deserves the title of revolution.

But, citizens, if our fathers have done much for liberty and fraternity, and have even more profoundly opened up the road of brotherhood, they have left it to us to do even more.

Justice did not speak its last word in '89, and who knows when it will speak it?

Are we not witnesses, our generation of 1848, to a corruption worse than that of the worst days of history, to a misery comparable to that of feudal times, an oppression of spirit and of conscience, and a degradation of all human faculties, which exceeds all that was seen in the epochs of most dreadful cruelty? Of what use are the conquests of the past, of religion and philosophy, and the constitutions and codes, when in virtue of the same rights that are guaranteed to us by those constitutions and codes, we find ourselves dispossessed of nature, excommunicated from the human species? What is politics, when we lack bread, when even the work which might give bread is taken from us? What to us is the freedom to go or to become, the liberty to think or not to think, the guarantees of the law, and the spectacles of the marvels of civilization? What is the meager education which is give to us, when by the withdrawal of all those objects on which we might practice human activity, we are ourselves plunged into an absolute void; when to the appeal of our senses, our hearts, and our reason, the universe and civilization reply: *Néant!* Nothing!

Citizens, I swear it by Christ and by our fathers! Justice has sounded its fourth hour, and misfortune to those who have not heard the call!

— Revolution of 1848, what do you call yourself?

— I am the *right to work!*

— What is your flag?

— *Association!*

— And your motto?

— *Equality before fortune!*

360

— Where are you taking us?

— *To Brotherhood!*

— *Salut* to you, Revolution! I will serve you as I have served God, as I have served Philosophy and Liberty, with all my heart, with all my soul, with all my intelligence and my courage, and will have no other sovereign and ruler than you!

Thus the revolution, having been by turns religious, philosophical and political, has become economic. And like all its predecessors it brings us nothing less than a contradiction of the past, a sort of reversal of the established order! Without this complete reversal of principles and beliefs, there is no revolution; there is only mystification. Let us continue to interrogate history, citizens.

Within the empire of polytheism, slavery had established and perpetuated itself in the name of what principle? In the name of religion. — Christ appeared, and slavery was abolished, precisely in the name of religion.

Christianity, in its turn, made reason subject to faith; philosophy reversed that order, and subordinated faith to reason.

Feudalism, in the name of politics, controlled everything, subjecting the laborer to the bourgeois, the bourgeois to the noble, the noble to the king, the king to the priest, and the priest to a dead letter. — In the name of politics again, '89 subjected everyone to the law, and recognized among men only citizens.

Today labor is at the discretion of capital. Well, then! The revolution tells you to change that order. It is time for capital to recognize the predominance of labor, for the tool to put itself at the disposition of the worker.

Such is this revolution, which has suffered sarcasm, calumny and persecution, just like any other. But, like the others, the Revolution of 1848 becomes more fertile by the blood of its martyrs. *Sanguis martyrun, semen christianorum!* exclaimed one of the greatest revolutionaries of times past, the indomitable Tertullien. Blood of republicans, seed of republicans.

361

Who does not dare to acknowledge this faith, sealed with the blood of our brothers, is not a revolutionary. The failure is an infidelity. He who dissembles regarding it is a renegade. To separate the Republic from socialism is to willfully confuse the freedom of mind and spirit with the slavery of the senses, the exercise of political rights with the deprivation of civil rights. It is contradictory, absurd.

Here, citizens, is the genealogy of social ideas: are we, or are we not, in the revolutionary tradition? It is a question of knowing if at present we are also engaged in revolutionary practice, if, like our fathers, we will be at once men of conservation and of progress, because it is only by this double title that we will be men of revolution.

We have the revolutionary principle, the revolutionary dogma, the revolutionary motto. What is it that we lack in order to accomplish the work entrusted to our hands by Providence? One thing only: revolutionary practice!

But what is that practice which distinguishes the epochs of revolution from ordinary times?

What constitutes revolutionary practice is that it no longer proceeds by technicality and diversity, or by imprescriptible transitions, but by simplifications and enjambments. It passes over, in broad equations, those middle terms which suggest the spirit of routine, whose application should normally have been made during the former time, but that the selfishness of the privilege or the inertia of the governments pushed back.

These great equitations of principles, these enormous shifts in mores, they also have their laws, not at all arbitrary, no more left to chance than the practice of revolutions.

But what, in the end, is that practice?

Suppose that the statesmen we have seen in power since February 24, that these short-sighted politicians of small means, of narrow and meticulous routines, had been in the place of the apostles. I ask you citizens, what would they have done?

They would have fallen into agreement with the innovators of the individual conferences, in secret consultations, that the plurality of gods was an absurdity. They would have said, like Cicero, that it is inconceivable that two augurs could look at one another without laughter; they would have condemned slavery very philosophically, and in a deep voice.

But they would have cried out against the bold propaganda which, denying the gods and all that society has sanctified, raised against it superstition and all the interests; they would have trusted in good policy, rather than tackling the old beliefs, and interpreting them; they would have knelt before Mercury the thief, before impudent Venus and incestuous Jupiter. They would have talked with respect and esteem of the Floralia and the Bacchanalia. They would have made a philosophy of polytheism, retold the history of the gods, renewed the personnel of the temples, published the payments for sacrifices and public ceremonies, according, as far as it was in them, reason and morality to the impure traditions of their fathers, by dint of attention, kindness and human respect; instead of saving the world, they would have caused it to perish.

There was, in the first centuries of the Christian era, a sect, a party powerful in genius and eloquence, which, in the face of the Christian revolution, undertook to continue the idolatry in the form of a moderate and progressive republic; they were the Neo-Platonists, to whom Apollonius of Tyana and the Emperor Julian attached themselves. It is in this fashion that we have seen with our own eyes certain preachers attempt the renovation of Catholicism, by interpreting its symbols from the point of view of modern ideas.

A vain attempt! Christian preaching, which is to say revolutionary practice, swept away all the gods and their hypocritical admirers; and Julian, the greatest politician and most beautiful spirit of his time, bears in the histories the name of *apostate*, for having been madly opposed to evangelical justice.

Let us cite one more example.

Let us suppose that in '89, the prudent counselors of despotism, the well-advised spirits of the nobility, the tolerant clergy, the wise men of the middle class, the most patient of the people — let us suppose, I say, that this elite of citizens, with the most upright vision and the most philanthropic views, but convinced of the dangers of abrupt innovations, had agreed to manage, following the rules of high policy, the transition from despotism to liberty. What would they have done?

They would have passed, after long discussion and mature deliberation, letting at least ten years elapse between each article, the promised charter; they would have negotiated with the pope, and with all manner of submissiveness, the civil constitution of the clergy; they would have negotiated with the convents, by amicable agreement, the repurchase of their goods; they would have opened an investigation into the value of feudal rights, and on the compensation to be accorded to the lords; they would have sought compensation to the privileged for the rights accorded to the people. They would have made the work of a thousand years what revolutionary practice might accomplish overnight.

All of this is not just empty talk: there was no lack of men in '89 willing to connect themselves to this false wisdom of revolution. The first of all was Louis XVI, who was as revolutionary at heart and in theory as anyone, but who did not understand that the revolution must also be practiced. Louis XVI set himself to haggle and quibble over everything, so much and so well, that they revolution, growing impatient, swept him away!

Here then is what I mean, today, by revolutionary practice.

The revolution of February proclaimed the *right to work*, the predominance of labor over capital.

On the basis of that principle, I say that before overriding all reforms, we have to occupy ourselves with a generalizing institution, which expresses, on all the points of social economy, the subordination of capital to labor; which, in lieu of making, as it has been, the capitalist the sponsor of the laborer, makes the laborer the arbiter and commander of the capitalist, an institution which changes the relation between the two great economic powers, labor and property, and from which follows, consequently, all other reforms.

Will it then be revolutionary to propose an agricultural bank serving, as always, the monopolizers of money; there to create a certified loan office, monument to stagnation and unemployment; elsewhere, to found an asylum, a pawn-shop, a hospital, a nursery, a penitentiary, or a prison, to increase pauperism by multiplying its sources?

Will it be a work of Revolution to finance a few millions, sometimes a company of tailors, sometimes of masons; to reduce the tax on drink and increase it on properties; to convert obligations into losses; to vote seeds and pick-axes for twelve thousand colonists leaving for Algeria, or to subsidize a trial phalanstery?

Will it be the speech or act of a revolutionary to argue for four months whether the people will work or will not, if capital hides or if it flees the country, if it awaits confidence or if it is confidence that awaits it, if the powers will be divided or only the functions, if the president will be the superior, the subordinate or the equal of the national assembly, if the first who will fill this role will be the nephew of the emperor or the son of the king, or if it would not be better, for that good use, to have a soldier or a poet; if the new sovereign will be named by the people or by the representatives, if the ministry of *reaction* which goes out merits more confidence than the ministry of *conciliation* which comes, if the Republic will be blue, white, red, or tricolor?

Will it be revolutionary, when it is a question of returning to labor the fictive production of capital, to declare the net revenue inviolable, rather than to seize it by a progressive tax; when it is necessary to organize equality in the acquisition of goods, to lay the blame on the mode of transmission; when 25,000 tradesmen implore a legal settlement, to answer them by bankruptcy; when property no longer receives rent or farm rent, to refuse it further credit; when the country demands the centralization of the banks, to deliver that credit to a financial oligarchy which only knows how to make a void in circulation and to maintain the crisis, while waiting for the discouragement of the people to bring back confidence?

Citizens, I accuse no one.

I know that to all except for us social democrats, who have envisioned and prepared for it, the Revolution of February has been a surprise; and if it is difficult for the old constitutionals to pass in so short a time from the monarchical faith to republican conviction, it is still more so for the politicians of the other century to comprehend anything of the practice of the new Revolution. Other times have other ideas. The great maneuvers of '93, good for the time, do not suit us now any more than the parliamentary tactics of the last thirty years; and if we want to abort the revolution, you have no surer means than to take up again these errors.

Citizens, you are still only a minority in this country. But already the revolutionary flood grows with the speed of the idea, with the majesty of the ocean. Again, some of that patience that made your success, and the triumph of the Revolution is assured. You have proven, since June, by you discipline, that you are politicians. From now on you will prove, by your acts, that you are organizers. The government will be enough, I hope, with the National Assembly, to maintain the republican form:

such at least is my conviction. But the revolutionary power, the power of conservation and of progress, is no longer today in the hands of the government; it is not in the National Assembly: it is in you. The people alone, acting upon themselves without intermediary, can achieve the economic Revolution begun in February. The people alone can save civilization and advance humanity!

What is Property? An Inquiry into the Principle of Right and of Government

P. J. Proudhon: His Life and His Works.

The correspondence[1] of P. J. Proudhon, the first volumes of which we publish to-day, has been collected since his death by the faithful and intelligent labors of his daughter, aided by a few friends. It was incomplete when submitted to Sainte Beuve, but the portion with which the illustrious academician became acquainted was sufficient to allow him to estimate it as a whole with that soundness of judgment which characterized him as a literary critic.

In an important work, which his habitual readers certainly have not forgotten, although death did not allow him to finish it, Sainte Beuve thus judges the correspondence of the great publicist: —

"The letters of Proudhon, even outside the circle of his particular friends, will always be of value; we can always learn something from them, and here is the proper place to determine the general character of his correspondence.

"It has always been large, especially since he became so celebrated; and, to tell the truth, I am persuaded that, in the future, the correspondence of Proudhon will be his principal, vital work, and that most of his books will be only accessory to and corroborative of this. At any rate, his books can be well understood only by the aid of his letters and the continual explanations which he makes to those who consult him in their doubt, and request him to define more clearly his position.

"There are, among celebrated people, many methods of correspondence. There are those to whom letter-writing is a bore, and who, assailed with questions and compliments, reply in the greatest haste, solely that the job may be over with, and who return politeness for politeness, mingling it with more or less wit. This kind of correspondence, though coming from celebrated people, is insignificant and unworthy of collection and classification.

"After those who write letters in performance of a disagreeable duty, and almost side by side with them in point of insignificance, I should put those who write in a manner wholly external, wholly superficial, devoted only to flattery, lavishing praise like gold, without counting it; and those also who weigh every word, who reply formally and pompously, with a view to fine phrases and effects. They exchange words only, and choose them solely for their brilliancy and show. You think it is you, individually, to whom they speak; but they are addressing themselves in your person to the four corners of Europe. Such letters are empty, and teach as nothing but theatrical execution and the favorite pose of their writers.

"I will not class among the latter the more prudent and sagacious authors who, when writing to individuals, keep one eye on posterity. We know that many who pursue this method have written long, finished, charming, flattering, and tolerably natural letters. Beranger furnishes us with the best example of this class.

"Proudhon, however, is a man of entirely different nature and habits. In writing, he thinks of nothing but his idea and the person whom he addresses: *ad rem et ad hominem*. A man of conviction and doctrine, to write does not weary him; to be questioned does not annoy him. When approached, he cares only to know that your motive is not one of futile curiosity, but the love of truth; he assumes you to be serious, he replies, he examines your objections, sometimes verbally, sometimes in writing; for, as he remarks, 'if there be some points which correspondence can never settle, but which can be made clear by conversation in two minutes, at other times just the opposite is the case: an objection clearly stated in writing, a doubt well expressed, which elicits a direct and positive reply, helps things along more than ten hours of oral intercourse!' In writing to you he does not hesitate to treat the subject anew; he unfolds to you the foundation and superstructure of his thought: rarely does he confess himself defeated — it is not his way; he holds to his position, but admits the breaks, the variations, in short, the *evolution* of his mind. The history of his mind is in his letters; there it must be sought.

"Proudhon, whoever addresses him, is always ready; he quits the page of the book on which he is at work to answer you with the same pen, and that without losing patience, without getting confused, without sparing or complaining of his ink; he is a public man, devoted to the propagation of his idea by all methods, and the best method, with him, is always the present one, the latest one. His very handwriting, bold, uniform, legible, even in the most tiresome passages, betrays no haste, no hurry to finish. Each line is accurate: nothing is left to chance; the punctuation, very correct and a little emphatic and decided, indicates with precision and delicate distinction all the links in the chain of his argument. He is devoted entirely to you, to his business and yours, while writing to you, and never to anything else. All the letters of his which I have seen are serious: not one is commonplace.

"But at the same time he is not at all artistic or affected; he does not *construct* his letters, he does not revise them, he spends no time in reading them over; we have a first draught, excellent and clear, a jet from the fountain-head, but that is all. The new arguments, which he discovers in support of his ideas and which opposition suggests to him, are an agreeable surprise, and shed a light which we should vainly search for even in his works. His correspondence differs essentially from his books, in that it gives you no uneasiness; it places you in the very heart of the man, explains him to you, and leaves you with an impression of moral esteem and almost of intellectual security. We feel his sincerity. I know of no one to whom he can be more fitly compared in this respect than George Sand, whose correspondence is large, and at the same time full of sincerity. His *rôle* and his nature correspond. If he is writing to a young man who unbosoms himself to him in sceptical anxiety, to a young woman who asks him to decide delicate questions of conduct for her, his letter takes the form of a short moral essay, of a father-confessor's advice. Has he perchance attended the theatre (a rare thing for him) to witness one of Ponsart's comedies, or a drama of Charles Edmond's, he feels bound to give an account of his impressions to the friend to whom he is indebted for this pleasure, and his letter becomes a literary and philosophical criticism, full of sense, and like no other. His familiarity is suited to his correspondent; he affects no rudeness. The terms of civility or affection which he employs towards his correspondents are sober, measured, appropriate to each, and honest in their simplicity and cordiality. When he speaks of morals and the family, he seems at times like the patriarchs of the Bible. His command of language is complete, and he never fails to avail himself of it. Now and then a coarse word, a few personalities, too bitter and quite unjust or injurious, will have to be suppressed in printing; time, however, as it passes away, permits many things and renders them inoffensive. Am I right in saying that Proudhon's correspondence, always substantial, will one day be the most accessible and attractive portion of his works?"

Almost the whole of Proudhon's real biography is included in his correspondence. Up to 1837, the date of the first letter which we have been able to collect, his life, narrated by Sainte Beuve, from whom we make numerous extracts, may be summed up in a few pages.

Pierre Joseph Proudhon was born on the 15th of January, 1809, in a suburb of Besançon, called Mouillère. His father and mother were employed in the great brewery belonging to M. Renaud. His father, though a cousin of the jurist Proudhon, the celebrated professor in the faculty of Dijon, was a journeyman brewer. His mother, a genuine peasant, was a common servant. She was an orderly person of great good sense; and, as they who knew her say, a superior woman of *heroic* character, — to use the expression of the venerable M. Weiss, the librarian at Besançon. She it was especially that Proudhon resembled: she and his grandfather Tournési, the soldier peasant of whom his mother told him, and whose courageous deeds he has described in his work on "Justice." Proudhon, who always felt a great veneration for his mother Catharine, gave her name to the elder of his daughters. In 1814, when Besançon was blockaded, Mouillère, which stood in front of the walls of the town, was destroyed in the defence of the place; and Proudhon's father established a cooper's shop in a suburb of Battant, called Vignerons. Very honest, but simple-minded and short-sighted, this cooper, the father of five children, of whom Pierre Joseph was the eldest, passed his life in poverty. At eight years of age, Proudhon either made himself useful in the house, or tended the cattle out of doors. No one should fail to read that beautiful and precious page of his work on "Justice," in which he describes the rural sports which he enjoyed when a neatherd. At the age of twelve, he was a cellar-boy in an inn. This, however, did not prevent him from studying. His mother was greatly aided by M. Renaud, the former owner of the brewery, who had at that time retired from business, and was engaged in the education of his children.

Proudhon entered school as a day-scholar in the sixth class. He was necessarily irregular in his attendance; domestic cares and restraints sometimes kept him from his classes. He succeeded nevertheless in his studies; he showed great perseverance. His family were so poor that they could not afford to furnish him with books; he was obliged to borrow them from his comrades, and copy the text of his lessons. He has himself told us that he was obliged to leave his wooden shoes outside the door, that he might not disturb the classes with his noise; and that, having no hat, he went to school bareheaded. One day, towards the close of his studies, on returning from the distribution of the prizes, loaded with crowns, he found nothing to eat in the house.

"In his eagerness for labor and his thirst for knowledge, Proudhon," says Sainte Beuve, "was not content with the instruction of his teachers. From his twelfth to his fourteenth year, he was a constant frequenter of the town library. One curiosity led to another, and he called for book after book, sometimes eight or ten at one sitting. The learned librarian, the friend and almost the brother of Charles Nodier, M. Weiss, approached him one day, and said, smiling, 'But, my little friend, what do you wish to do with all these books?' The child raised his head, eyed his questioner, and replied: 'What's that to you?' And the good M. Weiss remembers it to this day."

Forced to earn his living, Proudhon could not continue his studies. He entered a printing-office in Besançon as a proof-reader. Becoming, soon after, a compositor, he made a tour of France in this capacity. At Toulon, where he found himself without money and without work, he had a scene with the mayor, which he describes in his work on "Justice."

Sainte Beuve says that, after his tour of France, his service book being filled with good certificates, Proudhon was promoted to the position of foreman. But he does not tell us, for the reason that he had no knowledge of a letter written by Fallot, of which we never heard until six months since, that the printer at that time contemplated quitting his trade in order to become a teacher.

Towards 1829, Fallot, who was a little older than Proudhon, and who, after having obtained the Suard pension in 1832, died in his twenty-ninth year, while filling the position of assistant librarian at the Institute, was charged, Protestant though he was, with the revisal of a "Life of the Saints," which was published at Besançon. The book was in Latin, and Fallot added some notes which also were in Latin.

"But," says Sainte Beuve, "it happened that some errors escaped his attention, which Proudhon, then proof-reader in the printing office, did not fail to point out to him. Surprised at finding so good a Latin scholar in a workshop, he desired to make his acquaintance; and soon there sprung up between them a most earnest and intimate friendship: a friendship of the intellect and of the heart."

Addressed to a printer between twenty-two and twenty-three years of age, and predicting in formal terms his future fame, Fallot's letter seems to us so interesting that we do not hesitate to reproduce it entire.

"Paris, December 5, 1831.

"My dear Proudhon, — you have a right to be surprised at, and even dissatisfied with, my long delay in replying to your kind letter; I will tell you the cause of it. It became necessary to forward an account of your ideas to M. J. de Gray; to hear his objections, to reply to them, and to await his definitive response, which reached me but a short time ago; for M. J. is a sort of financial king, who takes no pains to be punctual in dealing with poor devils like ourselves. I, too, am careless in matters of business; I sometimes push my negligence even to disorder, and the metaphysical musings which continually occupy my mind, added to the amusements of Paris, render me the most incapable man in the world for conducting a negotiation with despatch.

"I have M. Jobard's decision; here it is: In his judgment, you are too learned and clever for his children; he fears that you could not accommodate your mind and character to the childish notions common to their age and station. In short. he is what the world calls a good father; that is, he wants to spoil his children, and, in order to do this easily, he thinks fit to retain his present instructor, who is not very learned, but who takes part in their games and joyous sports with wonderful facility, who points out the letters of the alphabet to the little girl, who takes the little boys to mass, and who, no less obliging than the worthy Abbé P. of our acquaintance, would readily dance for Madame's amusement. Such a profession would not suit you, you who have a free, proud, and manly soul: you are refused; let us dismiss the matter from our minds. Perhaps another time my solicitude will be less unfortunate. I can only ask your pardon for having thought of thus disposing of you almost without consulting you. I find my excuse in the motives which guided me; I had in view your well-being and advancement in the ways of this world.

"I see in your letter, my comrade, through its brilliant witticisms and beneath the frank and artless gayety with which you have sprinkled it, a tinge of sadness and despondency which pains me. You are unhappy, my friend: your present situation does not suit you; you cannot remain in it, it was not made for you, it is beneath you; you ought, by all means, to leave it, before its injurious influence begins to affect your faculties, and before you become settled, as they say, in the ways of your profession, were it possible that such a thing could ever happen, which I flatly deny. You are unhappy; you have not yet entered upon the path which Nature has marked out for you. But, faint-hearted soul, is that a cause for despondency? Ought you to feel discouraged? Struggle, *morbleu*, struggle persistently, and you will triumph. J. J. Rousseau groped about for forty years before his genius was revealed to him. You are not J. J Rousseau; but listen: I know not whether I should have divined the author of "Emile" when he was twenty years of age, supposing that I had been his contemporary, and had enjoyed the honor of his acquaintance. But I have known you, I have loved you, I have divined your future, if I may venture to say so; for the first time in my life, I am going to risk a prophecy. Keep this letter, read it again fifteen or twenty years hence, perhaps twenty-five, and if at that time the prediction which I am about to make has not been fulfilled, burn it as a piece of folly out of charity and respect for my memory. This is my prediction: you will be, Proudhon, in spite of yourself, inevitably, by the fact of your destiny, a writer, an author; you will be a philosopher; you will be one of the lights of the century, and your name will occupy a place in the annals of the nineteenth century, like those of Gassendi, Descartes, Malebranche, and Bacon in the seventeenth, and those of Diderot, Montesquieu, Helvetius. Locke, Hume, and Holbach in the eighteenth. Such will be your lot! Do now what you will, set type in a printing-office, bring up children, bury yourself in deep seclusion, seek obscure and lonely villages, it is all one to me; you cannot escape your destiny; you cannot divest yourself of your noblest feature, that active, strong, and inquiring mind, with which you are endowed; your place in the world has been appointed, and it cannot remain empty. Go where you please, I expect you in Paris, talking philosophy and the doctrines of Plato; you will have to come, whether you want to or not. I, who say this to you, must feel very sure of it in order to be willing to put it upon paper, since, without reward for my prophetic skill, — to which, I assure you, I make not the slightest claim, — I run the risk of passing for a hare-brained fellow, in case I prove to be mistaken: he plays a bold game who risks his good sense upon his cards, in return for the very trifling and insignificant merit of having divined a young man's future.

"When I say that I expect you in Paris, I use only a proverbial phrase which you must not allow to mislead you as to my projects and plans. To reside in Paris is disagreeable to me, very much so; and when this fine-art fever which possesses me has left me, I shall abandon the place without regret to seek a more peaceful residence in a provincial town, provided always the town shall afford me the means of living, bread, a bed, books, rest, and solitude. How I miss, my good Proudhon, that dark, obscure, smoky chamber in which I dwelt in Besançon, and where we spent so many pleasant hours in the discussion of philosophy! Do you remember it? But that is now far away. Will that happy time ever return? Shall we one day meet again? Here my life is restless, uncertain, precarious, and, what is worse, indolent, illiterate, and vagrant. I do no work, I live in idleness, I ramble about; I do not read, I no longer study; my books are forsaken; now and then I glance over a few metaphysical works, and after a days walk through dirty, filthy, crowded streets. I lie down with empty head and tired body, to repeat the performance on the following day. What is the object of these walks, you will ask. I make visits, my friend; I hold interviews with stupid people. Then a fit of curiosity seizes me, the least inquisitive of beings: there are museums, libraries, assemblies, churches, palaces, gardens, and theatres to visit. I am fond of pictures, fond of music, fond of sculpture; all these are beautiful and good, but they cannot appease hunger, nor take the place of my pleasant readings of Bailly, Hume, and Tennemann, which I used to enjoy by my fireside when I was able to read.

"But enough of complaints. Do not allow this letter to affect you too much, and do not think that I give way to dejection or despondency; no, I am a fatalist, and I believe in my star. I do not know yet what my calling is, nor for what branch of polite literature I am best fitted; I do not even know whether I am, or ever shall be, fitted for any: but what matters it? I suffer, I labor, I dream, I enjoy, I think; and, in a word, when my last hour strikes, I shall have lived.

"Proudhon, I love you, I esteem you; and, believe me, these are not mere phrases. What interest could I have in flattering and praising a poor printer? Are you rich, that you may pay for courtiers? Have you a sumptuous table, a dashing wife, and gold to scatter, in order to attract them to your suite? Have you the glory, honors, credit, which would render your acquaintance pleasing to their vanity and pride? No; you are poor, obscure, abandoned; but, poor, obscure, and abandoned, you have a friend, and a friend who knows all the obligations which that word imposes upon honorable people, when they venture to assume it. That friend is myself: put me to the test.

"GUSTAVE FALLOT."

It appears from this letter that if, at this period, Proudhon had already exhibited to the eyes of a clairvoyant friend his genius for research and investigation, it was in the direction of philosophical, rather than of economical and social, questions.

Having become foreman in the house of Gauthier & Co., who carried on a large printing establishment at Besançon, he corrected the proofs of ecclesiastical writers, the Fathers of the Church. As they were printing a Bible, a Vulgate, he was led to compare the Latin with the original Hebrew.

"In this way," says Sainte Beuve, "he learned Hebrew by himself, and, as everything was connected in his mind, he was led to the study of comparative philology. As the house of Gauthier published many works on Church history and theology, he came also to acquire, through this desire of his to investigate everything, an extensive knowledge of theology, which afterwards caused misinformed persons to think that he had been in an ecclesiastical seminary."

Towards 1836, Proudhon left the house of Gauthier, and, in company with an associate, established a small printing-office in Besançon. His contribution to the partnership consisted, not so much in capital, as in his knowledge of the trade. His partner committing suicide in 1838, Proudhon was obliged to wind up the business, an operation which he did not accomplish as quickly and as easily as he hoped. He was then urged by his friends to enter the ranks of the competitors for the Suard pension. This pension consisted of an income of fifteen hundred francs bequeathed to the Academy of Besançon by Madame Suard, the widow of the academician, to be given once in three years to the young man residing in the department of Doubs, a bachelor of letters or of science, and not possessing a fortune, whom the Academy of Besançon *should deem best fitted for a literary or scientific career, or for the study of law or of medicine.* The first to win the Suard pension was Gustave Fallot. Mauvais, who was a distinguished astronomer in the Academy of Sciences, was the second. Proudhon aspired to be the third. To qualify himself, he had to be received as a bachelor of letters, and was obliged to write a letter to the Academy of Besançon. In a phrase of this letter, the terms of which he had to modify, though he absolutely refused to change its spirit, Proudhon expressed his firm resolve to labor for the amelioration of the condition of his brothers, the working-men.

The only thing which he had then published was an "Essay on General Grammar," which appeared without the author's signature. While reprinting, at Besançon, the "Primitive Elements of Languages, Discovered by the Comparison of Hebrew roots with those of the Latin and French," by the Abbé Bergier, Proudhon had enlarged the edition of his "Essay on General Grammar."

The date of the edition, 1837, proves that he did not at that time think of competing for the Suard pension. In this work, which continued and completed that of the Abbé Bergier, Proudhon adopted the same point of view, that of Moses and of Biblical tradition. Two years later, in February, 1839, being already in possession of the Suard pension, he addressed to the Institute, as a competitor for the Volney prize, a memoir entitled: "Studies in Grammatical Classification and the Derivation of some French words." It was his first work, revised and presented in another form. Four memoirs only were sent to the Institute,

375

none of which gained the prize. Two honorable mentions were granted, one of them to memoir No. 4; that is, to P. J. Proudhon, printer at Besançon. The judges were MM. Amédée Jaubert, Reinaud, and Burnouf.

"The committee," said the report presented at the annual meeting of the five academies on Thursday, May 2, 1839, "has paid especial attention to manuscripts No. 1 and No. 4. Still, it does not feel able to grant the prize to either of these works, because they do not appear to be sufficiently elaborated. The committee, which finds in No. 4 some ingenious analyses, particularly in regard to the mechanism of the Hebrew language, regrets that the author has resorted to hazardous conjectures, and has sometimes forgotten the special recommendation of the committee to pursue the experimental and comparative method."

Proudhon remembered this. He attended the lectures of Eugène Burnouf, and, as soon as he became acquainted with the labors and discoveries of Bopp and his successors, he definitively abandoned an hypothesis which had been condemned by the Academy of Inscriptions and Belles-lettres. He then sold, for the value of the paper, the remaining copies of the "Essay" published by him in 1837. In 1850, they were still lying in a grocer's back-shop. A neighboring publisher then placed the edition on the market, with the attractive name of Proudhon upon it. A lawsuit ensued, in which the author was beaten. His enemies, and at that time there were many of them, would have been glad to have proved him a renegade and a recanter. Proudhon, in his work on "Justice," gives some interesting details of this lawsuit.

In possession of the Suard pension, Proudhon took part in the contest proposed by the Academy of Besançon on the question of the utility of the celebration of Sunday. His memoir obtained honorable mention, together with a medal which was awarded him, in open session, on the 24th of August, 1839. The reporter of the committee, the Abbé Doney, since made Bishop of Montauban, called attention to the unquestionable superiority of his talent.

"But," says Sainte Beuve, "he reproached him with having adopted dangerous theories, and with having touched upon questions of practical politics and social organization, where upright intentions and zeal for the public welfare cannot justify rash solutions."

Was it policy, we mean prudence, which induced Proudhon to screen his ideas of equality behind the Mosaic law? Sainte Beuve, like many others, seems to think so. But we remember perfectly well that, having asked Proudhon, in August, 1848, if he did not consider himself indebted in some respects to his fellow-countryman, Charles Fourier, we received from him the following reply: "I have certainly read Fourier, and have spoken of him more than once in my works; but, upon the whole, I do not think that I owe anything to him. My real masters, those who have caused fertile ideas to spring up in my mind, are three in number: first, the Bible; next, Adam Smith; and last, Hegel.

Freely confessed in the "Celebration of Sunday," the influence of the Bible on Proudhon is no less manifest in his first memoir on property. Proudhon undoubtedly brought to this work many ideas of his own; but is not the very foundation of ancient Jewish law to be found in its condemnation of usurious interest and its denial of the right of personal appropriation of land?

The first memoir on property appeared in 1840, under the title, "What is Property? or an Inquiry into the Principle of Right and of Government." Proudhon dedicated it, in a letter which served as the preface, to the Academy of Besançon. The latter, finding itself brought to trial by its pensioner, took the affair to heart, and evoked it, says Sainte Beuve, with all possible haste. The pension narrowly escaped being immediately withdrawn from the bold defender of the principle of equality of conditions. M. Vivien, then Minister of Justice, who was earnestly solicited to prosecute the author, wished first to obtain the opinion of the economist, Blanqui, a member of the Academy of Moral and Political Sciences. Proudhon having presented to this academy a copy of his book, M. Blanqui was appointed to review it. This review, though it opposed Proudhon's views, shielded him. Treated as a *savant* by M. Blanqui, the author was not prosecuted. He was always grateful to MM. Blanqui and Vivien for their handsome conduct in the matter.

M. Blanqui's review, which was partially reproduced by "Le Moniteur," on the 7th of September, 1840, naturally led Proudhon to address to him, in the form of a letter, his second memoir on property, which appeared in April, 1841. Proudhon had endeavored, in his first memoir, to demonstrate that the pursuit of equality of conditions is the true principle of right and of government. In the "Letter to M. Blanqui," he passes in review the numerous and varied methods by which this principle gradually becomes realized in all societies, especially in modern society.

In 1842, a third memoir appeared, entitled, "A Notice to Proprietors, or a Letter to M. Victor Considérant, Editor of 'La Phalange,' in Reply to a Defence of Property." Here the influence of Adam Smith manifested itself, and was frankly admitted. Did not Adam Smith find, in the principle of equality, the first of all the laws which govern wages? There are other laws, undoubtedly; but Proudhon considers them all as springing from the principle of property, as he defined it in his first memoir. Thus, in humanity, there are two principles, — one which leads us to equality, another which separates us from it. By the former, we treat each other as associates; by the latter, as strangers, not to say enemies. This distinction, which is constantly met with throughout the three memoirs, contained already, in germ, the idea which gave birth to the "System of Economical Contradictions," which appeared in 1846, the idea of antinomy or *contre-loi*.

The "Notice to Proprietors" was seized by the magistrates of Besançon; and Proudhon was summoned to appear before the assizes of Doubs within a week. He read his written defence to the jurors in person, and was acquitted. The jury, like M. Blanqui, viewed him only as a philosopher, an inquirer, a *savant*.

In 1843, Proudhon published the "Creation of Order in Humanity," a large volume, which does not deal exclusively with questions of social economy. Religion, philosophy, method, certainty, logic, and dialectics are treated at considerable length.

Released from his printing-office on the 1st of March of the same year, Proudhon had to look for a chance to earn his living. Messrs. Gauthier Bros., carriers by water between Mulhouse and Lyons, the eldest of whom was Proudhon's companion in childhood, conceived the happy thought of employing him, of utilizing his ability in their business, and in settling the numerous points of difficulty which daily arose. Besides the large number of accounts which his new duties required him to make out, and which retarded the publication of the "System of Economical Contradictions," until October, 1846, we ought to mention a work, which, before it appeared in pamphlet form, was published in the "Revue des Economistes," — "Competition between Railroads and Navigable Ways."

"Le Miserere, or the Repentance of a King," which he published in March, 1845, in the "Revue Indépendante," during that Lenten season when Lacordaire was preaching in Lyons, proves that, though devoting himself with ardor to the study of economical problems, Proudhon had not lost his interest in questions of religious history. Among his writings on these questions, which he was unfortunately obliged to leave unfinished, we may mention a nearly completed history of the early Christian heresies, and of the struggle of Christianity against Cæsarism.

We have said that, in 1848, Proudhon recognized three masters. Having no knowledge of the German language, he could not have read the works of Hegel, which at that time had not been translated into French. It was Charles Grün, a German, who had come to France to study the various philosophical and socialistic systems, who gave him the substance of the Hegelian ideas. During the winter of 1844–45, Charles Grün had some long conversations with Proudhon, which determined, very decisively, not the ideas, which belonged exclusively to the *bisontin* thinker, but the form of the important work on which he labored after 1843, and which was published in 1846 by Guillaumin.

Hegel's great idea, which Proudhon appropriated, and which he demonstrates with wonderful ability in the "System of Economical Contradictions," is as follows: Antinomy, that is, the existence of two laws or tendencies which are opposed to each other, is possible, not only with two different things, but with one and the same thing. Considered in their thesis, that is, in the law or tendency which created them, all the economical categories are rational, — competition, monopoly, the balance of trade, and property, as well as the division of labor, machinery, taxation, and credit. But, like communism and population, all these categories are antinomical; all are opposed, not only to each other, but to themselves. All is opposition, and disorder is born of this system of opposition. Hence, the sub-title of the work, — "Philosophy of Misery." No category can be suppressed; the opposition, antinomy, or *contre-tendance*, which exists in each of them, cannot be suppressed.

Where, then, lies the solution of the social problem? Influenced by the Hegelian ideas, Proudhon began to look for it in a superior synthesis, which should reconcile the thesis and antithesis. Afterwards, while at work upon his book on "Justice," he saw that the antinomical terms do not cancel each other, any more than the opposite poles of an electric pile destroy each other; that they are the procreative cause of motion, life, and progress; that the problem is to discover, not their fusion, which would be death, but their equilibrium, — an equilibrium for ever unstable, varying with the development of society.

On the cover of the "System of Economical Contradictions," Proudhon announced, as soon to appear, his "Solution of the Social Problem." This work, upon which he was engaged when the Revolution of 1848 broke out, had to be cut up into pamphlets and newspaper articles. The two pamphlets, which he published in March, 1848, before he became editor of "Le Représentant du Peuple," bear the same title, — "Solution of the Social Problem." The first, which is mainly a criticism of the early acts of the provisional government, is notable from the fact that in it Proudhon, in advance of all others, energetically opposed the establishment of national workshops. The second, "Organization of Credit and Circulation," sums up in a few pages his idea of economical progress: a gradual reduction of interest, profit, rent, taxes, and wages. All progress hitherto has been made in this manner; in this manner it must continue to be made. Those workingmen who favor a nominal increase of wages are, unconsciously. following a back-track, opposed to all their interests.

After having published in "Le Représentant du Peuple," the statutes of the Bank of Exchange, — a bank which was to make no profits, since it was to have no stockholders, and which, consequently, was to discount commercial paper with out interest, charging only a commission sufficient to defray its running expenses, — Proudhon endeavored, in a number of articles, to explain its mechanism and necessity. These articles have been collected in one volume, under the double title, "Résumé of the Social Question; Bank of Exchange." His other articles, those which up to December, 1848, were inspired by the progress of events, have been collected in another volume, — "Revolutionary Ideas."

Almost unknown in March, 1848, and struck off in April from the list of candidates for the Constituent Assembly by the delegation of workingmen which sat at the Luxembourg, Proudhon had but a very small number of votes at the general elections of April. At the complementary elections, which were held in the early days of June, he was elected in Paris by seventy-seven thousand votes.

After the fatal days of June, he published an article on *le terme*, which caused the first suspension of "Le Représentant du Peuple." It was at that time that he introduced a bill into the Assembly, which, being referred to the Committee on the Finances, drew forth, first, the report of M. Thiers, and then the speech which Proudhon delivered, on the 31st of July, in reply to this report. "Le Représentant du Peuple," reappearing a few days later, he wrote, *à propos* of the law requiring journals to give bonds, his famous article on "The Malthusians" (August 10, 1848). Ten days afterwards, "Le Représentant du Peuple," again suspended, definitively ceased to appear. "Le Peuple," of which he was the editor-in-chief, and the first number of which was issued in the early part of September, appeared weekly at first, for want of sufficient bonds; it afterwards appeared daily, with a double number once a week. Before "Le Peuple" had obtained its first bond, Proudhon published a remarkable pamphlet on the "Right to Labor," — a right which he denied in the form in which it was then affirmed. It was during the same period that he proposed, at the Poissonniere banquet, his *Toast to the Revolution*.

Proudhon, who had been asked to preside at the banquet, refused, and proposed in his stead, first, Ledru-Rollin, and then, in view of the reluctance of the organizers of the banquet, the illustrious president of the party of the Mountain, Lamennais. It was evidently his intention to induce the representatives of the Extreme Left to proclaim at last with him the Democratic and Social Republic. Lamennais being accepted by the organizers, the Mountain promised to be present at the banquet. The night before, all seemed right, when General Cavaignac replaced Minister Sénart by Minister Dufaure-Vivien. The Mountain, questioning the government, proposed a vote of confidence in the old minister, and, tacitly, of want of confidence in the new. Proudhon abstained from voting on this proposition. The Mountain declared that it would not attend the banquet, if Proudhon was to be present. Five Montagnards, Mathieu of Drôme at their head, went to the temporary office of "Le Peuple" to notify him of this. "Citizen Proudhon," said they to the organizers in his presence, "in abstaining from voting to-day on the proposition of the Mountain, has betrayed the Republican cause." Proudhon, vehemently questioned, began his defence by recalling, on the one hand, the treatment which he had received from the dismissed minister; and, on the other, the impartial conduct displayed towards him in 1840 by M. Vivien, the new minister. He then attacked the Mountain by telling its delegates that it sought only a pretext, and that really, in spite of its professions of Socialism in private conversation, whether with him or with the organizers of the banquet, it had not the courage to publicly declare itself Socialist.

On the following day, in his *Toast to the Revolution*, a toast which was filled with allusions to the exciting scene of the night before, Proudhon commenced his struggle against the Mountain. His duel with Félix Pyat was one of the episodes of this struggle, which became less bitter on Proudhon's side after the Mountain finally decided to publicly proclaim the Democratic and Social Republic. The campaign for the election of a President of the Republic had just begun. Proudhon made a very sharp attack on the candidacy of Louis Bonaparte in a pamphlet which is regarded as one of his literary *chefs-d'oeuvre*: the "Pamphlet on the Presidency." An opponent of this institution, against which he had voted in the Constituent Assembly, he at first decided to take no part in the campaign. But soon seeing that he was thus increasing the chances of Louis Bonaparte, and that if, as was not at all probable, the latter should not obtain an absolute majority of the votes, the Assembly would not fail to elect General Cavaignac, he espoused, for the sake of form, the candidacy of Raspail, who was supported by his friends in the Socialist Committee. Charles Delescluze, the editor-in-chief of "La Révolution Démocratique et Sociale," who could not forgive him for having preferred Raspail to Ledru-Rollin, the candidate of the Mountain, attacked him on the day after the election with a violence which overstepped all bounds. At first, Proudhon had the wisdom to refrain from answering him. At length, driven to an extremity, he became aggressive himself, and Delescluze sent him his seconds. This time, Proudhon positively refused to fight; he would not have fought with Félix Pyat, had not his courage been called in question.

On the 25th of January, 1849, Proudhon, rising from a sick bed, saw that the existence of the Constituent Assembly was endangered by the coalition of the monarchical parties with Louis Bonaparte, who was already planning his *coup d'Etat*. He did not hesitate to openly attack the man who had just received five millions of votes. He wanted to break the idol; he succeeded only in getting prosecuted and condemned himself. The prosecution demanded against him was authorized by a majority of the Constituent Assembly, in spite of the speech which he delivered on that occasion. Declared guilty by the jury, he was sentenced, in March, 1849, to three years' imprisonment and the payment of a fine of ten thousand francs.

Proudhon had not abandoned for a single moment his project of a Bank of Exchange, which was to operate without capital with a sufficient number of merchants and manufacturers for adherents. This bank, which he then called the *Bank of the People*, and around which he wished to gather the numerous working-people's associations which had been formed since the 24th of February, 1848, had already obtained a certain number of subscribers and adherents, the latter to the number of thirty-seven thousand. It was about to commence operations, when Proudhon's sentence forced him to choose between imprisonment and exile. He did not hesitate to abandon his project and return the money to the subscribers. He explained the motives which led him to this decision in an article in "Le Peuple."

Having fled to Belgium, he remained there but a few days, going thence to Paris, under an assumed name, to conceal himself in a house in the Rue de Chabrol. From his hiding-place he sent articles almost every day, signed and unsigned, to "Le Peuple." In the evening, dressed in a blouse, he went to some secluded spot to take the air. Soon, emboldened by habit, he risked an evening promenade upon the Boulevards, and afterwards carried his imprudence so far as to take a stroll by daylight in the neighborhood of the Gare du Nord. It was not long before he was recognized by the police, who arrested him on the 6th of June, 1849, in the Rue du Faubourg-Poissonniere.

Taken to the office of the prefect of police, then to Sainte — Pélagie, he was in the Conciergerie on the day of the 13th of June, 1849, which ended with the violent suppression of "Le Peuple." He then began to write the "Confessions of a Revolutionist," published towards the end of the year. He had been again transferred to Sainte-Pélagie, when he married, in December, 1849, Mlle. Euphrasie Piégard, a young working girl whose hand he had requested in 1847. Madame Proudhon bore him four daughters, of whom but two, Catherine and Stéphanie, survived their father. Stéphanie died in 1873.

In October, 1849, "Le Peuple" was replaced by a new journal, "La Voix du Peuple," which Proudhon edited from his prison cell. In it were published his discussions with Pierre Leroux and Bastiat. The political articles which he sent to "La Voix du Peuple" so displeased the government finally, that it transferred him to Doullens, where he was secretly confined for some time. Afterwards taken back to Paris, to appear before the assizes of the Seine in reference to an article in "La Voix du Peuple," he was defended by M. Cremieux and acquitted. From the Conciergerie he went again to Sainte-Pélagie, where he ended his three years in prison on the 6th of June, 1852.

"La Voix du Peuple," suppressed before the promulgation of the law of the 31st of May, had been replaced by a weekly sheet, "Le Peuple" of 1850. Established by the aid of the principal members of the Mountain, this journal soon met with the fate of its predecessors.

In 1851, several months before the *coup d'Etat*, Proudhon published the "General Idea of the Revolution of the Nineteenth Century," in which, after having shown the logical series of unitary governments, — from monarchy, which is the first term, to the direct government of the people, which is the last, — he opposes the ideal of an-archy or self-government to the communistic or governmental ideal.

At this period, the Socialist party, discouraged by the elections of 1849, which resulted in a greater conservative triumph than those of 1848, and justly angry with the national representative body which had just passed the law of the

31st of May, 1850, demanded direct legislation and direct government. Proudhon, who did not want, at any price, the plebiscitary system which he had good reason to regard as destructive of liberty, did not hesitate to point out, to those of his friends who expected every thing from direct legislation, one of the antinomies of universal suffrage. In so far as it is an institution intended to achieve, for the benefit of the greatest number, the social reforms to which landed suffrage is opposed, universal suffrage is powerless; especially if it pretends to legislate or govern directly. For, until the social reforms are accomplished, the greatest number is of necessity the least enlightened, and consequently the least capable of understanding and effecting reforms. In regard to the antinomy, pointed out by him, of liberty and government, — whether the latter be monarchic, aristocratic, or democratic in form, — Proudhon, whose chief desire was to preserve liberty, naturally sought the solution in the free contract. But though the free contract may be a practical solution of purely economical questions, it cannot be made use of in politics. Proudhon recognized this ten years later, when his beautiful study on "War and Peace" led him to find in the *federative principle* the exact equilibrium of liberty and government.

"The Social Revolution Demonstrated by the Coup d' Etat" appeared in 1852, a few months after his release from prison. At that time, terror prevailed to such an extent that no one was willing to publish his book without express permission from the government. He succeeded in obtaining this permission by writing to Louis Bonaparte a letter which he published at the same time with the work. The latter being offered for sale, Proudhon was warned that he would not be allowed to publish any more books of the same character. At that time he entertained the idea of writing a universal history entitled "Chronos." This project was never fulfilled.

Already the father of two children, and about to be presented with a third, Proudhon was obliged to devise some immediate means of gaining a living; he resumed his labors, and published, at first anonymously, the "Manual of a Speculator in the Stock-Exchange." Later, in 1857, after having completed the work, he did not hesitate to sign it, acknowledging in the preface his indebtedness to his collaborator, G. Duchêne.

Meantime, he vainly sought permission to establish a journal, or review. This permission was steadily refused him. The imperial government always suspected him after the publication of the "Social Revolution Demonstrated by the Coup d'Etat."

Towards the end of 1853, Proudhon issued in Belgium a pamphlet entitled "The Philosophy of Progress." Entirely inoffensive as it was, this pamphlet, which he endeavored to send into France, was seized on the frontier. Proudhon's complaints were of no avail.

The empire gave grants after grants to large companies. A financial society, having asked for the grant of a railroad in the east of France, employed Proudhon to write several memoirs in support of this demand. The grant was given to another company. The author was offered an indemnity as compensation, to be paid (as was customary in such cases) by the company which received the grant. It is needless to say that Proudhon would accept nothing. Then, wishing to explain to the public, as well as to the government, the end which he had in view, he published the work entitled "Reforms to be Effected in the Management of Railroads."

Towards the end of 1854, Proudhon had already begun his book on "Justice," when he had a violent attack of cholera, from which he recovered with great difficulty. Ever afterwards his health was delicate.

At last, on the 22d of April, 1858, he published, in three large volumes, the important work upon which he had labored since 1854. This work had two titles: the first, "Justice in the Revolution and in the Church;" the second, "New Principles of Practical Philosophy, addressed to His Highness Monseigneur Mathieu, Cardinal-Archbishop of Besançon." On the 27th of April, when there had scarcely been time to read the work, an order was issued by the magistrate for its seizure; on the 28th the seizure was effected. To this first act of the magistracy, the author of the incriminated book replied on the 11th of May in a strongly-motived petition, demanding a revision of the concordat of 1802; or, in other words, a new adjustment of the relations between Church and State. At bottom, this petition was but the logical consequence of the work itself. An edition of a thousand copies being published on the 17th of May, the "Petition to the Senate" was regarded by the public prosecutor as an aggravation of the offence or offences discovered in the body of the work to which it was an appendix, and was seized in its turn on the 23d. On the first of June, the author appealed to the Senate in a second "Petition," which was deposited with the first in the office of the Secretary of the Assembly, the guardian and guarantee, according to the constitution of 1852, of the principles of '89. On the 2d of June, the two processes being united, Proudhon appeared at the bar with his publisher, the printer of the book, and the printer of the petition, to receive the sentence of the police magistrate, which condemned him to three years' imprisonment, a fine of four thousand francs, and the suppression of his work. It is needless to say that the publisher and printers were also condemned by the sixth chamber.

Proudhon lodged an appeal; he wrote a memoir which the law of 1819, in the absence of which he would have been liable to a new prosecution, gave him the power to publish previous to the hearing. Having decided to make use of the means which the law permitted, he urged in vain the printers who were prosecuted with him to lend him their aid. He then demanded of Attorney-General Chaix d'Est Ange a statement to the effect that the twenty-third article of the law of the 17th of May, 1819, allows a written defence, and that a printer runs no risk in printing it. The attorney-general flatly refused. Proudhon then started for Belgium, where he printed his defence, which could not, of course, cross the French frontier. This memoir is entitled to rank with the best of Beaumarchais's; it is entitled: "Justice prosecuted by the Church; An Appeal from the Sentence passed upon P. J. Proudhon by the Police Magistrate of the Seine, on the 2d of June, 1858." A very close discussion of the grounds of the judgment of the sixth chamber, it was at the same time an excellent *résumé* of his great work.

Once in Belgium, Proudhon did not fail to remain there. In 1859, after the general amnesty which followed the Italian war, he at first thought himself included in it. But the imperial government, consulted by his friends, notified him that, in its opinion, and in spite of the contrary advice of M. Faustin Hélie, his condemnation was not of a political character. Proudhon, thus classed by the government with the authors of immoral works, thought it beneath his dignity to protest, and waited patiently for the advent of 1863 to allow him to return to France.

In Belgium, where he was not slow in forming new friendships, he published in 1859–60, in separate parts, a new edition of his great work on "Justice." Each number contained, in addition to the original text carefully reviewed and corrected, numerous explanatory notes and some "Tidings of the Revolution." In these tidings, which form a sort of review of the progress of ideas in Europe, Proudhon sorrowfully asserts that, after having for a long time marched at the head of the progressive nations, France has become, without appearing to suspect it, the most retrogressive of nations; and he considers her more than once as seriously threatened with moral death.

The Italian war led him to write a new work, which he published in 1861, entitled "War and Peace." This work, in which, running counter to a multitude of ideas accepted until then without examination, he pronounced for the first time against the restoration of an aristocratic and priestly Poland, and against the establishment of a unitary government in Italy, created for him a multitude of enemies. Most of his friends, disconcerted by his categorical affirmation of a right of force, notified him that they decidedly disapproved of his new publication. "You see," triumphantly cried those whom he had always combated, "this man is only a sophist."

Led by his previous studies to test every thing by the question of right, Proudhon asks, in his "War and Peace," whether there is a real right of which war is the vindication, and victory the demonstration. This right, which he roughly calls the right of the strongest or the right of force, and which is, after all, only the right of the most worthy to the preference in certain definite cases, exists, says Proudhon, independently of war. It cannot be legitimately vindicated except where necessity clearly demands the subordination of one will to another, and within the limits in which it exists; that is, without ever involving the enslavement of one by the other. Among nations, the right of the majority, which is only a corollary of the right of force, is as unacceptable as universal monarchy. Hence, until equilibrium is established and recognized between States or national forces, there must be war. War, says Proudhon, is not always necessary to determine which side is the strongest; and he has no trouble in proving this by examples drawn from the family, the workshop, and elsewhere. Passing then to the study of war, he proves that it by no means corresponds in practice to that which it ought to be according to his theory of the right of force. The systematic horrors of war naturally lead him to seek a cause for it other than the vindication of this right; and then only does the economist take it upon himself to denounce this cause to those who, like himself, want peace. The necessity of finding abroad a compensation for the misery resulting in every nation from the absence of economical equilibrium, is, according to Proudhon, the ever real, though ever concealed, cause of war. The pages devoted to this demonstration and to his theory of poverty, which he clearly distinguishes from misery and pauperism, shed entirely new light upon the philosophy of history. As for the author's conclusion, it is a very simple one. Since the treaty of Westphalia, and especially since the treaties of 1815, equilibrium has been the international law of Europe. It remains now, not to destroy it, but, while maintaining it, to labor peacefully, in every nation protected by it, for the equilibrium of economical forces. The last line of the book, evidently written to check imperial ambition, is: "Humanity wants no more war."

In 1861, after Garibaldi's expedition and the battle of Castelfidardo, Proudhon immediately saw that the establishment of Italian unity would be a severe blow to European equilibrium. It was chiefly in order to maintain this equilibrium that he pronounced so energetically in favor of Italian federation, even though it should be at first only a federation of monarchs. In vain was it objected that, in being established by France, Italian unity would break European equilibrium in our favor. Proudhon, appealing to history, showed that every State which breaks the equilibrium in its own favor only causes the other States to combine against it, and thereby diminishes its influence and power. He added that, nations being essentially selfish, Italy would not fail, when opportunity offered, to place her interest above her gratitude.

To maintain European equilibrium by diminishing great States and multiplying small ones; to unite the latter in organized federations, not for attack, but for defence; and with these federations, which, if they were not republican already, would quickly become so, to hold in check the great military monarchies, — such, in the beginning of 1861, was the political programme of Proudhon.

The object of the federations, he said, will be to guarantee, as far as possible, the beneficent reign of peace; and they will have the further effect of securing in every nation the triumph of liberty over despotism. Where the largest unitary State is, there liberty is in the greatest danger; further, if this State be democratic, despotism without the counterpoise of majorities is to be feared. With the federation, it is not so. The universal suffrage of the federal State is checked by the universal suffrage of the federated States; and the latter is offset in its turn by *property*, the stronghold of liberty, which it tends, not to destroy, but to balance with the institutions of *mutualism*.

All these ideas, and many others which were only hinted at in his work on "War and Peace," were developed by Proudhon in his subsequent publications, one of which has for its motto, "Reforms always, Utopias never." The thinker had evidently finished his evolution.

The Council of State of the canton of Vaud having offered prizes for essays on the question of taxation, previously discussed at a congress held at Lausanne, Proudhon entered the ranks and carried off the first prize. His memoir was published in 1861 under the title of "The Theory of Taxation."

About the same time, he wrote at Brussels, in "L'Office de Publicité," some remarkable articles on the question of literary property, which was discussed at a congress held in Belgium, These articles must not be confounded with "Literary Majorats," a more complete work on the same subject, which was published in 1863, soon after his return to France.

Arbitrarily excepted from the amnesty in 1859, Proudhon was pardoned two years later by a special act. He did not wish to take advantage of this favor, and seemed resolved to remain in Belgium until the 2d of June, 1863, the time when he was to acquire the privilege of prescription, when an absurd and ridiculous riot, excited in Brussels by an article published by him on federation and unity in Italy, induced him to hasten his return to France. Stones were thrown against the house in which he lived, in the Faubourg d'Ixelles. After having placed his wife and daughters in safety among his friends at Brussels, he arrived in Paris in September, 1862, and published there, "Federation and Italian Unity," a pamphlet which naturally commences with the article which served as a pretext for the rioters in Brussels.

Among the works begun by Proudhon while in Belgium, which death did not allow him to finish, we ought to mention a "History of Poland," which will be published later; and, "The Theory of Property," which appeared in 1865, before "The Gospels Annotated," and after the volume entitled "The Principle of Art and its Social Destiny."

The publications of Proudhon, in 1863, were: 1. "Literary Majorats: An Examination of a Bill having for its object the Creation of a Perpetual Monopoly for the Benefit of Authors, Inventors, and Artists;" 2. "The Federative Principle and the Necessity of Re-establishing the Revolutionary party;" 3. "The Sworn Democrats and the Refractories;" 4. "Whether the Treaties of 1815 have ceased to exist? Acts of the Future Congress."

The disease which was destined to kill him grew worse and worse; but Proudhon labored constantly! ... A series of articles, published in 1864 in "Le Messager de Paris," have been collected in a pamphlet under the title of "New Observations on Italian Unity." He hoped to publish during the same year his work on "The Political Capacity of the Working Classes," but was unable to write the last chapter... He grew weaker continually. His doctor prescribed rest. In the month of August he went to Franche-Comté, where he spent a month. Having returned to Paris, he resumed his labor with difficulty... From the month of December onwards, the heart disease made rapid progress; the oppression became insupportable, his legs were swollen, and he could not sleep...

On the 19th of January, 1865, he died, towards two o'clock in the morning, in the arms of his wife, his sister-in-law, and the friend who writes these lines...

The publication of his correspondence, to which his daughter Catherine is faithfully devoted, will tend, no doubt, to increase his reputation as a thinker, as a writer, and as an honest man.

J. A. LANGLOIS.

Preface.

The following letter served as a preface to the first edition of this memoir: —

"*To the Members of the Academy of Besançon.*

"PARIS, June 30, 1840.

"GENTLEMEN, — In the course of your debate of the 9th of May, 1833, in regard to the triennial pension established by Madame Suard, you expressed the following wish: —

" 'The Academy requests the titulary to present it annually, during the first fortnight in July, with a succinct and logical statement of the various studies which he has pursued during the year which has just expired.'

"I now propose, gentlemen, to discharge this duty.

"When I solicited your votes, I boldly avowed my intention to bend my efforts to the discovery of some means of *ameliorating the physical, moral, and intellectual condition of the mere numerous and poorer classes*. This idea, foreign as it may have seemed to the object of my candidacy, you received favorably; and, by the precious distinction with which it has been your pleasure to honor me, you changed this formal offer into an inviolable and sacred obligation. Thenceforth I understood with how worthy and honorable a society I had to deal: my regard for its enlightenment, my recognition of its benefits, my enthusiasm for its glory, were unbounded.

"Convinced at once that, in order to break loose from the beaten paths of opinions and systems, it was necessary to proceed in my study of man and society by scientific methods, and in a rigorous manner, I devoted one year to philology and grammar; linguistics, or the natural history of speech, being, of all the sciences, that which was best suited to the character of my mind, seemed to bear the closest relation to the researches which I was about to commence. A treatise, written at this period upon one of the most interesting questions of comparative grammar,[2] if it did not reveal the astonishing success, at least bore witness to the thoroughness, of my labors.

"Since that time, metaphysics and moral science have been my only studies; my perception of the fact that these sciences, though badly defined as to their object and not confined to their sphere, are, like the natural sciences, susceptible of demonstration and certainty, has already rewarded my efforts.

"But, gentlemen, of all the masters whom I have followed, to none do I owe so much as to you. Your co-operation, your programmes, your instructions, in agreement with my secret wishes and most cherished hopes, have at no time failed to enlighten me and to point out my road; this memoir on property is the child of your thought.

"In 1838, the Academy of Besançon proposed the following question: *To what causes must we attribute the continually increasing number of suicides, and what are the proper means for arresting the effects of this moral contagion?*

"Thereby it asked, in less general terms, what was the cause of the social evil, and what was its remedy? You admitted that yourselves, gentlemen when your committee reported that the competitors had enumerated with exactness the immediate and particular causes of suicide, as well as the means of preventing each of them; but that from this enumeration, chronicled with more or less skill, no positive information had been gained, either as to the primary cause of the evil, or as to its remedy.

"In 1839, your programme, always original and varied in its academical expression, became more exact. The investigations of 1838 had pointed out, as the causes or rather as the symptoms of the social malady, the neglect of the principles of religion and morality, the desire for wealth, the passion for enjoyment, and political disturbances. All these data were embodied by you in a single proposition: *The utility of the celebration of Sunday as regards hygiene, morality, and social and political relations.*

"In a Christian tongue you asked, gentlemen, what was the true system of society. A competitor[3] dared to maintain, and believed that he had proved, that the institution of a day of rest at weekly intervals is inseparably bound up with a political system based on the equality of conditions; that without equality this institution is an anomaly and an impossibility: that equality alone can revive this ancient and mysterious keeping of the seventh day. This argument did not meet with your approbation, since, without denying the relation pointed out by the competitor, you judged, and rightly gentlemen, that the principle of equality of conditions not being demonstrated, the ideas of the author were nothing more than hypotheses.

"Finally, gentlemen, this fundamental principle of equality you presented for competition in the following terms: *The economical and moral consequences in France up to the present time, and those which seem likely to appear in future, of the law concerning the equal division of hereditary property between the children.*

"Instead of confining one to common places without breadth or significance, it seems to me that your question should be developed as follows: —

"If the law has been able to render the right of heredity common to all the children of one father, can it not render it equal for all his grandchildren and great-grandchildren?

"If the law no longer heeds the age of any member of the family, can it not, by the right of heredity, cease to heed it in the race, in the tribe, in the nation?

"Can equality, by the right of succession, be preserved between citizens, as well as between cousins and brothers? In a word, can the principle of succession become a principle of equality?

"To sum up all these ideas in one inclusive question: What is the principle of heredity? What are the foundations of inequality? What is property?

"Such, gentlemen, is the object of the memoir that I offer you to day.

"If I have rightly grasped the object of your thought; if I succeed in bringing to light a truth which is indisputable, but, from causes which I am bold enough to claim to have explained, has always been misunderstood; if by an infallible method of investigation, I establish the dogma of equality of conditions; if I determine the principle of civil law, the essence of justice, and the form of society; if I annihilate property forever, — to you, gentlemen, will redound all the glory, for it is to your aid and your inspiration that I owe it.

"My purpose in this work is the application of method to the problems of philosophy; every other intention is foreign to and even abusive of it.

"I have spoken lightly of jurisprudence: I had the right; but I should be unjust did I not distinguish between this pretended science and the men who practise it. Devoted to studies both laborious and severe, entitled in all respects to the esteem of their fellow-citizens by their knowledge and eloquence our legists deserve but one reproach, that of an excessive deference to arbitrary laws.

"I have been pitiless in my criticism of the economists: for them I confess that, in general, I have no liking. The arrogance and the emptiness of their writings, their impertinent pride and their unwarranted blunders, have disgusted me. Whoever, knowing them, pardons them, may read them.

"I have severely blamed the learned Christian Church: it was my duty. This blame results from the facts which I call attention to: why has the Church decreed concerning things which it does not understand? The Church has erred in dogma and in morals; physics and mathematics testify against her. It may be wrong for me to say it, but surely it is unfortunate for Christianity that it is true. To restore religion, gentlemen, it is necessary to condemn the Church.

"Perhaps you will regret, gentlemen, that, in giving all my attention to method and evidence, I have too much neglected form and style: in vain should I have tried to do better. Literary hope and faith I have none. The nineteenth century is, in my eyes, a genesic era, in which new principles are elaborated, but in which nothing that is written shall endure. That is the reason, in my opinion, why, among so many men of talent, France to-day counts not one great writer. In a society like ours, to seek for literary glory seems to me an anachronism. Of what use is it to invoke an ancient sibyl when a muse is on the eve of birth? Pitiable actors in a tragedy nearing its end, that which it behooves us to do is to precipitate the catastrophe. The most deserving among us is he who plays best this part. Well, I no longer aspire to this sad success!

"Why should I not confess it, gentlemen? I have aspired to your suffrages and sought the title of your pensioner, hating all which exists and full of projects for its destruction; I shall finish this investigation in a spirit of calm and philosophical resignation. I have derived more peace from the knowledge of the truth, than anger from the feeling of oppression; and the most precious fruit that I could wish to gather from this memoir would be the inspiration of my readers with that tranquillity of soul which arises from the clear perception of evil and its cause, and which is much more powerful than passion and enthusiasm. My hatred of privilege and human authority was unbounded; perhaps at times I have been guilty, in my indignation, of confounding persons and things; at present I can only despise and complain; to cease to hate I only needed to know.

"It is for you now, gentlemen, whose mission and character are the proclamation of the truth, it is for you to instruct the people, and to tell them for what they ought to hope and what they ought to fear. The people, incapable as yet of sound judgment as to what is best for them, applaud indiscriminately the most opposite ideas, provided that in them they get a taste of flattery: to them the laws of thought are like the confines of the possible; to-day they can no more distinguish between a *savant* and a sophist, than formerly they could tell a physician from a sorcerer. 'Inconsiderately accepting, gathering together, and accumulating everything that is new, regarding all reports as true and indubitable, at the breath or ring of novelty they assemble like bees at the sound of a basin.'[4]

"May you, gentlemen, desire equality as I myself desire it; may you, for the eternal happiness of our country, become its propagators and its heralds; may I be the last of your pensioners! Of all the wishes that I can frame, that, gentlemen, is the most worthy of you and the most honorable for me.

"I am, with the profoundest respect and the most earnest gratitude,

"Your pensioner,

"P. J. PROUDHON."

Two months after the receipt of this letter, the Academy, in its debate of August 24th, replied to the address of its pensioner by a note, the text of which I give below: —

"A member calls the attention of the Academy to a pamphlet, published last June by the titulary of the Suard pension, entitled, "What is property?" and dedicated by the author to the Academy. He is of the opinion that the society owes it to justice, to example, and to its own dignity, to publicly disavow all responsibility for the anti-social doctrines contained in this publication. In consequence he demands:

"1. That the Academy disavow and condemn, in the most formal manner, the work of the Suard pensioner, as having been published without its assent, and as attributing to it opinions diametrically opposed to the principles of each of its members;

"2. That the pensioner be charged, in case he should publish a second edition of his book, to omit the dedication;

"3. That this judgment of the Academy be placed upon the records.

"These three propositions, put to vote, are adopted."

After this ludicrous decree, which its authors thought to render powerful by giving it the form of a contradiction, I can only beg the reader not to measure the intelligence of my compatriots by that of our Academy.

While my patrons in the social and political sciences were fulminating anathemas against my *brochure*, a man, who was a stranger to Franche-Comté, who did not know me, who might even have regarded himself as personally attacked by the too sharp judgment which I had passed upon the economists, a publicist as learned as he was modest, loved by the people whose sorrows he felt, honored by the power which he sought to enlighten without flattering or disgracing it, M. Blanqui — member of the Institute, professor of political economy, defender of property — took up my defence before his associates and before the ministry, and saved me from the blows of a justice which is always blind, because it is always ignorant.

It seems to me that the reader will peruse with pleasure the letter which M. Blanqui did me the honor to write to me upon the publication of my second memoir, a letter as honorable to its author as it is flattering to him to whom it is addressed.

"PARIS, May 1, 1841.

"MONSIEUR, — I hasten to thank you for forwarding to me your second memoir upon property. I have read it with all the interest that an acquaintance with the first would naturally inspire. I am very glad that you have modified somewhat the rudeness of form which gave to a work of such gravity the manner and appearance of a pamphlet; for you quite frightened me, sir, and your talent was needed to reassure me in regard to your intentions. One does not expend so much real knowledge with the purpose of inflaming his country. This proposition, now coming into notice — *property is robbery!* — was of a nature to repel from your book even those serious minds who do not judge by appearances, had you persisted in maintaining it in its rude simplicity. But if you have softened the form, you are none the less faithful to the ground-work of your doctrines; and although you have done me the honor to give me a share in this perilous teaching, I cannot accept a partnership which, as far as talent goes, would surely be a credit to me, but which would compromise me in all other respects.

"I agree with you in one thing only; namely, that all kinds of property get too frequently abused in this world. But I do not reason from the abuse to the abolition, — an heroic remedy too much like death, which cures all evils. I will go farther: I will confess that, of all abuses, the most hateful to me are those of property; but once more, there is a remedy for this evil without violating it, all the more without destroying it. If the present laws allow abuse, we can reconstruct them. Our civil code is not the Koran; it is not wrong to examine it. Change, then, the laws which govern the use of property, but be sparing of anathemas; for, logically, where is the honest man whose hands are entirely clean? Do you think that one can be a robber without knowing it, without wishing it, without suspecting it? Do you not admit that society in its present state, like every man, has in its constitution all kinds of virtues and vices inherited from our ancestors? Is property, then, in your eyes a thing so simple and so abstract that you can re-knead and equalize it, if I may so speak, in your metaphysical mill? One who has said as many excellent and practical things as occur in these two beautiful and paradoxical improvisations of yours cannot be a pure and unwavering utopist. You are too well acquainted with the economical and academical phraseology to play with the hard words of revolutions. I believe, then, that you have handled property as

Rousseau, eighty years ago, handled letters, with a magnificent and poetical display of wit and knowledge. Such, at least, is my opinion.

"That is what I said to the Institute at the time when I presented my report upon your book. I knew that they wished to proceed against you in the courts; you perhaps do not know by how narrow a chance I succeeded in preventing them.[5] What chagrin I should always have felt, if dress to me publicly and personally; I think I could offer some important criticisms. For the moment, I must content myself with thanking you for the kind words in which you have seen fit to speak of me. We each possess the merit of sincerity; I desire also the merit of prudence. You know how deep-seated is the disease under which the working-people are suffering; I know how many noble hearts beat under those rude garments, and I feel an irresistible and fraternal sympathy with the thousands of brave people who rise early in the morning to labor, to pay their taxes, and to make our country strong. I try to serve and enlighten them, whereas some endeavor to mislead them. You have not written directly for them. You have issued two magnificent manifestoes, the second more guarded than the first; issue a third more guarded than the second, and you will take high rank in science, whose first precept is calmness and impartiality.

"Farewell, sir! No man's esteem for another can exceed mine for you.

"BLANQUI."

I should certainly take some exceptions to this noble and eloquent letter; but I confess that I am more inclined to realize the prediction with which it terminates than to augment needlessly the number of my antagonists. So much controversy fatigues and wearies me. The intelligence expended in the warfare of words is like that employed in battle: it is intelligence wasted. M. Blanqui acknowledges that property is abused in many harmful ways; I call *property* the sum these abuses exclusively. To each of us property seems a polygon whose angles need knocking off; but, the operation performed, M. Blanqui maintains that the figure will still be a polygon (an hypothesis admitted in mathematics, although not proven), while I consider that this figure will be a circle. Honest people can at least understand one another.

For the rest, I allow that, in the present state of the question, the mind may legitimately hesitate before deciding in favor of the abolition of property. To gain the victory for one's cause, it does not suffice simply to overthrow a principle generally recognized, which has the indisputable merit of systematically recapitulating our political

397

theories; it is also necessary to establish the opposite principle, and to formulate the system which must proceed from it. Still further, it is necessary to show the method by which the new system will satisfy all the moral and political needs which induced the establishment of the first. On the following conditions, then, of subsequent evidence, depends the correctness of my preceding arguments: —

The discovery of a system of absolute equality in which all existing institutions, save property, or the sum of the abuses of property, not only may find a place, but may themselves serve as instruments of equality: individual liberty, the division of power, the public ministry, the jury system, administrative and judicial organization, the unity and completeness of instruction, marriage, the family, heredity in direct and collateral succession, the right of sale and exchange, the right to make a will, and even birthright, — a system which, better than property, guarantees the formation of capital and keeps up the courage of all; which, from a superior point of view, explains, corrects, and completes the theories of association hitherto proposed, from Plato and Pythagoras to Babeuf, Saint Simon, and Fourier; a system, finally, which, serving as a means of transition, is immediately applicable.

A work so vast requires, I am aware, the united efforts of twenty Montesquieus; nevertheless, if it is not given to a single man to finish, a single one can commence, the enterprise. The road that he shall traverse will suffice to show the end and assure the result.

First Memoir

Adversus hostem æterna auctertas esto.

Against the enemy, revendication is eternal.

Law of the twelve tables.

Chapter I. Method Pursued In This Work. — The Idea Of A Revolution.

If I were asked to answer the following question: *What is slavery?* and I should answer in one word, *It is murder*, my meaning would be understood at once. No extended argument would be required to show that the power to take from a man his thought, his will, his personality, is a power of life and death; and that to enslave a man is to kill him.

398

Why, then, to this other question: *What is property!* may I not likewise answer, *It is robbery*, without the certainty of being misunderstood; the second proposition being no other than a transformation of the first?

I undertake to discuss the vital principle of our government and our institutions, property: I am in my right. I may be mistaken in the conclusion which shall result from my investigations: I am in my right. I think best to place the last thought of my book first: still am I in my right.

Such an author teaches that property is a civil right, born of occupation and sanctioned by law; another maintains that it is a natural right, originating in labor, — and both of these doctrines, totally opposed as they may seem, are encouraged and applauded. I contend that neither labor, nor occupation, nor law, can create property; that it is an effect without a cause: am I censurable?

But murmurs arise!

Property is robbery! That is the war-cry of '93! That is the signal of revolutions!

Reader, calm yourself: I am no agent of discord, no firebrand of sedition. I anticipate history by a few days; I disclose a truth whose development we may try in vain to arrest; I write the preamble of our future constitution. This proposition which seems to you blasphemous — *property is robbery* — would, if our prejudices allowed us to consider it, be recognized as the lightning-rod to shield us from the coming thunderbolt; but too many interests stand in the way! ... Alas! philosophy will not change the course of events: destiny will fulfill itself regardless of prophecy. Besides, must not justice be done and our education be finished?

Property is robbery! ... What a revolution in human ideas! *Proprietor* and *robber* have been at all times expressions as contradictory as the beings whom they designate are hostile; all languages have perpetuated this opposition. On what authority, then, do you venture to attack universal consent, and give the lie to the human race? Who are you, that you should question the judgment of the nations and the ages?

Of what consequence to you, reader, is my obscure individuality? I live, like you, in a century in which reason submits only to fact and to evidence. My name, like yours, is TRUTH-SEEKER.[6] My mission is

399

written in these words of the law: *Speak without hatred and without fear; tell that which thou knowest!* The work of our race is to build the temple of science, and this science includes man and Nature. Now, truth reveals itself to all; to-day to Newton and Pascal, tomorrow to the herdsman in the valley and the journeyman in the shop. Each one contributes his stone to the edifice; and, his task accomplished, disappears. Eternity precedes us, eternity follows us: between two infinites, of what account is one poor mortal that the century should inquire about him?

Disregard then, reader, my title and my character, and attend only to my arguments. It is in accordance with universal consent that I undertake to correct universal error; from the *opinion* of the human race I appeal to its *faith*. Have the courage to follow me; and, if your will is untrammelled, if your conscience is free, if your mind can unite two propositions and deduce a third therefrom, my ideas will inevitably become yours. In beginning by giving you my last word, it was my purpose to warn you, not to defy you; for I am certain that, if you read me, you will be compelled to assent. The things of which I am to speak are so simple and clear that you will be astonished at not having perceived them before, and you will say: "I have neglected to think." Others offer you the spectacle of genius wresting Nature's secrets from her, and unfolding before you her sublime messages; you will find here only a series of experiments upon *justice* and *right* a sort of verification of the weights and measures of your conscience. The operations shall be conducted under your very eyes; and you shall weigh the result.

Nevertheless, I build no system. I ask an end to privilege, the abolition of slavery, equality of rights, and the reign of law. Justice, nothing else; that is the alpha and omega of my argument: to others I leave the business of governing the world.

One day I asked myself: Why is there so much sorrow and misery in society? Must man always be wretched? And not satisfied with the explanations given by the reformers, — these attributing the general distress to governmental cowardice and incapacity, those to conspirators and *émeutes*, still others to ignorance and general corruption, — and weary of the interminable quarrels of the tribune and the press, I sought to fathom the matter myself. I have consulted the masters of science; I have read a hundred volumes of philosophy, law, political economy, and history: would to God that I had lived in a century in which so much reading had been useless! I have made every effort to obtain exact information, comparing doctrines, replying to objections, continually constructing equations and reductions from arguments, and weighing thousands of syllogisms in the scales of the most rigorous logic. In this laborious work, I have collected many interesting facts which I shall share with my friends and the public as soon as I have leisure. But I must say that I recognized at once that we had never understood the meaning of these words, so common and yet so sacred: *Justice, equity, liberty;* that concerning each of these principles our ideas have been utterly obscure; and, in fact, that this ignorance was the sole cause, both of the poverty that devours us, and of all the calamities that have ever afflicted the human race.

My mind was frightened by this strange result: I doubted my reason. What! said I, that which eye has not seen, nor ear heard, nor insight penetrated, you have discovered!

Wretch, mistake not the visions of your diseased brain for the truths of science! Do you not know (great philosophers have said so) that in points of practical morality universal error is a contradiction?

I resolved then to test my arguments; and in entering upon this new labor I sought an answer to the following questions: Is it possible that humanity can have been so long and so universally mistaken in the application of moral principles? How and why could it be mistaken? How can its error, being universal, be capable of correction?

These questions, on the solution of which depended the certainty of my conclusions, offered no lengthy resistance to analysis. It will be seen, in chapter V. of this work, that in morals, as in all other branches of knowledge, the gravest errors are the dogmas of science; that, even in works of justice, to be mistaken is a privilege which ennobles man; and that whatever philosophical merit may attach to me is infinitely small. To name a thing is easy: the difficulty is to discern it before its appearance. In giving expression to the last stage of an idea, — an idea which permeates all minds, which to-morrow will be proclaimed by another if I fail to announce it to-day, — I can claim no merit save that of priority of utterance. Do we eulogize the man who first perceives the dawn?

Yes: all men believe and repeat that equality of conditions is identical with equality of rights; that *property* and *robbery* are synonymous terms; that every social advantage accorded, or rather usurped, in the name of superior talent or service, is iniquity and extortion. All men in their hearts, I say, bear witness to these truths; they need only to be made to understand it.

Before entering directly upon the question before me, I must say a word of the road that I shall traverse. When Pascal approached a geometrical problem, he invented a method of solution; to solve a problem in philosophy a method is equally necessary. Well, by how much do the problems of which philosophy treats surpass in the gravity of their results those discussed by geometry! How much more imperatively, then, do they demand for their solution a profound and rigorous analysis!

It is a fact placed for ever beyond doubt, say the modern psychologists, that every perception received by the mind is determined by certain general laws which govern the mind; is moulded, so to speak, in certain types pre-existing in our understanding, and which constitutes its original condition. Hence, say they, if the mind has no innate *ideas*, it has at least innate *forms*. Thus, for example, every phenomenon is of necessity conceived by us as happening in *time* and *space*, — that compels us to infer a *cause* of its occurrence; every thing which exists implies the ideas of *substance, mode, relation, number, &c.;* in a word, we form no idea which is not related to some one of the general principles of reason, independent of which nothing exists.

These axioms of the understanding, add the psychologists, these fundamental types, by which all our judgments and ideas are inevitably shaped, and which our sensations serve only to illuminate, are known in the schools as *categories*. Their primordial existence in the mind is to-day demonstrated; they need only to be systematized and catalogued. Aristotle recognized ten; Kant increased the number to fifteen; M. Cousin has reduced it to three, to two, to one; and the indisputable glory of this professor will be due to the fact that, if he has not discovered the true theory of categories, he has, at least, seen more clearly than any one else the vast importance of this question, — the greatest and perhaps the only one with which metaphysics has to deal.

I confess that I disbelieve in the innateness, not only of *ideas*, but also of *forms* or *laws* of our understanding; and I hold the metaphysics of Reid and Kant to be still farther removed from the truth than that of Aristotle. However, as I do not wish to enter here into a discussion of the mind, a task which would demand much labor and be of no interest to the public, I shall admit the hypothesis that our most general and most necessary ideas — such as time, space, substance, and cause — exist originally in the mind; or, at least, are derived immediately from its constitution.

402

But it is a psychological fact none the less true, and one to which the philosophers have paid too little attention, that habit, like a second nature, has the power of fixing in the mind new categorical forms derived from the appearances which impress us, and by them usually stripped of objective reality, but whose influence over our judgments is no less predetermining than that of the original categories. Hence we reason by the *eternal* and *absolute* laws of our mind, and at the same time by the secondary rules, ordinarily faulty, which are suggested to us by imperfect observation. This is the most fecund source of false prejudices, and the permanent and often invincible cause of a multitude of errors. The bias resulting from these prejudices is so strong that often, even when we are fighting against a principle which our mind thinks false, which is repugnant to our reason, and which our conscience disapproves, we defend it without knowing it, we reason in accordance with it, and we obey it while attacking it. Enclosed within a circle, our mind revolves about itself, until a new observation, creating within us new ideas, brings to view an external principle which delivers us from the phantom by which our imagination is possessed.

Thus, we know to-day that, by the laws of a universal magnetism whose cause is still unknown, two bodies (no obstacle intervening) tend to unite by an accelerated impelling force which we call *gravitation*. It is gravitation which causes unsupported bodies to fall to the ground, which gives them weight, and which fastens us to the earth on which we live. Ignorance of this cause was the sole obstacle which prevented the ancients from believing in the antipodes. "Can you not see," said St. Augustine after Lactantius, "that, if there were men under our feet, their heads would point downward, and that they would fall into the sky?" The bishop of Hippo, who thought the earth flat because it appeared so to the eye, supposed in consequence that, if we should connect by straight lines the zenith with the nadir in different places, these lines would be parallel with each other; and in the direction of these lines he traced every movement from above to below. Thence he naturally concluded that the stars were rolling torches set in the vault of the sky; that, if left to themselves, they would fall to the earth in a shower of fire; that the earth was one vast plain, forming the lower portion of the world, &c. If he had been asked by what the world itself was sustained, he would have answered that he did not know, but that to God nothing is impossible. Such were the ideas of St. Augustine in regard to space and movement, ideas fixed within him by a prejudice derived from an appearance, and which had become with him a general and categorical rule of judgment. Of the reason why bodies fall his mind knew nothing; he could only say that a body falls because it falls.

With us the idea of a fall is more complex: to the general ideas of space and movement which it implies, we add that of attraction or direction towards a centre, which gives us the higher idea of cause. But if physics has fully corrected our judgment in this respect, we still make use of the prejudice of St. Augustine; and when we say that a thing has *fallen*, we do not mean simply and in general that there has been an effect of gravitation, but specially and in particular that it is towards the earth, and *from above to below*, that this movement has taken place. Our mind is enlightened in vain; the imagination prevails, and our language remains forever incorrigible. To *descend from heaven* is as incorrect an expression as to *mount to heaven;* and yet this expression will live as long as men use language.

All these phrases — *from above to below; to descend from heaven; to fall from the clouds, &c.* — are henceforth harmless, because we know how to rectify them in practice; but let us deign to consider for a moment how much they have retarded the progress of science. If, indeed, it be a matter of little importance to statistics, mechanics, hydrodynamics, and ballistics, that the true cause of the fall of bodies should be known, and that our ideas of the general movements in space should be exact, it is quite otherwise when we undertake to explain the system of the universe, the cause of tides, the shape of the earth, and its position in the heavens: to understand these things we must leave the circle of appearances. In all ages there have been ingenious mechanicians, excellent architects, skilful artillerymen: any error, into which it was possible for them to fall in regard to the rotundity of the earth and gravitation, in no wise retarded the development of their art; the solidity of their buildings and accuracy of their aim was not affected by it. But sooner or later they were forced to grapple with phenomena, which the supposed parallelism of all perpendiculars erected from the earth's surface rendered inexplicable: then also commenced a struggle between the prejudices, which for centuries had sufficed in daily practice, and the unprecedented opinions which the testimony of the eyes seemed to contradict.

Thus, on the one hand, the falsest judgments, whether based on isolated facts or only on appearances, always embrace some truths whose sphere, whether large or small, affords room for a certain number of inferences, beyond which we fall into absurdity. The ideas of St. Augustine, for example, contained the following truths: that bodies fall towards the earth, that they fall in a straight line, that either the sun or the earth moves, that either the sky or the earth turns, &c. These general facts always have been true; our science has added nothing to them. But, on the other hand, it being necessary to account for every thing, we are obliged to seek for principles more and more comprehensive: that is why we have had to abandon successively, first the opinion that the world was flat, then the theory which regards it as the stationary centre of the universe, &c.

If we pass now from physical nature to the moral world, we still find ourselves subject to the same deceptions of appearance, to the same influences of spontaneity and habit. But the distinguishing feature of this second division of our knowledge is, on the one hand, the good or the evil which we derive from our opinions; and, on the other, the obstinacy with which we defend the prejudice which is tormenting and killing us.

Whatever theory we embrace in regard to the shape of the earth and the cause of its weight, the physics of the globe does not suffer; and, as for us, our social economy can derive therefrom neither profit nor damage. But it is in us and through us that the laws of our moral nature work; now, these laws cannot be executed without our deliberate aid, and, consequently, unless we know them. If, then, our science of moral laws is false, it is evident that, while desiring our own good, we are accomplishing our own evil; if it is only incomplete, it may suffice for a time for our social progress, but in the long run it will lead us into a wrong road, and will finally precipitate us into an abyss of calamities.

Then it is that we need to exercise our highest judgments; and, be it said to our glory, they are never found wanting: but then also commences a furious struggle between old prejudices and new ideas. Days of conflagration and anguish! We are told of the time when, with the same beliefs, with the same institutions, all the world seemed happy: why complain of these beliefs; why banish these institutions? We are slow to admit that that happy age served the precise purpose of developing the principle of evil which lay dormant in society; we accuse men and gods, the powers of earth and the forces of Nature. Instead of seeking the cause of the evil in his mind and heart, man blames his masters, his rivals, his neighbors, and himself; nations arm themselves, and slay and exterminate each other, until equilibrium is restored by the vast depopulation, and peace again arises from the ashes of the combatants. So loath is humanity to touch the customs of its ancestors, and to change the laws framed by the founders of communities, and confirmed by the faithful observance of the ages.

Nihil motum ex antiquo probabile est: Distrust all innovations, wrote Titus Livius. Undoubtedly it would be better were man not compelled to change: but what! because he is born ignorant, because he exists only on condition of gradual self-instruction, must he abjure the light, abdicate his reason, and abandon himself to fortune? Perfect health is better than convalescence: should the sick man, therefore, refuse to be cured? Reform, reform! cried, ages since, John the Baptist and Jesus Christ. Reform, reform! cried our fathers, fifty years ago; and for a long time to come we shall shout, Reform, reform!

Seeing the misery of my age, I said to myself: Among the principles that support society, there is one which it does not understand, which its ignorance has vitiated, and which causes all the evil that exists. This principle is the most ancient of all; for it is a characteristic of revolutions to tear down the most modern principles, and to respect those of long-standing. Now the evil by which we suffer is anterior to all revolutions. This principle, impaired by our ignorance, is honored and cherished; for if it were not cherished it would harm nobody, it would be without influence.

But this principle, right in its purpose, but misunderstood: this principle, as old as humanity, what is it? Can it be religion?

All men believe in God: this dogma belongs at once to their conscience and their mind. To humanity God is a fact as primitive, an idea as inevitable, a principle as necessary as are the categorical ideas of cause, substance, time, and space to our understanding. God is proven to us by the conscience prior to any inference of the mind; just as the sun is proven to us by the testimony of the senses prior to all the arguments of physics. We discover phenomena and laws by observation and experience; only this deeper sense reveals to us existence. Humanity believes that God is; but, in believing in God, what does it believe? In a word, what is God?

The nature of this notion of Divinity, — this primitive, universal notion, born in the race, — the human mind has not yet fathomed. At each step that we take in our investigation of Nature and of causes, the idea of God is extended and exalted; the farther science advances, the more God seems to grow and broaden. Anthropomorphism and idolatry constituted of necessity the faith of the mind in its youth, the theology of infancy and poesy. A harmless error, if they had not endeavored to make it a rule of conduct, and if they had been wise enough to respect the liberty of thought. But having made God in his own image, man wished to appropriate him still farther; not satisfied with disfiguring the Almighty, he treated him as his patrimony, his goods, his possessions. God, pictured in monstrous forms, became throughout the world the property of man and of the State. Such was the origin of the corruption of morals by religion, and the source of pious feuds and holy wars. Thank Heaven! we have learned to allow every one his own beliefs; we seek for moral laws outside the pale of religion. Instead of legislating as to the nature and attributes of God, the dogmas of theology, and the destiny of our souls, we wisely wait for science to tell us what to reject and what to accept. God, soul, religion, — eternal objects of our unwearied thought and our most fatal aberrations, terrible problems whose solution, for ever attempted, for ever remains unaccomplished, — concerning all these questions we may still be mistaken, but at least our error is harmless. With liberty in religion, and the separation of the spiritual from the temporal power, the influence of religious ideas upon the progress of society is purely negative; no law, no political or civil institution being founded on religion. Neglect of duties imposed by religion may increase the general corruption, but it is not the primary cause; it is only an auxiliary or result. It is universally admitted, and especially in the matter which now engages our attention, that the cause of the inequality of conditions among men — of pauperism, of universal misery, and of governmental embarrassments — can no longer be traced to religion: we must go farther back, and dig still deeper.

But what is there in man older and deeper than the religious sentiment?

There is man himself; that is, volition and conscience, free-will and law, eternally antagonistic. Man is at war with himself: why?

"Man," say the theologians, "transgressed in the beginning; our race is guilty of an ancient offence. For this transgression humanity has fallen; error and ignorance have become its sustenance. Read history, you will find universal proof of this necessity for evil in the permanent misery of nations. Man suffers and always will suffer; his disease is hereditary and constitutional. Use palliatives, employ emollients; there is no remedy."

Nor is this argument peculiar to the theologians; we find it expressed in equivalent language in the philosophical writings of the materialists, believers in infinite perfectibility. Destutt de Tracy teaches formally that poverty, crime, and war are the inevitable conditions of our social state; necessary evils, against which it would be folly to revolt. So, call it *necessity of evil* or *original depravity*, it is at bottom the same philosophy.

"The first man transgressed." If the votaries of the Bible interpreted it faithfully, they would say: *man originally transgressed*, that is, made a

407

mistake; for *to transgress, to fail, to make a mistake*, all mean the same thing.

"The consequences of Adam's transgression are inherited by the race; the first is ignorance." Truly, the race, like the individual, is born ignorant; but, in regard to a multitude of questions, even in the moral and political spheres, this ignorance of the race has been dispelled: who says that it will not depart altogether? Mankind makes continual progress toward truth, and light ever triumphs over darkness. Our disease is not, then, absolutely incurable, and the theory of the theologians is worse than inadequate; it is ridiculous, since it is reducible to this tautology: "Man errs, because he errs." While the true statement is this: "Man errs, because he learns." Now, if man arrives at a knowledge of all that he needs to know, it is reasonable to believe that, ceasing to err, he will cease to suffer.

But if we question the doctors as to this law, said to be engraved upon the heart of man, we shall immediately see that they dispute about a matter of which they know nothing; that, concerning the most important questions, there are almost as many opinions as authors; that we find no two agreeing as to the best form of government, the principle of authority, and the nature of right; that all sail hap-hazard upon a shoreless and bottomless sea, abandoned to the guidance of their private opinions which they modestly take to be right reason. And, in view of this medley of contradictory opinions, we say: "The object of our investigations is the law, the determination of the social principle. Now, the politicians, that is, the social scientists, do not understand each other; then the error lies in themselves; and, as every error has a reality for its object, we must look in their books to find the truth which they have unconsciously deposited there."

Now, of what do the lawyers and the publicists treat? Of *justice, equity, liberty, natural law, civil laws*, &c. But what is justice? What is its principle, its character, its formula? To this question our doctors evidently have no reply; for otherwise their science, starting with a principle clear and well defined, would quit the region of probabilities, and all disputes would end.

What is justice? The theologians answer: "All justice comes from God." That is true; but we know no more than before.

The philosophers ought to be better informed: they have argued so much about justice and injustice! Unhappily, an examination proves that their knowledge amounts to nothing, and that with them — as with

408

the savages whose every prayer to the sun is simply *O! O!* — it is a cry of admiration, love, and enthusiasm; but who does not know that the sun attaches little meaning to the interjection O! That is exactly our position toward the philosophers in regard to justice. Justice, they say, is a *daughter of Heaven; a light which illumines every man that comes into the world; the most beautiful prerogative of our nature; that which distinguishes us from the beasts and likens us to God* — and a thousand other similar things. What, I ask, does this pious litany amount to? To the prayer of the savages: O!

All the most reasonable teachings of human wisdom concerning justice are summed up in that famous adage: *Do unto others that which you would that others should do unto you; Do not unto others that which you would not that others should do unto you.* But this rule of moral practice is unscientific: what have I a right to wish that others should do or not do to me? It is of no use to tell me that my duty is equal to my right, unless I am told at the same time what my right is.

Let us try to arrive at something more precise and positive.

Justice is the central star which governs societies, the pole around which the political world revolves, the principle and the regulator of all transactions. Nothing takes place between men save in the name of *right;* nothing without the invocation of justice. Justice is not the work of the law: on the contrary, the law is only a declaration and application of *justice* in all circumstances where men are liable to come in contact. If, then, the idea that we form of justice and right were ill-defined, if it were imperfect or even false, it is clear that all our legislative applications would be wrong, our institutions vicious, our politics erroneous: consequently there would be disorder and social chaos.

This hypothesis of the perversion of justice in our minds, and, as a necessary result, in our acts, becomes a demonstrated fact when it is shown that the opinions of men have not borne a constant relation to the notion of justice and its applications; that at different periods they have undergone modifications: in a word, that there has been progress in ideas. Now, that is what history proves by the most overwhelming testimony.

Eighteen Hundred years ago, the world, under the rule of the Cæsars, exhausted itself in slavery, superstition, and voluptuousness. The people — intoxicated and, as it were, stupefied by their long-continued orgies — had lost the very notion of right and duty: war and dissipation by turns swept them away; usury and the labor of machines (that is of

409

slaves), by depriving them of the means of subsistence, hindered them from continuing the species. Barbarism sprang up again, in a hideous form, from this mass of corruption, and spread like a devouring leprosy over the depopulated provinces. The wise foresaw the downfall of the empire, but could devise no remedy. What could they think indeed? To save this old society it would have been necessary to change the objects of public esteem and veneration, and to abolish the rights affirmed by a justice purely secular; they said: "Rome has conquered through her politics and her gods; any change in theology and public opinion would be folly and sacrilege.

Rome, merciful toward conquered nations, though binding them in chains, spared their lives; slaves are the most fertile source of her wealth; freedom of the nations would be the negation of her rights and the ruin of her finances. Rome, in fact, enveloped in the pleasures and gorged with the spoils of the universe, is kept alive by victory and government; her luxury and her pleasures are the price of her conquests: she can neither abdicate nor dispossess herself." Thus Rome had the facts and the law on her side. Her pretensions were justified by universal custom and the law of nations. Her institutions were based upon idolatry in religion, slavery in the State, and epicurism in private life; to touch those was to shake society to its foundations, and, to use our modern expression, to open the abyss of revolutions. So the idea occurred to no one; and yet humanity was dying in blood and luxury.

All at once a man appeared, calling himself *The Word of God*. It is not known to this day who he was, whence he came, nor what suggested to him his ideas. He went about proclaiming everywhere that the end of the existing society was at hand, that the world was about to experience a new birth; that the priests were vipers, the lawyers ignoramuses, an I the philosophers hypocrites and liars; that master and slave were equals, that usury and every thing akin to it was robbery, that proprietors and idlers would one day burn, while the poor and pure in heart would find a haven of peace.

This man — *The Word of God* — was denounced and arrested as a public enemy by the priests and the lawyers, who well understood how to induce the people to demand his death. But this judicial murder, though it put the finishing stroke to their crimes, did not destroy the doctrinal seeds which *The Word of God* had sown. After his death, his original disciples travelled about in all directions, preaching what they called the *good news*, creating in their turn millions of missionaries; and, when their task seemed to be accomplished, dying by the sword of Roman justice. This persistent agitation, the war of the executioners

410

and martyrs, lasted nearly three centuries, ending in the conversion of the world. Idolatry was destroyed, slavery abolished, dissolution made room for a more austere morality, and the contempt for wealth was sometimes pushed almost to privation. Society was saved by the negation of its own principles, by a revolution in its religion, and by violation of its most sacred rights. In this revolution, the idea of justice spread to an extent that had not before been dreamed of, never to return to its original limits. Heretofore justice had existed only for the masters;[7] it then commenced to exist for the slaves.

Nevertheless, the new religion at that time had borne by no means all its fruits. There was a perceptible improvement of the public morals, and a partial release from oppression; but, other than that, the *seeds sown by the Son of Man*, having fallen into idolatrous hearts, had produced nothing save innumerable discords and a quasi-poetical mythology. Instead of developing into their practical consequences the principles of morality and government taught by *The Word of God*, his followers busied themselves in speculations as to his birth, his origin, his person, and his actions; they discussed his parables, and from the conflict of the most extravagant opinions upon unanswerable questions and texts which no one understood, was born *theology*, — which may be defined as the *science of the infinitely absurd*.

The truth of *Christianity* did not survive the age of the apostles; the *Gospel*, commented upon and symbolized by the Greeks and Latins, loaded with pagan fables, became literally a mass of contradictions; and to this day the reign of the *infallible Church* has been a long era of darkness. It is said that the *gates of hell* will not always prevail, that *The Word of God* will return, and that one day men will know truth and justice; but that will be the death of Greek and Roman Catholicism, just as in the light of science disappeared the caprices of opinion.

The monsters which the successors of the apostles were bent on destroying, frightened for a moment, reappeared gradually, thanks to the crazy fanaticism, and sometimes the deliberate connivance, of priests and theologians. The history of the enfranchisement of the French communes offers constantly the spectacle of the ideas of justice and liberty spreading among the people, in spite of the combined efforts of kings, nobles, and clergy. In the year 1789 of the Christian era, the French nation, divided by caste, poor and oppressed, struggled in the triple net of royal absolutism, the tyranny of nobles and parliaments, and priestly intolerance. There was the right of the king and the right of the priest, the right of the patrician and the right of the plebeian; there were the privileges of birth, province, communes, corporations, and trades; and, at the bottom of all, violence, immorality, and misery. For some time they talked of reformation; those who apparently desired it most favoring it only for their own profit, and the people who were to be the gainers expecting little and saying nothing. For a long time these poor people, either from distrust, incredulity, or despair, hesitated to ask for their rights: it is said that the habit of serving had taken the courage away from those old communes, which in the middle ages were so bold.

Finally a book appeared, summing up the whole matter in these two propositions: *What is thee third estate? — Nothing. What ought it to be? — Every thing.* Some one added by way of comment: *What is the king? — The servant of the people.*

This was a sudden revelation: the veil was torn aside, a thick bandage fell from all eyes. The people commenced to reason thus: —

If the king is our servant, he ought to report to us;

If he ought to report to us, he is subject to control;

If he can be controlled, he is responsible;

If he is responsible, he is punishable;

If he is punishable, he ought to be punished according to his merits;

If he ought to be punished according to his merits, he can be punished with death.

Five years after the publication of the *brochure* of Sieyès, the third estate was every thing; the king, the nobility, the clergy, were no more. In 1793, the nation, without stopping at the constitutional fiction of the inviolability of the sovereign, conducted Louis XVI. to the scaffold; in 1830, it accompanied Charles X. to Cherbourg. In each case, it may have erred, in fact, in its judgment of the offence; but, in right, the logic which led to its action was irreproachable. The people, in punishing their sovereign, did precisely that which the government of July was so severely censured for failing to do when it refused to execute Louis Bonaparte after the affair of Strasburg: they struck the true culprit. It was an application of the common law, a solemn decree of justice enforcing the penal laws.[8]

412

The spirit which gave rise to the movement of '89 was a spirit of negation; that, of itself, proves that the order of things which was substituted for the old system was not methodical or well-considered; that, born of anger and hatred, it could not have the effect of a science based on observation and study; that its foundations, in a word, were not derived from a profound knowledge of the laws of Nature and society. Thus the people found that the republic, among the so-called new institutions, was acting on the very principles against which they had fought, and was swayed by all the prejudices which they had intended to destroy. We congratulate ourselves, with inconsiderate enthusiasm, on the glorious French Revolution, the regeneration of 1789, the great changes that have been effected, and the reversion of institutions: a delusion, a delusion!

When our ideas on any subject, material, intellectual, or social, undergo a thorough change in consequence of new observations, I call that movement of the mind *revolution*. If the ideas are simply extended or modified, there is only *progress*. Thus the system of Ptolemy was a step in astronomical progress, that of Copernicus was a revolution. So, in 1789, there was struggle and progress; revolution there was none. An examination of the reforms which were attempted proves this.

The nation, so long a victim of monarchical selfishness, thought to deliver itself for ever by declaring that it alone was sovereign. But what was monarchy? The sovereignty of one man. What is democracy? The sovereignty of the nation, or, rather, of the national majority. But it is, in both cases, the sovereignty of man instead of the sovereignty of the law, the sovereignty of the will instead of the sovereignty of the reason; in one word, the passions instead of justice. Undoubtedly, when a nation passes from the monarchical to the democratic state, there is progress, because in multiplying the sovereigns we increase the opportunities of the reason to substitute itself for the will; but in reality there is no revolution in the government, since the principle remains the same. Now, we have the proof to-day that, with the most perfect democracy, we cannot be free.[9]

Nor is that all. The nation-king cannot exercise its sovereignty itself; it is obliged to delegate it to agents: this is constantly reiterated by those who seek to win its favor. Be these agents five, ten, one hundred, or a thousand, of what consequence is the number; and what matters the name? It is always the government of man, the rule of will and caprice. I ask what this pretended revolution has revolutionized?

We know, too, how this sovereignty was exercised; first by the Convention, then by the Directory, afterwards confiscated by the Consul. As for the Emperor, the strong man so much adored and mourned by the nation, he never wanted to be dependent on it; but, as if intending to set its sovereignty at defiance, he dared to demand its suffrage: that is, its abdication, the abdication of this inalienable sovereignty; and he obtained it.

But what is sovereignty? It is, they say, the *power to make laws.*[10] Another absurdity, a relic of despotism. The nation had long seen kings issuing their commands in this form: *for such is our pleasure;* it wished to taste in its turn the pleasure of making laws. For fifty years it has brought them forth by myriads; always, be it understood, through the agency of representatives. The play is far from ended.

The definition of sovereignty was derived from the definition of the law. The law, they said, is *the expression of the will of the sovereign:* then, under a monarchy, the law is the expression of the will of the king; in a republic, the law is the expression of the will of the people. Aside from the difference in the number of wills, the two systems are exactly identical: both share the same error, namely, that the law is the expression of a will; it ought to be the expression of a fact. Moreover they followed good leaders: they took the citizen of Geneva for their prophet, and the *contrat social* for their Koran.

Bias and prejudice are apparent in all the phrases of the new legislators. The nation had suffered from a multitude of exclusions and privileges; its representatives issued the following declaration: *All men are equal by nature and before the law*; an ambiguous and redundant declaration. *Men are equal by nature:* does that mean that they are equal in size, beauty, talents, and virtue? No; they meant, then, political and civil equality. Then it would have been sufficient to have said: *All men are equal before the law*.

But what is equality before the law? Neither the constitution of 1790, nor that of '93, nor the granted charter, nor the accepted charter, have defined it accurately. All imply an inequality in fortune and station incompatible with even a shadow of equality in rights. In this respect it may be said that all our constitutions have been faithful expressions of the popular will: I am going, to prove it.

Formerly the people were excluded from civil and military offices; it was considered a wonder when the following high-sounding article was inserted in the Declaration of Rights: "All citizens are equally eligible to office; free nations know no qualifications in their choice of officers save virtues and talents."

They certainly ought to have admired so beautiful an idea: they admired a piece of nonsense. Why! the sovereign people, legislators, and reformers, see in public offices, to speak plainly, only opportunities for pecuniary advancement. And, because it regards them as a source of profit, it decrees the eligibility of citizens. For of what use would this precaution be, if there were nothing to gain by it? No one would think of ordaining that none but astronomers and geographers should be pilots, nor of prohibiting stutterers from acting at the theatre and the opera. The nation was still aping the kings: like them it wished to award the lucrative positions to its friends and flatterers. Unfortunately, and this last feature completes the resemblance, the nation did not control the list of livings; that was in the hands of its agents and representatives. They, on the other hand, took care not to thwart the will of their gracious sovereign.

This edifying article of the Declaration of Rights, retained in the charters of 1814 and 1830, implies several kinds of civil inequality; that is, of inequality before the law: inequality of station, since the public functions are sought only for the consideration and emoluments which they bring; inequality of wealth, since, if it had been desired to equalize fortunes, public service would have been regarded as a duty, not as a reward; inequality of privilege, the law not stating what it means by *talents* and *virtues.* Under the empire, virtue and talent consisted simply in military bravery and devotion to the emperor; that was shown when Napoleon created his nobility, and attempted to connect it with the ancients. To-day, the man who pays taxes to the amount of two hundred francs is virtuous; the talented man is the honest pickpocket: such truths as these are accounted trivial.

The people finally legalized property. God forgive them, for they knew not what they did! For fifty years they have suffered for their miserable folly. But how came the people, whose voice, they tell us, is the voice of God, and whose conscience is infallible, — how came the people to err? How happens it that, when seeking liberty and equality, they fell back into privilege and slavery? Always through copying the ancient *régime.*

Formerly, the nobility and the clergy contributed towards the expenses of the State only by voluntary aid and gratuitous gift; their property could not be seized even for debt, — while the plebeian, overwhelmed by taxes and statute-labor, was continually tormented, now by the king's tax-gatherers, now by those of the nobles and clergy. He whose possessions were subject to mortmain could neither bequeath nor inherit property; he was treated like the animals, whose services and offspring belong to their master by right of accession. The people wanted the conditions of *ownership* to be alike for all; they thought that every one should *enjoy and freely dispose of his possessions his income and the fruit of his labor and industry.* The people did not invent property; but as they had not the same privileges in regard to it, which the nobles and clergy possessed, they decreed that the right should be exercised by all under the same conditions. The more obnoxious forms of property — statute-labor, mortmain, *maîtrise,* and exclusion from public office — have disappeared; the conditions of its enjoyment have been modified: the principle still remains the same. There has been progress in the regulation of the right; there has been no revolution.

These, then, are the three fundamental principles of modern society, established one after another by the movements of 1789 and 1830: 1. *Sovereignty of the human will;* in short, *despotism.* 2. *Inequality of wealth and rank.* 3. *Property* — above JUSTICE, always invoked as the guardian angel of sovereigns, nobles, and proprietors; JUSTICE, the general, primitive, categorical law of all society.

We must ascertain whether the ideas of *despotism, civil inequality* and *property,* are in harmony with the primitive notion of *justice,* and necessarily follow from it, — assuming various forms according to the condition, position, and relation of persons; or whether they are not rather the illegitimate result of a confusion of different things, a fatal association of ideas. And since justice deals especially with the questions of government, the condition of persons, and the possession of things, we must ascertain under what conditions, judging by universal opinion and the progress of the human mind, government is just, the condition of citizens is just, and the possession of things is just; then, striking out every thing which fails to meet these conditions, the result will at once tell us what legitimate government is, what the legitimate condition of citizens is, and what the legitimate possession of things is; and finally, as the last result of the analysis, what *justice* is.

Is the authority of man over man just?

Everybody answers, "No; the authority of man is only the authority of the law, which ought to be justice and truth." The private will counts for nothing in government, which consists, first, in discovering truth and justice in order to make the law; and, second, in superintending the execution of this law. I do not now inquire whether our constitutional form of government satisfies these conditions; whether, for example, the will of the ministry never influences the declaration and interpretation of the law; or whether our deputies, in their debates, are more intent on conquering by argument than by force of numbers: it is enough for me that my definition of a good government is allowed to be correct. This idea is exact. Yet we see that nothing seems more just to the Oriental nations than the despotism of their sovereigns; that, with the ancients and in the opinion of the philosophers themselves, slavery was just; that in the middle ages the nobles, the priests, and the bishops felt justified in holding slaves; that Louis XIV. thought that he was right when he said, "The State! I am the State;" and that Napoleon deemed it a crime for the State to oppose his will. The idea of justice, then, applied to sovereignty and government, has not always been what it is to-day; it has gone on developing and shaping itself by degrees, until it has arrived at its present state. But has it reached its last phase? I think not: only, as the last obstacle to be overcome arises from the institution of property which we have kept intact, in order to finish the reform in government and consummate the revolution, this very institution we must attack.

Is political and civil inequality just?

Some say yes; others no. To the first I would reply that, when the people abolished all privileges of birth and caste, they did it, in all probability, because it was for their advantage; why then do they favor the privileges of fortune more than those of rank and race? Because, say they, political inequality is a result of property; and without property society is impossible: thus the question just raised becomes a question of property. To the second I content myself with this remark: If you wish to enjoy political equality, abolish property; otherwise, why do you complain?

Is property just?

Everybody answers without hesitation, "Yes, property is just." I say everybody, for up to the present time no one who thoroughly understood the meaning of his words has answered no. For it is no easy thing to reply understandingly to such a question; only time and experience can furnish an answer. Now, this answer is given; it is for us to understand it. I undertake to prove it.

We are to proceed with the demonstration in the following order: —

I. We dispute not at all, we refute nobody, we deny nothing; we accept as sound all the arguments alleged in favor of property, and confine ourselves to a search for its principle, in order that we may then ascertain whether this principle is faithfully expressed by property. In fact, property being defensible on no ground save that of justice, the idea, or at least the intention, of justice must of necessity underlie all the arguments that have been made in defence of property; and, as on the other hand the right of property is only exercised over those things which can be appreciated by the senses, justice, secretly objectifying itself, so to speak, must take the shape of an algebraic formula. By this method of investigation, we soon see that every argument which has been invented in behalf of property, *whatever it may be*, always and of necessity leads to equality; that is, to the negation of property.

The first part covers two chapters: one treating of occupation, the foundation of our right; the other, of labor and talent, considered as causes of property and social inequality.

The first of these chapters will prove that the right of occupation *obstructs* property; the second that the right of labor *destroys* it.

II. Property, then, being of necessity conceived as existing only in connection with equality, it remains to find out why, in spite of this necessity of logic, equality does not exist. This new investigation also covers two chapters: in the first, considering the fact of property in itself, we inquire whether this fact is real, whether it exists, whether it is possible; for it would imply a contradiction, were these two opposite forms of society, equality and inequality, both possible. Then we discover, singularly enough, that property may indeed manifest itself accidentally; but that, as an institution and principle, it is mathematically impossible. So that the axiom of the school — *ab actu ad posse valet consecutio:* from the actual to the possible the inference is good — is given the lie as far as property is concerned.

Finally, in the last chapter, calling psychology to our aid, and probing man's nature to the bottom, we shall disclose the principle of *justice* — its formula and character; we shall state with precision the organic law of society; we shall explain the origin of property, the causes of its establishment, its long life, and its approaching death; we shall definitively establish its identity with robbery. And, after having shown that these three prejudices — *the sovereignty of man, the inequality of conditions, and property* — are one and the same; that they may be taken for each other, and are reciprocally convertible, — we shall have no trouble in inferring therefrom, by the principle of contradiction, the basis of government and right. There our investigations will end, reserving the right to continue them in future works.

The importance of the subject which engages our attention is recognized by all minds.

"Property," says M. Hennequin, "is the creative and conservative principle of civil society. Property is one of those basic institutions, new theories concerning which cannot be presented too soon; for it must not be forgotten, and the publicist and statesman must know, that on the answer to the question whether property is the principle or the result of social order, whether it is to be considered as a cause or an effect, depends all morality, and, consequently, all the authority of human institutions."

These words are a challenge to all men of hope and faith; but, although the cause of equality is a noble one, no one has yet picked up the gauntlet thrown down by the advocates of property; no one has been courageous enough to enter upon the struggle. The spurious learning of haughty jurisprudence, and the absurd aphorisms of a political economy controlled by property have puzzled the most generous minds; it is a sort of password among the most influential friends of liberty and the interests of the people that *equality is a chimera!* So many false theories and meaningless analogies influence minds otherwise keen, but which are unconsciously controlled by popular prejudice. Equality advances every day — *fit aequalitas.* Soldiers of liberty, shall we desert our flag in the hour of triumph?

A defender of equality, I shall speak without bitterness and without anger; with the independence becoming a philosopher, with the courage and firmness of a free man. May I, in this momentous struggle, carry into all hearts the light with which I am filled; and show, by the success of my argument, that equality failed to conquer by the sword only that it might conquer by the pen!

Chapter II. Property Considered As A Natural Right. — Occupation And Civil Law As Efficient Bases Of Property. Definitions.

The Roman law defined property as the right to use and abuse one's own within the limits of the law — *jus utendi et abutendi re suâ, guatenus juris ratio patitur*. A justification of the word *abuse* has been attempted, on the ground that it signifies, not senseless and immoral abuse, but only absolute domain. Vain distinction! invented as an excuse for property, and powerless against the frenzy of possession, which it neither prevents nor represses. The proprietor may, if he chooses, allow his crops to rot under foot; sow his field with salt; milk his cows on the sand; change his vineyard into a desert, and use his vegetable-garden as a park: do these things constitute abuse, or not? In the matter of property, use and abuse are necessarily indistinguishable.

According to the Declaration of Rights, published as a preface to the Constitution of '93, property is "the right to enjoy and dispose at will of one's goods, one's income, and the fruit of one's labor and industry."

Code Napoléon, article 544: "Property is the right to enjoy and dispose of things in the most absolute manner, provided we do not overstep the limits prescribed by the laws and regulations."

These two definitions do not differ from that of the Roman law: all give the proprietor an absolute right over a thing; and as for the restriction imposed by the code, — *provided we do not overstep the limits prescribed by the laws and regulations,* — its object is not to limit property, but to prevent the domain of one proprietor from interfering with that of another. That is a confirmation of the principle, not a limitation of it.

There are different kinds of property: 1. Property pure and simple, the dominant and seigniorial power over a thing; or, as they term it, *naked property.* 2. *Possession.* "Possession," says Duranton, "is a matter of fact, not of right." Toullier: "Property is a right, a legal power; possession is a fact." The tenant, the farmer, the *commandité,* the usufructuary, are possessors; the owner who lets and lends for use, the heir who is to come into possession on the death of a usufructuary, are proprietors. If I may venture the comparison: a lover is a possessor, a husband is a proprietor.

This double definition of property — domain and possession — is of the highest importance; and it must be clearly understood, in order to comprehend what is to follow.

From the distinction between possession and property arise two sorts of rights: the *jus in re,* the right in a thing, the right by which I may reclaim the property which I have acquired, in whatever hands I find it; and the *jus ad rem,* the right *to* a thing, which gives me a claim to become a proprietor. Thus the right of the partners to a marriage over each other's person is the *jus in re*; that of two who are betrothed is

420

only the *jus ad rem*. In the first, possession and property are united; the second includes only naked property. With me who, as a laborer, have a right to the possession of the products of Nature and my own industry, — and who, as a proletaire, enjoy none of them, — it is by virtue of the *jus ad rem* that I demand admittance to the *jus in re*.

This distinction between the *jus in re* and the *jus ad rem* is the basis of the famous distinction between *possessoire* and *petitoire*, — actual categories of jurisprudence, the whole of which is included within their vast boundaries. *Petitoire* refers to every thing relating to property; *possessoire* to that relating to possession. In writing this memoir against property, I bring against universal society an *action petitoire:* I prove that those who do not possess to-day are proprietors by the same title as those who do possess; but, instead of inferring therefrom that property should be shared by all, I demand, in the name of general security, its entire abolition. If I fail to win my case, there is nothing left for us (the proletarian class and myself) but to cut our throats: we can ask nothing more from the justice of nations; for, as the code of procedure (art 26) tells us in its energetic style, *the plaintiff who has been non-suited in an action petitoire, is debarred thereby from bringing an action possessoire.* If, on the contrary, I gain the case, we must then commence an *action possessoire*, that we may be reinstated in the enjoyment of the wealth of which we are deprived by property. I hope that we shall not be forced to that extremity; but these two actions cannot be prosecuted at once, such a course being prohibited by the same code of procedure.

Before going to the heart of the question, it will not be useless to offer a few preliminary remarks.

§ 1. — *Property as a Natural Right.*

The Declaration of Rights has placed property in its list of the natural and inalienable rights of man, four in all: *liberty, equality, property, security*. What rule did the legislators of

'93 follow in compiling this list? None. They laid down principles, just as they discussed sovereignty and the laws; from a general point of view, and according to their own opinion. They did every thing in their own blind way.

If we can believe Toullier: "The absolute rights can be reduced to three: *security, liberty, property*." Equality is eliminated by the Rennes professor; why? Is it because *liberty* implies it, or because property prohibits it? On this point the author of "Droit Civil Expliqué" is silent: it has not even occurred to him that the matter is under discussion.

Nevertheless, if we compare these three or four rights with each other, we find that property bears no resemblance whatever to the others; that for the majority of citizens it exists only potentially, and as a dormant faculty without exercise; that for the others, who do enjoy it, it is susceptible of certain transactions and modifications which do not harmonize with the idea of a natural right; that, in practice, governments, tribunals, and laws do not respect it; and finally that everybody, spontaneously and with one voice, regards it as chimerical.

Liberty is inviolable. I can neither sell nor alienate my liberty; every contract, every condition of a contract, which has in view the alienation or suspension of liberty, is null: the slave, when he plants his foot upon the soil of liberty, at that moment becomes a free man. When society seizes a malefactor and deprives him of his liberty, it is a case of legitimate defence: whoever violates the social compact by the commission of a crime declares himself a public enemy; in attacking the liberty of others, he compels them to take away his own. Liberty is the original condition of man; to renounce liberty is to renounce the nature of man: after that, how could we perform the acts of man?

Likewise, equality before the law suffers neither restriction nor exception. All Frenchmen are equally eligible to office: consequently, in the presence of this equality, condition and family have, in many cases, no influence upon choice. The poorest citizen can obtain judgment in the courts against one occupying the most exalted station. Let the millionaire, Ahab, build a château upon the vineyard of Naboth: the court will have the power, according to the circumstances, to order the destruction of the château, though it has cost millions; and to force the trespasser to restore the vineyard to its original state, and pay the damages. The law wishes all property, that has been legitimately acquired, to be kept inviolate without regard to value, and without respect for persons.

The charter demands, it is true, for the exercise of certain political rights, certain conditions of fortune and capacity; but all publicists know that the legislator's intention was not to establish a privilege, but to take security. Provided the conditions fixed by law are complied with, every citizen may be an elector, and every elector eligible. The right, once acquired, is the same for all; the law compares neither persons nor votes. I do not ask now whether this system is the best; it is enough that, in the opinion of the charter and in the eyes of every one, equality before the law is absolute, and, like liberty, admits of no compromise.

It is the same with the right of security. Society promises its members no half-way protection, no sham defence; it binds itself to them as they bind themselves to it. It does not say to them, "I will shield you, provided it costs me nothing; I will protect you, if I run no risks thereby." It says, "I will defend you against everybody; I will save and avenge you, or perish myself." The whole strength of the State is at the service of each citizen; the obligation which binds them together is absolute.

How different with property! Worshipped by all, it is acknowledged by none: laws, morals, customs, public and private conscience, all plot its death and ruin.

To meet the expenses of government, which has armies to support, tasks to perform, and officers to pay, taxes are needed. Let all contribute to these expenses: nothing more just. But why should the rich pay more than the poor? That is just, they say, because they possess more. I confess that such justice is beyond my comprehension.

Why are taxes paid? To protect all in the exercise of their natural rights — liberty, equality, security, and property; to maintain order in the State; to furnish the public with useful and pleasant conveniences.

Now, does it cost more to defend the rich man's life and liberty than the poor man's? Who, in time of invasion, famine, or plague, causes more trouble, — the large proprietor who escapes the evil without the assistance of the State, or the laborer who sits in his cottage unprotected from danger?

Is public order endangered more by the worthy citizen, or by the artisan and journeyman? Why, the police have more to fear from a few hundred laborers, out of work, than from two hundred thousand electors!

Does the man of large income appreciate more keenly than the poor man national festivities, clean streets, and beautiful monuments? Why, he prefers his country-seat to all the popular pleasures; and when he wants to enjoy himself, he does not wait for the greased pole!

One of two things is true: either the proportional tax affords greater security to the larger tax-payers, or else it is a wrong. Because, if property is a natural right, as the Declaration of '93 declares, all that belongs to me by virtue of this right is as sacred as my person; it is my blood, my life, myself: whoever touches it offends the apple of my eye. My income of one hundred thousand francs is as inviolable as the grisette's daily wage of seventy-five centimes; her attic is no more sacred than my suite of apartments. The tax is not levied in proportion to strength, size, or skill: no more should it be levied in proportion to property.

If, then, the State takes more from me, let it give me more in return, or cease to talk of equality of rights; for otherwise, society is established, not to defend property, but to destroy it. The State, through the proportional tax, becomes the chief of robbers; the State sets the example of systematic pillage: the State should be brought to the bar of justice at the head of those hideous brigands, that execrable mob which it now kills from motives of professional jealousy.

But, they say, the courts and the police force are established to restrain this mob; government is a company, not exactly for insurance, for it does not insure, but for vengeance and repression. The premium which this company exacts, the tax, is divided in proportion to property; that is, in proportion to the trouble which each piece of property occasions the avengers and repressers paid by the government.

This is any thing but the absolute and inalienable right of property. Under this system the poor and the rich distrust, and make war upon, each other. But what is the object of the war? Property. So that property is necessarily accompanied by war upon property. The liberty and security of the rich do not suffer from the liberty and security of the poor; far from that, they mutually strengthen and sustain each other. The rich man's right of property, on the contrary, has to be continually defended against the poor man's desire for property. What a contradiction! In England they have a poor-rate: they wish me to pay this tax. But what relation exists between my natural and inalienable right of property and the hunger from which ten million wretched people are suffering? When religion commands us to assist our fellows, it speaks in the name of charity, not in the name of law. The obligation of benevolence, imposed upon me by Christian morality, cannot be imposed upon me as a political tax for the benefit of any person or poor-house. I will give alms when I see fit to do so, when the sufferings of others excite in me that sympathy of which philosophers talk, and in which I do not believe: I will not be forced to bestow them. No one is

424

obliged to do more than comply with this injunction: *In the exercise of your own rights do not encroach upon the rights of another*; an injunction which is the exact definition of liberty. Now, my possessions are my own; no one has a claim upon them: I object to the placing of the third theological virtue in the order of the day.

Everybody, in France, demands the conversion of the five per cent. bonds; they demand thereby the complete sacrifice of one species of property. They have the right to do it, if public necessity requires it; but where is the just indemnity promised by the charter? Not only does none exist, but this indemnity is not even possible; for, if the indemnity were equal to the property sacrificed, the conversion would be useless.

The State occupies the same position to-day toward the bondholders that the city of Calais did, when besieged by Edward III., toward its notables. The English conqueror consented to spare its inhabitants, provided it would surrender to him its most distinguished citizens to do with as he pleased. Eustache and several others offered themselves; it was noble in them, and our ministers should recommend their example to the bondholders. But had the city the right to surrender them? Assuredly not. The right to security is absolute; the country can require no one to sacrifice himself. The soldier standing guard within the enemy's range is no exception to this rule. Wherever a citizen stands guard, the country stands guard with him: to-day it is the turn of the one, to-morrow of the other. When danger and devotion are common, flight is parricide. No one has the right to flee from danger; no one can serve as a scapegoat. The maxim of Caiaphas — *it is right that a man should die for his nation* — is that of the populace and of tyrants; the two extremes of social degradation.

It is said that all perpetual annuities are essentially redeemable. This maxim of civil law, applied to the State, is good for those who wish to return to the natural equality of labor and wealth; but, from the point of view of the proprietor, and in the mouth of conversionists, it is the language of bankrupts. The State is not only a borrower, it is an insurer and guardian of property; granting the best of security, it assures the most inviolable possession. How, then, can it force open the hands of its creditors, who have confidence in it, and then talk to them of public order and security of property? The State, in such an operation, is not a debtor who discharges his debt; it is a stock-company which allures its stockholders into a trap, and there, contrary to its authentic promise, exacts from them twenty, thirty, or forty per cent. of the interest on their capital.

425

That is not all. The State is a university of citizens joined together under a common law by an act of society. This act secures all in the possession of their property; guarantees to one his field, to another his vineyard, to a third his rents, and to the bondholder, who might have bought real estate but who preferred to come to the assistance of the treasury, his bonds. The State cannot demand, without offering an equivalent, the sacrifice of an acre of the field or a corner of the vineyard; still less can it lower rents: why should it have the right to diminish the interest on bonds? This right could not justly exist, unless the bondholder could invest his funds elsewhere to equal advantage; but being confined to the State, where can he find a place to invest them, since the cause of conversion, that is, the power to borrow to better advantage, lies in the State? That is why a government, based on the principle of property, cannot redeem its annuities without the consent of their holders. The money deposited with the republic is property which it has no right to touch while other kinds of property are respected; to force their redemption is to violate the social contract, and outlaw the bondholders.

The whole controversy as to the conversion of bonds finally reduces itself to this: —

Question. Is it just to reduce to misery forty-five thousand families who derive an income from their bonds of one hundred francs or less?

Answer. Is it just to compel seven or eight millions of tax-payers to pay a tax of five francs, when they should pay only three? It is clear, in the first place, that the reply is in reality no reply; but, to make the wrong more apparent, let us change it thus: Is it just to endanger the lives of one hundred thousand men, when we can save them by surrendering one hundred heads to the enemy? Reader, decide!

All this is clearly understood by the defenders of the present system. Yet, nevertheless, sooner or later, the conversion will be effected and property be violated, because no other course is possible; because property, regarded as a right, and not being a right, must of right perish; because the force of events, the laws of conscience, and physical and mathematical necessity must, in the end, destroy this illusion of our minds.

To sum up: liberty is an absolute right, because it is to man what impenetrability is to matter, — a *sine qua non* of existence; equality is an absolute right, because without equality there is no society; security is an absolute right, because in the eyes of every man his own liberty and life are as precious as another's. These three rights are absolute; that is, susceptible of neither increase nor diminution; because in society each associate receives as much as he gives, — liberty for liberty, equality for equality, security for security, body for body, soul for soul, in life and in death.

But property, in its derivative sense, and by the definitions of law, is a right outside of society; for it is clear that, if the wealth of each was social wealth, the conditions would be equal for all, and it would be a contradiction to say: *Property is a man's right to dispose at will of social property.* Then if we are associated for the sake of liberty, equality, and security, we are not associated for the sake of property; then if property is a *natural* right, this natural right is not *social*, but *anti-social*. Property and society are utterly irreconcilable institutions. It is as impossible to associate two proprietors as to join two magnets by their opposite poles. Either society must perish, or it must destroy property.

If property is a natural, absolute, imprescriptible, and inalienable right, why, in all ages, has there been so much speculation as to its origin? — for this is one of its distinguishing characteristics. The origin of a natural right! Good God! who ever inquired into the origin of the rights of liberty, security, or equality? They exist by the same right that we exist; they are born with us, they live and die with us. With property it is very different, indeed. By law, property can exist without a proprietor, like a quality without a subject. It exists for the human being who as yet is not, and for the octogenarian who is no more. And yet, in spite of these wonderful prerogatives which savor of the eternal and the infinite, they have never found the origin of property; the doctors still disagree. On one point only are they in harmony: namely, that the validity of the right of property depends upon the authenticity of its origin. But this harmony is their condemnation. Why have they acknowledged the right before settling the question of origin?

Certain classes do not relish investigation into the pretended titles to property, and its fabulous and perhaps scandalous history. They wish to hold to this proposition: that property is a fact; that it always has been, and always will be. With that proposition the *savant* Proudhon[11] commenced his "Treatise on the Right of Usufruct," regarding the origin of property as a useless question. Perhaps I would subscribe to this doctrine, believing it inspired by a commendable love of peace, were all my fellow-citizens in comfortable circumstances; but, no! I will not subscribe to it.

427

The titles on which they pretend to base the right of property are two in number: *occupation* and *labor*. I shall examine them successively, under all their aspects and in detail; and I remind the reader that, to whatever authority we appeal, I shall prove beyond a doubt that property, to be just and possible, must necessarily have equality for its condition.

§ 2. — *Occupation, as the Title to Property.*

It is remarkable that, at those meetings of the State Council at which the Code was discussed, no controversy arose as to the origin and principle of property. All the articles of Vol. II., Book 2, concerning property and the right of accession, were passed without opposition or amendment. Bonaparte, who on other questions had given his legists so much trouble, had nothing to say about property. Be not surprised at it: in the eyes of that man, the most selfish and wilful person that ever lived, property was the first of rights, just as submission to authority was the most holy of duties.

The right of *occupation*, or of the *first occupant*, is that which results from the actual, physical, real possession of a thing. I occupy a piece of land; the presumption is, that I am the proprietor, until the contrary is proved. We know that originally such a right cannot be legitimate unless it is reciprocal; the jurists say as much.

Cicero compares the earth to a vast theatre: *Quemadmodum theatrum cum commune sit, recte tamen dici potest ejus esse eum locum quem quisque occuparit.*

This passage is all that ancient philosophy has to say about the origin of property.

The theatre, says Cicero, is common to all; nevertheless, the place that each one occupies is called *his own*; that is, it is a place *possessed*, not a place *appropriated*. This comparison annihilates property; moreover, it implies equality. Can I, in a theatre, occupy at the same time one place in the pit, another in the boxes, and a third in the gallery? Not unless I have three bodies, like Geryon, or can exist in different places at the same time, as is related of the magician Apollonius.

According to Cicero, no one has a right to more than he needs: such is the true interpretation of his famous axiom — *suum quidque cujusque sit*, to each one that which belongs to him — an axiom that has been

428

strangely applied. That which belongs to each is not that which each *may* possess, but that which each *has a right* to possess. Now, what have we a right to possess? That which is required for our labor and consumption; Cicero's comparison of the earth to a theatre proves it. According to that, each one may take what place he will, may beautify and adorn it, if he can; it is allowable: but he must never allow himself to overstep the limit which separates him from another. The doctrine of Cicero leads directly to equality; for, occupation being pure toleration, if the toleration is mutual (and it cannot be otherwise) the possessions are equal.

Grotius rushes into history; but what kind of reasoning is that which seeks the origin of a right, said to be natural, elsewhere than in Nature? This is the method of the ancients: the fact exists, then it is necessary, then it is just, then its antecedents are just also. Nevertheless, let us look into it.

"Originally, all things were common and undivided; they were the property of all." Let us go no farther. Grotius tells us how this original communism came to an end through ambition and cupidity; how the age of gold was followed by the age of iron, &c. So that property rested first on war and conquest, then on treaties and agreements. But either these treaties and agreements distributed wealth equally, as did the original communism (the only method of distribution with which the barbarians were acquainted, and the only form of justice of which they could conceive; and then the question of origin assumes this form: how did equality afterwards disappear?) — or else these treaties and agreements were forced by the strong upon the weak, and in that case they are null; the tacit consent of posterity does not make them valid, and we live in a permanent condition of iniquity and fraud.

We never can conceive how the equality of conditions, having once existed, could afterwards have passed away. What was the cause of such degeneration? The instincts of the animals are unchangeable, as well as the differences of species; to suppose original equality in human society is to admit by implication that the present inequality is a degeneration from the nature of this society, — a thing which the defenders of property cannot explain. But I infer therefrom that, if Providence placed the first human beings in a condition of equality, it was an indication of its desires, a model that it wished them to realize in other forms; just as the religious sentiment, which it planted in their hearts, has developed and manifested itself in various ways. Man has but one nature, constant and unalterable: he pursues it through instinct, he wanders from it through reflection, he returns to it through judgment; who shall say that we are not returning now? According to Grotius, man has abandoned equality; according to me, he will yet return to it. How came he to abandon it? Why will he return to it? These are questions for future consideration.

Reid writes as follows: —

"The right of property is not innate, but acquired. It is not grounded upon the constitution of man, but upon his actions. Writers on jurisprudence have explained its origin in a manner that may satisfy every man of common understanding.

"The earth is given to men in common for the purposes of life, by the bounty of Heaven. But to divide it, and appropriate one part of its produce to one, another part to another, must be the work of men who have power and understanding given them, by which every man may accommodate himself, *without hurt to any other.*

"This common right of every man to what the earth produces, before it be occupied and appropriated by others, was, by ancient moralists, very properly compared to the right which every citizen had to the public theatre, where every man that came might occupy an empty seat, and thereby acquire a right to it while the entertainment lasted; but no man had a right to dispossess another.

"The earth is a great theatre, furnished by the Almighty, with perfect wisdom and goodness, for the entertainment and employment of all mankind. Here every man has a right to accommodate himself as a spectator, and to perform his part as an actor; but without hurt to others."

Consequences of Reid's doctrine.

1. That the portion which each one appropriates may wrong no one, it must be equal to the quotient of the total amount of property to be shared, divided by the number of those who are to share it;

2. The number of places being of necessity equal at all times to that of the spectators, no spectator can occupy two places, nor can any actor play several parts;

3. Whenever a spectator comes in or goes out, the places of all contract or enlarge correspondingly: for, says Reid, "*the right of property is not*

430

innate, but acquired;" consequently, it is not absolute; consequently, the occupancy on which it is based, being a conditional fact, cannot endow this right with a stability which it does not possess itself. This seems to have been the thought of the Edinburgh professor when he added: —

"A right to life implies a right to the necessary means of life; and that justice, which forbids the taking away the life of an innocent man, forbids no less the taking from him the necessary means of life. He has the same right to defend the one as the other. To hinder another man's innocent labor, or to deprive him of the fruit of it, is an injustice of the same kind, and has the same effect as to put him in fetters or in prison, and is equally a just object of resentment."

Thus the chief of the Scotch school, without considering at all the inequality of skill or labor, posits *a priori* the equality of the means of labor, abandoning thereafter to each laborer the care of his own person, after the eternal axiom: *Whoso does well, shall fare well.*

The philosopher Reid is lacking, not in knowledge of the principle, but in courage to pursue it to its ultimate. If the right of life is equal, the right of labor is equal, and so is the right of occupancy. Would it not be criminal, were some islanders to repulse, in the name of property, the unfortunate victims of a shipwreck struggling to reach the shore? The very idea of such cruelty sickens the imagination. The proprietor, like Robinson Crusoe on his island, wards off with pike and musket the proletaire washed overboard by the wave of civilization, and seeking to gain a foothold upon the rocks of property. "Give me work!" cries he with all his might to the proprietor: "don't drive me away, I will work for you at any price." "I do not need your services," replies the proprietor, showing the end of his pike or the barrel of his gun. "Lower my rent at least." "I need my income to live upon." "How can I pay you, when I can get no work?" "That is your business." Then the unfortunate proletaire abandons himself to the waves; or, if he attempts to land upon the shore of property, the proprietor takes aim, and kills him.

We have just listened to a spiritualist; we will now question a materialist, then an eclectic: and having completed the circle of philosophy, we will turn next to law.

According to Destutt de Tracy, property is a necessity of our nature. That this necessity involves unpleasant consequences, it would be folly to deny. But these consequences are necessary evils which do not invalidate the principle; so that it as unreasonable to rebel against property on account of the abuses which it generates, as to complain of life because it is sure to end in death. This brutal and pitiless philosophy promises at least frank and close reasoning. Let us see if it keeps its promise.

"We talk very gravely about the conditions of property, ... as if it was our province to decide what constitutes property... It would seem, to hear certain philosophers and legislators, that at a certain moment, spontaneously and without cause, people began to use the words *thine* and *mine;* and that they might have, or ought to have, dispensed with them. But *thine* and *mine* were never invented."

A philosopher yourself, you are too realistic. *Thine* and *mine* do not necessarily refer to self, as they do when I say your philosophy, and my equality; for your philosophy is you philosophizing, and my equality is I professing equality. *Thine* and *mine* oftener indicate a relation, — *your* country, *your* parish, *your* tailor, *your* milkmaid; *my* chamber, *my* seat at the theatre, *my* company and *my* battalion in the National Guard. In the former sense, we may sometimes say *my* labor, *my* skill, *my* virtue; never *my* grandeur nor *my* majesty: in the latter sense only, *my* field, *my* house, *my* vineyard, *my* capital, — precisely as the banker's clerk says *my* cash-box. In short, *thine* and *mine* are signs and expressions of personal, but equal, rights; applied to things outside of us, they indicate possession, function, use, not property.

It does not seem possible, but, nevertheless, I shall prove, by quotations, that the whole theory of our author is based upon this paltry equivocation.

"Prior to all covenants, men are, not exactly, as Hobbes says, in a state of *hostility*, but of *estrangement*. In this state, justice and injustice are unknown; the rights of one bear no relation to the rights of another. All have as many rights as needs, and all feel it their duty to satisfy those needs by any means at their command."

Grant it; whether true or false, it matters not. Destutt de Tracy cannot escape equality. On this theory, men, while in a state of *estrangement*, are under no obligations to each other; they all have the right to satisfy their needs without regard to the needs of others, and consequently the right to exercise their power over Nature, each according to his strength and ability. That involves the greatest inequality of wealth. Inequality of conditions, then, is the characteristic feature of estrangement or

432

barbarism: the exact opposite of Rousseau's idea. But let us look farther: —

"Restrictions of these rights and this duty commence at the time when covenants, either implied or expressed, are agreed upon. Then appears for the first time justice and injustice; that is, the balance between the rights of one and the rights of another, which up to that time were necessarily equal."

Listen: *rights were equal*; that means that each individual had the right to *satisfy his needs without reference to the needs of others*. In other words, that all had the right to injure each other; that there was no right save force and cunning. They injured each other, not only by war and pillage, but also by usurpation and appropriation. Now, in order to abolish this equal right to use force and stratagem, — this equal right to do evil, the sole source of the inequality of benefits and injuries, — they commenced to make *covenants either implied or expressed*, and established a balance. Then these agreements and this balance were intended to secure to all equal comfort; then, by the law of contradictions, if isolation is the principle of inequality, society must produce equality. The social balance is the equalization of the strong and the weak; for, while they are not equals, they are strangers; they can form no associations, they live as enemies. Then, if inequality of conditions is a necessary evil, so is isolation, for society and inequality are incompatible with each other. Then, if society is the true condition of man's existence, so is equality also. This conclusion cannot be avoided.

This being so, how is it that, ever since the establishment of this balance, inequality has been on the increase? How is it that justice and isolation always accompany each other? Destutt de Tracy shall reply: —

"*Needs* and *means, rights* and *duties*, are products of the will. If man willed nothing, these would not exist. But to have needs and means, rights and duties, is to *have*, to *possess*, something. They are so many kinds of property, using the word in its most general sense: they are things which belong to us."

Shameful equivocation, not justified by the necessity for generalization! The word *property* has two meanings: 1. It designates the quality which makes a thing what it is; the attribute which is peculiar to it, and especially distinguishes it. We use it in this sense when we say *the properties of the triangle* or of *numbers; the property of the magnet*, &c. 2. It expresses the right of absolute control over a thing by a free and intelligent being. It is used in this sense by writers on jurisprudence. Thus, in the phrase, *iron acquires the property of a magnet*, the word *property* does not convey the same idea that it does in this one: *I have acquired this magnet as my property*. To tell a poor man that he HAS property because he HAS arms and legs, — that the hunger from which he suffers, and his power to sleep in the open air are his property, — is to play upon words, and to add insult to injury.

"The sole basis of the idea of property is the idea of personality. As soon as property is born at all, it is born, of necessity, in all its fulness. As soon as an individual knows *himself*, — his moral personality, his capacities of enjoyment, suffering, and action, — he necessarily sees also that this *self* is exclusive proprietor of the body in which it dwells, its organs, their powers, faculties, &c... Inasmuch as artificial and conventional property exists, there must be natural property also; for nothing can exist in art without its counterpart in Nature."

We ought to admire the honesty and judgment of philosophers! Man has properties; that is, in the first acceptation of the term, faculties. He has property; that is, in its second acceptation, the right of domain. He has, then, the property of the property of being proprietor. How ashamed I should be to notice such foolishness, were I here considering only the authority of Destutt de Tracy! But the entire human race, since the origination of society and language, when metaphysics and dialectics were first born, has been guilty of this puerile confusion of thought. All which man could call his own was identified in his mind with his person. He considered it as his property, his wealth; a part of himself, a member of his body, a faculty of his mind. The possession of things was likened to property in the powers of the body and mind; and on this false analogy was based the right of property, — *the imitation of Nature by art*, as Destutt de Tracy so elegantly puts it.

But why did not this ideologist perceive that man is not proprietor even of his own faculties? Man has powers, attributes, capacities; they are given him by Nature that he may live, learn, and love: he does not own them, but has only the use of them; and he can make no use of them that does not harmonize with Nature's laws. If he had absolute mastery over his faculties, he could avoid hunger and cold; he could eat unstintedly, and walk through fire; he could move mountains, walk a hundred leagues in a minute, cure without medicines and by the sole force of his will, and could make himself immortal. He could say, "I wish to produce," and his tasks would be finished with the words; he could say. "I wish to know," and he would know; "I love," and he

434

would enjoy. What then? Man is not master of himself, but may be of his surroundings. Let him use the wealth of Nature, since he can live only by its use; but let him abandon his pretensions to the title of proprietor, and remember that he is called so only metaphorically.

To sum up: Destutt de Tracy classes together the external *productions* of Nature and art, and the *powers* or *faculties* of man, making both of them species of property; and upon this equivocation he hopes to establish, so firmly that it can never be disturbed, the right of property. But of these different kinds of property some are *innate*, as memory, imagination, strength, and beauty; while others are *acquired*, as land, water, and forests. In the state of Nature or isolation, the strongest and most skilful (that is, those best provided with innate property) stand the best chance of obtaining acquired property. Now, it is to prevent this encroachment and the war which results therefrom, that a balance (justice) has been employed, and covenants (implied or expressed) agreed upon: it is to correct, as far as possible, inequality of innate property by equality of acquired property. As long as the division remains unequal, so long the partners remain enemies; and it is the purpose of the covenants to reform this state of things. Thus we have, on the one hand, isolation, inequality, enmity, war, robbery, murder; on the other, society, equality, fraternity, peace, and love. Choose between them!

M. Joseph Dutens — a physician, engineer, and geometrician, but a very poor legist, and no philosopher at all — is the author of a "Philosophy of Political Economy," in which he felt it his duty to break lances in behalf of property. His reasoning seems to be borrowed from Destutt de Tracy. He commences with this definition of property, worthy of Sganarelle: "Property is the right by which a thing is one's own." Literally translated: Property is the right of property.

After getting entangled a few times on the subjects of will, liberty, and personality; after having distinguished between *immaterial-natural* property, and *material-natural* property, a distinction similar to Destutt de Tracy's of innate and acquired property, — M. Joseph Dutens concludes with these two general propositions: 1. Property is a natural and inalienable right of every man; 2. Inequality of property is a necessary result of Nature, — which propositions are convertible into a simpler one: All men have an equal right of unequal property.

He rebukes M. de Sismondi for having taught that landed property has no other basis than law and conventionality; and he says himself, speaking of the respect which people feel for property, that "their good

435

sense reveals to them the nature of the *original contract* made between society and proprietors."

He confounds property with possession, communism with equality, the just with the natural, and the natural with the possible. Now he takes these different ideas to be equivalents; now he seems to distinguish between them, so much so that it would be infinitely easier to refute him than to understand him. Attracted first by the title of the work, "Philosophy of Political Economy," I have found, among the author's obscurities, only the most ordinary ideas. For that reason I will not speak of him.

M. Cousin, in his "Moral Philosophy," page 15, teaches that all morality, all laws, all rights are given to man with this injunction: *"Free being, remain free."* Bravo! master; I wish to remain free if I can. He continues: —

"Our principle is true; it is good, it is social. Do not fear to push it to its ultimate.

"1. If the human person is sacred, its whole nature is sacred; and particularly its interior actions, its feelings, its thoughts, its voluntary decisions. This accounts for the respect due to philosophy, religion, the arts industry, commerce, and to all the results of liberty. I say respect, not simply toleration; for we do not tolerate a right, we respect it."

I bow my head before this philosophy.

"2. My liberty, which is sacred, needs for its objective action an instrument which we call the body: the body participates then in the sacredness of liberty; it is then inviolable. This is the basis of the principle of individual liberty.

"3. My liberty needs, for its objective action, material to work upon; in other words, property or a thing. This thing or property naturally participates then in the inviolability of my person. For instance, I take possession of an object which has become necessary and useful in the outward manifestation of my liberty. I say, 'This object is mine since it belongs to no one else; consequently, I possess it legitimately.' So the legitimacy of possession rests on two conditions. First, I possess only as a free being. Suppress free activity, you destroy my power to labor. Now it is only by labor that I can use this property or thing, and it is only by using it that I possess it. Free activity is then the principle of

436

the right of property. But that alone does not legitimate possession. All men are free; all can use property by labor. Does that mean that all men have a right to all property? Not at all. To possess legitimately, I must not only labor and produce in my capacity of a free being, but I must also be the first to occupy the property. In short, if labor and production are the principle of the right of property, the fact of first occupancy is its indispensable condition.

"4. I possess legitimately: then I have the right to use my property as I see fit. I have also the right to give it away. I have also the right to bequeath it; for if I decide to make a donation, my decision is as valid after my death as during my life."

In fact, to become a proprietor, in M. Cousin's opinion, one must take possession by occupation and labor. I maintain that the element of time must be considered also; for if the first occupants have occupied every thing, what are the newcomers to do? What will become of them, having an instrument with which to work, but no material to work upon? Must they devour each other? A terrible extremity, unforeseen by philosophical prudence; for the reason that great geniuses neglect little things.

Notice also that M. Cousin says that neither occupation nor labor, taken separately, can legitimate the right of property; and that it is born only from the union of the two. This is one of M. Cousin's eclectic turns, which he, more than any one else, should take pains to avoid. Instead of proceeding by the method of analysis, comparison, elimination, and reduction (the only means of discovering the truth amid the various forms of thought and whimsical opinions), he jumbles all systems together, and then, declaring each both right and wrong, exclaims: "There you have the truth."

But, adhering to my promise, I will not refute him. I will only prove, by all the arguments with which he justifies the right of property, the principle of equality which kills it. As I have already said, my sole intent is this: to show at the bottom of all these positions that inevitable major, *equality*; hoping hereafter to show that the principle of property vitiates the very elements of economical, moral, and governmental science, thus leading it in the wrong direction.

Well, is it not true, from M. Cousin's point of view, that, if the liberty of man is sacred, it is equally sacred in all individuals; that, if it needs property for its objective action, that is, for its life, the appropriation of material is equally necessary for all; that, if I wish to be respected in

437

my right of appropriation, I must respect others in theirs; and, consequently, that though, in the sphere of the infinite, a person's power of appropriation is limited only by himself, in the sphere of the finite this same power is limited by the mathematical relation between the number of persons and the space which they occupy? Does it not follow that if one individual cannot prevent another — his fellow-man — from appropriating an amount of material equal to his own, no more can he prevent individuals yet to come; because, while individuality passes away, universality persists, and eternal laws cannot be determined by a partial view of their manifestations? Must we not conclude, therefore, that whenever a person is born, the others must crowd closer together; and, by reciprocity of obligation, that if the new comer is afterwards to become an heir, the right of succession does not give him the right of accumulation, but only the right of choice?

I have followed M. Cousin so far as to imitate his style, and I am ashamed of it. Do we need such high-sounding terms, such sonorous phrases, to say such simple things? Man needs to labor in order to live; consequently, he needs tools to work with and materials to work upon. His need to produce constitutes his right to produce. Now, this right is guaranteed him by his fellows, with whom he makes an agreement to that effect. One hundred thousand men settle in a large country like France with no inhabitants: each man has a right to 1/100,000 of the land. If the number of possessors increases, each one's portion diminishes in consequence; so that, if the number of inhabitants rises to thirty-four millions, each one will have a right only to 1/34,000,000. Now, so regulate the police system and the government, labor, exchange, inheritance, &c., that the means of labor shall be shared by all equally, and that each individual shall be free; and then society will be perfect.

Of all the defenders of property, M. Cousin has gone the farthest. He has maintained against the economists that labor does not establish the right of property unless preceded by occupation, and against the jurists that the civil law can determine and apply a natural right, but cannot create it. In fact, it is not sufficient to say, "The right of property is demonstrated by the existence of property; the function of the civil law is purely declaratory." To say that, is to confess that there is no reply to those who question the legitimacy of the fact itself. Every right must be justifiable in itself, or by some antecedent right; property is no exception. For this reason, M. Cousin has sought to base it upon the *sanctity* of the human personality, and the act by which the will assimilates a thing. "Once touched by man," says one of M. Cousin's disciples, "things receive from him a character which transforms and

438

humanizes them." I confess, for my part, that I have no faith in this magic, and that I know of nothing less holy than the will of man. But this theory, fragile as it seems to psychology as well as jurisprudence, is nevertheless more philosophical and profound than those theories which are based upon labor or the authority of the law. Now, we have just seen to what this theory of which we are speaking leads, — to the equality implied in the terms of its statement.

But perhaps philosophy views things from too lofty a standpoint, and is not sufficiently practical; perhaps from the exalted summit of speculation men seem so small to the metaphysician that he cannot distinguish between them; perhaps, indeed, the equality of conditions is one of those principles which are very true and sublime as generalities, but which it would be ridiculous and even dangerous to attempt to rigorously apply to the customs of life and to social transactions. Undoubtedly, this is a case which calls for imitation of the wise reserve of moralists and jurists, who warn us against carrying things to extremes, and who advise us to suspect every definition; because there is not one, they say, which cannot be utterly destroyed by developing its disastrous results — *Omnis definitio in jure civili periculosa est: parum est enim ut non subverti possit.* Equality of conditions, — a terrible dogma in the ears of the proprietor, a consoling truth at the poor-man's sick-bed, a frightful reality under the knife of the anatomist, — equality of conditions, established in the political, civil, and industrial spheres, is only an alluring impossibility, an inviting bait, a satanic delusion.

It is never my intention to surprise my reader. I detest, as I do death, the man who employs subterfuge in his words and conduct. From the first page of this book, I have expressed myself so plainly and decidedly that all can see the tendency of my thought and hopes; and they will do me the justice to say, that it would be difficult to exhibit more frankness and more boldness at the same time. I do not hesitate to declare that the time is not far distant when this reserve, now so much admired in philosophers — this happy medium so strongly recommended by professors of moral and political science — will be regarded as the disgraceful feature of a science without principle, and as the seal of its reprobation. In legislation and morals, as well as in geometry, axioms are absolute, definitions are certain; and all the results of a principle are to be accepted, provided they are logically deduced. Deplorable pride! We know nothing of our nature, and we charge our blunders to it; and, in a fit of unaffected ignorance, cry out, "The truth is in doubt, the best definition defines nothing!" We shall know some time whether this distressing uncertainty of jurisprudence arises from the nature of its investigations, or from our prejudices; whether, to explain social phenomena, it is not enough to change our hypothesis, as did Copernicus when he reversed the system of Ptolemy.

But what will be said when I show, as I soon shall, that this same jurisprudence continually tries to base property upon equality? What reply can be made?

§ 3. — *Civil Law as the Foundation and Sanction of Property.*

Pothier seems to think that property, like royalty, exists by divine right. He traces back its origin to God himself — *ab Jove principium.* He begins in this way: —

"God is the absolute ruler of the universe and all that it contains: *Domini est terra et plenitudo ejus, orbis et universi qui habitant in eo.* For the human race he has created the earth and all its creatures, and has given it a control over them subordinate only to his own. 'Thou madest him to have dominion over the works of thy hands; thou hast put all things under his feet,' says the Psalmist. God accompanied this gift with these words, addressed to our first parents after the creation: 'Be fruitful, and multiply and replenish the earth,' " &c.

After this magnificent introduction, who would refuse to believe the human race to be an immense family living in brotherly union, and under the protection of a venerable father? But, heavens! are brothers enemies? Are fathers unnatural, and children prodigal?

God gave the earth to the human race: why then have I received none? *He has put all things under my feet,* — and I have not where to lay my head! *Multiply,* he tells us through his interpreter, Pothier. Ah, learned Pothier! that is as easy to do as to say; but you must give moss to the bird for its nest.

"The human race having multiplied, men divided among themselves the earth and most of the things upon it; that which fell to each, from that time exclusively belonged to him. That was the origin of the right of property."

Say, rather, the right of possession. Men lived in a state of communism; whether positive or negative it matters little. Then there was no property, not even private possession. The genesis and growth of possession gradually forcing people to labor for their support, they

440

agreed either formally or tacitly, — it makes no difference which, — that the laborer should be sole proprietor of the fruit of his labor; that is, they simply declared the fact that thereafter none could live without working. It necessarily followed that, to obtain equality of products, there must be equality of labor; and that, to obtain equality of labor, there must be equality of facilities for labor. Whoever without labor got possession, by force or by strategy, of another's means of subsistence, destroyed equality, and placed himself above or outside of the law. Whoever monopolized the means of production on the ground of greater industry, also destroyed equality. Equality being then the expression of right, whoever violated it was *unjust*.

Thus, labor gives birth to private possession; the right in a thing — *jus in re*. But in what thing? Evidently *in the product*, not *in the soil*. So the Arabs have always understood it; and so, according to Cæsar and Tacitus, the Germans formerly held. "The Arabs," says M. de Sismondi, "who admit a man's property in the flocks which he has raised, do not refuse the crop to him who planted the seed; but they do not see why another, his equal, should not have a right to plant in his turn. The inequality which results from the pretended right of the first occupant seems to them to be based on no principle of justice; and when all the land falls into the hands of a certain number of inhabitants, there results a monopoly in their favor against the rest of the nation, to which they do not wish to submit."

Well, they have shared the land. I admit that therefrom results a more powerful organization of labor; and that this method of distribution, fixed and durable, is advantageous to production: but how could this division give to each a transferable right of property in a thing to which all had an inalienable right of possession? In the terms of jurisprudence, this metamorphosis from possessor to proprietor is legally impossible; it implies in the jurisdiction of the courts the union of *possessoire* and *petitoire;* and the mutual concessions of those who share the land are nothing less than traffic in natural rights. The original cultivators of the land, who were also the original makers of the law, were not as learned as our legislators, I admit; and had they been, they could not have done worse: they did not foresee the consequences of the transformation of the right of private possession into the right of absolute property. But why have not those, who in later times have established the distinction between *jus in re* and *jus ad rem*, applied it to the principle of property itself?

Let me call the attention of the writers on jurisprudence to their own maxims.

The right of property, provided it can have a cause, can have but one —
Dominium non potest nisi ex una causa contingere. I can possess by
several titles; I can become proprietor by only one — *Non ut ex
pluribus causis idem nobis deberi potest, ita ex pluribus causis idem
potest nostrum esse.* The field which I have cleared, which I cultivate,
on which I have built my house, which supports myself, my family, and
my livestock, I can possess: 1st. As the original occupant; 2d. As a
laborer; 3d. By virtue of the social contract which assigns it to me as
my share. But none of these titles confer upon me the right of property.
For, if I attempt to base it upon occupancy, society can reply, "I am the
original occupant." If I appeal to my labor, it will say, "It is only on
that condition that you possess." If I speak of agreements, it will
respond, "These agreements establish only your right of use." Such,
however, are the only titles which proprietors advance. They never
have been able to discover any others. Indeed, every right — it is
Pothier who says it — supposes a producing cause in the person who
enjoys it; but in man who lives and dies, in this son of earth who passes
away like a shadow, there exists, with respect to external things, only
titles of possession, not one title of property. Why, then, has society
recognized a right injurious to itself, where there is no producing
cause? Why, in according possession, has it also conceded property?
Why has the law sanctioned this abuse of power?

The German Ancillon replies thus: —

"Some philosophers pretend that man, in employing his forces upon a
natural object, — say a field or a tree, — acquires a right only to the
improvements which he makes, to the form which he gives to the
object, not to the object itself. Useless distinction! If the form could be
separated from the object, perhaps there would be room for question;
but as this is almost always impossible, the application of man's
strength to the different parts of the visible world is the foundation of
the right of property, the primary origin of riches."

Vain pretext! If the form cannot be separated from the object, nor
property from possession, possession must be shared; in any case,
society reserves the right to fix the conditions of property. Let us
suppose that an appropriated farm yields a gross income of ten
thousand francs; and, as very seldom happens, that this farm cannot be
divided. Let us suppose farther that, by economical calculation, the
annual expenses of a family are three thousand francs: the possessor of
this farm should be obliged to guard his reputation as a good father of a
family, by paying to society ten thousand francs, — less the total costs

of cultivation, and the three thousand francs required for the maintenance of his family. This payment is not rent, it is an indemnity.

What sort of justice is it, then, which makes such laws as this: —

"Whereas, since labor so changes the form of a thing that the form and substance cannot be separated without destroying the thing itself, either society must be disinherited, or the laborer must lose the fruit of his labor; and

"Whereas, in every other case, property in raw material would give a title to added improvements, minus their cost; and whereas, in this instance, property in improvements ought to give a title to the principal;

"Therefore, the right of appropriation by labor shall never be admitted against individuals, but only against society."

In such a way do legislators always reason in regard to property. The law is intended to protect men's mutual rights, — that is, the rights of each against each, and each against all; and, as if a proportion could exist with less than four terms, the law-makers always disregard the latter. As long as man is opposed to man, property offsets property, and the two forces balance each other; as soon as man is isolated, that is, opposed to the society which he himself represents, jurisprudence is at fault: Themis has lost one scale of her balance.

Listen to the professor of Rennes, the learned Toullier: —

"How could this claim, made valid by occupation, become stable and permanent property, which might continue to stand, and which might be reclaimed after the first occupant had relinquished possession?

"Agriculture was a natural consequence of the multiplication of the human race, and agriculture, in its turn, favors population, and necessitates the establishment of permanent property; for who would take the trouble to plough and sow, if he were not certain that he would reap?"

To satisfy the husbandman, it was sufficient to guarantee him possession of his crop; admit even that he should have been protected in his right of occupation of land, as long as he remained its cultivator. That was all that he had a right to expect; that was all that the advance of civilization demanded. But property, property! the right of escheat

443

over lands which one neither occupies nor cultivates, — who had authority to grant it? who pretended to have it?

"Agriculture alone was not sufficient to establish permanent property; positive laws were needed, and magistrates to execute them; in a word, the civil State was needed.

"The multiplication of the human race had rendered agriculture necessary; the need of securing to the cultivator the fruit of his labor made permanent property necessary, and also laws for its protection. So we are indebted to property for the creation of the civil State."

Yes, of our civil State, as you have made it; a State which, at first, was despotism, then monarchy, then aristocracy, today democracy, and always tyranny.

"Without the ties of property it never would have been possible to subordinate men to the wholesome yoke of the law; and without permanent property the earth would have remained a vast forest. Let us admit, then, with the most careful writers, that if transient property, or the right of preference resulting from occupation, existed prior to the establishment of civil society, permanent property, as we know it to-day, is the work of civil law. It is the civil law which holds that, when once acquired, property can be lost only by the action of the proprietor, and that it exists even after the proprietor has relinquished possession of the thing, and it has fallen into the hands of a third party.

"Thus property and possession, which originally were confounded, became through the civil law two distinct and independent things; two things which, in the language of the law, have nothing whatever in common. In this we see what a wonderful change has been effected in property, and to what an extent Nature has been altered by the civil laws."

Thus the law, in establishing property, has not been the expression of a psychological fact, the development of a natural law, the application of a moral principle. It has literally *created* a right outside of its own province. It has realized an abstraction, a metaphor, a fiction; and that without deigning to look at the consequences, without considering the disadvantages, without inquiring whether it was right or wrong.

It has sanctioned selfishness; it has indorsed monstrous pretensions; it has received with favor impious vows, as if it were able to fill up a bottomless pit, and to satiate hell! Blind law; the law of the ignorant man; a law which is not a law; the voice of discord, deceit, and blood! This it is which, continually revived, reinstated, rejuvenated, restored, re-enforced — as the palladium of society — has troubled the consciences of the people, has obscured the minds of the masters, and has induced all the catastrophes which have befallen nations. This it is which Christianity has condemned, but which its ignorant ministers deify; who have as little desire to study Nature and man, as ability to read their Scriptures.

But, indeed, what guide did the law follow in creating the domain of property? What principle directed it? What was its standard?

Would you believe it? It was equality.

Agriculture was the foundation of territorial possession, and the original cause of property. It was of no use to secure to the farmer the fruit of his labor, unless the means of production were at the same time secured to him. To fortify the weak against the invasion of the strong, to suppress spoliation and fraud, the necessity was felt of establishing between possessors permanent lines of division, insuperable obstacles. Every year saw the people multiply, and the cupidity of the husbandman increase: it was thought best to put a bridle on ambition by setting boundaries which ambition would in vain attempt to overstep. Thus the soil came to be appropriated through need of the equality which is essential to public security and peaceable possession. Undoubtedly the division was never geographically equal; a multitude of rights, some founded in Nature, but wrongly interpreted and still more wrongly applied, inheritance, gift, and exchange; others, like the privileges of birth and position, the illegitimate creations of ignorance and brute force, — all operated to prevent absolute equality. But, nevertheless, the principle remained the same: equality had sanctioned possession; equality sanctioned property.

The husbandman needed each year a field to sow; what more convenient and simple arrangement for the barbarians, — instead of indulging in annual quarrels and fights, instead of continually moving their houses, furniture, and families from spot to spot, — than to assign to each individual a fixed and inalienable estate?

It was not right that the soldier, on returning from an expedition, should find himself dispossessed on account of the services which he had just rendered to his country; his estate ought to be restored to him. It became, therefore, customary to retain property by intent alone — *nudo*

445

animo; it could be sacrificed only with the consent and by the action of the proprietor.

It was necessary that the equality in the division should be kept up from one generation to another, without a new distribution of the land upon the death of each family; it appeared therefore natural and just that children and parents, according to the degree of relationship which they bore to the deceased, should be the heirs of their ancestors. Thence came, in the first place, the feudal and patriarchal custom of recognizing only one heir; then, by a quite contrary application of the principle of equality, the admission of all the children to a share in their father's estate, and, very recently also among us, the definitive abolition of the right of primogeniture.

But what is there in common between these rude outlines of instinctive organization and the true social science? How could these men, who never had the faintest idea of statistics, valuation, or political economy, furnish us with principles of legislation?

"The law," says a modern writer on jurisprudence, "is the expression of a social want, the declaration of a fact: the legislator does not make it, he declares it. 'This definition is not exact. The law is a method by which social wants must be satisfied; the people do not vote it, the legislator does not express it: the *savant* discovers and formulates it. But in fact, the law, according to M. Ch. Comte, who has devoted half a volume to its definition, was in the beginning only the *expression of a want*, and the indication of the means of supplying it; and up to this time it has been nothing else. The legists — with mechanical fidelity, full of obstinacy, enemies of philosophy, buried in literalities — have always mistaken for the last word of science that which was only the inconsiderate aspiration of men who, to be sure, were well-meaning, but wanting in foresight.

They did not foresee, these old founders of the domain of property, that the perpetual and absolute right to retain one's estate, — a right which seemed to them equitable, because it was common, — involves the right to transfer, sell, give, gain, and lose it; that it tends, consequently, to nothing less than the destruction of that equality which they established it to maintain. And though they should have foreseen it, they disregarded it; the present want occupied their whole attention, and, as ordinarily happens in such cases, the disadvantages were at first scarcely perceptible, and they passed unnoticed.

446

They did not foresee, these ingenuous legislators, that if property is retainable by intent alone — *nudo animo* — it carries with it the right to let, to lease, to loan at interest, to profit by exchange, to settle annuities, and to levy a tax on a field which intent reserves, while the body is busy elsewhere.

They did not foresee, these fathers of our jurisprudence, that, if the right of inheritance is any thing other than Nature's method of preserving equality of wealth, families will soon become victims of the most disastrous exclusions; and society, pierced to the heart by one of its most sacred principles, will come to its death through opulence and misery.[12]

They did not foresee... But why need I go farther?

Under whatever form of government we live, it can always be said that *le mort saisit le vif;* that is, that inheritance and succession will last for ever, whoever may be the recognized heir. But the St. Simonians wish the heir to be designated by the magistrate; others wish him to be chosen by the deceased, or assumed by the law to be so chosen: the essential point is that Nature's wish be satisfied, so far as the law of equality allows. To-day the real controller of inheritance is chance or caprice; now, in matters of legislation, chance and caprice cannot be accepted as guides. It is for the purpose of avoiding the manifold disturbances which follow in the wake of chance that Nature, after having created us equal, suggests to us the principle of heredity; which serves as a voice by which society asks us to choose, from among all our brothers, him whom we judge best fitted to complete our unfinished work.

The consequences are plain enough, and this is not the time to criticise the whole Code.

The history of property among the ancient nations is, then, simply a matter of research and curiosity. It is a rule of jurisprudence that the fact does not substantiate the right. Now, property is no exception to this rule: then the universal recognition of the right of property does not legitimate the right of property. Man is mistaken as to the constitution of society, the nature of right, and the application of justice; just as he was mistaken regarding the cause of meteors and the movement of the heavenly bodies. His old opinions cannot be taken for articles of faith. Of what consequence is it to us that the Indian race was divided into four classes; that, on the banks of the Nile and the Ganges, blood and position formerly determined the distribution of the land; that the

Greeks and Romans placed property under the protection of the gods; that they accompanied with religious ceremonies the work of partitioning the land and appraising their goods? The variety of the forms of privilege does not sanction injustice. The faith of Jupiter, the proprietor,[13] proves no more against the equality of citizens, than do the mysteries of Venus, the wanton, against conjugal chastity.

The authority of the human race is of no effect as evidence in favor of the right of property, because this right, resting of necessity upon equality, contradicts its principle; the decision of the religions which have sanctioned it is of no effect, because in all ages the priest has submitted to the prince, and the gods have always spoken as the politicians desired; the social advantages, attributed to property, cannot be cited in its behalf, because they all spring from the principle of equality of possession.

What means, then, this dithyramb upon property?

"The right of property is the most important of human institutions." ...

Yes; as monarchy is the most glorious.

"The original cause of man's prosperity upon earth."

Because justice was supposed to be its principle.

"Property became the legitimate end of his ambition, the hope of his existence, the shelter of his family; in a word, the corner-stone of the domestic dwelling, of communities, and of the political State."

Possession alone produced all that.

"Eternal principle, — "

Property is eternal, like every negation, —

"Of all social and civil institutions."

For that reason, every institution and every law based on property will perish.

"It is a boon as precious as liberty."

448

For the rich proprietor.

"In fact, the cause of the cultivation of the habitable earth."

If the cultivator ceased to be a tenant, would the land be worse cared for?

"The guarantee and the morality of labor."

Under the regime of property, labor is not a condition, but a privilege.

"The application of justice."

What is justice without equality of fortunes? A balance with false weights.

"All morality, — "

A famished stomach knows no morality, —

"All public order, — "

Certainly, the preservation of property, —

"Rest on the right of property."[14]

Corner-stone of all which is, stumbling-block of all which ought to be, — such is property.

To sum up and conclude: —

Not only does occupation lead to equality, it *prevents* property. For, since every man, from the fact of his existence, has the right of occupation, and, in order to live, must have material for cultivation on which he may labor; and since, on the other hand, the number of occupants varies continually with the births and deaths, — it follows that the quantity of material which each laborer may claim varies with the number of occupants; consequently, that occupation is always subordinate to population. Finally, that, inasmuch as possession, in right, can never remain fixed, it is impossible, in fact, that it can ever become property.

Every occupant is, then, necessarily a possessor or usufructuary, — a function which excludes proprietorship. Now, this is the right of the usufructuary: he is responsible for the thing entrusted to him; he must use it in conformity with general utility, with a view to its preservation and development; he has no power to transform it, to diminish it, or to change its nature; he cannot so divide the usufruct that another shall perform the labor while he receives the product. In a word, the usufructuary is under the supervision of society, submitted to the condition of labor and the law of equality.

Thus is annihilated the Roman definition of property — *the right of use and abuse* — an immorality born of violence, the most monstrous pretension that the civil laws ever sanctioned. Man receives his usufruct from the hands of society, which alone is the permanent possessor. The individual passes away, society is deathless.

What a profound disgust fills my soul while discussing such simple truths ! Do we doubt these things to-day? Will it be necessary to again take arms for their triumph? And can force, in default of reason, alone introduce them into our laws?

All have an equal right of occupancy.

The amount occupied being measured, not by the will, but by the variable conditions of space and number, property cannot exist.

This no code has ever expressed; this no constitution can admit! These are axioms which the civil law and the law of nations deny! ... .

But I hear the exclamations of the partisans of another system: "Labor, labor! that is the basis of property!"

Reader, do not be deceived. This new basis of property is worse than the first, and I shall soon have to ask your pardon for having demonstrated things clearer, and refuted pretensions more unjust, than any which we have yet considered.

Chapter III. Labor As The Efficient Cause Of The Domain Of Property

Nearly all the modern writers on jurisprudence, taking their cue from the economists, have abandoned the theory of first occupancy as a too dangerous one, and have adopted that which regards property as born of labor. In this they are deluded; they reason in a circle. To labor it is necessary to occupy, says M. Cousin. Consequently, I have added in my turn, all having an equal right of occupancy, to labor it is necessary to submit to equality. "The rich," exclaims Jean Jacques, "have the arrogance to say, 'I built this wall; I earned this land by my labor.' Who set you the tasks? we may reply, and by what right do you demand payment from us for labor which we did not impose upon you?" All sophistry falls to the ground in the presence of this argument.

But the partisans of labor do not see that their system is an absolute contradiction of the Code, all the articles and provisions of which suppose property to be based upon the fact of first occupancy. If labor, through the appropriation which results from it, alone gives birth to property, the Civil Code lies, the charter is a falsehood, our whole social system is a violation of right. To this conclusion shall we come, at the end of the discussion which is to occupy our attention in this chapter and the following one, both as to the right of labor and the fact of property. We shall see, on the one hand, our legislation in opposition to itself; and, on the other hand, our new jurisprudence in opposition both to its own principle and to our legislation.

I have asserted that the system which bases property upon labor implies, no less than that which bases it upon occupation, the equality of fortunes; and the reader must be impatient to learn how I propose to deduce this law of equality from the inequality of skill and faculties: directly his curiosity shall be satisfied. But it is proper that I should call his attention for a moment to this remarkable feature of the process; to wit, the substitution of labor for occupation as the principle of property; and that I should pass rapidly in review some of the prejudices to which proprietors are accustomed to appeal, which legislation has sanctioned, and which the system of labor completely overthrows.

Reader, were you ever present at the examination of a criminal? Have you watched his tricks, his turns, his evasions, his distinctions, his equivocations? Beaten, all his assertions overthrown, pursued like a fallow deer by the in exorable judge, tracked from hypothesis to hypothesis, — he makes a statement, he corrects it, retracts it, contradicts it, he exhausts all the tricks of dialectics, more subtle, more ingenious a thousand times than he who invented the seventy-two forms of the syllogism. So acts the proprietor when called upon to defend his right. At first he refuses to reply, he exclaims, he threatens, he defies; then, forced to accept the discussion, he arms himself with chicanery, he surrounds himself with formidable artillery, — crossing his fire, opposing one by one and all together occupation, possession,

451

limitation, covenants, immemorial custom, and universal consent. Conquered on this ground, the proprietor, like a wounded boar, turns on his pursuers. "I have done more than occupy," he cries with terrible emotion; "I have labored, produced, improved, transformed, *created*. This house, these fields, these trees are the work of my hands; I changed these brambles into a vineyard, and this bush into a fig-tree; and to-day I reap the harvest of my labors. I have enriched the soil with my sweat; I have paid those men who, had they not had the work which I gave them, would have died of hunger. No one shared with me the trouble and expense; no one shall share with me the benefits."

You have labored, proprietor! why then do you speak of original occupancy? What, were you not sure of your right, or did you hope to deceive men, and make justice an illusion? Make haste, then, to acquaint us with your mode of defence, for the judgment will be final; and you know it to be a question of restitution.

You have labored! but what is there in common between the labor which duty compels you to perform, and the appropriation of things in which there is a common interest? Do you not know that domain over the soil, like that over air and light, cannot be lost by prescription?

You have labored! have you never made others labor? Why, then, have they lost in laboring for you what you have gained in not laboring for them?

You have labored! very well; but let us see the results of your labor. We will count, weigh, and measure them. It will be the judgment of Balthasar; for I swear by balance, level, and square, that if you have appropriated another's labor in any way whatsoever, you shall restore it every stroke.

Thus, the principle of occupation is abandoned; no longer is it said, "The land belongs to him who first gets possession of it. Property, forced into its first intrenchment, repudiates its old adage; justice, ashamed, retracts her maxims, and sorrow lowers her bandage over her blushing cheeks. And it was but yesterday that this progress in social philosophy began: fifty centuries required for the extirpation of a lie! During this lamentable period, how many usurpations have been sanctioned, how many invasions glorified, how many conquests celebrated! The absent dispossessed, the poor banished, the hungry excluded by wealth, which is so ready and bold in action! Jealousies and wars, incendiarism and bloodshed, among the nations! But henceforth, thanks to the age and its spirit, it is to be admitted that the

452

earth is not a prize to be won in a race; in the absence of any other obstacle, there is a place for everybody under the sun. Each one may harness his goat to the bearn, drive his cattle to pasture, sow a corner of a field, and bake his bread by his own fireside.

But, no; each one cannot do these things. I hear it proclaimed on all sides, "Glory to labor and industry! to each according to his capacity; to each capacity according to its results!" And I see three-fourths of the human race again despoiled, the labor of a few being a scourge to the labor of the rest.

"The problem is solved," exclaims M. Hennequin. "Property, the daughter of labor, can be enjoyed at present and in the future only under the protection of the laws. It has its origin in natural law; it derives its power from civil law; and from the union of these two ideas, *labor* and *protection*, positive legislation results." ...

Ah! *the problem is solved! property is the daughter of labor!* What, then, is the right of accession, and the right of succession, and the right of donation, &c., if not the right to become a proprietor by simple occupancy? What are your laws concerning the age of majority, emancipation, guardianship, and interdiction, if not the various conditions by which he who is already a laborer gains or loses the right of occupancy; that is, property?

Being unable, at this time, to enter upon a detailed discussion of the Code, I shall content myself with examining the three arguments oftenest resorted to in support of property. 1. *Appropriation*, or the formation of property by possession; 2. *The consent of mankind*; 3. *Prescription*. I shall then inquire into the effects of labor upon the relative condition of the laborers and upon property.

§ 1. — *The Land cannot be Appropriated.*

"It would seem that lands capable of cultivation ought to be regarded as natural wealth, since they are not of human creation, but Nature's gratuitous gift to man; but inasmuch as this wealth is not fugitive, like the air and water, — inasmuch as a field is a fixed and limited space which certain men have been able to appropriate, to the exclusion of all others who in their turn have consented to this appropriation, — the land, which was a natural and gratuitous gift, has become social wealth, for the use of which we ought to pay." — *Say: Political Economy.*

Was I wrong in saying, at the beginning of this chapter, that the economists are the very worst authorities in matters of legislation and philosophy? It is the *father* of this class of men who clearly states the question, How can the supplies of Nature, the wealth created by Providence, become private property? and who replies by so gross an equivocation that we scarcely know which the author lacks, sense or honesty. What, I ask, has the fixed and solid nature of the earth to do with the right of appropriation? I can understand that a thing *limited* and *stationary*, like the land, offers greater chances for appropriation than the water or the sunshine; that it is easier to exercise the right of domain over the soil than over the atmosphere: but we are not dealing with the difficulty of the thing, and Say confounds the right with the possibility. We do not ask why the earth has been appropriated to a greater extent than the sea and the air; we want to know by what right man has appropriated wealth *which he did not create, and which Nature gave to him gratuitously.*

Say, then, did not solve the question which he asked. But if he had solved it, if the explanation which he has given us were as satisfactory as it is illogical, we should know no better than before who has a right to exact payment for the use of the soil, of this wealth which is not man's handiwork. Who is entitled to the rent of the land? The producer of the land, without doubt. Who made the land? God. Then, proprietor, retire!

But the creator of the land does not sell it: he gives it; and, in giving it, he is no respecter of persons. Why, then, are some of his children regarded as legitimate, while others are treated as bastards? If the equality of shares was an original right, why is the inequality of conditions a posthumous right?

Say gives us to understand that if the air and the water were not of a *fugitive* nature, they would have been appropriated. Let me observe in passing that this is more than an hypothesis; it is a reality. Men have appropriated the air and the water, I will not say as often as they could, but as often as they have been allowed to.

The Portuguese, having discovered the route to India by the Cape of Good Hope, pretended to have the sole right to that route; and Grotius, consulted in regard to this matter by the Dutch who refused to recognize this right, wrote expressly for this occasion his treatise on the "Freedom of the Seas," to prove that the sea is not liable to appropriation.

The right to hunt and fish used always to be confined to lords and proprietors; to-day it is leased by the government and communes to whoever can pay the license-fee and the rent. To regulate hunting and fishing is an excellent idea, but to make it a subject of sale is to create a monopoly of air and water.

What is a passport? A universal recommendation of the traveller's person; a certificate of security for himself and his property. The treasury, whose nature it is to spoil the best things, has made the passport a means of espionage and a tax. Is not this a sale of the right to travel?

Finally, it is permissible neither to draw water from a spring situated in another's grounds without the permission of the proprietor, because by the right of accession the spring belongs to the possessor of the soil, if there is no other claim; nor to pass a day on his premises without paying a tax; nor to look at a court, a garden, or an orchard, without the consent of the proprietor; nor to stroll in a park or an enclosure against the owner's will: every one is allowed to shut himself up and to fence himself in. All these prohibitions are so many positive interdictions, not only of the land, but of the air and water. We who belong to the proletaire class: property excommunicates us! *Terra, et aqua, et aere, et igne interdicti sumus.*

Men could not appropriate the most fixed of all the elements without appropriating the three others; since, by French and Roman law, property in the surface carries with it property from zenith to nadir — *Cujus est solum, ejus est usque ad cælum.* Now, if the use of water, air, and fire excludes property, so does the use of the soil. This chain of reasoning seems to have been presented by M. Ch. Comte, in his "Treatise on Property," chap. 5.

"If a man should be deprived of air for a few moments only, he would cease to exist, and a partial deprivation would cause him severe suffering; a partial or complete deprivation of food would produce like effects upon him though less suddenly; it would be the same, at least in certain climates! were he deprived of all clothing and shelter... To sustain life, then, man needs continually to appropriate many different things. But these things do not exist in like proportions. Some, such as the light of the stars, the atmosphere of the earth, the water composing the seas and oceans, exist in such large quantities that men cannot perceive any sensible increase or diminution; each one can appropriate as much as his needs require without detracting from the enjoyment of others, without causing them the least harm. Things of this sort are, so

455

to speak, the common property of the human race; the only duty imposed upon each individual in this regard is that of infringing not at all upon the rights of others."

Let us complete the argument of M. Ch. Comte. A man who should be prohibited from walking in the highways, from resting in the fields, from taking shelter in caves, from lighting fires, from picking berries, from gathering herbs and boiling them in a bit of baked clay, — such a man could not live. Consequently the earth — like water, air, and light — is a primary object of necessity which each has a right to use freely, without infringing another's right. Why, then, is the earth appropriated? M. Ch. Comte's reply is a curious one. Say pretends that it is because it is not *fugitive;* M. Ch. Comte assures us that it is because it is not *infinite.* The land is limited in amount. Then, according to M. Ch. Comte, it ought to be appropriated. It would seem, on the contrary, that he ought to say, Then it ought not to be appropriated. Because, no matter how large a quantity of air or light any one appropriates, no one is damaged thereby; there always remains enough for all. With the soil, it is very different. Lay hold who will, or who can, of the sun's rays, the passing breeze, or the sea's billows; he has my consent, and my pardon for his bad intentions. But let any living man dare to change his right of territorial possession into the right of property, and I will declare war upon him, and wage it to the death!

M. Ch. Comte's argument disproves his position. "Among the things necessary to the preservation of life," he says, "there are some which exist in such large quantities that they are inexhaustible; others which exist in lesser quantities, and can satisfy the wants of only a certain number of persons. The former are called *common*, the latter *private*."

This reasoning is not strictly logical. Water, air, and light are *common* things, not because they are *inexhaustible*, but because they are *indispensable;* and so indispensable that for that very reason Nature has created them in quantities almost infinite, in order that their plentifulness might prevent their appropriation. Likewise the land is indispensable to our existence, — consequently a common thing, consequently insusceptible of appropriation; but land is much scarcer than the other elements, therefore its use must be regulated, not for the profit of a few, but in the interest and for the security of all. In a word, equality of rights is proved by equality of needs. Now, equality of rights, in the case of a commodity which is limited in amount, can be realized only by equality of possession. An agrarian law underlies M. Ch. Comte's arguments.

From whatever point we view this question of property — provided we go to the bottom of it — we reach equality. I will not insist farther on the distinction between things which can, and things which cannot, be appropriated. On this point, economists and legists talk worse than nonsense. The Civil Code, after having defined property, says nothing about susceptibility of appropriation; and if it speaks of things which are in *the market*, it always does so without enumerating or describing them. However, light is not wanting. There are some few maxims such as these: *Ad reges potestas omnium pertinet, ad singulos proprietas; Omnia rex imperio possidet, singula dominio.* Social sovereignty opposed to private property! — might not that be called a prophecy of equality, a republican oracle? Examples crowd upon us: once the possessions of the church, the estates of the crown, the fiefs of the nobility were inalienable and imprescriptible. If, instead of abolishing this privilege, the Constituent had extended it to every individual; if it had declared that the right of labor, like liberty, can never be forfeited, — at that moment the revolution would have been consummated, and we could now devote ourselves to improvement in other directions.

§ 2. — *Universal Consent no Justification of Property.*

In the extract from Say, quoted above, it is not clear whether the author means to base the right of property on the stationary character of the soil, or on the consent which he thinks all men have granted to this appropriation. His language is such that it may mean either of these things, or both at once; which entitles us to assume that the author intended to say, "The right of property resulting originally from the exercise of the will, the stability of the soil permitted it to be applied to the land, and universal consent has since sanctioned this application."

However that may be, can men legitimate property by mutual consent? I say, no. Such a contract, though drafted by Grotius, Montesquieu, and J. J. Rousseau, though signed by the whole human race, would be null in the eyes of justice, and an act to enforce it would be illegal. Man can no more give up labor than liberty. Now, to recognize the right of territorial property is to give up labor, since it is to relinquish the means of labor; it is to traffic in a natural right, and divest ourselves of manhood.

But I wish that this consent, of which so much is made, had been given, either tacitly or formally. What would have been the result? Evidently, the surrenders would have been reciprocal; no right would have been abandoned without the receipt of an equivalent in exchange. We thus come back to equality again, — the *sine qua non* of appropriation; so that, after having justified property by universal consent, that is, by equality, we are obliged to justify the inequality of conditions by property. Never shall we extricate ourselves from this dilemma. Indeed, if, in the terms of the social compact, property has equality for its condition, at the moment when equality ceases to exist, the compact is broken and all property becomes usurpation. We gain nothing, then, by this pretended consent of mankind.

§ 3. — *Prescription gives no Title to Property.*

The right of property was the origin of evil on the earth, the first link in the long chain of crimes and misfortunes which the human race has endured since its birth. The delusion of prescription is the fatal charm thrown over the intellect, the death sentence breathed into the conscience, to arrest man's progress towards truth, and bolster up the worship of error.

The Code defines prescription thus: "The process of gaining and losing through the lapse of time." In applying this definition to ideas and beliefs, we may use the word *prescription* to denote the everlasting prejudice in favor of old superstitions, whatever be their object; the opposition, often furious and bloody, with which new light has always been received, and which makes the sage a martyr. Not a principle, not a discovery, not a generous thought but has met, at its entrance into the world, with a formidable barrier of preconceived opinions, seeming like a conspiracy of all old prejudices. Prescriptions against reason, prescriptions against facts, prescriptions against every truth hitherto unknown, — that is the sum and substance of the *statu quo* philosophy, the watchword of conservatives throughout the centuries.

When the evangelical reform was broached to the world, there was prescription in favor of violence, debauchery, and selfishness; when Galileo, Descartes, Pascal, and their disciples reconstructed philosophy and the sciences, there was prescription in favor of the Aristotelian philosophy; when our fathers of '89 demanded liberty and equality, there was prescription in favor of tyranny and privilege. "There always have been proprietors and there always will be:" it is with this profound utterance, the final effort of selfishness dying in its last ditch, that the friends of social inequality hope to repel the attacks of their adversaries; thinking undoubtedly that ideas, like property, can be lost by prescription.

Enlightened to-day by the triumphal march of science, taught by the most glorious successes to question our own opinions, we receive with favor and applause the observer of Nature, who, by a thousand experiments based upon the most profound analysis, pursues a new principle, a law hitherto undiscovered. We take care to repel no idea, no fact, under the pretext that abler men than ourselves lived in former days, who did not notice the same phenomena, nor grasp the same analogies. Why do we not preserve a like attitude towards political and philosophical questions? Why this ridiculous mania for affirming that every thing has been said, which means that we know all about mental and moral science? Why is the proverb, *There is nothing new under the sun*, applied exclusively to metaphysical investigations?

Because we still study philosophy with the imagination, instead of by observation and method; because fancy and will are universally regarded as judges, in the place of arguments and facts, — it has been impossible to this day to distinguish the charlatan from the philosopher, the *savant* from the impostor. Since the days of Solomon and Pythagoras, imagination has been exhausted in guessing out social and psychological laws; all systems have been proposed. Looked at in this light, it is probably true that *every thing has been said;* but it is no less true that *every thing remains to be proved.* In politics (to take only this branch of philosophy), in politics every one is governed in his choice of party by his passion and his interests; the mind is submitted to the impositions of the will, — there is no knowledge, there is not even a shadow of certainty. In this way, general ignorance produces general tyranny; and while liberty of thought is written in the charter, slavery of thought, under the name of *majority rule*, is decreed by the charter.

In order to confine myself to the civil prescription of which the Code speaks, I shall refrain from beginning a discussion upon this worn-out objection brought forward by proprietors; it would be too tiresome and declamatory. Everybody knows that there are rights which cannot be prescribed; and, as for those things which can be gained through the lapse of time, no one is ignorant of the fact that prescription requires certain conditions, the omission of one of which renders it null. If it is true, for example, that the proprietor's possession has been *civil, public, peaceable*, and *uninterrupted*, it is none the less true that it is not based on a just title; since the only titles which it can show — occupation and labor — prove as much for the proletaire who demands, as for the proprietor who defends. Further, this possession is *dishonest*, since it is founded on a violation of right, which prevents prescription, according to the saying of St. Paul — *Nunquam in usucapionibus juris error possessori prodest.* The violation of right lies either in the fact that the holder possesses as proprietor, while he should possess only as usufructuary; or in the fact that he has purchased a thing which no one had a right to transfer or sell.

Another reason why prescription cannot be adduced in favor of property (a reason borrowed from jurisprudence) is that the right to possess real estate is a part of a universal right which has never been totally destroyed even at the most critical periods; and the proletaire, in order to regain the power to exercise it fully, has only to prove that he has always exercised it in part. He, for example, who has the universal right to possess, give, exchange, loan, let, sell, transform, or destroy a thing, preserves the integrity of this right by the sole act of loaning, though he has never shown his authority in any other manner. Likewise we shall see that *equality of possessions, equality of rights, liberty, will, personality*, are so many identical expressions of one and the same idea, — the *right of preservation* and *development;* in a word, the right of life, against which there can be no prescription until the human race has vanished from the face of the earth.

Finally, as to the time required for prescription, it would be superfluous to show that the right of property in general cannot be acquired by simple possession for ten, twenty, a hundred, a thousand, or one hundred thousand years; and that, so long as there exists a human head capable of understanding and combating the right of property, this right will never be prescribed. For principles of jurisprudence and axioms of reason are different from accidental and contingent facts. One man's possession can prescribe against another man's possession; but just as the possessor cannot prescribe against himself, so reason has always the faculty of change and reformation. Past error is not binding on the future. Reason is always the same eternal force. The institution of property, the work of ignorant reason, may be abrogated by a more enlightened reason. Consequently, property cannot be established by prescription. This is so certain and so true, that on it rests the maxim that in the matter of prescription a violation of right goes for nothing.

But I should be recreant to my method, and the reader would have the right to accuse me of charlatanism and bad faith, if I had nothing further to advance concerning prescription. I showed, in the first place, that appropriation of land is illegal; and that, supposing it to be legal, it must be accompanied by equality of property. I have shown, in the second place, that universal consent proves nothing in favor of property; and that, if it proves any thing, it proves equality of property. I have yet to show that prescription, if admissible at all, presupposes equality of property.

This demonstration will be neither long nor difficult. I need only to call attention to the reasons why prescription was introduced.

"Prescription," says Dunod, "seems repugnant to natural equity, which permits no one either to deprive another of his possessions without his knowledge and consent, or to enrich himself at another's expense. But as it might often happen, in the absence of prescription, that one who had honestly earned would be ousted after long possession; and even that he who had received a thing from its rightful owner, or who had been legitimately relieved from all obligations, would, on losing his title, be liable to be dispossessed or subjected again, — the public welfare demanded that a term should be fixed, after the expiration of which no one should be allowed to disturb actual possessors, or reassert rights too long neglected... The civil law, in regulating prescription, has aimed, then, only to perfect natural law, and to supplement the law of nations; and as it is founded on the public good, which should always be considered before individual welfare, — *bono publico usucapio introducta est*, — it should be regarded with favor, provided the conditions required by the law are fulfilled."

Toullier, in his "Civil Law," says: "In order that the question of proprietorship may not remain too long unsettled, and thereby injure the public welfare, disturbing the peace of families and the stability of social transactions, the law has fixed a time when all claims shall be cancelled, and possession shall regain its ancient prerogative through its transformation into property."

Cassiodorus said of property, that it was the only safe harbor in which to seek shelter from the tempests of chicanery and the gales of avarice — *Hic unus inter humanas pro cellas portus, quem si homines fervida voluntate praeterierint; in undosis semper jurgiis errabunt.*

Thus, in the opinion of the authors, prescription is a means of preserving public order; a restoration in certain cases of the original mode of acquiring property; a fiction of the civil law which derives all its force from the necessity of settling differences which otherwise would never end. For, as Grotius says, time has no power to produce effects; all things happen in time, but nothing is done by time. Prescription, or the right of acquisition through the lapse of time, is, therefore, a fiction of the law, conventionally adopted.

But all property necessarily originated in prescription, or, as the Latins say, in *usucapion;* that is, in continued possession. I ask, then, in the first place, how possession can become property by the lapse of time?

461

Continue possession as long as you wish, continue it for years and for centuries, you never can give duration — which of itself creates nothing, changes nothing, modifies nothing — the power to change the usufructuary into a proprietor. Let the civil law secure against chance-comers the honest possessor who has held his position for many years, — that only confirms a right already respected; and prescription, applied in this way, simply means that possession which has continued for twenty, thirty, or a hundred years shall be retained by the occupant. But when the law declares that the lapse of time changes possessor into proprietor, it supposes that a right can be created without a producing cause; it unwarrantably alters the character of the subject; it legislates on a matter not open to legislation; it exceeds its own powers. Public order and private security ask only that possession shall be protected. Why has the law created property? Prescription was simply security for the future; why has the law made it a matter of privilege?

Thus the origin of prescription is identical with that of property itself; and since the latter can legitimate itself only when accompanied by equality, prescription is but another of the thousand forms which the necessity of maintaining this precious equality has taken. And this is no vain induction, no far-fetched inference. The proof is written in all the codes.

And, indeed, if all nations, through their instinct of justice and their conservative nature, have recognized the utility and the necessity of prescription; and if their design has been to guard thereby the interests of the possessor, — could they not do something for the absent citizen, separated from his family and his country by commerce, war, or captivity, and in no position to exercise his right of possession? No. Also, at the same time that prescription was introduced into the laws, it was admitted that property is preserved by intent alone, — *nudo animo.* Now, if property is preserved by intent alone, if it can be lost only by the action of the proprietor, what can be the use of prescription? How does the law dare to presume that the proprietor, who preserves by intent alone, intended to abandon that which he has allowed to be prescribed? What lapse of time can warrant such a conjecture; and by what right does the law punish the absence of the proprietor by depriving him of his goods? What then! we found but a moment since that prescription and property were identical; and now we find that they are mutually destructive!

Grotius, who perceived this difficulty, replied so singularly that his words deserve to be quoted: *Bene sperandum de hominibus, ac propterea non putandum eos hoc esse animo ut, rei caducae causa, hominem alterum velint in perpetuo peccato versari, quo d evitari saepe non poterit sine tali derelictione.* "Where is the man," he says, "with so unchristian a soul that, for a trifle, he would perpetuate the trespass of a possessor, which would inevitably be the result if he did not consent to abandon his right?" By the Eternal! I am that man. Though a million proprietors should burn for it in hell, I lay the blame on them for depriving me of my portion of this world's goods. To this powerful consideration Grotius rejoins, that it is better to abandon a disputed right than to go to law, disturb the peace of nations, and stir up the flames of civil war. I accept, if you wish it, this argument, provided you indemnify me. But if this indemnity is refused me, what do I, a proletaire, care for the tranquillity and security of the rich? I care as little for *public order* as for the proprietor's safety. I ask to live a laborer; otherwise I will die a warrior.

Whichever way we turn, we shall come to the conclusion that prescription is a contradiction of property; or rather that prescription and property are two forms of the same principle, but two forms which serve to correct each other; and ancient and modern jurisprudence did not make the least of its blunders in pretending to reconcile them. Indeed, if we see in the institution of property only a desire to secure to each individual his share of the soil and his right to labor; in the distinction between naked property and possession only an asylum for absentees, orphans, and all who do not know, or cannot maintain, their rights; in prescription only a means, either of defence against unjust pretensions and encroachments, or of settlement of the differences caused by the removal of possessors, — we shall recognize in these various forms of human justice the spontaneous efforts of the mind to come to the aid of the social instinct; we shall see in this protection of all rights the sentiment of equality, a constant levelling tendency. And, looking deeper, we shall find in the very exaggeration of these principles the confirmation of our doctrine; because, if equality of conditions and universal association are not soon realized, it will be owing to the obstacle thrown for the time in the way of the common sense of the people by the stupidity of legislators and judges; and also to the fact that, while society in its original state was illuminated with a flash of truth, the early speculations of its leaders could bring forth nothing but darkness.

After the first covenants, after the first draughts of laws and constitutions, which were the expression of man's primary needs, the legislator's duty was to reform the errors of legislation; to complete that which was defective; to harmonize, by superior definitions, those things which seemed to conflict. Instead of that, they halted at the literal meaning of the laws, content to play the subordinate part of commentators and scholiasts. Taking the inspirations of the human mind, at that time necessarily weak and faulty, for axioms of eternal and unquestionable truth, — influenced by public opinion, enslaved by the popular religion, — they have invariably started with the principle (following in this respect the example of the theologians) that that is infallibly true which has been admitted by all persons, in all places, and at all times — *quod ab omnibus, quod ubique, quod semper;* as if a general but spontaneous opinion was any thing more than an indication of the truth. Let us not be deceived: the opinion of all nations may serve to authenticate the perception of a fact, the vague sentiment of a law; it can teach us nothing about either fact or law. The consent of mankind is an indication of Nature; not, as Cicero says, a law of Nature. Under the indication is hidden the truth, which faith can believe, but only thought can know. Such has been the constant progress of the human mind in regard to physical phenomena and the creations of genius: how can it be otherwise with the facts of conscience and the rules of human conduct?

§ 4. — Labor — *That Labor has no Inherent Power to appropriate Natural Wealth.*

We shall show by the maxims of political economy and law, that is, by the authorities recognized by property, —

1. That labor has no inherent power to appropriate natural wealth.

2. That, if we admit that labor has this power, we are led directly to equality of property, — whatever the kind of labor, however scarce the product, or unequal the ability of the laborers.

3. That, in the order of justice, labor *destroys* property.

Following the example of our opponents, and that we may leave no obstacles in the path, let us examine the question in the strongest possible light.

M. Ch. Comte says, in his "Treatise on Property:" —

"France, considered as a nation, has a territory which is her own."

France, as an individuality, possesses a territory which she cultivates; it is not her property. Nations are related to each other as individuals are:

they are commoners and workers; it is an abuse of language to call them proprietors. The right of use and abuse belongs no more to nations than to men; and the time will come when a war waged for the purpose of checking a nation in its abuse of the soil will be regarded as a holy war.

Thus, M. Ch. Comte — who undertakes to explain how property comes into existence, and who starts with the supposition that a nation is a proprietor — falls into that error known as *begging the question;* a mistake which vitiates his whole argument.

If the reader thinks it is pushing logic too far to question a nation's right of property in the territory which it possesses, I will simply remind him of the fact that at all ages the results of the fictitious right of national property have been pretensions to suzerainty, tributes, monarchical privileges, statute-labor, quotas of men and money, supplies of merchandise, &c.; ending finally in refusals to pay taxes, insurrections, wars, and depopulations.

"Scattered through this territory are extended tracts of land, which have not been converted into individual property. These lands, which consist mainly of forests, belong to the whole population, and the government, which receives the revenues, uses or ought to use them in the interest of all."

Ought to use is well said: a lie is avoided thereby.

"Let them be offered for sale..."

Why offered for sale? Who has a right to sell them? Even were the nation proprietor, can the generation of to-day dispossess the generation of to-morrow? The nation, in its function of usufructuary, possesses them; the government rules, superintends, and protects them. If it also granted lands, it could grant only their use; it has no right to sell them or transfer them in any way whatever. Not being a proprietor, how can it transmit property?

"Suppose some industrious man buys a portion, a large swamp for example. This would be no usurpation, since the public would receive the exact value through the hands of the government, and would be as rich after the sale as before."

465

How ridiculous! What! because a prodigal, imprudent, incompetent official sells the State's possessions, while I, a ward of the State, — I who have neither an advisory nor a deliberative voice in the State councils, — while I am allowed to make no opposition to the sale, this sale is right and legal! The guardians of the nation waste its substance, and it has no redress! I have received, you tell me, through the hands of the government my share of the proceeds of the sale: but, in the first place, I did not wish to sell; and, had I wished to, I could not have sold. I had not the right. And then I do not see that I am benefited by the sale. My guardians have dressed up some soldiers, repaired an old fortress, erected in their pride some costly but worthless monument, — then they have exploded some fireworks and set up a greased pole! What does all that amount to in comparison with my loss?

The purchaser draws boundaries, fences himself in, and says, "This is mine; each one by himself, each one for himself." Here, then, is a piece of land upon which, henceforth, no one has a right to step, save the proprietor and his friends; which can benefit nobody, save the proprietor and his servants. Let these sales multiply, and soon the people — who have been neither able nor willing to sell, and who have received none of the proceeds of the sale — will have nowhere to rest, no place of shelter, no ground to till. They will die of hunger at the proprietor's door, on the edge of that property which was their birthright; and the proprietor, watching them die, will exclaim, "So perish idlers and vagrants!"

To reconcile us to the proprietor's usurpation, M. Ch. Comte assumes the lands to be of little value at the time of sale.

"The importance of these usurpations should not be exaggerated: they should be measured by the number of men which the occupied land would support, and by the means which it would furnish them. It is evident, for instance, that if a piece of land which is worth to-day one thousand francs was worth only five centimes when it was usurped, we really lose only the value of five centimes. A square league of earth would be hardly sufficient to support a savage in distress; to-day it supplies one thousand persons with the means of existence. Nine hundred and ninety-nine parts of this land is the legitimate property of the possessors; only one-thousandth of the value has been usurped."

A peasant admitted one day, at confession, that he had destroyed a document which declared him a debtor to the amount of three hundred francs. Said the father confessor, "You must return these three hundred francs." "No," replied the peasant, "I will return a penny to pay for the paper."

M. Ch. Comte's logic resembles this peasant's honesty. The soil has not only an integrant and actual value, it has also a potential value, — a value of the future, — which depends on our ability to make it valuable, and to employ it in our work. Destroy a bill of exchange, a promissory note, an annuity deed, — as a paper you destroy almost no value at all; but with this paper you destroy your title, and, in losing your title, you deprive yourself of your goods. Destroy the land, or, what is the same thing, sell it, — you not only transfer one, two, or several crops, but you annihilate all the products that you could derive from it; you and your children and your children's children.

When M. Ch. Comte, the apostle of property and the eulogist of labor, supposes an alienation of the soil on the part of the government, we must not think that he does so without reason and for no purpose; it is a necessary part of his position. As he rejected the theory of occupancy, and as he knew, moreover, that labor could not constitute the right in the absence of a previous permission to occupy, he was obliged to connect this permission with the authority of the government, which means that property is based upon the sovereignty of the people; in other words, upon universal consent. This theory we have already considered.

To say that property is the daughter of labor, and then to give labor material on which to exercise itself, is, if I am not mistaken, to reason in a circle. Contradictions will result from it.

"A piece of land of a certain size produces food enough to supply a man for one day. If the possessor, through his labor, discovers some method of making it produce enough for two days, he doubles its value. This new value is his work, his creation: it is taken from nobody; it is his property."

I maintain that the possessor is paid for his trouble and industry in his doubled crop, but that he acquires no right to the land. "Let the laborer have the fruits of his labor." Very good; but I do not understand that property in products carries with it property in raw material. Does the skill of the fisherman, who on the same coast can catch more fish than his fellows, make him proprietor of the fishing-grounds? Can the expertness of a hunter ever be regarded as a property-title to a game-forest? The analogy is perfect, — the industrious cultivator finds the reward of his industry in the abundancy and superiority of his crop. If

467

he has made improvements in the soil, he has the possessor's right of preference. Never, under any circumstances, can he be allowed to claim a property-title to the soil which he cultivates, on the ground of his skill as a cultivator.

To change possession into property, something is needed besides labor, without which a man would cease to be proprietor as soon as he ceased to be a laborer. Now, the law bases property upon immemorial, unquestionable possession; that is, prescription. Labor is only the sensible sign, the physical act, by which occupation is manifested. If, then, the cultivator remains proprietor after he has ceased to labor and produce; if his possession, first conceded, then tolerated, finally becomes inalienable, — it happens by permission of the civil law, and by virtue of the principle of occupancy. So true is this, that there is not a bill of sale, not a farm lease, not an annuity, but implies it. I will quote only one example.

How do we measure the value of land? By its product. If a piece of land yields one thousand francs, we say that at five per cent. it is worth twenty thousand francs; at four per cent. twenty-five thousand francs, &c.; which means, in other words, that in twenty or twenty-five years' time the purchaser would recover in full the amount originally paid for the land. If, then, after a certain length of time, the price of a piece of land has been wholly recovered, why does the purchaser continue to be proprietor? Because of the right of occupancy, in the absence of which every sale would be a redemption.

The theory of appropriation by labor is, then, a contradiction of the Code; and when the partisans of this theory pretend to explain the laws thereby, they contradict themselves.

"If men succeed in fertilizing land hitherto unproductive, or even death-producing, like certain swamps, they create thereby property in all its completeness."

What good does it do to magnify an expression, and play with equivocations, as if we expected to change the reality thereby? *They create property in all its completeness.* You mean that they create a productive capacity which formerly did not exist; but this capacity cannot be created without material to support it. The substance of the soil remains the same; only its qualities and modifications are changed. Man has created every thing — every thing save the material itself. Now, I maintain that this material he can only possess and use, on condition of permanent labor, — granting, for the time being, his right of property in things which he has produced.

This, then, is the first point settled: property in product, if we grant so much, does not carry with it property in the means of production; that seems to me to need no further demonstration. There is no difference between the soldier who possesses his arms, the mason who possesses the materials committed to his care, the fisherman who possesses the water, the hunter who possesses the fields and forests, and the cultivator who possesses the lands: all, if you say so, are proprietors of their products — not one is proprietor of the means of production. The right to product is exclusive — *jus in re;* the right to means is common — *jus ad rem.*

§ 5. — *That Labor leads to Equality of Property.*

Admit, however, that labor gives a right of property in material. Why is not this principle universal? Why is the benefit of this pretended law confined to a few and denied to the mass of laborers? A philosopher, arguing that all animals sprang up formerly out of the earth warmed by the rays of the sun, almost like mushrooms, on being asked why the earth no longer yielded crops of that nature, replied: "Because it is old, and has lost its fertility." Has labor, once so fecund, likewise become sterile? Why does the tenant no longer acquire through his labor the land which was formerly acquired by the labor of the proprietor?

"Because," they say, "it is already appropriated." That is no answer. A farm yields fifty bushels per *hectare;* the skill and labor of the tenant double this product: the increase is created by the tenant. Suppose the owner, in a spirit of moderation rarely met with, does not go to the extent of absorbing this product by raising the rent, but allows the cultivator to enjoy the results of his labor; even then justice is not satisfied. The tenant, by improving the land, has imparted a new value to the property; he, therefore, has a right to a part of the property. If the farm was originally worth one hundred thousand francs, and if by the labor of the tenant its value has risen to one hundred and fifty thousand francs, the tenant, who produced this extra value, is the legitimate proprietor of one-third of the farm. M. Ch. Comte could not have pronounced this doctrine false, for it was he who said: —

"Men who increase the fertility of the earth are no less useful to their fellow-men, than if they should create new land."

Why, then, is not this rule applicable to the man who im proves the land, as well as to him who clears it? The labor of the former makes the land worth one; that of the latter makes it worth two: both create equal values. Why not accord to both equal property? I defy any one to refute this argument, without again falling back on the right of first occupancy.

"But," it will be said, "even if your wish should be granted, property would not be distributed much more evenly than now. Land does not go on increasing in value for ever; after two or three seasons it attains its maximum fertility. That which is added by the agricultural art results rather from the progress of science and the diffusion of knowledge, than from the skill of the cultivator. Consequently, the addition of a few laborers to the mass of proprietors would be no argument against property."

This discussion would, indeed, prove a well-nigh useless one, if our labors culminated in simply extending land-privilege and industrial monopoly; in emancipating only a few hundred laborers out of the millions of proletaires. But this also is a misconception of our real thought, and does but prove the general lack of intelligence and logic.

If the laborer, who adds to the value of a thing, has a right of property in it, he who maintains this value acquires the same right. For what is maintenance? It is incessant addition, — continuous creation. What is it to cultivate? It is to give the soil its value every year; it is, by annually renewed creation, to prevent the diminution or destruction of the value of a piece of land. Admitting, then, that property is rational and legitimate, — admitting that rent is equitable and just, — I say that he who cultivates acquires property by as good a title as he who clears, or he who improves; and that every time a tenant pays his rent, he obtains a fraction of property in the land entrusted to his care, the denominator of which is equal to the proportion of rent paid. Unless you admit this, you fall into absolutism and tyranny; you recognize class privileges; you sanction slavery.

Whoever labors becomes a proprietor — this is an inevitable deduction from the acknowledged principles of political economy and jurisprudence. And when I say proprietor, I do not mean simply (as do our hypocritical economists) proprietor of his allowance, his salary, his wages, — I mean proprietor of the value which he creates, and by which the master alone profits.

470

As all this relates to the theory of wages and of the distribution of products, — and as this matter never has been even partially cleared up, — I ask permission to insist on it: this discussion will not be useless to the work in hand. Many persons talk of admitting working-people to a share in the products and profits; but in their minds this participation is pure benevolence: they have never shown — perhaps never suspected — that it was a natural, necessary right, inherent in labor, and inseparable from the function of producer, even in the lowest forms of his work.

This is my proposition: *The laborer retains, even after he has received his wages, a natural right of property in the thing which he has produced.*

I again quote M. Ch. Comte: —

"Some laborers are employed in draining marshes, in cutting down trees and brushwood, — in a word, in cleaning up the soil. They increase the value, they make the amount of property larger; they are paid for the value which they add in the form of food and daily wages: it then becomes the property of the capitalist."

The price is not sufficient: the labor of the workers has created a value; now this value is their property. But they have neither sold nor exchanged it; and you, capitalist, you have not earned it. That you should have a partial right to the whole, in return for the materials that you have furnished and the provisions that you have supplied, is perfectly just. You contributed to the production, you ought to share in the enjoyment. But your right does not annihilate that of the laborers, who, in spite of you, have been your colleagues in the work of production. Why do you talk of wages? The money with which you pay the wages of the laborers remunerates them for only a few years of the perpetual possession which they have abandoned to you. Wages is the cost of the daily maintenance and refreshment of the laborer. You are wrong in calling it the price of a sale. The workingman has sold nothing; he knows neither his right, nor the extent of the concession which he has made to you, nor the meaning of the contract which you pretend to have made with him. On his side, utter ignorance; on yours, error and surprise, not to say deceit and fraud.

Let us make this clearer by another and more striking example.

No one is ignorant of the difficulties that are met with in the conversion of untilled land into arable and productive land. These difficulties are so great, that usually an isolated man would perish before he could put the soil in a condition to yield him even the most meagre living. To that end are needed the united and combined efforts of society, and all the resources of industry. M. Ch. Comte quotes on this subject numerous and well-authenticated facts, little thinking that he is amassing testimony against his own system.

Let us suppose that a colony of twenty or thirty families establishes itself in a wild district, covered with underbrush and forests; and from which, by agreement, the natives consent to withdraw. Each one of these families possesses a moderate but sufficient amount of capital, of such a nature as a colonist would be apt to choose, — animals, seeds, tools, and a little money and food. The land having been divided, each one settles himself as comfortably as possible, and begins to clear away the portion allotted to him. But after a few weeks of fatigue, such as they never before have known, of inconceivable suffering, of ruinous and almost useless labor, our colonists begin to complain of their trade; their condition seems hard to them; they curse their sad existence.

Suddenly, one of the shrewdest among them kills a pig, cures a part of the meat; and, resolved to sacrifice the rest of his provisions, goes to find his companions in misery. "Friends," he begins in a very benevolent tone, "how much trouble it costs you to do a little work and live uncomfortably! A fortnight of labor has reduced you to your last extremity! ... Let us make an arrangement by which you shall all profit. I offer you provisions and wine: you shall get so much every day; we will work together, and, zounds! my friends, we will be happy and contented!"

Would it be possible for empty stomachs to resist such an invitation? The hungriest of them follow the treacherous tempter. They go to work; the charm of society, emulation, joy, and mutual assistance double their strength; the work can be seen to advance. Singing and laughing, they subdue Nature. In a short time, the soil is thoroughly changed; the mellowed earth waits only for the seed. That done, the proprietor pays his laborers, who, on going away, return him their thanks, and grieve that the happy days which they have spent with him are over.

Others follow this example, always with the same success.

Then, these installed, the rest disperse, — each one returns to his grubbing. But, while grubbing, it is necessary to live. While they have been clearing away for their neighbor, they have done no clearing for themselves. One year's seed-time and harvest is already gone. They had calculated that in lending their labor they could not but gain, since they would save their own provisions; and, while living better, would get still more money. False calculation! they have created for another the means wherewith to produce, and have created nothing for themselves. The difficulties of clearing remain the same; their clothing wears out, their provisions give out; soon their purse becomes empty for the profit of the individual for whom they have worked, and who alone can furnish the provisions which they need, since he alone is in a position to produce them. Then, when the poor grubber has exhausted his resources, the man with the provisions (like the wolf in the fable, who scents his victim from afar) again comes forward. One he offers to employ again by the day; from another he offers to buy at a favorable price a piece of his bad land, which is not, and never can be, of any use to him: that is, he uses the labor of one man to cultivate the field of another for his own benefit. So that at the end of twenty years, of thirty individuals originally equal in point of wealth, five or six have become proprietors of the whole district, while the rest have been philanthropically dispossessed!

In this century of *bourgeoisie* morality, in which I have had the honor to be born, the moral sense is so debased that I should not be at all surprised if I were asked, by many a worthy proprietor, what I see in this that is unjust and illegitimate? Debased creature! galvanized corpse! how can I expect to convince you, if you cannot tell robbery when I show it to you? A man, by soft and insinuating words, discovers the secret of taxing others that he may establish himself; then, once enriched by their united efforts, he refuses, on the very conditions which he himself dictated, to advance the well-being of those who made his fortune for him: and you ask how such conduct is fraudulent! Under the pretext that he has paid his laborers, that he owes them nothing more, that he has nothing to gain by putting himself at the service of others, while his own occupations claim his attention, — he refuses, I say, to aid others in getting a foothold, as he was aided in getting his own; and when, in the impotence of their isolation, these poor laborers are compelled to sell their birthright, he — this ungrateful proprietor, this knavish upstart — stands ready to put the finishing touch to their deprivation and their ruin. And you think that just? Take care! I read in your startled countenance the reproach of a guilty conscience, much more clearly than the innocent astonishment of involuntary ignorance.

"The capitalist," they say, "has paid the laborers their *daily wages*." To be accurate, it must be said that the capitalist has paid as many times one day's wage as he has employed laborers each day, — which is not at all the same thing. For he has paid nothing for that immense power which results from the union and harmony of laborers, and the convergence and simultaneousness of their efforts. Two hundred grenadiers stood the obelisk of Luxor upon its base in a few hours; do you suppose that one man could have accomplished the same task in two hundred days? Nevertheless, on the books of the capitalist, the amount of wages paid would have been the same. Well, a desert to prepare for cultivation, a house to build, a factory to run, — all these are obelisks to erect, mountains to move. The smallest fortune, the most insignificant establishment, the setting in motion of the lowest industry, demand the concurrence of so many different kinds of labor and skill, that one man could not possibly execute the whole of them. It is astonishing that the economists never have called attention to this fact. Strike a balance, then, between the capitalist's receipts and his payments.

The laborer needs a salary which will enable him to live while he works; for unless he consumes, he cannot produce. Whoever employs a man owes him maintenance and support, or wages enough to procure the same. That is the first thing to be done in all production. I admit, for the moment, that in this respect the capitalist has discharged his duty.

It is necessary that the laborer should find in his production, in addition to his present support, a guarantee of his future support; otherwise the source of production would dry up, and his productive capacity would become exhausted: in other words, the labor accomplished must give birth perpetually to new labor — such is the universal law of reproduction. In this way, the proprietor of a farm finds: 1. In his crops, means, not only of supporting himself and his family, but of maintaining and improving his capital, of feeding his live-stock — in a word, means of new labor and continual reproduction; 2. In his ownership of a productive agency, a permanent basis of cultivation and labor.

But he who lends his services, — what is his basis of cultivation? The proprietor's presumed need of him, and the unwarranted supposition that he wishes to employ him. Just as the commoner once held his land by the munificence and condescension of the lord, so to-day the working-man holds his labor by the condescension and necessities of the master and proprietor: that is what is called possession by a precarious[15] title. But this precarious condition is an injustice, for it implies an inequality in the bargain. The laborer's wages exceed but little his running expenses, and do not assure him wages for to-morrow;

while the capitalist finds in the instrument produced by the laborer a pledge of independence and security for the future.

Now, this reproductive leaven — this eternal germ of life, this preparation of the land and manufacture of implements for production — constitutes the debt of the capitalist to the producer, which he never pays; and it is this fraudulent denial which causes the poverty of the laborer, the luxury of idleness, and the inequality of conditions. This it is, above all other things, which has been so fitly named the exploitation of man by man.

One of three things must be done. Either the laborer must be given a portion of the product in addition to his wages; or the employer must render the laborer an equivalent in productive service; or else he must pledge himself to employ him for ever. Division of the product, reciprocity of service, or guarantee of perpetual labor, — from the adoption of one of these courses the capitalist cannot escape. But it is evident that he cannot satisfy the second and third of these conditions — he can neither put himself at the service of the thousands of working-men, who, directly or indirectly, have aided him in establishing himself, nor employ them all for ever. He has no other course left him, then, but a division of the property. But if the property is divided, all conditions will be equal — there will be no more large capitalists or large proprietors.

Consequently, when M. Ch. Comte — following out his hypothesis — shows us his capitalist acquiring one after another the products of his employees' labor, he sinks deeper and deeper into the mire; and, as his argument does not change, our reply of course remains the same.

"Other laborers are employed in building: some quarry the stone, others transport it, others cut it, and still others put it in place. Each of them adds a certain value to the material which passes through his hands; and this value, the product of his labor, is his property. He sells it, as fast as he creates it, to the proprietor of the building, who pays him for it in food and wages."

Divide et impera — divide, and you shall command; divide, and you shall grow rich; divide, and you shall deceive men, you shall daze their minds, you shall mock at justice! Separate laborers from each other, perhaps each one's daily wage exceeds the value of each individual's product; but that is not the question under consideration. A force of one thousand men working twenty days has been paid the same wages that one would be paid for working fifty-five years; but this force of one

475

thousand has done in twenty days what a single man could not have accomplished, though he had labored for a million centuries. Is the exchange an equitable one? Once more, no; when you have paid all the individual forces, the collective force still remains to be paid. Consequently, there remains always a right of collective property which you have not acquired, and which you enjoy unjustly.

Admit that twenty days' wages suffice to feed, lodge, and clothe this multitude for twenty days: thrown out of employment at the end of that time, what will become of them, if, as fast as they create, they abandon their creations to the proprietors who will soon discharge them? While the proprietor, firm in his position (thanks to the aid of all the laborers), dwells in security, and fears no lack of labor or bread, the laborer's only dependence is upon the benevolence of this same proprietor, to whom he has sold and surrendered his liberty. If, then, the proprietor, shielding himself behind his comfort and his rights, refuses to employ the laborer, how can the laborer live? He has ploughed an excellent field, and cannot sow it; he has built an elegant and commodious house, and cannot live in it; he has produced all, and can enjoy nothing

Labor leads us to equality. Every step that we take brings us nearer to it; and if laborers had equal strength, diligence, and industry, clearly their fortunes would be equal also. Indeed, if, as is pretended, — and as we have admitted, — the laborer is proprietor of the value which he creates, it follows: —

1. That the laborer acquires at the expense of the idle proprietor;

2. That all production being necessarily collective, the laborer is entitled to a share of the products and profits commensurate with his labor;

3. That all accumulated capital being social property, no one can be its exclusive proprietor.

These inferences are unavoidable; these alone would suffice to revolutionize our whole economical system, and change our institutions and our laws. Why do the very persons, who laid down this principle, now refuse to be guided by it? Why do the Says, the Comtes, the Hennequins, and others — after having said that property is born of labor — seek to fix it by occupation and prescription?

But let us leave these sophists to their contradictions and blindness. The good sense of the people will do justice to their equivocations. Let us make haste to enlighten it, and show it the true path. Equality approaches; already between it and us but a short distance intervenes: to-morrow even this distance will have been traversed.

§ 6. — *That in Society all Wages are Equal.*

When the St. Simonians, the Fourierists, and, in general, all who in our day are connected with social economy and reform, inscribe upon their banner, —

"To each according to his capacity, to each capacity according to its results" *(St. Simon)*;

"To each according to his capital, his labor, and his skill" (*Fourier*), — they mean — although they do not say so in so many words — that the products of Nature procured by labor and industry are a reward, a palm, a crown offered to all kinds of preeminence and superiority. They regard the land as an immense arena in which prizes are contended for, — no longer, it is true, with lances and swords, by force and by treachery; but by acquired wealth, by knowledge, talent, and by virtue itself. In a word, they mean — and everybody agrees with them — that the greatest capacity is entitled to the greatest reward; and, to use the mercantile phraseology, — which has, at least, the merit of being straightforward, — that salaries must be governed by capacity and its results.

The disciples of these two self-styled reformers cannot deny that such is their thought; for, in doing so, they would contradict their official interpretations, and would destroy the unity of their systems. Furthermore, such a denial on their part is not to be feared. The two sects glory in laying down as a principle inequality of conditions, — reasoning from Nature, who, they say, intended the inequality of capacities. They boast only of one thing; namely, that their political system is so perfect, that the social inequalities always correspond with the natural inequalities. They no more trouble themselves to inquire whether inequality of conditions — I mean of salaries — is possible, than they do to fix a measure of capacity.[16]

"To each according to his capacity, to each capacity according to its results."

477

"To each according to his capital, his labor, and his skill."

Since the death of St. Simon and Fourier, not one among their numerous disciples has attempted to give to the public a scientific demonstration of this grand maxim; and I would wager a hundred to one that no Fourierist even suspects that this biform aphorism is susceptible of two interpretations.

"To each according to his capacity, to each capacity according to its results."

"To each according to his capital, his labor, and his skill."

This proposition, taken, as they say, *in sensu obvio* — in the sense usually attributed to it — is false, absurd, unjust, contradictory, hostile to liberty, friendly to tyranny, anti-social, and was unluckily framed under the express influence of the property idea.

And, first, *capital* must be crossed off the list of elements which are entitled to a reward. The Fourierists — as far as I have been able to learn from a few of their pamphlets — deny the right of occupancy, and recognize no basis of property save labor. Starting with a like premise, they would have seen — had they reasoned upon the matter — that capital is a source of production to its proprietor only by virtue of the right of occupancy, and that this production is therefore illegitimate. Indeed, if labor is the sole basis of property, I cease to be proprietor of my field as soon as I receive rent for it from another. This we have shown beyond all cavil. It is the same with all capital; so that to put capital in an enterprise, is, by the law's decision, to exchange it for an equivalent sum in products. I will not enter again upon this now useless discussion, since I propose, in the following chapter, to exhaust the subject of *production by capital.*

Thus, capital can be exchanged, but cannot be a source of income.

Labor and *skill* remain; or, as St. Simon puts it, *results* and *capacities.* I will examine them successively.

Should wages be governed by labor? In other words, is it just that he who does the most should get the most? I beg the reader to pay the closest attention to this point.

To solve the problem with one stroke, we have only to ask ourselves the following question: "Is labor a *condition* or a *struggle*? "The reply seems plain.

God said to man, "In the sweat of thy face shalt thou eat bread," — that is, thou shalt produce thy own bread: with more or less ease, according to thy skill in directing and combining thy efforts, thou shalt labor. God did not say, "Thou shalt quarrel with thy neighbor for thy bread;" but, "Thou shalt labor by the side of thy neighbor, and ye shall dwell together in harmony." Let us develop the meaning of this law, the extreme simplicity of which renders it liable to misconstruction.

In labor, two things must be noticed and distinguished: *association* and *available material.*

In so far as laborers are associated, they are equal; and it involves a contradiction to say that one should be paid more than another. For, as the product of one laborer can be paid for only in the product of another laborer, if the two products are unequal, the remainder — or the difference between the greater and the smaller — will not be acquired by society; and, therefore, not being exchanged, will not affect the equality of wages. There will result, it is true, in favor of the stronger laborer a natural inequality, but not a social inequality; no one having suffered by his strength and productive energy. In a word, society exchanges only equal products — that is, rewards no labor save that performed for her benefit; consequently, she pays all laborers equally: with what they produce outside of her sphere she has no more to do, than with the difference in their voices and their hair.

I seem to be positing the principle of inequality: the reverse of this is the truth. The total amount of labor which can be performed for society (that is, of labor susceptible of exchange), being, within a given space, as much greater as the laborers are more numerous, and as the task assigned to each is less in magnitude, — it follows that natural inequality neutralizes itself in proportion as association extends, and as the quantity of consumable values produced thereby increases. So that in society the only thing which could bring back the inequality of labor would be the right of occupancy, — the right of property.

Now, suppose that this daily social task consists in the ploughing, hoeing, or reaping of two square decameters, and that the average time required to accomplish it is seven hours: one laborer will finish it in six hours, another will require eight; the majority, however, will work seven. But provided each one furnishes the quantity of labor demanded

479

of him, whatever be the time he employs, they are entitled to equal wages.

Shall the laborer who is capable of finishing his task in six hours have the right, on the ground of superior strength and activity, to usurp the task of the less skilful laborer, and thus rob him of his labor and bread? Who dares maintain such a proposition? He who finishes before the others may rest, if he chooses; he may devote himself to useful exercise and labors for the maintenance of his strength, and the culture of his mind, and the pleasure of his life. This he can do without injury to any one: but let him confine himself to services which affect him solely. Vigor, genius, diligence, and all the personal advantages which result therefrom, are the work of Nature and, to a certain extent, of the individual; society awards them the esteem which they merit: but the wages which it pays them is measured, not by their power, but by their production. Now, the product of each is limited by the right of all.

If the soil were infinite in extent, and the amount of available material were exhaustless, even then we could not accept this maxim, — *To each according to his labor*. And why? Because society, I repeat, whatever be the number of its subjects, is forced to pay them all the same wages, since she pays them only in their own products. Only, on the hypothesis just made, inasmuch as the strong cannot be prevented from using all their advantages, the inconveniences of natural inequality would reappear in the very bosom of social equality. But the land, considering the productive power of its inhabitants and their ability to multiply, is very limited; further, by the immense variety of products and the extreme division of labor, the social task is made easy of accomplishment. Now, through this limitation of things producible, and through the ease of producing them, the law of absolute equality takes effect.

Yes, life is a struggle. But this struggle is not between man and man — it is between man and Nature; and it is each one's duty to take his share in it. If, in the struggle, the strong come to the aid of the weak, their kindness deserves praise and love; but their aid must be accepted as a free gift, — not imposed by force, nor offered at a price. All have the same career before them, neither too long nor too difficult; whoever finishes it finds his reward at the end: it is not necessary to get there first.

In printing-offices, where the laborers usually work by the job, the compositor receives so much per thousand letters set; the pressman so much per thousand sheets printed. There, as elsewhere, inequalities of talent and skill are to be found. When there is no prospect of dull times (for printing and typesetting, like all other trades, sometimes come to a stand-still), every one is free to work his hardest, and exert his faculties to the utmost: he who does more gets more; he who does less gets less. When business slackens, compositors and pressmen divide up their labor; all monopolists are detested as no better than robbers or traitors.

There is a philosophy in the action of these printers, to which neither economists nor legists have ever risen. If our legislators had introduced into their codes the principle of distributive justice which governs printing-offices; if they had observed the popular instincts, — not for the sake of servile imitation, but in order to reform and generalize them, — long ere this liberty and equality would have been established on an immovable basis, and we should not now be disputing about the right of property and the necessity of social distinctions.

It has been calculated that if labor were equally shared by the whole number of able-bodied individuals, the average working-day of each individual, in France, would not exceed five hours. This being so, how can we presume to talk of the inequality of laborers? It is the *labor* of Robert Macaire that causes inequality.

The principle, *To each according to his labor*, interpreted to mean, *Who works most should receive most*, is based, therefore, on two palpable errors: one, an error in economy, that in the labor of society tasks must necessarily be unequal; the other, an error in physics, that there is no limit to the amount of producible things.

"But," it will be said, "suppose there are some people who wish to perform only half of their task?" ... Is that very embarrassing? Probably they are satisfied with half of their salary. Paid according to the labor that they had performed, of what could they complain? and what injury would they do to others? In this sense, it is fair to apply the maxim, — *To each according to his results*. It is the law of equality itself.

Further, numerous difficulties, relative to the police system and the organization of industry, might be raised here. I will reply to them all with this one sentence, — that they must all be solved by the principle of equality. Thus, some one might observe, "Here is a task which cannot be postponed without detriment to production. Ought society to suffer from the negligence of a few? and will she not venture — out of respect for the right of labor — to assure with her own hands the product which they refuse her? In such a case, to whom will the salary belong?"

481

To society; who will be allowed to perform the labor, either herself, or through her representatives, but always in such a way that the general equality shall never be violated, and that only the idler shall be punished for his idleness. Further, if society may not use excessive severity towards her lazy members, she has a right, in self-defence, to guard against abuses.

But every industry needs — they will add — leaders, instructors, superintendents, &c. Will these be engaged in the general task? No; since their task is to lead, instruct, and superintend. But they must be chosen from the laborers by the laborers themselves, and must fulfil the conditions of eligibility. It is the same with all public functions, whether of administration or instruction.

Then, article first of the universal constitution will be: —

"The limited quantity of available material proves the necessity of dividing the labor among the whole number of laborers. The capacity, given to all, of accomplishing a social task, — that is, an equal task, — and the impossibility of paying one laborer save in the products of another, justify the equality of wages."

§ 7. — *That Inequality of Powers is the Necessary Condition of Equality of Fortunes.*

It is objected, — and this objection constitutes the second part of the St. Simonian, and the third part of the Fourierstic, maxims, —

"That all kinds of labor cannot be executed with equal ease. Some require great superiority of skill and intelligence; and on this superiority is based the price. The artist, the *savant*, the poet, the statesman, are esteemed only because of their excellence; and this excellence destroys all similitude between them and other men: in the presence of these heights of science and genius the law of equality disappears. Now, if equality is not absolute, there is no equality. From the poet we descend to the novelist; from the sculptor to the stonecutter; from the architect to the mason; from the chemist to the cook, &c. Capacities are classified and subdivided into orders, genera, and species. The extremes of talent are connected by intermediate talents. Humanity is a vast hierarchy, in which the individual estimates himself by comparison, and fixes his price by the value placed upon his product by the public."

This objection always has seemed a formidable one. It is the stumbling-block of the economists, as well as of the defenders of equality. It has led the former into egregious blunders, and has caused the latter to utter incredible platitudes. Gracchus Babeuf wished all superiority to be *stringently repressed*, and even *persecuted as a social calamity*. To establish his communistic edifice, he lowered all citizens to the stature of the smallest. Ignorant eclectics have been known to object to the inequality of knowledge, and I should not be surprised if some one should yet rebel against the inequality of virtue. Aristotle was banished, Socrates drank the hemlock, Epaminondas was called to account, for having proved superior in intelligence and virtue to some dissolute and foolish demagogues. Such follies will be re-enacted, so long as the inequality of fortunes justifies a populace, blinded and oppressed by the wealthy, in fearing the elevation of new tyrants to power.

Nothing seems more unnatural than that which we examine too closely, and often nothing seems less like the truth than the truth itself. On the other hand, according to J. J. Rousseau, "it takes a great deal of philosophy to enable us to observe once what we see every day;" and, according to d'Alembert, "the ordinary truths of life make but little impression on men, unless their attention is especially called to them." The father of the school of economists (Say), from whom I borrow these two quotations, might have profited by them; but he who laughs at the blind should wear spectacles, and he who notices him is near-sighted.

Strange! that which has frightened so many minds is not, after all, an objection to equality — it is the very condition on which equality exists! ...

Natural inequality the condition of equality of fortunes! ... What a paradox! ... I repeat my assertion, that no one may think I have blundered — inequality of powers is the *sine qua non* of equality of fortunes.

There are two things to be considered in society — *functions* and *relations*.

I. *Functions*. Every laborer is supposed to be capable of performing the task assigned to him; or, to use a common expression, "every workman must know his trade." The workman equal to his work, — there is an equation between functionary and function.

In society, functions are not alike; there must be, then, different capacities. Further, — certain functions demand greater intelligence and powers; then there are people of superior mind and talent. For the performance of work necessarily involves a workman: from the need springs the idea, and the idea makes the producer. We only know what our senses long for and our intelligence demands; we have no keen desire for things of which we cannot conceive, and the greater our powers of conception, the greater our capabilities of production.

Thus, functions arising from needs, needs from desires, and desires from spontaneous perception and imagination, the same intelligence which imagines can also produce; consequently, no labor is superior to the laborer. In a word, if the function calls out the functionary, it is because the functionary exists before the function.

Let us admire Nature's economy. With regard to these various needs which she has given us, and which the isolated man cannot satisfy unaided, Nature has granted to the race a power refused to the individual. This gives rise to the principle of the *division of labor*, — a principle founded on the *speciality of vocations*.

The satisfaction of some needs demands of man continual creation; while others can, by the labor of a single individual, be satisfied for millions of men through thousands of centuries. For example, the need of clothing and food requires perpetual reproduction; while a knowledge of the system of the universe may be acquired for ever by two or three highly-gifted men. The perpetual current of rivers supports our commerce, and runs our machinery; but the sun, alone in the midst of space, gives light to the whole world. Nature, who might create Platos and Virgils, Newtons and Cuviers, as she creates husbandmen and shepherds, does not see fit to do so; choosing rather to proportion the rarity of genius to the duration of its products, and to balance the number of capacities by the competency of each one of them.

I do not inquire here whether the distance which separates one man from another, in point of talent and intelligence, arises from the deplorable condition of civilization, nor whether that which is now called the *inequality of powers* would be in an ideal society any thing more than a *diversity of powers*. I take the worst view of the matter; and, that I may not be accused of tergiversation and evasion of difficulties, I acknowledge all the inequalities that any one can desire.[17]

Certain philosophers, in love with the levelling idea, maintain that all minds are equal, and that all differences are the result of education. I am no believer, I confess, in this doctrine; which, even if it were true, would lead to a result directly opposite to that desired. For, if capacities are equal, whatever be the degree of their power (as no one can be coerced), there are functions deemed coarse, low, and degrading, which deserve higher pay, — a result no less repugnant to equality than to the principle, *to each capacity according to its results*. Give me, on the contrary, a society in which every kind of talent bears a proper numerical relation to the needs of the society, and which demands from each producer only that which his special function requires him to produce; and, without impairing in the least the hierarchy of functions, I will deduce the equality of fortunes.

This is my second point.

II. *Relations*. In considering the element of labor, I have shown that in the same class of productive services, the capacity to perform a social task being possessed by all, no inequality of reward can be based upon an inequality of individual powers. However, it is but fair to say that certain capacities seem quite incapable of certain services; so that, if human industry were entirely confined to one class of products, numerous incapacities would arise, and, consequently, the greatest social inequality. But every body sees, without any hint from me, that the variety of industries avoids this difficulty; so clear is this that I shall not stop to discuss it. We have only to prove, then, that functions are equal to each other; just as laborers, who perform the same function, are equal to each other. — — Property makes man a eunuch, and then reproaches him for being nothing but dry wood, a decaying tree.

Are you astonished that I refuse to genius, to knowledge, to courage, — in a word, to all the excellences admired by the world, — the homage of dignities, the distinctions of power and wealth? It is not I who refuse it: it is economy, it is justice, it is liberty. Liberty! for the first time in this discussion I appeal to her. Let her rise in her own defence, and achieve her victory.

Every transaction ending in an exchange of products or services may be designated as a *commercial operation*.

Whoever says commerce, says exchange of equal values; for, if the values are not equal, and the injured party perceives it, he will not consent to the exchange, and there will be no commerce.

Commerce exists only among free men. Transactions may be effected between other people by violence or fraud, but there is no commerce.

A free man is one who enjoys the use of his reason and his faculties; who is neither blinded by passion, nor hindered or driven by oppression, nor deceived by erroneous opinions.

So, in every exchange, there is a moral obligation that neither of the contracting parties shall gain at the expense of the other; that is, that, to be legitimate and true, commerce must be exempt from all inequality. This is the first condition of commerce. Its second condition is, that it be voluntary; that is, that the parties act freely and openly.

I define, then, commerce or exchange as an act of society.

The negro who sells his wife for a knife, his children for some bits of glass, and finally himself for a bottle of brandy, is not free. The dealer in human flesh, with whom he negotiates, is not his associate; he is his enemy.

The civilized laborer who bakes a loaf that he may eat a slice of bread, who builds a palace that he may sleep in a stable, who weaves rich fabrics that he may dress in rags, who produces every thing that he may dispense with every thing, — is not free. His employer, not becoming his associate in the exchange of salaries or services which takes place between them, is his enemy.

The soldier who serves his country through fear instead of through love is not free; his comrades and his officers, the ministers or organs of military justice, are all his enemies.

The peasant who hires land, the manufacturer who borrows capital, the tax-payer who pays tolls, duties, patent and license fees, personal and property taxes, &c., and the deputy who votes for them, — all act neither intelligently nor freely. Their enemies are the proprietors, the capitalists, the government.

Give men liberty, enlighten their minds that they may know the meaning of their contracts, and you will see the most perfect equality in exchanges without regard to superiority of talent and knowledge; and you will admit that in commercial affairs, that is, in the sphere of society, the word superiority is void of sense.

Let Homer sing his verse. I listen to this sublime genius in comparison with whom I, a simple herdsman, an humble farmer, am as nothing. What, indeed, — if product is to be compared with product, — are my cheeses and my beans in the presence of his "Iliad"? But, if Homer wishes to take from me all that I possess, and make me his slave in return for his inimitable poem, I will give up the pleasure of his lays, and dismiss him. I can do without his "Iliad," and wait, if necessary, for the "æneid." Homer cannot live twenty-four hours without my products. Let him accept, then, the little that I have to offer; and then his muse may instruct, encourage, and console me.

"What! do you say that such should be the condition of one who sings of gods and men? Alms, with the humiliation and suffering which they bring with them! — what barbarous generosity!" ... Do not get excited, I beg of you. Property makes of a poet either a Croesus or a beggar; only equality knows how to honor and to praise him. What is its duty? To regulate the right of the singer and the duty of the listener. Now, notice this point, which is a very important one in the solution of this question: both are free, the one to sell, the other to buy. Henceforth their respective pretensions go for nothing; and the estimate, whether fair or unfair, that they place, the one upon his verse, the other upon his liberality, can have no influence upon the conditions of the contract. We must no longer, in making our bargains, weigh talent; we must consider products only.

In order that the bard of Achilles may get his due reward, he must first make himself wanted: that done, the exchange of his verse for a fee of any kind, being a free act, must be at the same time a just act; that is, the poet's fee must be equal to his product. Now, what is the value of this product?

Let us suppose, in the first place, that this "Iliad" — this *chef-d' oeuvre* that is to be equitably rewarded — is really above price, that we do not know how to appraise it. If the public, who are free to purchase it, refuse to do so, it is clear that, the poem being unexchangeable, its intrinsic value will not be diminished; but that its exchangeable value, or its productive utility, will be reduced to zero, will be nothing at all. Then we must seek the amount of wages to be paid between infinity on the one hand and nothing on the other, at an equal distance from each, since all rights and liberties are entitled to equal respect; in other words, it is not the intrinsic value, but the relative value, of the thing sold that needs to be fixed. The question grows simpler: what is this rela tive value? To what reward does a poem like the "Iliad" entitle its author?

The first business of political economy, after fixing its definitions, was the solution of this problem; now, not only has it not been solved, but it has been declared insoluble. According to the economists, the relative or exchangeable value of things cannot be absolutely determined; it necessarily varies.

"The value of a thing," says Say, "is a positive quantity, but only for a given moment. It is its nature to perpetually vary, to change from one point to another. Nothing can fix it absolutely, because it is based on needs and means of production which vary with every moment. These variations complicate economical phenomena, and often render them very difficult of observation and solution. I know no remedy for this; it is not in our power to change the nature of things."

Elsewhere Say says, and repeats, that value being based on utility, and utility depending entirely on our needs, whims, customs, &c., value is as variable as opinion. Now, political economy being the science of values, of their production, distribution, exchange, and consumption, — if exchangeable value cannot be absolutely determined, how is political economy possible? How can it be a science? How can two economists look each other in the face without laughing? How dare they insult metaphysicians and psychologists? What! that fool of a Descartes imagined that philosophy needed an immovable base — an *aliquid inconcussum* — on which the edifice of science might be built, and he was simple enough to search for it! And the Hermes of economy, Trismegistus Say, devoting half a volume to the amplification of that solemn text, *political economy is a science*, has the courage to affirm immediately afterwards that this science cannot determine its object, — which is equivalent to saying that it is without a principle or foundation! He does not know, then, the illustrious Say, the nature of a science; or rather, he knows nothing of the subject which he discusses.

Say's example has borne its fruits. Political economy, as it exists at present, resembles ontology: discussing effects and causes, it knows nothing, explains nothing, decides nothing. The ideas honored with the name of economic laws are nothing more than a few trifling generalities, to which the economists thought to give an appearance of depth by clothing them in high-sounding words. As for the attempts that have been made by the economists to solve social problems, all that can be said of them is, that, if a glimmer of sense occasionally appears in their lucubrations, they immediately fall back into absurdity. For twenty-five years political economy, like a heavy fog, has weighed upon France, checking the efforts of the mind, and setting limits to liberty.

Has every creation of industry a venal, absolute, unchangeable, and consequently legitimate and true value? — Yes.

Can every product of man be exchanged for some other product of man? — Yes, again.

How many nails is a pair of shoes worth?

If we can solve this appalling problem, we shall have the key of the social system for which humanity has been searching for six thousand years. In the presence of this problem, the economist recoils confused; the peasant who can neither read nor write replies without hesitation: "As many as can be made in the same time, and with the same expense."

The absolute value of a thing, then, is its cost in time and expense. How much is a diamond worth which costs only the labor of picking it up? — Nothing; it is not a product of man. How much will it be worth when cut and mounted? — The time and expense which it has cost the laborer. Why, then, is it sold at so high a price? — Because men are not free. Society must regulate the exchange and distribution of the rarest things, as it does that of the most common ones, in such a way that each may share in the enjoyment of them. What, then, is that value which is based upon opinion? — Delusion, injustice, and robbery.

By this rule, it is easy to reconcile every body. If the mean term, which we are searching for, between an infinite value and no value at all is expressed in the case of every product, by the amount of time and expense which the product cost, a poem which has cost its author thirty years of labor and an outlay of ten thousand francs in journeys, books, &c., must be paid for by the ordinary wages received by a laborer during thirty years, *plus* ten thousand francs indemnity for expense incurred. Suppose the whole amount to be fifty thousand francs; if the society which gets the benefit of the production include a million of men, my share of the debt is five centimes.

This gives rise to a few observations.

1. The same product, at different times and in different places, may cost more or less of time and outlay; in this view, it is true that value is a variable quantity. But this variation is not that of the economists, who place in their list of the causes of the variation of values, not only the means of production, but taste, caprice, fashion, and opinion. In short,

489

the true value of a thing is invariable in its algebraic expression, although it may vary in its monetary expression.

2. The price of every product in demand should be its cost in time and outlay — neither more nor less: every product not in demand is a loss to the producer — a commercial non-value.

3. The ignorance of the principle of evaluation, and the difficulty under many circumstances of applying it, is the source of commercial fraud, and one of the most potent causes of the inequality of fortunes.

4. To reward certain industries and pay for certain products, a society is needed which corresponds in size with the rarity of talents, the costliness of the products, and the variety of the arts and sciences. If, for example, a society of fifty farmers can support a schoolmaster, it requires one hundred for a shoemaker, one hundred and fifty for a blacksmith, two hundred for a tailor, &c. If the number of farmers rises to one thousand, ten thousand, one hundred thousand, &c., as fast as their number increases, that of the functionaries which are earliest required must increase in the same proportion; so that the highest functions become possible only in the most powerful societies.[18] That is the peculiar feature of capacities; the character of genius, the seal of its glory, cannot arise and develop itself, except in the bosom of a great nation. But this physiological condition, necessary to the existence of genius, adds nothing to its social rights: far from that, — the delay in its appearance proves that, in economical and civil affairs, the loftiest intelligence must submit to the equality of possessions; an equality which is anterior to it, and of which it constitutes the crown.

This is severe on our pride, but it is an inexorable truth. And here psychology comes to the aid of social economy, giving us to understand that talent and material recompense have no common measure; that, in this respect, the condition of all producers is equal: consequently, that all comparison between them, and all distinction in fortunes, is impossible.

In fact, every work coming from the hands of man — compared with the raw material of which it is composed — is beyond price. In this respect, the distance is as great between a pair of wooden shoes and the trunk of a walnut-tree, as between a statue by Scopas and a block of marble. The genius of the simplest mechanic exerts as much influence over the materials which he uses, as does the mind of a Newton over the inert spheres whose distances, volumes, and revolutions he calculates. You ask for talent and genius a corresponding degree of honor and reward. Fix for me the value of a wood-cutter's talent, and I will fix that of Homer. If any thing can reward intelligence, it is intelligence itself. That is what happens, when various classes of producers pay to each other a reciprocal tribute of admiration and praise. But if they contemplate an exchange of products with a view to satisfying mutual needs, this exchange must be effected in accordance with a system of economy which is indifferent to considerations of talent and genius, and whose laws are deduced, not from vague and meaningless admiration, but from a just balance between *debit* and *credit;* in short, from commercial accounts.

Now, that no one may imagine that the liberty of buying and selling is the sole basis of the equality of wages, and that society's sole protection against superiority of talent lies in a certain force of inertia which has nothing in common with right, I shall proceed to explain why all capacities are entitled to the same reward, and why a corresponding difference in wages would be an injustice. I shall prove that the obligation to stoop to the social level is inherent in talent; and on this very superiority of genius I will found the equality of fortunes. I have just given the negative argument in favor of rewarding all capacities alike; I will now give the direct and positive argument.

Listen, first, to the economist: it is always pleasant to see how he reasons, and how he understands justice. Without him, moreover, without his amusing blunders and his wonderful arguments, we should learn nothing. Equality, so odious to the economist, owes every thing to political economy.

"When the parents of a physician [the text says a lawyer, which is not so good an example] have expended on his education forty thousand francs, this sum may be regarded as so much capital invested in his head. It is therefore permissible to consider it as yielding an annual income of four thousand francs. If the physician earns thirty thousand, there remains an income of twenty-six thousand francs due to the personal talents given him by Nature. This natural capital, then, if we assume ten per cent. as the rate of interest, amounts to two hundred and sixty thousand francs; and the capital given him by his parents, in defraying the expenses of his education, to forty thousand francs. The union of these two kinds of capital constitutes his fortune." — *Say: Complete Course, &c..*

Say divides the fortune of the physician into two parts: one is composed of the capital which went to pay for his education, the other represents his personal talents. This division is just; it is in conformity with the nature of things; it is universally admitted; it serves as the major premise of that grand argument which establishes the inequality of capacities. I accept this premise without qualification; let us look at the consequences.

1. Say *credits* the physician with forty thousand francs, — the cost of his education. This amount should be entered upon the *debit* side of the account. For, although this expense was incurred for him, it was not incurred by him. Then, instead of appropriating these forty thousand francs, the physician should add them to the price of his product, and repay them to those who are entitled to them. Notice, further, that Say speaks of *income* instead of *reimbursement;* reasoning on the false principle of the productivity of capital.

The expense of educating a talent is a debt contracted by this talent. From the very fact of its existence, it becomes a debtor to an amount equal to the cost of its production. This is so true and simple that, if the education of some one child in a family has cost double or triple that of its brothers, the latter are entitled to a proportional amount of the property previous to its division. There is no difficulty about this in the case of guardianship, when the estate is administered in the name of the minors.

2. That which I have just said of the obligation incurred by talent of repaying the cost of its education does not embarrass the economist. The man of talent, he says, inheriting from his family, inherits among other things a claim to the forty thousand francs which his education costs; and he becomes, in consequence, its proprietor. But this is to abandon the right of talent, and to fall back upon the right of occupancy; which again calls up all the questions asked in Chapter II. What is the right of occupancy? what is inheritance? Is the right of succession a right of accumulation or only a right of choice? how did the physician's father get his fortune? was he a proprietor, or only a usufructuary? If he was rich, let him account for his wealth; if he was poor, how could he incur so large an expense? If he received aid, what right had he to use that aid to the disadvantage of his benefactors, &c.?

3. "There remains an income of twenty-six thousand francs due to the personal talents given him by Nature." *(Say,* — as above quoted.) Reasoning from this premise, Say concludes that our physician's talent is equivalent to a capital of two hundred and sixty thousand francs. This skilful calculator mistakes a consequence for a principle. The talent must not be measured by the gain, but rather the gain by the talent; for it may happen, that, notwithstanding his merit, the physician in

492

question will gain nothing at all, in which case will it be necessary to conclude that his talent or fortune is equivalent to zero? To such a result, however, would Say's reasoning lead; a result which is clearly absurd.

Now, it is impossible to place a money value on any talent whatsoever, since talent and money have no common measure. On what plausible ground can it be maintained that a physician should be paid two, three, or a hundred times as much as a peasant? An unavoidable difficulty, which has never been solved save by avarice, necessity, and oppression. It is not thus that the right of talent should be determined. But how is it to be determined?

4. I say, first, that the physician must be treated with as much favor as any other producer, that he must not be placed below the level of others. This I will not stop to prove. But I add that neither must he be lifted above that level; because his talent is collective property for which he did not pay, and for which he is ever in debt.

Just as the creation of every instrument of production is the result of collective force, so also are a man's talent and knowledge the product of universal intelligence and of general knowledge slowly accumulated by a number of masters, and through the aid of many inferior industries. When the physician has paid for his teachers, his books, his diplomas, and all the other items of his educational expenses, he has no more paid for his talent than the capitalist pays for his house and land when he gives his employees their wages. The man of talent has contributed to the production in himself of a useful instrument. He has, then, a share in its possession; he is not its proprietor. There exist side by side in him a free laborer and an accumulated social capital. As a laborer, he is charged with the use of an instrument, with the superintendence of a machine; namely, his capacity. As capital, he is not his own master; he uses himself, not for his own benefit, but for that of others.

Even if talent did not find in its own excellence a reward for the sacrifices which it costs, still would it be easier to find reasons for lowering its reward than for raising it above the common level. Every producer receives an education; every laborer is a talent, a capacity, — that is, a piece of collective property. But all talents are not equally costly. It takes but few teachers, but few years, and but little study, to make a farmer or a mechanic: the generative effort and — if I may venture to use such language — the period of social gestation are proportional to the loftiness of the capacity. But while the physician,

493

the poet, the artist, and the *savant* produce but little, and that slowly, the productions of the farmer are much less uncertain, and do not require so long a time. Whatever be then the capacity of a man, — when this capacity is once created, — it does not belong to him. Like the material fashioned by an industrious hand, it had the power of *becoming*, and society has given it *being*. Shall the vase say to the potter, "I am that I am, and I owe you nothing"?

The artist, the *savant*, and the poet find their just recompense in the permission that society gives them to devote themselves exclusively to science and to art: so that in reality they do not labor for themselves, but for society, which creates them, and requires of them no other duty. Society can, if need be, do without prose and verse, music and painting, and the knowledge of the movements of the moon and stars; but it cannot live a single day without food and shelter.

Undoubtedly, man does not live by bread alone; he must, also (according to the Gospel), *live by the word of God;* that is, he must love the good and do it, know and admire the beautiful, and study the marvels of Nature. But in order to cultivate his mind, he must first take care of his body, — the latter duty is as necessary as the former is noble. If it is glorious to charm and instruct men, it is honorable as well to feed them. When, then, society — faithful to the principle of the division of labor — intrusts a work of art or of science to one of its members, allowing him to abandon ordinary labor, it owes him an indemnity for all which it prevents him from producing industrially; but it owes him nothing more. If he should demand more, society should, by refusing his services, annihilate his pretensions. Forced, then, in order to live, to devote himself to labor repugnant to his nature, the man of genius would feel his weakness, and would live the most distasteful of lives.

They tell of a celebrated singer who demanded of the Empress of Russia (Catherine II.) twenty thousand roubles for his services: "That is more than I give my field-marshals," said Catherine. "Your majesty," replied the other, "has only to make singers of her field-marshals."

If France (more powerful than Catherine II.) should say to Mademoiselle Rachel, "You must act for one hundred louis, or else spin cotton;" to M. Duprez, "You must sing for two thousand four hundred francs, or else work in the vineyard," — do you think that the actress Rachel, and the singer Duprez, would abandon the stage? If they did, they would be the first to repent it.

Mademoiselle Rachel receives, they say, sixty thousand francs annually from the Comédie-Française. For a talent like hers, it is a slight fee. Why not one hundred thousand francs, two hundred thousand francs? Why! not a civil list? What meanness! Are we really guilty of chaffering with an artist like Mademoiselle Rachel?

It is said, in reply, that the managers of the theatre cannot give more without incurring a loss; that they admit the superior talent of their young associate; but that, in fixing her salary, they have been compelled to take the account of the company's receipts and expenses into consideration also.

That is just, but it only confirms what I have said; namely, that an artist's talent may be infinite, but that its mercenary claims are necessarily limited, — on the one hand, by its usefulness to the society which rewards it; on the other, by the resources of this society: in other words, that the demand of the seller is balanced by the right of the buyer.

Mademoiselle Rachel, they say, brings to the treasury of the Théâtre-Français more than sixty thousand francs. I admit it; but then I blame the theatre. From whom does the Théâtre-Français take this money? From some curious people who are perfectly free. Yes; but the workingmen, the lessees, the tenants, those who borrow by pawning their possessions, from whom these curious people recover all that they pay to the theatre, — are they free? And when the better part of their products are consumed by others at the play, do you assure me that their families are not in want? Until the French people, reflecting on the salaries paid to all artists, *savants*, and public functionaries, have plainly expressed their wish and judgment as to the matter, the salaries of Mademoiselle Rachel and all her fellow-artists will be a compulsory tax extorted by violence, to reward pride, and support libertinism.

It is because we are neither free nor sufficiently enlightened, that we submit to be cheated in our bargains; that the laborer pays the duties levied by the prestige of power and the selfishness of talent upon the curiosity of the idle, and that we are perpetually scandalized by these monstrous inequalities which are encouraged and applauded by public opinion.

The whole nation, and the nation only, pays its authors, its *savants*, its artists, its officials, whatever be the hands through which their salaries pass. On what basis should it pay them? On the basis of equality. I have proved it by estimating the value of talent. I shall confirm it in the following chapter, by proving the impossibility of all social inequality.

What have we shown so far? Things so simple that really they seem silly: —

That, as the traveller does not appropriate the route which he traverses, so the farmer does not appropriate the field which he sows;

That if, nevertheless, by reason of his industry, a laborer may appropriate the material which he employs, every employer of material becomes, by the same title, a proprietor;

That all capital, whether material or mental, being the result of collective labor, is, in consequence, collective property;

That the strong have no right to encroach upon the labor of the weak, nor the shrewd to take advantage of the credulity of the simple;

Finally, that no one can be forced to buy that which he does not want, still less to pay for that which he has not bought; and, consequently, that the exchangeable value of a product, being measured neither by the opinion of the buyer nor that of the seller, but by the amount of time and outlay which it has cost, the property of each always remains the same.

Are not these very simple truths? Well, as simple as they seem to you, reader, you shall yet see others which surpass them in dullness and simplicity. For our course is the reverse of that of the geometricians: with them, the farther they advance, the more difficult their problems become; we, on the contrary, after having commenced with the most abstruse propositions, shall end with the axioms.

But I must close this chapter with an exposition of one of those startling truths which never have been dreamed of by legists or economists.

§ 8. — *That, from the Stand-point of Justice, Labor destroys Property.*

This proposition is the logical result of the two preceding sections, which we have just summed up.

The isolated man can supply but a very small portion of his wants; all his power lies in association, and in the intelligent combination of universal effort. The division and co-operation of labor multiply the quantity and the variety of products; the individuality of functions improves their quality.

There is not a man, then, but lives upon the products of several thousand different industries; not a laborer but receives from society at large the things which he consumes, and, with these, the power to reproduce. Who, indeed, would venture the assertion, "I produce, by my own effort, all that I consume; I need the aid of no one else"? The farmer, whom the early economists regarded as the only real producer — the farmer, housed, furnished, clothed, fed, and assisted by the mason, the carpenter, the tailor, the miller, the baker, the butcher, the grocer, the blacksmith, &c., — the farmer, I say, can he boast that he produces by his own unaided effort?

The various articles of consumption are given to each by all; consequently, the production of each involves the production of all. One product cannot exist without another; an isolated industry is an impossible thing. What would be the harvest of the farmer, if others did not manufacture for him barns, wagons, ploughs, clothes, &c.? Where would be the *savant* without the publisher; the printer without the typecaster and the machinist; and these, in their turn, without a multitude of other industries? ... Let us not prolong this catalogue — so easy to extend — lest we be accused of uttering commonplaces. All industries are united by mutual relations in a single group; all productions do reciprocal service as means and end; all varieties of talent are but a series of changes from the inferior to the superior.

Now, this undisputed and indisputable fact of the general participation in every species of product makes all individual productions common; so that every product, coming from the hands of the producer, is mortgaged in advance by society. The producer himself is entitled to only that portion of his product, which is expressed by a fraction whose denominator is equal to the number of individuals of which society is composed. It is true that in return this same producer has a share in all the products of others, so that he has a claim upon all, just as all have a claim upon him; but is it not clear that this reciprocity of mortgages, far from authorizing property, destroys even possession? The laborer is not even possessor of his product; scarcely has he finished it, when society claims it.

"But," it will be answered, "even if that is so — even if the product does not belong to the producer — still society gives each laborer an equivalent for his product; and this equivalent, this salary, this reward, this allowance, becomes his property. Do you deny that this property is legitimate?

And if the laborer, instead of consuming his entire wages, chooses to economize, — who dare question his right to do so?"

The laborer is not even proprietor of the price of his labor, and cannot absolutely control its disposition. Let us not be blinded by a spurious justice. That which is given the laborer in exchange for his product is not given him as a reward for past labor, but to provide for and secure future labor. We consume before we produce. The laborer may say at the end of the day, "I have paid yesterday's expenses; to-morrow I shall pay those of today." At every moment of his life, the member of society is in debt; he dies with the debt unpaid: — how is it possible for him to accumulate?

They talk of economy — it is the proprietor's hobby. Under a system of equality, all economy which does not aim at subsequent reproduction or enjoyment is impossible — why? Because the thing saved, since it cannot be converted into capital, has no object, and is without a *final cause*. This will be explained more fully in the next chapter.

To conclude: —

The laborer, in his relation to society, is a debtor who of necessity dies insolvent. The proprietor is an unfaithful guardian who denies the receipt of the deposit committed to his care, and wishes to be paid for his guardianship down to the last day.

Lest the principles just set forth may appear to certain readers too metaphysical, I shall reproduce them in a more concrete form, intelligible to the dullest brains, and pregnant with the most important consequences.

Hitherto, I have considered property as a power of *exclusion;* hereafter, I shall examine it as a power of *invasion.*

498

Chapter IV. That Property Is Impossible.

The last resort of proprietors, — the overwhelming argument whose invincible potency reassures them, — is that, in their opinion, equality of conditions is impossible. "Equality of conditions is a chimera," they cry with a knowing air; "distribute wealth equally to-day — to-morrow this equality will have vanished."

To this hackneyed objection, which they repeat everywhere with the most marvellous assurance, they never fail to add the following comment, as a sort of *Glory be to the Father*: "If all men were equal, nobody would work." This anthem is sung with variations.

"If all were masters, nobody would obey."

"If nobody were rich, who would employ the poor?"

And, "If nobody were poor, who would labor for the rich?"

But let us have done with invective — we have better arguments at our command.

If I show that property itself is impossible — that it is property which is a contradiction, a chimera, a utopia; and if I show it no longer by metaphysics and jurisprudence, but by figures, equations, and calculations, — imagine the fright of the astounded proprietor! And you, reader; what do you think of the retort?

Numbers govern the world — *mundum regunt numeri*. This proverb applies as aptly to the moral and political, as to the sidereal and molecular, world. The elements of justice are identical with those of algebra; legislation and government are simply the arts of classifying and balancing powers; all jurisprudence falls within the rules of arithmetic. This chapter and the next will serve to lay the foundations of this extraordinary doctrine. Then will be unfolded to the reader's vision an immense and novel career; then shall we commence to see in numerical relations the synthetic unity of philosophy and the sciences; and, filled with admiration and enthusiasm for this profound and majestic simplicity of Nature, we shall shout with the apostle: "Yes, the Eternal has made all things by number, weight, and measure!" We shall understand not only that equality of conditions is possible, but that all else is impossible; that this seeming impossibility which we charge upon it arises from the fact that we always think of it in connection either with the proprietary or the communistic *régime*, — political systems equally irreconcilable with human nature. We shall see finally that equality is constantly being realized without our knowledge, even at the very moment when we are pronouncing it incapable of realization; that the time draws near when, without any effort or even wish of ours, we shall have it universally established; that with it, in it, and by it, the natural and true political order must make itself manifest.

It has been said, in speaking of the blindness and obstinacy of the passions, that, if man had any thing to gain by denying the truths of arithmetic, he would find some means of unsettling their certainty: here is an opportunity to try this curious experiment. I attack property, no longer with its own maxims, but with arithmetic. Let the proprietors prepare to verify my figures; for, if unfortunately for them the figures prove accurate, the proprietors are lost.

In proving the impossibility of property, I complete the proof of its injustice. In fact, —

That which is *just* must be *useful;*

That which is useful must be *true;*

That which is true must be *possible;*

Therefore, every thing which is impossible is untrue, useless, unjust. Then, — *a priori,* — we may judge of the justice of any thing by its possibility; so that if the thing were absolutely impossible, it would be absolutely unjust.

Property is physically and mathematically impossible.

Demonstration.

Axiom. — *Property is the Right of Increase claimed by the Proprietor over any thing which he has stamped as his own.*

This proposition is purely an axiom, because, —

1. It is not a definition, since it does not express all that is included in the right of property — the right of sale, of exchange, of gift; the right to transform, to alter, to consume, to destroy, to use and abuse, &c. All

these rights are so many different powers of property, which we may consider separately; but which we disregard here, that we may devote all our attention to this single one, — the right of increase.

2. It is universally admitted. No one can deny it without denying the facts, without being instantly belied by universal custom.

3. It is self-evident, since property is always accompanied (either actually or potentially) by the fact which this axiom expresses; and through this fact, mainly, property manifests, establishes, and asserts itself.

4. Finally, its negation involves a contradiction. The right of increase is really an inherent right, so essential a part of property, that, in its absence, property is null and void.

Observations. — Increase receives different names according to the thing by which it is yielded: if by land, *farm-rent;* if by houses and furniture, *rent;* if by life-investments, *revenue;* if by money, *interest;* if by exchange, *advantage gain, profit* (three things which must not be confounded with the wages or legitimate price of labor).

Increase — a sort of royal prerogative, of tangible and consumable homage — is due to the proprietor on account of his nominal and metaphysical occupancy. His seal is set upon the thing; that is enough to prevent any one else from occupying it without *his* permission.

This permission to use his things the proprietor may, if he chooses, freely grant. Commonly he sells it. This sale is really a stellionate and an extortion; but by the legal fiction of the right of property, this same sale, severely punished, we know not why, in other cases, is a source of profit and value to the proprietor.

The amount demanded by the proprietor, in payment for this permission, is expressed in monetary terms by the dividend which the supposed product yields in nature. So that, by the right of increase, the proprietor reaps and does not plough; gleans and does not till; consumes and does not produce; enjoys and does not labor. Very different from the idols of the Psalmist are the gods of property: the former had hands and felt not; the latter, on the contrary, *manus habent et palpabunt.*

501

The right of increase is conferred in a very mysterious and supernatural manner. The inauguration of a proprietor is accompanied by the awful ceremonies of an ancient initiation. First, comes the *consecration* of the article; a consecration which makes known to all that they must offer up a suitable sacrifice to the proprietor, whenever they wish, by his permission obtained and signed, to use his article.

Second, comes the *anathema*, which prohibits — except on the conditions aforesaid — all persons from touching the article, even in the proprietor's absence; and pronounces every violator of property sacrilegious, infamous, amenable to the secular power, and deserving of being handed over to it.

Finally, the *dedication*, which enables the proprietor or patron saint — the god chosen to watch over the article — to inhabit it mentally, like a divinity in his sanctuary. By means of this dedication, the substance of the article — so to speak — becomes converted into the person of the proprietor, who is regarded as ever present in its form.

This is exactly the doctrine of the writers on jurisprudence. "Property," says Toullier, "is a *moral quality* inherent in a thing; *an actual bond* which fastens it to the proprietor, and which cannot be broken save by his act." Locke humbly doubted whether God could make matter *intelligent*. Toullier asserts that the proprietor renders it *moral*. How much does he lack of being a God? These are by no means exaggerations.

Property is the right of increase; that is, the power to produce without labor. Now, to produce without labor is to make something from nothing; in short, to create. Surely it is no more difficult to do this than to moralize matter. The jurists are right, then, in applying to proprietors this passage from the Scriptures, — *Ego dixi: Dii estis et filii Excelsi omnes,* — "I have said, Ye are gods; and all of you are children of the Most High."

Property is the right of increase. To us this axiom shall be like the name of the beast in the Apocalypse, — a name in which is hidden the complete explanation of the whole mystery of this beast. It was known that he who should solve the mystery of this name would obtain a knowledge of the whole prophecy, and would succeed in mastering the beast. Well! by the most careful interpretation of our axiom we shall kill the sphinx of property. Starting from this eminently characteristic fact — the *right of increase* — we shall pursue the old serpent through his coils; we shall count the murderous entwinings of this frightful tænia, whose head, with its thousand suckers, is always hidden from the sword of its most violent enemies, though abandoning to them immense fragments of its body. It requires something more than courage to subdue this monster. It was written that it should not die until a proletaire, armed with a magic wand, had fought with it.

Corollaries

1. *The amount of increase is proportional to the thing increased.* Whatever be the rate of interest, — whether it rise to three, five, or ten per cent., or fall to one-half, one-fourth, one-tenth, — it does not matter; the law of increase remains the same. The law is as follows: —

All capital — the cash value of which can be estimated — may be considered as a term in an arithmetical series which progresses in the ratio of one hundred, and the revenue yielded by this capital as the corresponding term of another arithmetical series which progresses in a ratio equal to the rate of interest. Thus, a capital of five hundred francs being the fifth term of the arithmetical progression whose ratio is one hundred, its revenue at three per cent. will be indicated by the fifth term of the arithmetical progression whose ratio is three: — 100 . 200 . 300 . 400 . 500. 3 . 6 . 9 . 12 . 15.

An acquaintance with this sort of *logarithms* — tables of which, calculated to a very high degree, are possessed by proprietors — will give us the key to the most puzzling problems, and cause us to experience a series of surprises.

By this *logarithmic* theory of the right of increase, a piece of property, together with its income, may be defined as *a number whose logarithm is equal to the sum of its units divided by one hundred, and multiplied by the rate of interest.* For instance; a house valued at one hundred thousand francs, and leased at five per cent., yields a revenue of five thousand francs, according to the formula $100,000 \times 5 / 100 =$ five thousand. *vice versa,* a piece of land which yields, at two and a half per cent., a revenue of three thousand francs is worth one hundred and twenty thousand francs, according to this other formula; $3,000 \times 100 / 2 \ 1/2 =$ one hundred and twenty thousand.

In the first case, the ratio of the progression which marks the increase of interest is five; in the second, it is two and a half.

Observation. — The forms of increase known as farm-rent, income, and interest are paid annually; rent is paid by the week, the month, or the year; profits and gains are paid at the time of exchange. Thus, the amount of increase is proportional both to the thing increased, and the time during which it increases; in other words, usury grows like a cancer — *foenus serpit sicut cancer*.

2. *The increase paid to the proprietor by the occupant is a dead loss to the latter.* For if the proprietor owed, in exchange for the increase which he receives, some thing more than the permission which he grants, his right of property would not be perfect — he would not possess *jure optimo, jure perfecto;* that is, he would not be in reality a proprietor. Then, all which passes from the hands of the occupant into those of the proprietor in the name of increase, and as the price of the permission to occupy, is a permanent gain for the latter, and a dead loss and annihilation for the former; to whom none of it will return, save in the forms of gift, alms, wages paid for his services, or the price of merchandise which he has delivered. In a word, increase perishes so far as the borrower is concerned; or to use the more energetic Latin phrase, — *res perit solventi.*

3. *The right of increase oppresses the proprietor as well as the stranger.* The master of a thing, as its proprietor, levies a tax for the use of his property upon himself as its possessor, equal to that which he would receive from a third party; so that capital bears interest in the hands of the capitalist, as well as in those of the borrower and the *commandité.* If, indeed, rather than accept a rent of five hundred francs for my apartment, I prefer to occupy and enjoy it, it is clear that I shall become my own debtor for a rent equal to that which I deny myself. This principle is universally practised in business, and is regarded as an axiom by the economists. Manufacturers, also, who have the advantage of being proprietors of their floating capital, although they owe no interest to any one, in calculating their profits subtract from them, not only their running expenses and the wages of their employees, but also the interest on their capital. For the same reason, money-lenders retain in their own possession as little money as possible; for, since all capital necessarily bears interest, if this interest is supplied by no one, it comes out of the capital, which is to that extent diminished. Thus, by the right of increase, capital eats itself up. This is, doubtless, the idea that Papinius intended to convey in the phrase, as elegant as it is forcible — *Foenus mordet solidam.* I beg pardon for using Latin so frequently in discussing this subject; it is an homage which I pay to the most usurious nation that ever existed.

First Proposition. *Property is impossible, because it demands Something for Nothing.*

The discussion of this proposition covers the same ground as that of the origin of farm-rent, which is so much debated by the economists. When I read the writings of the greater part of these men, I cannot avoid a feeling of contempt mingled with anger, in view of this mass of nonsense, in which the detestable vies with the absurd. It would be a repetition of the story of the elephant in the moon, were it not for the atrocity of the consequences. To seek a rational and legitimate origin of that which is, and ever must be, only robbery, extortion, and plunder — that must be the height of the proprietor's folly; the last degree of bedevilment into which minds, otherwise judicious, can be thrown by the perversity of selfishness.

"A farmer," says Say, "is a wheat manufacturer who, among other tools which serve him in modifying the material from which he makes the wheat, employs one large tool, which we call a field. If he is not the proprietor of the field, if he is only a tenant, he pays the proprietor for the productive service of this tool. The tenant is reimbursed by the purchaser, the latter by another, until the product reaches the consumer; who redeems the first payment, *plus* all the others, by means of which the product has at last come into his hands."

Let us lay aside the subsequent payments by which the product reaches the consumer, and, for the present, pay attention only to the first one of all, — the rent paid to the proprietor by the tenant. On what ground, we ask, is the proprietor entitled to this rent?

According to Ricardo, MacCulloch, and Mill, farm-rent, properly speaking, is simply the *excess of the product of the most fertile land over that of lands of an inferior quality;* so that farm-rent is not demanded for the former until the increase of population renders necessary the cultivation of the latter.

It is difficult to see any sense in this. How can a right to the land be based upon a difference in the quality of the land? How can varieties of soil engender a principle of legislation and politics? This reasoning is either so subtle, or so stupid, that the more I think of it, the more bewildered I become. Suppose two pieces of land of equal area; the one, A, capable of supporting ten thousand inhabitants; the other, B, capable of supporting nine thousand only: when, owing to an increase in their number, the inhabitants of A shall be forced to cultivate B, the landed proprietors of A will exact from their tenants in A a rent

505

proportional to the difference between ten and nine. So say, I think, Ricardo, Macculloch, and Mill. But if A supports as many inhabitants as it can contain, — that is, if the inhabitants of A, by our hypothesis, have only just enough land to keep them alive, — how can they pay farm-rent?

If they had gone no farther than to say that the difference in land has *occasioned* farm-rent, instead of *caused* it, this observation would have taught us a valuable lesson; namely, that farm-rent grew out of a desire for equality. Indeed, if all men have an equal right to the possession of good land, no one can be forced to cultivate bad land without indemnification. Farm-rent — according to Ricardo, Macculloch, and Mill — would then have been a compensation for loss and hardship. This system of practical equality is a bad one, no doubt; but it sprang from good intentions. What argument can Ricardo, Maculloch [sic] , and Mill develop therefrom in favor of property? Their theory turns against themselves, and strangles them.

Malthus thinks that farm-rent has its source in the power possessed by land of producing more than is necessary to supply the wants of the men who cultivate it. I would ask Malthus why successful labor should entitle the idle to a portion of the products?

But the worthy Malthus is mistaken in regard to the fact. Yes; land has the power of producing more than is needed by those who cultivate it, if by *cultivators* is meant tenants only. The tailor also makes more clothes than he wears, and the cabinet-maker more furniture than he uses. But, since the various professions imply and sustain one another, not only the farmer, but the followers of all arts and trades — even to the doctor and the school-teacher — are, and ought to be, regarded as *cultivators of the land*. Malthus bases farm-rent upon the principle of commerce. Now, the fundamental law of commerce being equivalence of the products exchanged, any thing which destroys this equivalence violates the law. There is an error in the estimate which needs to be corrected.

Buchanan — a commentator on Smith — regarded farm-rent as the result of a monopoly, and maintained that labor alone is productive. Consequently, he thought that, without this monopoly, products would rise in price; and he found no basis for farm-rent save in the civil law. This opinion is a corollary of that which makes the civil law the basis of property. But why has the civil law — which ought to be the written expression of justice — authorized this monopoly? Whoever says monopoly, necessarily excludes justice. Now, to say that farm-rent is a monopoly sanctioned by the law, is to say that injustice is based on justice, — a contradiction in terms.

Say answers Buchanan, that the proprietor is not a monopolist, because a monopolist "is one who does not increase the utility of the merchandise which passes through his hands."

How much does the proprietor increase the utility of his tenant's products? Has he ploughed, sowed, reaped, mowed, winnowed, weeded? These are the processes by which the tenant and his employees increase the utility of the material which they consume for the purpose of reproduction.

"The landed proprietor increases the utility of products by means of his implement, the land. This implement receives in one state, and returns in another the materials of which wheat is composed. The action of the land is a chemical process, which so modifies the material that it multiplies it by destroying it. The soil is then a producer of utility; and when it [the soil?] asks its pay in the form of profit, or farm rent, for its proprietor, it at the same time gives something to the consumer in exchange for the amount which the consumer pays it. It gives him a produced utility; and it is the production of this utility which warrants us in calling land productive, as well as labor."

Let us clear up this matter.

The blacksmith who manufactures for the farmer implements of husbandry, the wheelwright who makes him a cart, the mason who builds his barn, the carpenter, the basket-maker, &c., — all of whom contribute to agricultural production by the tools which they provide, — are producers of utility; consequently, they are entitled to a part of the products.

"Undoubtedly," says Say; "but the land also is an implement whose service must be paid for, then..."

I admit that the land is an implement; but who made it? Did the proprietor? Did he — by the efficacious virtue of the right of property, by this *moral quality* infused into the soil — endow it with vigor and fertility? Exactly there lies the monopoly of the proprietor; in the fact that, though he did not make the implement, he asks pay for its use. When the Creator shall present himself and claim farm-rent, we will consider the matter with him; or even when the proprietor — his pretended representative — shall exhibit his power-of-attorney.

"The proprietor's service," adds Say, "is easy, I admit."

It is a frank confession.

"But we cannot disregard it. Without property, one farmer would contend with another for the possession of a field without a proprietor, and the field would remain uncultivated..."

Then the proprietor's business is to reconcile farmers by robbing them. O logic! O justice! O the marvellous wisdom of economists! The proprietor, if they are right, is like Perrin-Dandin who, when summoned by two travellers to settle a dispute about an oyster, opened it, gobbled it, and said to them: —

"The Court awards you each a shell."

Could any thing worse be said of property?

Will Say tell us why the same farmers, who, if there were no proprietors, would contend with each other for possession of the soil, do not contend to-day with the proprietors for this possession? Obviously, because they think them legitimate possessors, and because their respect for even an imaginary right exceeds their avarice. I proved, in Chapter II., that possession is sufficient, without property, to maintain social order. Would it be more difficult, then, to reconcile possessors without masters than tenants controlled by proprietors? Would laboring men, who respect — much to their own detriment — the pretended rights of the idler, violate the natural rights of the producer and the manufacturer? What! if the husbandman forfeited his right to the land as soon as he ceased to occupy it, would he become more covetous? And would the impossibility of demanding increase, of taxing another's labor, be a source of quarrels and law-suits? The economists use singular logic. But we are not yet through. Admit that the proprietor is the legitimate master of the land.

"The land is an instrument of production," they say. That is true. But when, changing the noun into an adjective, they alter the phrase, thus, "The land is a productive instrument," they make a wicked blunder.

According to Quesnay and the early economists, all production comes from the land. Smith, Ricardo, and de Tracy, on the contrary, say that labor is the sole agent of production. Say, and most of his successors, teach that *both* land *and* labor *and* capital are productive. The latter constitute the eclectic school of political economy. The truth is, that *neither* land *nor* labor *nor* capital is productive. Production results from the co-operation of these three equally necessary elements, which, taken separately, are equally sterile.

Political economy, indeed, treats of the production, distribution, and consumption of wealth or values. But of what values? Of the values produced by human industry; that is, of the changes made in matter by man, that he may appropriate it to his own use, and not at all of Nature's spontaneous productions. Man's labor consists in a simple laying on of hands. When he has taken that trouble, he has produced a value. Until then, the salt of the sea, the water of the springs, the grass of the fields, and the trees of the forests are to him as if they were not. The sea, without the fisherman and his line, supplies no fish. The forest, without the wood-cutter and his axe, furnishes neither fuel nor timber.

The meadow, without the mower, yields neither hay nor aftermath. Nature is a vast mass of material to be cultivated and converted into products; but Nature produces nothing for herself: in the economical sense, her products, in their relation to man, are not yet products.

Capital, tools, and machinery are likewise unproductive. The hammer and the anvil, without the blacksmith and the iron, do not forge. The mill, without the miller and the grain, does not grind, &c. Bring tools and raw material together; place a plough and some seed on fertile soil; enter a smithy, light the fire, and shut up the shop, — you will produce nothing. The following remark was made by an economist who possessed more good sense than most of his fellows: "Say credits capital with an active part unwarranted by its nature; left to itself, it is an idle tool." (*J. Droz: Political Economy*.)

Finally, labor and capital together, when unfortunately combined, produce nothing. Plough a sandy desert, beat the water of the rivers, pass type through a sieve, — you will get neither wheat, nor fish, nor books. Your trouble will be as fruitless as was the immense labor of the army of Xerxes; who, as Herodotus says, with his three million soldiers, scourged the Hellespont for twenty-four hours, as a punishment for having broken and scattered the pontoon bridge which the great king had thrown across it.

509

Tools and capital, land and labor, considered individually and abstractly, are not, literally speaking, productive. The proprietor who asks to be rewarded for the use of a tool, or the productive power of his land, takes for granted, then, that which is radically false; namely, that capital produces by its own effort, — and, in taking pay for this imaginary product, he literally receives something for nothing.

Objection. — But if the blacksmith, the wheelwright, all manufacturers in short, have a right to the products in return for the implements which they furnish; and if land is an implement of production, — why does not this implement entitle its proprietor, be his claim real or imaginary, to a portion of the products; as in the case of the manufacturers of ploughs and wagons?

Reply. — Here we touch the heart of the question, the mystery of property; which we must clear up, if we would understand any thing of the strange effects of the right of increase.

He who manufactures or repairs the farmer's tools receives the price *once*, either at the time of delivery, or in several payments; and when this price is once paid to the manufacturer, the tools which he has delivered belong to him no more. Never does he claim double payment for the same tool, or the same job of repairs. If he annually shares in the products of the farmer, it is owing to the fact that he annually makes something for the farmer.

The proprietor, on the contrary, does not yield his implement; eternally he is paid for it, eternally he keeps it.

In fact, the rent received by the proprietor is not intended to defray the expense of maintaining and repairing the implement; this expense is charged to the borrower, and does not concern the proprietor except as he is interested in the preservation of the article. If he takes it upon himself to attend to the repairs, he takes care that the money which he expends for this purpose is repaid.

This rent does not represent the product of the implement, since of itself the implement produces nothing; we have just proved this, and we shall prove it more clearly still by its consequences.

Finally, this rent does not represent the participation of the proprietor in the production; since this participation could consist, like that of the blacksmith and the wheelwright, only in the surrender of the whole or a part of his implement, in which case he would cease to be its proprietor, which would involve a contradiction of the idea of property.

Then, between the proprietor and his tenant there is no exchange either of values or services; then, as our axiom says, farm-rent is real increase, — an extortion based solely upon fraud and violence on the one hand, and weakness and ignorance upon the other. *Products* say the economists, *are bought only by products*. This maxim is property's condemnation. The proprietor, producing neither by his own labor nor by his implement, and receiving products in exchange for nothing, is either a parasite or a thief. Then, if property can exist only as a right, property is impossible.

Corollaries. — 1. The republican constitution of 1793, which defined property as "the right to enjoy the fruit of one's labor," was grossly mistaken. It should have said, "Property is the right to enjoy and dispose at will of another's goods, — the fruit of another's industry and labor."

2. Every possessor of lands, houses, furniture, machinery, tools, money, &c., who lends a thing for a price exceeding the cost of repairs (the repairs being charged to the lender, and representing products which he exchanges for other products), is guilty of swindling and extortion. In short, all rent received (nominally as damages, but really as payment for a loan) is an act of property, — a robbery.

Historical Comment. — The tax which a victorious nation levies upon a conquered nation is genuine farm-rent. The seigniorial rights abolished by the Revolution of 1789, — tithes, mortmain, statute-labor, &c., — were different forms of the rights of property; and they who under the titles of nobles, seigneurs, prebendaries, &c. enjoyed these rights, were neither more nor less than proprietors. To defend property to-day is to condemn the Revolution.

Second Proposition. *Property is impossible because wherever it exists Production costs more than it is worth.*

The preceding proposition was legislative in its nature; this one is economical. It serves to prove that property, which originates in violence, results in waste.

"Production," says Say, "is exchange on a large scale. To render the exchange productive the value of the whole amount of service must be

511

balanced by the value of the product. If this condition is not complied with, the exchange is unequal; the producer gives more than he receives."

Now, value being necessarily based upon utility, it follows that every useless product is necessarily valueless, — that it cannot be exchanged; and, consequently, that it cannot be given in payment for productive services.

Then, though production may equal consumption, it never can exceed it; for there is no real production save where there is a production of utility, and there is no utility save where there is a possibility of consumption. Thus, so much of every product as is rendered by excessive abundance inconsumable, becomes useless, valueless, unexchangeable, — consequently, unfit to be given in payment for any thing whatever, and is no longer a product.

Consumption, on the other hand, to be legitimate, — to be true consumption, — must be reproductive of utility; for, if it is unproductive, the products which it destroys are cancelled values — things produced at a pure loss; a state of things which causes products to depreciate in value. Man has the power to destroy, but he consumes only that which he reproduces. Under a right system of economy, there is then an equation between production and consumption.

These points established, let us suppose a community of one thousand families, enclosed in a territory of a given circumference, and deprived of foreign intercourse. Let this community represent the human race, which, scattered over the face of the earth, is really isolated. In fact, the difference between a community and the human race being only a numerical one, the economical results will be absolutely the same in each case.

Suppose, then, that these thousand families, devoting themselves exclusively to wheat-culture, are obliged to pay to one hundred individuals, chosen from the mass, an annual revenue of ten per cent. on their product. It is clear that, in such a case, the right of increase is equivalent to a tax levied in advance upon social production. Of what use is this tax?

It cannot be levied to supply the community with provisions, for between that and farm-rent there is nothing in common; nor to pay for services and products, — for the proprietors, laboring like the others, have labored only for themselves. Finally, this tax is of no use to its recipients who, having harvested wheat enough for their own consumption, and not being able in a society without commerce and manufactures to procure any thing else in exchange for it, thereby lose the advantage of their income.

In such a society, one-tenth of the product being inconsumable, one-tenth of the labor goes unpaid — production costs more than it is worth.

Now, change three hundred of our wheat-producers into artisans of all kinds: one hundred gardeners and wine-growers, sixty shoemakers and tailors, fifty carpenters and blacksmiths, eighty of various professions, and, that nothing may be lacking, seven school-masters, one mayor, one judge, and one priest; each industry furnishes the whole community with its special product. Now, the total production being one thousand, each laborer's consumption is one; namely, wheat, meat, and grain, 0.7; wine and vegetables, 0.1; shoes and clothing, 0.06; iron-work and furniture, 0.05; sundries, 0.08; instruction, 0.007; administration, 0.002; mass, 0.001, Total 1.

But the community owes a revenue of ten per cent.; and it matters little whether the farmers alone pay it, or all the laborers are responsible for it, — the result is the same. The farmer raises the price of his products in proportion to his share of the debt; the other laborers follow his example. Then, after some fluctuations, equilibrium is established, and all pay nearly the same amount of the revenue. It would be a grave error to assume that in a nation none but farmers pay farm-rent — the whole nation pays it.

I say, then, that by this tax of ten per cent. each laborer's consumption is reduced as follows: wheat, 0.63; wine and vegetables, 0.09; clothing and shoes, 0.054; furniture and iron-work, 0.045; other products, 0.072; schooling, 0.0063; administration, 0.0018; mass, 0.0009. Total 0.9.

The laborer has produced 1; he consumes only 0.9. He loses, then, one-tenth of the price of his labor; his production still costs more than it is worth. On the other hand, the tenth received by the proprietors is no less a waste; for, being laborers themselves, they, like the others, possess in the nine-tenths of their product the wherewithal to live: they want for nothing. Why should they wish their proportion of bread, wine, meat, clothes, shelter, &c., to be doubled, if they can neither consume nor exchange them? Then farm-rent, with them as with the rest of the laborers, is a waste, and perishes in their hands. Extend the hypothesis, increase the number and variety of the products, you still have the same result.

Hitherto, we have considered the proprietor as taking part in the production, not only (as Say says) by the use of his instrument, but in an effective manner and by the labor of his hands. Now, it is easy to see that, under such circumstances, property will never exist. What happens?

The proprietor — an essentially libidinous animal, without virtue or shame — is not satisfied with an orderly and disciplined life. He loves property, because it enables him to do at leisure what he pleases and when he pleases. Having obtained the means of life, he gives himself up to trivialities and indolence; he enjoys, he fritters away his time, he goes in quest of curiosities and novel sensations. Property — to enjoy itself — has to abandon ordinary life, and busy itself in luxurious occupations and unclean enjoyments.

Instead of giving up a farm-rent, which is perishing in their hands, and thus lightening the labor of the community, our hundred proprietors prefer to rest. In consequence of this withdrawal, — the absolute production being diminished by one hundred, while the consumption remains the same, — production and consumption seem to balance. But, in the first place, since the proprietors no longer labor, their consumption is, according to economical principles, unproductive; consequently, the previous condition of the community — when the labor of one hundred was rewarded by no products — is superseded by one in which the products of one hundred are consumed without labor. The deficit is always the same, whichever the column of the account in which it is expressed. Either the maxims of political economy are false, or else property, which contradicts them, is impossible.

The economists — regarding all unproductive consumption as an evil, as a robbery of the human race — never fail to exhort proprietors to moderation, labor, and economy; they preach to them the necessity of making themselves useful, of remunerating production for that which they receive from it; they launch the most terrible curses against luxury and laziness. Very beautiful morality, surely; it is a pity that it lacks common sense. The proprietor who labors, or, as the economists say, *who makes himself useful*, is paid for this labor and utility; is he, therefore, any the less idle as concerns the property which he does not use, and from which he receives an income? His condition, whatever he may do, is an unproductive and *felonious* one; he cannot cease to waste and destroy without ceasing to be a proprietor.

514

But this is only the least of the evils which property engenders. Society has to maintain some idle people, whether or no. It will always have the blind, the maimed, the insane, and the idiotic. It can easily support a few sluggards. At this point, the impossibilities thicken and become complicated.

Third Proposition. *Property is impossible, because, with a given capital, Production is proportional to labor, not to property.*

To pay a farm-rent of one hundred at the rate of ten per cent. of the product, the product must be one thousand; that the product may be one thousand, a force of one thousand laborers is needed. It follows, that in granting a furlough, as we have just done, to our one hundred laborer-proprietors, all of whom had an equal right to lead the life of men of income, — we have placed ourselves in a position where we are unable to pay their revenues. In fact, the productive power, which at first was one thousand, being now but nine hundred, the production is also reduced to nine hundred, one-tenth of which is ninety. Either, then, ten proprietors out of the one hundred cannot be paid, — provided the remaining ninety are to get the whole amount of their farm-rent, — or else all must consent to a decrease of ten per cent. For it is not for the laborer, who has been wanting in no particular, who has produced as in the past, to suffer by the withdrawal of the proprietor. The latter must take the consequences of his own idleness. But, then, the proprietor becomes poorer for the very reason that he wishes to enjoy; by exercising his right, he loses it; so that property seems to decrease and vanish in proportion as we try to lay hold of it, — the more we pursue it, the more it eludes our grasp. What sort of a right is that which is governed by numerical relations, and which an arithmetical calculation can destroy?

The laborer-proprietor received, first, as laborer, 0.9 in wages; second, as proprietor, 1 in farm-rent. He said to himself, "My farm-rent is sufficient; I have enough and to spare without my labor." And thus it is that the income upon which he calculated gets diminished by one-tenth, — he at the same time not even suspecting the cause of this diminution. By taking part in the production, he was himself the creator of this tenth which has vanished; and while he thought to labor only for himself, he unwittingly suffered a loss in exchanging his products, by which he was made to pay to himself one-tenth of his own farm-rent. Like every one else, he produced 1, and received but 0.9

515

If, instead of nine hundred laborers, there had been but five hundred, the whole amount of farm-rent would have been reduced to fifty; if there had been but one hundred, it would have fallen to ten. We may posit, then, the following axiom as a law of proprietary economy: *Increase must diminish as the number of idlers augments.*

This first result will lead us to another more surprising still. Its effect is to deliver us at one blow from all the evils of property, without abolishing it, without wronging proprietors, and by a highly conservative process.

We have just proved that, if the farm-rent in a community of one thousand laborers is one hundred, that of nine hundred would be ninety, that of eight hundred, eighty, that of one hundred, ten, &c. So that, in a community where there was but one laborer, the farm-rent would be but 0.1; no matter how great the extent and value of the land appropriated. Therefore, *with a given landed capital, production is proportional to labor, not to property.*

Guided by this principle, let us try to ascertain the maximum increase of all property whatever.

What is, essentially, a farm-lease? It is a contract by which the proprietor yields to a tenant possession of his land, in consideration of a portion of that which it yields him, the proprietor. If, in consequence of an increase in his household, the tenant becomes ten times as strong as the proprietor, he will produce ten times as much. Would the proprietor in such a case be justified in raising the farm-rent tenfold? His right is not, The more you produce, the more I demand. It is, The more I sacrifice, the more I demand. The increase in the tenant's household, the number of hands at his disposal, the resources of his industry, — all these serve to increase production, but bear no relation to the proprietor. His claims are to be measured by his own productive capacity, not that of others. Property is the right of increase, not a poll-tax. How could a man, hardly capable of cultivating even a few acres by himself, demand of a community, on the ground of its use of ten thousand acres of his property, ten thousand times as much as he is incapable of producing from one acre? Why should the price of a loan be governed by the skill and strength of the borrower, rather than by the utility sacrificed by the proprietor? We must recognize, then, this second economical law: *Increase is measured by a fraction of the proprietors production.*

Now, this production, what is it? In other words, What can the lord and master of a piece of land justly claim to have sacrificed in lending it to a tenant?

The productive capacity of a proprietor, like that of any laborer, being one, the product which he sacrifices in surrendering his land is also one. If, then, the rate of increase is ten per cent., the maximum increase is 0.1.

But we have seen that, whenever a proprietor withdraws from production, the amount of products is lessened by 1. Then the increase which accrues to him, being equal to 0.1 while he remains among the laborers, will be equal after his withdrawal, by the law of the decrease of farm-rent, to 0.09. Thus we are led to this final formula: *The maximum income of a proprietor is equal to the square root of the product of one laborer* (some number being agreed upon to express this product). *The diminution which this income suffers, if the proprietor is idle, is equal to a fraction whose numerator is 1, and whose denominator is the number which expresses the product.*

Thus the maximum income of an idle proprietor, or of one who labors in his own behalf outside of the community, figured at ten per cent. on an average production of one thousand francs per laborer, would be ninety francs. If, then, there are in France one million proprietors with an income of one thousand francs each, which they consume unproductively, instead of the one thousand millions which are paid them annually, they are entitled in strict justice, and by the most accurate calculation, to ninety millions only.

It is something of a reduction, to take nine hundred and ten millions from the burdens which weigh so heavily upon the laboring class! Nevertheless, the account is not finished, and the laborer is still ignorant of the full extent of his rights.

What is the right of increase when confined within just limits? A recognition of the right of occupancy. But since all have an equal right of occupancy, every man is by the same title a proprietor. Every man has a right to an income equal to a fraction of his product. If, then, the laborer is obliged by the right of property to pay a rent to the proprietor, the proprietor is obliged by the same right to pay the same amount of rent to the laborer; and, since their rights balance each other, the difference between them is zero.

Scholium. — If farm-rent is only a fraction of the supposed product of the proprietor, whatever the amount and value of the property, the same is true in the case of a large number of small and distinct proprietors. For, although one man may use the property of each separately, he cannot use the property of all at the same time.

To sum up. The right of increase, which can exist only within very narrow limits, defined by the laws of production, is annihilated by the right of occupancy. Now, without the right of increase, there is no property. Then property is impossible.

Fourth Proposition. *Property is impossible, because it is Homicide.*

If the right of increase could be subjected to the laws of reason and justice, it would be reduced to an indemnity or reward whose *maximum* never could exceed, for a single laborer, a certain fraction of that which he is capable of producing. This we have just shown. But why should the right of increase — let us not fear to call it by its right name, the right of robbery — be governed by reason, with which it has nothing in common? The proprietor is not content with the increase allotted him by good sense and the nature of things: he demands ten times, a hundred times, a thousand times, a million times as much. By his own labor, his property would yield him a product equal only to one; and he demands of society, no longer a right proportional to his productive capacity, but a *per capita* tax. He taxes his fellows in proportion to their strength, their number, and their industry. A son is born to a farmer. "Good!" says the proprietor; "one more chance for increase!" By what process has farm-rent been thus changed into a poll-tax? Why have our jurists and our theologians failed, with all their shrewdness, to check the extension of the right of increase?

The proprietor, having estimated from his own productive capacity the number of laborers which his property will accommodate, divides it into as many portions, and says: "Each one shall yield me revenue." To increase his income, he has only to divide his property. Instead of reckoning the interest due him on his labor, he reckons it on his capital; and, by this substitution, the same property, which in the hands of its owner is capable of yielding only one, is worth to him ten, a hundred, a thousand, a million. Consequently, he has only to hold himself in readiness to register the names of the laborers who apply to him — his task consists in drafting leases and receipts.

Not satisfied with the lightness of his duties, the proprietor does not intend to bear even the deficit resulting from his idleness; he throws it upon the shoulders of the producer, of whom he always demands the same reward. When the farm-rent of a piece of land is once raised to its highest point, the proprietor never lowers it; high prices, the scarcity of labor, the disadvantages of the season, even pestilence itself, have no effect upon him — why should he suffer from hard times when he does not labor?

Here commences a new series of phenomena.

Say — who reasons with marvellous clearness whenever he assails taxation, but who is blind to the fact that the proprietor, as well as the tax-gatherer, steals from the tenant, and in the same manner — says in his second letter to Malthus: —

"If the collector of taxes and those who employ him consume one-sixth of the products, they thereby compel the producers to feed, clothe, and support themselves on five-sixths of what they produce. They admit this, but say at the same time that it is possible for each one to live on five-sixths of what he produces. I admit that, if they insist upon it; but I ask if they believe that the producer would live as well, in case they demanded of him, instead of one-sixth, two-sixths, or one-third, of their products? No; but he would still live. Then I ask whether he would still live, in case they should rob him of two-thirds, ... then three-quarters? But I hear no reply."

If the master of the French economists had been less blinded by his proprietary prejudices, he would have seen that farm-rent has precisely the same effect.

Take a family of peasants composed of six persons, — father, mother, and four children, — living in the country, and cultivating a small piece of ground. Let us suppose that by hard labor they manage, as the saying is, to make both ends meet; that, having lodged, warmed, clothed, and fed themselves, they are clear of debt, but have laid up nothing. Taking the years together, they contrive to live. If the year is prosperous, the father drinks a little more wine, the daughters buy themselves a dress, the sons a hat; they eat a little cheese, and, occasionally, some meat. I say that these people are on the road to wreck and ruin.

For, by the third corollary of our axiom, they owe to themselves the interest on their own capital. Estimating this capital at only eight thousand francs at two and a half per cent., there is an annual interest of two hundred francs to be paid. If, then, these two hundred francs, instead of being subtracted from the gross product to be saved and capitalized, are consumed, there is an annual deficit of two hundred francs in the family assets; so that at the end of forty years these good people, without suspecting it, will have eaten up their property and become bankrupt!

This result seems ridiculous — it is a sad reality.

The conscription comes. What is the conscription? An act of property exercised over families by the government without warning — a robbery of men and money. The peasants do not like to part with their sons, — in that I do not think them wrong. It is hard for a young man of twenty to gain any thing by life in the barracks; unless he is depraved, he detests it. You can generally judge of a soldier's morality by his hatred of his uniform. Unfortunate wretches or worthless scamps, — such is the make-up of the French army. This ought not to be the case, — but so it is. Question a hundred thousand men, and not one will contradict my assertion.

Our peasant, in redeeming his two conscripted sons, expends four thousand francs, which he borrows for that purpose; the interest on this, at five per cent., is two hundred francs; — a sum equal to that referred to above. If, up to this time, the production of the family, constantly balanced by its consumption, has been one thousand two hundred francs, or two hundred francs per persons — in order to pay this interest, either the six laborers must produce as much as seven, or must consume as little as five. Curtail consumption they cannot — how can they curtail necessity? To produce more is impossible; they can work neither harder nor longer. Shall they take a middle course, and consume five and a half while producing six and a half? They would soon find that with the stomach there is no compromise — that beyond a certain degree of abstinence it is impossible to go — that strict necessity can be curtailed but little without injury to the health; and, as for increasing the product, — there comes a storm, a drought, an epizootic, and all the hopes of the farmer are dashed. In short, the rent will not be paid, the interest will accumulate, the farm will be seized, and the possessor ejected.

Thus a family, which lived in prosperity while it abstained from exercising the right of property, falls into misery as soon as the exercise of this right becomes a necessity. Property requires of the husbandman the double power of enlarging his land, and fertilizing it by a simple command. While a man is simply possessor of the land, he finds in it means of subsistence; as soon as he pretends to proprietorship, it suffices him no longer. Being able to produce only that which he consumes, the fruit of his labor is his recompense for his trouble — nothing is left for the instrument.

Required to pay what he cannot produce, — such is the condition of the tenant after the proprietor has retired from social production in order to speculate upon the labor of others by new methods.

Let us now return to our first hypothesis.

The nine hundred laborers, sure that their future production will equal that of the past, are quite surprised, after paying their farm-rent, to find themselves poorer by one-tenth than they were the previous year. In fact, this tenth — which was formerly produced and paid by the proprietor-laborer who then took part in the production, and paid part of the — public expenses — now has not been produced, and has been paid. It must then have been taken from the producer's consumption. To choke this inexplicable deficit, the laborer borrows, confident of his intention and ability to return, — a confidence which is shaken the following year by a new loan, *plus* the interest on the first. From whom does he borrow? From the proprietor. The proprietor lends his surplus to the laborer; and this surplus, which he ought to return, becomes — being lent at interest — a new source of profit to him. Then debts increase indefinitely; the proprietor makes advances to the producer who never returns them; and the latter, constantly robbed and constantly borrowing from the robbers, ends in bankruptcy, defrauded of all that he had.

Suppose that the proprietor — who needs his tenant to furnish him with an income — then releases him from his debts. He will thus do a very benevolent deed, which will procure for him a recommendation in the curate's prayers; while the poor tenant, overwhelmed by this unstinted charity, and taught by his catechism to pray for his benefactors, will promise to redouble his energy, and suffer new hardships that he may discharge his debt to so kind a master.

This time he takes precautionary measures; he raises the price of grains. The manufacturer does the same with his products. The reaction comes, and, after some fluctuation, the farm-rent — which the tenant thought to put upon the manufacturer's shoulders — becomes nearly balanced. So that, while he is congratulating himself upon his success, he finds himself again impoverished, but to an extent somewhat smaller than before. For the rise having been general, the proprietor suffers with the

521

rest; so that the laborers, instead of being poorer by one-tenth, lose only nine-hundredths. But always it is a debt which necessitates a loan, the payment of interest, economy, and fasting. Fasting for the nine-hundredths which ought not to be paid, and are paid; fasting for the redemption of debts; fasting to pay the interest on them. Let the crop fail, and the fasting becomes starvation. They say, "*It is necessary to work more.*" That means, obviously, that *it is necessary to produce more.* By what conditions is production effected? By the combined action of labor, capital, and land. As for the labor, the tenant undertakes to furnish it; but capital is formed only by economy. Now, if the tenant could accumulate any thing, he would pay his debts. But granting that he has plenty of capital, of what use would it be to him if the extent of the land which he cultivates always remained the same? He needs to enlarge his farm.

Will it be said, finally, that he must work harder and to better advantage? But, in our estimation of farm-rent, we have assumed the highest possible average of production. Were it not the highest, the proprietor would increase the farm-rent. Is not this the way in which the large landed proprietors have gradually raised their rents, as fast as they have ascertained by the increase in population and the development of industry how much society can produce from their property? The proprietor is a foreigner to society; but, like the vulture, his eyes fixed upon his prey, he holds himself ready to pounce upon and devour it.

The facts to which we have called attention, in a community of one thousand persons, are reproduced on a large scale in every nation and wherever human beings live, but with infinite variations and in innumerable forms, which it is no part of my intention to describe.

In fine, property — after having robbed the laborer by usury — murders him slowly by starvation. Now, without robbery and murder, property cannot exist; with robbery and murder, it soon dies for want of support. Therefore it is impossible.

Fifth Proposition. *Property is impossible, because, if it exists, Society devours itself.*

When the ass is too heavily loaded, he lies down; man always moves on. Upon this indomitable courage, the proprietor — well knowing that it exists — bases his hopes of speculation. The free laborer produces ten; for me, thinks the proprietor, he will produce twelve.

522

Indeed, — before consenting to the confiscation of his fields, before bidding farewell to the paternal roof, — the peasant, whose story we have just told, makes a desperate effort; he leases new land; he will sow one-third more; and, taking half of this new product for himself, he will harvest an additional sixth, and thereby pay his rent. What an evil! To add one-sixth to his production, the farmer must add, not one-sixth, but two-sixths to his labor. At such a price, he pays a farm-rent which in God's eyes he does not owe.

The tenant's example is followed by the manufacturer. The former tills more land, and dispossesses his neighbors; the latter lowers the price of his merchandise, and endeavors to monopolize its manufacture and sale, and to crush out his competitors. To satisfy property, the laborer must first produce beyond his needs. Then, he must produce beyond his strength; for, by the withdrawal of laborers who become proprietors, the one always follows from the other. But to produce beyond his strength and needs, he must invade the production of another, and consequently diminish the number of producers. Thus the proprietor — after having lessened production by stepping outside — lessens it still further by encouraging the monopoly of labor. Let us calculate it.

The laborer's deficit, after paying his rent, being, as we have seen, one-tenth, he tries to increase his production by this amount. He sees no way of accomplishing this save by increasing his labor: this also he does. The discontent of the proprietors who have not received the full amount of their rent; the advantageous offers and promises made them by other farmers, whom they suppose more diligent, more industrious, and more reliable; the secret plots and intrigues, — all these give rise to a movement for the re-division of labor, and the elimination of a certain number of producers. Out of nine hundred, ninety will be ejected, that the production of the others may be increased one-tenth. But will the total product be increased? Not in the least: there will be eight hundred and ten laborers producing as nine hundred, while, to accomplish their purpose, they would have to produce as one thousand. Now, it having been proved that farm-rent is proportional to the landed capital instead of to labor, and that it never diminishes, the debts must continue as in the past, while the labor has increased. Here, then, we have a society which is continually decimating itself, and which would destroy itself, did not the periodical occurrence of failures, bankruptcies, and political and economical catastrophes re-establish equilibrium, and distract attention from the real causes of the universal distress.

The monopoly of land and capital is followed by economical processes which also result in throwing laborers out of employment. Interest being a constant burden upon the shoulders of the farmer and the manufacturer, they exclaim, each speaking for himself, "I should have the means wherewith to pay my rent and interest, had I not to pay so many hands." Then those admirable inventions, intended to assure the easy and speedy performance of labor, become so many infernal machines which kill laborers by thousands.

"A few years ago, the Countess of Strafford ejected fifteen thousand persons from her estate, who, as tenants, added to its value. This act of private administration was repeated in 1820, by another large Scotch proprietor, towards six hundred tenants and their families." — *Tissot: on Suicide and Revolt.*

The author whom I quote, and who has written eloquent words concerning the revolutionary spirit which prevails in modern society, does not say whether he would have disapproved of a revolt on the part of these exiles. For myself, I avow boldly that in my eyes it would have been the first of rights, and the holiest of duties; and all that I desire to-day is that my profession of faith be understood.

Society devours itself, — 1. By the violent and periodical sacrifice of laborers: this we have just seen, and shall see again; 2. By the stoppage of the producer's consumption caused by property. These two modes of suicide are at first simultaneous; but soon the first is given additional force by the second, famine uniting with usury to render labor at once more necessary and more scarce.

By the principles of commerce and political economy, that an industrial enterprise may be successful, its product must furnish, — 1. The interest on the capital employed; 2. Means for the preservation of this capital; 3. The wages of all the employees and contractors. Further, as large a profit as possible must be realized.

The financial shrewdness and rapacity of property is worthy of admiration. Each different name which increase takes affords the proprietor an opportunity to receive it, — 1. In the form of interest; 2. In the form of profit. For, it says, a part of the income derived from manufactures consists of interest on the capital employed. If one hundred thousand francs have been invested in a manufacturing enterprise, and in a year's time five thousand francs have been received therefrom in addition to the expenses, there has been no profit, but only interest on the capital. Now, the proprietor is not a man to labor for nothing. Like the lion in the fable, he gets paid in each of his capacities; so that, after he has been served, nothing is left for his associates.

Ego primam tollo, nominor quia leo.
Secundam quia sum fortis tribuctis mihi.
Tum quia plus valeo, me sequetur tertia.
Malo adficietur, si quis quartam tetigerit.

I know nothing prettier than this fable.

"I am the contractor. I take the first share.
I am the laborer, I take the second.
I am the capitalist, I take the third.
I am the proprietor, I take the whole."

In four lines, Phaedrus has summed up all the forms of property.

I say that this interest, all the more then this profit, is impossible.

What are laborers in relation to each other? So many members of a large industrial society, to each of whom is assigned a certain portion of the general production, by the principle of the division of labor and functions. Suppose, first, that this society is composed of but three individuals, — a cattle-raiser, a tanner, and a shoemaker. The social industry, then, is that of shoemaking. If I should ask what ought to be each producer's share of the social product, the first schoolboy whom I should meet would answer, by a rule of commerce and association, that it should be one-third. But it is not our duty here to balance the rights of laborers conventionally associated: we have to prove that, whether associated or not, our three workers are obliged to act as if they were; that, whether they will or no, they are associated by the force of things, by mathematical necessity.

Three processes are required in the manufacture of shoes, — the rearing of cattle, the preparation of their hides, and the cutting and sewing. If the hide, on leaving the farmer's stable, is worth one, it is worth two on leaving the tanner's pit, and three on leaving the shoemaker's shop. Each laborer has produced a portion of the utility; so that, by adding all these portions together, we get the value of the article. To obtain any quantity whatever of this article, each producer must pay, then, first for his own labor, and second for the labor of the other producers. Thus, to obtain as many shoes as can be made from ten hides, the farmer will give thirty raw hides, and the tanner twenty tanned hides. For, the shoes that are made from ten hides are worth thirty raw hides, in consequence of the extra labor bestowed upon them; just as twenty tanned hides are worth thirty raw hides, on account of the tanner's labor. But if the shoemaker demands thirty-three in the farmer's product, or twenty-two in the tanner's, for ten in his own, there will be no exchange; for, if there were, the farmer and the tanner, after having paid the shoemaker ten for his labor, would have to pay eleven for that which they had themselves sold for ten, — which, of course, would be impossible.[19]

Well, this is precisely what happens whenever an emolument of any kind is received; be it called revenue, farm-rent, interest, or profit. In the little community of which we are speaking, if the shoemaker — in order to procure tools, buy a stock of leather, and support himself until he receives something from his investment — borrows money at interest, it is clear that to pay this interest he will have to make a profit off the tanner and the farmer. But as this profit is impossible unless fraud is used, the interest will fall back upon the shoulders of the unfortunate shoemaker, and ruin him.

I have imagined a case of unnatural simplicity. There is no human society but sustains more than three vocations. The most uncivilized society supports numerous industries; to-day, the number of industrial functions (I mean by industrial functions all useful functions) exceeds, perhaps, a thousand. However numerous the occupations, the economic law remains the same, — *That the producer may live, his wages must repurchase his product.*

The economists cannot be ignorant of this rudimentary principle of their pretended science: why, then, do they so obstinately defend property, and inequality of wages, and the legitimacy of usury, and the honesty of profit, — all of which contradict the economic law, and make exchange impossible? A contractor pays one hundred thousand francs for raw material, fifty thousand francs in wages, and then expects to receive a product of two hundred thousand francs, — that is, expects to make a profit on the material and on the labor of his employees; but if the laborers and the purveyor of the material cannot, with their combined wages, repurchase that which they have produced for the contractor, how can they live? I will develop my question. Here details become necessary.

If the workingman receives for his labor an average of three francs per day, his employer (in order to gain any thing beyond his own salary, if only interest on his capital) must sell the day's labor of his employee, in the form of merchandise, for more than three francs. The workingman cannot, then, repurchase that which he has produced for his master. It is thus with all trades whatsoever. The tailor, the hatter, the cabinet-maker, the blacksmith, the tanner, the mason, the jeweller,

526

the printer, the clerk, &c., even to the farmer and wine-grower, cannot repurchase their products; since, producing for a master who in one form or another makes a profit, they are obliged to pay more for their own labor than they get for it.

In France, twenty millions of laborers, engaged in all the branches of science, art, and industry, produce every thing which is useful to man. Their annual wages amount, it is estimated. to twenty thousand millions; but, in consequence of the right of property, and the multifarious forms of increase, premiums, tithes, interests, fines, profits, farm-rents, house-rents, revenues, emoluments of every nature and description, their products are estimated by the proprietors and employers at twenty-five thousand millions. What does that signify? That the laborers, who are obliged to repurchase these products in order to live, must either pay five for that which they produced for four, or fast one day in five.

If there is an economist in France able to show that this calculation is false, I summon him to appear; and I promise to retract all that I have wrongfully and wickedly uttered in my attacks upon property.

Let us now look at the results of this profit.

If the wages of the workingmen were the same in all pursuits, the deficit caused by the proprietor's tax would be felt equally everywhere; but also the cause of the evil would be so apparent, that it would soon be discovered and suppressed. But, as there is the same inequality of wages (from that of the scavenger up to that of the minister of state) as of property, robbery continually rebounds from the stronger to the weaker; so that, since the laborer finds his hardships increase as he descends in the social scale, the lowest class of people are literally stripped naked and eaten alive by the others.

The laboring people can buy neither the cloth which they weave, nor the furniture which they manufacture, nor the metal which they forge, nor the jewels which they cut, nor the prints which they engrave. They can procure neither the wheat which they plant, nor the wine which they grow, nor the flesh of the animals which they raise. They are allowed neither to dwell in the houses which they build, nor to attend the plays which their labor supports, nor to enjoy the rest which their body requires. And why? Because the right of increase does not permit these things to be sold at the cost-price, which is all that laborers can afford to pay. On the signs of those magnificent warehouses which he in his poverty admires, the laborer reads in large letters: "This is thy work, and thou shalt not have it." *Sic vos non vobis*!

Every manufacturer who employs one thousand laborers, and gains from them daily one sou each, is slowly pushing them into a state of misery. Every man who makes a profit has entered into a conspiracy with famine. But the whole nation has not even this labor, by means of which property starves it. And why? Because the workers are forced by the insufficiency of their wages to monopolize labor; and because, before being destroyed by dearth, they destroy each other by competition. Let us pursue this truth no further.

If the laborer's wages will not purchase his product, it follows that the product is not made for the producer. For whom, then, is it intended? For the richer consumer; that is, for only a fraction of society. But when the whole society labors, it produces for the whole society. If, then, only a part of society consumes, sooner or later a part of society will be idle. Now, idleness is death, as well for the laborer as for the proprietor. This conclusion is inevitable.

The most distressing spectacle imaginable is the sight of producers resisting and struggling against this mathematical necessity, this power of figures to which their prejudices blind them.

If one hundred thousand printers can furnish reading-matter enough for thirty-four millions of men, and if the price of books is so high that only one-third of that number can afford to buy them, it is clear that these one hundred thousand printers will produce three times as much as the booksellers can sell. That the products of the laborers may never exceed the demands of the consumers, the laborers must either rest two days out of three, or, separating into three groups, relieve each other three times a week, month, or quarter; that is, during two-thirds of their life they must not live. But industry, under the influence of property, does not proceed with such regularity. It endeavors to produce a great deal in a short time, because the greater the amount of products, and the shorter the time of production, the less each product costs. As soon as a demand begins to be felt, the factories fill up, and everybody goes to work. Then business is lively, and both governors and governed rejoice. But the more they work to-day, the more idle will they be hereafter; the more they laugh, the more they shall weep. Under the rule of property, the flowers of industry are woven into none but funeral wreaths. The laborer digs his own grave.

If the factory stops running, the manufacturer has to pay interest on his capital the same as before. He naturally tries, then, to continue production by lessening expenses. Then comes the lowering of wages; the introduction of machinery; the employment of women and children to do the work of men; bad workmen, and wretched work. They still produce, because the decreased cost creates a larger market; but they do not produce long, because, the cheapness being due to the quantity and rapidity of production, the productive power tends more than ever to outstrip consumption. It is when laborers, whose wages are scarcely sufficient to support them from one day to another, are thrown out of work, that the consequences of the principle of property become most frightful. They have not been able to economize, they have made no savings, they have accumulated no capital whatever to support them even one day more. Today the factory is closed. To-morrow the people starve in the streets. Day after tomorrow they will either die in the hospital, or eat in the jail.

And still new misfortunes come to complicate this terrible situation. In consequence of the cessation of business, and the extreme cheapness of merchandise, the manufacturer finds it impossible to pay the interest on his borrowed capital; whereupon his frightened creditors hasten to withdraw their funds. Production is suspended, and labor comes to a standstill. Then people are astonished to see capital desert commerce, and throw itself upon the Stock Exchange; and I once heard M. Blanqui bitterly lamenting the blind ignorance of capitalists. The cause of this movement of capital is very simple; but for that very reason an economist could not understand it, or rather must not explain it. The cause lies solely in *competition*.

I mean by competition, not only the rivalry between two parties engaged in the same business, but the general and simultaneous effort of all kinds of business to get ahead of each other. This effort is to-day so strong, that the price of merchandise scarcely covers the cost of production and distribution; so that, the wages of all laborers being lessened, nothing remains, not even interest for the capitalists.

The primary cause of commercial and industrial stagnations is, then, interest on capital, — that interest which the ancients with one accord branded with the name of usury, whenever it was paid for the use of money, but which they did not dare to condemn in the forms of house-rent, farm-rent, or profit: as if the nature of the thing lent could ever warrant a charge for the lending; that is, robbery.

In proportion to the increase received by the capitalist will be the frequency and intensity of commercial crises, — the first being given, we always can determine the two others; and *vice versa*. Do you wish to know the regulator of a society? Ascertain the amount of active capital; that is, the capital bearing interest, and the legal rate of this interest.

The course of events will be a series of overturns, whose number and violence will be proportional to the activity of capital.

In 1839, the number of failures in Paris alone was one thousand and sixty-four. This proportion was kept up in the early months of 1840; and, as I write these lines, the crisis is not yet ended. It is said, further, that the number of houses which have wound up their business is greater than the number of declared failures. By this flood, we may judge of the waterspout's power of suction.

The decimation of society is now imperceptible and permanent, now periodical and violent; it depends upon the course which property takes. In a country where the property is pretty evenly distributed, and where little business is done, — the rights and claims of each being balanced by those of others, — the power of invasion is destroyed. There — it may be truly said — property does not exist, since the right of increase is scarcely exercised at all. The condition of the laborers — as regards security of life — is almost the same as if absolute equality prevailed among them. They are deprived of all the advantages of full and free association, but their existence is not endangered in the least. With the exception of a few isolated victims of the right of property — of this misfortune whose primary cause no one perceives — the society appears to rest calmly in the bosom of this sort of equality. But have a care; it is balanced on the edge of a sword: at the slightest shock, it will fall and meet with death!

Ordinarily, the whirlpool of property localizes itself. On the one hand, farm-rent stops at a certain point; on the other, in consequence of competition and over-production, the price of manufactured goods does not rise, — so that the condition of the peasant varies but little, and depends mainly on the seasons. The devouring action of property bears, then, principally upon business. We commonly say *commercial crises*, not *agricultural crises;* because, while the farmer is eaten up slowly by the right of increase, the manufacturer is swallowed at a single mouthful. This leads to the cessation of business, the destruction of fortunes, and the inactivity of the working people; who die one after another on the highways, and in the hospitals, prisons, and galleys.

To sum up this proposition: —

Property sells products to the laborer for more than it pays him for them; therefore it is impossible.

Appendix To The Fifth Proposition.

I. Certain reformers, and even the most of the publicists — who, though belonging to no particular school, busy themselves in devising means for the amelioration of the lot of the poorer and more numerous class — lay much stress now-a-days on a better organization of labor. The disciples of Fourier, especially, never stop shouting, *"On to the phalanx!"* declaiming in the same breath against the foolishness and absurdity of other sects. They consist of half-a-dozen incomparable geniuses who have discovered that *five and four make nine; take two away, and nine remain,* — and who weep over the blindness of France, who refuses to believe in this astonishing arithmetic.[20]

In fact, the Fourierists proclaim themselves, on the one hand, defenders of property, of the right of increase, which they have thus formulated: *To each according to his capital, his labor, and his skill.* On the other hand, they wish the workingman to come into the enjoyment of all the wealth of society; that is, — abridging the expression, — into the undivided enjoyment of his own product. Is not this like saying to the workingman, "Labor, you shall have three francs per day; you shall live on fifty-five sous; you shall give the rest to the proprietor, and thus you will consume three francs"?

If the above speech is not an exact epitome of Charles Fourier's system, I will subscribe to the whole phalansterian folly with a pen dipped in my own blood.

Of what use is it to reform industry and agriculture, — of what use, indeed, to labor at all, — if property is maintained, and labor can never meet its expenses? Without the abolition of property, the organization of labor is neither more nor less than a delusion. If production should be quadrupled, — a thing which does not seem to me at all impossible, — it would be labor lost: if the additional product was not consumed, it would be of no value, and the proprietor would decline to receive it as interest; if it was consumed, all the disadvantages of property would reappear. It must be confessed that the theory of passional attraction is gravely at fault in this particular, and that Fourier, when he tried to harmonize the *passion* for property, — a bad passion, whatever he may say to the contrary, — blocked his own chariot-wheels.

The absurdity of the phalansterian economy is so gross, that many people suspect Fourier, in spite of all the homage paid by him to proprietors, of having been a secret enemy of property. This opinion might be supported by plausible arguments; still it is not mine. Charlatanism was too important a part for such a man to play, and sincerity too insignificant a one. I would rather think Fourier ignorant (which is generally admitted) than disingenuous. As for his disciples, before they can formulate any opinion of their own, they must declare once for all, unequivocally and with no mental reservation, whether they mean to maintain property or not, and what they mean by their famous motto, — "To each according to his capital, his labor, and his skill."

II. But, some half-converted proprietor will observe, "Would it not be possible, by suppressing the bank, incomes, farm-rent, house-rent, usury of all kinds, and finally property itself, to proportion products to capacities? That was St. Simon's idea; it was also Fourier's; it is the desire of the human conscience; and no decent person would dare maintain that a minister of state should live no better than a peasant."

O Midas! your ears are long! What! will you never understand that disparity of wages and the right of increase are one and the same? Certainly, St. Simon, Fourier, and their respective flocks committed a serious blunder in attempting to unite, the one, inequality and communism; the other, inequality and property: but you, a man of figures, a man of economy, — you, who know by heart your *logarithmic* tables, — how can you make so stupid a mistake? Does not political economy itself teach you that the product of a man, whatever be his individual capacity, is never worth more than his labor, and that a man's labor is worth no more than his consumption? You remind me of that great constitution-framer, poor Pinheiro-Ferreira, the Sieyès of the nineteenth century, who, dividing the citizens of a nation into twelve classes, — or, if you prefer, into twelve grades, — assigned to some a salary of one hundred thousand francs each; to others, eighty thousand; then twenty-five thousand, fifteen thousand, ten thousand, &c., down to one thousand five hundred, and one thousand francs, the minimum allowance of a citizen. Pinheiro loved distinctions, and could no more conceive of a State without great dignitaries than of an army without drum-majors; and as he also loved, or thought he loved, liberty, equality, and fraternity, he combined the good and the evil of our old society in an eclectic philosophy which he embodied in a constitution.

Excellent Pinheiro! Liberty even to passive submission, fraternity even to identity of language, equality even in the jury-box and at the guillotine, — such was his ideal republic. Unappreciated genius, of whom the present century was unworthy, but whom the future will avenge!

Listen, proprietor. Inequality of talent exists in fact; in right it is not admissible, it goes for nothing, it is not thought of. One Newton in a century is equal to thirty millions of men; the psychologist admires the rarity of so fine a genius, the legislator sees only the rarity of the function. Now, rarity of function bestows no privilege upon the functionary; and that for several reasons, all equally forcible.

1. Rarity of genius was not, in the Creator's design, a motive to compel society to go down on its knees before the man of superior talents, but a providential means for the performance of all functions to the greatest advantage of all.

2. Talent is a creation of society rather than a gift of Nature; it is an accumulated capital, of which the receiver is only the guardian. Without society, — without the education and powerful assistance which it furnishes, — the finest nature would be inferior to the most ordinary capacities in the very respect in which it ought to shine. The more extensive a man's knowledge, the more luxuriant his imagination, the more versatile his talent, — the more costly has his education been, the more remarkable and numerous were his teachers and his models, and the greater is his debt. The farmer produces from the time that he leaves his cradle until he enters his grave: the fruits of art and science are late and scarce; frequently the tree dies before the fruit ripens. Society, in cultivating talent, makes a sacrifice to hope.

3. Capacities have no common standard of comparison: the conditions of development being equal, inequality of talent is simply speciality of talent.

4. Inequality of wages, like the right of increase, is economically impossible. Take the most favorable case, — that where each laborer has furnished his maximum production; that there may be an equitable distribution of products, the share of each must be equal to the quotient of the total production divided by the number of laborers. This done, what remains wherewith to pay the higher wages? Nothing whatever.

Will it be said that all laborers should be taxed? But, then, their consumption will not be equal to their production, their wages will not

533

pay for their productive service, they will not be able to repurchase their product, and we shall once more be afflicted with all the calamities of property. I do not speak of the injustice done to the defrauded laborer, of rivalry, of excited ambition, and burning hatred, — these may all be important considerations, but they do not hit the point.

On the one hand, each laborer's task being short and easy, and the means for its successful accomplishment being equal in all cases, how could there be large and small producers? On the other hand, all functions being equal, either on account of the actual equivalence of talents and capacities, or on account of social co-operation, how could a functionary claim a salary proportional to the worth of his genius?

But, what do I say? In equality wages are always proportional to talents. What is the economical meaning of wages? The reproductive consumption of the laborer. The very act by which the laborer produces constitutes, then, this consumption, exactly equal to his production, of which we are speaking. When the astronomer produces observations, the poet verses, or the *savant* experiments, they consume instruments, books, travels, &c., &c.; now, if society supplies this consumption, what more can the astronomer, the *savant*, or the poet demand? We must conclude, then, that in equality, and only in equality, St. Simon's adage — *To each according to his capacity to each capacity according to its results* — finds its full and complete application.

III. The great evil — the horrible and ever-present evil — arising from property, is that, while property exists, population, however reduced, is, and always must be, over-abundant. Complaints have been made in all ages of the excess of population; in all ages property has been embarrassed by the presence of pauperism, not perceiving that it caused it. Further, — nothing is more curious than the diversity of the plans proposed for its extermination. Their atrocity is equalled only by their absurdity.

The ancients made a practice of abandoning their children. The wholesale and retail slaughter of slaves, civil and foreign wars, also lent their aid. In Rome (where property held full sway), these three means were employed so effectively, and for so long a time, that finally the empire found itself without inhabitants. When the barbarians arrived, nobody was to be found; the fields were no longer cultivated; grass grew in the streets of the Italian cities.

In China, from time immemorial, upon famine alone has devolved the task of sweeping away the poor. The people living almost exclusively upon rice, if an accident causes the crop to fail, in a few days hunger kills the inhabitants by myriads; and the Chinese historian records in the annals of the empire, that in such a year of such an emperor twenty, thirty, fifty, one hundred thousand inhabitants died of starvation. Then they bury the dead, and recommence the production of children until another famine leads to the same result. Such appears to have been, in all ages, the Confucian economy.

I borrow the following facts from a modern economist: —

"Since the fourteenth and fifteenth centuries, England has been preyed upon by pauperism. At that time beggars were punished by law." Nevertheless, she had not one-fourth as large a population as she has to-day.

"Edward prohibits alms-giving, on pain of imprisonment... The laws of 1547 and 1656 prescribe a like punishment, in case of a second offence. Elizabeth orders that each parish shall support its own paupers. But what is a pauper? Charles II. decides that an *undisputed* residence of forty days constitutes a settlement in a parish; but, if disputed, the new-comer is forced to pack off. James II. modifies this decision, which is again modified by William. In the midst of trials, reports, and modifications, pauperism increases, and the workingman languishes and dies.

"The poor-tax in 1774 exceeded forty millions of francs; in 1783-4-5, it averaged fifty-three millions; 1813, more than a hundred and eighty-seven millions five hundred thousand francs; 1816, two hundred and fifty millions; in 1817, it is estimated at three hundred and seventeen millions.

"In 1821, the number of paupers enrolled upon the parish lists was estimated at four millions, nearly one-third of the population.

"*France*. In 1544, Francis I. establishes a compulsory tax in behalf of the poor. In 1566 and 1586, the same principle is applied to the whole kingdom.

"Under Louis XIV., forty thousand paupers infested the capital [as many in proportion as to-day]. Mendicity was punished severely. In

535

1740, the Parliament of Paris re-establishes within its own jurisdiction the compulsory assessment.

"The Constituent Assembly, frightened at the extent of the evil and the difficulty of curing it, ordains the *statu quo*.

"The Convention proclaims assistance of the poor to be a *national debt*. Its law remains unexecuted.

"Napoleon also wishes to remedy the evil: his idea is imprisonment. 'In that way,' said he, 'I shall protect the rich from the importunity of beggars, and shall relieve them of the disgusting sight of abject poverty.' " O wonderful man!

From these facts, which I might multiply still farther, two things are to be inferred, — the one, that pauperism is independent of population; the other, that all attempts hitherto made at its extermination have proved abortive.

Catholicism founds hospitals and convents, and commands charity; that is, she encourages mendicity. That is the extent of her insight as voiced by her priests.

The secular power of Christian nations now orders taxes on the rich, now banishment and imprisonment for the poor; that is, on the one hand, violation of the right of property, and, on the other, civil death and murder.

The modern economists — thinking that pauperism is caused by the excess of population, exclusively — have devoted themselves to devising checks. Some wish to prohibit the poor from marrying; thus, — having denounced religious celibacy, — they propose compulsory celibacy, which will inevitably become licentious celibacy.

Others do not approve this method, which they deem too violent; and which, they say, deprives the poor man of *the only pleasure which he knows in this world*. They would simply recommend him to be *prudent*. This opinion is held by Malthus, Sismondi, Say, Droz, Duchatel, &c. But if the poor are to be *prudent*, the rich must set the example. Why should the marriageable age of the latter be fixed at eighteen years, while that of the former is postponed until thirty?

Again, they would do well to explain clearly what they mean by this matrimonial prudence which they so urgently recommend to the laborer; for here equivocation is especially dangerous, and I suspect that the economists are not thoroughly understood. "Some half-enlightened ecclesiastics are alarmed when they hear prudence in marriage advised; they fear that the divine injunction — *increase and multiply* — is to be set aside. To be logical, they must anathematize bachelors." (*J. Droz: Political Economy.*)

M. Droz is too honest a man, and too little of a theologian, to see why these casuists are so alarmed; and this chaste ignorance is the very best evidence of the purity of his heart. Religion never has encouraged early marriages; and the kind of *prudence* which it condemns is that described in this Latin sentence from Sanchez, — *An licet ob metum liberorum semen extra vas ejicere*?

Destutt de Tracy seems to dislike prudence in either form. He says: "I confess that I no more share the desire of the moralists to diminish and restrain our pleasures, than that of the politicians to increase our procreative powers, and accelerate reproduction." He believes, then, that we should love and marry when and as we please. Widespread misery results from love and marriage, but this our philosopher does not heed. True to the dogma of the necessity of evil, to evil he looks for the solution of all problems. He adds: "The multiplication of men continuing in all classes of society, the surplus members of the upper classes are supported by the lower classes, and those of the latter are destroyed by poverty." This philosophy has few avowed partisans; but it has over every other the indisputable advantage of demonstration in practice. Not long since France heard it advocated in the Chamber of Deputies, in the course of the discussion on the electoral reform, — *Poverty will always exist*. That is the political aphorism with which the minister of state ground to powder the arguments of M. Arago. *Poverty will always exist*! Yes, so long as property does.

The Fourierists — *inventors* of so many marvellous contrivances — could not, in this field, belie their character. They invented four methods of checking increase of population at will.

1. *The vigor of women*. On this point they are contradicted by experience; for, although vigorous women may be less likely to conceive, nevertheless they give birth to the healthiest children; so that the advantage of maternity is on their side.

2. *Integral exercise*, or the equal development of all the physical powers. If this development is equal, how is the power of reproduction lessened?

3. *The gastronomic regime;* or, in plain English, the philosophy of the belly. The Fourierists say, that abundance of rich food renders women sterile; just as too much sap — while enhancing the beauty of flowers — destroys their reproductive capacity. But the analogy is a false one. Flowers become sterile when the stamens — or male organs — are changed into petals, as may be seen by inspecting a rose; and when through excessive dampness the pollen loses its fertilizing power. Then, — in order that the gastronomic *régime* may produce the results claimed for it, — not only must the females be fattened, but the males must be rendered impotent.

4. *Phanerogamic morality*, or public concubinage. I know not why the phalansterians use Greek words to convey ideas which can be expressed so clearly in French. This method — like the preceding one — is copied from civilized customs. Fourier, himself, cites the example of prostitutes as a proof.

Now we have no certain knowledge yet of the facts which he quotes. So states Parent Duchatelet in his work on "Prostitution."

From all the information which I have been able to gather, I find that all the remedies for pauperism and fecundity — sanctioned by universal practice, philosophy, political economy, and the latest reformers — may be summed up in the following list: masturbation, onanism,[21] sodomy, *tribadie*, polyandry,[22] prostitution, castration, continence, abortion, and infanticide.[23]

All these methods being proved inadequate, there remains proscription.

Unfortunately, proscription, while decreasing the number of the poor, increases their proportion. If the interest charged by the proprietor upon the product is equal only to one-twentieth of the product (by law it is equal to one-twentieth of the capital), it follows that twenty laborers produce for nineteen only; because there is one among them, called proprietor, who eats the share of two. Suppose that the twentieth laborer — the poor one — is killed: the production of the following year will be diminished one-twentieth; consequently the nineteenth will have to yield his portion, and perish. For, since it is not one-twentieth of the product of nineteen which must be paid to the proprietor, but one-twentieth of the product of twenty (see third proposition), each surviving laborer must sacrifice one-twentieth *plus* one four-hundredth of his product; in other words, one man out of nineteen must be killed. Therefore, while property exists, the more poor people we kill, the more there are born in proportion.

Malthus, who proved so clearly that population increases in geometrical progression, while production increases only in arithmetical progression, did not notice this *pauperizing* power of property. Had he observed this, he would have understood that, before trying to check reproduction, the right of increase should be abolished; because, wherever that right is tolerated, there are always too many inhabitants, whatever the extent or fertility of the soil.

It will be asked, perhaps, how I would maintain a balance between population and production; for sooner or later this problem must be solved. The reader will pardon me, if I do not give my method here. For, in my opinion, it is useless to say a thing unless we prove it. Now, to explain my method fully would require no less than a formal treatise. It is a thing so simple and so vast, so common and so extraordinary, so true and so misunderstood, so sacred and so profane, that to name it without developing and proving it would serve only to excite contempt and incredulity. One thing at a time. Let us establish equality, and this remedy will soon appear; for truths follow each other, just as crimes and errors do.

Sixth Proposition. *Property is impossible, because it is the Mother of Tyranny.*

What is government? Government is public economy, the supreme administrative power over public works and national possessions.

Now, the nation is like a vast society in which all the, citizens are stockholders. Each one has a deliberative voice in the assembly; and, if the shares are equal, has one vote at his disposal. But, under the *régime* of property, there is great inequality between the shares of the stockholders; therefore, one may have several hundred votes, while another has only one. If, for example, I enjoy an income of one million; that is, if I am the proprietor of a fortune of thirty or forty millions well invested, and if this fortune constitutes 1/30000 of the national capital, — it is clear that the public administration of my property would form 1/30000 of the duties of the government; and, if the nation had a population of thirty-four millions, that I should have as many votes as one thousand one hundred and thirty-three simple stockholders.

Thus, when M. Arago demands the right of suffrage for all members of the National Guard, he is perfectly right; since every citizen is enrolled for at least one national share, which entitles him to one vote. But the illustrious orator ought at the same time to demand that each elector shall have as many votes as he has shares; as is the case in commercial associations. For to do otherwise is to pretend that the nation has a right to dispose of the property of individuals without consulting them; which is contrary to the right of property. In a country where property exists, equality of electoral rights is a violation of property.

Now, if each citizen's sovereignty must and ought to be proportional to his property, it follows that the small stock holders are at the mercy of the larger ones; who will, as soon as they choose, make slaves of the former, marry them at pleasure, take from them their wives, castrate their sons, prostitute their daughters, throw the aged to the sharks, — and finally will be forced to serve themselves in the same way, unless they prefer to tax themselves for the support of their servants. In such a condition is Great Britain to-day. John Bull — caring little for liberty, equality, or dignity — prefers to serve and beg. But you, *bonhomme Jacques*?

Property is incompatible with political and civil equality; then property is impossible.

Historical Comments. — 1. When the vote of the third estate was doubled by the States-General of 1789, property was grossly violated. The nobility and the clergy possessed three-fourths of the soil of France; they should have controlled three-fourths of the votes in the national representation. To double the vote of the third estate was just, it is said, since the people paid nearly all the taxes. This argument would be sound, if there were nothing to be voted upon but taxes. But it was a question at that time of reforming the government and the constitution; consequently, the doubling of the vote of the third estate was a usurpation, and an attack on property.

2. If the present representatives of the radical opposition should come into power, they would work a reform by which every National Guard should be an elector, and every elector eligible for office, — an attack on property.

They would lower the rate of interest on public funds, — an attack on property.

They would, in the interest of the public, pass laws to regulate the exportation of cattle and wheat, — an attack on property.

They would alter the assessment of taxes, — an attack on property.

They would educate the people gratuitously, — a conspiracy against property.

They would organize labor; that is, they would guarantee labor to the workingman, and give him a share in the profits, — the abolition of property.

Now, these same radicals are zealous defenders of property, — a radical proof that they know not what they do, nor what they wish.

3. Since property is the grand cause of privilege and despotism, the form of the republican oath should be changed. Instead of, "I swear hatred to royalty," henceforth the new member of a secret society should say, "I swear hatred to property."

Seventh Proposition. *Property is impossible, because, in consuming its Receipts, it loses them; in hoarding them, it nullifies them; and in using them as Capital, it turns them against Production.*

I. If, with the economists, we consider the laborer as a living machine, we must regard the wages paid to him as the amount necessary to support this machine, and keep it in repair. The head of a manufacturing establishment — who employs laborers at three, five, ten, and fifteen francs per day, and who charges twenty francs for his superintendence — does not regard his disbursements as losses, because he knows they will return to him in the form of products. Consequently, *labor* and *reproductive consumption* are identical.

What is the proprietor? He is a machine which does not work; or, which working for its own pleasure, and only when it sees fit, produces nothing.

What is it to consume as a proprietor? It is to consume without working, to consume without reproducing. For, once more, that which the proprietor consumes as a laborer comes back to him; he does not give his labor in exchange for his property, since, if he did, he would thereby cease to be a proprietor. In consuming as a laborer, the proprietor gains, or at least does not lose, since he recovers that which he consumes; in consuming as a proprietor, he impoverishes himself. To enjoy property, then, it is necessary to destroy it; to be a real proprietor, one must cease to be a proprietor.

The laborer who consumes his wages is a machine which destroys and reproduces; the proprietor who consumes his income is a bottomless gulf, — sand which we water, a stone which we sow. So true is this, that the proprietor — neither wishing nor knowing how to produce, and perceiving that as fast as he uses his property he destroys it for ever — has taken the precaution to make some one produce in his place. That is what political economy, speaking in the name of eternal justice, calls *producing by his capital, — producing by his tools*. And that is what ought to be called *producing by a slave — producing as a thief and as a tyrant*. He, the proprietor, produce! ... The robber might say, as well: "I produce."

The consumption of the proprietor has been styled luxury, in opposition to *useful* consumption. From what has just been said, we see that great luxury can prevail in a nation which is not rich, — that poverty even increases with luxury, and *vice versâ*. The economists (so much credit must be given them, at least) have caused such a horror of luxury, that to-day a very large number of proprietors — not to say almost all — ashamed of their idleness — labor, economize, and capitalize. They have jumped from the frying-pan into the fire.

I cannot repeat it too often: the proprietor who thinks to deserve his income by working, and who receives wages for his labor, is a functionary who gets paid twice; that is the only difference between an idle proprietor and a laboring proprietor. By his labor, the proprietor produces his wages only — not his income. And since his condition enables him to engage in the most lucrative pursuits, it may be said that the proprietor's labor harms society more than it helps it. Whatever the proprietor does, the consumption of his income is an actual loss, which his salaried functions neither repair nor justify; and which would annihilate property, were it not continually replenished by outside production.

II. Then, the proprietor who consumes annihilates the product: he does much worse if he lays it up. The things which he lays by pass into another world; nothing more is seen of them, not even the *caput mortuum*, — the smoke. If we had some means of transportation by which to travel to the moon, and if the proprietors should be seized with a sudden fancy to carry their savings thither, at the end of a certain

542

time our terraqueous planet would be transported by them to its satellite!

The proprietor who lays up products will neither allow others to enjoy them, nor enjoy them himself; for him there is neither possession nor property. Like the miser, he broods over his treasures: he does not use them. He may feast his eyes upon them; he may lie down with them; he may sleep with them in his arms: all very fine, but coins do not breed coins. No real property without enjoyment; no enjoyment without consumption; no consumption without loss of property, — such is the inflexible necessity to which

God's judgment compels the proprietor to bend. A curse upon property !

III. The proprietor who, instead of consuming his income, uses it as capital, turns it against production, and thereby makes it impossible for him to exercise his right. For the more he increases the amount of interest to be paid upon it, the more he is compelled to diminish wages. Now, the more he diminishes wages, — that is, the less he devotes to the maintenance and repair of the machines, — the more he diminishes the quantity of labor; and with the quantity of labor the quantity of product, and with the quantity of product the very source of his income. This is clearly shown by the following example: —

Take an estate consisting of arable land, meadows, and vineyards, containing the dwellings of the owner and the tenant; and worth, together with the farming implements, one hundred thousand francs, the rate of increase being three per cent. If, instead of consuming his revenue, the proprietor uses it, not in enlarging but in beautifying his estate, can he annually demand of his tenant an additional ninety francs on account of the three thousand francs which he has thus added to his capital? Certainly not; for on such conditions the tenant, though producing no more than before, would soon be obliged to labor for nothing, — what do I say? to actually suffer loss in order to hold his lease.

In fact, revenue can increase only as productive soil increases: it is useless to build walls of marble, and work with plows of gold. But, since it is impossible to go on acquiring for ever, to add estate to estate, to *continue one's possessions*, as the Latins said; and since, moreover, the proprietor always has means wherewith to capitalize, — it follows that the exercise of his right finally becomes impossible.

Well, in spite of this impossibility, property capitalizes, and in capitalizing increases its revenue; and, without stopping to look at the particular cases which occur in commerce, manufacturing operations, and banking, I will cite a graver fact, — one which directly affects all citizens. I mean the indefinite increase of the budget.

The taxes increase every year. It would be difficult to tell in which department of the government the expenses increase; for who can boast of any knowledge as to the budget? On this point, the ablest financiers continually disagree. What is to be thought, I ask, of the science of government, when its professors cannot understand one another's figures? Whatever be the immediate causes of this growth of the budget, it is certain that taxation increases at a rate which causes everybody to despair. Everybody sees it, everybody acknowledges it; but nobody seems to understand the primary cause.[24] Now, I say that it cannot be otherwise, — that it is necessary and inevitable.

A nation is the tenant of a rich proprietor called the *government*, to whom it pays, for the use of the soil, a farm-rent called a tax. Whenever the government makes war, loses or gains a battle, changes the outfit of its army, erects a monument, digs a canal, opens a road, or builds a railway, it borrows money, on which the tax-payers pay interest; that is, the government, without adding to its productive capacity, increases its active capital, — in a word, capitalizes after the manner of the proprietor of whom I have just spoken.

Now, when a governmental loan is once contracted, and the interest is once stipulated, the budget cannot be reduced. For, to accomplish that, either the capitalists must relinquish their interest, which would involve an abandonment of property; or the government must go into bankruptcy, which would be a fraudulent denial of the political principle; or it must pay the debt, which would require another loan; or it must reduce expenses, which is impossible, since the loan was contracted for the sole reason that the ordinary receipts were insufficient; or the money expended by the government must be reproductive, which requires an increase of productive capacity, — a condition excluded by our hypothesis; or, finally, the tax-payers must submit to a new tax in order to pay the debt, — an impossible thing. For, if this new tax were levied upon all citizens alike, half, or even more, of the citizens would be unable to pay it; if the rich had to bear the whole, it would be a forced contribution, — an invasion of property. Long financial experience has shown that the method of loans, though exceedingly dangerous, is much surer, more convenient, and less costly than any other method; consequently the government borrows, — that is, goes on capitalizing, — and increases the budget.

Then, a budget, instead of ever diminishing, must necessarily and continually increase. It is astonishing that the economists, with all their learning, have failed to perceive a fact so simple and so evident. If they have perceived it, why have they neglected to condemn it?

Historical Comment. — Much interest is felt at present in a financial operation which is expected to result in a reduction of the budget. It is proposed to change the present rate of increase, five per cent. Laying aside the politico-legal question to deal only with the financial question, — is it not true that, when five per cent. is changed to four per cent., it will then be necessary, for the same reasons, to change four to three; then three to two, then two to one, and finally to sweep away increase altogether? But that would be the advent of equality of conditions and the abolition of property. Now it seems to me, that an intelligent nation should voluntarily meet an inevitable revolution half way, instead of suffering itself to be dragged after the car of inflexible necessity.

Eighth Proposition. *Property is impossible, because its power of Accumulation is infinite, and is exercised only over finite quantities.*

If men, living in equality, should grant to one of their number the exclusive right of property; and this sole proprietor should lend one hundred francs to the human race at compound interest, payable to his descendants twenty-four generations hence, — at the end of six hundred years this sum of one hundred francs, at five per cent., would amount to 107,854,010,777,600 francs; two thousand six hundred and ninety-six and one-third times the capital of France (supposing her capital to be 40,000,000,000), or more than twenty times the value of the terrestrial globe!

Suppose that a man, in the reign of St. Louis, had borrowed one hundred francs, and had refused, — he and his heirs after him, — to return it. Even though it were known that the said heirs were not the rightful possessors, and that prescription had been interrupted always at the right moment, — nevertheless, by our laws, the last heir would be obliged to return the one hundred francs with interest, and interest on the interest; which in all would amount, as we have seen, to nearly one hundred and eight thousand billions.

Every day, fortunes are growing in our midst much more rapidly than this. The preceding example supposed the interest equal to one-twentieth of the capital, — it often equals one-tenth, one-fifth, one-half of the capital; and sometimes the capital itself.

The Fourierists — irreconcilable enemies of equality, whose partisans they regard as *sharks* — intend, by quadrupling production, to satisfy all the demands of capital, labor, and skill. But, should production be multiplied by four, ten, or even one hundred, property would soon absorb, by its power of accumulation and the effects of its capitalization, both products and capital, and the land, and even the laborers. Is the phalanstery to be prohibited from capitalizing and lending at interest? Let it explain, then, what it means by property.

I will carry these calculations no farther. They are capable of infinite variation, upon which it would be puerile for me to insist. I only ask by what standard judges, called upon to decide a suit for possession, fix the interest? And, developing the question, I ask, —

Did the legislator, in introducing into the Republic the principle of property, weigh all the consequences? Did he know the law of the possible? If he knew it, why is it not in the Code? Why is so much latitude allowed to the proprietor in accumulating property and charging interest, — to the judge in recognizing and fixing the domain of property, — to the State in its power to levy new taxes continually? At what point is the nation justified in repudiating the budget, the tenant his farm-rent, and the manufacturer the interest on his capital? How far may the idler take advantage of the laborer? Where does the right of spoliation begin, and where does it end? When may the producer say to the proprietor, "I owe you nothing more"? When is property satisfied? When must it cease to steal?

If the legislator did know the law of the possible, and disregarded it, what must be thought of his justice? If he did not know it, what must be thought of his wisdom? Either wicked or foolish, how can we recognize his authority?

If our charters and our codes are based upon an absurd hypothesis, what is taught in the law-schools? What does a judgment of the Court of Appeal amount to? About what do our Chambers deliberate? What is *politics*? What is our definition of a *statesman*? What is the meaning of *jurisprudence*? Should we not rather say *jurisignorance*?

If all our institutions are based upon an error in calculation, does it not follow that these institutions are so many shams? And if the entire social structure is built upon this absolute impossibility of property, is it not true that the government under which we live is a chimera, and our present society a utopia?

Ninth Proposition. *Property is impossible, because it is powerless against Property.*

I. By the third corollary of our axiom, interest tells against the proprietor as well as the stranger. This economical principle is universally admitted. Nothing simpler at first blush; yet, nothing more absurd, more contradictory in terms, or more absolutely impossible.

The manufacturer, it is said, pays himself the rent on his house and capital. *He pays himself;* that is, he gets paid by the public who buy his products. For, suppose the manufacturer, who seems to make this profit on his property, wishes also to make it on his merchandise, can he then pay himself one franc for that which cost him ninety centimes, and make money by the operation? No: such a transaction would transfer the merchant's money from his right hand to his left, but without any profit whatever.

Now, that which is true of a single individual trading with himself is true also of the whole business world. Form a chain of ten, fifteen, twenty producers; as many as you wish. If the producer A makes a profit out of the producer B. B's loss must, according to economical principles, be made up by C, C's by D; and so on through to Z.

But by whom will Z be paid for the loss caused him by the profit charged by A in the beginning? *By the consumer*, replies Say. Contemptible equivocation! Is this consumer any other, then, than A, B. C, D, &c., or Z? By whom will Z be paid? If he is paid by A, no one makes a profit; consequently, there is no property. If, on the contrary, Z bears the burden himself, he ceases to be a member of society; since it refuses him the right of property and profit, which it grants to the other associates.

Since, then, a nation, like universal humanity, is a vast industrial association which cannot act outside of itself, it is clear that no man can enrich himself without impoverishing another. For, in order that the right of property, the right of increase, may be respected in the case of A, it must be denied to Z; thus we see how equality of rights, separated

547

from equality of conditions, may be a truth. The iniquity of political economy in this respect is flagrant. "When I, a manufacturer, purchase the labor of a workingman, I do not include his wages in the net product of my business; on the contrary, I deduct them. But the workingman includes them in his net product... "(*Say: Political Economy.*)

That means that all which the workingman gains is *net product;* but that only that part of the manufacturer's gains is *net product,* which remains after deducting his wages. But why is the right of profit confined to the manufacturer? Why is this right, which is at bottom the right of property itself, denied to the workingman? In the terms of economical science, the workingman is capital. Now, all capital, beyond the cost of its maintenance and repair, must bear interest. This the proprietor takes care to get, both for his capital and for himself. Why is the workingman prohibited from charging a like interest for his capital, which is himself?

Property, then, is inequality of rights; for, if it were not inequality of rights, it would be equality of goods, — in other words, it would not exist. Now, the charter guarantees to all equality of rights. Then, by the charter, property is impossible.

II. Is A, the proprietor of an estate, entitled by the fact of his proprietorship to take possession of the field belonging to B. his neighbor? "No," reply the proprietors; "but what has that to do with the right of property?" That I shall show you by a series of similar propositions.

Has C, a hatter, the right to force D, his neighbor and also a hatter, to close his shop, and cease his business? Not the least in the world.

But C wishes to make a profit of one franc on every hat, while D is content with fifty centimes. It is evident that D's moderation is injurious to C's extravagant claims. Has the latter a right to prevent D from selling? Certainly not.

Since D is at liberty to sell his hats fifty centimes cheaper than C if he chooses, C in his turn is free to reduce his price one franc. Now, D is poor, while C is rich; so that at the end of two or three years D is ruined by this intolerable competition, and C has complete control of the market. Can the proprietor D get any redress from the proprietor C? Can he bring a suit against him to recover his business and property?

No; for D could have done the same thing, had he been the richer of the two.

On the same ground, the large proprietor A may say to the small proprietor B: "Sell me your field, otherwise you shall not sell your wheat," — and that without doing him the least wrong, or giving him ground for complaint. So that A can devour B if he likes, for the very reason that A is stronger than B. Consequently, it is not the right of property which enables A and C to rob B and D, but the right of might. By the right of property, neither the two neighbors A and B, nor the two merchants C and D, could harm each other. They could neither dispossess nor destroy one another, nor gain at one another's expense. The power of invasion lies in superior strength.

But it is superior strength also which enables the manufacturer to reduce the wages of his employees, and the rich merchant and well-stocked proprietor to sell their products for what they please. The manufacturer says to the laborer, "You are as free to go elsewhere with your services as I am to receive them. I offer you so much." The merchant says to the customer, "Take it or leave it; you are master of your money, as I am of my goods. I want so much." Who will yield? The weaker.

Therefore, without force, property is powerless against property, since without force it has no power to increase; therefore, without force, property is null and void.

Historical Comment. — The struggle between colonial and native sugars furnishes us a striking example of this impossibility of property. Leave these two industries to themselves, and the native manufacturer will be ruined by the colonist. To maintain the beet-root, the cane must be taxed: to protect the property of the one, it is necessary to injure the property of the other. The most remarkable feature of this business is precisely that to which the least attention is paid; namely, that, in one way or another, property has to be violated. Impose on each industry a proportional tax, so as to preserve a balance in the market, and you create a *maximum price*, — you attack property in two ways. On the one hand, your tax interferes with the liberty of trade; on the other, it does not recognize equality of proprietors. Indemnify the beet-root, you violate the property of the tax-payer. Cultivate the two varieties of sugar at the nation's expense, just as different varieties of tobacco are cultivated, — you abolish one species of property. This last course would be the simpler and better one; but, to induce the nations to adopt it, requires such a co-operation of able minds and generous hearts as is at present out of the question.

Competition, sometimes called liberty of trade, — in a word, property in exchange, — will be for a long time the basis of our commercial legislation; which, from the economical point of view, embraces all civil laws and all government. Now, what is competition? A duel in a closed field, where arms are the test of right.

"Who is the liar, — the accused or the accuser?" said our barbarous ancestors. "Let them fight it out," replied the still more barbarous judge; "the stronger is right."

Which of us two shall sell spices to our neighbor? "Let each offer them for sale," cries the economist; "the sharper, or the more cunning, is the more honest man, and the better merchant."

Such is the exact spirit of the Code Napoleon.

Tenth Proposition. *Property is impossible, because it is the Negation of equality.*

The development of this proposition will be the *résumé* of the preceding ones.

1. It is a principle of economical justice, that *products are bought only by products*. Property, being capable of defence only on the ground that it produces utility, is, since it produces nothing, for ever condemned.

2. It is an economical law, that *labor must be balanced by product*. It is a fact that, with property, production costs more than it is worth.

3. Another economical law: *The capital being given, production is measured, not by the amount of capital, but by productive capacity.* Property, requiring income to be always proportional to capital without regard to labor, does not recognize this relation of equality between effect and cause.

4 and 5. Like the insect which spins its silk, the laborer never produces for himself alone. Property, demanding a double product and unable to obtain it, robs the laborer, and kills him.

550

6. Nature has given to every man but one mind, one heart, one will. Property, granting to one individual a plurality of votes, supposes him to have a plurality of minds.

7. All consumption which is not reproductive of utility is destruction. Property, whether it consumes or hoards or capitalizes, is productive of *inutility*, — the cause of sterility and death.

8. The satisfaction of a natural right always gives rise to an equation; in other words, the right to a thing is necessarily balanced by the possession of the thing. Thus, between the right to liberty and the condition of a free man there is a balance, an equation; between the right to be a father and paternity, an equation; between the right to security and the social guarantee, an equation. But between the right of increase and the receipt of this increase there is never an equation; for every new increase carries with it the right to another, the latter to a third, and so on for ever. Property, never being able to accomplish its object, is a right against Nature and against reason.

9. Finally, property is not self-existent. An extraneous cause — either *force* or *fraud* — is necessary to its life and action. In other words, property is not equal to property: it is a negation — a delusion — NOTHING.

Chapter V. Psychological Exposition Of The Idea Of Justice And Injustice, And A Determination Of The Principle Of Government And Of Right.

Property is impossible; equality does not exist. We hate the former, and yet wish to possess it; the latter rules all our thoughts, yet we know not how to reach it. Who will explain this profound antagonism between our conscience and our will? Who will point out the causes of this pernicious error, which has become the most sacred principle of justice and society?

I am bold enough to undertake the task, and I hope to succeed.

But before explaining why man has violated justice, it is necessary to determine what justice is.

Part First.

§ 1. — *Of the Moral Sense in Man and the Animals.*

The philosophers have endeavored often to locate the line which separates man's intelligence from that of the brutes; and, according to their general custom, they gave utterance to much foolishness before resolving upon the only course possible for them to take, — observation. It was reserved for an unpretending *savant* — who perhaps did not pride himself on his philosophy — to put an end to the interminable controversy by a simple distinction; but one of those luminous distinctions which are worth more than systems. Frederic Cuvier separated *instinct* from *intelligence*.

But, as yet, no one has proposed this question: —

Is the difference between man's moral sense and that of the brute a difference in kind or only in degree?

If, hitherto, any one had dared to maintain the latter alternative, his arguments would have seemed scandalous, blasphemous, and offensive to morality and religion. The ecclesiastical and secular tribunals would have condemned him with one voice. And, mark the style in which they would have branded the immoral paradox! "Conscience," — they would have cried, — "conscience, man's chief glory, was given to him exclusively; the notion of justice and injustice, of merit and demerit, is his noble privilege; to man, alone, — the lord of creation, — belongs the sublime power to resist his worldly propensities, to choose between good and evil, and to bring himself more and more into the resemblance of God through liberty and justice... No; the holy image of virtue was never graven save on the heart of man." Words full of feeling, but void of sense.

Man is a rational and social animal — *zwon logikon kai politikon* — said Aristotle. This definition is worth more than all which have been given since. I do not except even M. de Bonald's celebrated definition, — *man is an intellect served by organs* — a definition which has the double fault of explaining the known by the unknown; that is, the living being by the intellect; and of neglecting man's essential quality, — animality.

Man, then, is an animal living in society. Society means the sum total of relationships; in short, system. Now, all systems exist only on certain conditions. What, then, are the conditions, the *laws*, of human society?

What are the *rights* of men with respect to each other; what is *justice*?

It amounts to nothing to say, — with the philosophers of various schools, — "It is a divine instinct, an immortal and heavenly voice, a guide given us by Nature, a light revealed unto every man on coming into the world, a law engraved upon our hearts; it is the voice of conscience, the *dictum* of reason, the inspiration of sentiment, the *penchant* of feeling; it is the love of self in others; it is enlightened self-interest; or else it is an innate idea, the imperative command of applied reason, which has its source in the concepts of pure reason; it is a passional attraction," &c., &c. This may be as true as it seems beautiful; but it is utterly meaningless. Though we should prolong this litany through ten pages (it has been filtered through a thousand volumes), we should be no nearer to the solution of the question.

"Justice is public utility," says Aristotle. That is true, but it is a tautology. "The principle that the public welfare ought to be the object of the legislator" — says M. Ch. Comte in his "Treatise on Legislation" — "cannot be overthrown. But legislation is advanced no farther by its announcement and demonstration, than is medicine when it is said that it is the business of physicians to cure the sick."

Let us take another course. *Right* is the sum total of the principles which govern society. Justice, in man, is the respect and observation of those principles. To practise justice is to obey the social instinct; to do an act of justice is to do a social act. If, then, we watch the conduct of men towards each other under different circumstances, it will be easy for us to distinguish between the presence and absence of society; from the result we may inductively infer the law.

Let us commence with the simplest and least doubtful cases.

The mother, who protects her son at the peril of her life, and sacrifices every thing to his support, is in society with him — she is a good mother. She, on the contrary, who abandons her child, is unfaithful to the social instinct, — maternal love being one of its many features; she is an unnatural mother.

If I plunge into the water to rescue a drowning man, I am his brother, his associate; if, instead of aiding him, I sink him, I am his enemy, his murderer.

Whoever bestows alms treats the poor man as his associate; not thoroughly, it is true, but only in respect to the amount which he shares with him. Whoever takes by force or stratagem that which is not the product of his labor, destroys his social character — he is a brigand.

The Samaritan who relieves the traveller lying by the wayside, dresses his wounds, comforts him, and supplies him with money, thereby declares himself his associate — his neighbor; the priest, who passes by on the other side, remains unassociated, and is his enemy.

In all these cases, man is moved by an internal attraction towards his fellow, by a secret sympathy which causes him to love, congratulate, and condole; so that, to resist this attraction, his will must struggle against his nature.

But in these respects there is no decided difference between man and the animals. With them, as long as the weakness of their young endears them to their mothers, — in a word, associates them with their mothers, — the latter protect the former, at the peril of their lives, with a courage which reminds us of our heroes dying for their country. Certain species unite for hunting purposes, seek each other, call each other (a poet would say invite each other), to share their prey; in danger they aid, protect, and warn each other. The elephant knows how to help his companion out of the ditch into which the latter has fallen. Cows form a circle, with their horns outward and their calves in the centre, in order to repel the attacks of wolves. Horses and pigs, on hearing a cry of distress from one of their number, rush to the spot whence it comes. What descriptions I might give of their marriages, the tenderness of the males towards the females, and the fidelity of their loves! Let us add, however, — to be entirely just — that these touching demonstrations of society, fraternity, and love of neighbor, do not prevent the animals from quarrelling, fighting, and outrageously abusing one another while gaining their livelihood and showing their gallantry; the resemblance between them and ourselves is perfect.

The social instinct, in man and beast, exists to a greater or less degree — its nature is the same. Man has the greater need of association, and employs it more; the animal seems better able to endure isolation. In man, social needs are more imperative and complex; in the beast, they seem less intense, less diversified, less regretted. Society, in a word, aims, in the case of man, at the preservation of the race and the individual; with the animals, its object is more exclusively the preservation of the race.

554

As yet, we have met with no claim which man can make for himself alone. The social instinct and the moral sense he shares with the brutes; and when he thinks to become god-like by a few acts of charity, justice, and devotion, he does not perceive that in so acting he simply obeys an instinct wholly animal in its nature. As we are good, loving, tender, just, so we are passionate, greedy, lewd, and vindictive; that is, we are like the beasts. Our highest virtues appear, in the last analysis, as blind, impulsive instincts. What subjects for canonization and apotheosis!

There is, however, a difference between us two-handed bipeds and other living creatures — what is it?

A student of philosophy would hasten to reply: "This difference lies in the fact that we are conscious of our social faculty, while the animals are unconscious of theirs — in the fact that while we reflect and reason upon the operation of our social instinct, the animals do nothing of the kind."

I will go farther. It is by our reflective and reasoning powers, with which we seem to be exclusively endowed, that we know that it is injurious, first to others and then to ourselves, to resist the social instinct which governs us, and which we call *justice*. It is our reason which teaches us that the selfish man, the robber, the murderer — in a word, the traitor to society — sins against Nature, and is guilty with respect to others and himself, when he does wrong wilfully. Finally, it is our social sentiment on the one hand, and our reason on the other, which cause us to think that beings such as we should take the responsibility of their acts. Such is the principle of remorse, revenge, and penal justice.

But this proves only an intellectual diversity between the animals and man, not at all an affectional one; for, although we reason upon our relations with our fellows, we likewise reason upon our most trivial actions, — such as drinking, eating, choosing a wife, or selecting a dwelling-place. We reason upon things earthly and things heavenly; there is nothing to which our reasoning powers are not applicable. Now, just as the knowledge of external phenomena, which we acquire, has no influence upon their causes and laws, so reflection, by illuminating our instinct, enlightens us as to our sentient nature, but does not alter its character; it tells us what our morality is, but neither changes nor modifies it. Our dissatisfaction with ourselves after doing wrong, the indignation which we feel at the sight of injustice, the idea of deserved punishment and due remuneration, are effects of reflection, and not immediate effects of instinct and emotion. Our appreciation (I

555

do not say exclusive appreciation, for the animals also realize that they have done wrong, and are indignant when one of their number is attacked, but), our infinitely superior appreciation of our social duties, our knowledge of good and evil, does not establish, as regards morality, any vital difference between man and the beasts.

§ 2. — *Of the first and second degrees of Sociability.*

I insist upon the fact, which I have just pointed out, as one of the most important facts of anthropology.

The sympathetic attraction, which causes us to associate, is, by reason of its blind, unruly nature, always governed by temporary impulse, without regard to higher rights, and without distinction of merit or priority. The bastard dog follows indifferently all who call it; the suckling child regards every man as its father and every woman as its nurse; every living creature, when deprived of the society of animals of its species, seeks companionship in its solitude. This fundamental characteristic of the social instinct renders intolerable and even hateful the friendship of frivolous persons, liable to be infatuated with every new face, accommodating to all whether good or bad, and ready to sacrifice, for a passing *liaison*, the oldest and most honorable affections. The fault of such beings is not in the heart — it is in the judgment. Sociability, in this degree, is a sort of magnetism awakened in us by the contemplation of a being similar to ourselves, but which never goes beyond the person who feels it; it may be reciprocated, but not communicated. Love, benevolence, pity, sympathy, call it what you will, there is nothing in it which deserves esteem, — nothing which lifts man above the beast.

The second degree of sociability is justice, which may be defined as the *recognition of the equality between another's personality and our own.* The sentiment of justice we share with the animals; we alone can form an exact idea of it; but our idea, as has been said already, does not change its nature. We shall soon see how man rises to a third degree of sociability which the animals are incapable of reaching. But I must first prove by metaphysics that *society, justice,* and *equality,* are three equivalent terms, — three expressions meaning the same thing, — whose mutual conversion is always allowable.

If, amid the confusion of a shipwreck, having escaped in a boat with some provisions, I see a man struggling with the waves, am I bound to go to his assistance? Yes, I am bound under penalty of being adjudged guilty of murder and treason against society.

556

But am I also bound to share with him my provisions?

To settle this question, we must change the phraseology. If society is binding on the boat, is it also binding on the provisions? Undoubtedly. The duty of an associate is absolute. Man's occupancy succeeds his social nature, and is subordinate to it; possession can become exclusive only when permission to occupy is granted to all alike. That which in this instance obscures our duty is our power of foresight, which, causing us to fear an eventual danger, impels us to usurpation, and makes us robbers and murderers. Animals do not calculate the duty of instinct any more than the disadvantages resulting to those who exercise it; it would be strange if the intellect of man — the most sociable of animals — should lead him to disobey the law. He betrays society who attempts to use it only for his own advantage; better that God should deprive us of prudence, if it is to serve as the tool of our selfishness.

"What!" you will say, "must I share my bread, the bread which I have earned and which belongs to me, with the stranger whom I do not know; whom I may never see again, and who, perhaps, will reward me with ingratitude? If we had earned this bread together, if this man had done something to obtain it, he might demand his share, since his co-operation would entitle him to it; but as it is, what claim has he on me? We have not produced together — we shall not eat together."

The fallacy in this argument lies in the false supposition, that each producer is not necessarily associated with every other producer.

When two or more individuals have regularly organized a society, — when the contracts have been agreed upon, drafted, and signed, — there is no difficulty about the future. Everybody knows that when two men associate — for instance — in order to fish, if one of them catches no fish, he is none the less entitled to those caught by his associate. If two merchants form a partnership, while the partnership lasts, the profits and losses are divided between them; since each produces, not for himself, but for the society: when the time of distribution arrives, it is not the producer who is considered, but the associate. That is why the slave, to whom the planter gives straw and rice; and the civilized laborer, to whom the capitalist pays a salary which is always too small, — not being associated with their employers, although producing with them, — are disregarded when the product is divided. Thus, the horse who draws our coaches, and the ox who draws our carts produce with us, but are not associated with us; we take their product, but do not share it with them. The animals and laborers whom we employ hold the same relation to us. Whatever we do for them, we do, not from a sense of justice, but out of pure benevolence.[25]

But is it possible that we are not all associated? Let us call to mind what was said in the last two chapters, That even though we do not want to be associated, the force of things, the necessity of consumption, the laws of production, and the mathematical principle of exchange combine to associate us. There is but a single exception to this rule, — that of the proprietor, who, producing by his right of increase, is not associated with any one, and consequently is not obliged to share his product with any one; just as no one else is bound to share with him. With the exception of the proprietor, we labor for each other; we can do nothing by ourselves unaided by others, and we continually exchange products and services with each other. If these are not social acts, what are they?

Now, neither a commercial, nor an industrial, nor an agricultural association can be conceived of in the absence of equality; equality is its *sine qua non*. So that, in all matters which concern this association, to violate society is to violate justice and equality. Apply this principle to humanity at large. After what has been said, I assume that the reader has sufficient insight to enable him to dispense with any aid of mine.

By this principle, the man who takes possession of a field, and says, "This field is mine," will not be unjust so long as every one else has an equal right of possession; nor will he be unjust, if, wishing to change his location, he exchanges this field for an equivalent. But if, putting another in his place, he says to him, "Work for me while I rest," he then becomes unjust, unassociated, *unequal*. He is a proprietor.

Reciprocally, the sluggard, or the rake, who, without performing any social task, enjoys like others — and often more than others — the products of society, should be proceeded against as a thief and a parasite. We owe it to ourselves to give him nothing; but, since he must live, to put him under supervision, and compel him to labor.

Sociability is the attraction felt by sentient beings for each other. Justice is this same attraction, accompanied by thought and knowledge. But under what general concept, in what category of the understanding, is justice placed? In the category of equal quantities. Hence, the ancient definition of justice — *Justum æquale est, injustum inæquale*. What is it, then, to practise justice? It is to give equal wealth to each, on condition of equal labor. It is to act socially. Our selfishness may complain; there is no escape from evidence and necessity.

What is the right of occupancy? It is a natural method of dividing the earth, by reducing each laborer's share as fast as new laborers present themselves. This right disappears if the public interest requires it; which, being the social interest, is also that of the occupant.

What is the right of labor? It is the right to obtain one's share of wealth by fulfilling the required conditions. It is the right of society, the right of equality.

Justice, which is the product of the combination of an idea and an instinct, manifests itself in man as soon as he is capable of feeling, and of forming ideas. Consequently, it has been regarded as an innate and original sentiment; but this opinion is logically and chronologically false. But justice, by its composition hybrid — if I may use the term, — justice, born of emotion and intellect combined, seems to me one of the strongest proofs of the unity and simplicity of the *ego;* the organism being no more capable of producing such a mixture by itself, than are the combined senses of hearing and sight of forming a binary sense, half auditory and half visual.

This double nature of justice gives us the definitive basis of all the demonstrations in Chapters II., III., and IV. On the one hand, the idea of *justice* being identical with that of society, and society necessarily implying equality, equality must underlie all the sophisms invented in defence of property; for, since property can be defended only as a just and social institution, and property being inequality, in order to prove that property is in harmony with society, it must be shown that injustice is justice, and that inequality is equality, — a contradiction in terms. On the other hand, since the idea of equality — the second element of justice — has its source in the mathematical proportions of things; and since property, or the unequal distribution of wealth among laborers, destroys the necessary balance between labor, production, and consumption, — property must be impossible.

All men, then, are associated; all are entitled to the same justice; all are equal. Does it follow that the preferences of love and friendship are unjust?

This requires explanation. I have already supposed the case of a man in peril, I being in a position to help him. Now, I suppose myself appealed to at the same time by two men exposed to danger. Am I not allowed — am I not commanded even — to rush first to the aid of him who is endeared to me by ties of blood, friendship, acquaintance, or esteem, at the risk of leaving the other to perish? Yes. And why? Because within universal society there exist for each of us as many special societies as there are individuals; and we are bound, by the principle of sociability itself, to fulfil the obligations which these impose upon us, according to the intimacy of our relations with them. Therefore we must give our father, mother, children, friends, relatives, &c., the preference over all others. But in what consists this preference?

A judge has a case to decide, in which one of the parties is his friend, and the other his enemy. Should he, in this instance, prefer his *intimate associate* to his *distant associate;* and decide the case in favor of his friend, in spite of evidence to the contrary? No: for, if he should favor his friend's injustice, he would become his accomplice in his violation of the social compact; he would form with him a sort of conspiracy against the social body. Preference should be shown only in personal matters, such as love, esteem, confidence, or intimacy, when all cannot be considered at once. Thus, in case of fire, a father would save his own child before thinking of his neighbor's; but the recognition of a right not being an optional matter with a judge, he is not at liberty to favor one person to the detriment of another.

The theory of these special societies — which are formed concentrically, so to speak, by each of us inside of the main body — gives the key to all the problems which arise from the opposition and conflict of the different varieties of social duty, — problems upon which the ancient tragedies are based.

The justice practised among animals is, in a certain degree, negative. With the exception of protecting their young, hunting and plundering in troops, uniting for common defence and sometimes for individual assistance, it consists more in prevention than in action. A sick animal who cannot arise from the ground, or an imprudent one who has fallen over a precipice, receives neither medicine nor nourishment. If he cannot cure himself, nor relieve himself of his trouble, his life is in danger: he will neither be cared for in bed, nor fed in a prison. Their neglect of their fellows arises as much from the weakness of their intellect as from their lack of resources. Still, the degrees of intimacy common among men are not unknown to the animals. They have friendships of habit and of choice; friendships neighborly, and friendships parental. In comparison with us, they have feeble memories, sluggish feelings, and are almost destitute of intelligence; but the identity of these faculties is preserved to some extent, and our superiority in this respect arises entirely from our understanding.

It is our strength of memory and penetration of judgment which enable us to multiply and combine the acts which our social instinct impels us to perform, and which teaches us how to render them more effective, and how to distribute them justly. The beasts who live in society practise justice, but are ignorant of its nature, and do not reason upon it; they obey their instinct without thought or philosophy. They know not how to unite the social sentiment with the idea of equality, which they do not possess; this idea being an abstract one. We, on the contrary, starting with the principle that society implies equality, can, by our reasoning faculty, understand and agree with each other in settling our rights; we have even used our judgment to a great extent. But in all this our conscience plays a small part, as is proved by the fact that the idea of *right* — of which we catch a glimpse in certain animals who approach nearer than any others to our standard of intelligence — seems to grow, from the low level at which it stands in savages, to the lofty height which it reaches in a Plato or a Franklin. If we trace the development of the moral sense in individuals, and the progress of laws in nations, we shall be convinced that the ideas of justice and legislative perfection are always proportional to intelligence. The notion of justice — which has been regarded by some philosophers as simple — is then, in reality, complex. It springs from the social instinct on the one hand, and the idea of equality on the other; just as the notion of guilt arises from the feeling that justice has been violated, and from the idea of free-will.

In conclusion, instinct is not modified by acquaintance with its nature; and the facts of society, which we have thus far observed, occur among beasts as well as men. We know the meaning of justice; in other words, of sociability viewed from the standpoint of equality. We have met with nothing which separates us from the animals.

§ 3. — *Of the third degree of Sociability.*

The reader, perhaps, has not forgotten what was said in the third chapter concerning the division of labor and the speciality of talents. The sum total of the talents and capacities of the race is always the same, and their nature is always similar. We are all born poets, mathematicians, philosophers, artists, artisans, or farmers, but we are not born equally endowed; and between one man and another in society, or between one faculty and another in the same individual, there is an infinite difference. This difference of degree in the same faculties, this predominance of talent in certain directions, is, we have said, the very foundation of our society. Intelligence and natural genius have been distributed by Nature so economically, and yet so liberally, that in society there is no danger of either a surplus or a scarcity of special talents; and that each laborer, by devoting himself to his function, may always attain to the degree of proficiency necessary to enable him to benefit by the labors and discoveries of his fellows. Owing to this simple and wise precaution of Nature, the laborer is not isolated by his task. He communicates with his fellows through the mind, before he is united with them in heart; so that with him love is born of intelligence.

It is not so with societies of animals. In every species, the aptitudes of all the individuals — though very limited — are equal in number and (when they are not the result of instinct) in intensity. Each one does as well as all the others what all the others do; provides his food, avoids the enemy, burrows in the earth, builds a nest, &c. No animal, when free and healthy, expects or requires the aid of his neighbor; who, in his turn, is equally independent.

Associated animals live side by side without any intellectual intercourse or intimate communication, — all doing the same things, having nothing to learn or to remember; they see, feel, and come in contact with each other, but never penetrate each other. Man continually exchanges with man ideas and feelings, products and services. Every discovery and act in society is necessary to him. But of this immense quantity of products and ideas, that which each one has to produce and acquire for himself is but an atom in the sun. Man would not be man were it not for society, and society is supported by the balance and harmony of the powers which compose it.

Society, among the animals, is *simple;* with man it is *complex.* Man is associated with man by the same instinct which associates animal with animal; but man is associated differently from the animal, and it is this difference in association which constitutes the difference in morality.

I have proved, — at too great length, perhaps, — both by the spirit of the laws which regard property as the basis of society, and by political economy, that inequality of conditions is justified neither by priority of occupation nor superiority of talent, service, industry, and capacity. But, although equality of conditions is a necessary consequence of natural right, of liberty, of the laws of production, of the capacity of physical nature, and of the principle of society itself, — it does not prevent the social sentiment from stepping over the boundaries of *debt* and *credit.* The fields of benevolence and love extend far beyond; and when economy has adjusted its balance, the mind begins to benefit by its own justice, and the heart expands in the boundlessness of its affection.

The social sentiment then takes on a new character, which varies with different persons. In the strong, it becomes the pleasure of generosity; among equals, frank and cordial friendship; in the weak, the pleasure of admiration and gratitude.

The man who is superior in strength, skill, or courage, knows that he owes all that he is to society, without which he could not exist. He knows that, in treating him precisely as it does the lowest of its members, society discharges its whole duty towards him. But he does not underrate his faculties; he is no less conscious of his power and greatness; and it is this voluntary reverence which he pays to humanity, this avowal that he is but an instrument of Nature, — who is alone worthy of glory and worship, — it is, I say, this simultaneous confession of the heart and the mind, this genuine adoration of the Great Being, that distinguishes and elevates man, and lifts him to a degree of social morality to which the beast is powerless to attain. Hercules destroying the monsters and punishing brigands for the safety of Greece, Orpheus teaching the rough and wild Pelasgians, — neither of them putting a price upon their services, — there we see the noblest creations of poetry, the loftiest expression of justice and virtue.

The joys of self-sacrifice are ineffable.

If I were to compare human society to the old Greek tragedies, I should say that the phalanx of noble minds and lofty souls dances the *strophe*, and the humble multitude the *antistrophe*. Burdened with painful and disagreeable tasks, but rendered omnipotent by their number and the harmonic arrangement of their functions, the latter execute what the others plan. Guided by them, they owe them nothing; they honor them, however, and lavish upon them praise and approbation.

Gratitude fills people with adoration and enthusiasm.

But equality delights my heart. Benevolence degenerates into tyranny, and admiration into servility. Friendship is the daughter of equality. O my friends! may I live in your midst without emulation, and without glory; let equality bring us together, and fate assign us our places. May I die without knowing to whom among you I owe the most esteem!

Friendship is precious to the hearts of the children of men.

Generosity, gratitude (I mean here only that gratitude which is born of admiration of a superior power), and friendship are three distinct shades of a single sentiment which I will call

équité, or *social proportionality*.[26] *Equité* does not change justice: but, always taking *équité* for the base, it superadds esteem, and thereby forms in man a third degree of sociability. *Equité* makes it at once our duty and our pleasure to aid the weak who have need of us, and to make them our equals; to pay to the strong a just tribute of gratitude and honor, without enslaving ourselves to them; to cherish our neighbors, friends, and equals, for that which we receive from them, even by right of exchange. *Equité* is sociability raised to its ideal by reason and justice; its commonest manifestation is *urbanity* or *politeness*, which, among certain nations, sums up in a single word nearly all the social duties.

Now, this feeling is unknown among the beasts, who love and cling to each other, and show their preferences, but who cannot conceive of esteem, and who are incapable of generosity, admiration, or politeness.

This feeling does not spring from intelligence, which calculates, computes, and balances, but does not love; which sees, but does not feel. As justice is the product of social instinct and reflection combined, so *équité* is a product of justice and taste combined — that is, of our powers of judging and of idealizing.

This product — the third and last degree of human sociability — is determined by our complex mode of association; in which inequality, or rather the divergence of faculties, and the speciality of functions — tending of themselves to isolate laborers — demand a more active sociability.

That is why the force which oppresses while protecting is execrable; why the silly ignorance which views with the same eye the marvels of art, and the products of the rudest industry, excites unutterable contempt; why proud mediocrity, which glories in saying, "I have paid you — I owe you nothing," is especially odious.

Sociability, justice, équité — such, in its triplicity, is the exact definition of the instinctive faculty which leads us into communication with our fellows, and whose physical manifestation is expressed by the formula: *Equality in natural wealth, and the products of labor*.

These three degrees of sociability support and imply each other. *Equité* cannot exist without justice; society without justice is a solecism. If, in order to reward talent, I take from one to give to another, in unjustly stripping the first, I do not esteem his talent as I ought; if, in society, I award more to myself than to my associate, we are not really associated. Justice is sociability as manifested in the division of material things, susceptible of weight and measure; *equité* is justice accompanied by admiration and esteem, — things which cannot be measured.

From this several inferences may be drawn.

1. Though we are free to grant our esteem to one more than to another, and in all possible degrees, yet we should give no one more than his proportion of the common wealth; because the duty of justice, being imposed upon us before that of *equité*, must always take precedence of it. The woman honored by the ancients, who, when forced by a tyrant to choose between the death of her brother and that of her husband, sacrificed the latter on the ground that she could find another husband but not another brother, — that woman, I say, in obeying her sense of *equité*, failed in point of justice, and did a bad deed, because conjugal association is a closer relation than fraternal association, and because the life of our neighbor is not our property.

By the same principle, inequality of wages cannot be admitted by law on the ground of inequality of talents; because the just distribution of wealth is the function of economy, — not of enthusiasm.

Finally, as regards donations, wills, and inheritance, society, careful both of the personal affections and its own rights, must never permit love and partiality to destroy justice. And, though it is pleasant to think that the son, who has been long associated with his father in business, is more capable than any one else of carrying it on; and that the citizen, who is surprised in the midst of his task by death, is best fitted, in consequence of his natural taste for his occupation, to designate his successor; and though the heir should be allowed the right of choice in case of more than one inheritance, — nevertheless, society can tolerate no concentration of capital and industry for the benefit of a single man, no monopoly of labor, no encroachment.[27]

2. *Equité*, justice, and society, can exist only between individuals of the same species. They form no part of the relations of different races to each other, — for instance, of the wolf to the goat, of the goat to man, of man to God, much less of God to man. The attribution of justice,

equity, and love to the Supreme Being is pure anthropomorphism; and the adjectives just, merciful, pitiful, and the like, should be stricken from our litanies. God can be regarded as just, equitable, and good, only to another God. Now, God has no associate; consequently, he cannot experience social affections, — such as goodness, *équité*, and justice. Is the shepherd said to be just to his sheep and his dogs? No: and if he saw fit to shear as much wool from a lamb six months old, as from a ram of two years; or, if he required as much work from a young dog as from an old one, — they would say, not that he was unjust, but that he was foolish. Between man and beast there is no society, though there may be affection. Man loves the animals as *things*, — as *sentient things*, if you will, — but not as *persons*. Philosophy, after having eliminated from the idea of God the passions ascribed to him by superstition, will then be obliged to eliminate also the virtues which our liberal piety awards to him.[28]

If God should come down to earth, and dwell among us, we could not love him unless he became like us; nor give him any thing unless he produced something; nor listen to him unless he proved us mistaken; nor worship him unless he manifested his power. All the laws of our nature, affectional, economical, and intellectual, would prevent us from treating him as we treat our fellow-men, — that is, according to reason, justice, and *équité*. I infer from this that, if God should wish ever to put himself into immediate communication with man, he would have to become a man.

Now, if kings are images of God, and executors of his will, they cannot receive love, wealth, obedience, and glory from us, unless they consent to labor and associate with us — produce as much as they consume, reason with their subjects, and do wonderful things. Still more; if, as some pretend, kings are public functionaries, the love which is due them is measured by their personal amiability; our obligation to obey them, by the wisdom of their commands; and their civil list, by the total social production divided by the number of citizens.

Thus, jurisprudence, political economy, and psychology agree in admitting the law of equality. Right and duty — the due reward of talent and labor — the outbursts of love and enthusiasm, — all are regulated in advance by an invariable standard; all depend upon number and balance. Equality of conditions is the law of society, and universal solidarity is the ratification of this law.

Equality of conditions has never been realized, thanks to our passions and our ignorance; but our opposition to this law has made it all the more a necessity. To that fact history bears perpetual testimony, and the course of events reveals it to us. Society advances from equation to equation. To the eyes of the economist, the revolutions of empires seem now like the reduction of algebraical quantities, which are inter-deducible; now like the discovery of unknown quantities, induced by the inevitable influence of time. Figures are the providence of history. Undoubtedly there are other elements in human progress; but in the multitude of hidden causes which agitate nations, there is none more powerful or constant, none less obscure, than the periodical explosions of the proletariat against property. Property, acting by exclusion and encroachment, while population was increasing, has been the life-principle and definitive cause of all revolutions. Religious wars, and wars of conquest, when they have stopped short of the extermination of races, have been only accidental disturbances, soon repaired by the mathematical progression of the life of nations. The downfall and death of societies are due to the power of accumulation possessed by property.

In the middle ages, take Florence, — a republic of merchants and brokers, always rent by its well-known factions, the Guelphs and Ghibellines, who were, after all, only the people and the proprietors fighting against each other, — Florence, ruled by bankers, and borne down at last by the weight of her debts;[29] in ancient times, take Rome, preyed upon from its birth by usury, flourishing, nevertheless, as long as the known world furnished its terrible proletaires with *labor*, stained with blood by civil war at every interval of rest, and dying of exhaustion when the people lost, together with their former energy, their last spark of moral sense; Carthage, a commercial and financial city, continually divided by internal competition; Tyre, Sidon, Jerusalem, Nineveh, Babylon, ruined, in turn, by commercial rivalry and, as we now express it, by panics in the market, — do not these famous examples show clearly enough the fate which awaits modern nations, unless the people, unless France, with a sudden burst of her powerful voice, proclaims in thunder-tones the abolition of the *régime* of property?

Here my task should end. I have proved the right of the poor; I have shown the usurpation of the rich. I demand justice; it is not my business to execute the sentence. If it should be argued — in order to prolong for a few years an illegitimate privilege — that it is not enough to demonstrate equality, that it is necessary also to organize it, and above all to establish it peacefully, I might reply: The welfare of the oppressed is of more importance than official composure. Equality of conditions is a natural law upon which public economy and jurisprudence are based. The right to labor, and the principle of equal distribution of wealth, cannot give way to the anxieties of power. It is not for the proletaire to reconcile the contradictions of the codes, still less to suffer for the errors of the government. On the contrary, it is the duty of the civil and administrative power to reconstruct itself on the basis of political equality. An evil, when known, should be condemned and destroyed. The legislator cannot plead ignorance as an excuse for upholding a glaring iniquity. Restitution should not be delayed. Justice, justice! recognition of right! reinstatement of the proletaire! — when these results are accomplished, then, judges and consuls, you may attend to your police, and provide a government for the Republic!

For the rest, I do not think that a single one of my readers accuses me of knowing how to destroy, but of not knowing how to construct. In demonstrating the principle of equality, I have laid the foundation of the social structure I have done more. I have given an example of the true method of solving political and legislative problems. Of the science itself, I confess that I know nothing more than its principle; and I know of no one at present who can boast of having penetrated deeper. Many people cry, "Come to me, and I will teach you the truth!" These people mistake for the truth their cherished opinion and ardent conviction, which is usually any thing but the truth. The science of society — like all human sciences — will be for ever incomplete. The depth and variety of the questions which it embraces are infinite. We hardly know the A B C of this science, as is proved by the fact that we have not yet emerged from the period of systems, and have not ceased to put the authority of the majority in the place of facts. A certain philological society decided linguistic questions by a plurality of votes. Our parliamentary debates — were their results less pernicious — would be even more ridiculous. The task of the true publicist, in the age in which we live, is to close the mouths of quacks and charlatans, and to teach the public to demand demonstrations, instead of being contented with symbols and programmes. Before talking of the science itself, it is necessary to ascertain its object, and discover its method and principle. The ground must be cleared of the prejudices which encumber it. Such is the mission of the nineteenth century.

For my part, I have sworn fidelity to my work of demolition, and I will not cease to pursue the truth through the ruins and rubbish. I hate to see a thing half done; and it will be believed without any assurance of mine, that, having dared to raise my hand against the Holy Ark, I shall not rest contented with the removal of the cover. The mysteries of the sanctuary of iniquity must be unveiled, the tables of the old alliance broken, and all the objects of the ancient faith thrown in a heap to the swine. A charter has been given to us, — a *résumé* of political science, the monument of twenty legislatures. A code has been written, — the pride of a conqueror, and the summary of ancient wisdom. Well! of this charter and this code not one article shall be left standing upon another! The time has come for the wise to choose their course, and prepare for reconstruction.

But, since a destroyed error necessarily implies a counter-truth, I will not finish this treatise without solving the first problem of political science, — that which receives the attention of all minds.

When property is abolished, what will be the form of society! Will it be communism?

Part Second.

§ 1. — *Of the Causes of our Mistakes. The Origin of Property.*

The true form of human society cannot be determined until the following question has been solved: —

Property not being our natural condition, how did it gain a foothold? Why has the social instinct, so trustworthy among the animals, erred in the case of man? Why is man, who was born for society, not yet associated?

I have said that human society is *complex* in its nature. Though this expression is inaccurate, the fact to which it refers is none the less true; namely, the classification of talents and capacities. But who does not see that these talents and capacities, owing to their infinite variety, give rise to an infinite variety of wills, and that the character, the inclinations, and — if I may venture to use the expression — the form of the *ego*, are necessarily changed; so that in the order of liberty, as in the order of intelligence, there are as many types as individuals, as many characters as heads, whose tastes, fancies, and propensities, being modified by dissimilar ideas, must necessarily conflict? Man, by his nature and his instinct, is predestined to society; but his personality, ever varying, is adverse to it.

In societies of animals, all the members do exactly the same things. The same genius directs them; the same will animates them. A society of beasts is a collection of atoms, round, hooked, cubical, or triangular, but always perfectly identical. These personalities do not vary, and we might say that a single *ego* governs them all. The labors which animals perform, whether alone or in society, are exact reproductions of their character. Just as the swarm of bees is composed of individual bees, alike in nature and equal in value, so the honeycomb is formed of individual cells, constantly and invariably repeated.

But man's intelligence, fitted for his social destiny and his personal needs, is of a very different composition, and therefore gives rise to a wonderful variety of human wills. In the bee, the will is constant and uniform, because the instinct which guides it is invariable, and constitutes the animal's whole life and nature. In man, talent varies, and the mind wavers; consequently, his will is multiform and vague. He seeks society, but dislikes constraint and monotony; he is an imitator, but fond of his own ideas, and passionately in love with his works.

If, like the bees, every man were born possessed of talent, perfect knowledge of certain kinds, and, in a word, an innate acquaintance with the functions he has to perform, but destitute of reflective and reasoning faculties, society would organize itself. We should see one man plowing a field, another building houses; this one forging metals, that one cutting clothes; and still others storing the products, and superintending their distribution. Each one, without inquiring as to the object of his labor, and without troubling himself about the extent of his task, would obey orders, bring his product, receive his salary, and would then rest for a time; keeping meanwhile no accounts, envious of nobody, and satisfied with the distributor, who never would be unjust to any one. Kings would govern, but would not reign; for to reign is to be a *proprietor à l'engrais*, as Bonaparte said: and having no commands to give, since all would be at their posts, they would serve rather as rallying centres than as authorities or counsellors. It would be a state of ordered communism, but not a society entered into deliberately and freely.

But man acquires skill only by observation and experiment. He reflects, then, since to observe and experiment is to reflect; he reasons, since he cannot help reasoning. In reflecting, he becomes deluded; in reasoning, he makes mistakes, and, thinking himself right, persists in them. He is wedded to his opinions; he esteems himself, and despises others. Consequently, he isolates himself; for he could not submit to the majority without renouncing his will and his reason, — that is, without disowning himself, which is impossible. And this isolation, this intellectual egotism, this individuality of opinion, lasts until the truth is demonstrated to him by observation and experience. A final illustration will make these facts still clearer.

570

If to the blind but convergent and harmonious instincts of a swarm of bees should be suddenly added reflection and judgment, the little society could not long exist. In the first place, the bees would not fail to try some new industrial process; for instance, that of making their cells round or square. All sorts of systems and inventions would be tried, until long experience, aided by geometry, should show them that the hexagonal shape is the best. Then insurrections would occur. The drones would be told to provide for themselves, and the queens to labor; jealousy would spread among the laborers; discords would burst forth; soon each one would want to produce on his own account; and finally the hive would be abandoned, and the bees would perish. Evil would be introduced into the honey-producing republic by the power of reflection, — the very faculty which ought to constitute its glory.

Thus, moral evil, or, in this case, disorder in society, is naturally explained by our power of reflection. The mother of poverty, crime, insurrection, and war was inequality of conditions; which was the daughter of property, which was born of selfishness, which was engendered by private opinion, which descended in a direct line from the autocracy of reason. Man, in his infancy, is neither criminal nor barbarous, but ignorant and inexperienced. Endowed with imperious instincts which are under the control of his reasoning faculty, at first he reflects but little, and reasons inaccurately; then, benefiting by his mistakes, he rectifies his ideas, and perfects his reason. In the first place, it is the savage sacrificing all his possessions for a trinket, and then repenting and weeping; it is Esau selling his birthright for a mess of pottage, and afterwards wishing to cancel the bargain; it is the civilized workman laboring in insecurity, and continually demanding that his wages be increased, neither he nor his employer understanding that, in the absence of equality, any salary, however large, is always insufficient. Then it is Naboth dying to defend his inheritance; Cato tearing out his entrails that he might not be enslaved; Socrates drinking the fatal cup in defence of liberty of thought; it is the third estate of '89 reclaiming its liberty: soon it will be the people demanding equality of wages and an equal division of the means of production.

Man is born a social being, — that is, he seeks equality and justice in all his relations, but he loves independence and praise. The difficulty of satisfying these various desires at the same time is the primary cause of the despotism of the will, and the appropriation which results from it. On the other hand, man always needs a market for his products; unable to compare values of different kinds, he is satisfied to judge approximately, according to his passion and caprice; and he engages in dishonest commerce, which always results in wealth and poverty. Thus, the greatest evils which man suffers arise from the misuse of his social nature, of this same justice of which he is so proud, and which he applies with such deplorable ignorance. The practice of justice is a science which, when once discovered and diffused, will sooner or later put an end to social disorder, by teaching us our rights and duties.

This progressive and painful education of our instinct, this slow and imperceptible transformation of our spontaneous perceptions into deliberate knowledge, does not take place among the animals, whose instincts remain fixed, and never become enlightened.

"According to Frederic Cuvier, who has so clearly distinguished between instinct and intelligence in animals, 'instinct is a natural and inherent faculty, like feeling, irritability, or intelligence. The wolf and the fox who recognize the traps in which they have been caught, and who avoid them; the dog and the horse, who understand the meaning of several of our words, and who obey us, — thereby show *intelligence*. The dog who hides the remains of his dinner, the bee who constructs his cell, the bird who builds his nest, act only from *instinct*. Even man has instincts: it is a special instinct which leads the new-born child to suck. But, in man, almost every thing is accomplished by intelligence; and intelligence supplements instinct. The opposite is true of animals: their instinct is given them as a supplement to their intelligence.' " — *Flourens: Analytical Summary of the Observations of F. Cuvier.*

"We can form a clear idea of instinct only by admitting that animals have in their *sensorium*, images or innate and constant sensations, which influence their actions in the same manner that ordinary and accidental sensations commonly do. It is a sort of dream, or vision, which always follows them and in all which relates to instinct they may be regarded as somnambulists." — *F. Cuvier: Introduction to the Animal Kingdom.*

Intelligence and instinct being common, then, though in different degrees, to animals and man, what is the distinguishing characteristic of the latter? According to F. Cuvier, it is *reflection or the power of intellectually considering our own modifications by a survey of ourselves.*

This lacks clearness, and requires an explanation.

If we grant intelligence to animals, we must also grant them, in some degree, reflection; for, the first cannot exist without the second, as F. Cuvier himself has proved by numerous examples. But notice that the

572

learned observer defines the kind of reflection which distinguishes us from the animals as the *power of considering our own modifications*. This I shall endeavour to interpret, by developing to the best of my ability the laconism of the philosophical naturalist.

The intelligence acquired by animals never modifies the operations which they perform by instinct: it is given them only as a provision against unexpected accidents which might disturb these operations. In man, on the contrary, instinctive action is constantly changing into deliberate action. Thus, man is social by instinct, and is every day becoming social by reflection and choice. At first, he formed his words by instinct;[30] he was a poet by inspiration: to-day, he makes grammar a science, and poetry an art. His conception of God and a future life is spontaneous and instinctive, and his expressions of this conception have been, by turns, monstrous, eccentric, beautiful, comforting, and terrible. All these different creeds, at which the frivolous irreligion of the eighteenth century mocked, are modes of expression of the religious sentiment. Some day, man will explain to himself the character of the God whom he believes in, and the nature of that other world to which his soul aspires.

All that he does from instinct man despises; or, if he admires it, it is as Nature's work, not as his own. This explains the obscurity which surrounds the names of early inventors; it explains also our indifference to religious matters, and the ridicule heaped upon religious customs. Man esteems only the products of reflection and of reason. The most wonderful works of instinct are, in his eyes, only lucky *god-sends;* he reserves the name *discovery* — I had almost said creation — for the works of intelligence. Instinct is the source of passion and enthusiasm; it is intelligence which causes crime and virtue.

In developing his intelligence, man makes use of not only his own observations, but also those of others. He keeps an account of his experience, and preserves the record; so that the race, as well as the individual, becomes more and more intelligent. The animals do not transmit their knowledge; that which each individual accumulates dies with him.

It is not enough, then, to say that we are distinguished from the animals by reflection, unless we mean thereby the *constant tendency of our instinct to become intelligence*. While man is governed by instinct, he is unconscious of his acts. He never would deceive himself, and never would be troubled by errors, evils, and disorder, if, like the animals, instinct were his only guide. But the Creator has endowed us with

573

reflection, to the end that our instinct might become intelligence; and since this reflection and resulting knowledge pass through various stages, it happens that in the beginning our instinct is opposed, rather than guided, by reflection; consequently, that our power of thought leads us to act in opposition to our nature and our end; that, deceiving ourselves, we do and suffer evil, until instinct which points us towards good, and reflection which makes us stumble into evil, are replaced by the science of good and evil, which invariably causes us to seek the one and avoid the other.

Thus, evil — or error and its consequences — is the firstborn son of the union of two opposing faculties, instinct and reflection; good, or truth, must inevitably be the second child. Or, to again employ the figure, evil is the product of incest between adverse powers; good will sooner or later be the legitimate child of their holy and mysterious union.

Property, born of the reasoning faculty, intrenches itself behind comparisons. But, just as reflection and reason are subsequent to spontaneity, observation to sensation, and experience to instinct, so property is subsequent to communism. Communism — or association in a simple form — is the necessary object and original aspiration of the social nature, the spontaneous movement by which it manifests and establishes itself. It is the first phase of human civilization. In this state of society, — which the jurists have called *negative communism* — man draws near to man, and shares with him the fruits of the field and the milk and flesh of animals. Little by little this communism — negative as long as man does not produce — tends to become positive and organic through the development of labor and industry. But it is then that the sovereignty of thought, and the terrible faculty of reasoning logically or illogically, teach man that, if equality is the *sine qua non* of society, communism is the first species of slavery. To express this idea by an Hegelian formula, I will say:

Communism — the first expression of the social nature — is the first term of social development, — the *thesis;* property, the reverse of communism, is the second term, — the *antithesis*. When we have discovered the third term, the *synthesis*, we shall have the required solution. Now, this synthesis necessarily results from the correction of the thesis by the antithesis. Therefore it is necessary, by a final examination of their characteristics, to eliminate those features which are hostile to sociability. The union of the two remainders will give us the true form of human association.

§ 2. — *Characteristics of Communism and of Property.*

574

I. I ought not to conceal the fact that property and communism have been considered always the only possible forms of society. This deplorable error has been the life of property. The disadvantages of communism are so obvious that its critics never have needed to employ much eloquence to thoroughly disgust men with it. The irreparability of the injustice which it causes, the violence which it does to attractions and repulsions, the yoke of iron which it fastens upon the will, the moral torture to which it subjects the conscience, the debilitating effect which it has upon society; and, to sum it all up, the pious and stupid uniformity which it enforces upon the free, active, reasoning, unsubmissive personality of man, have shocked common sense, and condemned communism by an irrevocable decree.

The authorities and examples cited in its favor disprove it. The communistic republic of Plato involved slavery; that of Lycurgus employed Helots, whose duty it was to produce for their masters, thus enabling the latter to devote themselves exclusively to athletic sports and to war. Even J. J. Rousseau — confounding communism and equality — has said somewhere that, without slavery, he did not think equality of conditions possible. The communities of the early Church did not last the first century out, and soon degenerated into monasteries. In those of the Jesuits of Paraguay, the condition of the blacks is said by all travellers to be as miserable as that of slaves; and it is a fact that the good Fathers were obliged to surround themselves with ditches and walls to prevent their new converts from escaping. The followers of Baboeuf — guided by a lofty horror of property rather than by any definite belief — were ruined by exaggeration of their principles; the St. Simonians, lumping communism and inequality, passed away like a masquerade. The greatest danger to which society is exposed to-day is that of another shipwreck on this rock.

Singularly enough, systematic communism — the deliberate negation of property — is conceived under the direct influence of the proprietary prejudice; and property is the basis of all communistic theories.

The members of a community, it is true, have no private property; but the community is proprietor, and proprietor not only of the goods, but of the persons and wills. In consequence of this principle of absolute property, labor, which should be only a condition imposed upon man by Nature, becomes in all communities a human commandment, and therefore odious. Passive obedience, irreconcilable with a reflecting will, is strictly enforced. Fidelity to regulations, which are always defective, however wise they may be thought, allows of no complaint. Life, talent, and all the human faculties are the property of the State, which has the right to use them as it pleases for the common good. Private associations are sternly prohibited, in spite of the likes and dislikes of different natures, because to tolerate them would be to introduce small communities within the large one, and consequently private property; the strong work for the weak, although this ought to be left to benevolence, and not enforced, advised, or enjoined; the industrious work for the lazy, although this is unjust; the clever work for the foolish, although this is absurd; and, finally, man — casting aside his personality, his spontaneity, his genius, and his affections — humbly annihilates himself at the feet of the majestic and inflexible Commune!

Communism is inequality, but not as property is. Property is the exploitation of the weak by the strong. Communism is the exploitation of the strong by the weak. In property, inequality of conditions is the result of force, under whatever name it be disguised: physical and mental force; force of events, chance, *fortune;* force of accumulated property, &c. In communism, inequality springs from placing mediocrity on a level with excellence. This damaging equation is repellent to the conscience, and causes merit to complain; for, although it may be the duty of the strong to aid the weak, they prefer to do it out of generosity, — they never will endure a comparison. Give them equal opportunities of labor, and equal wages, but never allow their jealousy to be awakened by mutual suspicion of unfaithfulness in the performance of the common task.

Communism is oppression and slavery. Man is very willing to obey the law of duty, serve his country, and oblige his friends; but he wishes to labor when he pleases, where he pleases, and as much as he pleases. He wishes to dispose of his own time, to be governed only by necessity, to choose his friendships, his recreation, and his discipline; to act from judgment, not by command; to sacrifice himself through selfishness, not through servile obligation. Communism is essentially opposed to the free exercise of our faculties, to our noblest desires, to our deepest feelings. Any plan which could be devised for reconciling it with the demands of the individual reason and will would end only in changing the thing while preserving the name. Now, if we are honest truth-seekers, we shall avoid disputes about words.

Thus, communism violates the sovereignty of the conscience, and equality: the first, by restricting spontaneity of mind and heart, and freedom of thought and action; the second, by placing labor and laziness, skill and stupidity, and even vice and virtue on an equality in point of comfort. For the rest, if property is impossible on account of

576

the desire to accumulate, communism would soon become so through the desire to shirk.

II. Property, in its turn, violates equality by the rights of exclusion and increase, and freedom by despotism. The former effect of property having been sufficiently developed in the last three chapters, I will content myself here with establishing by a final comparison, its perfect identity with robbery.

The Latin words for robber are *fur* and *latro;* the former taken from the Greek *for*, from GREEK *iþþþ or fhrw*, Latin *fero*, I carry away; the latter from *laqrw*, I play the part of a brigand, which is derived from *lhqw*, Latin *lateo*, I conceal myself. The Greeks have also *klepths*, from *kleptw*, I filch, whose radical consonants are the same as those of *kalnptw*, I cover, I conceal. Thus, in these languages, the idea of a robber is that of a man who conceals, carries away, or diverts, in any manner whatever, a thing which does not belong to him.

The Hebrews expressed the same idea by the word *gannab*, — robber, — from the verb *ganab*, which means to put away, to turn aside: *lo thignob (Decalogue: Eighth Commandment)*, thou shalt not steal, — that is, thou shalt not hold back, thou shalt not put away any thing for thyself. That is the act of a man who, on entering into a society into which he agrees to bring all that he has, secretly reserves a portion, as did the celebrated disciple Ananias.

The etymology of the French verb *voler* is still more significant. *Voler*, or *faire la vole* (from the Latin *vola*, palm of the hand), means to take all the tricks in a game of ombre; so that *le voleur*, the robber, is the capitalist who takes all, who gets the lion's share. Probably this verb *voler* had its origin in the professional slang of thieves, whence it has passed into common use, and, consequently into the phraseology of the law.

Robbery is committed in a variety of ways, which have been very cleverly distinguished and classified by legislators according to their heinousness or merit, to the end that some robbers may be honored, while others are punished.

We rob, — 1. By murder on the highway; 2. Alone, or in a band; 3. By breaking into buildings, or scaling walls; 4. By abstraction; 5. By fraudulent bankruptcy; 6. By forgery of the handwriting of public officials or private individuals; 7. By manufacture of counterfeit money.

This species includes all robbers who practise their profession with no other aid than force and open fraud. Bandits, brigands, pirates, rovers by land and sea, — these names were gloried in by the ancient heroes, who thought their profession as noble as it was lucrative. Nimrod, Theseus, Jason and his Argonauts; Jephthah, David, Cacus, Romulus, Clovis and all his Merovingian descendants; Robert Guiscard, Tancred de Hauteville, Bohemond, and most of the Norman heroes, — were brigands and robbers. The heroic character of the robber is expressed in this line from Horace, in reference to Achilles, — *"Jura neget sibi nata, nihil non arroget armis,"*[31] and by this sentence from the dying words of Jacob (Gen. xlviii.), which the Jews apply to David, and the Christians to their Christ: *Manus ejus contra omnes.* In our day, the robber — the warrior of the ancients — is pursued with the utmost vigor. His profession, in the language of the code, entails ignominious and corporal penalties, from imprisonment to the scaffold. A sad change in opinions here below!

We rob, — 8. By cheating; 9. By swindling; 10. By abuse of trust; 11. By games and lotteries.

This second species was encouraged by the laws of Lycurgus, in order to sharpen the wits of the young. It is the kind practised by Ulysses, Solon, and Sinon; by the ancient and modern Jews, from Jacob down to Deutz; and by the Bohemians, the Arabs, and all savage tribes. Under Louis XIII. and Louis XIV., it was not considered dishonorable to cheat at play. To do so was a part of the game; and many worthy people did not scruple to correct the caprice of Fortune by dexterous jugglery. To-day even, and in all countries, it is thought a mark of merit among peasants, merchants, and shopkeepers to *know how to make a bargain,* — that is, to deceive one's man. This is so universally accepted, that the cheated party takes no offence. It is known with what reluctance our government resolved upon the abolition of lotteries. It felt that it was dealing a stab thereby at property. The pickpocket, the blackleg, and the charlatan make especial use of their dexterity of hand, their subtlety of mind, the magic power of their eloquence, and their great fertility of invention. Sometimes they offer bait to cupidity. Therefore the penal code — which much prefers intelligence to muscular vigor — has made, of the four varieties mentioned above, a second category, liable only to correctional, not to Ignominious, punishments.

Let them now accuse the law of being materialistic and atheistic.

We rob, — 12. By usury.

578

This species of robbery, so odious and so severely punished since the publication of the Gospel, is the connecting link between forbidden and authorized robbery. Owing to its ambiguous nature, it has given rise to a multitude of contradictions in the laws and in morals, — contradictions which have been very cleverly turned to account by lawyers, financiers, and merchants. Thus the usurer, who lends on mortgage at ten, twelve, and fifteen per cent., is heavily fined when detected; while the banker, who receives the same interest (not, it is true, upon a loan, but in the way of exchange or discount, — that is, of sale), is protected by royal privilege. But the distinction between the banker and the usurer is a purely nominal one. Like the usurer, who lends on property, real or personal, the banker lends on business paper; like the usurer, he takes his interest in advance; like the usurer, he can recover from the borrower if the property is destroyed (that is, if the note is not redeemed), — a circumstance which makes him a money-lender, not a money-seller. But the banker lends for a short time only, while the usurer's loan may be for one, two, three, or more years. Now, a difference in the duration of the loan, or the form of the act, does not alter the nature of the transaction. As for the capitalists who invest their money, either with the State or in commercial operations, at three, four, and five per cent., — that is, who lend on usury at a little lower rate than the bankers and usurers, — they are the flower of society, the cream of honesty! Moderation in robbery is the height of virtue![32]

We rob, — 13. By farm-rent, house-rent, and leases of all kinds.

The author of the "Provincial Letters" entertained the honest Christians of the seventeenth century at the expense of Escobar, the Jesuit, and the contract *Mohatra*." The contract *Mohatra*," said Escobar, "is a contract by which goods are bought, at a high price and on credit, to be again sold at the same moment to the same person, cash down, and at a lower price." Escobar found a way to justify this kind of usury. Pascal and all the Jansenists laughed at him. But what would the satirical Pascal, the learned Nicole, and the invincible Arnaud have said, if Father Antoine Escobar de Valladolid had answered them thus: "A lease is a contract by which real estate is bought, at a high price and on credit, to be again sold, at the expiration of a certain time, to the same person, at a lower price; only, to simplify the transaction, the buyer is content to pay the difference between the first sale and the second. Either deny the identity of the lease and the contract *Mohatra*, and then I will annihilate you in a moment; or, if you admit the similarity, admit also the soundness of my doctrine: otherwise you proscribe both interest and rent at one blow"?

In reply to this overwhelming argument of the Jesuit, the sire of Montalte would have sounded the tocsin, and would have shouted that society was in peril, — that the Jesuits were sapping its very foundations.

We rob, — 14. By commerce, when the profit of the merchant exceeds his legitimate salary.

Everybody knows the definition of commerce — *The art of buying for three francs that which is worth six, and of selling for six that which is worth three.* Between commerce thus defined and *vol a l'americaine,* the only difference is in the relative proportion of the values exchanged, — in short, in the amount of the profit.

We rob, — 15. By making profit on our product, by accepting sinecures, and by exacting exorbitant wages.

The farmer, who sells a certain amount of corn to the consumer, and who during the measurement thrusts his hand into the bushel and takes out a handful of grains, robs; the professor, whose lectures are paid for by the State, and who through the intervention of a bookseller sells them to the public a second time, robs; the sinecurist, who receives an enormous product in exchange for his vanity, robs; the functionary, the laborer, whatever he may be, who produces only one and gets paid four, one hundred, or one thousand, robs; the publisher of this book, and I, its author, — we rob, by charging for it twice as much as it is worth.

In recapitulation: —

Justice, after passing through the state of negative communism, called by the ancient poets the *age of gold,* commences as the right of the strongest. In a society which is trying to organize itself, inequality of faculties calls up the idea of merit; *équité* suggests the plan of proportioning not only esteem, but also material comforts, to personal merit; and since the highest and almost the only merit then recognized is physical strength, the strongest, *apistos,* and consequently the best, *apistos,* is entitled to the largest share; and if it is refused him, he very naturally takes it by force. From this to the assumption of the right of property in all things, it is but one step.

Such was justice in the heroic age, preserved, at least by tradition, among the Greeks and Romans down to the last days of their republics.

Plato, in the "Gorgias," introduces a character named Callicles, who spiritedly defends the right of the strongest, which Socrates, the advocate of equality, *ton ison*, seriously refutes. It is related of the great Pompey, that he blushed easily, and, nevertheless, these words once escaped his lips: "Why should I respect the laws, when I have arms in my hand?" This shows him to have been a man in whom the moral sense and ambition were struggling for the mastery, and who sought to justify his violence by the motto of the hero and the brigand.

From the right of the strongest springs the exploitation of man by man, or bondage; usury, or the tribute levied upon the conquered by the conqueror; and the whole numerous family of taxes, duties, monarchical prerogatives, house-rents, farm-rents, &c.; in one word, — property.

Force was followed by artifice, the second manifestation of justice, which was detested by the ancient heroes, who, not excelling in that direction, were heavy losers by it. Force was still employed, but mental force instead of physical. Skill in deceiving an enemy by treacherous propositions seemed deserving of reward; nevertheless, the strong always prided themselves upon their honesty. In those days, oaths were observed and promises kept according to the letter rather than the spirit: *Uti lingua nuncupassit, ita jus esto,* — "As the tongue has spoken, so must the right be," says the law of the Twelve Tables. Artifice, or rather perfidy, was the main element in the politics of ancient Rome. Among other examples, Vico cites the following, also quoted by Montesquieu: The Romans had guaranteed to the Carthaginians the preservation of their goods and their *city*, — intentionally using the word *civitas*, that is, the society, the State; the Carthaginians, on the contrary, understood them to mean the material city, *urbs*, and accordingly began to rebuild their walls. They were immediately attacked on account of their violation of the treaty, by the Romans, who, acting upon the old heroic idea of right, did not imagine that, in taking advantage of an equivocation to surprise their enemies, they were waging unjust war.

From artifice sprang the profits of manufactures, commerce, and banking, mercantile frauds, and pretensions which are honored with the beautiful names of *talent* and *genius*, but which ought to be regarded as the last degree of knavery and deception; and, finally, all sorts of social inequalities.

In those forms of robbery which are prohibited by law, force and artifice are employed alone and undisguised; in the authorized forms, they conceal themselves within a useful product, which they use as a tool to plunder their victim.

The direct use of violence and stratagem was early and universally condemned; but no nation has yet got rid of that kind of robbery which acts through talent, labor, and possession, and which is the source of all the dilemmas of casuistry and the innumerable contradictions of jurisprudence.

The right of force and the right of artifice — glorified by the rhapsodists in the poems of the "Iliad" and the "Odyssey" — inspired the legislation of the Greeks and Romans, from which they passed into our morals and codes. Christianity has not changed at all. The Gospel should not be blamed, because the priests, as stupid as the legists, have been unable either to expound or to understand it. The ignorance of councils and popes upon all questions of morality is equal to that of the market-place and the money-changers; and it is this utter ignorance of right, justice, and society, which is killing the Church, and discrediting its teachings for ever. The infidelity of the Roman church and other Christian churches is flagrant; all have disregarded the precept of Jesus; all have erred in moral and doctrinal points; all are guilty of teaching false and absurd dogmas, which lead straight to wickedness and murder. Let it ask pardon of God and men, — this church which called itself infallible, and which has grown so corrupt in morals; let its reformed sisters humble themselves, ... and the people, undeceived, but still religious and merciful, will begin to think.[33]

The development of right has followed the same order, in its various expressions, that property has in its forms. Every where we see justice driving robbery before it and confining it within narrower and narrower limits. Hitherto the victories of justice over injustice, and of equality over inequality, have been won by instinct and the simple force of things; but the final triumph of our social nature will be due to our reason, or else we shall fall back into feudal chaos. Either this glorious height is reserved for our intelligence, or this miserable depth for our baseness.

The second effect of property is despotism. Now, since despotism is inseparably connected with the idea of legitimate authority, in explaining the natural causes of the first, the principle of the second will appear.

What is to be the form of government in the future? hear some of my younger readers reply: "Why, how can you ask such a question? You are a republican." "A republican! Yes; but that word specifies nothing. *Res publica;* that is, the public thing. Now, whoever is interested in public affairs — no matter under what form of government — may call himself a republican. Even kings are republicans." —

"Well! you are a democrat?" — "No." — "What! you would have a monarchy." — "No." — "A constitutionalist?" — "God forbid!" — "You are then an aristocrat?" — "Not at all." — "You want a mixed government?" — "Still less." — "What are you, then?" — "I am an anarchist."

"Oh! I understand you; you speak satirically. This is a hit at the government." — "By no means. I have just given you my serious and well-considered profession of faith. Although a firm friend of order, I am (in the full force of the term) an anarchist. Listen to me."

In all species of sociable animals, "the weakness of the young is the principle of their obedience to the old, who are strong; and from habit, which is a kind of conscience with them, the power remains with the oldest, although he finally becomes the weakest. Whenever the society is under the control of a chief, this chief is almost always the oldest of the troop. I say almost always, because the established order may be disturbed by violent outbreaks. Then the authority passes to another; and, having been re-established by force, it is again maintained by habit. Wild horses go in herds: they have a chief who marches at their head, whom they confidently follow, and who gives the signal for flight or battle.

"The sheep which we have raised follows us, but it follows in company with the flock in the midst of which it was born. It regards man *as the chief of its flock*... Man is regarded by domestic animals as a member of their society. All that he has to do is to get himself accepted by them as an associate: he soon becomes their chief, in consequence of his superior intelligence. He does not, then, change the *natural condition* of these animals, as Buffon has said. On the contrary, he uses this natural condition to his own advantage; in other words, he finds *sociable* animals, and renders them *domestic* by becoming their associate and chief. Thus, the *domesticity* of animals is only a special condition, a simple modification, a definitive consequence of their *sociability*. All domestic animals are by nature sociable animals." ... — *Flourens: Summary of the Observations of F. Cuvier.*

Sociable animals follow their chief by *instinct;* but take notice of the fact (which F. Cuvier omitted to state), that the function of the chief is altogether one of *intelligence.* The chief does not teach the others to associate, to unite under his lead, to reproduce their kind, to take to flight, or to defend themselves. Concerning each of these particulars, his subordinates are as well informed as he. But it is the chief who, by his accumulated experience, provides against accidents; he it is whose private intelligence supplements, in difficult situations, the general instinct; he it is who deliberates, decides, and leads; he it is, in short, whose enlightened prudence regulates the public routine for the greatest good of all.

Man (naturally a sociable being) naturally follows a chief. Originally, the chief is the father, the patriarch, the elder; in other words, the good and wise man, whose functions, consequently, are exclusively of a reflective and intellectual nature. The human race — like all other races of sociable animals — has its instincts, its innate faculties, its general ideas, and its categories of sentiment and reason. Its chiefs, legislators, or kings have devised nothing, supposed nothing, imagined nothing. They have only guided society by their accumulated experience, always however in conformity with opinions and beliefs.

Those philosophers who (carrying into morals and into history their gloomy and factious whims) affirm that the human race had originally neither chiefs nor kings, know nothing of the nature of man. Royalty, and absolute royalty, is — as truly and more truly than democracy — a primitive form of government. Perceiving that, in the remotest ages, crowns and kingships were worn by heroes, brigands, and knight-errants, they confound the two things, — royalty and despotism. But royalty dates from the creation of man; it existed in the age of negative communism. Ancient heroism (and the despotism which it engendered) commenced only with the first manifestation of the idea of justice; that is, with the reign of force. As soon as the strongest, in the comparison of merits, was decided to be the best, the oldest had to abandon his position, and royalty became despotic.

The spontaneous, instinctive, and — so to speak — physiological origin of royalty gives it, in the beginning, a superhuman character. The nations connected it with the gods, from whom they said the first kings descended. This notion was the origin of the divine genealogies of royal families, the incarnations of gods, and the messianic fables. From it sprang the doctrine of divine right, which is still championed by a few singular characters.

Royalty was at first elective, because — at a time when man produced but little and possessed nothing — property was too weak to establish the principle of heredity, and secure to the son the throne of his father; but as soon as fields were cleared, and cities built, each function was, like every thing else, appropriated, and hereditary kingships and priesthoods were the result. The principle of heredity was carried into even the most ordinary professions, — a circumstance which led to class distinctions, pride of station, and abjection of the common people, and which confirms my assertion, concerning the principle of patrimonial succession, that it is a method suggested by Nature of filling vacancies in business, and completing unfinished tasks.

From time to time, ambition caused usurpers, or *supplanters* of kings, to start up; and, in consequence, some were called kings by right, or legitimate kings, and others *tyrants*. But we must not let these names deceive us. There have been execrable kings, and very tolerable tyrants. Royalty may always be good, when it is the only possible form of government; legitimate it is never. Neither heredity, nor election, nor universal suffrage, nor the excellence of the sovereign, nor the consecration of religion and of time, can make royalty legitimate. Whatever form it takes, — monarchic, oligarchic, or democratic, — royalty, or the government of man by man, is illegitimate and absurd.

Man, in order to procure as speedily as possible the most thorough satisfaction of his wants, seeks *rule*. In the beginning, this rule is to him living, visible, and tangible. It is his father, his master, his king. The more ignorant man is, the more obedient he is, and the more absolute is his confidence in his guide. But, it being a law of man's nature to conform to rule, — that is, to discover it by his powers of reflection and reason, — man reasons upon the commands of his chiefs. Now, such reasoning as that is a protest against authority, — a beginning of disobedience. At the moment that man inquires into the motives which govern the will of his sovereign, — at that moment man revolts. If he obeys no longer because the king commands, but because the king demonstrates the wisdom of his commands, it may be said that henceforth he will recognize no authority, and that he has become his own king. Unhappy he who shall dare to command him, and shall offer, as his authority, only the vote of the majority; for, sooner or later, the minority will become the majority, and this imprudent despot will be overthrown, and all his laws annihilated.

In proportion as society becomes enlightened, royal authority diminishes. That is a fact to which all history bears witness. At the birth of nations, men reflect and reason in vain. Without methods, without principles, not knowing how to use their reason, they cannot judge of the justice of their conclusions. Then the authority of kings is immense, no knowledge having been acquired with which to contradict it. But, little by little, experience produces habits, which develop into customs; then the customs are formulated in maxims, laid down as principles, — in short, transformed into laws, to which the king, the living law, has to bow. There comes a time when customs and laws are so numerous that the will of the prince is, so to speak, entwined by the public will; and that, on taking the crown, he is obliged to swear that he will govern in conformity with established customs and usages; and that he is but the executive power of a society whose laws are made independently of him.

Up to this point, all is done instinctively, and, as it were, unconsciously; but see where this movement must end.

By means of self-instruction and the acquisition of ideas, man finally acquires the idea of *science*, — that is, of a system of knowledge in harmony with the reality of things, and inferred from observation. He searches for the science, or the system, of inanimate bodies, — the system of organic bodies, the system of the human mind, and the system of the universe: why should he not also search for the system of society? But, having reached this height, he comprehends that political truth, or the science of politics, exists quite independently of the will of sovereigns, the opinion of majorities, and popular beliefs, — that kings, ministers, magistrates, and nations, as wills, have no connection with the science, and are worthy of no consideration. He comprehends, at the same time, that, if man is born a sociable being, the authority of his father over him ceases on the day when, his mind being formed and his education finished, he becomes the associate of his father; that his true chief and his king is the demonstrated truth; that politics is a science, not a stratagem; and that the function of the legislator is reduced, in the last analysis, to the methodical search for truth.

Thus, in a given society, the authority of man over man is inversely proportional to the stage of intellectual development which that society has reached; and the probable duration of that authority can be calculated from the more or less general desire for a true government, — that is, for a scientific government. And just as the right of force and the right of artifice retreat before the steady advance of justice, and must finally be extinguished in equality, so the sovereignty of the will yields to the sovereignty of the reason, and must at last be lost in scientific socialism. Property and royalty have been crumbling to pieces ever since the world began. As man seeks justice in equality, so society seeks order in anarchy.

Anarchy, — the absence of a master, of a sovereign,[34] — such is the form of government to which we are every day approximating, and which our accustomed habit of taking man for our rule, and his will for law, leads us to regard as the height of disorder and the expression of chaos. The story is told, that a citizen of Paris in the seventeenth century having heard it said that in Venice there was no king, the good man could not recover from his astonishment, and nearly died from laughter at the mere mention of so ridiculous a thing. So strong is our prejudice. As long as we live, we want a chief or chiefs; and at this very moment I hold in my hand a *brochure*, whose author — a zealous communist — dreams, like a second Marat, of the dictatorship. The most advanced among us are those who wish the greatest possible number of sovereigns, — their most ardent wish is for the royalty of the National Guard. Soon, undoubtedly, some one, jealous of the citizen militia, will say, "Everybody is king." But, when he has spoken, I will say, in my turn, "Nobody is king; we are, whether we will or no, associated." Every question of domestic politics must be decided by departmental statistics; every question of foreign politics is an affair of international statistics. The science of government rightly belongs to one of the sections of the Academy of Sciences, whose permanent secretary is necessarily prime minister; and, since every citizen may address a memoir to the Academy, every citizen is a legislator. But, as the opinion of no one is of any value until its truth has been proven, no one can substitute his will for reason, — nobody is king.

All questions of legislation and politics are matters of science, not of opinion. The legislative power belongs only to the reason, methodically recognized and demonstrated. To attribute to any power whatever the right of veto or of sanction, is the last degree of tyranny. Justice and legality are two things as independent of our approval as is mathematical truth. To compel, they need only to be known; to be known, they need only to be considered and studied. What, then, is the nation, if it is not the sovereign, — if it is not the source of the legislative power? The nation is the guardian of the law — the nation is the *executive power*. Every citizen may assert: "This is true; that is just; "but his opinion controls no one but himself. That the truth which he proclaims may become a law, it must be recognized. Now, what is it to recognize a law? It is to verify a mathematical or a metaphysical calculation; it is to repeat an experiment, to observe a phenomenon, to establish a fact. Only the nation has the right to say, "Be it known and decreed."

I confess that this is an overturning of received ideas, and that I seem to be attempting to revolutionize our political system; but I beg the reader

587

to consider that, having begun with a paradox, I must, if I reason correctly, meet with paradoxes at every step, and must end with paradoxes. For the rest, I do not see how the liberty of citizens would be endangered by entrusting to their hands, instead of the pen of the legislator, the sword of the law. The executive power, belonging properly to the will, cannot be confided to too many proxies. That is the true sovereignty of the nation.[35]

The proprietor, the robber, the hero, the sovereign — for all these titles are synonymous — imposes his will as law, and suffers neither contradiction nor control; that is, he pretends to be the legislative and the executive power at once. Accordingly, the substitution of the scientific and true law for the royal will is accomplished only by a terrible struggle; and this constant substitution is, after property, the most potent element in history, the most prolific source of political disturbances. Examples are too numerous and too striking to require enumeration.

Now, property necessarily engenders despotism, — the government of caprice, the reign of libidinous pleasure. That is so clearly the essence of property that, to be convinced of it, one need but remember what it is, and observe what happens around him. Property is the right to *use* and *abuse*. If, then, government is economy, — if its object is production and consumption, and the distribution of labor and products, — how is government possible while property exists? And if goods are property, why should not the proprietors be kings, and despotic kings — kings in proportion to their *facultés bonitaires*? And if each proprietor is sovereign lord within the sphere of his property, absolute king throughout his own domain, how could a government of proprietors be any thing but chaos and confusion?

§ 3. — *Determination of the third form of Society. Conclusion.*

Then, no government, no public economy, no administration, is possible, which is based upon property.

Communism seeks *equality* and *law*. Property, born of the sovereignty of the reason, and the sense of personal merit, wishes above all things *independence* and *proportionality*.

But communism, mistaking uniformity for law, and levelism for equality, becomes tyrannical and unjust. Property, by its despotism and encroachments, soon proves itself oppressive and anti-social.

The objects of communism and property are good — their results are bad. And why? Because both are exclusive, and each disregards two elements of society. Communism rejects independence and proportionality; property does not satisfy equality and law.

Now, if we imagine a society based upon these four principles, — equality, law, independence, and proportionality, — we find: —

1. That *equality*, consisting only in *equality of conditions*, that is, *of means*, and not in *equality of comfort*, — which it is the business of the laborers to achieve for themselves, when provided with equal means, — in no way violates justice and *équité*.

2. That *law*, resulting from the knowledge of facts, and consequently based upon necessity itself, never clashes with independence.

3. That individual *independence*, or the autonomy of the private reason, originating in the difference in talents and capacities, can exist without danger within the limits of the law.

4. That *proportionality*, being admitted only in the sphere of intelligence and sentiment, and not as regards material objects, may be observed without violating justice or social equality.

This third form of society, the synthesis of communism and property, we will call *liberty*.[36]

In determining the nature of liberty, we do not unite communism and property indiscriminately; such a process would be absurd eclecticism. We search by analysis for those elements in each which are true, and in harmony with the laws of Nature and society, disregarding the rest altogether; and the result gives us an adequate expression of the natural form of human society, — in one word, liberty.

Liberty is equality, because liberty exists only in society; and in the absence of equality there is no society.

Liberty is anarchy, because it does not admit the government of the will, but only the authority of the law; that is, of necessity.

Liberty is infinite variety, because it respects all wills within the limits of the law.

Liberty is proportionality, because it allows the utmost latitude to the ambition for merit, and the emulation of glory.

We can now say, in the words of M. Cousin: "Our principle is true; it is good, it is social; let us not fear to push it to its ultimate."

Man's social nature becoming *justice* through reflection, *équité* through the classification of capacities, and having *liberty* for its formula, is the true basis of morality, — the principle and regulator of all our actions. This is the universal motor, which philosophy is searching for, which religion strengthens, which egotism supplants, and whose place pure reason never can fill. *Duty* and *right* are born of *need*, which, when considered in connection with others, is a *right*, and when considered in connection with ourselves, a *duty*.

We need to eat and sleep. It is our right to procure those things which are necessary to rest and nourishment. It is our duty to use them when Nature requires it.

We need to labor in order to live. To do so is both our right and our duty.

We need to love our wives and children. It is our duty to protect and support them. It is our right to be loved in preference to all others. Conjugal fidelity is justice. Adultery is high treason against society.

We need to exchange our products for other products. It is our right that this exchange should be one of equivalents; and since we consume before we produce, it would be our duty, if we could control the matter, to see to it that our last product shall follow our last consumption. Suicide is fraudulent bankruptcy.

We need to live our lives according to the dictates of our reason. It is our right to maintain our freedom. It is our duty to respect that of others.

We need to be appreciated by our fellows. It is our duty to deserve their praise. It is our right to be judged by our works.

Liberty is not opposed to the rights of succession and bequest. It contents itself with preventing violations of equality. "Choose," it tells us, "between two legacies, but do not take them both." All our legislation concerning transmissions, entailments, adoptions, and, if I may venture to use such a word, *coadjutoreries*, requires remodelling.

Liberty favors emulation, instead of destroying it. In social equality, emulation consists in accomplishing under like conditions; it is its own reward. No one suffers by the victory.

Liberty applauds self-sacrifice, and honors it with its votes, but it can dispense with it. Justice alone suffices to maintain the social equilibrium. Self-sacrifice is an act of supererogation. Happy, however, the man who can say, "I sacrifice myself."[37]

Liberty is essentially an organizing force. To insure equality between men and peace among nations, agriculture and industry, and the centres of education, business, and storage, must be distributed according to the climate and the geographical position of the country, the nature of the products, the character and natural talents of the inhabitants, &c., in proportions so just, so wise, so harmonious, that in no place shall there ever be either an excess or a lack of population, consumption, and products. There commences the science of public and private right, the true political economy. It is for the writers on jurisprudence, henceforth unembarrassed by the false principle of property, to describe the new laws, and bring peace upon earth. Knowledge and genius they do not lack; the foundation is now laid for them.[38]

I have accomplished my task; property is conquered, never again to arise. Wherever this work is read and discussed, there will be deposited the germ of death to property; there, sooner or later, privilege and servitude will disappear, and the despotism of will will give place to the reign of reason. What sophisms, indeed, what prejudices (however obstinate) can stand before the simplicity of the following propositions: —

I. Individual *possession*[39] is the condition of social life; five thousand years of property demonstrate it. *Property* is the suicide of society. Possession is a right; property is against right. Suppress property while maintaining possession, and, by this simple modification of the principle, you will revolutionize law, government, economy, and institutions; you will drive evil from the face of the earth.

II. All having an equal right of occupancy, possession varies with the number of possessors; property cannot establish itself.

III. The effect of labor being the same for all, property is lost in the common prosperity.

IV. All human labor being the result of collective force, all property becomes, in consequence, collective and unitary. To speak more exactly, labor destroys property.

V. Every capacity for labor being, like every instrument of labor, an accumulated capital, and a collective property, inequality of wages and fortunes (on the ground of inequality of capacities) is, therefore, injustice and robbery.

VI. The necessary conditions of commerce are the liberty of the contracting parties and the equivalence of the products exchanged. Now, value being expressed by the amount of time and outlay which each product costs, and liberty being inviolable, the wages of laborers (like their rights and duties) should be equal.

VII. Products are bought only by products. Now, the condition of all exchange being equivalence of products, profit is impossible and unjust. Observe this elementary principle of economy, and pauperism, luxury, oppression, vice, crime, and hunger will disappear from our midst.

VIII. Men are associated by the physical and mathematical law of production, before they are voluntarily associated by choice. Therefore, equality of conditions is demanded by justice; that is, by strict social law: esteem, friendship, gratitude, admiration, all fall within the domain of *equitable* or *proportional* law only.

IX. Free association, liberty — whose sole function is to maintain equality in the means of production and equivalence in exchanges — is the only possible, the only just, the only true form of society.

X. Politics is the science of liberty. The government of man by man (under whatever name it be disguised) is oppression. Society finds its highest perfection in the union of order with anarchy.

The old civilization has run its race; a new sun is rising, and will soon renew the face of the earth. Let the present generation perish, let the old prevaricators die in the desert! the holy earth shall not cover their bones. Young man, exasperated by the corruption of the age, and absorbed in your zeal for justice! — if your country is dear to you, and if you have the interests of humanity at heart, have the courage to espouse the cause of liberty! Cast off your old selfishness, and plunge into the rising flood of popular equality! There your regenerate soul will acquire new life and vigor; your enervated genius will recover unconquerable energy; and your heart, perhaps already withered, will be rejuvenated! Every thing will wear a different look to your illuminated vision; new sentiments will engender new ideas within you; religion, morality, poetry, art, language will appear before you in nobler and fairer forms; and thenceforth, sure of your faith, and thoughtfully enthusiastic, you will hail the dawn of universal regeneration!

And you, sad victims of an odious law! — you, whom a jesting world despoils and outrages! — you, whose labor has always been fruitless, and whose rest has been without hope, — take courage! your tears are numbered! The fathers have sown in affliction, the children shall reap in rejoicings!

O God of liberty! God of equality! Thou who didst place in my heart the sentiment of justice, before my reason could comprehend it, hear my ardent prayer! Thou hast dictated all that I have written; Thou hast shaped my thought; Thou hast directed my studies; Thou hast weaned my mind from curiosity and my heart from attachment, that I might publish Thy truth to the master and the slave. I have spoken with what force and talent Thou hast given me: it is Thine to finish the work. Thou knowest whether I seek my welfare or Thy glory, O God of liberty! Ah! perish my memory, and let humanity be free! Let me see from my obscurity the people at last instructed; let noble teachers enlighten them; let generous spirits guide them! Abridge, if possible, the time of our trial; stifle pride and avarice in equality; annihilate this love of glory which enslaves us; teach these poor children that in the bosom of liberty there are neither heroes nor great men! Inspire the powerful man, the rich man, him whose name my lips shall never pronounce in Thy presence, with a horror of his crimes; let him be the first to apply for admission to the redeemed society; let the promptness of his repentance be the ground of his forgiveness! Then, great and small, wise and foolish, rich and poor, will unite in an ineffable fraternity; and, singing in unison a new hymn, will rebuild Thy altar, O God of liberty and equality!

Second Memoir

A Letter to M. Blanqui. Paris, April 1, 1841.

Monsieur, — Before resuming my "Inquiries into Government and Property," it is fitting, for the satisfaction of some worthy people, and also in the interest of order, that I should make to you a plain, straightforward explanation. In a much-governed State, no one would be allowed to attack the external form of the society, and the groundwork of its institutions, until he had established his right to do so, — first, by his morality; second, by his capacity; and, third, by the purity of his intentions. Any one who, wishing to publish a treatise upon the constitution of the country, could not satisfy this threefold condition, would be obliged to procure the endorsement of a responsible patron possessing the requisite qualifications.

But we Frenchmen have the liberty of the press. This grand right — the sword of thought, which elevates the virtuous citizen to the rank of legislator, and makes the malicious citizen an agent of discord — frees us from all preliminary responsibility to the law; but it does not release us from our internal obligation to render a public account of our sentiments and thoughts. I have used, in all its fulness, and concerning an important question, the right which the charter grants us. I come to-day, sir, to submit my conscience to your judgment, and my feeble insight to your discriminating reason. You have criticised in a kindly spirit — I had almost said with partiality for the writer — a work which teaches a doctrine that you thought it your duty to condemn. "The Academy of Moral and Political Sciences," said you in your report, "can accept the conclusions of the author only as far as it likes." I venture to hope, sir, that, after you have read this letter, if your prudence still restrains you, your fairness will induce you to do me justice.

Men, equal in the dignity of their persons and equal before the law, should be equal in their conditions, — such is the thesis which I maintained and developed in a memoir bearing the title, "What is Property? or, An Inquiry into the Principle of Right and of Government."

The idea of social equality, even in individual fortunes, has in all ages besieged, like a vague presentiment, the human imagination. Poets have sung of it in their hymns; philosophers have dreamed of it in their Utopias; priests teach it, but only for the spiritual world. The people, governed by it, never have had faith in it; and the civil power is never

594

more disturbed than by the fables of the age of gold and the reign of Astrea. A year ago, however, this idea received a scientific demonstration, which has not yet been satisfactorily answered, and, permit me to add, never will be. This demonstration, owing to its slightly impassioned style, its method of reasoning, — which was so at variance with that employed by the generally recognized authorities, — and the importance and novelty of its conclusions, was of a nature to cause some alarm; and might have been dangerous, had it not been — as you, sir, so well said — a sealed letter, so far as the general public was concerned, addressed only to men of intelligence. I was glad to see that through its metaphysical dress you recognized the wise foresight of the author; and I thank you for it. May God grant that my intentions, which are wholly peaceful, may never be charged upon me as treasonable!

Like a stone thrown into a mass of serpents, the First Memoir on Property excited intense animosity, and aroused the passions of many. But, while some wished the author and his work to be publicly denounced, others found in them simply the solution of the fundamental problems of society; a few even basing evil speculations upon the new light which they had obtained. It was not to be expected that a system of inductions abstractly gathered together, and still more abstractly expressed, would be understood with equal accuracy in its *ensemble* and in each of its parts.

To find the law of equality, no longer in charity and self-sacrifice (which are not binding in their nature), but in justice; to base equality of functions upon equality of persons; to determine the absolute principle of exchange; to neutralize the inequality of individual faculties by collective force; to establish an equation between property and robbery; to change the law of succession without destroying the principle; to maintain the human personality in a system of absolute association, and to save liberty from the chains of communism; to synthetize the monarchical and democratic forms of government; to reverse the division of powers; to give the executive power to the nation, and to make legislation a positive, fixed, and absolute science, — what a series of paradoxes! what a string of delusions! if I may not say, what a chain of truths! But it is not my purpose here to pass upon the theory of the right of possession. I discuss no dogmas. My only object is to justify my views, and to show that, in writing as I did, I not only exercised a right, but performed a duty.

Yes, I have attacked property, and shall attack it again; but, sir, before demanding that I shall make the *amende honorable* for having obeyed my conscience and spoken the exact truth, condescend, I beg of you, to cast a glance at the events which are happening around us; look at our deputies, our magistrates, our philosophers, our ministers, our professors, and our publicists; examine their methods of dealing with the matter of property; count up with me the restrictions placed upon it every day in the name of the public welfare; measure the breaches already made; estimate those which society thinks of making hereafter; add the ideas concerning property held by all theories in common; interrogate history, and then tell me what will be left, half a century hence, of this old right of property; and, thus perceiving that I have so many accomplices, you will immediately declare me innocent.

What is the law of expropriation on the ground of public utility, which everybody favors, and which is even thought too lenient?[40] A flagrant violation of the right of property. Society indemnifies, it is said, the dispossessed proprietor; but does it return to him the traditional associations, the poetic charm, and the family pride which accompany property? Naboth, and the miller of Sans-Souci, would have protested against French law, as they protested against the caprice of their kings. "It is the field of our fathers," they would have cried, "and we will not sell it!" Among the ancients, the refusal of the individual limited the powers of the State. The Roman law bowed to the will of the citizen, and an emperor — Commodus, if I remember rightly — abandoned the project of enlarging the forum out of respect for the rights of the occupants who refused to abdicate. Property is a real right, *jus in re*, — a right inherent in the thing, and whose principle lies in the external manifestation of man's will. Man leaves his imprint, stamps his character, upon the objects of his handiwork. This plastic force of man, as the modern jurists say, is the seal which, set upon matter, makes it holy. Whoever lays hands upon it, against the proprietor's will, does violence to the latter's personality. And yet, when an administrative committee saw fit to declare that public utility required it, property had to give way to the general will. Soon, in the name of public utility, methods of cultivation and conditions of enjoyment will be prescribed; inspectors of agriculture and manufactures will be appointed; property will be taken away from unskilful hands, and entrusted to laborers who are more deserving of it; and a general superintendence of production will be established. It is not two years since I saw a proprietor destroy a forest more than five hundred acres in extent. If public utility had interfered, that forest — the only one for miles around — would still be standing.

But, it is said, expropriation on the ground of public utility is only an exception which confirms the principle, and bears testimony in favor of the right. Very well; but from this exception we will pass to another, from that to a third, and so on from exceptions to exceptions, until we have reduced the rule to a pure abstraction.

How many supporters do you think, sir, can be claimed for the project of the conversion of the public funds? I venture to say that everybody favors it, except the fund-holders.

Now, this so-called conversion is an extensive expropriation, and in this case with no indemnity whatever. The public funds are so much real estate, the income from which the proprietor counts upon with perfect safety, and which owes its value to the tacit promise of the government to pay interest upon it at the established rate, until the fund-holder applies for redemption. For, if the income is liable to diminution, it is less profitable than house-rent or farm-rent, whose rates may rise or fall according to the fluctuations in the market; and in that case, what inducement has the capitalist to invest his money in the State? When, then, you force the fund-holder to submit to a diminution of interest, you make him bankrupt to the extent of the diminution; and since, in consequence of the conversion, an equally profitable investment becomes impossible, you depreciate his property.

That such a measure may be justly executed, it must be generalized; that is, the law which provides for it must decree also that interest on sums lent on deposit or on mortgage throughout the realm, as well as house and farm-rents, shall be reduced to three per cent. This simultaneous reduction of all kinds of income would be not a whit more difficult to accomplish than the proposed conversion; and, further, it would offer the advantage of forestalling at one blow all objections to it, at the same time that it would insure a just assessment of the land-tax. See! If at the moment of conversion a piece of real estate yields an income of one thousand francs, after the new law takes effect it will yield only six hundred francs. Now, allowing the tax to be an aliquot part — one-fourth for example — of the income derived from each piece of property, it is clear on the one hand that the proprietor would not, in order to lighten his share of the tax, underestimate the value of his property; since, house and farm-rents being fixed by the value of the capital, and the latter being measured by the tax, to depreciate his real estate would be to reduce his revenue. On the other hand, it is equally evident that the same proprietors could not overestimate the value of their property, in order to increase their incomes beyond the limits of the law, since the tenants and farmers, with their old leases in their hands, would enter a protest.

Such, sir, must be the result sooner or later of the conversion which has been so long demanded; otherwise, the financial operation of which we are speaking would be a crying injustice, unless intended as a stepping-stone. This last motive seems the most plausible one; for in spite of the clamors of interested parties, and the flagrant violation of certain rights, the public conscience is bound to fulfil its desire, and is no more affected when charged with attacking property, than when listening to the complaints of the bondholders. In this case, instinctive justice belies legal justice.

Who has not heard of the inextricable confusion into which the Chamber of Deputies was thrown last year, while discussing the question of colonial and native sugars? Did they leave these two industries to themselves? The native manufacturer was ruined by the colonist. To maintain the beet-root, the cane had to be taxed. To protect the property of the one, it became necessary to violate the property of the other. The most remarkable feature of this business was precisely that to which the least attention was paid; namely, that, in one way or another, property had to be violated. Did they impose on each industry a proportional tax, so as to preserve a balance in the market? They created a maximum *price* for each variety of sugar; and, as this maximum *price* was not the same, they attacked property in two ways, — on the one hand, interfering with the liberty of trade; on the other, disregarding the equality of proprietors. Did they suppress the beet-root by granting an indemnity to the manufacturer? They sacrificed the property of the tax-payer. Finally, did they prefer to cultivate the two varieties of sugar at the nation's expense, just as different varieties of tobacco are cultivated? They abolished, so far as the sugar industry was concerned, the right of property. This last course, being the most social, would have been certainly the best; but, if property is the necessary basis of civilization, how is this deep-seated antagonism to be explained?[41]

Not satisfied with the power of dispossessing a citizen on the ground of public utility, they want also to dispossess him on the ground of *private utility*. For a long time, a revision of the law concerning mortgages was clamored for; a process was demanded, in behalf of all kinds of credit and in the interest of even the debtors themselves, which would render the expropriation of real estate as prompt, as easy, and as effective as that which follows a commercial protest. The Chamber of Deputies, in the early part of this year, 1841, discussed this project, and the law was passed almost unanimously. There is nothing more just, nothing more reasonable, nothing more philosophical apparently, than the motives which gave rise to this reform.

I. Formerly, the small proprietor whose obligation had arrived at maturity, and who found himself unable to meet it, had to employ all that he had left, after being released from his debt, in defraying the legal costs. Henceforth, the promptness of expropriation will save him from total ruin. 2. The difficulties in the way of payment arrested credit, and prevented the employment of capital in agricultural enterprises. This cause of distrust no longer existing, capitalists will find new markets, agriculture will rapidly develop, and farmers will be the first to enjoy the benefit of the new law. 3. Finally, it was iniquitous and absurd, that, on account of a protested note, a poor manufacturer should see in twenty-four hours his business arrested, his labor suspended, his merchandise seized, his machinery sold at auction, and finally himself led off to prison, while two years were sometimes necessary to expropriate the most miserable piece of real estate. These arguments, and others besides, you clearly stated, sir, in your first lectures of this academic year.

But, when stating these excellent arguments, did you ask yourself, sir, whither would tend such a transformation of our system of mortgages? ... To monetize, if I may say so, landed property; to accumulate it within portfolios; to separate the laborer from the soil, man from Nature; to make him a wanderer over the face of the earth; to eradicate from his heart every trace of family feeling, national pride, and love of country; to isolate him more and more; to render him indifferent to all around him; to concentrate his love upon one object, — money; and, finally, by the dishonest practices of usury, to monopolize the land to the profit of a financial aristocracy, — a worthy auxiliary of that industrial feudality whose pernicious influence we begin to feel so bitterly. Thus, little by little, the subordination of the laborer to the idler, the restoration of abolished castes, and the distinction between patrician and plebeian, would be effected; thus, thanks to the new privileges granted to the property of the capitalists, that of the small and intermediate proprietors would gradually disappear, and with it the whole class of free and honest laborers. This certainly is not my plan for the abolition of property. Far from mobilizing the soil, I would, if possible, immobilize even the functions of pure intelligence, so that society might be the fulfilment of the intentions of Nature, who gave us our first possession, the land. For, if the instrument or capital of production is the mark of the laborer, it is also his pedestal, his support, his country, and, as the Psalmist says, *the place of his activity and his rest.*[42]

Let us examine more closely still the inevitable and approaching result of the last law concerning judicial sales and mortgages. Under the system of competition which is killing us, and whose necessary expression is a plundering and tyrannical government, the farmer will need always capital in order to repair his losses, and will be forced to contract loans. Always depending upon the future for the payment of his debts, he will be deceived in his hope, and surprised by maturity. For what is there more prompt, more unexpected, more abbreviatory of space and time, than the maturity of an obligation? I address this question to all whom this pitiless Nemesis pursues, and even troubles in their dreams. Now, under the new law, the expropriation of a debtor will be effected a hundred times more rapidly; then, also, spoliation will be a hundred times surer, and the free laborer will pass a hundred times sooner from his present condition to that of a serf attached to the soil. Formerly, the length of time required to effect the seizure curbed the usurer's avidity, gave the borrower an opportunity to recover himself, and gave rise to a transaction between him and his creditor which might result finally in a complete release. Now, the debtor's sentence is irrevocable: he has but a few days of grace.

And what advantages are promised by this law as an offset to this sword of Damocles, suspended by a single hair over the head of the unfortunate husbandman? The expenses of seizure will be much less, it is said; but will the interest on the borrowed capital be less exorbitant? For, after all, it is interest which impoverishes the peasant and leads to his expropriation. That the law may be in harmony with its principle, that it may be truly inspired by that spirit of justice for which it is commended, it must — while facilitating expropriation — lower the legal price of money. Otherwise, the reform concerning mortgages is but a trap set for small proprietors, — a legislative trick.

Lower interest on money! But, as we have just seen, that is to limit property. Here, sir, you shall make your own defence. More than once, in your learned lectures, I have heard you deplore the precipitancy of the Chambers, who, without previous study and without profound knowledge of the subject, voted almost unanimously to maintain the statutes and privileges of the Bank. Now these privileges, these statutes, this vote of the Chambers, mean simply this, — that the market price of specie, at five or six per cent., is not too high, and that the conditions of exchange, discount, and circulation, which generally double this interest, are none too severe. So the government thinks. M. Blanqui — a professor of political economy, paid by the State — maintains the contrary, and pretends to demonstrate, by decisive arguments, the necessity of a reform. Who, then, best understands the interests of property, — the State, or M. Blanqui?

600

If specie could be borrowed at half the present rate, the revenues from all sorts of property would soon be reduced one-half also. For example: when it costs less to build a house than to hire one, when it is cheaper to clear a field than to procure one already cleared, competition inevitably leads to a reduction of house and farm-rents, since the surest way to depreciate active capital is to increase its amount. But it is a law of political economy that an increase of production augments the mass of available capital, consequently tends to raise wages, and finally to annihilate interest. Then, proprietors are interested in maintaining the statutes and privileges of the Bank; then, a reform in this matter would compromise the right of increase; then, the peers and deputies are better informed than Professor Blanqui.

But these same deputies, — so jealous of their privileges whenever the equalizing effects of a reform are within their intellectual horizon, — what did they do a few days before they passed the law concerning judicial sales? They formed a conspiracy against property! Their law to regulate the labor of children in factories will, without doubt, prevent the manufacturer from compelling a child to labor more than so many hours a day; but it will not force him to increase the pay of the child, nor that of its father. To-day, in the interest of health, we diminish the subsistence of the poor; to-morrow it will be necessary to protect them by fixing their *minimum* wages. But to fix their minimum wages is to compel the proprietor, is to force the master to accept his workman as an associate, which interferes with freedom and makes mutual insurance obligatory. Once entered upon this path, we never shall stop. Little by little the government will become manufacturer, commission-merchant, and retail dealer. It will be the sole proprietor. Why, at all epochs, have the ministers of State been so reluctant to meddle with the question of wages? Why have they always refused to interfere between the master and the workman? Because they knew the touchy and jealous nature of property, and, regarding it as the principle of all civilization, felt that to meddle with it would be to unsettle the very foundations of society. Sad condition of the proprietary *régime*, — one of inability to exercise charity without violating justice![43]

And, sir, this fatal consequence which necessity forces upon the State is no mere imagination. Even now the legislative power is asked, no longer simply to regulate the government of factories, but to create factories itself. Listen to the millions of voices shouting on all hands for *the organisation of labor, the creation of national workshops!* The whole laboring class is agitated: it has its journals, organs, and representatives. To guarantee labor to the workingman, to balance production with sale, to harmonize industrial proprietors, it advocates to-day — as a sovereign remedy — one sole head, one national wardenship, one huge manufacturing company. For, sir, all this is included in the idea of national workshops. On this subject I wish to quote, as proof, the views of an illustrious economist, a brilliant mind, a progressive intellect, an enthusiastic soul, a true patriot, and yet an official defender of the right of property.[44]

The honorable professor of the Conservatory proposes then, —

1. *To check the continual emigration of laborers from the country into the cities.*

But, to keep the peasant in his village, his residence there must be made endurable: to be just to all, the proletaire of the country must be treated as well as the proletaire of the city. Reform is needed, then, on farms as well as in factories; and, when the government enters the workshop, the government must seize the plough! What becomes, during this progressive invasion, of independent cultivation, exclusive domain, property?

2. *To fix for each profession a moderate salary, varying with time and place and based upon certain data.*

The object of this measure would be to secure to laborers their subsistence, and to proprietors their profits, while obliging the latter to sacrifice from motives of prudence, if for no other reason, a portion of their income. Now, I say, that this portion, in the long run, would swell until at last there would be an equality of enjoyment between the proletaire and the proprietor. For, as we have had occasion to remark several times already, the interest of the capitalist — in other words the increase of the idler — tends, on account of the power of labor, the multiplication of products and exchanges, to continually diminish, and, by constant reduction, to disappear. So that, in the society proposed by M. Blanqui, equality would not be realized at first, but would exist potentially; since property, though outwardly seeming to be industrial feudality, being no longer a principle of exclusion and encroachment, but only a privilege of division, would not be slow, thanks to the intellectual and political emancipation of the proletariat, in passing into absolute equality, — as absolute at least as any thing can be on this earth.

I omit, for the sake of brevity, the numerous considerations which the professor adduces in support of what he calls, too modestly in my opinion, his Utopia. They would serve only to prove beyond all

602

question that, of all the charlatans of radicalism who fatigue the public ear, no one approaches, for depth and clearness of thought, the audacious M. Blanqui.

3. *National workshops should be in operation only during periods of stagnation in ordinary industries; at such times they should be opened as vast outlets to the flood of the laboring population.*

But, sir, the stoppage of private industry is the result of over-production, and insufficient markets. If, then, production continues in the national workshops, how will the crisis be terminated? Undoubtedly, by the general depreciation of merchandise, and, in the last analysis, by the conversion of private workshops into national workshops. On the other hand, the government will need capital with which to pay its workmen; now, how will this capital be obtained? By taxation. And upon what will the tax be levied? Upon property. Then you will have proprietary industry sustaining against itself, and at its own expense, another industry with which it cannot compete. What, think you, will become, in this fatal circle, of the possibility of profit, — in a word, of property?

Thank Heaven! equality of conditions is taught in the public schools; let us fear revolutions no longer. The most implacable enemy of property could not, if he wished to destroy it, go to work in a wiser and more effective way. Courage, then, ministers, deputies, economists! make haste to seize this glorious initiative; let the watchwords of equality, uttered from the heights of science and power, be repeated in the midst of the people; let them thrill the breasts of the proletaires, and carry dismay into the ranks of the last representatives of privilege!

The tendency of society in favor of compelling proprietors to support national workshops and public manufactories is so strong that for several years, under the name of *electoral reform*, it has been exclusively the question of the day. What is, after all, this electoral reform which the people grasp at, as if it were a bait, and which so many ambitious persons either call for or denounce? It is the acknowledgment of the right of the masses to a voice in the assessment of taxes, and the making of the laws; which laws, aiming always at the protection of material interests, affect, in a greater or less degree, all questions of taxation or wages. Now the people, instructed long since by their journals, their dramas,[45] and their songs,[46] know to-day that taxation, to be equitably divided, must be graduated, and must be borne mainly by the rich, — that it must be levied upon luxuries, &c. And be sure that the people, once in the majority in the Chamber, will not fail to apply these lessons. Already we have a minister of public works. National workshops will follow; and soon, as a consequence, the excess of the proprietor's revenue over the workingman's wages will be swallowed up in the coffers of the laborers of the State. Do you not see that in this way property is gradually reduced, as nobility was formerly, to a nominal title, to a distinction purely honorary in its nature?

Either the electoral reform will fail to accomplish that which is hoped from it, and will disappoint its innumerable partisans, or else it will inevitably result in a transformation of the absolute right under which we live into a right of possession; that is, that while, at present, property makes the elector, after this reform is accomplished, the citizen, the producer will be the possessor.[47] Consequently, the radicals are right in saying that the electoral reform is in their eyes only a means; but, when they are silent as to the end, they show either profound ignorance, or useless dissimulation. There should be no secrets or reservations from peoples and powers. He disgraces himself and fails in respect for his fellows, who, in publishing his opinions, employs evasion and cunning. Before the people act, they need to know the whole truth. Unhappy he who shall dare to trifle with them! For the people are credulous, but they are strong. Let us tell them, then, that this reform which is proposed is only a means, — a means often tried, and hitherto without effect, — but that the logical object of the electoral reform is equality of fortunes; and that this equality itself is only a new means having in view the superior and definitive object of the salvation of society, the restoration of morals and religion, and the revival of poetry and art.

It would be an abuse of the reader's patience to insist further upon the tendency of our time towards equality. There are, moreover, so many people who denounce the present age, that nothing is gained by exposing to their view the popular, scientific, and representative tendencies of the nation. Prompt to recognize the accuracy of the inferences drawn from observation, they confine themselves to a general censure of the facts, and an absolute denial of their legitimacy. "What wonder," they say, "that this atmosphere of equality intoxicates us, considering all that has been said and done during the past ten years! ... Do you not see that society is dissolving, that a spirit of infatuation is carrying us away? All these hopes of regeneration are but forebodings of death; your songs of triumph are like the prayers of the departing, your trumpet peals announce the baptism of a dying man. Civilization is falling in ruin: *Imus, imus, præcipites*!"

Such people deny God. I might content myself with the reply that the spirit of 1830 was the result of the maintenance of the violated charter; that this charter arose from the Revolution of '89; that '89 implies the States-General's right of remonstrance, and the enfranchisement of the communes; that the communes suppose feudalism, which in its turn supposes invasion, Roman law, Christianity, &c.

But it is necessary to look further. We must penetrate to the very heart of ancient institutions, plunge into the social depths, and uncover this indestructible leaven of equality which the God of justice breathed into our souls, and which manifests itself in all our works.

Labor is man's contemporary; it is a duty, since it is a condition of existence: "In the sweat of thy face shalt thou eat bread." It is more than a duty, it is a mission: "God put the man into the garden to dress it." I add that labor is the cause and means of equality.

Cast away upon a desert island two men: one large, strong, and active; the other weak, timid, and domestic. The latter will die of hunger; while the other, a skilful hunter, an expert fisherman, and an indefatigable husbandman, will overstock himself with provisions. What greater inequality, in this state of Nature so dear to the heart of Jean Jacques, could be imagined! But let these two men meet and associate themselves: the second immediately attends to the cooking, takes charge of the household affairs, and sees to the provisions, beds, and clothes; provided the stronger does not abuse his superiority by enslaving and ill-treating his companion, their social condition will be perfectly equal. Thus, through exchange of services, the inequalities of Nature neutralize each other, talents associate, and forces balance. Violence and inertia are found only among the poor and the aristocratic. And in that lies the philosophy of political economy, the mystery of human brotherhood. *Hic est sapientia.* Let us pass from the hypothetical state of pure Nature into civilization.

The proprietor of the soil, who produces, I will suppose with the economists, by lending his instrument, receives at the foundation of a society so many bushels of grain for each acre of arable land. As long as labor is weak, and the variety of its products small, the proprietor is powerful in comparison with the laborers; he has ten times, one hundred times, the portion of an honest man. But let labor, by multiplying its inventions, multiply its enjoyments and wants, and the proprietor, if he wishes to enjoy the new products, will be obliged to reduce his income every day; and since the first products tend rather to depreciate than to rise in value, — in consequence of the continual addition of the new ones, which may be regarded as supplements of the first ones, — it follows that the idle proprietor grows poor as fast as public prosperity increases. "Incomes" (I like to quote you, sir, because it is impossible to give too good an authority for these elementary principles of economy, and because I cannot express them better myself), "incomes," you have said, "tend to disappear as capital increases. He who possesses to-day an income of twenty thousand pounds is not nearly as rich as he who possessed the same amount fifty years ago. The time is coming when all property will be a burden to the idle, and will necessarily pass into the hands of the able and industrious.[48] ..."

In order to live as a proprietor, or to consume without producing, it is necessary, then, to live upon the labor of another; in other words, it is necessary to kill the laborer. It is upon this principle that proprietors of those varieties of capital which are of primary necessity increase their farm-rents as fast as industry develops, much more careful of their privileges in that respect, than those economists who, in order to strengthen property, advocate a reduction of interest. But the crime is unavailing: labor and production increase; soon the proprietor will be forced to labor, and then property is lost.

The proprietor is a man who, having absolute control of an instrument of production, claims the right to enjoy the product of the instrument without using it himself. To this end he lends it; and we have just seen that from this loan the laborer derives a power of exchange, which sooner or later will destroy the right of increase. In the first place, the proprietor is obliged to allow the laborer a portion of the product, for without it the laborer could not live. Soon the latter, through the development of his industry, finds a means of regaining the greater portion of that which he gives to the proprietor; so that at last, the objects of enjoyment increasing continually, while the income of the idler remains the same, the proprietor, having exhausted his resources, begins to think of going to work himself. Then the victory of the producer is certain. Labor commences to tip the balance towards its own side, and commerce leads to equilibrium.

Man's instinct cannot err; as, in liberty, exchange of functions leads inevitably to equality among men, so commerce — or exchange of products, which is identical with exchange of functions — is a new cause of equality. As long as the proprietor does not labor, however small his income, he enjoys a privilege; the laborer's welfare may be equal to his, but equality of conditions does not exist. But as soon as the proprietor becomes a producer, — since he can exchange his special product only with his tenant or his *commandité*, — sooner or later this tenant, this *exploited* man, if violence is not done him, will make a profit out of the proprietor, and will oblige him to restore — in the exchange of their respective products — the interest on his capital. So that, balancing one injustice by another, the contracting parties will be equal. Labor and exchange, when liberty prevails, lead, then, to equality of fortunes; mutuality of services neutralizes privilege. That is why despots in all ages and countries have assumed control of commerce; they wished to prevent the labor of their subjects from becoming an obstacle to the rapacity of tyrants.

Up to this point, all takes place in the natural order; there is no premeditation, no artifice. The whole proceeding is governed by the laws of necessity alone. Proprietors and laborers act only in obedience to their wants. Thus, the exercise of the right of increase, the art of robbing the producer, depends — during this first period of civilization — upon physical violence, murder, and war. But at this point a gigantic and complicated conspiracy is hatched against the capitalists. The weapon of the *exploiters* is met by the *exploited* with the instrument of commerce, — a marvellous invention, denounced at its origin by the moralists who favored property, but inspired without doubt by the genius of labor, by the Minerva of the proletaires.

The principal cause of the evil lay in the accumulation and immobility of capital of all sorts, — an immobility which prevented labor, enslaved and subalternized by haughty idleness, from ever acquiring it. The necessity was felt of dividing and mobilizing wealth, of rendering it portable, of making it pass from the hands of the possessor into those of the worker. Labor invented *money*. Afterwards, this invention was revived and developed by the *bill of exchange* and the *Bank*. For all these things are substantially the same, and proceed from the same mind. The first man who conceived the idea of representing a value by a shell, a precious stone, or a certain weight of metal, was the real inventor of the Bank. What is a piece of money, in fact? It is a bill of exchange written upon solid and durable material, and carrying with it its own redemption. By this means, oppressed equality was enabled to laugh at the efforts of the proprietors, and the balance of justice was adjusted for the first time in the tradesman's shop. The trap was cunningly set, and accomplished its purpose so thoroughly that in idle hands money became only dissolving wealth, a false symbol, a shadow of riches. An excellent economist and profound philosopher was that miser who took as his motto, "*When a guinea is exchanged, it evaporates.*" So it may be said, "When real estate is converted into money, it is lost." This explains the constant fact of history, that the nobles — the unproductive proprietors of the soil — have every where been dispossessed by industrial and commercial plebeians. Such was especially the case in the formation of the Italian republics, born, during the middle ages, of the impoverishment of the seigniors. I will not pursue the interesting considerations which this matter suggests; I could only repeat the testimony of historians, and present economical demonstrations in an altered form.

The greatest enemy of the landed and industrial aristocracy to-day, the incessant promoter of equality of fortunes, is the *banker*. Through him immense plains are divided, mountains change their positions, forests are grown upon the public squares, one hemisphere produces for another, and every corner of the globe has its usufructuaries. By means of the Bank new wealth is continually created, the use of which (soon becoming indispensable to selfishness) wrests the dormant capital from the hands of the jealous proprietor. The banker is at once the most potent creator of wealth, and the main distributor of the products of art and Nature. And yet, by the strangest antinomy, this same banker is the most relentless collector of profits, increase, and usury ever inspired by the demon of property. The importance of the services which he renders leads us to endure, though not without complaint, the taxes which he imposes. Nevertheless, since nothing can avoid its providential mission, since nothing which exists can escape the end for which it exists the banker (the modern Croesus) must some day become the restorer of equality. And following in your footsteps, sir, I have already given the reason; namely, that profit decreases as capital multiplies, since an increase of capital — calling for more laborers, without whom it remains unproductive — always causes an increase of wages. Whence it follows that the Bank, to-day the suction-pump of wealth, is destined to become the steward of the human race.

The phrase *equality of fortunes* chafes people, as if it referred to a condition of the other world, unknown here below. There are some persons, radicals as well as moderates, whom the very mention of this idea fills with indignation. Let, then, these silly aristocrats abolish mercantile societies and insurance companies, which are founded by prudence for mutual assistance. For all these social facts, so spontaneous and free from all levelling intentions, are the legitimate fruits of the instinct of equality.

When the legislator makes a law, properly speaking he does not *make* it, — he does not *create* it: he *describes* it. In legislating upon the moral, civil, and political relations of citizens, he does not express an arbitrary notion: he states the general idea, — the higher principle which governs the matter which he is considering; in a word, he is the proclaimer, not the inventor, of the law. So, when two or more men form among themselves, by synallagmatic contract, an industrial or an insurance association, they recognize that their interests, formerly isolated by a false spirit of selfishness and independence, are firmly connected by their inner natures, and by the mutuality of their relations. They do not really bind themselves by an act of their private will: they swear to conform henceforth to a previously existing social law hitherto disregarded by them. And this is proved by the fact that these same men, could they avoid association, would not associate. Before they can be induced to unite their interests, they must acquire full knowledge of the dangers of competition and isolation; hence the experience of evil is the only thing which leads them into society.

Now I say that, to establish equality among men, it is only necessary to generalize the principle upon which insurance, agricultural, and commercial associations are based. I say that competition, isolation of interests, monopoly, privilege, accumulation of capital, exclusive enjoyment, subordination of functions, individual production, the right of profit or increase, the exploitation of man by man, and, to sum up all these species under one head, that PROPERTY is the principal cause of misery and crime. And, for having arrived at this offensive and anti-proprietary conclusion, I am an abhorred monster; radicals and conservatives alike point me out as a fit subject for prosecution; the academies shower their censures upon me; the most worthy people regard me as mad; and those are excessively tolerant who content themselves with the assertion that I am a fool. Oh, unhappy the writer who publishes the truth otherwise than as a performance of a duty! If he has counted upon the applause of the crowd; if he has supposed that avarice and self-interest would forget themselves in admiration of him; if he has neglected to encase himself within three thicknesses of brass, — he will fail, as he ought, in his selfish undertaking. The unjust criticisms, the sad disappointments, the despair of his mistaken ambition, will kill him.

But, if I am no longer permitted to express my own personal opinion concerning this interesting question of social equilibrium, let me, at least, make known the thought of my masters, and develop the doctrines advocated in the name of the government.

It never has been my intention, sir, in spite of the vigorous censure which you, in behalf of your academy, have pronounced upon the doctrine of equality of fortunes, to contradict and cope with you. In listening to you, I have felt my inferiority too keenly to permit me to enter upon such a discussion. And then, — if it must be said, — however different your language is from mine, we believe in the same principles; you share all my opinions. I do not mean to insinuate thereby, sir, that you have (to use the phraseology of the schools) an *esoteric* and an *exoteric* doctrine, — that, secretly believing in equality, you defend property only from motives of prudence and by command. I am not rash enough to regard you as my colleague in my revolutionary projects; and I esteem you too highly, moreover, to suspect you of dissimulation. I only mean that the truths which methodical investigation and laborious metaphysical speculation have painfully demonstrated to me, a profound acquaintance with political economy and a long experience reveal to you. While I have reached my belief in equality by long reflection, and almost in spite of my desires, you hold yours, sir, with all the zeal of faith, — with all the spontaneity of genius. That is why your course of lectures at the Conservatory is a perpetual war upon property and inequality of fortunes; that is why your most learned investigations, your most ingenious analyses, and your innumerable observations always conclude in a formula of progress and equality; that is why, finally, you are never more admired and applauded than at those moments of inspiration when, borne upon the wings of science, you ascend to those lofty truths which cause plebeian hearts to beat with enthusiasm, and which chill with horror men whose intentions are evil. How many times, from the place where I eagerly drank in your eloquent words, have I inwardly thanked Heaven for exempting you from the judgment passed by St. Paul upon the philosophers of his time, — "They have known the truth, and have not made it known"! How many times have I rejoiced at finding my own justification in each of your discourses! No, no; I neither wish nor ask for any thing which you do not teach yourself. I appeal to your numerous audience; let it belie me if, in commenting upon you, I pervert your meaning.

A disciple of Say, what in your eyes is more anti-social than the custom-houses; or, as you correctly call them, the barriers erected by monopoly between nations? What is more annoying, more unjust, or more absurd, than this prohibitory system which compels us to pay forty sous in France for that which in England or Belgium would bring us but fifteen? It is the custom-house, you once said,[49] which arrests the development of civilization by preventing the specialization of industries; it is the custom-house which enriches a hundred monopolists by impoverishing millions of citizens; it is the custom-house which produces famine in the midst of abundance, which makes labor sterile by prohibiting exchange, and which stifles production in a mortal embrace. It is the custom-house which renders nations jealous of, and hostile to, each other; four-fifths of the wars of all ages were

610

caused originally by the custom-house. And then, at the highest pitch of your enthusiasm, you shouted: "Yes, if to put an end to this hateful system, it should become necessary for me to shed the last drop of my blood, I would joyfully spring into the gap, asking only time enough to give thanks to God for having judged me worthy of martyrdom!"

And, at that solemn moment, I said to myself: "Place in every department of France such a professor as that, and the revolution is avoided."

But, sir, by this magnificent theory of liberty of commerce you render military glory impossible, — you leave nothing for diplomacy to do; you even take away the desire for conquest, while abolishing profit altogether. What matters it, indeed, who restores Constantinople, Alexandria, and Saint Jean d'Acre, if the Syrians, Egyptians, and Turks are free to choose their masters; free to exchange their products with whom they please? Why should Europe get into such a turmoil over this petty Sultan and his old Pasha, if it is only a question whether we or the English shall civilize the Orient, — shall instruct Egypt and Syria in the European arts, and shall teach them to construct machines, dig canals, and build railroads? For, if to national independence free trade is added, the foreign influence of these two countries is thereafter exerted only through a voluntary relationship of producer to producer, or apprentice to journeyman.

Alone among European powers, France cheerfully accepted the task of civilizing the Orient, and began an invasion which was quite apostolic in its character, — so joyful and high-minded do noble thoughts render our nation! But diplomatic rivalry, national selfishness, English avarice, and Russian ambition stood in her way. To consummate a long-meditated usurpation, it was necessary to crush a too generous ally: the robbers of the Holy Alliance formed a league against dauntless and blameless France. Consequently, at the news of this famous treaty, there arose among us a chorus of curses upon the principle of property, which at that time was acting under the hypocritical formulas of the old political system. The last hour of property seemed to have struck by the side of Syria; from the Alps to the ocean, from the Rhine to the Pyrenees, the popular conscience was aroused. All France sang songs of war, and the coalition turned pale at the sound of these shuddering cries: "War upon the autocrat, who wishes to be proprietor of the old world! War upon the English perjurer, the devourer of India, the poisoner of China, the tyrant of Ireland, and the eternal enemy of France! War upon the allies who have conspired against liberty and equality! War! war! war upon property!"

611

By the counsel of Providence the emancipation of the nations is postponed. France is to conquer, not by arms, but by example. Universal reason does not yet understand this grand equation, which, commencing with the abolition of slavery, and advancing over the ruins of aristocracies and thrones, must end in equality of rights and fortunes; but the day is not far off when the knowledge of this truth will be as common as that of equality of origin. Already it seems to be understood that the Oriental question is only a question of custom-houses. Is it, then, so difficult for public opinion to generalize this idea, and to comprehend, finally, that if the suppression of custom-houses involves the abolition of national property, it involves also, as a consequence, the abolition of individual property?

In fact, if we suppress the custom-houses, the alliance of the nations is declared by that very act; their solidarity is recognized, and their equality proclaimed. If we suppress the custom-houses, the principle of association will not be slow in reaching from the State to the province, from the province to the city, and from the city to the workshop. But, then, what becomes of the privileges of authors and artists? Of what use are the patents for invention, imagination, amelioration, and improvement? When our deputies write a law of literary property by the side of a law which opens a large breach in the custom-house they contradict themselves, indeed, and pull down with one hand what they build up with the other. Without the custom-house. literary property does not exist, and the hopes of our starving authors are frustrated. For, certainly you do not expect, with the good man Fourier, that literary property will exercise itself in China to the profit of a French writer; and that an ode of Lamartine, sold by privilege all over the world, will bring in millions to its author! The poet's work is peculiar to the climate in which he lives; every where else the reproduction of his works, having no market value, should be frank and free. But what! will it be necessary for nations to put themselves under mutual surveillance for the sake of verses, statues, and elixirs? We shall always have, then, an excise, a city-toll, rights of entrance and transit, custom-houses finally; and then, as a reaction against privilege, smuggling.

Smuggling! That word reminds me of one of the most horrible forms of property. "Smuggling," you have said, sir,[50] "is an offence of political creation; it is the exercise of natural liberty, defined as a crime in certain cases by the will of the sovereign. The smuggler is a gallant man, — a man of spirit, who gaily busies himself in procuring for his neighbor, at a very low price, a jewel, a shawl, or any other object of necessity or luxury, which domestic monopoly renders excessively dear." Then, to a very poetical monograph of the smuggler, you add this dismal conclusion, — that the smuggler belongs to the family of Mandrin, and that the galleys should be his home!

But, sir, you have not called attention to the horrible exploitation which is carried on in this way in the name of property.

It is said, — and I give this report only as an hypothesis and an illustration, for I do not believe it, — it is said that the present minister of finances owes his fortune to smuggling. M. Humann, of Strasbourg, sent out of France, it is said, enormous quantities of sugar, for which he received the bounty on exportation promised by the State; then, smuggling this sugar back again, he exported it anew, receiving the bounty on exportation a second time, and so on. Notice, sir, that I do not state this as a fact; I give it only as it is told, not endorsing or even believing it. My sole design is to fix the idea in the mind by an example. If I believed that a minister had committed such a crime, that is, if I had personal and authentic knowledge that he had, I would denounce M. Humann, the minister of finances, to the Chamber of Deputies, and would loudly demand his expulsion from the ministry.

But that which is undoubtedly false of M. Humann is true of many others, as rich and no less honorable than he. Smuggling, organized on a large scale by the eaters of human flesh, is carried on to the profit of a few pashas at the risk and peril of their imprudent victims. The inactive proprietor offers his merchandise for sale; the actual smuggler risks his liberty, his honor, and his life. If success crowns the enterprise, the courageous servant gets paid for his journey; the profit goes to the coward. If fortune or treachery delivers the instrument of this execrable traffic into the hands of the custom-house officer, the master-smuggler suffers a loss which a more fortunate voyage will soon repair. The agent, pronounced a scoundrel, is thrown into prison in company with robbers; while his glorious patron, a juror, elector, deputy, or minister, makes laws concerning expropriation, monopoly, and custom-houses!

I promised, at the beginning of this letter, that no attack on property should escape my pen, my only object being to justify myself before the public by a general recrimination. But I could not refrain from branding so odious a mode of exploitation, and I trust that this short digression will be pardoned.

Property does not avenge, I hope, the injuries which smuggling suffers.

The conspiracy against property is general; it is flagrant; it takes possession of all minds, and inspires all our laws; it lies at the bottom of all theories. Here the proletaire pursues property in the street, there the legislator lays an interdict upon it; now, a professor of political economy or of industrial legislation,[51] paid to defend it, undermines it with redoubled blows; at another — time, an academy calls it in question,[52] or inquires as to the progress of its demolition.[53] To-day there is not an idea, not an opinion, not a sect, which does not dream of muzzling property. None confess it, because none are yet conscious of it; there are too few minds capable of grasping spontaneously this *ensemble* of causes and effects, of principles and consequences, by which I try to demonstrate the approaching disappearance of property; on the other hand, the ideas that are generally formed of this right are too divergent and too loosely determined to allow an admission, so soon, of the contrary theory. Thus, in the middle and lower ranks of literature and philosophy, no less than among the common people, it is thought that, when property is abolished, no one will be able to enjoy the fruit of his labor; that no one will have any thing peculiar to himself, and that tyrannical communism will be established on the ruins of family and liberty! — chimeras, which are to support for a little while longer the cause of privilege.

But, before determining precisely the idea of property, before seeking amid the contradictions of systems for the common element which must form the basis of the new right, let us cast a rapid glance at the changes which, at the various periods of history, property has undergone. The political forms of nations are the expression of their beliefs. The mobility of these forms, their modification and their destruction, are solemn experiences which show us the value of ideas, and gradually eliminate from the infinite variety of customs the absolute, eternal, and immutable truth. Now, we shall see that every political institution tends, necessarily, and on pain of death, to equalize conditions; that every where and always equality of fortunes (like equality of rights) has been the social aim, whether the plebeian classes have endeavored to rise to political power by means of property, or whether — rulers already — they have used political power to overthrow property. We shall see, in short, by the progress of society, that the consummation of justice lies in the extinction of individual domain.

For the sake of brevity, I will disregard the testimony of ecclesiastical history and Christian theology: this subject deserves a separate treatise, and I propose hereafter to return to it. Moses and Jesus Christ proscribed, under the names of usury and inequality,[54] all sorts of profit and increase. The church itself, in its purest teachings, has always condemned property; and when I attacked, not only the authority of the church, but also its infidelity to justice, I did it to the glory of religion. I wanted to provoke a peremptory reply, and to pave the way for Christianity's triumph, in spite of the innumerable attacks of which it is at present the object. I hoped that an apologist would arise forthwith, and, taking his stand upon the Scriptures, the Fathers, the canons, and the councils and constitutions of the Popes, would demonstrate that the church always has maintained the doctrine of equality, and would attribute to temporary necessity the contradictions of its discipline. Such a labor would serve the cause of religion as well as that of equality. We must know, sooner or later, whether Christianity is to be regenerated in the church or out of it, and whether this church accepts the reproaches cast upon it of hatred to liberty and antipathy to progress. Until then we will suspend judgment, and content ourselves with placing before the clergy the teachings of history.

When Lycurgus undertook to make laws for Sparta, in what condition did he find this republic? On this point all historians agree. The people and the nobles were at war. The city was in a confused state, and divided by two parties, — the party of the poor, and the party of the rich. Hardly escaped from the barbarism of the heroic ages, society was rapidly declining. The proletariat made war upon property, which, in its turn, oppressed the proletariat. What did Lycurgus do? His first measure was one of general security, at the very idea of which our legislators would tremble. He abolished all debts; then, employing by turns persuasion and force, he induced the nobles to renounce their privileges, and re-established equality. Lycurgus, in a word, hunted property out of Lacedæmon, seeing no other way to harmonize liberty, equality, and law. I certainly should not wish France to follow the example of Sparta; but it is remarkable that the most ancient of Greek legislators, thoroughly acquainted with the nature and needs of the people, more capable than any one else of appreciating the legitimacy of the obligations which he, in the exercise of his absolute authority, cancelled; who had compared the legislative systems of his time, and whose wisdom an oracle had proclaimed, — it is remarkable, I say, that Lycurgus should have judged the right of property incompatible with free institutions, and should have thought it his duty to preface his legislation by a *coup d'état* which destroyed all distinctions of fortune.

Lycurgus understood perfectly that the luxury, the love of enjoyments, and the inequality of fortunes, which property engenders, are the bane of society; unfortunately the means which he employed to preserve his republic were suggested to him by false notions of political economy, and by a superficial knowledge of the human heart. Accordingly,

615

property, which this legislator wrongly confounded with wealth, reentered the city together with the swarm of evils which he was endeavoring to banish; and this time Sparta was hopelessly corrupted.

"The introduction of wealth," says M. Pastoret, "was one of the principal causes of the misfortunes which they experienced. Against these, however, the laws had taken extraordinary precautions, the best among which was the inculcation of morals which tended to suppress desire."

The best of all precautions would have been the anticipation of desire by satisfaction. Possession is the sovereign remedy for cupidity, a remedy which would have been the less perilous to Sparta because fortunes there were almost equal, and conditions were nearly alike. As a general thing, fasting and abstinence are bad teachers of moderation.

"There was a law," says M. Pastoret again, "to prohibit the rich from wearing better clothing than the poor, from eating more delicate food, and from owning elegant furniture, vases, carpets, fine houses," &c. Lycurgus hoped, then, to maintain equality by rendering wealth useless. How much wiser he would have been if, in accordance with his military discipline, he had organized industry and taught the people to procure by their own labor the things which he tried in vain to deprive them of. In that case, enjoying happy thoughts and pleasant feelings, the citizen would have known no other desire than that with which the legislator endeavored to inspire him, — love of honor and glory, the triumphs of talent and virtue.

"Gold and all kinds of ornaments were forbidden the women." Absurd. After the death of Lycurgus, his institutions became corrupted; and four centuries before the Christian era not a vestige remained of the former simplicity. Luxury and the thirst for gold were early developed among the Spartans in a degree as intense as might have been expected from their enforced poverty and their inexperience in the arts. Historians have accused Pausanias, Lysander, Agesilaus, and others of having corrupted the morals of their country by the introduction of wealth obtained in war. It is a slander. The morals of the Spartans necessarily grew corrupt as soon as the Lacedæmonian poverty came in contact with Persian luxury and Athenian elegance. Lycurgus, then, made a fatal mistake in attempting to inspire generosity and modesty by enforcing vain and proud simplicity.

"Lycurgus was not frightened at idleness! A Lacedæmonian, happening to be in Athens (where idleness was forbidden) during the punishment of a citizen who had been found guilty, asked to see the Athenian thus condemned for having exercised the rights of a free man... It was one of the principles of Lycurguss, acted upon for several centuries, that free men should not follow lucrative professions... The women disdained domestic labor; they did not spin their wool themselves, as did the other Greeks [they did not, then, read Homer!]; they left their slaves to make their clothing for them." — *Pastoret: History of Legislation.*

Could any thing be more contradictory? Lycurgus proscribed property among the citizens, and founded the means of subsistence on the worst form of property, — on property obtained by force. What wonder, after that, that a lazy city, where no industry was carried on, became a den of avarice? The Spartans succumbed the more easily to the allurements of luxury and Asiatic voluptuousness, being placed entirely at their mercy by their own coarseness. The same thing happened to the Romans, when military success took them out of Italy, — a thing which the author of the prosopopoeia of Fabricius could not explain. It is not the cultivation of the arts which corrupts morals, but their degradation, induced by inactive and luxurious opulence. The instinct of property is to make the industry of Dædalus, as well as the talent of Phidias, subservient to its own fantastic whims and disgraceful pleasures. Property, not wealth, ruined the Spartans.

When Solon appeared, the anarchy caused by property was at its height in the Athenian republic. "The inhabitants of Attica were divided among themselves as to the form of government. Those who lived on the mountains (the poor) preferred the popular form; those of the plain (the middle class), the oligarchs; those by the sea coast, a mixture of oligarchy and democracy. Other dissensions were arising from the inequality of fortunes. The mutual antagonism of the rich and poor had become so violent, that the one-man power seemed the only safe-guard against the revolution with which the republic was threatened." (*Pastoret: History of Legislation.*)

Quarrels between the rich and the poor, which seldom occur in monarchies, because a well established power suppresses dissensions, seem to be the life of popular governments. Aristotle had noticed this. The oppression of wealth submitted to agrarian laws, or to excessive taxation; the hatred of the lower classes for the upper class, which is exposed always to libellous charges made in hopes of confiscation, — these were the features of the Athenian government which were especially revolting to Aristotle, and which caused him to favor a limited monarchy. Aristotle, if he had lived in our day, would have supported the constitutional government. But, with all deference to the

Stagirite, a government which sacrifices the life of the proletaire to that of the proprietor is quite as irrational as one which supports the former by robbing the latter; neither of them deserve the support of a free man, much less of a philosopher.

Solon followed the example of Lycurgus. He celebrated his legislative inauguration by the abolition of debts, — that is, by bankruptcy. In other words, Solon wound up the governmental machine for a longer or shorter time depending upon the rate of interest. Consequently, when the spring relaxed and the chain became unwound, the republic had either to perish, or to recover itself by a second bankruptcy. This singular policy was pursued by all the ancients. After the captivity of Babylon, Nehemiah, the chief of the Jewish nation, abolished debts; Lycurgus abolished debts; Solon abolished debts; the Roman people, after the expulsion of the kings until the accession of the Cæsars, struggled with the Senate for the abolition of debts. Afterwards, towards the end of the republic, and long after the establishment of the empire, agriculture being abandoned, and the provinces becoming depopulated in consequence of the excessive rates of interest, the emperors freely granted the lands to whoever would cultivate them, — that is, they abolished debts. No one, except Lycurgus, who went to the other extreme, ever perceived that the great point was, not to release debtors by a *coup d'état*, but to prevent the contraction of debts in future. On the contrary, the most democratic governments were always exclusively based upon individual property; so that the social element of all these republics was war between the citizens.

Solon decreed that a census should be taken of all fortunes, regulated political rights by the result, granted to the larger proprietors more influence, established the balance of powers, — in a word, inserted in the constitution the most active leaven of discord; as if, instead of a legislator chosen by the people, he had been their greatest enemy. Is it not, indeed, the height of imprudence to grant equality of political rights to men of unequal conditions? If a manufacturer, uniting all his workmen in a joint-stock company, should give to each of them a consultative and deliberative voice, — that is, should make all of them masters, — would this equality of mastership secure continued inequality of wages? That is the whole political system of Solon, reduced to its simplest expression.

"In giving property a just preponderance," says M. Pastoret, "Solon repaired, as far as he was able, his first official act, — the abolition of debts... He thought he owed it to public peace to make this great sacrifice of acquired rights and natural equity. But the violation of

618

individual property and written contracts is a bad preface to a public code."

In fact, such violations are always cruelly punished. In '89 and '93, the possessions of the nobility and the clergy were confiscated, the clever proletaires were enriched; and to-day the latter, having become aristocrats, are making us pay dearly for our fathers' robbery. What, therefore, is to be done now? It is not for us to violate right, but to restore it. Now, it would be a violation of justice to dispossess some and endow others, and then stop there. We must gradually lower the rate of interest, organize industry, associate laborers and their functions, and take a census of the large fortunes, not for the purpose of granting privileges, but that we may effect their redemption by settling a life-annuity upon their proprietors. We must apply on a large scale the principle of collective production, give the State eminent domain over all capital! make each producer responsible, abolish the custom-house, and transform every profession and trade into a public function. Thereby large fortunes will vanish without confiscation or violence; individual possession will establish itself, without communism, under the inspection of the republic; and equality of conditions will no longer depend simply on the will of citizens.

Of the authors who have written upon the Romans, Bossuet and Montesquieu occupy prominent positions in the first rank; the first being generally regarded as the father of the philosophy of history, and the second as the most profound writer upon law and politics. Nevertheless, it could be shown that these two great writers, each of them imbued with the prejudices of their century and their cloth, have left the question of the causes of the rise and fall of the Romans precisely where they found it.

Bossuet is admirable as long as he confines himself to description: witness, among other passages, the picture which he has given us of Greece before the Persian War, and which seems to have inspired "Telemachus;" the parallel between Athens and Sparta, drawn twenty times since Bossuet; the description of the character and morals of the ancient Romans; and, finally, the sublime peroration which ends the "Discourse on Universal History." But when the famous historian deals with causes, his philosophy is at fault.

"The tribunes always favored the division of captured lands, or the proceeds of their sale, among the citizens. The Senate steadfastly opposed those laws which were damaging to the State, and wanted the price of lands to be awarded to the public treasury."

Thus, according to Bossuet, the first and greatest wrong of civil wars was inflicted upon the people, who, dying of hunger, demanded that the lands, which they had shed their blood to conquer, should be given to them for cultivation. The patricians, who bought them to deliver to their slaves, had more regard for justice and the public interests. How little affects the opinions of men! If the *rôles* of Cicero and the Gracchi had been inverted, Bossuet, whose sympathies were aroused by the eloquence of the great orator more than by the clamors of the tribunes, would have viewed the agrarian laws in quite a different light. He then would have understood that the interest of the treasury was only a pretext; that, when the captured lands were put up at auction, the patricians hastened to buy them, in order to profit by the revenues from them, — certain, moreover, that the price paid would come back to them sooner or later, in exchange either for supplies furnished by them to the republic, or for the subsistence of the multitude, who could buy only of them, and whose services at one time, and poverty at another, were rewarded by the State. For a State does not hoard; on the contrary, the public funds always return to the people. If, then, a certain number of men are the sole dealers in articles of primary necessity, it follows that the public treasury, in passing and repassing through their hands, deposits and accumulates real property there.

When Menenius related to the people his fable of the limbs and the stomach, if any one had remarked to this story-teller that the stomach freely gives to the limbs the nourishment which it freely receives, but that the patricians gave to the plebeians only for cash, and lent to them only at usury, he undoubtedly would have silenced the wily senator, and saved the people from a great imposition. The Conscript Fathers were fathers only of their own line. As for the common people, they were regarded as an impure race, exploitable, taxable, and workable at the discretion and mercy of their masters.

As a general thing, Bossuet shows little regard for the people. His monarchical and theological instincts know nothing but authority, obedience, and alms-giving, under the name of charity. This unfortunate disposition constantly leads him to mistake symptoms for causes; and his depth, which is so much admired, is borrowed from his authors, and amounts to very little, after all. When he says, for instance, that "the dissensions in the republic, and finally its fall, were caused by the jealousies of its citizens, and their love of liberty carried to an extreme and intolerable extent," are we not tempted to ask him what caused those *jealousies*? — what inspired the people with that *love of liberty, extreme and intolerable*? It would be useless to reply, The corruption of morals; the disregard for the ancient poverty; the

620

debaucheries, luxury, and class jealousies; the seditious character of the Gracchi, &c. Why did the morals become corrupt, and whence arose those eternal dissensions between the patricians and the plebeians?

In Rome, as in all other places, the dissension between the rich and the poor was not caused directly by the desire for wealth (people, as a general thing, do not covet that which they deem it illegitimate to acquire), but by a natural instinct of the plebeians, which led them to seek the cause of their adversity in the constitution of the republic. So we are doing to-day; instead of altering our public economy, we demand an electoral reform. The Roman people wished to return to the social compact; they asked for reforms, and demanded a revision of the laws, and a creation of new magistracies. The patricians, who had nothing to complain of, opposed every innovation. Wealth always has been conservative. Nevertheless, the people overcame the resistance of the Senate; the electoral right was greatly extended; the privileges of the plebeians were increased, — they had their representatives, their tribunes, and their consuls; but, notwithstanding these reforms, the republic could not be saved. When all political expedients had been exhausted, when civil war had depleted the population, when the Cæsars had thrown their bloody mantle over the cancer which was consuming the empire, — inasmuch as accumulated property always was respected, and since the fire never stopped, the nation had to perish in the flames. The imperial power was a compromise which protected the property of the rich, and nourished the proletaires with wheat from Africa and Sicily: a double error, which destroyed the aristocrats by plethora and the commoners by famine. At last there was but one real proprietor left, — the emperor, — whose dependent, flatterer, parasite, or slave, each citizen became; and when this proprietor was ruined, those who gathered the crumbs from under his table, and laughed when he cracked his jokes, perished also.

Montesquieu succeeded no better than Bossuet in fathoming the causes of the Roman decline; indeed, it may be said that the president has only developed the ideas of the bishop. If the Romans had been more moderate in their conquests, more just to their allies, more humane to the vanquished; if the nobles had been less covetous, the emperors less lawless, the people less violent, and all classes less corrupt; if ... &c., — perhaps the dignity of the empire might have been preserved, and Rome might have retained the sceptre of the world! That is all that can be gathered from the teachings of Montesquieu. But the truth of history does not lie there; the destinies of the world are not dependent upon such trivial causes. The passions of men, like the contingencies of time and the varieties of climate, serve to maintain the forces which move

621

humanity and produce all historical changes; but they do not explain them. The grain of sand of which Pascal speaks would have caused the death of one man only, had not prior action ordered the events of which this death was the precursor.

Montesquieu has read extensively; he knows Roman history thoroughly, is perfectly well acquainted with the people of whom he speaks, and sees very clearly why they were able to conquer their rivals and govern the world. While reading him we admire the Romans, but we do not like them; we witness their triumphs without pleasure, and we watch their fall without sorrow. Montesquieu's work, like the works of all French writers, is skilfully composed, — spirited, witty, and filled with wise observations. He pleases, interests, instructs, but leads to little reflection; he does not conquer by depth of thought; he does not exalt the mind by elevated reason or earnest feeling. In vain should we search his writings for knowledge of antiquity, the character of primitive society, or a description of the heroic ages, whose morals and prejudices lived until the last days of the republic. Vico, painting the Romans with their horrible traits, represents them as excusable, because he shows that all their conduct was governed by preexisting ideas and customs, and that they were informed, so to speak, by a superior genius of which they were unconscious; in Montesquieu, the Roman atrocity revolts, but is not explained. Therefore, as a writer, Montesquieu brings greater credit upon French literature; as a philosopher, Vico bears away the palm.

Originally, property in Rome was national, not private. Numa was the first to establish individual property by distributing the lands captured by Romulus. What was the dividend of this distribution effected by Numa? What conditions were imposed upon individuals, what powers reserved to the State? None whatever. Inequality of fortunes, absolute abdication by the republic of its right of eminent domain over the property of citizens, — such were the first results of the division of Numa, who justly may be regarded as the originator of Roman revolutions. He it was who instituted the worship of the god Terminus, — the guardian of private possession, and one of the most ancient gods of Italy. It was Numa who placed property under the protection of Jupiter; who, in imitation of the Etrurians, wished to make priests of the land-surveyors; who invented a liturgy for cadastral operations, and ceremonies of consecration for the marking of boundaries, — who, in short, made a religion of property.[55] All these fancies would have been more beneficial than dangerous, if the holy king had not forgotten one essential thing; namely, to fix the amount that each citizen could possess, and on what conditions he could possess it. For, since it is the essence of property to continually increase by accession and profit, and since the lender will take advantage of every opportunity to apply this principle inherent in property, it follows that properties tend, by means of their natural energy and the religious respect which protects them, to absorb each other, and fortunes to increase or diminish to an indefinite extent, — a process which necessarily results in the ruin of the people, and the fall of the republic. Roman history is but the development of this law.

Scarcely had the Tarquins been banished from Rome and the monarchy abolished, when quarrels commenced between the orders. In the year 494 B.C., the secession of the commonalty to the Mons Sacer led to the establishment of the tribunate. Of what did the plebeians complain? That they were poor, exhausted by the interest which they paid to the proprietors, — *foeneratoribus;* that the republic, administered for the benefit of the nobles, did nothing for the people; that, delivered over to the mercy of their creditors, who could sell them and their children, and having neither hearth nor home, they were refused the means of subsistence, while the rate of interest was kept at its highest point, &c. For five centuries, the sole policy of the Senate was to evade these just complaints; and, notwithstanding the energy of the tribunes, notwithstanding the eloquence of the Gracchi, the violence of Marius, and the triumph of Cæsar, this execrable policy succeeded only too well. The Senate always temporized; the measures proposed by the tribunes might be good, but they were inopportune. It admitted that something should be done; but first it was necessary that the people should resume the performance of their duties, because the Senate could not yield to violence, and force must be employed only by the law. If the people — out of respect for legality — took this beautiful advice, the Senate conjured up a difficulty; the reform was postponed, and that was the end of it. On the contrary, if the demands of the proletaires became too pressing, it declared a foreign war, and neighboring nations were deprived of their liberty, to maintain the Roman aristocracy.

But the toils of war were only a halt for the plebeians in their onward march towards pauperism. The lands confiscated from the conquered nations were immediately added to the domain of the State, to the *ager publicus;* and, as such, cultivated for the benefit of the treasury; or, as was more often the case, they were sold at auction. None of them were granted to the proletaires, who, unlike the patricians and knights, were not supplied by the victory with the means of buying them. War never enriched the soldier; the extensive plundering has been done always by the generals. The vans of Augereau, and of twenty others, are famous in our armies; but no one ever heard of a private getting rich. Nothing was more common in Rome than charges of peculation, extortion, embezzlement, and brigandage, carried on in the provinces at the head of armies, and in other public capacities. All these charges were quieted by intrigue, bribery of the judges, or desistance of the accuser. The culprit was allowed always in the end to enjoy his spoils in peace; his son was only the more respected on account of his father's crimes. And, in fact, it could not be otherwise. What would become of us, if every deputy, peer, or public functionary should be called upon to show his title to his fortune!

"The patricians arrogated the exclusive enjoyment of the *ager publicus;* and, like the feudal seigniors, granted some portions of their lands to their dependants, — a wholly precarious concession, revocable at the will of the grantor. The plebeians, on the contrary, were entitled to the enjoyment of only a little pasture-land left to them in common: an utterly unjust state of things, since, in consequence of it, taxation — *census* — weighed more heavily upon the poor than upon the rich. The patrician, in fact, always exempted himself from the tithe which he owed as the price and as the acknowledgment of the concession of domain; and, on the other hand, paid no taxes on his *possessions*, if, as there is good reason to believe, only citizens' property was taxed." — *Laboulaye: History of Property*.

In order thoroughly to understand the preceding quotation, we must know that the estates of *citizens* — that is, estates independent of the public domain, whether they were obtained in the division of Numa, or had since been sold by the questors — were alone regarded as *property;* upon these a tax, or *cense*, was imposed. On the contrary, the estates obtained by concessions of the public domain, of the *ager publicus* (for which a light rent was paid), were called *possessions*. Thus, among the Romans, there was a *right of property* and a *right of possession* regulating the administration of all estates. Now, what did the proletaires wish? That the *jus possessionis* — the simple right of possession — should be extended to them at the expense, as is evident, not of private property, but of the public domain, — *agri publici*. The proletaires, in short, demanded that they should be tenants of the land which they had conquered. This demand, the patricians in their avarice never would accede to. Buying as much of this land as they could, they afterwards found means of obtaining the rest as *possessions*. Upon this land they employed their slaves. The people, who could not buy, on account of the competition of the rich, nor hire, because — cultivating with their own hands — they could not promise a rent equal to the revenue which the land would yield when cultivated by slaves, were always deprived of possession and property.

Civil wars relieved, to some extent, the sufferings of the multitude. "The people enrolled themselves under the banners of the ambitious, in order to obtain by force that which the law refused them, — property. A colony was the reward of a victorious legion. But it was no longer the *ager publicus* only; it was all Italy that lay at the mercy of the legions. The *ager publicus* disappeared almost entirely, ... but the cause of the evil — accumulated property — became more potent than ever." (*Laboulaye: History of Property.*)

The author whom I quote does not tell us why this division of territory which followed civil wars did not arrest the encroachments of accumulated property; the omission is easily supplied. Land is not the only requisite for cultivation; a working-stock is also necessary, — animals, tools, harnesses, a house, an advance, &c. Where did the colonists, discharged by the dictator who rewarded them, obtain these things? From the purse of the usurers; that is, of the patricians, to whom all these lands finally returned, in consequence of the rapid increase of usury, and the seizure of estates. Sallust, in his account of the conspiracy of Catiline, tells us of this fact. The conspirators were old soldiers of Sylla, who, as a reward for their services, had received from him lands in Cisalpine Gaul, Tuscany, and other parts of the peninsula Less than twenty years had elapsed since these colonists, free of debt, had left the service and commenced farming; and already they were crippled by usury, and almost ruined. The poverty caused by the exactions of creditors was the life of this conspiracy which well-nigh inflamed all Italy, and which, with a worthier chief and fairer means, possibly would have succeeded. In Rome, the mass of the people were favorable to the conspirators — *cuncta plebes Catilinæ incepta probabat;* the allies were weary of the patricians' robberies; deputies from the Allobroges (the Savoyards) had come to Rome to appeal to the Senate in behalf of their fellow-citizens involved in debt; in short, the complaint against the large proprietors was universal. "We call men and gods to witness," said the soldiers of Catiline, who were Roman citizens with not a slave among them, "that we have taken arms neither against the country, nor to attack any one, but in defence of our lives and liberties. Wretched, poor, most of us deprived of country, all of us of fame and fortune, by the violence and cruelty of usurers, we have no rights, no property, no liberty."[56]

The bad reputation of Catiline, and his atrocious designs, the imprudence of his accomplices, the treason of several, the strategy of

Cicero, the angry outbursts of Cato, and the terror of the Senate, baffled this enterprise, which, in furnishing a precedent for expeditions against the rich, would perhaps have saved the republic, and given peace to the world. But Rome could not evade her destiny; the end of her expiations had not come. A nation never was known to anticipate its punishment by a sudden and unexpected conversion. Now, the long-continued crimes of the Eternal City could not be atoned for by the massacre of a few hundred patricians. Catiline came to stay divine vengeance; therefore his conspiracy failed.

The encroachment of large proprietors upon small proprietors, by the aid of usury, farm-rent, and profits of all sorts, was common throughout the empire. The most honest citizens invested their money at high rates of interest.[57] Cato, Cicero, Brutus, all the stoics so noted for their frugality, *viri frugi*, — Seneca, the teacher of virtue, — levied enormous taxes in the provinces, under the name of usury; and it is something remarkable, that the last defenders of the republic, the proud Pompeys, were all usurious aristocrats, and oppressors of the poor. But the battle of Pharsalus, having killed men only, without touching institutions, the encroachments of the large domains became every day more active. Ever since the birth of Christianity, the Fathers have opposed this invasion with all their might. Their writings are filled with burning curses upon this crime of usury, of which Christians are not always innocent. St. Cyprian complains of certain bishops of his time, who, absorbed in disgraceful stock-jobbing operations, abandoned their churches, and went about the provinces appropriating lands by artifice and fraud, while lending money and piling up interests upon interests.[58] Why, in the midst of this passion for accumulation, did not the possession of the public land, like private property, become concentrated in a few hands?

By law, the domain of the State was inalienable, and consequently possession was always revocable; but the edict of the praetor continued it indefinitely, so that finally the possessions of the patricians were transformed into absolute property, though the name, possessions, was still applied to them. This conversion, instigated by senatorial avarice; owed its accomplishment to the most deplorable and indiscreet policy. If, in the time of Tiberius Gracchus, who wished to limit each citizen's possession of the *ager publicus* to five hundred acres, the amount of this possession had been fixed at as much as one family could cultivate, and granted on the express condition that the possessor should cultivate it himself, and should lease it to no one, the empire never would have been desolated by large estates; and possession, instead of increasing property, would have absorbed it. On what, then, depended the establishment and maintenance of equality in conditions and fortunes? On a more equitable division of the *ager publicus*, a wiser distribution of the right of possession.

I insist upon this point, which is of the utmost importance, because it gives us an opportunity to examine the history of this individual possession, of which I said so much in my first memoir, and which so few of my readers seem to have understood. The Roman republic — having, as it did, the power to dispose absolutely of its territory, and to impose conditions upon possessors — was nearer to liberty and equality than any nation has been since. If the Senate had been intelligent and just, — if, at the time of the retreat to the Mons Sacer, instead of the ridiculous farce enacted by Menenius Agrippa, a solemn renunciation of the right to acquire had been made by each citizen on attaining his share of possessions, — the republic, based upon equality of possessions and the duty of labor, would not, in attaining its wealth, have degenerated in morals; Fabricius would have enjoyed the arts without controlling artists; and the conquests of the ancient Romans would have been the means of spreading civilization, instead of the series of murders and robberies that they were.

But property, having unlimited power to amass and to lease, was daily increased by the addition of new possessions. From the time of Nero, six individuals were the sole proprietors of one-half of Roman Africa. In the fifth century, the wealthy families had incomes of no less than two millions: some possessed as many as twenty thousand slaves. All the authors who have written upon the causes of the fall of the Roman republic concur. M. Giraud of Aix[59] quotes the testimony of Cicero, Seneca, Plutarch, Olympiodorus, and Photius. Under Vespasian and Titus, Pliny, the naturalist, exclaimed: "Large estates have ruined Italy, and are ruining the provinces."

But it never has been understood that the extension of property was effected then, as it is to-day, under the aegis of the law, and by virtue of the constitution. When the Senate sold captured lands at auction, it was in the interest of the treasury and of public welfare. When the patricians bought up possessions and property, they realized the purpose of the Senate's decrees; when they lent at high rates of interest, they took advantage of a legal privilege. "Property," said the lender, "is the right to enjoy even to the extent of abuse, *jus utendi et abutendi*; that is, the right to lend at interest, — to lease, to acquire, and then to lease and lend again." But property is also the right to exchange, to transfer, and to sell. If, then, the social condition is such that the proprietor, ruined by usury, may be compelled to sell his possession, the means of his subsistence, he will sell it; and, thanks to the law, accumulated property — devouring and anthropophagous property — will be established.[60]

The immediate and secondary cause of the decline of the Romans was, then, the internal dissensions between the two orders of the republic, — the patricians and the plebeians, — dissensions which gave rise to civil wars, proscriptions, and loss of liberty, and finally led to the empire; but the primary and mediate cause of their decline was the establishment by Numa of the institution of property.

I end with an extract from a work which I have quoted several times already, and which has recently received a prize from the Academy of Moral and Political Sciences: —

"The concentration of property," says M. Laboulaye, "while causing extreme poverty, forced the emperors to feed and amuse the people, that they might forget their misery. *Panem et circenses:* that was the Roman law in regard to the poor; a dire and perhaps a necessary evil wherever a landed aristocracy exists.

"To feed these hungry mouths, grain was brought from Africa and the provinces, and distributed gratuitously among the needy. In the time of Cæsar, three hundred and twenty thousand people were thus fed. Augustus saw that such a measure led directly to the destruction of husbandry; but to abolish these distributions was to put a weapon within the reach of the first aspirant for power. The emperor shrank at the thought.

"While grain was gratuitous, agriculture was impossible. Tillage gave way to pasturage, another cause of depopulation, even among slaves.

"Finally, luxury, carried further and further every day, covered the soil of Italy with elegant *villas*, which occupied whole cantons. Gardens and groves replaced the fields, and the free population fled to the towns. Husbandry disappeared almost entirely, and with husbandry the husbandman. Africa furnished the wheat, and Greece the wine. Tiberius complained bitterly of this evil, which placed the lives of the Roman people at the mercy of the winds and waves: that was his anxiety. One day later, and three hundred thousand starving men walked the streets of Rome: that was a revolution.

"This decline of Italy and the provinces did not stop. After the reign of Nero, depopulation commenced in towns as noted as Antium and

Tarentum. Under the reign of Pertinax, there was so much desert land that the emperor abandoned it, even that which belonged to the treasury, to whoever would cultivate it, besides exempting the farmers from taxation for a period of ten years. Senators were compelled to invest one-third of their fortunes in real estate in Italy; but this measure served only to increase the evil which they wished to cure. To force the rich to possess in Italy was to increase the large estates which had ruined the country. And must I say, finally, that Aurelian wished to send the captives into the desert lands of Etruria, and that Valentinian was forced to settle the Alamanni on the fertile banks of the Po?"

If the reader, in running through this book, should complain of meeting with nothing but quotations from other works, extracts from journals and public lectures, comments upon laws, and interpretations of them, I would remind him that the very object of this memoir is to establish the conformity of my opinion concerning property with that universally held; that, far from aiming at a paradox, it has been my main study to follow the advice of the world; and, finally, that my sole pretension is to clearly formulate the general belief. I cannot repeat it too often, — and I confess it with pride, — I teach absolutely nothing that is new; and I should regard the doctrine which I advocate as radically erroneous, if a single witness should testify against it.

Let us now trace the revolutions in property among the Barbarians.

As long as the German tribes dwelt in their forests, it did not occur to them to divide and appropriate the soil. The land was held in common: each individual could plow, sow, and reap. But, when the empire was once invaded, they bethought themselves of sharing the land, just as they shared spoils after a victory. "Hence," says M. Laboulaye, "the expressions *sortes Burgundiorum Gothorum* and *klhroi Ouandigwn*; hence the German words *allod*, allodium, and *loos*, lot, which are used in all modern languages to designate the gifts of chance."

Allodial property, at least with the mass of coparceners, was originally held, then, in equal shares; for all of the prizes were equal, or, at least, equivalent. This property, like that of the Romans, was wholly individual, independent, exclusive, transferable, and consequently susceptible of accumulation and invasion. But, instead of its being, as was the case among the Romans, the large estate which, through increase and usury, subordinated and absorbed the small one, among the Barbarians — fonder of war than of wealth, more eager to dispose of persons than to appropriate things — it was the warrior who, through superiority of arms, enslaved his adversary. The Roman wanted matter;

629

the Barbarian wanted man. Consequently, in the feudal ages, rents were almost nothing, — simply a hare, a partridge, a pie, a few pints of wine brought by a little girl, or a Maypole set up within the suzerain's reach. In return, the vassal or incumbent had to follow the seignior to battle (a thing which happened almost every day), and equip and feed himself at his own expense. "This spirit of the German tribes — this spirit of companionship and association — governed the territory as it governed individuals. The lands, like the men, were secured to a chief or seignior by a bond of mutual protection and fidelity. This subjection was the labor of the German epoch which gave birth to feudalism. By fair means or foul, every proprietor who could not be a chief was forced to be a vassal." (*Laboulaye: History of Property*.)

By fair means or foul, every mechanic who cannot be a master has to be a journeyman; every proprietor who is not an invader will be invaded; every producer who cannot, by the exploitation of other men, furnish products at less than their proper value, will lose his labor. Corporations and masterships, which are hated so bitterly, but which will reappear if we are not careful, are the necessary results of the principle of competition which is inherent in property; their organization was patterned formerly after that of the feudal hierarchy, which was the result of the subordination of men and possessions.

The times which paved the way for the advent of feudalism and the reappearance of large proprietors were times of carnage and the most frightful anarchy. Never before had murder and violence made such havoc with the human race. The tenth century, among others, if my memory serves me rightly, was called the *century of iron*. His property, his life, and the honor of his wife and children always in danger the small proprietor made haste to do homage to his seignior, and to bestow something on the church of his freehold, that he might receive protection and security.

"Both facts and laws bear witness that from the sixth to the tenth century the proprietors of small freeholds were gradually plundered, or reduced by the encroachments of large proprietors and counts to the condition of either vassals or tributaries. The Capitularies are full of repressive provisions; but the incessant reiteration of these threats only shows the perseverance of the evil and the impotency of the government. Oppression, moreover, varies but little in its methods. The complaints of the free proprietors, and the groans of the plebeians at the time of the Gracchi, were one and the same. It is said that, whenever a poor man refused to give his estate to the bishop, the curate, the count, the judge, or the centurion, these immediately sought an opportunity to ruin him. They made him serve in the army until, completely ruined, he was induced, by fair means or foul, to give up his freehold." — *Laboulaye: History of Property.*

How many small proprietors and manufacturers have not been ruined by large ones through chicanery, law-suits, and competition? Strategy, violence, and usury, — such are the proprietor's methods of plundering the laborer.

Thus we see property, at all ages and in all its forms, oscillating by virtue of its principle between two opposite terms, — extreme division and extreme accumulation.

Property, at its first term, is almost null. Reduced to personal exploitation, it is property only potentially. At its second term, it exists in its perfection; then it is truly property.

When property is widely distributed, society thrives, progresses, grows, and rises quickly to the zenith of its power. Thus, the Jews, after leaving Babylon with Esdras and Nehemiah, soon became richer and more powerful than they had been under their kings. Sparta was in a strong and prosperous condition during the two or three centuries which followed the death of Lycurgus. The best days of Athens were those of the Persian war; Rome, whose inhabitants were divided from the beginning into two classes, — the exploiters and the exploited, — knew no such thing as peace.

When property is concentrated, society, abusing itself, polluted, so to speak, grows corrupt, wears itself out — how shall I express this horrible idea? — plunges into long-continued and fatal luxury.

When feudalism was established, society had to die of the same disease which killed it under the Cæsars, — I mean accumulated property. But humanity, created for an immortal destiny, is deathless; the revolutions which disturb it are purifying crises, invariably followed by more vigorous health. In the fifth century, the invasion of the Barbarians partially restored the world to a state of natural equality. In the twelfth century, a new spirit pervading all society gave the slave his rights, and through justice breathed new life into the heart of nations. It has been said, and often repeated, that Christianity regenerated the world. That is true; but it seems to me that there is a mistake in the date. Christianity had no influence upon Roman society; when the Barbarians came, that society had disappeared. For such is God's curse upon property; every political organization based upon the exploitation of man . shall perish:

631

slave-labor is death to the race of tyrants. The patrician families became extinct, as the feudal families did, and as all aristocracies must.

It was in the middle ages, when a reactionary movement was beginning to secretly undermine accumulated property, that the influence of Christianity was first exercised to its full extent. The destruction of feudalism, the conversion of the serf into the commoner, the emancipation of the communes, and the admission of the Third Estate to political power, were deeds accomplished by Christianity exclusively. I say Christianity, not ecclesiasticism; for the priests and bishops were themselves large proprietors, and as such often persecuted the villeins. Without the Christianity of the middle ages, the existence of modern society could not be explained, and would not be possible. The truth of this assertion is shown by the very facts which M. Laboulaye quotes, although this author inclines to the opposite opinion.[61]

1. *Slavery among the Romans.* — "The Roman slave was, in the eyes of the law, only a thing, — no more than an ox or a horse. He had neither property, family, nor personality; he was defenceless against his master's cruelty, folly, or cupidity. 'Sell your oxen that are past use,' said Cato, 'sell your calves, your lambs, your wool, your hides, your old ploughs, your old iron, your old slave, and your sick slave, and all that is of no use to you.' When no market could be found for the slaves that were worn out by sickness or old age, they were abandoned to starvation. Claudius was the first defender of this shameful practice."

"Discharge your old workman," says the economist of the proprietary school; "turn off that sick domestic, that toothless and worn-out servant. Put away the unserviceable beauty; to the hospital with the useless mouths!"

"The condition of these wretched beings improved but little under the emperors; and the best that can be said of the goodness of Antoninus is that he prohibited intolerable cruelty, as an *abuse of property. Expedit enim reipublicæ ne quis re re sua male utatur*, says Gaius.

"As soon as the Church met in council, it launched an anathema against the masters who had exercised over their slaves this terrible right of life and death. Were not the slaves, thanks to the right of sanctuary and to their poverty, the dearest *protégés* of religion? Constantine, who embodied in the laws the grand ideas of Christianity, valued the life of a slave as highly as that of a freeman, and declared the master, who had intentionally brought death upon his slave, guilty of murder. Between

632

this law and that of Antoninus there is a complete revolution in moral ideas: the slave was a thing; religion has made him a man."

Note the last words: "Between the law of the Gospel and that of Antoninus there is a complete revolution in moral ideas: the slave was a thing; religion has made him a man." The moral revolution which transformed the slave into a fructified them. Most of the emancipation charters begin with these words: "For the love of God and the salvation of my soul." Now, we did not commence to love God and to think of our salvation until after the promulgation of the Gospel.

2. *Of Servitude.* — "I see, in the lord's manor, slaves charged with domestic duties. Some are employed in the personal service of the master; others are charged with household cares. The women spin the wool; the men grind the grain, make the bread, or practise, in the interest of the seignior, what little they know of the industrial arts. The master punishes them when he chooses, kills them with impunity, and sells them and theirs like so many cattle. The slave has no personality, and consequently no *wehrgeld*[62] peculiar to himself: he is a thing. The *wehrgeld* belongs to the master as a compensation for the loss of his property. Whether the slave is killed or stolen, the indemnity does not change, for the injury is the same; but the indemnity increases or diminishes according to the value of the serf. In all these particulars Germanic slavery and Roman servitude are alike."

This similarity is worthy of notice. Slavery is always the same, whether in a Roman villa or on a Barbarian farm. The man, like the ox and the ass, is a part of the live-stock; a price is set upon his head; he is a tool without a conscience, a chattel without personality, an impeccable, irresponsible being, who has neither rights nor duties.

Why did his condition improve?

"In good season ..." [when ?] "the serf began to be regarded as a man; and, as such, the law of the Visigoths, under the influence of Christian ideas, punished with fine or banishment any one who maimed or killed him."

Always Christianity, always religion, though we should like to speak of the laws only. Did the philanthropy of the Visigoths make its first appearance before or after the preaching of the Gospel? This point must be cleared up.

"After the conquest, the serfs were scattered over the large estates of the Barbarians, each having his house, his lot, and his peculium, in return for which he paid rent and performed service. They were rarely separated from their homes when their land was sold; they and all that they had became the property of the purchaser. The law favored this realization of the serf, in not allowing him to be sold out of the country."

What inspired this law, destructive not only of slavery, but of property itself? For, if the master cannot drive from his domain the slave whom he has once established there, it follows that the slave is proprietor, as well as the master.

"The Barbarians," again says M. Laboulaye, "were the first to recognize the slave's rights of family and property, — two rights which are incompatible with slavery."

But was this recognition the necessary result of the mode of servitude in vogue among the Germanic nations previous to their conversion to Christianity, or was it the immediate effect of that spirit of justice infused with religion, by which the seignior was forced to respect in the serf a soul equal to his own, a brother in Jesus Christ, purified by the same baptism, and redeemed by the same sacrifice of the Son of God in the form of man? For we must not close our eyes to the fact that, though the Barbarian morals and the ignorance and carelessness of the seigniors, who busied themselves mainly with wars and battles, paying little or no attention to agriculture, may have been great aids in the emancipation of the serfs, still the vital principle of this emancipation was essentially Christian. Suppose that the Barbarians had remained Pagans in the midst of a Pagan world. As they did not change the Gospel, so they would not have changed the polytheistic customs; slavery would have remained what it was; they would have continued to kill the slaves who were desirous of liberty, family, and property; whole nations would have been reduced to the condition of Helots; nothing would have changed upon the terrestrial stage, except the actors. The Barbarians were less selfish, less imperious, less dissolute, and less cruel than the Romans. Such was the nature upon which, after the fall of the empire and the renovation of society, Christianity was to act. But this nature, grounded as in former times upon slavery and war, would, by its own energy, have produced nothing but war and slavery.

"*Gradually* the serfs obtained the privilege of being judged by the same standard as their masters..."

When, how, and by what title did they obtain this privilege?

Gradually their duties were regulated."

Whence came the regulations? Who had the authority to introduce them?

"The master took a part of the labor of the serf, — three days, for instance, — and left the rest to him. As for Sunday, that belonged to God."

And what established Sunday, if not religion? Whence I infer, that the same power which took it upon itself to suspend hostilities and to lighten the duties of the serf was also that which regulated the judiciary and created a sort of law for the slave.

But this law itself, on what did it bear? — what was its principle? — what was the philosophy of the councils and popes with reference to this matter? The reply to all these questions, coming from me alone, would be distrusted. The authority of M. Laboulaye shall give credence to my words. This holy philosophy, to which the slaves were indebted for every thing, this invocation of the Gospel, was an anathema against property.

The proprietors of small freeholds, that is, the freemen of the middle class, had fallen, in consequence of the tyranny of the nobles, into a worse condition than that of the tenants and serfs. "The expenses of war weighed less heavily upon the serf than upon the freeman; and, as for legal protection, the seigniorial court, where the serf was judged by his peers, was far preferable to the cantonal assembly. It was better to have a noble for a seignior than for a judge."

So it is better to-day to have a man of large capital for an associate than for a rival. The honest tenant — the laborer who earns weekly a moderate but constant salary — is more to be envied than the independent but small farmer, or the poor licensed mechanic.

At that time, all were either seigniors or serfs, oppressors or oppressed. "Then, under the protection of convents, or of the seigniorial turret, new societies were formed, which silently spread over the soil made fertile by their hands, and which derived their power from the annihilation of the free classes whom they enlisted in their behalf. As tenants, these men acquired, from generation to generation, sacred

635

rights over the soil which they cultivated in the interest of lazy and pillaging masters. As fast as the social tempest abated, it became necessary to respect the union and heritage of these villeins, who by their labor had truly prescribed the soil for their own profit."

I ask how prescription could take effect where a contrary title and possession already existed? M. Laboulaye is a lawyer. Where, then, did he ever see the labor of the slave and the cultivation by the tenant prescribe the soil for their own profit, to the detriment of a recognized master daily acting as a proprietor? Let us not disguise matters. As fast as the tenants and the serfs grew rich, they wished to be independent and free; they commenced to associate, unfurl their municipal banners, raise belfries, fortify their towns, and refuse to pay their seigniorial dues. In doing these things they were perfectly right; for, in fact, their condition was intolerable. But in law — I mean in Roman and Napoleonic law — their refusal to obey and pay tribute to their masters was illegitimate.

Now, this imperceptible usurpation of property by the commonalty was inspired by religion.

The seignior had attached the serf to the soil; religion granted the serf rights over the soil. The seignior imposed duties upon the serf; religion fixed their limits. The seignior could kill the serf with impunity, could deprive him of his wife, violate his daughter, pillage his house, and rob him of his savings; religion checked his invasions: it excommunicated the seignior. Religion was the real cause of the ruin of feudal property. Why should it not be bold enough to-day to resolutely condemn capitalistic property? Since the middle ages, there has been no change in social economy except in its forms; its relations remain unaltered.

The only result of the emancipation of the serfs was that property changed hands; or, rather, that new proprietors were created. Sooner or later the extension of privilege, far from curing the evil, was to operate to the disadvantage of the plebeians. Nevertheless, the new social organization did not meet with the same end in all places. In Lombardy, for example, where the people rapidly growing rich through commerce and industry soon conquered the authorities, even to the exclusion of the nobles, — first, the nobility became poor and degraded, and were forced, in order to live and maintain their credit, to gain admission to the guilds; then, the ordinary subalternization of property leading to inequality of fortunes, to wealth and poverty, to jealousies and hatreds, the cities passed rapidly from the rankest democracy under the yoke of a few ambitious leaders. Such was the fate of most of the Lombardic

636

cities, — Genoa, Florence, Bologna, Milan, Pisa, &c,. — which afterwards changed rulers frequently, but which have never since risen in favor of liberty. The people can easily escape from the tyranny of despots, but they do not know how to throw off the effects of their own despotism; just as we avoid the assassin's steel, while we succumb to a constitutional malady. As soon as a nation becomes proprietor, either it must perish, or a foreign invasion must force it again to begin its evolutionary round.[63]

In France, the Revolution was much more gradual. The communes, in taking refuge under the protection of the kings, had found them masters rather than protectors. Their liberty had long since been lost, or, rather, their emancipation had been suspended, when feudalism received its death-blow at the hand of Richelieu. Then liberty halted; the prince of the feudatories held sole and undivided sway. The nobles, the clergy, the commoners, the parliaments, every thing in short except a few seeming privileges, were controlled by the king; who, like his early predecessors, consumed regularly, and nearly always in advance, the revenues of his domain, — and that domain was France. Finally, '89 arrived; liberty resumed its march; a century and a half had been required to wear out the last form of feudal property, — monarchy.

The French Revolution may be defined as *the substitution of real right for personal right;* that is to say, in the days of feudalism, the value of property depended upon the standing of the proprietor, while, after the Revolution, the regard for the man was proportional to his property. Now, we have seen from what has been said in the preceding pages, that this recognition of the right of laborers had been the constant aim of the serfs and communes, the secret motive of their efforts. The movement of '89 was only the last stage of that long insurrection. But it seems to me that we have not paid sufficient attention to the fact that the Revolution of 1789, instigated by the same causes, animated by the same spirit, triumphing by the same struggles, was consummated in Italy four centuries ago. Italy was the first to sound the signal of war against feudalism; France has followed; Spain and England are beginning to move; the rest still sleep. If a grand example should be given to the world, the day of trial would be much abridged.

Note the following summary of the revolutions of property, from the days of the Roman Empire down to the present time: — 1. *Fifth Century.* — Barbarian invasions; division of the lands of the empire into independent portions or freeholds. 2. *From the fifth to the eighth Century.* — Gradual concentration of freeholds, or transformation of the small freeholds into fiefs, feuds, tenures, &c. Large properties, small possessions. Charlemagne (771–814) decrees that all freeholds are dependent upon the king of France. 3. *From the eighth to the tenth Century.* — The relation between the crown and the superior dependents is broken; the latter becoming freeholders, while the smaller dependents cease to recognize the king, and adhere to the nearest suzerain. Feudal system. 4. *Twelfth Century.* — Movement of the serfs towards liberty; emancipation of the communes. 5. *Thirteenth Century.* — Abolition of personal right, and of the feudal system in Italy. Italian Republics. 6. *Seventeenth Century.* — Abolition of feudalism in France during Richelieu's ministry. Despotism.

7. 1789. — Abolition of all privileges of birth, caste, provinces, and corporations; equality of persons and of rights. French democracy. 8. 1830. — The principle of concentration inherent in individual property is *remarked.* Development of the idea of association.

The more we reflect upon this series of transformations and changes, the more clearly we see that they were necessary in their principle, in their manifestations, and in their result.

It was necessary that inexperienced conquerors, eager for liberty, should divide the Roman Empire into a multitude of estates, as free and independent as themselves.

It was necessary that these men, who liked war even better than liberty, should submit to their leaders; and, as the freehold represented the man, that property should violate property.

It was necessary that, under the rule of a nobility always idle when not fighting, there should grow up a body of laborers, who, by the power of production, and by the division and circulation of wealth, would gradually gain control over commerce, industry, and a portion of the land, and who, having become rich, would aspire to power and authority also.

It was necessary, finally, that liberty and equality of rights having been achieved, and individual property still existing, attended by robbery, poverty, social inequality, and oppression, there should be an inquiry into the cause of this evil, and an idea of universal association formed, whereby, on condition of labor, all interests should be protected and consolidated.

"Evil, when carried too far," says a learned jurist, "cures itself; and the political innovation which aims to increase the power of the State, finally succumbs to the effects of its own work. The Germans, to secure their independence, chose chiefs; and soon they were oppressed by their kings and noblemen. The monarchs surrounded themselves with volunteers, in order to control the freemen; and they found themselves dependent upon their proud vassals. The *missi dominici* were sent into the provinces to maintain the power of the emperors, and to protect the people from the oppressions of the noblemen; and not only did they usurp the imperial power to a great extent, but they dealt more severely with the inhabitants. The freemen became vassals, in order to get rid of military service and court duty; and they were immediately involved in all the personal quarrels of their seigniors, and compelled to do jury duty in their courts... The kings protected the cities and the communes, in the hope of freeing them from the yoke of the grand vassals, and of rendering their own power more absolute; and those same communes have, in several European countries, procured the establishment of a constitutional power, are now holding royalty in check, and are giving rise to a universal desire for political reform." — *Meyer: Judicial Institutions of Europe.*

In recapitulation.

What was feudalism? A confederation of the grand seign iors against the villeins, and against the king.[64] What is constitutional government? A confederation of the *bourgeoisie* against the laborers, and against the king.[65]

How did feudalism end? In the union of the communes and the royal authority. How will the *bourgeoisie* aristocracy end? In the union of the proletariat and the sovereign power.

What was the immediate result of the struggle of the communes and the king against the seigniors? The monarchical unity of Louis XIV. What will be the result of the struggle of the proletariat and the sovereign power combined against the *bourgeoisie*? The absolute unity of the nation and the government.

It remains to be seen whether the nation, one and supreme, will be represented in its executive and central power by *one*, by *five*, by *one hundred*, or *one thousand;* that is, it remains to be seen, whether the royalty of the barricades intends to maintain itself by the people, or without the people, and whether Louis Philippe wishes his reign to be the most famous in all history.

639

I have made this statement as brief, but at the same time as accurate as I could, neglecting facts and details, that I might give the more attention to the economical relations of society. For the study of history is like the study of the human organism; just as the latter has its system, its organs, and its functions, which can be treated separately, so the former has its *ensemble*, its instruments, and its causes. Of course I do not pretend that the principle of property is a complete *résumé* of all the social forces; but, as in that wonderful machine which we call our body, the harmony of the whole allows us to draw a general conclusion from the consideration of a single function or organ, so, in discussing historical causes, I have been able to reason with absolute accuracy from a single order of facts, certain as I was of the perfect correlation which exists between this special order and universal history. As is the property of a nation, so is its family, its marriage, its religion, its civil and military organization, and its legislative and judicial institutions. History, viewed from this standpoint, is a grand and sublime psychological study.

Well, sir, in writing against property, have I done more than quote the language of history? I have said to modern society, — the daughter and heiress of all preceding societies, — *Age guod agis:* complete the task which for six thousand years you have been executing under the inspiration and by the command of God; hasten to finish your journey; turn neither to the right nor the left, but follow the road which lies before you. You seek reason, law, unity, and discipline; but hereafter you can find them only by stripping off the veils of your infancy, and ceasing to follow instinct as a guide. Awaken your sleeping conscience; open your eyes to the pure light of reflection and science; behold the phantom which troubled your dreams, and so long kept you in a state of unutterable anguish. Know thyself, O long-deluded society[66] know thy enemy! ... And I have denounced property.

We often hear the defenders of the right of domain quote in defence of their views the testimony of nations and ages. We can judge, from what has just been said, how far this historical argument conforms to the real facts and the conclusions of science.

To complete this apology, I must examine the various theories.

Neither politics, nor legislation, nor history, can be explained and understood, without a positive theory which defines their elements, and discovers their laws; in short, without a philosophy. Now, the two principal schools, which to this day divide the attention of the world, do not satisfy this condition.

640

The first, essentially *practical* in its character, confined to a statement of facts, and buried in learning, cares very little by what laws humanity develops itself. To it these laws are the secret of the Almighty, which no one can fathom without a commission from on high. In applying the facts of history to government, this school does not reason; it does not anticipate; it makes no comparison of the past with the present, in order to predict the future. In its opinion, the lessons of experience teach us only to repeat old errors, and its whole philosophy consists in perpetually retracing the tracks of antiquity, instead of going straight ahead forever in the direction in which they point.

The second school may be called either *fatalistic* or *pantheistic*. To it the movements of empires and the revolutions of humanity are the manifestations, the incarnations, of the Almighty. The human race, identified with the divine essence, wheels in a circle of appearances, informations, and destructions, which necessarily excludes the idea of absolute truth, and destroys providence and liberty.

Corresponding to these two schools of history, there are two schools of jurisprudence, similarly opposed, and possessed of the same peculiarities.

1. The practical and conventional school, to which the law is always a creation of the legislator, an expression of his will, a privilege which he condescends to grant, — in short, a gratuitous affirmation to be regarded as judicious and legitimate, no matter what it declares.

2. The fatalistic and pantheistic school, sometimes called the historical school, which opposes the despotism of the first, and maintains that law, like literature and religion, is always the expression of society, — its manifestation, its form, the external realization of its mobile spirit and its ever-changing inspirations.

Each of these schools, denying the absolute, rejects thereby all positive and *à priori* philosophy.

Now, it is evident that the theories of these two schools, whatever view we take of them, are utterly unsatisfactory: for, opposed, they form no dilemma, — that is, if one is false, it does not follow that the other is true; and, united, they do not constitute the truth, since they disregard the absolute, without which there is no truth. They are respectively a *thesis* and an *antithesis*. There remains to be found, then, a *synthesis*, which, predicating the absolute, justifies the will of the legislator, explains the variations of the law, annihilates the theory of the circular movement of humanity, and demonstrates its progress.

The legists, by the very nature of their studies and in spite of their obstinate prejudices, have been led irresistibly to suspect that the absolute in the science of law is not as chimerical as is commonly supposed; and this suspicion arose from their comparison of the various relations which legislators have been called upon to regulate.

M. Laboulaye, the laureate of the Institute, begins his "History of Property" with these words: —

"While the law of contract, which regulates only the mutual interests of men, has not varied for centuries (except in certain forms which relate more to the proof than to the character of the obligation), the civil law of property, which regulates the mutual relations of citizens, has undergone several radical changes, and has kept pace in its variations with all the vicissitudes of society. The law of contract, which holds essentially to those principles of eternal justice which are engraven upon the depths of the human heart, is the immutable element of jurisprudence, and, in a certain sense, its philosophy. Property, on the contrary, is the variable element of jurisprudence, its history, its policy."

Marvellous! There is in law, and consequently in politics, something variable and something invariable. The invariable element is obligation, the bond of justice, duty; the variable element is property, — that is, the external form of law, the subject-matter of the contract. Whence it follows that the law can modify, change, reform, and judge property. Reconcile that, if you can, with the idea of an eternal, absolute, permanent, and indefectible right.

However, M. Laboulaye is in perfect accord with himself when he adds, "Possession of the soil rests solely upon force until society takes it in hand, and espouses the cause of the possessor;"[67] and, a little farther, "The right of property is not natural, but social. The laws not only protect property: they give it birth," &c. Now, that which the law has made the law can unmake; especially since, according to M. Laboulaye, — an avowed partisan of the historical or pantheistic school, — the law is not absolute, is not an idea, but a form.

But why is it that property is variable, and, unlike obligation, incapable of definition and settlement? Before affirming, somewhat boldly without doubt, that in right there are no absolute principles (the most dangerous, most immoral, most tyrannical — in a word, most anti-social — assertion imaginable), it was proper that the right of property should be subjected to a thorough examination, in order to put in evidence its variable, arbitrary, and contingent elements, and those which are eternal, legitimate, and absolute; then, this operation performed, it became easy to account for the laws, and to correct all the codes.

Now, this examination of property I claim to have made, and in the fullest detail; but, either from the public's lack of interest in an unrecommended and unattractive pamphlet, or — which is more probable — from the weakness of exposition and want of genius which characterize the work, the First Memoir on Property passed unnoticed; scarcely would a few communists, having turned its leaves, deign to brand it with their disapprobation. You alone, sir, in spite of the disfavor which I showed for your economical predecessors in too severe a criticism of them, — you alone have judged me justly; and although I cannot accept, at least literally, your first judgment, yet it is to you alone that I appeal from a decision too equivocal to be regarded as final.

It not being my intention to enter at present into a discussion of principles, I shall content myself with estimating, from the point of view of this simple and intelligible absolute, the theories of property which our generation has produced.

The most exact idea of property is given us by the Roman law, faithfully followed in this particular by the ancient legists. It is the absolute, exclusive, autocratic domain of a man over a thing, — a domain which begins by *usucaption*, is maintained by *possession*, and finally, by the aid of *prescription*, finds its sanction in the civil law; a domain which so identifies the man with the thing, that the proprietor can say, "He who uses my field, virtually compels me to labor for him; therefore he owes me compensation."

I pass in silence the secondary modes by which property can be acquired, — *tradition, sale, exchange, inheritance,* &c., — which have nothing in common with the origin of property.

Accordingly, Pothier said *the domain of property*, and not simply *property*. And the most learned writers on jurisprudence — in imitation of the Roman praetor who recognized a *right of property* and a *right of possession* — have carefully distinguished between the *domain* and the right of *usufruct, use,* and *habitation*, which, reduced to its natural limits, is the very expression of justice; and which is, in my opinion, to supplant domanial property, and finally form the basis of all jurisprudence.

But, sir, admire the clumsiness of systems, or rather the fatality of logic! While the Roman law and all the *savants* inspired by it teach that property in its origin is the right of first occupancy sanctioned by law, the modern legists, dissatisfied with this brutal definition, claim that property is based upon *labor*. Immediately they infer that he who no longer labors, but makes another labor in his stead, loses his right to the earnings of the latter. It is by virtue of this principle that the serfs of the middle ages claimed a legal right to property, and consequently to the enjoyment of political rights; that the clergy were despoiled in '89 of their immense estates, and were granted a pension in exchange; that at the restoration the liberal deputies opposed the indemnity of one billion francs. "The nation," said they, "has acquired by twenty-five years of labor and possession the property which the emigrants forfeited by abandonment and long idleness: why should the nobles be treated with more favor than the priests?"[68]

All usurpations, not born of war, have been caused and supported by labor. All modern history proves this, from the end of the Roman empire down to the present day. And as if to give a sort of legal sanction to these usurpations, the doctrine of labor, subversive of property, is professed at great length in the Roman law under the name of *prescription*.

The man who cultivates, it has been said, makes the land his own; consequently, no more property. This was clearly seen by the old jurists, who have not failed to denounce this novelty; while on the other hand the young school hoots at the absurdity of the first-occupant theory. Others have presented themselves, pretending to reconcile the two opinions by uniting them. They have failed, like all the *juste-milieux* of the world, and are laughed at for their eclecticism. At present, the alarm is in the camp of the old doctrine; from all sides pour in *defences of property, studies regarding property, theories of property*, each one of which, giving the lie to the rest, inflicts a fresh wound upon property.

Consider, indeed, the inextricable embarrassments, the contradictions, the absurdities, the incredible nonsense, in which the bold defenders of property so lightly involve themselves. I choose the eclectics, because, those killed, the others cannot survive.

644

M. Troplong, jurist, passes for a philosopher in the eyes of the editors of "Le Droit." I tell the gentlemen of "Le Droit" that, in the judgment of philosophers, M. Troplong is only an advocate; and I prove my assertion.

M. Troplong is a defender of progress. "The words of the code," says he, "are fruitful sap with which the classic works of the eighteenth century overflow. To wish to suppress them ... is to violate the law of progress, and to forget that a science which moves is a science which grows."[69]

Now, the only mutable and progressive portion of law, as we have already seen, is that which concerns property. If, then, you ask what reforms are to be introduced into the right of property? M. Troplong makes no reply; what progress is to be hoped for? no reply; what is to be the destiny of property in case of universal association? no reply; what is the absolute and what the contingent, what the true and what the false, in property? no reply. M. Troplong favors quiescence and *in statu quo* in regard to property. What could be more unphilosophical in a progressive philosopher?

Nevertheless, M. Troplong has thought about these things. "There are," he says, "many weak points and antiquated ideas in the doctrines of modern authors concerning property: witness the works of MM. Toullier and Duranton." The doctrine of M. Troplong promises, then, strong points, advanced and progressive ideas. Let us see; let us examine: —

"Man, placed in the presence of matter, is conscious of a power over it, which has been given to him to satisfy the needs of his being. King of inanimate or unintelligent nature, he feels that he has a right to modify it, govern it, and fit it for his use. There it is, the subject of property, which is legitimate only when exercised over things, never when over persons."

M. Troplong is so little of a philosopher, that he does not even know the import of the philosophical terms which he makes a show of using. He says of matter that it is the *subject* of property; he should have said the *object*. M. Troplong uses the language of the anatomists, who apply the term *subject* to the human matter used in their experiments.

This error of our author is repeated farther on: "Liberty, which overcomes matter, the subject of property, &c." The *subject* of property

645

is man; its *object* is matter. But even this is but a slight mortification; directly we shall have some crucifixions.

Thus, according to the passage just quoted, it is in the conscience and personality of man that the principle of property must be sought. Is there any thing new in this doctrine? Apparently it never has occurred to those who, since the days of Cicero and Aristotle, and earlier, have maintained that *things belong to the first occupant*, that occupation may be exercised by beings devoid of conscience and personality. The human personality, though it may be the principle or the subject of property, as matter is the object, is not the *condition*. Now, it is this condition which we most need to know. So far, M. Troplong tells us no more than his masters, and the figures with which he adorns his style add nothing to the old idea.

Property, then, implies three terms: The subject, the object, and the condition. There is no difficulty in regard to the first two terms. As to the third, the condition of property down to this day, for the Greek as for the Barbarian, has been that of first occupancy. What now would you have it, progressive doctor?

"When man lays hands for the first time upon an object without a master, he performs an act which, among individuals, is of the greatest importance. The thing thus seized and occupied participates, so to speak, in the personality of him who holds it. It becomes sacred, like himself. It is impossible to take it without doing violence to his liberty, or to remove it without rashly invading his person. Diogenes did but express this truth of intuition, when he said: 'Stand out of my light!' "

Very good! but would the prince of cynics, the very personal and very haughty Diogenes, have had the right to charge another cynic, as rent for this same place in the sunshine, a bone for twenty-four hours of possession? It is that which constitutes the proprietor; it is that which you fail to justify. In reasoning from the human personality and individuality to the right of property, you unconsciously construct a syllogism in which the conclusion includes more than the premises, contrary to the rules laid down by Aristotle. The individuality of the human person proves *individual possession*, originally called *proprietas*, in opposition to collective possession, *communio*. It gives birth to the distinction between *thine* and *mine*, true signs of equality, not, by any means, of subordination. "From equivocation to equivocation," says M. Michelet,[70] "property would crawl to the end of the world; man could not limit it, were not he himself its limit. Where they clash, there will be its frontier." In short, individuality of being destroys the hypothesis of communism, but it does not for that reason give birth to domain, — that domain by virtue of which the holder of a thing exercises over the person who takes his place a right of prestation and suzerainty, that has always been identified with property itself.

Further, that he whose legitimately acquired possession injures nobody cannot be nonsuited without flagrant injustice, is a truth, not of *intuition*, as M. Troplong says, but of *inward sensation*,[71] which has nothing to do with property.

M. Troplong admits, then, occupancy as a condition of property. In that, he is in accord with the Roman law, in accord with MM. Toullier and Duranton; but in his opinion this condition is not the only one, and it is in this particular that his doctrine goes beyond theirs.

"But, however exclusive the right arising from sole occupancy, does it not become still more so, when man has moulded matter by his labor; when he has deposited in it a portion of himself, re-creating it by his industry, and setting upon it the seal of his intelligence and activity? Of all conquests, that is the most legitimate, for it is the price of labor.

He who should deprive a man of the thing thus remodelled, thus humanized, would invade the man himself, and would inflict the deepest wounds upon his liberty."

I pass over the very beautiful explanations in which M. Troplong, discussing labor and industry, displays the whole wealth of his eloquence. M. Troplong is not only a philosopher, he is an orator, an artist. *He abounds with appeals to the conscience and the passions.* I might make sad work of his rhetoric, should I undertake to dissect it; but I confine myself for the present to his philosophy.

If M. Troplong had only known how to think and reflect, before abandoning the original fact of occupancy and plunging into the theory of labor, he would have asked himself: "What is it to occupy?" And he would have discovered that *occupancy* is only a generic term by which all modes of possession are expressed, — seizure, station, immanence, habitation, cultivation, use, consumption, &c.; that labor, consequently, is but one of a thousand forms of occupancy. He would have understood, finally, that the right of possession which is born of labor is governed by the same general laws as that which results from the simple seizure of things. What kind of a legist is he who declaims when he ought to reason, who continually mistakes his metaphors for legal

647

axioms, and who does not so much as know how to obtain a universal by induction, and form a category?

If labor is identical with occupancy, the only benefit which it secures to the laborer is the right of individual possession of the object of his labor; if it differs from occupancy, it gives birth to a right equal only to itself, — that is, a right which begins, continues, and ends, with the labor of the occupant. It is for this reason, in the words of the law, that one cannot acquire a just title to a thing by labor alone. He must also hold it for a year and a day, in order to be regarded as its possessor; and possess it twenty or thirty years, in order to become its proprietor.

These preliminaries established, M. Troplong's whole structure falls of its own weight, and the inferences, which he attempts to draw, vanish.

"Property once acquired by occupation and labor, it naturally preserves itself, not only by the same means, but also by the refusal of the holder to abdicate; for from the very fact that it has risen to the height of a right, it is its nature to perpetuate itself and to last for an indefinite period... Rights, considered from an ideal point of view, are imperishable and eternal; and time, which affects only the contingent, can no more disturb them than it can injure God himself." It is astonishing that our author, in speaking of the *ideal, time*, and *eternity*, did not work into his sentence the *divine wings* of Plato, — so fashionable to-day in philosophical works.

With the exception of falsehood, I hate nonsense more than any thing else in the world. *Property once acquired*! Good, if it is acquired; but, as it is not acquired, it cannot be preserved. *Rights are eternal*! Yes, in the sight of God, like the archetypal ideas of the Platonists. But, on the earth, rights exist only in the presence of a subject, an object, and a condition. Take away one of these three things, and rights no longer exist. Thus, individual possession ceases at the death of the subject, upon the destruction of the object, or in case of exchange or abandonment.

Let us admit, however, with M. Troplong, that property is an absolute and eternal right, which cannot be destroyed save by the deed and at the will of the proprietor. What are the consequences which immediately follow from this position?

To show the justice and utility of prescription, M. Troplong supposes the case of a *bona fide* possessor whom a proprietor, long since forgotten or even unknown, is attempting to eject from his possession.

"At the start, the error of the possessor was excusable but not irreparable. Pursuing its course and growing old by degrees, it has so completely clothed itself in the colors of truth, it has spoken so loudly the language of right, it has involved so many confiding interests, that it fairly may be asked whether it would not cause greater confusion to go back to the reality than to sanction the fictions which it (an error, without doubt) has sown on its way? Well, yes; it must be confessed, without hesitation, that the remedy would prove worse than the disease, and that its application would lead to the most outrageous injustice."

How long since utility became a principle of law? When the Athenians, by the advice of Aristides, rejected a proposition eminently advantageous to their republic, but also utterly unjust, they showed finer moral perception and greater clearness of intellect than M. Troplong. Property is an eternal right, independent of time, indestructible except by the act and at the will of the proprietor; and here this right is taken from the proprietor, and on what ground? Good God! on the ground of *absence*! Is it not true that legists are governed by caprice in giving and taking away rights? When it pleases these gentlemen, idleness, unworthiness, or absence can invalidate a right which, under quite similar circumstances, labor, residence, and virtue are inadequate to obtain. Do not be astonished that legists reject the absolute. Their good pleasure is law, and their disordered imaginations are the real cause of the *evolutions* in jurisprudence.

"If the nominal proprietor should plead ignorance, his claim would be none the more valid. Indeed, his ignorance might arise from inexcusable carelessness, etc."

What! in order to legitimate dispossession through prescription, you suppose faults in the proprietor! You blame his absence, — which may have been involuntary; his neglect, — not knowing what caused it; his carelessness, — a gratuitous supposition of your own! It is absurd. One very simple observation suffices to annihilate this theory. Society, which, they tell us, makes an exception in the interest of order in favor of the possessor as against the old proprietor, owes the latter an indemnity; since the privilege of prescription is nothing but expropriation for the sake of public utility.

But here is something stronger: —

"In society a place cannot remain vacant with impunity. A new man arises in place of the old one who disappears or goes away; he brings here his existence, becomes entirely absorbed, and devotes himself to this post which he finds abandoned. Shall the deserter, then, dispute the honor of the victory with the soldier who fights with the sweat standing on his brow, and bears the burden of the day, in behalf of a cause which he deems just?"

When the tongue of an advocate once gets in motion, who can tell where it will stop? M. Troplong admits and justifies usurpation in case of the *absence* of the proprietor, and on a mere presumption of his *carelessness*. But when the neglect is authenticated; when the abandonment is solemnly and voluntarily set forth in a contract in the presence of a magistrate; when the proprietor dares to say, "I cease to labor, but I still claim a share of the product," — then the absentee's right of property is protected; the usurpation of the possessor would be criminal; farm-rent is the reward of idleness.

Where is, I do not say the consistency, but, the honesty of this law?

Prescription is a result of the civil law, a creation of the legislator. Why has not the legislator fixed the conditions differently? — why, instead of twenty and thirty years, is not a single year sufficient to prescribe? — why are not voluntary absence and confessed idleness as good grounds for dispossession as involuntary absence, ignorance, or apathy?

But in vain should we ask M. Troplong, the philosopher, to tell us the ground of prescription. Concerning the code, M. Troplong does not reason. "The interpreter," he says, "must take things as they are, society as it exists, laws as they are made: that is the only sensible starting-point." Well, then, write no more books; cease to reproach your predecessors — who, like you, have aimed only at interpretation of the law — for having remained in the rear; talk no more of philosophy and progress, for the lie sticks in your throat.

M. Troplong denies the reality of the right of possession; he denies that possession has ever existed as a principle of society; and he quotes M. de Savigny, who holds precisely the opposite position, and whom he is content to leave unanswered. At one time, M. Troplong asserts that possession and property are *contemporaneous*, and that they exist *at the same time*, which implies that the *right* of property is based on the *fact* of possession, — a conclusion which is evidently absurd; at another, he denies that possession *had any historical existence prior to property*, — an assertion which is contradicted by the customs of many nations which cultivate the land without appropriating it; by the Roman law, which distinguished so clearly between *possession* and *property;* and

650

by our code itself, which makes possession for twenty or thirty years the condition of property. Finally, M. Troplong goes so far as to maintain that the Roman maxim, *Nihil comune habet proprietas cum possessione* — which contains so striking an allusion to the possession of the *ager publicus*, and which, sooner or later, will be again accepted without qualification — expresses in French law only a judicial axiom, a simple rule forbidding the union of an *action possessoire* with an *action petitoire*, — an opinion as retrogressive as it is unphilosophical.

In treating of *actions possessoires*, M. Troplong is so unfortunate or awkward that he mutilates economy through failure to grasp its meaning "Just as property," he writes, "gave rise to the action for revendication, so possession — the *jus possessionis* — was the cause of possessory interdicts... There were two kinds of interdicts, — the interdict *recuperandæ possessionis*, and the interdict *retinendæ possessionis*, — which correspond to our *complainte en cas de saisine et nouvelete*. There is also a third, — *adipiscendæ possessionis*, — of which the Roman law-books speak in connection with the two others. But, in reality, this interdict is not possessory: for he who wishes to acquire possession by this means does not possess, and has not possessed; and yet acquired possession is the condition of possessory interdicts." Why is not an action to acquire possession equally conceivable with an action to be reinstated in possession? When the Roman plebeians demanded a division of the conquered territory; when the proletaires of Lyons took for their motto, *Vivre en travaillant, ou mourir en combattant* (to live working, or die fighting); when the most enlightened of the modern economists claim for every man the right to labor and to live, — they only propose this interdict, *adipiscendæ possessionis*, which embarrasses M. Troplong so seriously. And what is my object in pleading against property, if not to obtain possession?

How is it that M. Troplong — the legist, the orator, the philosopher — does not see that logically this interdict must be admitted, since it is the necessary complement of the two others, and the three united form an indivisible trinity, — to *recover*, to *maintain*, to *acquire*? To break this series is to create a blank, destroy the natural synthesis of things, and follow the example of the geometrician who tried to conceive of a solid with only two dimensions. But it is not astonishing that M. Troplong rejects the third class of *actions possessoires*, when we consider that he rejects possession itself. He is so completely controlled by his prejudices in this respect, that he is unconsciously led, not to unite (that would be horrible in his eyes), but to identify the *action possessoire* with the *action petitoire*. This could be easily proved, were it not too tedious to plunge into these metaphysical obscurities.

651

As an interpreter of the law, M. Troplong is no more successful than as a philosopher. One specimen of his skill in this direction, and I am done with him: —

Code of Civil Procedure, Art. 23: "*Actions possessoires* are only when commenced within the year of trouble by those who have held possession for at least a year by an irrevocable title."

M. Troplong's comments: —

"Ought we to maintain — as Duparc, Poullain, and Lanjuinais would have us — the rule *spoliatus ante omnia restituendus*, when an individual, who is neither proprietor nor annual possessor, is expelled by a third party, who has no right to the estate? I think not. Art. 23 of the Code is general: it absolutely requires that the plaintiff in *actions possessoires* shall have been in peaceable possession for a year at least. That is the invariable principle: it can in no case be modified. And why should it be set aside? The plaintiff had no seisin; he had no privileged possession; he had only a temporary occupancy, insufficient to warrant in his favor the presumption of property, which renders the annual possession so valuable. Well! this *ae facto* occupancy he has lost; another is invested with it: possession is in the hands of this new-comer. Now, is not this a case for the application of the principle, *In pari causa possesser potior habetur*? Should not the actual possessor be preferred to the evicted possessor? Can he not meet the complaint of his adversary by saying to him: 'Prove that you were an annual possessor before me, for you are the plaintiff. As far as I am concerned, it is not for me to tell you how I possess, nor how long I have possessed. *Possideo quia possideo.* I have no other reply, no other defence. When you have shown that your action is admissible, then we will see whether you are entitled to lift the veil which hides the origin of my possession.' "

And this is what is honored with the name of jurisprudence and philosophy, — the restoration of force. What! when I have "moulded matter by my labor" [I quote M. Troplong]; when I have "deposited in it a portion of myself" [M. Troplong]; when I have "re-created it by my industry, and set upon it the seal of my intelligence" [M. Troplong], — on the ground that I have not possessed it for a year, a stranger may dispossess me, and the law offers me no protection! And if M. Troplong is my judge, M. Troplong will condemn me! And if I resist my adversary, — if, for this bit of mud which I may call *my field*, and of which they wish to rob me, a war breaks out between the two competitors, — the legislator will gravely wait until the stronger, having killed the other, has had possession for a year! No, no, Monsieur Troplong! you do not understand the words of the law; for I prefer to call in question your intelligence rather than the justice of the legislator. You are mistaken in your application of the principle, *In pari causa possessor potior habetur:* the actuality of possession here refers to him who possessed at the time when the difficulty arose, not to him who possesses at the time of the complaint. And when the code prohibits the reception of *actions possessoires*, in cases where the possession is not of a year's duration, it simply means that if, before a year has elapsed, the holder relinquishes possession, and ceases actually to occupy *in propria persona*, he cannot avail himself of an *action possessoire* against his successor. In a word, the code treats possession of less than a year as it ought to treat all possession, however long it has existed, — that is, the condition of property ought to be, not merely seisin for a year, but perpetual seisin.

I will not pursue this analysis farther. When an author bases two volumes of quibbles on foundations so uncertain, it may be boldly declared that his work, whatever the amount of learning displayed in it, is a mess of nonsense unworthy a critic's attention.

At this point, sir, I seem to hear you reproaching me for this conceited dogmatism, this lawless arrogance, which respects nothing, claims a monopoly of justice and good sense, and assumes to put in the pillory any one who dares to maintain an opinion contrary to its own. This fault, they tell me, more odious than any other in an author, was too prominent a characteristic of my First Memoir, and I should do well to correct it.

It is important to the success of my defence, that I should vindicate myself from this reproach; and since, while perceiving in myself other faults of a different character, I still adhere in this particular to my disputatious style, it is right that I should give my reasons for my conduct. I act, not from inclination, but from necessity.

I say, then, that I treat my authors as I do for two reasons: a *reason of right*, and a *reason of intention;* both peremptory.

1. Reason of right. When I preach equality of fortunes, I do not advance an opinion more or less probable, a utopia more or less ingenious, an idea conceived within my brain by means of imagination only. I lay down an absolute truth, concerning which hesitation is impossible, modesty superfluous, and doubt ridiculous.

But, do you ask, what assures me that that which I utter is true? What assures me, sir? The logical and metaphysical processes which I use, the correctness of which I have demonstrated by *à priori* reasoning; the fact that I possess an infallible method of investigation and verification with which my authors are unacquainted; and finally, the fact that for all matters relating to property and justice I have found a formula which explains all legislative variations, and furnishes a key for all problems. Now, is there so much as a shadow of method in M. Toullier, M. Troplong, and this swarm of insipid commentators, almost as devoid of reason and moral sense as the code itself? Do you give the name of method to an alphabetical, chronological, analogical, or merely nominal classification of subjects? Do you give the name of method to these lists of paragraphs gathered under an arbitrary head, these sophistical vagaries, this mass of contradictory quotations and opinions, this nauseous style, this spasmodic rhetoric, models of which are so common at the bar, though seldom found elsewhere? Do you take for philosophy this twaddle, this intolerable pettifoggery adorned with a few scholastic trimmings? No, no! a writer who respects himself, never will consent to enter the balance with these manipulators of law, misnamed *jurists*; and for my part I object to a comparison.

2. Reason of intention. As far as I am permitted to divulge this secret, I am a conspirator in an immense revolution, terrible to charlatans and despots, to all exploiters of the poor and credulous, to all salaried idlers, dealers in political panaceas and parables, tyrants in a word of thought and of opinion. I labor to stir up the reason of individuals to insurrection against the reason of authorities.

According to the laws of the society of which I am a member, all the evils which afflict humanity arise from faith in external teachings and submission to authority. And not to go outside of our own century, is it not true, for instance, that France is plundered, scoffed at, and tyrannized over, because she speaks in masses, and not by heads? The French people are penned up in three or four flocks, receiving their signal from a chief, responding to the voice of a leader, and thinking just as he says. A certain journal, it is said, has fifty thousand subscribers; assuming six readers to every subscriber, we have three hundred thousand sheep browsing and bleating at the same cratch. Apply this calculation to the whole periodical press, and you find that, in our free and intelligent France, there are two millions of creatures receiving every morning from the journals spiritual pasturage. Two millions! In other words, the entire nation allows a score of little fellows to lead it by the nose.

654

By no means, sir, do I deny to journalists talent, science, love of truth, patriotism, and what you please. They are very worthy and intelligent people, whom I undoubtedly should wish to resemble, had I the honor to know them. That of which I complain, and that which has made me a conspirator, is that, instead of enlightening us, these gentlemen command us, impose upon us articles of faith, and that without demonstration or verification. When, for example, I ask why these fortifications of Paris, which, in former times, under the influence of certain prejudices, and by means of a concurrence of extraordinary circumstances supposed for the sake of the argument to have existed, may perhaps have served to protect us, but which it is doubtful whether our descendants will ever use, — when I ask, I say, on what grounds they assimilate the future to a hypothetical past, they reply that M. Thiers, who has a great mind, has written upon this subject a report of admirable elegance and marvellous clearness. At this I become angry, and reply that M. Thiers does not know what he is talking about. Why, having wanted no detached forts seven years ago, do we want them to-day?

"Oh! damn it," they say, "the difference is great; the first forts were too near to us; with these we cannot be bom-barded." You cannot be bombarded; but you can be blockaded, and will be, if you stir. What! to obtain blockade forts from the Parisians, it has sufficed to prejudice them against bombardment forts! And they thought to outwit the government! Oh, the sovereignty of the people! ...

"Damn it! M. Thiers, who is wiser than you, says that it would be absurd to suppose a government making war upon citizens, and maintaining itself by force and in spite of the will of the people. That would be absurd!" Perhaps so: such a thing has happened more than once, and may happen again. Besides, when despotism is strong, it appears almost legitimate. However that may be, they lied in 1833, and they lie again in 1841, — those who threaten us with the bomb-shell. And then, if M. Thiers is so well assured of the intentions of the government, why does he not wish the forts to be built before the circuit is extended? Why this air of suspicion of the government, unless an intrigue has been planned between the government and M. Thiers?

"Damn it! we do not wish to be again invaded. If Paris had been fortified in 1815, Napoleon would not have been conquered!" But I tell you that Napoleon was not conquered, but sold; and that if, in 1815, Paris had had fortifications, it would have been with them as with the thirty thousand men of Grouchy, who were misled during the battle. It is still easier to surrender forts than to lead soldiers.

Would the selfish and the cowardly ever lack reasons for yielding to the enemy?

"But do you not see that the absolutist courts are provoked at our fortifications? — a proof that they do not think as you do." You believe that; and, for my part, I believe that in reality they are quite at ease about the matter; and, if they appear to tease our ministers, they do so only to give the latter an opportunity to decline. The absolutist courts are always on better terms with our constitutional monarchy, than our monarchy with us. Does not M. Guizot say that France needs to be defended within as well as without? Within! against whom? Against France. O Parisians! it is but six months since you demanded war, and now you want only barricades. Why should the allies fear your doctrines, when you cannot even control yourselves? ... How could you sustain a siege, when you weep over the absence of an actress?

"But, finally, do you not understand that, by the rules of modern warfare, the capital of a country is always the objective point of its assailants? Suppose our army defeated on the Rhine, France invaded, and defenceless Paris falling into the hands of the enemy. It would be the death of the administrative power; without a head it could not live. The capital taken, the nation must submit. What do you say to that?"

The reply is very simple. Why is society constituted in such a way that the destiny of the country depends upon the safety of the capital? Why, in case our territory be invaded and Paris besieged, cannot the legislative, executive, and military powers act outside of Paris? Why this localization of all the vital forces of France? ... Do not cry out upon decentralization. This hackneyed reproach would discredit only your own intelligence and sincerity. It is not a question of decentralization; it is your political fetichism which I attack. Why should the national unity be attached to a certain place, to certain functionaries, to certain bayonets? Why should the Place Maubert and the Palace of the Tuileries be the palladium of France?

Now let me make an hypothesis.

Suppose it were written in the charter, "In case the country be again invaded, and Paris forced to surrender, the government being annihilated and the national assembly dissolved, the electoral colleges shall reassemble spontaneously and without other official notice, for the purpose of appointing new deputies, who shall organize a provisional government at Orleans. If Orleans succumbs, the government shall reconstruct itself in the same way at Lyons; then at

Bordeaux, then at Bayonne, until all France be captured or the enemy driven from the land. For the government may perish, but the nation never dies. The king, the peers, and the deputies massacred, *Vive la France!*"

Do you not think that such an addition to the charter would be a better safeguard for the liberty and integrity of the country than walls and bastions around Paris? Well, then! do henceforth for administration, industry, science, literature, and art that which the charter ought to prescribe for the central government and common defence. Instead of endeavoring to render Paris impregnable, try rather to render the loss of Paris an insignificant matter. Instead of accumulating about one point academies, faculties, schools, and political, administrative, and judicial centres; instead of arresting intellectual development and weakening public spirit in the provinces by this fatal agglomeration, — can you not, without destroying unity, distribute social functions among places as well as among persons? Such a system — in allowing each province to participate in political power and action, and in balancing industry, intelligence, and strength in all parts of the country — would equally secure, against enemies at home and enemies abroad, the liberty of the people and the stability of the government.

Discriminate, then, between the centralization of functions and the concentration of organs; between political unity and its material symbol.

"Oh! that is plausible; but it is impossible!" — which means that the city of Paris does not intend to surrender its privileges, and that there it is still a question of property.

Idle talk! The country, in a state of panic which has been cleverly worked upon, has asked for fortifications. I dare to affirm that it has abdicated its sovereignty. All parties are to blame for this suicide, — the conservatives, by their acquiescence in the plans of the government; the friends of the dynasty, because they wish no opposition to that which pleases them, and because a popular revolution would annihilate them; the democrats, because they hope to rule in their turn.[72] That which all rejoice at having obtained is a means of future repression. As for the defence of the country, they are not troubled about that. The idea of tyranny dwells in the minds of all, and brings together into one conspiracy all forms of selfishness. We wish the regeneration of society, but we subordinate this desire to our ideas and convenience. That our approaching marriage may take place, that our business may succeed, that our opinions may triumph, we postpone reform.

657

Intolerance and selfishness lead us to put fetters upon liberty; and, because we cannot wish all that God wishes, we would, if it rested with us, stay the course of destiny rather than sacrifice our own interests and self-love. Is not this an instance where the words of Solomon apply, — "*L'iniquité a menti à elle-même*"?

For this reason, sir, I have enlisted in a desperate war against every form of authority over the multitude. Advance sentinel of the proletariat, I cross bayonets with the celebrities of the day, as well as with spies and charlatans. Well, when I am fighting with an illustrious adversary, must I stop at the end of every phrase, like an orator in the tribune, to say "the learned author," "the eloquent writer," "the profound publicist," and a hundred other platitudes with which it is fashionable to mock people? These civilities seem to me no less insulting to the man attacked than dishonorable to the aggressor. But when, rebuking an author, I say to him, "Citizen, your doctrine is absurd, and, if to prove my assertion is an offence against you, I am guilty of it," immediately the listener opens his ears; he is all attention; and, if I do not succeed in convincing him, at least I give his thought an impulse, and set him the wholesome example of doubt and free examination.

Then do not think, sir, that, in tripping up the philosophy of your very learned and very estimable *confrère*, M. Troplong, I fail to appreciate his talent as a writer (in my opinion, he has too much for a jurist); nor his knowledge, though it is too closely confined to the letter of the law, and the reading of old books. In these particulars, M. Troplong offends on the side of excess rather than deficiency. Further, do not believe that I am actuated by any personal animosity towards him, or that I have the slightest desire to wound his self-love. I know M. Troplong only by his "Treatise on Prescription," which I wish he had not written; and as for my critics, neither M. Troplong, nor any of those whose opinion I value, will ever read me. Once more, my only object is to prove, as far as I am able, to this unhappy French nation, that those who make the laws, as well as those who interpret them, are not infallible organs of general, impersonal, and absolute reason.

I had resolved to submit to a systematic criticism the semi-official defence of the right of property recently put forth by M. Wolowski, your colleague at the Conservatory. With this view, I had commenced to collect the documents necessary for each of his lectures, but, soon perceiving that the ideas of the professor were incoherent, that his arguments contradicted each other, that one affirmation was sure to be overthrown by another, and that in M. Wolowski's lucubrations the good was always mingled with the bad, and being by nature a little suspicious, it suddenly occurred to me that M. Wolowski was an advocate of equality in disguise, thrown in spite of himself into the position in which the patriarch Jacob pictures one of his sons, — *inter duas clitellas*, between two stools, as the proverb says. In more parliamentary language, I saw clearly that M. Wolowski was placed between his profound convictions on the one hand and his official duties on the other, and that, in order to maintain his position, he had to assume a certain slant. Then I experienced great pain at seeing the reserve, the circumlocution, the figures, and the irony to which a professor of legislation, whose duty it is to teach dogmas with clearness and precision, was forced to resort; and I fell to cursing the society in which an honest man is not allowed to say frankly what he thinks. Never, sir, have you conceived of such torture: I seemed to be witnessing the martyrdom of a mind. I am going to give you an idea of these astonishing meetings, or rather of these scenes of sorrow.

Monday, Nov. 20, 1840. — The professor declares, in brief, — 1. That the right of property is not founded upon occupation, but upon the impress of man; 2. That every man has a natural and inalienable right to the use of matter.

Now, if matter can be appropriated, and if, notwithstanding, all men retain an inalienable right to the use of this matter, what is property? — and if matter can be appropriated only by labor, how long is this appropriation to continue? — questions that will confuse and confound all jurists whatsoever.

Then M. Wolowski cites his authorities. Great God! what witnesses he brings forward! First, M. Troplong, the great metaphysician, whom we have discussed; then, M. Louis Blanc, editor of the "Revue du Progres," who came near being tried by jury for publishing his "Organization of Labor," and who escaped from the clutches of the public prosecutor only by a juggler's trick;[73] Corinne, — I mean Madame de Stael, — who, in an ode, making a poetical comparison of the land with the waves, of the furrow of a plough with the wake of a vessel, says "that property exists only where man has left his trace," which makes property dependent upon the solidity of the elements; Rousseau, the apostle of liberty and equality, but who, according to M. Wolowski, attacked property only *as a joke*, and in order to point a paradox; Robespierre, who prohibited a division of the land, because he regarded such a measure as a rejuvenescence of property, and who, while awaiting the definitive organization of the republic, placed all property in the care of the people, — that is, transferred the right of

659

eminent domain from the individual to society; Babeuf, who wanted property for the nation, and communism for the citizens; M. Considérant, who favors a division of landed property into shares, — that is, who wishes to render property nominal and fictitious: the whole being intermingled with jokes and witticisms (intended undoubtedly to lead people away from the *hornets' nests*) at the expense of the adversaries of the right of property!

November 26. — M. Wolowski supposes this objection: Land, like water, air, and light, is necessary to life, therefore it cannot be appropriated; and he replies: The importance of landed property diminishes as the power of industry increases.

Good! this importance *diminishes*, but it does not *disappear*; and this, of itself, shows landed property to be illegitimate. Here M. Wolowski pretends to think that the opponents of property refer only to property in land, while they merely take it as a term of comparison; and, in showing with wonderful clearness the absurdity of the position in which he places them, he finds a way of drawing the attention of his hearers to another subject without being false to the truth which it is his office to contradict.

"Property," says M. Wolowski, "is that which distinguishes man from the animals." That may be; but are we to regard this as a compliment or a satire?

"Mahomet," says M. Wolowski, "decreed property." And so did Genghis Khan, and Tamerlane, and all the ravagers of nations. What sort of legislators were they?

"Property has been in existence ever since the origin of the human race." Yes, and so has slavery, and despotism also; and likewise polygamy and idolatry. But what does this antiquity show?

The members of the Council of the State — M. Portalis at their head — did not raise, in their discussion of the Code, the question of the legitimacy of property. "Their silence," says M. Wolowski, "is a precedent in favor of this right." I may regard this reply as personally addressed to me, since the observation belongs to me. I reply, "As long as an opinion is universally admitted, the universality of belief serves of itself as argument and proof. When this same opinion is attacked, the former faith proves nothing; we must resort to reason. Ignorance, however old and pardonable it may be, never outweighs reason."

660

Property has its abuses, M. Wolowski confesses. "But," he says, "these abuses gradually disappear. To-day their cause is known. They all arise from a false theory of prop-erty. In principle, property is inviolable, but it can and must be checked and disciplined." Such are the conclusions of the professor.

When one thus remains in the clouds, he need not fear to equivocate. Nevertheless, I would like him to define these *abuses* of property, to show their cause, to explain this true theory from which no abuse is to spring; in short, to tell me how, without destroying property, it can be governed for the greatest good of all. "Our civil code," says M. Wolowski, in speaking of this subject, "leaves much to be desired." I think it leaves every thing undone.

Finally, M. Wolowski opposes, on the one hand, the concentration of capital, and the absorption which results therefrom; and, on the other, he objects to the extreme division of the land. Now I think that I have demonstrated in my First Memoir, that large accumulation and minute division are the first two terms of an economical trinity, — a *thesis* and an *antithesis*. But, while M. Wolowski says nothing of the third term, the *synthesis*, and thus leaves the inference in suspense, I have shown that this third term is ASSOCIATION, which is the annihilation of property.

November 30. — LITERARY PROPERTY. M. Wolowski grants that it is just to recognize the rights of talent (which is not in the least hostile to equality); but he seriously objects to perpetual and absolute property in the works of genius, to the profit of the authors' heirs. His main argument is, that society has a right of collective production over every creation of the mind. Now, it is precisely this principle of collective power that I developed in my "Inquiries into Property and Government," and on which I have established the complete edifice of a new social organization. M. Wolowski is, as far as I know, the first jurist who has made a legislative application of this economical law. Only, while I have extended the principle of collective power to every sort of product, M. Wolowski, more prudent than it is my nature to be, confines it to neutral ground. So, that that which I am bold enough to say of the whole, he is contented to affirm of a part, leaving the intelligent hearer to fill up the void for himself. However, his arguments are keen and close. One feels that the professor, finding himself more at ease with one aspect of property, has given the rein to his intellect, and is rushing on towards liberty.

661

1. Absolute literary property would hinder the activity of other men, and obstruct the development of humanity. It would be the death of progress; it would be suicide. What would have happened if the first inventions, — the plough, the level, the saw, &c., — had been appropriated?

Such is the first proposition of M. Wolowski.

I reply: Absolute property in land and tools hinders human activity, and obstructs progress and the free development of man. What happened in Rome, and in all the ancient nations? What occurred in the middle ages? What do we see to-day in England, in consequence of absolute property in the sources of production? The suicide of humanity.

2. Real and personal property is in harmony with the social interest. In consequence of literary property, social and individual interests are perpetually in conflict.

The statement of this proposition contains a rhetorical figure, common with those who do not enjoy full and complete liberty of speech. This figure is the *anti-phrasis* or *contre-vérité*. It consists, according to Dumarsais and the best humanists, in saying one thing while meaning another. M. Wolowski's proposition, naturally expressed, would read as follows: "Just as real and personal property is essentially hostile to society, so, in consequence of literary property, social and individual interests are perpetually in conflict."

3. M. de Montalembert, in the Chamber of Peers, vehemently protested against the assimilation of authors to inventors of machinery; an assimilation which he claimed to be injurious to the former. M. Wolowski replies, that the rights of authors, without machinery, would be nil; that, without paper-mills, type foundries, and printing-offices, there could be no sale of verse and prose; that many a mechanical invention, — the compass, for instance, the telescope, or the steam-engine, — is quite as valuable as a book.

Prior to M. Montalembert, M. Charles Comte had laughed at the inference in favor of mechanical inventions, which logical minds never fail to draw from the privileges granted to authors. "He," says M. Comte, "who first conceived and executed the idea of transforming a piece of wood into a pair of *sabots*, or an animal's hide into a pair of sandals, would thereby have acquired an exclusive right to make shoes for the human race!" Undoubtedly, under the system of property. For, in fact, this pair of *sabots*, over which you make so merry, is the creation of the shoemaker, the work of his genius, the expression of his thought; to him it is his poem, quite as much as "Le Roi s'amuse," is M. Victor Hugo's drama. Justice for all alike. If you refuse a patent to a perfecter of boots, refuse also a privilege to a maker of rhymes.

4. That which gives importance to a book is a fact external to the author and his work. Without the intelligence of society, without its development, and a certain community of ideas, passions, and interests between it and the authors, the works of the latter would be worth nothing. The exchangeable value of a book is due even more to the *social condition* than to the talent displayed in it.

Indeed, it seems as if I were copying my own words. This proposition of M. Wolowski contains a special expression of a general and absolute idea, one of the strongest and most conclusive against the right of property. Why do artists, like mechanics, find the means to live? Because society has made the fine arts, like the rudest industries, objects of consumption and exchange, governed consequently by all the laws of commerce and political economy. Now, the first of these laws is the equipoise of functions; that is, the equality of associates.

5. M. Wolowski indulges in sarcasm against the petitioners for literary property. "There are authors," he says, "who crave the privileges of authors, and who for that purpose point out the power of the melodrama. They speak of the niece of Corneille, begging at the door of a theatre which the works of her uncle had enriched... To satisfy the avarice of literary people, it would be necessary to create literary majorats, and make a whole code of exceptions."

I like this virtuous irony. But M. Wolowski has by no means exhausted the difficulties which the question involves. And first, is it just that MM. Cousin, Guizot, Villemain, Damiron, and company, paid by the State for delivering lectures, should be paid a second time through the booksellers? — that I, who have the right to report their lectures, should not have the right to print them? Is it just that MM. Noel and Chapsal, overseers of the University, should use their influence in selling their selections from literature to the youth whose studies they are instructed to superintend in consideration of a salary? And, if that is not just, is it not proper to refuse literary property to every author holding public offices, and receiving pensions or sinecures?

Again, shall the privilege of the author extend to irreligious and immoral works, calculated only to corrupt the heart, and obscure the understanding? To grant this privilege is to sanction immorality by law;

to refuse it is to censure the author. And since it is impossible, in the present imperfect state of society, to prevent all violations of the moral law, it will be necessary to open a license-office for books as well as morals. But, then, three-fourths of our literary people will be obliged to register; and, recognized thenceforth on their own declaration as *prostitutes*, they will necessarily belong to the public. We pay toll to the prostitute; we do not endow her.

Finally, shall plagiarism be classed with forgery? If you reply "Yes," you appropriate in advance all the subjects of which books treat; if you say "No," you leave the whole matter to the decision of the judge. Except in the case of a clandestine reprint, how will he distinguish forgery from quotation, imitation, plagiarism, or even coincidence? A *savant* spends two years in calculating a table of logarithms to nine or ten decimals. He prints it. A fortnight after his book is selling at half-price; it is impossible to tell whether this result is due to forgery or competition. What shall the court do? In case of doubt, shall it award the property to the first occupant? As well decide the question by lot.

These, however, are trifling considerations; but do we see that, in granting a perpetual privilege to authors and their heirs, we really strike a fatal blow at their interests? We think to make booksellers dependent upon authors, — a delusion. The booksellers will unite against works, and their proprietors. Against works, by refusing to push their sale, by replacing them with poor imitations, by reproducing them in a hundred indirect ways; and no one knows how far the science of plagiarism, and skilful imitation may be carried. Against proprietors. Are we ignorant of the fact, that a demand for a dozen copies enables a bookseller to sell a thousand; that with an edition of five hundred he can supply a kingdom for thirty years? What will the poor authors do in the presence of this omnipotent union of booksellers? I will tell them what they will do. They will enter the employ of those whom they now treat as pirates; and, to secure an advantage, they will become wage laborers. A fit reward for ignoble avarice, and insatiable pride.[74]

6. *Objection.* — Property in occupied land passes to the heirs of the occupant. "Why," say the authors, "should not the work of genius pass in like manner to the heirs of the man of genius?" M. Wolowski's reply: "Because the labor of the first occupant is continued by his heirs, while the heirs of an author neither change nor add to his works. In landed property, the continuance of labor explains the continuance of the right."

Yes, when the labor is continued; but if the labor is not continued, the right ceases. Thus is the right of possession, founded on personal labor, recognized by M. Wolowski.

M. Wolowski decides in favor of granting to authors property in their works for a certain number of years, dating from the day of their first publication.

The succeeding lectures on patents on inventions were no less instructive, although intermingled with shocking contradictions inserted with a view to make the useful truths more palatable. The necessity for brevity compels me to terminate this examination here, not without regret.

Thus, of two eclectic jurists, who attempt a defence of property, one is entangled in a set of dogmas without principle or method, and is constantly talking nonsense; and the other designedly abandons the cause of property, in order to present under the same name the theory of individual possession. Was I wrong in claiming that confusion reigned among legists, and ought I to be legally prosecuted for having said that their science henceforth stood convicted of falsehood, its glory eclipsed?

The ordinary resources of the law no longer sufficing, philosophy, political economy, and the framers of systems have been consulted. All the oracles appealed to have been discouraging.

The philosophers are no clearer to-day than at the time of the eclectic efflorescence; nevertheless, through their mystical apothegms, we can distinguish the words *progress, unity, association, solidarity, fraternity,* which are certainly not reassuring to proprietors. One of these philosophers, M. Pierre Leroux, has written two large books, in which he claims to show by all religious, legislative, and philosophical systems that, since men are responsible to each other, equality of conditions is the final law of society. It is true that this philosopher admits a kind of property; but as he leaves us to imagine what property would become in presence of equality, we may boldly class him with the opponents of the right of increase.

I must here declare freely — in order that I may not be suspected of secret connivance, which is foreign to my nature — that M. Leroux has my full sympathy. Not that I am a believer in his quasi-Pythagorean philosophy (upon this subject I should have more than one observation to submit to him, provided a veteran covered with stripes would not despise the remarks of a conscript); not that I feel bound to this author by any special consideration for his opposition to property. In my opinion, M. Leroux could, and even ought to, state his position more explicitly and logically. But I like, I admire, in M. Leroux, the antagonist of our philosophical demigods, the demolisher of usurped reputations, the pitiless critic of every thing that is respected because of its antiquity. Such is the reason for my high esteem of M. Leroux; such would be the principle of the only literary association which, in this century of coteries, I should care to form. We need men who, like M. Leroux, call in question social principles, — not to diffuse doubt concerning them, but to make them doubly sure; men who excite the mind by bold negations, and make the conscience tremble by doctrines of annihilation. Where is the man who does not shudder on hearing M. Leroux exclaim, "There is neither a paradise nor a hell; the wicked will not be punished, nor the good rewarded. Mortals! cease to hope and fear; you revolve in a circle of appearances; humanity is an immortal tree, whose branches, withering one after another, feed with their *débris* the root which is always young!" Where is the man who, on hearing this desolate confession of faith, does not demand with terror, "Is it then true that I am only an aggregate of elements organized by an unknown force, an idea realized for a few moments, a form which passes and disappears? Is it true that my mind is only a harmony, and my soul a vortex? What is the *ego*? what is God? what is the sanction of society?"

In former times, M. Leroux would have been regarded as a great culprit, worthy only (like Vanini) of death and universal execration. To-day, M. Leroux is fulfilling a mission of salvation, for which, whatever he may say, he will be rewarded. Like those gloomy invalids who are always talking of their approaching death, and who faint when the doctor's opinion confirms their pretence, our materialistic society is agitated and loses countenance while listening to this startling decree of the philosopher, "Thou shalt die!" Honor then to M. Leroux, who has revealed to us the cowardice of the Epicureans; to M. Leroux, who renders new philosophical solutions necessary! Honor to the anti-eclectic, to the apostle of equality!

In his work on "Humanity," M. Leroux commences by positing the necessity of property: "You wish to abolish property; but do you not see that thereby you would annihilate man and even the name of man? ... You wish to abolish property; but could you live without a body? I will not tell you that it is necessary to support this body; ... I will tell you that this body is itself a species of property."

In order clearly to understand the doctrine of M. Leroux, it must be borne in mind that there are three necessary and primitive forms of society, — communism, property, and that which to-day we properly call association. M. Leroux rejects in the first place communism, and combats it with all his might. Man is a personal and free being, and therefore needs a sphere of independence and individual activity. M. Leroux emphasizes this in adding: "You wish neither family, nor country, nor property; therefore no more fathers, no more sons, no more brothers. Here you are, related to no being in time, and therefore without a name; here you are, alone in the midst of a billion of men who to-day inhabit the earth. How do you expect me to distinguish you in space in the midst of this multitude?"

If man is indistinguishable, he is nothing. Now, he can be distinguished, individualized, only through a devotion of certain things to his use, — such as his body, his faculties, and the tools which he uses. "Hence," says M. Leroux, "the necessity of appropriation;" in short, property.

But property on what condition? Here M. Leroux, after having condemned communism, denounces in its turn the right of domain. His whole doctrine can be summed up in this single proposition, — *Man may be made by property a slave or a despot by turns.*

That posited, if we ask M. Leroux to tell us under what system of property man will be neither a slave nor a despot, but free, just, and a citizen, M. Leroux replies in the third volume of his work on "Humanity:" —

"There are three ways of destroying man's communion with his fellows and with the universe: ... 1. By separating man in time; 2. by separating him in space; 3. by dividing the land, or, in general terms, the instruments of production; by attaching men to things, by subordinating man to property, by making man a proprietor."

This language, it must be confessed, savors a little too strongly of the metaphysical heights which the author frequents, and of the school of M. Cousin. Nevertheless, it can be seen, clearly enough it seems to me, that M. Leroux opposes the exclusive appropriation of the instruments of production; only he calls this non-appropriation of the instruments of production a *new method* of establishing property, while I, in accordance with all precedent, call it a destruction of property. In fact, without the appropriation of instruments, property is nothing.

"Hitherto. we have confined ourselves to pointing out and combating the despotic features of property, by considering property alone. We have failed to see that the despotism of property is a correlative of the division of the human race; ... that property, instead of being organized in such a way as to facilitate the unlimited communion of man with his fellows and with the universe, has been, on the contrary, turned against this communion."

Let us translate this into commercial phraseology. In order to destroy despotism and the inequality of conditions, men must cease from competition and must associate their interests. Let employer and employed (now enemies and rivals) become associates.

Now, ask any manufacturer, merchant, or capitalist, whether he would consider himself a proprietor if he were to share his revenue and profits with this mass of wage-laborers whom it is proposed to make his associates.

"Family, property, and country are finite things, which ought to be organized with a view to the infinite. For man is a finite being, who aspires to the infinite. To him, absolute finiteness is evil. The infinite is his aim, the indefinite his right."

Few of my readers would understand these hierophantic words, were I to leave them unexplained. M. Leroux means, by this magnificent formula, that humanity is a single immense society, which, in its collective unity, represents the infinite; that every nation, every tribe, every commune, and every citizen are, in different degrees, fragments or finite members of the infinite society, the evil in which results solely from individualism and privilege, — in other words, from the subordination of the infinite to the finite; finally, that, to attain humanity's end and aim, each part has a right to an indefinitely progressive development.

"All the evils which afflict the human race arise from caste. The family is a blessing; the family caste (the nobility) is an evil. Country is a blessing; the country caste (supreme, domineering, conquering) is an evil; property (individual possession) is a blessing; the property caste (the domain of property of Pothier, Toullier, Troplong, &c.) is an evil."

Thus, according to M. Leroux, there is property and property, — the one good, the other bad. Now, as it is proper to call different things by different names, if we keep the name "property" for the former, we must call the latter robbery, rapine, brigandage. If, on the contrary, we reserve the name "property" for the latter, we must designate the former by the term *possession*, or some other equivalent; otherwise we should be troubled with an unpleasant synonymy.

What a blessing it would be if philosophers, daring for once to say all that they think, would speak the language of ordinary mortals! Nations and rulers would derive much greater profit from their lectures, and, applying the same names to the same ideas, would come, perhaps, to understand each other. I boldly declare that, in regard to property, I hold no other opinion than that of M. Leroux; but, if I should adopt the style of the philosopher, and repeat after him, "Property is a blessing, but the property caste — the *statu quo* of property — is an evil," I should be extolled as a genius by all the bachelors who write for the reviews.[75] If, on the contrary, I prefer the classic language of Rome and the civil code, and say accordingly, "Possession is a blessing, but property is robbery," immediately the aforesaid bachelors raise a hue and cry against the monster, and the judge threatens me. Oh, the power of language!

The economists, questioned in their turn, propose to associate capital and labor. You know, sir, what that means. If we follow out the doctrine, we soon find that it ends in an absorption of property, not by the community, but by a general and indissoluble *commandite [sic]* , so that the condition of the proprietor would differ from that of the workingman only in receiving larger wages. This system, with some peculiar additions and embellishments, is the idea of the phalanstery. But it is clear that, if inequality of conditions is one of the attributes of property, it is not the whole of property. That which makes property a *delightful thing*, as some philosopher (I know not who) has said, is the power to dispose at will, not only of one's own goods, but of their specific nature; to use them at pleasure; to confine and enclose them; to excommunicate mankind, as M. Pierre Leroux says; in short, to make such use of them as passion, interest, or even caprice, may suggest. What is the possession of money, a share in an agricultural or industrial enterprise, or a government-bond coupon, in comparison with the infinite charm of being master of one's house and grounds, under one's vine and fig-tree? "*Beati possidentes!*" says an author quoted by M. Troplong. Seriously, can that be applied to a man of income, who has no other possession under the sun than the market, and in his pocket his money? As well maintain that a trough is a coward. A nice method of reform! They never cease to condemn the thirst for gold, and the growing individualism of the century; and yet, most inconceivable of contradictions, they prepare to turn all kinds of property into one, — property in coin.

669

I must say something further of a theory of property lately put forth with some ado: I mean the theory of M. Considérant.

The Fourierists are not men who examine a doctrine in order to ascertain whether it conflicts with their system. On the contrary, it is their custom to exult and sing songs of triumph whenever an adversary passes without perceiving or noticing them. These gentlemen want direct refutations, in order that, if they are beaten, they may have, at least, the selfish consolation of having been spoken of. Well, let their wish be gratified.

M. Considérant makes the most lofty pretensions to logic. His method of procedure is always that of *major, minor*, and *conclusion*. He would willingly write upon his hat, *"Argumentator in barbara."* But M. Considérant is too intelligent and quick-witted to be a good logician, as is proved by the fact that he appears to have taken the syllogism for logic.

The syllogism, as everybody knows who is interested in philosophical curiosities, is the first and perpetual sophism of the human mind, — the favorite tool of falsehood, the stumbling-block of science, the advocate of crime. The syllogism has produced all the evils which the fabulist so eloquently condemned, and has done nothing good or useful: it is as devoid of truth as of justice. We might apply to it these words of Scripture: *"Celui qui met en lui sa confiance, périra."* Consequently, the best philosophers long since condemned it; so that now none but the enemies of reason wish to make the syllogism its weapon.

M. Considérant, then, has built his theory of property upon a syllogism. Would he be disposed to stake the system of Fourier upon his arguments, as I am ready to risk the whole doctrine of equality upon my refutation of that system?

Such a duel would be quite in keeping with the warlike and chivalric tastes of M. Considérant, and the public would profit by it; for, one of the two adversaries falling, no more would be said about him, and there would be one grumbler less in the world.

The theory of M. Considérant has this remarkable feature, that, in attempting to satisfy at the same time the claims of both laborers and proprietors, it infringes alike upon the rights of the former and the privileges of the latter. In the first place, the author lays it down as a principle: "1. That the use of the land belongs to each member of the race; that it is a natural and imprescriptible right, similar in all respects

670

to the right to the air and the sunshine. 2. That the right to labor is equally fundamental, natural, and imprescriptible." I have shown that the recognition of this double right would be the death of property. I denounce M. Considérant to the proprietors!

But M. Considérant maintains that the right to labor creates the right of property, and this is the way he reasons: —

Major Premise. — "Every man legitimately possesses the thing which his labor, his skill, — or, in more general terms, his action, — has created."

To which M. Considérant adds, by way of comment: "Indeed, the land not having been created by man, it follows from the fundamental principle of property, that the land, being given to the race in common, can in no wise be the exclusive and legitimate property of such and such individuals, who were not the creators of this value."

If I am not mistaken, there is no one to whom this proposition, at first sight and in its entirety, does not seem utterly irrefutable. Reader, distrust the syllogism.

First, I observe that the words *legitimately possesses* signify to the author's mind is *legitimate proprietor;* otherwise the argument, being intended to prove the legitimacy of property, would have no meaning. I might here raise the question of the difference between property and possession, and call upon M. Considérant, before going further, to define the one and the other; but I pass on.

This first proposition is doubly false. 1. In that it asserts the act of *creation* to be the only basis of property. 2. In that it regards this act as sufficient in all cases to authorize the right of property.

And, in the first place, if man may be proprietor of the game which he does not create, but which he *kills;* of the fruits which he does not create, but which he *gathers;* of the vegetables which he does not create, but which he *plants;* of the animals which he does not create, but which he *rears,* — it is conceivable that men may in like manner become proprietors of the land which they do not create, but which they clear and fertilize. The act of creation, then, is not *necessary* to the acquisition of the right of property. I say further, that this act alone is not always sufficient, and I prove it by the second premise of M. Considérant: —

Minor Premise. — "Suppose that on an isolated island, on the soil of a nation, or over the whole face of the earth (the extent of the scene of action does not affect our judgment of the facts), a generation of human beings devotes itself for the first time to industry, agriculture, manufactures, &c. This generation, by its labor, intelligence, and activity, creates products, develops values which did not exist on the uncultivated land. Is it not perfectly clear that the property of this industrious generation will stand on a basis of right, if the value or wealth produced by the activity of all be distributed among the producers, according to each one's assistance in the creation of the general wealth? That is unquestionable."

That is quite questionable. For this value or wealth, *produced by the activity of all*, is by the very fact of its creation *collective* wealth, the use of which, like that of the land, may be divided, but which as property remains *undivided.* And why this undivided ownership? Because the society which creates is itself indivisible, — a permanent unit, incapable of reduction to fractions. And it is this unity of society which makes the land common property, and which, as M. Considérant says, renders its use imprescriptible in the case of every individual. Suppose, indeed, that at a given time the soil should be equally divided; the very next moment this division, if it allowed the right of property, would become illegitimate. Should there be the slightest irregularity in the method of transfer, men, members of society, imprescriptible possessors of the land, might be deprived at one blow of property, possession, and the means of production. In short, property in capital is indivisible, and consequently inalienable, not necessarily when the capital is *uncreated*, but when it is *common* or *collective.*

I confirm this theory against M. Considérant, by the third term of his syllogism: —

Conclusion. — "The results of the labor performed by this generation are divisible into two classes, between which it is important clearly to distinguish. The first class includes the products of the soil which belong to this first generation in its usufructuary capacity, augmented, improved and refined by its labor and industry. These products consist either of objects of consumption or instruments of labor. It is clear that these products are the legitimate property of those who have created them by their activity... Second class. — Not only has this generation created the products just mentioned (objects of consumption and instruments of labor), but it has also added to the original value of the soil by cultivation, by the erection of buildings, by all the labor producing permanent results, which it has performed. This additional

672

value evidently constitutes a product — a value created by the activity of the first generation; and if, *by any means whatever*, the ownership of this value be distributed among the members of society equitably, — that is, in pro-portion to the labor which each has performed, — each will legitimately possess the portion which he receives. He may then dispose of this legitimate and private property as he sees fit, — exchange it, give it away, or transfer it; and no other individual, or collection of other individuals, — that is, society, — can lay any claim to these values."

Thus, by the distribution of collective capital, to the use of which each associate, either in his own right or in right of his authors, has an imprescriptible and undivided title, there will be in the phalanstery, as in the France of 1841, the poor and the rich; some men who, to live in luxury, have only, as Figaro says, to take the trouble to be born, and others for whom the fortune of life is but an opportunity for long-continued poverty; idlers with large incomes, and workers whose fortune is always in the future; some privileged by birth and caste, and others pariahs whose sole civil and political rights are *the right to labor, and the right to land.* For we must not be deceived; in the phalanstery every thing will be as it is to-day, an object of property, — machines, inventions, thought, books, the products of art, of agriculture, and of industry; animals, houses, fences, vineyards, pastures, forests, fields, — every thing, in short, except the *uncultivated land.* Now, would you like to know what uncultivated land is worth, according to the advocates of property? "A square league hardly suffices for the support of a savage," says M. Charles Comte. Estimating the wretched subsistence of this savage at three hundred francs per year, we find that the square league necessary to his life is, relatively to him, faithfully represented by a rent of fifteen francs. In France there are twenty-eight thousand square leagues, the total rent of which, by this estimate, would be four hundred and twenty thousand francs, which, when divided among nearly thirty-four millions of people, would give each an *income of a centime and a quarter.*

That is the new right which the great genius of Fourier has invented *in behalf of the French people*, and with which his first disciple hopes to reform the world. I denounce M. Considérant to the proletariat!

If the theory of M. Considérant would at least really guar-antee this property which he cherishes so jealously, I might pardon him the flaws in his syllogism, certainly the best one he ever made in his life. But, no: that which M. Considérant takes for property is only a privilege of extra pay. In Fourier's system, neither the created capital nor the increased value of the soil are divided and appropriated in any effective manner: the instruments of labor, whether created or not, remain in the hands of the phalanx; the pretended proprietor can touch only the income. He is permitted neither to realize his share of the stock, nor to possess it exclusively, nor to administer it, whatever it be. The cashier throws him his dividend; and then, proprietor, eat the whole if you can!

The system of Fourier would not suit the proprietors, since it takes away the most delightful feature of property, — the free disposition of one's goods. It would please the communists no better, since it involves unequal conditions. It is repugnant to the friends of free association and equality, in consequence of its tendency to wipe out human character and individuality by suppressing possession, family, and country, — the threefold expression of the human personality.

Of all our active publicists, none seem to me more fertile in resources, richer in imagination, more luxuriant and varied in style, than M. Considérant. Nevertheless, I doubt if he will undertake to reestablish his theory of property. If he has this courage, this is what I would say to him: "Before writing your reply, consider well your plan of action; do not scour the country; have recourse to none of your ordinary expedients; no complaints of civilization; no sarcasms upon equality; no glorification of the phalanstery. Leave Fourier and the departed in peace, and endeavor only to re-adjust the pieces of your syllogism. To this end, you ought, first, to analyze closely each proposition of your adversary; second, to show the error, either by a direct refutation, or by proving the converse; third, to oppose argument to argument, so that, objection and reply meeting face to face, the stronger may break down the weaker, and shiver it to atoms. By that method only can you boast of having conquered, and compel me to regard you as an honest reasoner, and a good artillery-man."

I should have no excuse for tarrying longer with these phal-ansterian crotchets, if the obligation which I have imposed upon myself of making a clean sweep, and the necessity of vindicating my dignity as a writer, did not prevent me from passing in silence the reproach uttered against me by a correspondent of "La Phalange." "We have seen but lately," says this journalist,[76] "that M. Proudhon, enthusiast as he has been for the science created by Fourier, is, or will be, an enthusiast for any thing else whatsoever."

If ever sectarians had the right to reproach another for changes in his beliefs, this right certainly does not belong to the disciples of Fourier, who are always so eager to administer the phalansterian baptism to the deserters of all parties. But why regard it as a crime, if they are sincere? Of what consequence is the constancy or inconstancy of an individual to the truth which is always the same? It is better to enlighten men's minds than to teach them to be obstinate in their prejudices. Do we not know that man is frail and fickle, that his heart is full of delusions, and that his lips are a distillery of falsehood? *Omnis homo meudax.* Whether we will or no, we all serve for a time as instruments of this truth, whose kingdom comes every day. God alone is immutable, because he is eternal.

That is the reply which, as a general rule, an honest man is entitled always to make, and which I ought perhaps to be content to offer as an excuse; for I am no better than my fathers. But, in a century of doubt and apostasy like ours, when it is of importance to set the small and the weak an example of strength and honesty of utterance, I must not suffer my character as a public assailant of property to be dishonored. I must render an account of my old opinions.

Examining myself, therefore, upon this charge of Fourierism, and endeavoring to refresh my memory, I find that, having been connected with the Fourierists in my studies and my friendships, it is possible that, without knowing it, I have been one of Fourier's partisans. Jérôme Lalande placed Napoleon and Jesus Christ in his catalogue of atheists. The Fourierists resemble this astronomer: if a man happens to find fault with the existing civilization, and to admit the truth of a few of their criticisms, they straightway enlist him, willy-nilly, in their school. Nevertheless, I do not deny that I have been a Fourierist; for, since they say it, of course it may be so. But, sir, that of which my ex-associates are ignorant, and which doubtless will astonish you, is that I have been many other things, — in religion, by turns a Protestant, a Papist, an Arian and Semi-Arian, a Manichean, a Gnostic, an Adamite even and a Pre-Adamite, a Sceptic, a Pelagian, a Socinian, an Anti-Trinitarian, and a Neo-Christian;[77] in philosophy and politics, an Idealist, a Pantheist, a Platonist, a Cartesian, an Eclectic (that is, a sort of *juste-milieu*), a Monarchist, an Aristocrat, a Constitutionalist, a follower of Babeuf, and a Communist. I have wandered through a whole encyclopaedia of systems. Do you think it surprising, sir, that, among them all, I was for a short time a Fourierist?

For my part, I am not at all surprised, although at present I have no recollection of it. One thing is sure, — that my superstition and credulity reached their height at the very period of my life which my critics reproachfully assign as the date of my Fourieristic beliefs. Now I hold quite other views. My mind no longer admits that which is demonstrated by syllogisms, analogies, or metaphors, which are the methods of the phalanstery, but demands a process of generalization and induction which excludes error. Of my past *opinions*, I retain absolutely none. I have acquired some *knowledge*. I no longer *believe*. I either *know*, or am *igno-rant*. In a word, in seeking for the reason of things, I saw that I was a *rationalist*.

Undoubtedly, it would have been simpler to begin where I have ended. But then, if such is the law of the human mind; if all society, for six thousand years, has done nothing but fall into error; if all mankind are still buried in the darkness of faith, deceived by their prejudices and passions, guided only by the instinct of their leaders; if my accusers, themselves, are not free from sectarianism (for they call themselves *Fourierists*), — am I alone inexcusable for having, in my inner self, at the secret tribunal of my conscience, begun anew the journey of our poor humanity?

I would by no means, then, deny my errors; but, sir, that which distinguishes me from those who rush into print is the fact that, though my thoughts have varied much, my writings do not vary. To-day, even, and on a multitude of questions, I am beset by a thousand extravagant and contradictory opinions; but my opinions I do not print, for the public has nothing to do with them. Before addressing my fellow-men, I wait until light breaks in upon the chaos of my ideas, in order that what I may say may be, not the whole truth (no man can know that), but nothing but the truth.

This singular disposition of my mind to first identify itself with a system in order to better understand it, and then to reflect upon it in order to test its legitimacy, is the very thing which disgusted me with Fourier, and ruined in my esteem the societary school. To be a faithful Fourierist, in fact, one must abandon his reason and accept every thing from a master, — doctrine, interpretation, and application. M. Considérant, whose excessive intolerance anathematizes all who do not abide by his sovereign decisions, has no other conception of Fourierism. Has he not been appointed Fourier's vicar on earth and pope of a Church which, unfortunately for its apostles, will never be of this world? Passive belief is the theological virtue of all sectarians, especially of the Fourierists.

Now, this is what happened to me. While trying to demonstrate by argument the religion of which I had become a follower in studying Fourier, I suddenly perceived that by reasoning I was becoming incredulous; that on each article of the creed my reason and my faith

676

were at variance, and that my six weeks' labor was wholly lost. I saw that the Fourierists — in spite of their inexhaustible gabble, and their extravagant pretension to decide in all things — were neither *savants*, nor logicians, nor even believers; that they were *scientific quacks*, who were led more by their self-love than their conscience to labor for the triumph of their sect, and to whom all means were good that would reach that end. I then understood why to the Epicureans they promised women, wine, music, and a sea of luxury; to the rigorists, maintenance of marriage, purity of morals, and temperance; to laborers, high wages; to proprietors, large incomes; to philosophers, solutions the secret of which Fourier alone possessed; to priests, a costly religion and magnificent festivals; to *savants*, knowledge of an unimaginable nature; to each, indeed, that which he most desired. In the beginning, this seemed to me droll; in the end, I regarded it as the height of impudence. No, sir; no one yet knows of the foolishness and infamy which the phalansterian system contains. That is a subject which I mean to treat as soon as I have balanced my accounts with property.[78]

It is rumored that the Fourierists think of leaving France and going to the new world to found a phalanstery. When a house threatens to fall, the rats scamper away; that is because they are rats. Men do better; they rebuild it. Not long since, the St. Simonians, despairing of their country which paid no heed to them, proudly shook the dust from their feet, and started for the Orient to fight the battle of free woman. Pride, wilfulness, mad selfishness! True charity, like true faith, does not worry, never despairs; it seeks neither its own glory, nor its interest, nor empire; it does every thing for all, speaks with indulgence to the reason and the will, and desires to conquer only by persuasion and sacrifice. Remain in France, Fourierists, if the progress of humanity is the only thing which you have at heart! There is more to do here than in the new world. Otherwise, go! you are nothing but liars and hypocrites!

The foregoing statement by no means embraces all the political elements, all the opinions and tendencies, which threaten the future of property; but it ought to satisfy any one who knows how to classify facts, and to deduce their law or the idea which governs them. Existing society seems abandoned to the demon of falsehood and discord; and it is this sad sight which grieves so deeply many distinguished minds who lived too long in a former age to be able to understand ours. Now, while the short-sighted spectator begins to despair of humanity, and, distracted and cursing that of which he is ignorant, plunges into scepticism and fatalism, the true observer, certain of the spirit which governs the world, seeks to comprehend and fathom Providence. The memoir on "Property," published last year by the pensioner of the Academy of Besançon, is simply a study of this nature.

The time has come for me to relate the history of this unlucky treatise, which has already caused me so much chagrin, and made me so unpopular; but which was on my part so involuntary and unpremeditated, that I would dare to affirm that there is not an economist, not a philosopher, not a jurist, who is not a hundred times guiltier than I. There is something so singular in the way in which I was led to attack property, that if, on hearing my sad story, you persist, sir, in your blame, I hope at least you will be forced to pity me.

I never have pretended to be a great politician; far from that, I always have felt for controversies of a political nature the greatest aversion; and if, in my "Essay on Property," I have sometimes ridiculed our politicians, believe, sir, that I was governed much less by my pride in the little that I know, than by my vivid consciousness of their ignorance and excessive vanity. Relying more on Providence than on men; not suspecting at first that politics, like every other science, contained an absolute truth; agreeing equally well with Bossuet and Jean Jacques, — I accepted with resignation my share of human misery, and contented myself with praying to God for good deputies, upright ministers, and an honest king. By taste as well as by discretion and lack of confidence in my powers, I was slowly pursuing some commonplace studies in philology, mingled with a little metaphysics, when I suddenly fell upon the greatest problem that ever has occupied philosophical minds: I mean the *criterion* of certainty.

Those of my readers who are unacquainted with the philosophical terminology will be glad to be told in a few words what this *criterion* is, which plays so great a part in my work.

The *criterion* of certainty, according to the philosophers, will be, when discovered, an infallible method of establishing the truth of an opinion, a judgment, a theory, or a system, in nearly the same way as gold is recognized by the touchstone, as iron approaches the magnet, or, better still, as we verify a mathematical operation by applying the *proof*. *Time* has hitherto served as a sort of *criterion* for society. Thus, the primitive men — having observed that they were not all equal in strength, beauty, and labor — judged, and rightly, that certain ones among them were called by nature to the performance of simple and common functions; but they concluded, and this is where their error lay, that these same individuals of duller intellect, more restricted genius, and weaker personality, were predestined to *serve* the others; that is, to

678

labor while the latter rested, and to have no other will than theirs: and from this idea of a natural subordination among men sprang domesticity, which, voluntarily accepted at first, was imperceptibly converted into horrible slavery. Time, making this error more palpable, has brought about justice. Nations have learned at their own cost that the subjection of man to man is a false idea, an erroneous theory, pernicious alike to master and to slave. And yet such a social system has stood several thousand years, and has been defended by celebrated philosophers; even to-day, under somewhat mitigated forms, sophists of every description uphold and extol it. But experience is bringing it to an end.

Time, then, is the *criterion* of societies; thus looked at, history is the demonstration of the errors of humanity by the argument *reductio ad absurdum*.

Now, the *criterion* sought for by metaphysicians would have the advantage of discriminating at once between the true and the false in every opinion; so that in politics, religion, and morals, for example, the true and the useful being immediately recognized, we should no longer need to await the sorrowful experience of time. Evidently such a secret would be death to the sophists, — that cursed brood, who, under different names, excite the curiosity of nations, and, owing to the difficulty of separating the truth from the error in their artistically woven theories, lead them into fatal ventures, disturb their peace, and fill them with such extraordinary prejudice.

Up to this day, the *criterion* of certainty remains a mystery; this is owing to the multitude of *criteria* that have been successively proposed. Some have taken for an absolute and definite *criterion* the testimony of the senses; others intui-tion; these evidence; those argument. M. Lamennais affirms that there is no other *criterion* than universal reason. Before him, M. de Bonald thought he had discovered it in language. Quite recently, M. Buchez has proposed morality; and, to harmonize them all, the eclectics have said that it was absurd to seek for an absolute *criterion*, since there were as many *criteria* as special orders of knowledge.

Of all these hypotheses it may be observed, That the testimony of the senses is not a *criterion*, because the senses, relating us only to phenomena, furnish us with no ideas; that intuition needs external confirmation or objective certainty; that evidence requires proof, and argument verification; that universal reason has been wrong many a time; that language serves equally well to express the true or the false;

that morality, like all the rest, needs demonstration and rule; and finally, that the eclectic idea is the least reasonable of all, since it is of no use to say that there are several *criteria* if we cannot point out one. I very much fear that it will be with the *cri-terion* as with the philosopher's stone; that it will finally be abandoned, not only as insolvable, but as chimerical. Consequently, I entertain no hopes of having found it; nevertheless, I am not sure that some one more skilful will not discover it.

Be it as it may with regard to a *criterion* or *criteria*, there are methods of demonstration which, when applied to certain subjects, may lead to the discovery of unknown truths, bring to light relations hitherto unsuspected, and lift a paradox to the highest degree of certainty. In such a case, it is not by its novelty, nor even by its content, that a system should be judged, but by its method. The critic, then, should follow the example of the Supreme Court, which, in the cases which come before it, never examines the facts, but only the form of procedure. Now, what is the form of procedure? A method.

I then looked to see what philosophy, in the absence of a *criterion*, had accomplished by the aid of special methods, and I must say that I could not discover — in spite of the loudly-proclaimed pretensions of some — that it had produced any thing of real value; and, at last, wearied with the philosophical twaddle, I resolved to make a new search for the *criterion*. I confess it, to my shame, this folly lasted for two years, and I am not yet entirely rid of it. It was like seeking a needle in a haystack. I might have learned Chinese or Arabic in the time that I have lost in considering and reconsidering syllogisms, in rising to the summit of an induction as to the top of a ladder, in inserting a proposition between the horns of a dilemma, in decomposing, distinguishing, separating, denying, affirming, admitting, as if I could pass abstractions through a sieve.

I selected justice as the subject-matter of my experiments. Finally, after a thousand decompositions, recompositions, and double compositions, I found at the bottom of my analytical crucible, not the *criterion* of certainty, but a metaphysico-economico-political treatise, whose conclusions were such that I did not care to present them in a more artistic or, if you will, more intelligible form. The effect which this work produced upon all classes of minds gave me an idea of the spirit of our age, and did not cause me to regret the prudent and scientific obscurity of my style. How happens it that to-day I am obliged to defend my intentions, when my conduct bears the evident impress of such lofty morality?

You have read my work, sir, and you know the gist of my tedious and scholastic lucubrations. Considering the revolutions of humanity, the vicissitudes of empires, the transformations of property, and the innumerable forms of justice and of right, I asked, "Are the evils which afflict us inherent in our condition as men, or do they arise only from an error? This inequality of fortunes which all admit to be the cause of society's embarrassments, is it, as some assert, the effect of Nature; or, in the division of the products of labor and the soil, may there not have been some error in calculation? Does each laborer receive all that is due him, and only that which is due him? In short, in the present conditions of labor, wages, and exchange, is no one wronged? — are the accounts well kept? — is the social balance accurate?"

Then I commenced a most laborious investigation. It was necessary to arrange informal notes, to discuss contradictory titles, to reply to captious allegations, to refute absurd pretensions, and to describe fictitious debts, dishonest transactions, and fraudulent accounts. In order to triumph over quibblers, I had to deny the authority of custom, to examine the arguments of legislators, and to oppose science with science itself. Finally, all these operations completed, I had to give a judicial decision.

I therefore declared, my hand upon my heart, before God and men, that the causes of social inequality are three in number: 1. *Gratuitous appropriation of collective wealth*; 2. *Inequality in exchange*; 3. *The right of profit or increase*.

And since this threefold method of extortion is the very essence of the domain of property, I denied the legitimacy of property, and proclaimed its identity with robbery.

That is my only offence. I have reasoned upon property; I have searched for the *criterion* of justice; I have demonstrated, not the possibility, but the necessity, of equality of fortunes; I have allowed myself no attack upon persons, no assault upon the government, of which I, more than any one else, am a provisional adherent. If I have sometimes used the word *proprietor*, I have used it as the abstract name of a metaphysical being, whose reality breathes in every individual, — not alone in a privileged few.

Nevertheless, I acknowledge — for I wish my confession to be sincere — that the general tone of my book has been bitterly censured. They complain of an atmosphere of passion and invective unworthy of an

681

honest man, and quite out of place in the treatment of so grave a subject.

If this reproach is well founded (which it is impossible for me either to deny or admit, because in my own cause I cannot be judge), — if, I say, I deserve this charge, I can only humble myself and acknowledge myself guilty of an involuntary wrong; the only excuse that I could offer being of such a nature that it ought not to be communicated to the public. All that I can say is, that I understand better than any one how the anger which injustice causes may render an author harsh and violent in his criticisms. When, after twenty years of labor, a man still finds himself on the brink of starvation, and then suddenly discovers in an equivocation, an error in calculation, the cause of the evil which torments him in common with so many millions of his fellows, he can scarcely restrain a cry of sorrow and dismay.

But, sir, though pride be offended by my rudeness, it is not to pride that I apologize, but to the proletaires, to the simple-minded, whom I perhaps have scandalized. My angry dialectics may have produced a bad effect on some peaceable minds. Some poor workingman — more affected by my sarcasm than by the strength of my arguments — may, perhaps, have concluded that property is the result of a perpetual Machiavelianism on the part of the governors against the governed, — a deplorable error of which my book itself is the best refutation. I devoted two chapters to showing how property springs from human personality and the comparison of individuals. Then I explained its perpetual limitation; and, following out the same idea, I predicted its approaching disappearance. How, then, could the editors of the "Revue Démocratique," after having borrowed from me nearly the whole substance of their economical articles, dare to say: "The holders of the soil, and other productive capital, are more or less wilful accomplices in a vast robbery, they being the exclusive receivers and sharers of the stolen goods"?

The proprietors *wilfully* guilty of the crime of robbery!

Never did that homicidal phrase escape my pen; never did my heart conceive the frightful thought. Thank Heaven! I know not how to calumniate my kind; and I have too strong a desire to seek for the reason of things to be willing to believe in criminal conspiracies. The millionnaire is no more tainted by property than the journeyman who works for thirty sous per day. On both sides the error is equal, as well as the intention. The effect is also the same, though positive in the former, and negative in the latter. I accused property; I did not denounce the proprietors, which would have been absurd: and I am sorry that there are among us wills so perverse and minds so shattered that they care for only so much of the truth as will aid them in their evil designs. Such is the only regret which I feel on account of my indignation, which, though expressed perhaps too bitterly, was at least honest, and legitimate in its source.

However, what did I do in this essay which I voluntarily submitted to the Academy of Moral Sciences? Seeking a fixed axiom amid social uncertainties, I traced back to one fundamental question all the secondary questions over which, at present, so keen and diversified a conflict is raging This question was the right of property. Then, comparing all existing theories with each other, and extracting from them that which is common to them all, I endeavored to discover that element in the idea of property which is necessary, immutable, and absolute; and asserted, after authentic verification, that this idea is reducible to that of *individual and transmissible possession; susceptible of exchange, but not of alienation; founded on labor, and not on fictitious occupancy, or idle caprice.* I said, further, that this idea was the result of our revolutionary movements, — the culminating point towards which all opinions, gradually divesting themselves of their contradictory elements, converge. And I tried to demonstrate this by the spirit of the laws, by political economy, by psychology and history.

A Father of the Church, finishing a learned exposition of the Catholic doctrine, cried, in the enthusiasm of his faith, *"Domine, si error est, a te decepti sumus* (if my religion is false, God is to blame)." I, as well as this theologian, can say, "If equality is a fable, God, through whom we act and think and are; God, who governs society by eternal laws, who rewards just nations, and punishes proprietors, — God alone is the author of evil; God has lied. The fault lies not with me."

But, if I am mistaken in my inferences, I should be shown my error, and led out of it. It is surely worth the trouble, and I think I deserve this honor. There is no ground for proscription. For, in the words of that member of the Convention who did not like the guillotine, *to kill is not to reply.* Until then, I persist in regarding my work as useful, social, full of instruction for public officials, — worthy, in short, of reward and encouragement.

For there is one truth of which I am profoundly convinced, — nations live by absolute ideas, not by approximate and partial conceptions; therefore, men are needed who define principles, or at least test them in the fire of controversy. Such is the law, — the idea first, the pure idea, the understanding of the laws of God, the theory: practice follows with slow steps, cautious, attentive to the succession of events; sure to seize, towards this eternal meridian, the indications of supreme reason. The co-operation of theory and practice produces in humanity the realization of order, — the absolute truth.[79]

All of us, as long as we live, are called, each in proportion to his strength, to this sublime work. The only duty which it imposes upon us is to refrain from appropriating the truth to ourselves, either by concealing it, or by accommodating it to the temper of the century, or by using it for our own interests. This principle of conscience, so grand and so simple, has always been present in my thought.

Consider, in fact, sir, that which I might have done, but did not wish to do. I reason on the most honorable hypothesis. What hindered me from concealing, for some years to come, the abstract theory of the equality of fortunes, and, at the same time, from criticising constitutions and codes; from showing the absolute and the contingent, the immutable and the ephemeral, the eternal and the transitory, in laws present and past; from constructing a new system of legislation, and establishing on a solid foundation this social edifice, ever destroyed and as often rebuilt? Might I not, taking up the definitions of casuists, have clearly shown the cause of their contradictions and uncertainties, and supplied, at the same time, the inadequacies of their conclusions? Might I not have confirmed this labor by a vast historical exposition, in which the principle of exclusion, and of the accumulation of property, the appropriation of collective wealth, and the radical vice in exchanges, would have figured as the constant causes of tyranny, war, and revolution?

"It should have been done," you say. Do not doubt, sir, that such a task would have required more patience than genius. With the principles of social economy which I have analyzed, I would have had only to break the ground, and follow the furrow. The critic of laws finds nothing more difficult than to determine justice: the labor alone would have been longer. Oh, if I had pursued this glittering prospect, and, like the man of the burning bush, with inspired counte-nance and deep and solemn voice, had presented myself some day with new tables, there would have been found fools to admire, boobies to applaud, and cowards to offer me the dictatorship; for, in the way of popular infatuations, nothing is impossible.

But, sir, after this monument of insolence and pride, what should I have deserved in your opinion, at the tribunal of God, and in the judgment of free men? Death, sir, and eternal reprobation!

I therefore spoke the truth as soon as I saw it, waiting only long enough to give it proper expression. I pointed out error in order that each might reform himself, and render his labors more useful. I announced the existence of a new political element, in order that my associates in reform, developing it in concert, might arrive more promptly at that unity of principles which alone can assure to society a better day. I expected to receive, if not for my book, at least for my commendable conduct, a small republican ovation. And, behold! journalists denounce me, academicians curse me, political adventurers (great God!) think to make themselves tolerable by protesting that they are not like me! I give the formula by which the whole social edifice may be scientifically reconstructed, and the strongest minds reproach me for being able only to destroy. The rest despise me, because I am unknown. When the "Essay on Property" fell into the reformatory camp, some asked: "Who has spoken? Is it Arago? Is it Lamennais? Michel de Bourges or Garnier-Pagès?" And when they heard the name of a new man: "We do not know him," they would reply. Thus, the monopoly of thought, property in reason, oppresses the proletariat as well as the *bourgeoisie*. The worship of the infamous prevails even on the steps of the tabernacle.

But what am I saying? May evil befall me, if I blame the poor creatures! Oh! let us not despise those generous souls, who in the excitement of their patriotism are always prompt to identify the voice of their chiefs with the truth. Let us encourage rather their simple credulity, enlighten complacently and tenderly their precious sincerity, and reserve our shafts for those vain-glorious spirits who are always admiring their genius, and, in different tongues, caressing the people in order to govern them.

These considerations alone oblige me to reply to the strange and superficial conclusions of the "Journal du Peuple" (issue of Oct. 11, 1840), on the question of property. I leave, therefore, the journalist to address myself only to his readers. I hope that the self-love of the writer will not be offended, if, in the presence of the masses, I ignore an individual.

You say, proletaires of the "Peuple," "For the very reason that men and things exist, there always will be men who will possess things; nothing, therefore, can destroy property."

In speaking thus, you unconsciously argue exactly after the manner of M. Cousin, who always reasons from *possession* to *property*. This coincidence, however, does not surprise me. M. Cousin is a philosopher of much mind, and you, proletaires, have still more. Certainly it is honorable, even for a philosopher, to be your companion in error.

Originally, the word *property* was synonymous with *proper* or *individual possession*. It designated each individual's special right to the use of a thing. But when this right of use, inert (if I may say so) as it was with regard to the other usufructuaries, became active and paramount, — that is, when the usufructuary converted his right to personally use the thing into the right to use it by his neighbor's labor, — then property changed its nature, and its idea became complex. The legists knew this very well, but instead of opposing, as they ought, this accumulation of profits, they accepted and sanctioned the whole. And as the right of farm-rent necesarily [sic] implies the right of use, — in other words, as the right to cultivate land by the labor of a slave supposes one's power to cultivate it himself, according to the principle that the greater includes the less, — the name property was reserved to designate this double right, and that of possession was adopted to designate the right of use. Whence property came to be called the perfect right, the right of domain, the eminent right, the heroic or *quiritaire* right, — in Latin, *jus perfectum, jus optimum, jus quiritarium, jus dominii*, — while possession became assimilated to farm-rent.

Now, that individual possession exists of right, or, better, from natural necessity, all philosophers admit, and can easily e demonstrated; but when, in imitation of M. Cousin, we assume it to be the basis of the domain of property, we fall into the sophism called *sophisma amphibolic vel ambiguitatis*, which consists in changing the meaning by a verbal equivocation.

People often think themselves very profound, because, by the aid of expressions of extreme generality, they appear to rise to the height of absolute ideas, and thus deceive inexperienced minds; and, what is worse, this is commonly called *examining abstractions*. But the abstraction formed by the comparison of identical facts is one thing, while that which is deduced from different acceptations of the same term is quite another. The first gives the universal idea, the axiom, the law; the second indicates the order of generation of ideas. All our errors arise from the constant confusion of these two kinds of abstractions. In this particular, languages and philosophies are alike deficient. The less common an idiom is, and the more obscure its terms, the more prolific is it as a source of error: a philosopher is sophistical in proportion to his ignorance of any method of neutralizing this imperfection in language. If the art of correcting the errors of speech by scientific methods is ever discovered, then philosophy will have found its *criterion* of certainty.

Now, then, the difference between property and possession being well established, and it being settled that the former, for the reasons which I have just given, must necessarily disappear, is it best, for the slight advantage of restoring an etymology, to retain the word *property*? My opinion is that it would be very unwise to do so, and I will tell why. I quote from the "Journal du Peuple:" —

"To the legislative power belongs the right to regulate property, to prescribe the conditions of acquiring, possessing, and transmitting it... It cannot be denied that inheritance, assessment, commerce, industry, labor, and wages require the most important modifications."

You wish, proletaires, to *regulate property;* that is, you wish to destroy it and reduce it to the right of possession. For to regulate property without the consent of the proprietors is to deny the right *of domain;* to associate employees with proprietors is to destroy the *eminent* right; to suppress or even reduce farm-rent, house-rent, revenue, and increase generally, is to annihilate *perfect* property. Why, then, while laboring with such laudable enthusiasm for the establishment of equality, should you retain an expression whose equivocal meaning will always be an obstacle in the way of your success?

There you have the first reason — a wholly philosophical one — for rejecting not only the thing, but the name, property. Here now is the political, the highest reason.

Every social revolution — M. Cousin will tell you — is effected only by the realization of an idea, either political, moral, or religious. When Alexander conquered Asia, his idea was to avenge Greek liberty against the insults of Oriental despotism; when Marius and Cæsar overthrew the Roman patricians, their idea was to give bread to the people; when Christianity revolutionized the world, its idea was to emancipate mankind, and to substitute the worship of one God for the deities of Epicurus and Homer; when France rose in '89, her idea was liberty and equality before the law. There has been no true revolution, says M. Cousin, with out its idea; so that where an idea does not exist, or even fails of a formal expression, revolution is impossible. There are mobs, conspirators, rioters, regicides. There are no revolutionists. Society, devoid of ideas, twists and tosses about, and dies in the midst of its fruitless labor.

Nevertheless, you all feel that a revolution is to come, and that you alone can accomplish it. What, then, is the idea which governs you, proletaires of the nineteenth century? — for really I cannot call you revolutionists. What do you think? — what do you believe? — what do you want? Be guarded in your reply. I have read faithfully your favorite journals, your most esteemed authors. I find everywhere only vain and puerile *entités;* nowhere do I discover an idea.

I will explain the meaning of this word *entité,* — new, without doubt, to most of you.

By *entité* is generally understood a substance which the imagination grasps, but which is incognizable by the senses and the reason. Thus the *soporific power* of opium, of which Sganarelle speaks, and the *peccant humors* of ancient medicine, are *entités*. The *entité* is the support of those who do not wish to confess their ignorance. It is incomprehensible; or, as St. Paul says, the *argumentum non apparentium*. In philosophy, the *entité* is often only a repetition of words which add nothing to the thought.

For example, when M. Pierre Leroux — who says so many excellent things, but who is too fond, in my opinion, of his Platonic formulas — assures us that the evils of humanity are due to our *ignorance of life*, M. Pierre Leroux utters an *entité;* for it is evident that if we are evil it is because we do not know how to live; but the knowledge of this fact is of no value to us.

When M. Edgar Quinet declares that France suffers and declines because there is an *antagonism* of men and of interests, he declares an *entité;* for the problem is to discover the cause of this antagonism.

When M. Lamennais, in thunder tones, preaches self-sacrifice and love, he proclaims two *entités*; for we need to know on what conditions self-sacrifice and love can spring up and exist.

So also, proletaires, when you talk of *liberty, progress*, and *the sovereignty of the people*, you make of these naturally intelligible things so many *entités* in space: for, on the one hand, we need a new definition of liberty, since that of '89 no longer suffices; and, on the other, we must know in what direction society should proceed in order to be in progress. As for the sovereignty of the people, that is a grosser *entité* than the sovereignty of reason; it is the *entité* of *entités*. In fact, since sovereignty can no more be conceived of outside of the people than outside of reason, it remains to be ascertained who, among the people, shall exercise the sovereignty; and, among so many minds, which shall be the sovereigns. To say that the people should elect their representatives is to say that the people should recognize their sovereigns, which does not remove the difficulty at all.

But suppose that, equal by birth, equal before the law, equal in personality, equal in social functions, you wish also to be equal in conditions.

Suppose that, perceiving all the mutual relations of men, whether they produce or exchange or consume, to be relations of commutative justice, — in a word, social relations; suppose, I say, that, perceiving this, you wish to give this natural society a legal existence, and to establish the fact by law, —

I say that then you need a clear, positive, and exact expression of your whole idea, — that is, an expression which states at once the principle, the means, and the end; and I add that that expression is *association.*

And since the association of the human race dates, at least rightfully, from the beginning of the world, and has gradually established and perfected itself by successively divesting itself of its negative elements, slavery, nobility, despotism, aristocracy, and feudalism, — I say that, to eliminate the last negation of society, to formulate the last revolutionary idea, you must change your old rallying-cries, *no more absolutism, no more nobility, no more slaves*! into that of *no more property*! ...

But I know what astonishes you, poor souls, blasted by the wind of poverty, and crushed by your patrons' pride: it is *equality*, whose consequences frighten you. How, you have said in your journal, — how can we "dream of a level which, being unnatural, is therefore unjust? How shall we pay the day's labor of a Cormenin or a Lamennais?"

Plebeians, listen! When, after the battle of Salamis, the Athenians assembled to award the prizes for courage, after the ballots had been collected, it was found that each combatant had one vote for the first prize, and Themistocles all the votes for the second. The people of Minerva were crowned by their own hands. Truly heroic souls! all were worthy of the olive-branch, since all had ventured to claim it for

689

themselves. Antiquity praised this sublime spirit. Learn, proletaires, to esteem yourselves, and to respect your dignity. You wish to be free, and you know not how to be citizens. Now, whoever says "citizens" necessarily says equals.

If I should call myself Lamennais or Cormenin, and some journal, speaking of me, should burst forth with these hyperboles, *incomparable genius, superior mind, consummate virtue, noble character*, I should not like it, and should complain, — first, because such eulogies are never deserved; and, second, because they furnish a bad example. But I wish, in order to reconcile you to equality, to measure for you the greatest literary personage of our century. Do not accuse me of envy, proletaires, if I, a defender of equality, estimate at their proper value talents which are universally admired, and which I, better than any one, know how to recognize. A dwarf can always measure a giant: all that he needs is a yardstick.

You have seen the pretentious announcements of "*L'Esquisse d'une Philosophie*," and you have admired the work on trust; for either you have not read it, or, if you have, you are incapable of judging it. Acquaint yourselves, then, with this speculation more brilliant than sound; and, while admiring the enthusiasm of the author, cease to pity those useful labors which only habit and the great number of the persons engaged in them render contemptible. I shall be brief; for, notwithstanding the importance of the subject and the genius of the author, what I have to say is of but little moment.

M. Lamennais starts with the existence of God. How does he demonstrate it? By Cicero's argument, — that is, by the consent of the human race. There is nothing new in that. We have still to find out whether the belief of the human race is legitimate; or, as Kant says, whether our subjective certainty of the existence of God corresponds with the objective truth. This, however, does not trouble M. Lamennais. He says that, if the human race believes, it is because it has a reason for believing. Then, having pronounced the name of God, M. Lamennais sings a hymn; and that is his demonstration!

This first hypothesis admitted, M. Lamennais follows it with a second; namely, that there are three persons in God. But, while Christianity teaches the dogma of the Trinity only on the authority of revelation, M. Lamennais pretends to arrive at it by the sole force of argument; and he does not perceive that his pretended demonstration is, from beginning to end, anthropomorphism, — that is, an ascription of the faculties of the human mind and the powers of nature to the Divine substance. New songs, new hymns!

God and the Trinity thus *demonstrated*, the philosopher passes to the creation, — a third hypothesis, in which M. Lamennais, always eloquent, varied, and sublime, *demonstrates* that God made the world neither of nothing, nor of something, nor of himself; that he was free in creating, but that nevertheless he could not but create; that there is in matter a matter which is not matter; that the archetypal ideas of the world are separated from each other, in the Divine mind, by a division which is obscure and unintelligible, and yet substantial and real, which involves intelligibility, &c. We meet with like contradictions concerning the origin of evil. To explain this problem, — one of the profoundest in philosophy, — M. Lamennais at one time denies evil, at another makes God the author of evil, and at still another seeks outside of God a first cause which is not God, — an amalgam of *entités* more or less incoherent, borrowed from Plato, Proclus, Spinoza, I might say even from all philosophers.

Having thus established his trinity of hypotheses, M. Lamennais deduces therefrom, by a badly connected chain of analogies, his whole philosophy. And it is here especially that we notice the syncretism which is peculiar to him. The theory of M. Lamennais embraces all systems, and supports all opinions. Are you a materialist? Suppress, as useless *entités*, the three persons in God; then, starting directly from heat, light, and electro-magnetism, — which, according to the author, are the three original fluids, the three primary external manifestations of Will, Intelligence, and Love, — you have a materialistic and atheistic cosmogony. On the contrary, are you wedded to spiritualism? With the theory of the immateriality of the body, you are able to see everywhere nothing but spirits. Finally, if you incline to pantheism, you will be satisfied by M. Lamennais, who formally teaches that the world is not an *emanation* from Divinity, — which is pure pantheism, — but a *flow* of Divinity.

I do not pretend, however, to deny that "L'Esquisse" contains some excellent things; but, by the author's declaration, these things are not original with him; it is the system which is his. That is undoubtedly the reason why M. Lamennais speaks so contemptuously of his predecessors in philosophy, and disdains to quote his originals. He thinks that, since "L'Esquisse" contains all true philosophy, the world will lose nothing when the names and works of the old philosophers perish. M. Lamennais, who renders glory to God in beautiful songs, does not know how as well to render justice to his fellows. His fatal

691

fault is this appropriation of knowledge, which the theologians call the *philosophical sin*, or the *sin against the Holy Ghost* — a sin which will not damn you, proletaires, nor me either.

In short, "L'Esquisse," judged as a system, and divested of all which its author borrows from previous systems, is a commonplace work, whose method consists in constantly explaining the known by the unknown, and in giving *entités* for abstractions, and tautologies for proofs. Its whole theodicy is a work not of genius but of imagination, a patching up of neo-Platonic ideas. The psychological portion amounts to nothing, M. Lamennais openly ridiculing labors of this character, without which, however, metaphysics is impossible. The book, which treats of logic and its methods, is weak, vague, and shallow. Finally, we find in the physical and physiological speculations which M. Lamennais deduces from his trinitarian cosmogony grave errors, the preconceived design of accommodating facts to theory, and the substitution in almost every case of hypothesis for reality. The third volume on industry and art is the most interesting to read, and the best. It is true that M. Lamennais can boast of nothing but his style. As a philosopher, he has added not a single idea to those which existed before him.

Why, then, this excessive mediocrity of M. Lamennais considered as a thinker, a mediocrity which disclosed itself at the time of the publication of the "Essai sur l'Indifférence"? It is because (remember this well, proletaires!) Nature makes no man truly complete, and because the development of certain faculties almost always excludes an equal development of the opposite faculties; it is because M. Lamennais is preeminently a poet, a man of feeling and sentiment. Look at his style, — exuberant, sonorous, picturesque, vehement, full of exaggeration and invective, — and hold it for certain that no man pos-sessed of such a style was ever a true metaphysician. This wealth of expression and illustration, which everybody admires, becomes in M Lamennais the incurable cause of his philosophical impotence. His flow of language, and his sensitive nature misleading his imagination, he thinks that he is reasoning when he is only repeating himself, and readily takes a description for a logical deduction. Hence his horror of positive ideas, his feeble powers of analysis, his pronounced taste for indefinite analogies, verbal abstractions, hypothetical generalities, in short, all sorts of *entités*.

Further, the entire life of M. Lamennais is conclusive proof of his anti-philosophical genius. Devout even to mysticism, an ardent ultramontane, an intolerant theocrat, he at first feels the double influence of the religious reaction and the literary theories which marked the beginning of this century, and falls back to the middle ages and Gregory VII.; then, suddenly becoming a progressive Christian and a democrat, he gradually leans towards rationalism, and finally falls into deism. At present, everybody waits at the trap-door. As for me, though I would not swear to it, I am inclined to think that M. Lamennais, already taken with scepticism, will die in a state of indifference. He owes to individual reason and methodical doubt this expiation of his early essays.

It has been pretended that M. Lamennais, preaching now a theocracy, now universal democracy, has been always consistent; that, under different names, he has sought invariably one and the same thing, — unity. Pitiful excuse for an author surprised in the very act of contradiction! What would be thought of a man who, by turns a servant of despotism under Louis XVI., a demagogue with Robespierre, a courtier of the Emperor, a bigot during fifteen years of the Restoration, a conservative since 1830, should dare to say that he ever had wished for but one thing, — public order? Would he be regarded as any the less a renegade from all parties? Public order, unity, the world's welfare, social harmony, the union of the nations, — concerning each of these things there is no possible difference of opinion. Everybody wishes them; the character of the publicist depends only upon the means by which he proposes to arrive at them. But why look to M. Lamennais for a steadfastness of opinion, which he himself repudiates? Has he not said, "The mind has no law; that which I believe to-day, I did not believe yesterday; I do not know that I shall believe it to-morrow"?

No; there is no real superiority among men, since all talents and capacities are combined never in one individual. This man has the power of thought, that one imagination and style, still another industrial and commercial capacity. By our very nature and education, we possess only special aptitudes which are limited and confined, and which become consequently more necessary as they gain in depth and strength. Capacities are to each other as functions and persons; who would dare to classify them in ranks? The finest genius is, by the laws of his existence and development, the most dependent upon the society which creates him. Who would dare to make a god of the glorious child?

"It is not strength which makes the man," said a Hercules of the market-place to the admiring crowd; "it is character." That man, who had only his muscles, held force in contempt. The lesson is a good one,

693

proletaires; we should profit by it. It is not talent (which is also a force), it is not knowledge, it is not beauty which makes the man. It is heart, courage, will, virtue. Now, if we are equal in that which makes us men, how can the accidental distribution of secondary faculties detract from our manhood?

Remember that privilege is naturally and inevitably the lot of the weak; and do not be misled by the fame which accompanies certain talents whose greatest merit consists in their rarity, and a long and toilsome apprenticeship. It is easier for M. Lamennais to recite a philippic, or sing a humanitarian ode after the Platonic fashion, than to discover a single useful truth; it is easier for an economist to apply the laws of production and distribution than to write ten lines in the style of M. Lamennais; it is easier for both to speak than to act. You, then, who put your hands to the work, who alone truly create, why do you wish me to admit your inferiority? But, what am I saying? Yes, you are inferior, for you lack virtue and will! Ready for labor and for battle, you have, when liberty and equality are in question, neither courage nor character!

In the preface to his pamphlet on "Le Pays et le Gouverne-ment," as well as in his defence before the jury, M. Lamennais frankly declared himself an advocate of property. Out of regard for the author and his misfortune, I shall abstain from characterizing this declaration, and from examining these two sorrowful performances. M. Lamennais seems to be only the tool of a quasi-radical party, which flatters him in order to use him, without respect for a glorious, but hence forth powerless, old age. What means this profession of faith? From the first number of "L'Avenir" to "L'Esquisse d'une Philosophie," M. Lamennais always favors equality, association, and even a sort of vague and indefinite communism. M. Lamennais, in recognizing the right of property, gives the lie to his past career, and renounces his most generous tendencies. Can it, then, be true that in this man, who has been too roughly treated, but who is also too easily flattered, strength of talent has already outlived strength of will?

It is said that M. Lamennais has rejected the offers of several of his friends to try to procure for him a commutation of his sentence. M. Lamennais prefers to serve out his time. May not this affectation of a false stoicism come from the same source as his recognition of the right of property? The Huron, when taken prisoner, hurls insults and threats at his conqueror, — that is the heroism of the savage; the martyr prays for his executioners, and is willing to receive from them his life, — that is the heroism of the Christian. Why has the apostle of love become an apostle of anger and revenge? Has, then, the translator of "L'Imitation" forgotten that he who offends charity cannot honor virtue? Galileo, retracting on his knees before the tribunal of the inquisition his heresy in regard to the movement of the earth, and recovering at that price his liberty, seems to me a hundred times grander than M. Lamennais. What! if we suffer for truth and justice, must we, in retaliation, thrust our persecutors outside the pale of human society; and, when sentenced to an unjust punishment, must we decline exemption if it is offered to us, because it pleases a few base satellites to call it a pardon? Such is not the wisdom of Christianity. But I forgot that in the presence of M. Lamennais this name is no longer pronounced. May the prophet of "L'Avenir" be soon restored to liberty and his friends; but, above all, may he henceforth derive his inspiration only from his genius and his heart!

O proletaires, proletaires! how long are you to be victimized by this spirit of revenge and implacable hatred which your false friends kindle, and which, perhaps, has done more harm to the development of reformatory ideas than the corruption, ignorance, and malice of the government? Believe me, at the present time everybody is to blame. In fact, in intention, or in example, all are found wanting; and you have no right to accuse any one. The king himself (God forgive me! I do not like to justify a king), — the king himself is, like his predecessors, only the personification of an idea, and an idea, proletaires, which possesses you yet. His greatest wrong consists in wishing for its complete realization, while you wish it realized only partially, — consequently, in being logical in his government; while you, in your complaints, are not at all so. You clamor for a second regicide. He that is without sin among you, — let him cast at the prince of property the first stone!

How successful you would have been if, in order to influence men, you had appealed to the self-love of men, — if, in order to alter the constitution and the law, you had placed yourselves within the constitution and the law! Fifty thousand laws, they say, make up our political and civil codes. Of these fifty thousand laws, twenty-five thousand are for you, twenty-five thousand against you. Is it not clear that your duty is to oppose the former to the latter, and thus, by the argument of contradiction, drive privilege into its last ditch? This method of action is henceforth the only useful one, being the only moral and rational one.

For my part, if I had the ear of this nation, to which I am attached by birth and predilection, with no intention of playing the leading part in the future republic, I would instruct the laboring masses to conquer property through institutions and judicial pleadings; to seek auxiliaries and accomplices in the highest ranks of society, and to ruin all privileged classes by taking advantage of their common desire for power and popularity. The petition for the electoral reform has already received two hundred thousand signatures, and the illustrious Arago threatens us with a million. Surely, that will be well done; but from this million of citizens, who are as willing to vote for an emperor as for equality, could we not select ten thousand signatures — I mean *bonâ fide* signatures — whose authors can read, write, cipher, and even think a little, and whom we could invite, after due perusal and verbal explanation, to sign such a petition as the following: —

"To his Excellency the Minister of the interior: —

"MONSIEUR LE MINISTRE, — On the day when a royal ordinance, decreeing the establishment of model national workshops, shall appear in the 'Moniteur,' the undersigned, to the number of *ten thousand*, will repair to the Palace of the Tuileries, and there, with all the power of their lungs, will shout, 'Long live Louis Philippe!'

"On the day when the 'Moniteur' shall inform the public that this petition is refused, the undersigned, to the number of *ten thousand*, will say secretly in their hearts, 'Down with Louis Philippe!' "

If I am not mistaken, such a petition would have some effect.[80] The pleasure of a popular ovation would be well worth the sacrifice of a few millions. They sow so much to reap unpopularity! Then, if the nation, its hopes of 1830 restored, should feel it its duty to keep its promise, — and it would keep it, for the word of the nation is, like that of God, sacred, — if, I say, the nation, reconciled by this act with the public-spirited monarchy, should bear to the foot of the throne its cheers and its vows, and should at that solemn moment choose me to speak in its name, the following would be the substance of my speech: —

"SIRE, — This is what the nation wishes to say to your Majesty: —

"O King! you see what it costs to gain the applause of the citizens. Would you like us henceforth to take for our motto: 'Let us help the King, the King will help us'? Do you wish the people to cry: 'THE KING AND THE FRENCH NATION'? Then abandon these grasping bankers, these quarrelsome lawyers, these miserable *bourgeois*, these infamous writers, these dishonored men. All these, Sire, hate you, and continue to support you only because they fear us. Finish the work of our kings; wipe out aristocracy and privilege; consult with these

696

faithful proletaires, with the nation, which alone can honor a sovereign and sincerely shout, 'Long live the king!' "

The rest of what I have to say, sir, is for you alone; others would not understand me. You are, I perceive, a republican as well as an economist, and your patriotism revolts at the very idea of addressing to the authorities a petition in which the government of Louis Philippe should be tacitly recognized. "National workshops! it were well to have such institutions established," you think; "but patriotic hearts never will accept them from an aristocratic ministry, nor by the courtesy of a king." Already, undoubtedly, your old prejudices have returned, and you now regard me only as a sophist, as ready to flatter the powers that be as to dishonor, by pushing them to an extreme, the principles of equality and universal fraternity.

What shall I say to you? ... That I should so lightly compromise the future of my theories, either this clever sophistry which is attributed to me must be at bottom a very trifling affair, or else my convictions must be so firm that they deprive me of free-will.

But, not to insist further on the necessity of a compromise between the executive power and the people, it seems to me, sir, that, in doubting my patriotism, you reason very capriciously, and that your judgments are exceedingly rash. You, sir, ostensibly defending government and property, are allowed to be a republican, reformer, phalansterian, any thing you wish; I, on the contrary, demanding distinctly enough a slight reform in public economy, am foreordained a conservative, and likewise a friend of the dynasty. I cannot explain myself more clearly. So firm a believer am I in the philosophy of accomplished facts and the *statu quo* of governmental forms that, instead of destroying that which exists and beginning over again the past, I prefer to render every thing legitimate by correcting it. It is true that the corrections which I propose, though respecting the form, tend to finally change the nature of the things corrected. Who denies it? But it is precisely that which constitutes my system of *statu quo*. I make no war upon symbols, figures, or phantoms. I respect scarecrows, and bow before bugbears. I ask, on the one hand, that property be left as it is, but that interest on all kinds of capital be gradually lowered and finally abolished; on the other hand, that the charter be maintained in its present shape, but that method be introduced into administration and politics. That is all. Nevertheless, submitting to all that is, though not satisfied with it, I endeavor to conform to the established order, and to render unto Cæsar the things that are Cæsar's. Is it thought, for instance, that I love property? ... Very well; I am myself a proprietor and do homage to the

697

right of increase, as is proved by the fact that I have creditors to whom I faithfully pay, every year, a large amount of interest. The same with politics. Since we are a monarchy, I would cry, *"Long live the king,"* rather than suffer death; which does not prevent me, however, from demanding that the irremovable, inviolable, and hereditary representative of the nation shall act with the proletaires against the privileged classes; in a word, that the king shall become the leader of the radical party. Thereby we proletaires would gain every thing; and I am sure that, at this price, Louis Philippe might secure to his family the perpetual presidency of the republic. And this is why I think so.

If there existed in France but one great functional inequality, the duty of the functionary being, from one end of the year to the other, to hold full court of *savants*, artists, soldiers, deputies, inspectors, &c., it is evident that the expenses of the presidency then would be the national expenses; and that, through the reversion of the civil list to the mass of consumers, the great inequality of which I speak would form an exact equation with the whole nation. Of this no econo-mist needs a demonstration. Consequently, there would be no more fear of cliques, courtiers, and appanages, since no new inequality could be established. The king, as king, would have friends (unheard-of thing), but no family. His relatives or kinsmen, — *agnats et cognats*, — if they were fools, would be nothing to him; and in no case, with the exception of the heir apparent, would they have, even in court, more privileges than others. No more nepotism, no more favor, no more baseness. No one would go to court save when duty required, or when called by an honorable distinction; and as all conditions would be equal and all functions equally honored, there would be no other emulation than that of merit and virtue. I wish the king of the French could say without shame, "My brother the gardener, my sister-in-law the milk-maid, my son the prince-royal, and my son the blacksmith." His daughter might well be an artist. That would be beautiful, sir; that would be royal; no one but a buffoon could fail to understand it.

In this way, I have come to think that the forms of royalty may be made to harmonize with the requirements of equality, and have given a monarchical form to my republican spirit.

I have seen that France contains by no means as many democrats as is generally supposed, and I have compromised with the monarchy. I do not say, however, that, if France wanted a republic, I could not accommodate myself equally well, and perhaps better. By nature, I hate all signs of distinction, crosses of honor, gold lace, liveries, costumes, honorary titles, &c., and, above all, parades. If I had my way, no general should be distinguished from a soldier, nor a peer of France from a peasant. Why have I never taken part in a review? for I am happy to say, sir, that I am a national guard; I have nothing else in the world but that. Because the review is always held at a place which I do not like, and because they have fools for officers whom I am compelled to obey. You see, — and this is not the best of my history, — that, in spite of my conservative opinions, my life is a perpetual sacrifice to the republic.

Nevertheless, I doubt if such simplicity would be agreeable to French vanity, to that inordinate love of distinction and flattery which makes our nation the most frivolous in the world. M. Lamartine, in his grand "Meditation on Bonaparte," calls the French *a nation of Brutuses.* We are merely a nation of Narcissuses. Previous to '89, we had the aristocracy of blood; then every *bourgeois* looked down upon the commonalty, and wished to be a nobleman. Afterwards, distinction was based on wealth, and the *bourgeoisie* jealous of the nobility, and proud of their money, used 1830 to promote, not liberty by any means, but the aristocracy of wealth. When, through the force of events, and the natural laws of society, for the development of which France offers such free play, equality shall be established in functions and fortunes, then the beaux and the belles, the *savants* and the artists, will form new classes. There is a universal and innate desire in this Gallic country for fame and glory. We must have distinctions, be they what they may, — nobility, wealth, talent, beauty, or dress. I suspect MM. Arage and Garnier-Pagès of having aristocratic manners, and I picture to myself our great journalists, in their columns so friendly to the people, administering rough kicks to the compositors in their printing offices.

"This man," once said "Le National" in speaking of Carrel, "whom we had proclaimed *first consul*! ... Is it not true that the monarchical principle still lives in the hearts of our democrats, and that they want universal suffrage in order to make themselves kings? Since "Le National" prides itself on holding more fixed opinions than "Le Journal des Debats," I presume that, Armand Carrel being dead, M. Armand Marrast is now first consul, and M. Garnier-Pagès second consul. In every thing the deputy must give way to the journalist. I do not speak of M. Arago, whom I believe to be, in spite of calumny, too learned for the consulship. Be it so. Though we have consuls, our position is not much altered. I am ready to yield my share of sovereignty to MM. Armand Marrast and Garnier-Pagès, the appointed consuls, provided they will swear on entering upon the duties of their office, to abolish property and not be haughty.

Forever promises! Forever oaths! Why should the people trust in tribunes, when kings perjure themselves? Alas! truth and honesty are no longer, as in the days of King John, in the mouth of princes. A whole senate has been convicted of felony, and, the interest of the governors always being, for some mysterious reason, opposed to the interest of the governed, parliaments follow each other while the nation dies of hunger. No, no! No more protectors, no more emperors, no more consuls. Better manage our affairs ourselves than through agents. Better associate our industries than beg from monopolies; and, since the republic cannot dispense with virtues, we should labor for our reform.

This, therefore, is my line of conduct. I preach emancipation to the proletaires; association to the laborers; equality to the wealthy. I push forward the revolution by all means in my power, — the tongue, the pen, the press, by action, and example. My life is a continual apostleship.

Yes, I am a reformer; I say it as I think it, in good faith, and that I may be no longer reproached for my vanity. I wish to convert the world. Very likely this fancy springs from an enthusiastic pride which may have turned to delirium; but it will be admitted at least that I have plenty of company, and that my madness is not monomania. At the present day, everybody wishes to be reckoned among the lunatics of Beranger. To say nothing of the Babeufs, the Marats, and the Robespierres, who swarm in our streets and workshops, all the great reformers of antiquity live again in the most illustrious personages of our time. One is Jesus Christ, another Moses, a third Mahomet; this is Orpheus, that Plato, or Pythagoras. Gregory VII., himself, has risen from the grave together with the evangelists and the apostles; and it may turn out that even I am that slave who, having escaped from his master's house, was forthwith made a bishop and a reformer by St. Paul. As for the virgins and holy women, they are expected daily; at present, we have only Aspasias and courtesans.

Now, as in all diseases, the diagnostic varies according to the temperament, so my madness has its peculiar aspects and distinguishing characteristic.

Reformers, as a general thing, are jealous of their *rôle*; they suffer no rivals, they want no partners; they have disciples, but no co-laborers. It is my desire, on the contrary, to communicate my enthusiasm, and to make it, as far as I can, epidemic. I wish that all were, like myself, reformers, in order that there might be no more sects; and that Christs,

Anti-Christs, and false Christs might be forced to understand and agree with each other.

Again, every reformer is a magician, or at least desires to become one. Thus Moses, Jesus Christ, and the apostles, proved their mission by miracles. Mahomet ridiculed miracles after having endeavored to perform them. Fourier, more cunning, promises us wonders when the globe shall be covered with phalansteries. For myself, I have as great a horror of miracles as of authorities, and aim only at logic. That is why I continually search after the *criterion* of certainty. I work for the reformation of ideas. Little matters it that they find me dry and austere. I mean to conquer by a bold struggle, or die in the attempt; and whoever shall come to the defence of property, I swear that I will force him to argue like M. Considérant, or philosophize like M. Troplong.

Finally, — and it is here that I differ most from my compeers, — I do not believe it necessary, in order to reach equality, to turn every thing topsy-turvy. To maintain that nothing but an overturn can lead to reform is, in my judgment, to construct a syllogism, and to look for the truth in the regions of the unknown. Now, I am for generalization, induction, and progress. I regard general disappropriation as impossible: attacked from that point, the problem of universal association seems to me insolvable. Property is like the dragon which Hercules killed: to destroy it, it must be taken, not by the head, but by the tail, — that is, by profit and interest.

I stop. I have said enough to satisfy any one who can read and understand. The surest way by which the government can baffle intrigues and break up parties is to take possession of science, and point out to the nation, at an already appreciable distance, the rising oriflamme of equality; to say to those politicians of the tribune and the press, for whose fruitless quarrels we pay so dearly, "You are rushing forward, blind as you are, to the abolition of property; but the government marches with its eyes open. You hasten the future by unprincipled and insincere controversy; but the government, which knows this future, leads you thither by a happy and peaceful transition. The present generation will not pass away before France, the guide and model of civilized nations, has regained her rank and legitimate influence."

But, alas! the government itself, — who shall enlighten it? Who can induce it to accept this doctrine of equality, whose terrible but decisive formula the most generous minds hardly dare to acknowledge? ... I feel my whole being tremble when I think that the testimony of three men

701

— yes, of three men who make it their business to teach and define —
would suffice to give full play to public opinion, to change beliefs, and
to fix destinies. Will not the three men be found? ...

May we hope, or not? What must we think of those who govern us? In
the world of sorrow in which the proletaire moves, and where nothing
is known of the intentions of power, it must be said that despair
prevails. But you, sir, — you, who by function belong to the official
world; you, in whom the people recognize one of their noblest friends,
and property its most prudent adversary, — what say you of our
deputies, our ministers, our king? Do you believe that the authorities
are friendly to us? Then let the government declare its position; let it
print its profession of faith in equality, and I am dumb. Otherwise, I
shall continue the war; and the more obstinacy and malice is shown, the
oftener will I redouble my energy and audacity. I have said before, and
I repeat it, — I have sworn, not on the dagger and the death's-head,
amid the horrors of a catacomb, and in the presence of men besmeared
with blood; but I have sworn on my conscience to pursue property, to
grant it neither peace nor truce, until I see it everywhere execrated. I
have not yet published half the things that I have to say concerning the
right of domain, nor the best things. Let the knights of property, if there
are any who fight otherwise than by retreating, be prepared every day
for a new demonstration and accusation; let them enter the arena armed
with reason and knowledge, not wrapped up in sophisms, for justice
will be done.

"To become enlightened, we must have liberty. That alone suffices; but
it must be the liberty to use the reason in regard to all public matters.

"And yet we hear on every hand authorities of all kinds and degrees
crying: 'Do not reason!'

"If a distinction is wanted, here is one: —

"The *public* use of the reason always should be free, but the *private* use
ought always to be rigidly restricted. By public use, I mean the
scientific, literary use; by private, that which may be taken advantage
of by civil officials and public functionaries. Since the governmental
machinery must be kept in motion, in order to preserve unity and attain
our object, we must not reason; we must obey. But the same individual
who is bound, from this point of view, to passive obedience, has the
right to speak in his capacity of citizen and scholar. He can make an
appeal to the public, submit to it his observations on events which

702

occur around him and in the ranks above him, taking care, however, to avoid offences which are punishable.

"Reason, then, as much as you like; only, obey." — *Kant: Fragment on the Liberty of Thought and of the Press. Tissot's Translation.*

These words of the great philosopher outline for me my duty. I have delayed the reprint of the work entitled "What is Property?" in order that I might lift the discussion to the philosophical height ·from which ridiculous clamor has dragged it down; and that, by a new presentation of the question, I might dissipate the fears of good citizens. I now reenter upon the public use of my reason, and give truth full swing. The second edition of the First Memoir on Property will immediately follow the publication of this letter. Before issuing any thing further, I shall await the observations of my critics, and the co-operation of the friends of the people and of equality.

Hitherto, I have spoken in my own name, and on my own personal responsibility. It was my duty. I was endeavoring to call attention to principles which antiquity could not discover, because it knew nothing of the science which reveals them, — political economy. I have, then, testified as to *facts;* in short, I have been a *witness.* Now my *rôle* changes. It remains for me to deduce the practical consequences of the facts proclaimed. The position of *public prosecutor* is the only one which I am henceforth fitted to fill, and I shall sum up the case in the name of the *people.*

I am, sir, with all the consideration that I owe to your talent and your character,

Your very humble and most obedient servant,

P. J. PROUDHON,

Pensioner of the Academy of Besançon.

P.S. During the session of April 2, the Chamber of Deputies rejected, by a very large majority, the literary-property bill, *because it did not understand it.* Nevertheless, literary property is only a special form of the right of property, which everybody claims to understand. Let us hope that this legislative precedent will not be fruitless for the cause of equality. The consequence of the vote of the Chamber is the abolition of capitalistic property, — property incomprehensible, contradictory, impossible, and absurd.

[1] In the French edition of Proudhon's works, the above sketch of his life is prefixed to the first volume of his correspondence, but the translator prefers to insert it here as the best method of introducing the author to the American public. He would, however, caution readers against accepting the biographer's interpretation of the author's views as in any sense authoritative; advising them, rather, to await the publication of the remainder of Proudhon's writings, that they may form an opinion for themselves. — *Translator*

[2] "An Inquiry into Grammatical Classifications." By P. J. Proudhon. A treatise which received honorable mention from the Academy of Inscriptions, May 4, 1839. Out of print.

[3] "The Utility of the Celebration of Sunday," &c. By P. J. Proudhon. Besançon, 1839, 12mo; 2d edition, Paris, 1841, 18mo.

[4] Charron, on "Wisdom," Chapter xviii.

[5] M. Vivien, Minister of Justice, before commencing proceedings against the "Memoir upon Property," asked the opinion of M. Blanqui; and it was on the strength of the observations of this honorable academician that he spared a book the king's counsel, that is to say, the intellectual executioner, had followed in my very tracks to attack your book and annoy your person! I actually passed two terrible nights, and I succeeded in restraining the secular arm only by showing that your book was an academical dissertation, and not the manifesto of an incendiary. Your style is too lofty ever to be of service to the madmen who in discussing the gravest questions of our social order, use paving-stones as their weapons. But see to it, sir, that ere long they do not come, in spite of you, to seek for ammunition in this formidable arsenal, and that your vigorous metaphysics falls not into the hands of some sophist of the market-place, who might discuss the question in the presence of a starving audience: we should have pillage for conclusion and   peroration.
"I feel as deeply as you, sir, the abuses which you point out; but I have so great an affection for order, — not that common and strait-laced order with which the police are satisfied, but the majestic and imposing order of human societies, — that I sometimes find myself embarrassed in attacking certain abuses. I like to rebuild with one hand when I am

compelled to destroy with the other. In pruning an old tree, we guard against destruction of the buds and fruit. You know that as well as any one. You are a wise and learned man; you have a thoughtful mind. The terms by which you characterize the fanatics of our day are strong enough to reassure the most suspicious imaginations as to your intentions; but you conclude in favor of the abolition of property! You wish to abolish the most powerful motor of the human mind; you attack the paternal sentiment in its sweetest illusions; with one word you arrest the formation of capital, and we build henceforth upon the sand instead of on a rock. That I cannot agree to; and for that reason I have criticised your book, so full of beautiful pages, so brilliant with knowledge   and   fervor!

"I wish, sir, that my impaired health would permit me to examine with you, page by page, the memoir which you have done me the honor to ad- which had already excited the indignation of the magistrates. M. Vivien is not the only official to whom I have been indebted, since my first publication, for assistance and protection; but such generosity in the political arena is so rare that one may acknowledge it graciously and freely. I have always thought, for my part, that bad institutions made bad magistrates; just as the cowardice and hypocrisy of certain bodies results solely from the spirit which governs them. Why, for instance, in spite of the virtues and talents for which they are so noted, are the academies generally centres of intellectual repression, stupidity, and base intrigue? That question ought to be proposed by an academy: there would be no lack of competitors.

[6] In Greek, *skeptikos* examiner; a philosopher whose business is to seek the truth.

[7] Religion, laws, marriage, were the privileges of freemen, and, in the beginning, of nobles only. *Dii majorum gentium* — gods of the patrician families; *jus gentium* — right of nations; that is, of families or nobles. The slave and the plebeian had no families; their children were treated as the offspring of animals. *Beasts* they were born, *beasts* they must live.

[8] If the chief of the executive power is responsible, so must the deputies be also. It is astonishing that this idea has never occurred to any one; it might be made the subject of an interesting essay. But I declare that I would not, for all the world, maintain it; the people are yet much too logical for me to furnish them with arguments.

[9] See De Tocqueville, "Democracy in the United States;" and Michel Chevalier, "Letters on North America." Plutarch tells us, "Life of

Pericles," that in Athens honest people were obliged to conceal themselves while studying, fearing they would be regarded as aspirants for office.

[10] "Sovereignty," according to Toullier, "is human omnipotence." A materialistic definition: if sovereignty is any thing, it is a *right* not a *force* or a faculty. And what is human omnipotence?

[11] The Proudhon here referred to is J. B. V. Proudhon; a distinguished French jurist, and distant relative of the Translator.

[12] Here, especially, the simplicity of our ancestors appears in all its rudeness. After having made first cousins heirs, where there were no legitimate children, they could not so divide the property between two different branches as to prevent the simultaneous existence of extreme wealth and extreme poverty in the same family. For example: — James, dying, leaves two sons, Peter and John, heirs of his fortune: James's property is divided equally between them. But Peter has only one daughter, while John, his brother, leaves six sons. It is clear that, to be true to the principle of equality, and at the same time to that of heredity, the two estates must be divided in seven equal portions among the children of Peter and John; for otherwise a stranger might marry Peter's daughter, and by this alliance half of the property of James, the grandfather, would be transferred to another family, which is contrary to the principle of heredity. Furthermore, John's children would be poor on account of their number, while their cousin, being an only child, would be rich, which is contrary to the principle of equality. If we extend this combined application of two principles apparently opposed to each other, we shall become convinced that the right of succession, which is assailed with so little wisdom in our day, is no obstacle to the maintenance of equality.

[13] *Zeus klésios.*

[14] Giraud, "Investigations into the Right of Property among the Romans."

[15] Precarious, from precor, "I pray;" because the act of concession expressly signified that the lord, in answer to the prayers of his men or slaves, had granted them permission to labor.

[16] In St. Simon's system, the St.-Simonian priest determines the capacity of each by virtue of his pontifical infallibility, in imitation of

706

the Roman Church: in Fourier's, the ranks and merits are decided by vote, in imitation of the constitutional *régime*. Clearly, the great man is an object of ridicule to the reader; he did not mean to tell his secret.

[17] I cannot conceive how any one dares to justify the inequality of conditions, by pointing to the base inclinations and propensities of certain men. Whence comes this shameful degradation of heart and mind to which so many fall victims, if not from the misery and abjection into which property plunges them?

[18] How many citizens are needed to support a professor of philosophy? — Thirty-five millions. How many for an economist? — Two billions. And for a literary man, who is neither a *savant*, nor an artist, nor a philosopher, nor an economist, and who writes newspaper novels? — None.

[19] There is an error in the author's calculation here; but the translator, feeling sure that the reader will understand Proudhon's meaning, prefers not to alter his figures. — *Translator*.

[20] Fourier, having to multiply a whole number by a fraction, never failed, they say, to obtain a product much greater than the multiplicand. He affirmed that under his system of harmony the mercury would solidify when the temperature was above zero. He might as well have said that the Harmonians would make burning ice. I once asked an intelligent phalansterian what he thought of such physics. "I do not know," he answered; "but I believe." And yet the same man disbelieved in the doctrine of the Real Presence.

[21] *Hoc inter se differunt onanismus et manuspratio, nempe quod hæc a solitario exercetur, ille autem a duobus reciprocatur, masculo scilicet et faemina. Porro foedam hanc onanismi venerem ludentes uxoria mariti habent nunc omnigm suavissimam*

[22] Polyandry, — plurality of husbands.

[23] Infanticide has just been publicly advocated in England, in a pamphlet written by a disciple of Malthus. He proposes an *annual massacre of the innocents* in all families containing more children than the law allows; and he asks that a magnificent cemetery, adorned with statues, groves, fountains, and flowers, be set apart as a special burying-place for the superfluous children. Mothers would resort to this delightful spot to dream of the happiness of these little angels, and

would return, quite comforted, to give birth to others, to be buried in their turn.

[24] "The financial situation of the English government was shown up in the House of Lords during the session of January 23. It is not an encouraging one. For several years the expenses have exceeded the receipts, and the Minister has been able to re-establish the balance only by loans renewed annually. The combined deficits of the years 1838 and 1839 amount to forty-seven million five hundred thousand francs. In 1840, the excess of expenses over receipts is expected to be twenty-two million five hundred thousand francs. Attention was called to these figures by Lord Ripon. Lord Melbourne replied: 'The noble earl unhappily was right in declaring that the public expenses continually increase, and with him I must say that there is no room for hope that they can be diminished or met in any way.' " — *National: January* 26, 1840.

[25] To perform an act of benevolence towards one's neighbor is called, in Hebrew, *to do justice;* in Greek, *to take compassion* or *pity* (*elehmosunh*,from which is derived the French *aumone*); in Latin, *to perform an act of love* or *charity;* in French, *give alms.* We can trace the degradation of this principle through these various expressions: the first signifies duty; the second only sympathy; the third, affection, a matter of choice, not an obligation; the fourth, caprice.

[26] I mean here by *équité* what the Latins called *humanitas,* — that is, the kind of sociability which is peculiar to man. Humanity, gentle and courteous to all, knows how to distinguish ranks, virtues, and capacities without injury to any. It is the just distribution of social sympathy and universal love.

[27] Justice and *équité* never have been understood. "Suppose that some spoils, taken from the enemy, and equal to twelve, are to be divided between Achilles and Ajax. If the two persons were equal, their respective shares would be arithmetically equal: Achilles would have six, Ajax six. And if we should carry out this arithmetical equality, Thersites would be entitled to as much as Achilles, which would be unjust in the extreme. To avoid this injustice, the worth of the persons should be estimated, and the spoils divided accordingly. Suppose that the worth of Achilles is double that of Ajax: the former's share is eight, the latter four. There is no arithmetical equality, but a proportional equality. It is this comparison of merits, *rationum,* that Aristotle calls distributive justice. It is a geometrical proportion." — Toullier: *French Law according to the Code.*

708

Are Achilles and Ajax associated, or are they not? Settle that, and you settle the whole question. If Achilles and Ajax, instead of being associated, are themselves in the service of Agamemnon who pays them, there is no objection to Aristotle's method. The slave-owner, who controls his slaves, may give a double allowance of brandy to him who does double work. That is the law of despotism; the right of slavery. But if Achilles and Ajax are associated, they are equals. What matters it that Achilles has a strength of four, while that of Ajax is only two? The latter may always answer that he is free; that if Achilles has a strength of four, five could kill him; finally, that in doing personal service he incurs as great a risk as Achilles. The same argument applies to Thersites. If he is unable to fight, let him be cook, purveyor, or butler. If he is good for nothing, put him in the hospital. In no case wrong him, or   impose   upon   him   laws.
Man must live in one of two states: either in society, or out of it. In society, conditions are necessarily equal, except in the degree of esteem and consideration which each one may receive. Out of society, man is so much raw material, a capitalized tool, and often an incommodious and useless piece of furniture.

[28] Between woman and man there may exist love, passion, ties of custom, and the like; but there is no real society. Man and woman are not companions. The difference of the sexes places a barrier between them, like that placed between animals by a difference of race. Consequently, far from advocating what is now called the emancipation of woman, I should incline, rather, if there were no other alternative, to exclude   her   from   society.
The rights of woman and her relations with man are yet to be determined Matrimonial legislation, like civil legislation, is a matter for the future to settle.

[29] "The strong-box of Cosmo de Medici was the grave of Florentine liberty," said M. Michelet to the College of France.

[30] "The problem of the origin of language is solved by the distinction made by Frederic Cuvier between instinct and intelligence. Language is not a premeditated, arbitrary, or conventional device; nor is it communicated or revealed to us by God. Language is an instinctive and unpremeditated creation of man, as the hive is of the bee. In this sense, it may be said that language is not the work of man, since it is not the work of his mind. Further, the mechanism of language seems more wonderful and ingenious when it is not regarded as the result of reflection. This fact is one of the most curious and indisputable which philology has observed. See, among other works, a Latin essay by F. G.

Bergmann (Strasbourg, 1839), in which the learned author explains how the phonetic germ is born of sensation; how language passes through three successive stages of development; why man, endowed at birth with the instinctive faculty of creating a language, loses this faculty as fast as his mind develops; and that the study of languages is real natural history, — in fact, a science. France possesses to-day several philologists of the first rank, endowed with rare talents and deep philosophic insight, — modest *savants* developing a science almost without the knowledge of the public; devoting themselves to studies which are scornfully looked down upon, and seeming to shun applause as much as others seek it."

[31] "My right is my lance and my buckler." General de Brossard said, like Achilles: "I get wine, gold, and women with my lance and my buckler."

[32] It would be interesting and profitable to review the authors who have written on usury, or, to use the gentler expression which some prefer, lending at interest. The theologians always have opposed usury; but, since they have admitted always the legitimacy of rent, and since rent is evidently identical with interest, they have lost themselves in a labyrinth of subtle distinctions, and have finally reached a pass where they do not know what to think of usury. The Church — the teacher of morality, so jealous and so proud of the purity of her doctrine — has always been ignorant of the real nature of property and usury. She even has proclaimed through her pontiffs the most deplorable errors. *Non potest mutuum*, said Benedict XIV., *locationi ullo pacto comparari.* "Rent," says Bossuet, "is as far from usury as heaven is from the earth." How, on [sic] such a doctrine, condemn lending at interest? how justify the Gospel, which expressly forbids usury? The difficulty of theologians is a very serious one. Unable to refute the economical demonstrations, which rightly assimilate interest to rent, they no longer dare to condemn interest, and they can say only that there must be such a thing as usury, since the Gospel forbids it. But what, then, is usury? Nothing is more amusing than to see these *instructors of nations* hesitate between the authority of the Gospel, which, they say, *never can have spoken in vain*, and the authority of economical demonstrations. Nothing, to my mind, is more creditable to the Gospel than this old infidelity of its pretended teachers. Salmasius, having assimilated interest to rent, was *refuted* by Grotius, Pufendorf, Burlamaqui, Wolf, and Heineccius; and, what is more curious still, Salmasius *admitted his error*. Instead of inferring from this doctrine of Salmasius that all increase is illegitimate, and proceeding straight on to the demonstration of Gospel equality, they arrived at just the opposite conclusion; namely,

that since everybody acknowledges that rent is permissible, if we allow that interest does not differ from rent, there is nothing left which can be called usury. and, consequently, that the commandment of Jesus Christ is an *illusion*, and amounts to *nothing*, which is an impious conclusion. If this memoir had appeared in the time of Bossuet, that great theologian would have *proved* by scripture, the fathers, traditions, councils, and popes, that property exists by Divine right, while usury is an invention of the devil; and the heretical work would have been burned, and the author imprisoned.

[33] "I preach the Gospel, I live by the Gospel," said the Apostle; meaning thereby that he lived by his labor. The Catholic clergy prefer to live by property. The struggles in the communes of the middle ages between the priests and bishops and the large proprietors and seigneurs are famous. The papal excommunications fulminated in defence of ecclesiastical revenues are no less so. Even to-day, the official organs of the Gallican clergy still maintain that the pay received by the clergy is not a salary, but an indemnity for goods of which they were once proprietors, and which were taken from them in '89 by the Third Estate. The clergy prefer to live by the right of increase rather than by labor.
One of the main causes of Ireland's poverty to-day is the immense revenues of the English clergy. So heretics and orthodox — Protestants and Papists — cannot reproach each other. All have strayed from the path of justice; all have disobeyed the eighth commandment of the Decalogue: "Thou shalt not steal."

[34] The meaning ordinarily attached to the word "anarchy" is absence of principle, absence of rule; consequently, it has been regarded as synonymous with "disorder."

[35] If such ideas are ever forced into the minds of the people, it will be by representative government and the tyranny of talkers. Once science, thought, and speech were characterized by the same expression. To designate a thoughtful and a learned man, they said, "a man quick to speak and powerful in discourse. "For a long time, speech has been abstractly distinguished from science and reason. Gradually, this abstraction is becoming realized, as the logicians say, in society; so that we have to-day *savants* of many kinds who talk but little, and *talkers* who are not even *savants* in the science of speech. Thus a philosopher is no longer a *savant:* he is a talker. Legislators and poets were once profound and sublime characters: now they are talkers. A talker is a sonorous bell, whom the least shock suffices to set in perpetual motion. With the talker, the flow of speech is always directly proportional to the

poverty of thought. Talkers govern the world; they stun us, they bore us, they worry us, they suck our blood, and laugh at us. As for the *savants*, they keep silence: if they wish to say a word, they are cut short. Let them write.

[36] *libertas, librare, libratio, libra,* — liberty, to liberate, libration, balance (pound), — words which have a common derivation. Liberty is the balance of rights and duties. To make a man free is to balance him with others, — that is, to put him or their level.

[37] In a monthly publication, the first number of which has just appeared under the name of "L'Egalitaire," self-sacrifice is laid down as a principle of equality. This is a confusion of ideas. Self-sacrifice, taken alone, is the last degree of inequality. To seek equality in self-sacrifice is to confess that equality is against nature. Equality must be based upon justice, upon strict right, upon the principles invoked by the proprietor himself; otherwise it will never exist. Self-sacrifice is superior to justice; but it cannot be imposed as law, because it is of such a nature as to admit of no reward. It is, indeed, desirable that everybody shall recognize the necessity of self-sacrifice, and the idea of "L'Egalitaire" is an excellent example. Unfortunately, it can have no effect. What would you reply, indeed, to a man who should say to you, "I do not want to sacrifice myself"? Is he to be compelled to do so? When self-sacrifice is forced, it becomes oppression, slavery, the exploitation of man by man. Thus have the proletaires sacrificed themselves to property.

[38] The disciples of Fourier have long seemed to me the most advanced of all modern socialists, and almost the only ones worthy of the name. If they had understood the nature of their task, spoken to the people, awakened their sympathies, and kept silence when they did not understand; if they had made less extravagant pretensions, and had shown more respect for public intelligence, — perhaps the reform would now, thanks to them, be in progress. But why are these earnest reformers continually bowing to power and wealth, — that is, to all that is anti-reformatory? How, in a thinking age, can they fail to see that the world must be converted by *demonstration*, not by myths and allegories? Why do they, the deadly enemies of civilization, borrow from it, nevertheless, its most pernicious fruits, — property, inequality of fortune and rank, gluttony, concubinage, prostitution, what do I know? theurgy, magic, and sorcery? Why these endless denunciations of morality, metaphysics, and psychology, when the abuse of these sciences, which they do not understand, constitutes their whole system? Why this mania for deifying a man whose principal merit consisted in

talking nonsense about things whose names, even, he did not know, in the strongest language ever put upon paper? Whoever admits the infallibility of a man becomes thereby incapable of instructing others. Whoever denies his own reason will soon proscribe free thought. The phalansterians would not fail to do it if they had the power. Let them condescend to reason, let them proceed systematically, let them give us demonstrations instead of revelations, and we will listen willingly. Then let them organize manufactures, agriculture, and commerce; let them make labor attractive, and the most humble functions honorable, and our praise shall be theirs. Above all, let them throw off that Illuminism which gives them the appearance of impostors or dupes, rather than believers and apostles.

[39] Individual possession is no obstacle to extensive cultivation and unity of exploitation. If I have not spoken of the drawbacks arising from small estates, it is because I thought it useless to repeat what so many others have said, and what by this time all the world must know. But I am surprised that the economists, who have so clearly shown the disadvantages of spade-husbandry, have failed to see that it is caused entirely by property; above all, that they have not perceived that their plan for mobilizing the soil is a first step towards the abolition of property.

[40] In the Chamber of Deputies, during the session of the fifth of January, 1841, M. Dufaure moved to renew the expropriation bill, on the ground of public utility.

[41] "What is Property?" Chap. IV., Ninth Proposition.

[42] *Tu cognovisti sessionem meam et resurrectionem meam.* Psalm 139.

[43] The emperor Nicholas has just compelled all the manufacturers in his empire to maintain, at their own expense, within their establishments, small hospitals for the reception of sick workmen, — the number of beds in each being proportional to the number of laborers in the factory. "You profit by man's labor," the Czar could have said to his proprietors; "you shall be responsible for man's life." M. Blanqui has said that such a measure could not succeed in France. It would be an attack upon property, — a thing hardly conceivable even in Russia, Scythia, or among the Cossacks; but among us, the oldest sons of civilization! ... I fear very much that this quality of age may prove in the end a mark of decrepitude.

[44] Course of M. Blanqui. Lecture of Nov. 27,1840.

[45] In "Mazaniello," the Neapolitan fisherman demands, amid the applause of the galleries, that a tax be levied upon luxuries.

[46] *Sème le champ, prolétaire;*
C'est l l'oisif qui récoltera.

[47] "In some countries, the enjoyment of certain political rights depends upon the amount of property. But, in these same countries, property is expressive, rather than attributive, of the qualifications necessary to the exercise of these rights. It is rather a conjectural proof than the cause of these qualifications." — *Rossi: Treatise on Penal Law.*
This assertion of M. Rossi is not borne out by history. Property is the cause of the electoral right, not as a *presumption of capacity*, — an idea which never prevailed until lately, and which is extremely absurd, — but as a *guarantee of devotion to the established order*. The electoral body is a league of those interested in the maintenance of property, against those not interested. There are thousands of documents, even official documents, to prove this, if necessary. For the rest, the present system is only a continuation of the municipal system, which, in the middle ages, sprang up in connection with feudalism, — an oppressive, mischief-making system, full of petty passions and base intrigues.

[48] Lecture of December 22.

[49] Lecture of Jan. 15, 1841.

[50] Lecture of Jan. 15, 1841.

[51] MM. Blanqui and Wolowski.

[52] Subject proposed by the Fourth Class of the Institute, the Academy of Moral and Political Sciences: "What would be the effect upon the working-class of the organization of labor, according to the modern ideas of association?"

[53] Subject proposed by the Academy of Besançon: "The economical and moral consequences in France, up to the present time, and those which seem likely to appear in future, of the law concerning the equal division of hereditary property between the children."

[54] *Pleonexia, — greater property.* The Vulgate translates it avaritia.

[55] Similar or analogous customs have existed among all nations. Consult, among other works, "Origin of French Law," by M. Michelet; and "Antiquities of German Law," by Grimm.

[56] *Dees hominesque testamur, nos arma neque contra patriam cepisse neque quo periculum aliis faceremus, sed uti corpora nostra ab injuria tuta forent, qui miseri, egentes, violentia atque crudelitate foeneraterum, plerique patriae, sed omncsfarna atque fortunis expertes sumus; neque cuiquam nostrum licuit, more majorum, lege uti, neque, amisso patrimonio, libferum corpus habere. — Sallus: Bellum Catilinarium.*

[57] Fifty, sixty, and eighty per cent. — *Course of M. Blanqui.*

[58] *Episcopi plurimi, quos et hortamento esse oportet cœteris et exemplo, divina prouratione contempta, procuratores rerum sœularium fieri, derelicta cathedra, plebe leserta, per alienas provincias oberrantes, negotiationis quaestuosae nundinas au uucu-, pari, esurientibus in ecclesia fratribus habere argentum largitur velle, fundos insidi.sis fraudibus rapere, usuris multiplicantibus foenus augere. — Cyprian: De Lapsis.* In this passage, St. Cyprian alludes to lending on mortgages and to compound interest.

[59] "Inquiries concerning Property among the Romans."

[60] "Its acquisitive nature works rapidly in the sleep of the law. It is ready, at the word, to absorb every thing. Witness the famous equivocation about the ox-hide which, when cut up into thongs, was large enough to enclose the site of Carthage... The legend has reappeared several times since Dido... Such is the love of man for the land. Limited by tombs, measured by the members of the human body, by the thumb, the foot, and the arm, it harmonizes, as far as possible, with the very proportions of man. Nor is be satisfied yet: he calls Heaven to witness that it is his; he tries to or his land, to give it the form of heaven... In his titanic intoxication, he describes property in the very terms which he employs in describing the Almighty — *fundus optimus maximus...* He shall make it his couch, and they shall be separated no more, — *kai emignunto Figothti.*" — *Michelet: Origin of French Law.*

[61] M. Guizot denies that Christianity alone is entitled to the glory of the abolition of slavery. "To this end," he says, "many causes were necessary, — the evolution of other ideas and other principles of civilization." So general an assertion cannot be refuted. Some of these ideas and causes should have been pointed out, that we might judge whether their source was not wholly Christian, or whether at least the Christian spirit had not penetrated and thus citizen was effected, then, by Christianity before the Barbarians set foot upon the soil of the empire. We have only to trace the progress of this *moral* revolution in the *personnel* of society. "But," M. Laboulaye rightly says, "it did not change the condition of men in a moment, any more than that of things; between slavery and liberty there was an abyss which could not be filled in a day; the transitional step was servitude." Now, what was servitude? In what did it differ from Roman slavery, and whence came this difference? Let the same author answer.

[62] *Weregild,* — the fine paid for the murder of a man. So much for a count, so much for a baron, so much for a freeman, so much for a priest; for a slave, nothing. His value was restored to the proprietor.

[63] The spirit of despotism and monopoly which animated the communes has not escaped the attention of historians. "The formation of the commoners' associations," says Meyer, "did not spring from the true spirit of liberty, but from the desire for exemption from the charges of the seigniors, from individual interests, and jealousy of the welfare of others... Each commune or corporation opposed the creation of every other; and this spirit increased to such an extent that the King of England, Henry V., having established a university at Caen, in 1432, the city and university of Paris opposed the registration of the edict. "The communes once organized, the kings treated them as superior vassals. Now, just as the under vassal had no communication with the king except through the direct vassal, so also the commoners could enter no complaints except through the commune. "Like causes produce like effects. Each commune became a small and separate State, governed by a few citizens, who sought to extend their authority over the others; who, in their turn, revenged themselves upon the unfortunate inhabitants who had not the right of citizenship. Feudalism in unemancipated countries, and oligarchy in the communes, made nearly the same ravages. There were sub-associations, fraternities, tradesmen's associations in the communes, and colleges in the universities. The oppression was so great, that it was no rare thing to see the inhabitants of a commune demanding its suppression..." — *Meyer: Judicial Institutions of Europe.*

[64] Feudalism was, in spirit and in its providential destiny, a long protest of the human personality against the monkish communism with which Europe, in the middle ages, was overrun. After the orgies of Pagan selfishness, society — carried to the opposite extreme by the Christian religion — risked its life by unlimited self-denial and absolute indifference to the pleasures of the world. Feudalism was the balance-weight which saved Europe from the combined influence of the religious communities and the Manlchean sects which had sprung up since the fourth century under different names and in different countries. Modern civilization is indebted to feudalism for the definitive establishment of the person, of marriage, of the family, and of country. (See, on this subject, Guizot, "History of Civilization in Europe.")

[65] This was made evident in July, 1830, and the years which followed it, when the electoral *bourgeoisie* effected a revolution in order to get control over the king, and suppressed the *émeutes* in order to restrain the people. The *bourgeoisie*, through the jury, the magistracy, its position in the army, and its municipal despotism, governs both royalty and the people. It is the *bourgeoisie* which, more than any other class, is conservative and retrogressive. It is the *bourgeoisie* which makes and unmakes ministries. It is the *bourgeoisie* which has destroyed the influence of the Upper Chamber, and which will dethrone the King whenever he shall become unsatisfactory to it. It is to please the *bourgeoisie* that royalty makes itself unpopular. It is the *bourgeoisie* which is troubled at the hopes of the people, and which hinders reform. The journals of the *bourgeoisie* are the ones which preach morality and religion to us, while reserving scepticism and indifference for themselves; which attack personal government, and favor the denial of the electoral privilege to those who have no property. The *bourgeoisie* will accept any thing rather than the emancipation of the proletariat. As soon as it thinks its privileges threatened, it will unite with royalty; and who does not know that at this very moment these two antagonists have suspended their quarrels? ... It has been a question of property.

[66] *Missing footnote*

[67] The same opinion was recently expressed from the tribune by one of our most honorable Deputies, M. Gauguier. "Nature," said he, "has not endowed man with landed property." Changing the adjective *landed*, which designates only a species into *capitalistic*, which denotes the genus, — M. Gauguier made an *égalitaire* profession of faith.

[68] A professor of comparative legislation, M. Lerminier, has gone still farther. He has dared to say that the nation took from the clergy all their possessions, not because of *idleness*, but because of *unworthiness*. "You have civilized the world," cries this apostle of equality, speaking to the priests; "and for that reason your possessions were given you. In your hands they were at once an instrument and a reward. But you do not now deserve them, for you long since ceased to civilize any thing whatever..."

This position is quite in harmony with my principles, and I heartily applaud the indignation of M. Lerminier; but I do not know that a proprietor was ever deprived of his property because *unworthy;* and as reasonable, social, and even useful as the thing may seem, it is quite contrary to the uses and customs of property.

[69] "Treatise on Prescription."

[70] "Origin of French Law."

[71] To honor one's parents, to be grateful to one's benefactors, to neither kill nor steal, — truths of inward sensation. To obey God rather than men, to render to each that which is his; the whole is greater than a part, a straight line is the shortest road from one point to another, — truths of intuition. All are *à priori* but the first are felt by the conscience, and imply only a simple act of the soul; the second are perceived by the reason, and imply comparison and relation. In short, the former are sentiments, the latter are ideas.

[72] Armand Carrel would have favored the fortification of the capital. "Le National" has said, again and again, placing the name of its old editor by the side of the names of Napoleon and Vauban. What signifies this exhumation of an anti-popular politician? It signifies that Armand Carrel wished to make government an individual and irremovable, but elective, property, and that he wished this property to be elected, not by the people, but by the army. The political system of Carrel was simply a reorganization of the pretorian guards. Carrel also hated the *péquins*. That which he deplored in the revolution of July was not, they say, the insurrection of the people, but the victory of the people over the soldiers. That is the reason why Carrel, after 1830, would never support the patriots. "Do you answer me with a few regiments?" he asked. Armand Carrel regarded the army — the military power — as the basis of law and government. This man undoubtedly had a moral sense within him, but he surely had no sense of justice. Were he still in this world, I declare it boldly, liberty would have no greater enemy than Carrel.

It is said that on this question of the fortification of Paris the staff of "Le National" are not agreed. This would prove, if proof were needed, that a journal may blunder and falsify, without entitling any one to accuse its editors. A journal is a metaphysical being, for which no one is really responsible, and which owes its existence solely to mutual concessions. This idea ought to frighten those worthy citizens who, because they borrow their opinions from a journal, imagine that they belong to a political party, and who have not the faintest suspicion that they are really without a head.

[73] In a very short article, which was read by M. Wolowski, M. Louis Blanc declares, in substance, that he is not a communist (which I easily believe); that one must be a fool to attack property (but he does not say why); and that it is very necessary to guard against confounding property with its abuses. When Voltaire overthrew Christianity, he repeatedly avowed that he had no spite against religion, but only against its abuses.

[74] The property fever is at its height among writers and artists, and it is curious to see the complacency with which our legislators and men of letters cherish this devouring passion. An artist sells a picture, and then, the merchandise delivered, assumes to prevent the purchaser from selling engravings, under the pretext that he, the painter, in selling the original, has not sold his *design*. A dispute arises between the amateur and the artist in regard to both the fact and the law. M. Villemain, the Minister of Public Instruction, being consulted as to this particular case, finds that the painter is right; only the property in the design should have been specially reserved in the contract: so that, in reality, M. Villemain recognizes in the artist a power to surrender his work and prevent its communication; thus contradicting the legal axiom, One *cannot give and keep at the same time*. A strange reasoner is M. Villemain! An ambiguous principle leads to a false conclusion. Instead of rejecting the principle, M. Villemain hastens to admit the conclusion. With him the *reductio ad absurdum* is a convincing argument. Thus he is made official defender of literary property, sure of being understood and sustained by a set of loafers, the disgrace of literature and the plague of public morals. Why, then, does M. Villemain feel so strong an interest in setting himself up as the chief of the literary classes, in playing for their benefit the *rôle* of *Trissotin* in the councils of the State, and in becoming the accomplice and associate of a band of profli-gates, — *soi-disant* men of letters, — who for more than ten years have labored with such deplorable success to ruin public spirit, and corrupt the heart by warping the mind? Contradictions of contradictions!" Genius is the great leveller of the

719

world," cries M. de Lamartine; "then genius should be a proprietor. Literary property is the fortune of democracy." This unfortunate poet thinks himself profound when he is only puffed up. His eloquence consists solely in coupling ideas which clash with each other: *round square, dark sun, fallen angel, priest* and *love, thought* and *poetry, gunius* and *fortune, leveling* and *property*. Let us tell him, in reply, that his mind is a dark luminary; that each of his discourses is a disordered harmony; and that all his successes, whether in verse or prose, are due to the use of the extraordinary in the treatment of the most ordinary subjects.

"Le National," in reply to the report of M. Lamartine, endeavors to prove that literary property is of quite a different nature from landed property; as if the nature of the right of property depended on the object to which it is applied, and not on the mode of its exercise and the condition of its existence. But the main object of "Le National" is to please a class of proprietors whom an extension of the right of property vexes: that is why "Le National" opposes literary property. Will it tell us, once for all, whether it is for equality or against it?

[75] M. Leroux has been highly praised in a review for having defended property. I do not know whether the industrious encyclopedist is pleased with the praise, but I know very well that in his place I should mourn for reason and for truth.

"Le National," on the other hand, has laughed at M. Leroux and his ideas on property, charging him with *tautology* and *childishness*. "Le National" does not wish to understand. Is it necessary to remind this journal that it has no right to deride a dogmatic philosopher, because it is without a doctrine itself? From its foundation, "Le National" has been a nursery of intriguers and renegades. From time to time it takes care to warn its readers. Instead of lamenting over all its defections, the democratic sheet would do better to lay the blame on itself, and confess the shallowness of its theories. When will this organ of popular interests and the electoral reform cease to hire sceptics and spread doubt? I will wager, without going further, that M. Leon Durocher, the critic of M. Leroux, is an anonymous or pseudonymous editor of some *bourgeois*, or even aristocratic, journal.

[76] "Impartial," of Besançon.

[77] The Arians deny the divinity of Christ. The Semi-Arians differ from the Arians only by a few subtle distinctions. M. Pierre Leroux, who regards Jesus as a man, but claims that the Spirit of God was infused into him, is a true Semi-Arian.

720

The Manicheans admit two co-existent and eternal principles, — God and matter, spirit and flesh, light and darkness, good and evil; but, unlike the Phalansterians, who pretend to reconcile the two, the Manicheans make war upon matter, and labor with all their might for the destruction of the flesh, by condemning marriage and forbidding reproduction, — which does not prevent them, however, from indulging in all the carnal pleasures which the intensest lust can conceive of. In this last particular, the tendency of the Fourieristic morality is quite Manichean.

The Gnostics do not differ from the early Christians. As their name indicates, they regarded themselves as inspired. Fourier, who held peculiar ideas concerning the visions of somnambulists, and who believed in the possibility of developing the magnetic power to such an extent as to enable us to commune with invisible beings, might, if he were living, pass also for a Gnostic.

The Adamites attend mass entirely naked, from motives of chastity. Jean Jacques Rousseau, who took the sleep of the senses for chastity, and who saw in modesty only a refinement of pleasure, inclined towards Adamism. I know such a sect, whose members usually celebrate their mysteries in the costume of Venus coming from the bath.

The Pre-Adamites believe that men existed before the first man. I once met a Pre-Adamite. True, he was deaf and a Fourierist.

The Pelagians deny grace, and attribute all the merit of good works to liberty. The Fourierists, who teach that man's nature and passions are good, are reversed Pelagians; they give all to grace, and nothing to liberty.

The Socinians, deists in all other respects, admit an original revelation. Many people are Socinians to-day, who do not suspect it, and who regard their opinions as new.

The Neo-Christians are those simpletons who admire Christianity because it has produced bells and cathedrals. Base in soul, corrupt in heart, dissolute in mind and senses, the Neo-Christians seek especially after the external form, and admire religion, as they love women, for its physical beauty. They believe in a coming revelation, as well as a transfiguration of Catholicism. They will sing masses at the grand spectacle in the phalanstery.

[78] It should be understood that the above refers only to the moral and political doctrines of Fourier, — doctrines which, like all philosophical and religious systems, have their root and *raison d'existence* in society itself, and for this reason deserve to be examined. The peculiar

speculations of Fourier and his sect concerning cosmogony, geology, natural history, physiology, and psychology, I leave to the attention of those who would think it their duty to seriously refute the fables of Blue Beard and the Ass's Skin.

[79] A writer for the radical press, M. Louis Raybaud, said, in the preface to his "Studies of Contemporary Reformers:" "Who does not know that morality is relative? Aside from a few grand sentiments which are strikingly instinctive, the measure of human acts varies with nations and climates, and only civilization — the progressive education of the race — can lead to a universal morality... The absolute escapes our contingent and finite nature; the absolute is the secret of God." God keep from evil M. Louis Raybaud! But I cannot help remarking that all political apostates begin by the negation of the absolute, which is really the negation of truth. What can a writer, who professes scepticism, have in common with radical views? What has he to say to his readers? What judgment is he entitled to pass upon contemporary reformers? M. Raybaud thought it would seem wise to repeat an old impertinence of the legist, and that may serve him for an excuse. We all have these weaknesses. But I am surprised that a man of so much intelligence as M. Raybaud, who *studies systems*, fails to see the very thing he ought first to recognize, — namely, that systems are the progress of the mind towards the absolute.

[80] The electoral reform, it is continually asserted, is not an *end*, but a *means*. Undoubtedly; but what, then, is the end? Why not furnish an unequivocal explanation of its object? How can the people choose their representatives, unless they know in advance the purpose for which they choose them, and the object of the commission which they entrust to   them?
But, it is said, the very business of those chosen by the people is to find out the object of the reform.

That is a quibble. What is to hinder these persons, who are to be elected in future, from first seeking for this object, and then, when they have found it, from communicating it to the people? The reformers have well said, that, while the object of the electoral reform remains in the least indefinite, it will be only a means of transferring power from the hands of petty tyrants to the hands of other tyrants. We know already how a nation may be oppressed by being led to believe that it is obeying only its own laws. The history of universal suffrage, among all nations, is the history of the restrictions of liberty by and in the name of the multitude.

Still, if the electoral reform, in its present shape, were rational, practical, acceptable to clean consciences and upright minds, perhaps one might be excused, though ignorant of its object, for supporting it. But, no; the text of the petition determines nothing, makes no distinctions, requires no conditions, no guarantee; it establishes the right without the duty. "Every Frenchman is a voter, and eligible to office." As well say: "Every bayonet is intelligent, every savage is civilized, every slave is free." In its vague generality, the reformatory petition is the weakest of abstractions, or the highest form of political treason. Consequently, the enlightened patriots distrust and despise each other. The most radical writer of the time, — he whose economical and social theories are, without comparison, the most advanced, — M. Leroux, has taken a bold stand against universal suffrage and democratic government, and has written an exceedingly keen criticism of J. J. Rousseau. That is undoubtedly the reason why M. Leroux is no longer the philosopher of "Le National." That journal, like Napoleon, does not like men of ideas. Nevertheless, "Le National" ought to know that he who fights against ideas will perish by ideas.

2637955R00364

Printed in Great Britain
by Amazon.co.uk, Ltd.,
Marston Gate.